The Routledge Sociolinguistics Reader

Both a companion to *Introducing Sociolinguistics*, Miriam Meyerhoff's bestselling textbook, and a stand-alone Reader in sociolinguistics, this collection includes classic foundational readings and more recent innovative articles.

Intended to be highly user-friendly, *The Routledge Sociolinguistics Reader* includes substantial section introductions, further reading, a reader's guide on how to use the book and an introductory chapter providing advice on how to undertake qualitative and quantitative research. This introduction is supplemented by exercises focusing on data handling and collection.

The *Reader* is divided into six sections and each section is thematically organised. Each reading is accessible to beginning students of sociolinguistics but the entire selection is assembled to also help advanced students focus on themes, principles and concepts that cut across different researchers' work. Beginning and advanced students are supported by Content Questions to assist understanding of essential features in the readings, and Concept Questions which help advanced students make connections across readings, apply theory to data, and critically engage with the readings. A companion website supports and connects the *Reader* and textbook with structured exercises, links to associated websites and video examples, plus an online glossary.

The Routledge Sociolinguistics Reader is essential reading for students on courses in sociolinguistics, language and society and language and variation.

Miriam Meyerhoff is Professor of Linguistics at the University of Auckland. Her work investigates language variation and the interplay between language and social identities, using qualitative and quantitative methods. She is author of *Introducing Sociolinguistics*, and co-editor of the *Handbook of Language and Gender*, as well as *Social Lives in Language* and the Creole Language Library.

Erik Schleef is lecturer in the Department of Linguistics and English Language at the University of Manchester. His research interests include language variation and change, language and gender, and language acquisition in immigrant contexts. He has lived and taught in the US, the UK, Germany, and Switzerland.

The Routledge Sociolinguistics Reader

Edited by

Miriam Meyerhoff and Erik Schleef

LONDON AND NEW YORK

First published 2010
by Routledge
2 Park Square, Milton Park, Abingdon, Oxon OX14 4RN

Simultaneously published in the USA and Canada
by Routledge
270 Madison Avenue, New York, NY 10016

Routledge is an imprint of the Taylor & Francis Group, an informa business

Typeset in Perpetua and AkzidenzGroteskBE by
RefineCatch Limited, Bungay, Suffolk

British Library Cataloguing in Publication Data
A catalogue record for this book is available from the British Library

Library of Congress Cataloging in Publication Data
The Routledge sociolinguistics reader / edited by Miriam Meyerhoff and Erik Schleef.
    p. cm.
Includes bibliographical references and index.
1. Sociolinguistics.   I. Meyerhoff, Miriam.   II. Schleef, Erik, 1971–
P40.S5657 2010
306.44–dc22
2010000220

ISBN10: 0-415-46956-2 (hbk)
ISBN10: 0-415-46957-0 (pbk)

ISBN13: 978-0-415-46956-2 (hbk)
ISBN13: 978-0-415-46957-9 (pbk)

CONTENTS

INTRODUCTION

PART ONE
Identities, Style and Politeness   27

     VOWELS AND NAIL POLISH: THE EMERGENCE OF LINGUISTIC STYLE
     IN THE PREADOLESCENT HETEROSEXUAL MARKETPLACE

28   Janet Holmes and Stephanie Schnurr   448
     'DOING FEMININITY' AT WORK: MORE THAN JUST RELATIONAL PRACTICE

PART SIX
Gender   461

Editors' Introduction to Part Six   463

29   Niloofar Haeri   466
     A LINGUISTIC INNOVATION OF WOMEN IN CAIRO

30   Elinor Ochs   483
     INDEXING GENDER

31   Scott Fabius Kiesling   498
     POWER AND THE LANGUAGE OF MEN

32   Rusty Barrett   514
     MARKEDNESS AND STYLESWITCHING IN PERFORMANCES BY AFRICAN
     AMERICAN DRAG QUEENS

     Notes on Concept Questions   532
     Index   550

FIGURES

TABLES

USER'S GUIDE TO *THE ROUTLEDGE SOCIOLINGUISTICS READER*

THIS BOOK IS INTENDED to serve as a companion, a guide and a conversation on the topic of sociolinguistics. The purpose of a Reader is to compile important and/or helpful sources from a field of enquiry, sources that enable students to explore and critique the methods and principles that are associated with that field, and sources that provide the scaffolding on which a teacher can build a coherent course of study. In *The Routledge Sociolinguistics Reader*, we have tried to gather together some of the readings we have enjoyed and learnt much from over the years, both as learners and teachers in the field. You will find some classic readings, but many more recent ones that in our opinion embody some of the best work illustrating good ways of doing sociolinguistic research, and that have highlighted important principles that inform the collection of sociolinguistic data, how such data is handled and analysed once it has been collected, and how it is then related to other work.

An ideal Reader on any topic would be one that could stand alone – independently modelling key methods and illuminating central principles in a field – and we hope that any-one who is studying independently and who might pick this volume up will profit from it as it stands. We have divided *The Routledge Sociolinguistics Reader* (*TRSR*) into six parts that create a spiral curriculum through key concepts in sociolinguistics. We have tried to get away from representing research as either "top-down" or "bottom-up". Instead *TRSR* tries to forge a spiral, which emphasises the connections between different practitioners and different sub-fields in sociolinguistics. The six parts are:

- Identities, style and politeness – how people present themselves to others through language
- Perceptions and language attitudes – how people perceive others through language
- Multilingualism and language contact – how people organise their communities around language norms
- Variation and change – how the influence of intersecting and independent factors can be seen in language
- Social class, networks and communities of practice – how the specific effects of who we associate with influence language; and

- Gender – how one of the most socially salient identities in society is reproduced and contested through language.

Users of *TRSR* who work through each part in turn will find that their journey takes them from perspectives on individual style, through individuals' place in society, and then gradually unpacks community-wide patterns of variation and change, highlighting properties and identities that have specifically local meaning.

However, the real world is generally less than ideal, and it may be helpful for a Reader to be supported with another text that can spell out methodological issues and the central principles in the field. When we have piloted the material in *The Routledge Sociolinguistics Reader* prior to publication, we have used it in conjunction with readings from an introductory text in sociolinguistics. The six parts complement the structure of Routledge's *Introducing Sociolinguistics* text (Meyerhoff 2006) and the two volumes should work together very well as a basis for an introductory course. But experienced teachers will see ways in which *The Routledge Sociolinguistics Reader* could be supplemented with readings from other introductory volumes.

The Routledge Sociolinguistics Reader provides a number of questions and exercises at the end of each reading. There are always two distinct types of questions, which we call **Content Questions** and **Concept Questions**. Content Questions provide a guided check on aspects of the article that we think are essential foundational knowledge in order to be able to get the most out of the reading. They are a good basis for checking comprehension of the main points. Concept Questions probe a little further; they explore more complicated issues raised by the author(s) in the reading and they encourage readers to make connections between articles in different sections of the Reader.

Over the years, we have found that a division of questions along these lines best suits the kinds of diverse needs that many large classes in sociolinguistics have, and the diverse kinds of audiences that may be approaching sociolinguistics as beginners. For example, even very talented (post-)graduate students may want reassurance that they have understood the key points in an article if they are reading in a second (or third…) language. Equally, an introductory class in sociolinguistics at any level may include some students who are already firmly committed to a degree in linguistics, and others who are taking the course because it complements their main subject of study. For a committed linguistics major (or someone who is considering making the jump), Concept Questions are an excellent basis around which informal study groups, or discussions in tutorial sections can be organised. We hope that as well as providing ready-made topics for in-depth discussion, they also suggest other discussion topics and other ways of relating readings to each other that reflect readers' own interests.

Concept Questions are supplemented at the end of the book with brief notes on what we were thinking about when we created these questions. This is not to say they are answers; in fact, we tried to resist the temptation to offer answers to Concept Questions. Instead, we have used the notes as a way of suggesting how you might go about answering the Concept Questions and where you might look for relevant information.

If you find you like the Concept Questions, you may like to visit the **web site** associated with *The Routledge Sociolinguistics Reader* (www.routledge.com/textbooks/meyerhoff). The web site contains links to supplementary exercises (including some interactive ones which are beyond the scope of a print book) and links to other useful web-based resources relevant to the topics covered in *The Routledge Sociolinguistics Reader*. In addition, the exercises scattered throughout *Introducing Sociolinguistics* are a good source of materials that will extend users' ability to test their understanding of key concepts in sociolinguistics and to apply them to unfamiliar data sets.

Another feature of *The Routledge Sociolinguistics Reader* that we hope will be useful to students starting out in the field is the "how-to" chapter we have written specifically for this volume. "Sociolinguistic methods for data collection and interpretation" started out as a two hour workshop for (post-)graduate students, who might or might not be already working in socio-linguistics. It has subsequently been adapted to the needs of various audiences, including a one hour fast-track version for undergraduates, a workshop for formal and experimental linguistics students to familiarise them with what sociolinguists do and what kinds of questions they ask about language. As well as including answers to (or guidance on) some of the questions our students and our colleagues' students have asked over the years, we conclude with several exercises as we do with the articles throughout the Reader. In this case, the exercises are very clearly focused on methods, and can be broken up to suit the needs and interests of different audiences. (To complete all the exercises, you will probably need a two hour class.)

Representing other people's research is a fearsome responsibility. In almost all cases, the copyright holders were kind enough to give us permission to excerpt from their original work, and this adds an additional responsibility of care. We hope we have been sensitive in our treatment of their original ideas. Where we have omitted something from the original text we show this with ellipsis, so: [. . .]. Likewise, any editorial comments of our own are enclosed in square brackets. We have made some minor changes to the original texts, e.g. renumbering tables, figures and examples, and truncating the original references to reflect our editing, but we have retained the conventions the original authors used to name people in their references. We have also retained the original numbering for footnotes, even if this means they end up being non-sequential in our extracts. In some cases, we have identified typographical errors in the original and where we have been able to confirm this with the author(s) we have made an amendment to the text. Where an original text cited works that were "in press" or "forthcoming" we have endeavoured to find the details for these works. Unfortunately, this has not always been possible. Where references were missing in the original, they have perforce continued to be missing in this volume.

By excerpting from some of the writing that we have found most inspirational, we hope we are able to introduce a wider range of readers to the complex and intellectually rewarding field of sociolinguistics. The paradoxical world of editing a reader is that on the one hand, we hope we have done a satisfactory job and that you will enjoy *The Routledge Sociolinguistics Reader*, as it stands. But on the other hand, we particuarly hope that our selections here inspire you to seek out and read these excellent articles in their entirety, and go on to the other works they refer to.

Miriam Meyerhoff   Erik Schleef
Auckland, 2010   *Manchester, 2010*

ACKNOWLEDGEMENTS

THE EDITORS ARE VERY grateful to Abigail Candelas de la Ossa, Robert Pollard and Chie Adachi for their advice and help in preparing this volume. Our thanks also go to the reviewers of our original book proposal, in particular to Hanne Andersen, Bill Haddican and Robin Queen, and to those who provided us with comments on the introductory sections and our methods chapter, especially Dave Britain, Yuni Kim, Naomi Nagy and Nuria Yañez-Bouza. The insights of all these people have enriched this volume tremendously. Exercise five in our methods article is courtesy of Agata Daleszyńska. For financial support for administrative assistance, we thank Routledge and the University of Manchester Faculty of Humanities. We would also like to thank the staff at Routledge for their invaluable support, in particular Louisa Semlyen, Nadia Seemungal and Moira Taylor.

Allan Bell (2001) Back in style: reworking audience design. In Penelope Eckert and John R. Rickford (eds) *Style and Sociolinguistic Variation*. Cambridge: Cambridge University Press, 139–169. © Cambridge University Press 2001, reproduced with permission.

Figures 9.1, 9.2 and 9.3 from Allan Bell (1984) Language style as audience design. *Language in Society* 13: 145–204. © Cambridge University Press 1994, reproduced with permission.

Jennifer Hay, Stefanie Jannedy and Norma Mendoza-Denton (1999) Oprah and /ay/: lexical frequency, referee design, and style. In *Proceedings of the 14th International Congress of Phonetic Sciences*, San Francisco, August 1999.

Qing Zhang (2005) A Chinese yuppie in Beijing: phonological variation and the construction of a new professional identity. *Language in Society* 34: 431–466. © Cambridge University Press 2005, reproduced with permission.

John Laver (1981): Linguistic routines and politeness in greeting and parting. In: Florian Coulmas (ed.) *Conversational Routine*. The Hague: Mouton, 289–305. By permission of Walter De Gruyter GMBH & Co.KG.

Sachiko Ide (1989) Formal forms and discernment: two neglected aspects of universals of linguistic politeness. *Multilingua* 8: 223–248. By permission of Walter de Gruyter GMBH & Co. KG.

Dennis Preston (2003) Language with an attitude. In Jack K. Chambers, Peter Trudgill and Natalie Schilling-Estes (eds) *The Handbook of Language Variation and Change*. Oxford: Wiley-Blackwell. 40–66. © Wiley-Blackwell 2003, reproduced with permission.

Table 2.1 from Thomas Purnell, William Idsardi and John Baugh (1999). Perceptual and phonetic experiments on American English dialect identification. *Journal of Language and Social Pyschology*. 18: 10–30. Used by permission of the publisher, Sage.

Table 2.2 from Peter Trudgill (1972) Sex, covert prestige and linguistic change in the urban British English of Norwich. *Language in Society* 1: 179–95. © Cambridge University Press 2005, reproduced with permission.

Figure 2.3 from Ahmed Al-Banyan and Dennis R. Preston (1998) What is Standard American English? *Studia Anglica Posnaniensia* 33: 29–46. Used by permission of the publisher.

Dennis Preston (1985) The Li'l Abner syndrome: written representations of speech. *American Speech*. 60: 328–336. Copyright, 1985, the American Dialect Society. All rights reserved. Used by permission of the publisher, Duke University Press.

Thomas Purnell, William Idsardi and John Baugh (1999) Perceptual and phonetic experiments on American English dialect identification. *Journal of Language and Social Psychology* 18: 10–30. Used by permission of the publisher, Sage.

Gibson Ferguson (2006) Language education policy and the medium of instruction issue in post-colonial Africa. In: Gibson Ferguson *Language Planning and Education*. Edinburgh: Edinburgh University Press, 179–198. Used by permission of the publisher, Edinburgh University Press, www.euppublishing.com.

Isabelle Buchstaller (2006) Social stereotypes, personality traits and regional perceptions displaced: attitudes towards the new quotative in the UK. *Journal of Sociolinguistics* 10: 362–381. Used by permission of the publisher, Blackwell.

Jinny K. Choi (2005) Bilingualism in Paraguay: forty years after Rubin's study. *Journal of Multilingual and Multicultural Development* 26: 233–248. Taylor & Francis Ltd, reprinted by permission of the publisher.

Don Kulick and Christopher Stroud (1990) Code-switching in Gapun: social and linguistic aspects of language use in a language shifting community. In: John W.M. Verhaar (ed.) *Melanesian Pidgin and Tok Pisin*. Amsterdam/Philadelphia: John Benjamins, 205–234. By kind permission of John Benjamins.

Jan-Peter Blom and John Gumperz (1972) Social meaning in linguistic structure: code-switching in Norway. In John Gumperz and Dell Hymes (eds) *Directions in Sociolinguistics*. New York: Holt, Rinehart and Winston, 407–434. Second edition, Blackwell. Reproduced with permission of Blackwell Publishing Ltd.

David Britain (1997) Dialect contact, focusing and phonological rule complexity: the koineisation of Fenland English. *Penn Working Papers in Linguistics: A Selection of Papers from NWAVE 25*, 4: 141–169. Reproduced by permission of David Britain.

Monica Heller (2001) Legitimate language in a multilingual school. In: Monica Heller and Marilyn Martin-Jones (eds) *Voices of Authority: Education and Linguistic Difference*. Westport: Ablex, 381–402. © 2001. Reproduced with permission of ABC-Clio, LLC.

Ben Rampton (1998) Language crossing and the redefinition of reality. In Peter Auer (ed.) *Code-switching in Conversation: Language, Interaction and Identity*. London/New York: Routledge, 290–317. Reproduced by permission of Taylor & Francis Books UK.

Miriam Meyerhoff and Nancy Niedzielski (2003) The globalisation of vernacular variation. *Journal of Sociolinguistics* 7: 534–555. Blackwell. Reproduced with permission of Blackwell Publishing Ltd.

Table 2 from Miriam Meyerhoff (1993) Lexical shift in working class New Zealand English. *English World-Wide* 14: 231–248. Reproduced with permission of John Benjamins.

Table 3 from Janet Holmes (1995) Two for /t/: flapping and glottal stops in New Zealand English. *Te Reo* 38: 53–72. Reproduced with permission of the publisher.

William Labov (1972) The social motivation of a sound change. In William Labov *Sociolinguistic Patterns*. Philadelphia: University of Pennsylvania Press, 1–42. Reproduced with permission of University of Pennsylvania Press.

Table 1.1 from US Bureau of Census (*U.S. Census of Population: 1960. Number of Inhabitants. Massachusetts.* Final Report PC(1)–23A (Washington, D.C.: GPO, 1962), Table 7, 23–11.

Rika Ito and Sali Tagliamonte (2003) *Well* weird, *right* dodgy, *very* strange, *really* cool: layering and recycling in English intensifiers. *Language in Society* 32: 257–279. © Cambridge University Press 2003. Reproduced with permission.

Table 1 abstracted from Tauno F. Mustanoja (1960) *A Middle English syntax.* Helsinki: Société Néophilologique, 319–28. Reproduced with permission of Tauno F. Mustanoja.

Table 2 from Sali A. Tagliamonte (1998) *Was/were* variation across the generations: view from the city of York. *Language Variation and Change* 10:153–91. Reproduced with permission of Cambridge University Press and Sali A. Tagliamonte.

Gillian Sankoff and Hélène Blondeau (2007) Language change across the lifespan: /r/ in Montreal French. *Language*, 83: 560–588. Reproduced with permission of the LSA.

Table 1 adapted from William Labov (1994) *Principles of Linguistic Change, Vol. 1: Internal Factors.* Oxford: Blackwell, 83. Reproduced with permission of Blackwell.

Figure 1 from Jean Clermont and Henrietta Cedergreen (1979) Les 'R' de ma mere sont perdus dans l'air. In Pierrette Thibault *Le Français Parlé: Etudes Sociolinguistiques.* Edmonton, AB: Linguistic Research, 13–28.

Peter Trudgill (1988) Norwich revisited: recent linguistic changes in an English urban dialect. *English World Wide* 9: 33–49. By kind permission of John Benjamins.

Figures 1 and 2 from Peter Trudgill (1974) *The Social Differentiation of English in Norwich.* Cambridge: Cambridge University Press. Reproduced with permission of Cambridge University Press and Peter Trudgill.

Richard Cameron (2005) Aging and gendering. *Language in Society* 34: 23–61. © Cambridge University Press 2005. Reproduced with permission.

Lesley Milroy and James Milroy (1992) Social network and social class: toward an integrated sociolinguistic model. *Language in Society* 21: 1–26. © Cambridge University Press 1992. Reproduced with permission.

Figure 2 adapted from Sharon Ash and John Myhill (1986) Linguistic correlates of inter-ethnic contact. In David Sankoff (1986) *Diversity and Diachrony.* Amsterdam: Benjamins, 33–44. Reproduced with permission of John Benjamins.

Paul Kerswill and Ann Williams (2000) Mobility versus social class in dialect levelling: evidence from new and old towns in England. In Klaus Mattheier (ed.) *Dialect and Migration in a Changing Europe.* Frankfurt/M, Berlin, Bern, Bruxelles, New York, Oxford, Wien: Peter Lang 2000.

Terttu Nevalainen (1999) Making the best of 'bad' data. *Neuphilologische Mitteilungen*

100: 499–533. Reproduced with permission of the Modern Language Society and Terttu Nevalainen.

Table 1 from Merja Kytö (1993) Third-person present singular verb inflection in Early British and American English. *Language Variation and Change* 5: 113–139. Reproduced with permission of Cambridge University Press and Merja Kytö.

Penelope Eckert (1998) Vowels and nail polish: the emergence of linguistic style in the preadolescent heterosexual marketplace. In Nancy Warner et al (eds) *Proceedings of the 1996 Berkeley Women and Language Conference*. Berkeley: Berkeley Women and Language Group, 183–190. Reproduced with permission of Penelope Eckert.

Janet Holmes and Stephanie Schnurr (2006) 'Doing femininity' at work: more than just relational practice. *Journal of Sociolinguistics* 10: 31–51. Blackwell. Reproduced with permission of Blackwell Publishing Ltd.

Niloofar Haeri (1994) A linguistic innovation of women in Cairo. *Language Variation and Change* 6: 87–112. © Cambridge University Press 1994. Reproduced with permission.

Elinor Ochs (1992) Indexing gender. In Alessandro Duranti and Charles Goodwin (eds) *Rethinking Context: Language as an Interactive Phenomenon*. Cambridge: Cambridge University Press, 335–358. © Cambridge University Press 1992. Reproduced with permission.

Scott F. Kiesling (1997) Power and the language of men. In Ulrike Hanna Meinhof and Sally Johnson (eds) *Language and Masculinity*. Oxford: Blackwell, 65–85. Reproduced with permission of Blackwell Publishing Ltd.

Rusty Barrett (1998) Markedness and style-switching in performances by African-American drag queens. In Carol Myers-Scotton (ed.) *Codes and Consequences: Choosing Linguistic Varieties*. New York/Oxford: Oxford University Press, 139–161. By permission of Oxford University Press.

Every effort has been made to obtain permission to reproduce copyright material. If any proper acknowledgement has not been made, or permission not received, we would invite copyright holders to inform us of this oversight.

Chapter 1

Erik Schleef and Miriam Meyerhoff

SOCIOLINGUISTIC METHODS FOR DATA COLLECTION AND INTERPRETATION

S O H E R E Y O U A R E, a sizeable collection of previous sociolinguistic research sitting in your lap, and the promise of happy hours poring over other people's findings. Inspired by this prior work in the field, and fired up with questions of your own that you would like to answer, you resolve to try your hand at finding the answers. But how to start? And how to get it finished for the end of semester? Over the years, a number of our students in sociolinguistics classes have told us that reading about other people's research is very interesting, but what they really miss is a sense of *how-to*. A field guide for sociolinguists.

Some introductory texts are very helpful in this regard. Milroy and Gordon (2003) provide accounts of tried and tested methods and accepted ethical practice for socio-linguistics researchers. Their accounts run parallel to their introduction of concepts and theory in sociolinguistics, and their book is highly recommended particularly for a detailed exploration of how sociolinguistic methodologies are linked to the fine art of asking and answering research questions. Tagliamonte (2006) also provides guidelines for collecting data suitable for a quantitative analysis, and then walks the reader through steps by which you can subject the resulting corpus to multivariate statistical analysis. Walker (2010) also works through numerous examples of different variables, and provides a valuable model of how an analysis of variation can incorporate linguistic argumentation at all points.

This chapter is a much shorter attempt to provide key concepts and methods and is intended to complement the primary research that is showcased in many individual research articles. It covers a range of problematic issues relating to data collection and data interpretation that independent researchers often need to face. It is in particular aimed at students designing their first research projects. The scope of these projects will be somewhat narrower and the time constraints even more severe than they are for the academics whose work you can read about in research articles.

The first half of the chapter deals primarily with data collection. Several different types of data and sampling techniques are outlined and related practical issues are discussed. The second half of the chapter focuses on data interpretation. There, we discuss issues that are associated with identifying meaningful patterns and analysing sociolinguistic data. Key concepts include: the range of linguistic features that can be analysed as "variables", the concept of "variants" and the "envelope of variation". The chapter is by no means solely focused on quantitative, variationist methods. We'll briefly discuss arguments for and against exhaustive transcription of a corpus and provide practice in mapping out a plan of action – qualitative and quantitative – for an unseen data set. For the quantitative researcher, we will go one step further and outline how you extract tokens from a corpus into a spreadsheet and what you might do with them next.

It's worth stressing at the outset that no method for collecting and analysing linguistic data is fail-safe. For most students, planning and methodology involves compromises: compromises between what you would like to replicate from other people's work, and what you have the time and resources to achieve; compromises between what you expected to find out and what you eventually get. What this chapter can do is provide you with enough information about methods to enable you to make reasoned compromises and to enable you to justify the decisions you've made about how to collect and analyse your data when you write up your research report.

1. DATA COLLECTION

In the initial phase of any sociolinguistic project you have to identify a sociolinguistic problem that concerns a particular linguistic phenomenon. This is common to all good academic research projects. For example, you might be struck by conflicting claims in the literature and want to see which one(s) appear to be better supported by actual talk in action. Or you might have observed people engaging in some form of speech event, or using certain forms that (for some reason) strike you as distinctive or unexpected. Once such a problem and its linguistic phenomenon or variable(s) (more on variables under 2.1) have been identified, you need to collect appropriate data to address the problem. The particular issue you're investigating will naturally influence how you go about your data collection. The process of data collection brings up several questions that we'll deal with in turn. They include: How do you gain access to informants? What data do you want to collect? In what context? What variable(s) or linguistic phenomena do you want to focus on? What social factors do you want to investigate? How much data do you need from how many speakers? What ethical issues do you need to consider?

We begin by looking at the important initial steps in a research project: entering the community of speakers.

1.1 First contact: Gaining access to informants and entering the community

Gaining access to informants and entering the community can be quite a challenge. You will need some kind of contact to the community you want to study. Researchers often work in communities they belong to, and many students want to replicate previous sociolinguistic studies in their own community. In this case, a friend, a family member, a former workmate, or a friend of a friend may be able to help you. These are the optimal starting points for many student projects. If you do not have such a contact, you will have to find one by talking to, writing, or e-mailing a member of the community you want to study. Some communities are particularly well-suited as points of access to a range of speakers because they have well-established networks in place that you can use, for example schools, churches, societies or internet interest groups.

If you are not already a member of the community you're interested in, you can become one, e.g. through volunteer work or by making personal contacts in societies. We have had several students undertake research on the speech and interaction patterns among members of sports teams. Sometimes the best way to do this is to join the team.

When entering the community and talking to informants always be honest, polite and interested. Do your homework. Make sure you know what your consultants' interests are so that you can talk to them. Every group of speakers, even small groups in "your own" speech community, has their own norms and values. That's part of what defines them as a group. It is a very good idea to make sure that you find out a bit about their values, culture and social norms so that you can conduct your research in a context of mutual respect. You will almost certainly be learning as you go, so openness and humility are crucial attributes. Most importantly, this will enable you to pose questions in terms of the consultants' cultural perspectives, which may be very different from your own.

1.2 Data types

There are at least four different kinds of data that you can collect for a sociolinguistic study and each of these can help you answer particular questions.

Naturally occurring data (conversations, broadcast media, etc.) is speech that would have occurred (in a similar form), whether you would have recorded it or not. This is a great source of data as it is often very unmonitored speech. However, if you want to answer a particular question you may need a lot of naturally occurring data to get the information you want (e.g. if you investigate non-phonological variables, such as how and when people give compliments, or specific questions, such as where people think "the North" starts linguistically). Holmes & Schnurr (2006) and Eckert (1998) are studies that use naturally occurring data of this kind. Holmes and Schnurr (2006) draw on data that they collected in workplace settings such as offices and meetings, and Eckert (1998) investigated talk that occurred in school settings such as the playground or the school yard.

Interview data, on the other hand, allows you to focus your data collection a little more. You set up a meeting for an interview with one or more people and record it. This also allows you to ask specific questions if you are interested in certain factual information or opinions. Zhang's (2005) study is based on interview data. Her sociolinguistic interviews at the workplaces of managerial professionals in Beijing focused on two general topics: professional experiences and Beijing society and culture.

Ideally, an interview is structured around a prepared set of topics which you have made yourself very familiar with, so you can pose them as naturally as possible and give the interview the feeling of a chat rather than an interview – perhaps even approximating the unmonitored, casual norms of speech that are targeted in naturally occurring data (to this end, you may want to avoid the term "interview" and keep the list of questions out of your informants' sight). Alternatively, you can use certain tools that you have designed prior to the interview and which you think will elicit a structured set of the linguistic features you're interested in. Following Labov (1966), a common structure for socio-linguistic interviews may involve a range of activities such as reading a word list, reading a text passage or a question-answer session that then evolves into casual speech.

These non-conversational tasks allow you to extract an equal number of tokens of the linguistic feature you're interested in from every person recorded and to control the context in which the variables you may be interested in occur. Concerning this issue, interviews have a clear advantage over naturally occurring speech, which is great for giving us an insight into speakers' everyday norms, but it can provide a patchy sample of some variables. Even phonetic features are not all equally likely to be spontaneously produced in natural conversation (at the end of this chapter we give an old, but indicative, count of the frequency of phonemes in southern British English – as you can see you may have to listen and record a lot of naturally occurring speech to get a good sample of voiceless interdental fricatives!).

Manipulating tasks is also a useful way of varying how much attention the speaker is paying to the recording process and continues to be a fairly quick and replicable way of eliciting stylistic differences in speech. You may want to combine certain tools and start with the most structured one in order to reduce the attention the interviewee pays to his or her speech bit by bit.

Other tried and tested means for eliciting spontaneous speech (which again allow you to control some of the vocabulary people will use) include asking interviewees to tell you a story, possibly based on pictures you brought with you, or giving them a map task to get them talking. The classic map task involves two maps, one with a route plotted on it and one without and two speakers: one speaker describes to the other how to get from point A to point B via the route printed on their map, negotiating various obstacles printed on the maps.

When conducting interviews, there are a couple of practical issues that you may want to keep in mind. Some of these are summarised in Figure 1.1 (for more information see Tagliamonte 2006).

Questionnaire data is sometimes used by sociolinguists as well, usually not to elicit actual language data but often in order to collect data on attitudes about language or qualitative sociolinguistic information. It can be very helpful, for instance, if you are trying to determine when certain varieties are used and by whom. Choi's (2005) study on bilingualism in Paraguay is a study that uses questionnaires to collect such language use data. Occasionally, actual language data is collected in questionnaires but this is mostly restricted to the lexicon (*What would you say: "faucet" or "tap"?*).

When designing your questionnaires, there are a couple of issues that are worth thinking about. Some of these are summarised in Figure 1.2 (for more information, see De Vaus 2002).

Experimental data is also occasionally used by sociolinguists. This kind of data is elicited in an experimental setting and often involves listening to specific linguistic stimuli or to particular sounds. Matched guise tests are a classic method for eliciting language attitude data and involve an informant listening to the same person using two different languages or accents. See for example Purnell, Idsardi and Baugh (1999) for a study that uses experimental data to detect language attitudes.

When collecting data, you want to reduce the observer's paradox as much as possible (observing an event is often influenced by the presence of an observer/interviewer),

- Collect demographic data and at least 1 hour of speech for each speaker.
- The interviewer should sound natural, show interest, volunteer experience, respond to new issues and follow subjects' interests but always with a view to letting the interviewee speak most of the time, not the interviewer.
- Prepare an interview schedule, i.e. hierarchically structured sets of questions. Ask short questions.
- Start with general, impersonal questions and progress to specific and personal questions. Questions on language should be at the end of the interview.
- Avoid yes/no questions, vague questions, and questions that might be too personal.
- Use questions like: *Tell me about where you were born?*, *What's been your best holiday?*, *What do you like best about living in X?*; ask for elaboration e.g. *What happened then?*, backchannel, give and ask for examples and pick up on local culture (where possible, take an insider's point of view).
- Avoid leading questions in interviews and do not be blinded by your initial assumptions. Don't ask *Isn't it sad that your grandparents' dialect is dying out?* But ask *What do you think about X being used less now than 30 years ago?* Note here the avoidance of an emotionally charged question that suggests a particular answer, and also note the avoidance of the term dialect, which may offend speakers who consider their variety a language. Use the local term whenever you can.
- Think about where to put your recording equipment to get the best sound and tell people where to sit. Avoid recording outdoors. The best room in the house is usually the living room but make sure to turn off televisions and stay away from any other noisy machines in the room, such as fridges or clocks.
- Practise your interviewing and recording techniques with a friend beforehand!

Figure 1.1   Practical issues in conducting a sociolinguistic interview.

for example, by using relatively unobtrusive recording equipment, by employing interviewers with in-group status and by conducting interviews in self-selected dyads.

There are of course other sources of data that can be included in sociolinguistic studies. Corpora based on written or spoken language, for example, have been used for sociolinguistic analyses of language (see for example Nevalainen 1999), and other sources of data such as official documents, printed media text, census data, etc. can be used to explore the social aspects of language. In fact, many sociolinguistic studies combine data from different sources, a practice we recommend as it allows you to triangulate your data analysis and explore an issue from different angles.

1.3 Sampling techniques

Once you've made a decision on the type of data you want to collect, you will have to think about a technique to collect the data. At this stage it is very important to keep in mind that different research questions require different sampling techniques and that sampling techniques can of course be combined. Four different sampling techniques have been used quite frequently in sociolinguistic studies, and we introduce each of them briefly below (for a more detailed discussion see Starks and McRobbie-Utasi 2001,

- Write a brief introduction of what the project is about. Indicate that participation is voluntary and that informants will remain anonymous.
- Use closed and open questions (both have advantages and disadvantages when it comes to categorisation, quantification and time).
- Group questions into sections which structure the questionnaire and will make it easier for the informant to follow.
- Introduce a variety of question formats so that the questionnaire remains interesting (open, closed, rating scales, multiple choice).
- For closed questions, ensure that the range of possible responses is exhaustive to avoid biasing the responses in a certain direction. Where it makes sense, you should include the category 'other (please specify)' to capture unanticipated responses.
- In some cases, it might be wise to include a 'no commitment' response option. This is especially true in cases when there is only a handful of options available, none of which the informants may really believe. However, be careful: there's also a danger of informants relying too much on the 'no opinion' option.
- Possible responses for closed questions are best found by designing a test questionnaire with open questions, using these to elicit possible answers, and then including these answers in the final research questionnaire. Unfortunately, you may not always have time and funding for this method.
- For open questions, leave enough space for the informants to write a few lines but not so much space that the task of answering appears daunting.
- Ask several questions about the same issue if you can. As De Vaus (2002: 50) points out, "opinions are complex and are best measured with a number of questions to capture the scope of the concept".
- Word questions as clearly and unambiguously as possible so that questions are interpreted by the informants in the intended way.
  - ☐ E.g. try to avoid using "not" in any of your questions. De Vaus (2002: 98) points out that this can make questions hard to understand, in particular when asking an informant whether they agree or disagree with a statement.
- Think about the ordering of questions (e.g. do you want to start with general biographical questions and leave very specific linguistic questions for the end, or keep biography backgrounded till the end?).
- Write a brief closing in which you thank informants for their participation, invite them to add any other comments (below or on the next page) they might have and give them your (e-mail) address, should they wish to contact you later to provide you with more information or to withdraw their consent to use the data.
- Test your questionnaire on a friend before you use it!

Figure 1.2   Some issues in questionnaire design.

Tagliamonte 2006). They are random sampling, stratified random sampling, the ethnographic approach, and social networks including the "friend of a friend" technique.

Random sampling: When the goal of a study is to provide a snapshot of variation in a city as a whole, random sampling may be appropriate. A random sample of a targeted group (e.g. Chicago) means that everyone in the group (here, everyone in Chicago) would have an equal chance of being chosen as an interviewee, for instance because their name was randomly picked out of a telephone book. Interviewer and interviewees in such a set up are usually strangers. Labov's original study of New York City's Lower East Side

(Labov 1966, 1972) piggybacked off a random sample being undertaken for other research purposes.

Stratified random sampling: Usually, sociolinguists have specific social or linguistic questions in mind when they start their research, and in order to ensure that their research adequately addresses those questions, they *stratify* their sample somewhat. In stratified random sampling the sample is manipulated according to several secondary variables. The population is divided into strata, i.e. groups of individuals that may be important to the study. From each stratum a separate random sample is then collected and combined with the samples from other strata to form the full sample. Notice that even in the case of Labov's New York City study, his sample was constrained by area. Tagliamonte (2006: 23) proposes that as a minimum requirement a sample should be representative on the bases of age, sex, social class and/or educational level. That's not always possible for a student project, but as a desideratum, it's something you can be aware of. Once the target population has been defined, selection should ideally be random. Trudgill's study of speakers in Norwich is based on a stratified random sample of four wards in Norwich which resembled the city as a whole in its social characteristics (Trudgill 1988). Trudgill randomly chose names from voter registration lists to select speakers for his study.

Ethnographic research: The ethnographic approach is an entirely different approach from the two discussed above. In the course of data collection, the researcher often develops personal associations with members of a community and becomes a member of it, i.e. collects data as a participant-observer. Scott Kiesling's (1997) study is a good example of this technique. He integrated himself within a fraternity at a university in the United States and became a participant observer while also recording data and collecting qualitative information about the community (US fraternities and sororities are a bit mysterious to people from other countries – they're kind of like clubs university students compete to be members of. They have their own initiation rituals and an internal structure and some have enough accommodation for all members to live in one clubhouse throughout their college years).

Participant observation is often combined with other survey techniques as it enables the researcher to collect information about the cultural context of the group of speakers being investigated, and this kind of information can be invaluable when you start interpreting the data. The importance of understanding not only what is said, but how people respond to that (and equally their attitudes to what is not said) inform research conducted within communities of practice. A community of practice is characterised by mutual engagement, a jointly negotiated enterprise, and a shared repertoire (see Meyerhoff 2006 for more information).

Social networks, "friend of a friend" sampling: Rather than studying more abstract social categories, such as social class or age, the network approach focuses on some pre-existing social group (a social network) to which researchers attach themselves to collect large amounts of spontaneous speech. The "friend of a friend" technique is often used to make contacts within the group. You can ask your contacts in a group to introduce you to friends of theirs who may be willing to be recorded. With time, you may become a participant observer within this network of friends and acquaintances (so the work shifts subtly into a more ethnographic mode). Lesley and James Milroy conducted what is now regarded as a classic study, based on a network analysis and recordings made by pursuing friend of a friend contacts in Belfast (Milroy and Milroy 1992).

Tagliamonte (2006: 22) recommends avoiding people with official status such as priests, teachers, and community leaders as initial contacts since they are most likely to introduce the researcher to people within their social network of contacts who tend to use standard speech styles; however, from a practical point of view, these may be very good initial contacts in a community and in some cases it may be impossible to do research without having a local community leader approve your work. If you use such initial contacts, just be aware of the kind of network they introduce you to and try to branch out if it doesn't match your target population.

Whichever sampling technique you choose, it is important to keep in mind that different research questions require different sampling techniques and that sampling techniques are often combined (see exercises below).

1.4 Sample design

The next step in designing your study is making a decision about the type and number of people you want to collect data from. Suppose you decide to investigate several linguistic variables as used by young people between 18 and 28 who live in different neighbour-hoods which more or less overlap with two different socioeconomic classes. Depending on your research question, you might devise the following template for sample design:

Table 1.1   Data grid

Age	Working class		Middle class	
	Male	Female	Male	Female
18–23	5	5	5	5
23–28	5	5	5	5
Subtotal	10	10	10	10
				Grand total: 40

Using a data grid like this obviously helps you when using a stratified random sample, but even if you conduct a network study, a data grid can help you get an idea of how many speakers you will need data from. It is usually recommended to have at least 5 or 6 speakers per cell if you want to be able to make statistically sound generalisations about (say) middle class males between 23 and 28 years old. So if you were to add another age group to this grid, your grand total would rise to 60! This is quite substantial and shows that it is worth thinking about sample design in advance, as you may simply not have the funds and time to collect that much data, not to mention analyse it all at the end. Adding another social factor, such as ethnicity, would increase the grand total by a further order of magnitude.

How much data you need from every single individual does of course depend on your research question. If you ask informants to fill in questionnaires, the answer is one questionnaire per person; if you are looking at phonological variables and only use word lists and reading passages, you may need just 15 minutes of speech per person. If you're after casual speech, you will need substantially more. If you're interested in syntactic variables (which occur less frequently than certain phonological variables), much more data is needed (see exercises below).

For the quantitative analysis of variables, *each cell* in the grid should have at least 30 tokens, i.e. occurrences of a particular variable. With fewer than that, you won't be able to say anything quantitatively meaningful about your data. An appropriate target for undergraduate student projects is more than the 30 tokens per cell minimum. (Sometimes you have to take what you can get, of course. If you are committed to working with spontaneous speech and your variable is not terribly frequent, you may have fewer tokens in a given cell. In this case, your generalisations should be very tentative.)

1.5 Ethical considerations of data collection

First of all, never record covertly! It is deceptive and high-handed, and it shows scant regard for other people's wants, and for their right to privacy. In some places, it is quite simply illegal.

The people you are recording must be informed about being recorded, and they should also be informed about what you are going to do with the recordings afterwards, so that they can give their informed consent to your work. Most universities or colleges in the West will want you to devise a form that explains the purpose of the research (in general terms, don't be too specific as you may bias your participants' responses), what the data will be used for and what will happen to the data after it has been collected. You should also indicate that the anonymity of people being recorded is guaranteed, that participation is voluntary (people can opt out at any stage), and you should allow and enable access to you, the researcher, and the research findings by at least giving your contact details at the end of the form. So prepare an information sheet for your participants and (in most cases) also a consent form that your participants can sign. Alternatively you can have all of this in just one document. Your department, school, or college may very well have a standard consent form available that you may be able to use. Especially if you're located in North America, you may have to submit your data collection plans, questionnaires, etc. to an institutionalised board first that will have to approve your research plans. Some general guidelines can be found on the web (see also exercises below):

1. American Anthropological Association Code of Ethics [*Extremely helpful in outlining rights and responsibilities for all parties in longer-term research, or research where the researcher is a member in good standing of the community they are examining.*]
2. British Association for Applied Linguistics – Recommendations on Good Practice [*Useful starting point for most sociolinguistic research.*]
3. British Psychological Society – Code of Conduct [*Well-suited for experiments, including those testing not only linguistic skills but other aspects of cognition and perception.*]
4. The Linguistic Society of America Ethics Statement [*Very useful as a basic, highly general, ethical framework for linguists of all subdisciplines.*]

Once you have thought about all of this, made the necessary decisions and have prepared all the material, you can finally start collecting your data!

2. DATA INTERPRETATION

2.1 The sociolinguistic variable

Once you have collected all your data, analysis starts. If your sociolinguistic analysis focuses on a set of particular linguistic items (rather than other sociolinguistic issues, such as language planning or attitudes), you will have given some thought to your selection of variables and variants before starting data collection. A variable can be described as an abstract representation of the source of variation. It is the main object of your investigation. A variable is represented by two or more variants (Meyerhoff 2006, Wolfram 1993).

What variable(s) you analyse depends on your research questions so it will most likely evolve out of previous research or personal observations and should also influence the way you collect data (e.g. by designing a word list that focuses on particular variables). This is why you should choose your (potential) variables before you collect your data; you can of course refine them during and after data collection. Previous studies on a particular variety (such as academic articles, dialect maps), personal observation of features, comments by speakers themselves, or even an informal pilot study of this variety can be very helpful in selecting variables.

Variables can be of a phonetic nature, e.g. variation of vowels in PRICE and MOUTH in Labov's study of Martha's Vineyard (Labov 1972), but they can also be of a syntactic or morphological nature, e.g. negation and third person singular-s, as in Nevalainen's historical, sociolinguistic study of language use and the factors of social status and gender in the Early Modern English period (Nevalainen 1999). Variables can also be of a lexical/ discourse nature, e.g. variation in the use of intensifiers in Ito and Tagliamonte (2003) and of lexical pairs in New Zealand English discussed in Meyerhoff and Niedzielski (2003).

It is very important to be aware of the envelope of variation in which a variable occurs, i.e. all and only the contexts where it can possibly occur. This is easier to circumscribe for phonological variables as we usually know when they could occur (e.g. the word *butter* can be realised with an intervocalic [t] or a glottal stop or an alveolar flap), but it is much harder for other types of variables. For example passive meaning can be realised in different ways, e.g. through the get-passive, the be-passive, or an active sentence (*Peter got hit by a car, Peter was hit by a car, A car hit Peter*): but are passive and active equivalents of a sentence really "the same" thing under the surface? (Many functional linguists would say they are not.) Which variants are you going to include and which ones will be excluded and why? What is the context of occurrence of certain variables anyway? Can their occurrence be predicted? If the occurrence of a variant can be reliably predicted (as for example the distribution of the linking r-sound in RP) then you want to set them aside and discuss those contexts separately: you can't analyse variation where there is no variation.

Defining the envelope of variation requires you to do some homework (what have other people said about this variable?) and also to apply critically the knowledge you gain as a researcher – the variety you are working on may be different. Dave Britain gives a good example of this with respect to (t)-glottaling, a common variant in British English. Most of the literature will tell you [t] and [ʔ] vary word finally (perhaps followed by a consonant or a vowel, and sometimes, though less frequently, when they are turn-final tokens), and there may be some mention of intervocalic contexts for words like *butter*. But in some British English dialects /t/ can be rendered as a glottal in many other contexts (e.g. before and after an /n/ or /l/ – *enter*, *alter*, *bottle*, *button*) and in words like *atlas* and *Gatwick*. In some East Anglian dialects it can even be a glottalised word initially. So you must draw on what you know from a range of sources to define the envelope of variation appropriately.

The difficulties of how to deal with variables other than phonological ones have been widely discussed in the literature, e.g. Lavandera (1978), Dines (1980), and some helpful guidelines for phonological, morphosyntactic and discourse variables are available, e.g. in Milroy and Gordon (2003) and Llamas, Mullany and Stockwell (2007).

Once you've identified the variable and its variants you will want to find out what determines speakers' choice of variants – the social and linguistic constraints of variation. Is this variation rooted in the linguistic system, or are there any social factors which influence variation such as age of speakers, their occupation, or gender? Determining the relationship between the distribution of variants and these linguistic or non-linguistic factors is the core of variation analysis.

2.2 To transcribe or not to transcribe?

You've got your data, you've made a decision on your variables. What next? In a best case scenario, you have plenty of time and funding and are able to transcribe all your data (or you may even have the money to pay somebody to do it for you). Being able to access transcriptions of all your data is the easiest way to analyse your corpus, and we highly recommend it. It takes about an hour to transcribe 10 to 15 minutes of recorded speech, depending on the quality of the recording. Unfortunately, time and money are often in short supply. In such a case you may have to resort to partial transcription or no transcription at all and only note selected tokens. The last two methods are particularly appropriate if you know exactly what you're looking for and are only interested in very specific linguistic items, e.g. the pronunciation of intervocalic (t). However, if your interest is of a qualitative nature and you may want to conduct a discourse analysis, or if you have a wider quantitative interest, you should make sure to transcribe all your data.

As for transcription conventions, it's a good idea to make use of a commonly used system, such as Gail Jefferson's, which is widely used in conversation analysis (most accessibly summarised in Atkinson and Heritage 1999). There is no need to use all existing transcription conventions and to be detailed in all respects (for example transcribing a noticeable breath or timing pauses to the tenths of a second). Transcribe what you think you need. If pause is not important for your study, just mark pauses in a very general way rather than timing them to the millisecond. Whatever you do, you should list your transcription conventions in the methods section of your essay or in the appendix, similarly to how Holmes & Schnurr (2006) and Kiesling (1997) have done. Due to space constraints, we cannot go into the politics of transcription here; consult Cameron (2001), Bucholtz (2000), or Preston (1985) if you want to find out more about how your choice of non-standard transcription conventions may influence the social perception of the speakers whose speech you have transcribed.

We strongly recommend that you consider the merits of using one of the freeware programmes that are available for making your transcriptions time-aligned to the recording. The advantages of having your transcription linked directly to sound are enormous. It's clearly helpful for phonetic variation not to be switching back and forth between sound files and transcription, but at all levels of linguistic structure, we benefit from staying as close as possible to what the speaker originally uttered. The best-known of the freeware packages are ELAN and Praat (ELAN 2009; Boersma and Weeninck 2009). ELAN and Praat run on PC, Mac and Linux operating systems. Both programmes also allow you more or less freedom to keep your coding of specific variants time-aligned (see 2.3). ELAN works successfully for multi-party conversations and also allows video input. Both need .wav file input, so if you plan to use them you should record interviews and conversation as .wav, and not, for instance, .mp3.

In partial transcription, you only transcribe the sentences or sections in which your variable occurs, the speaker and the time point at which it occurred. This may be just a sentence in the case of intervocalic (t), or a thematically coherent discourse unit if you're looking at discourse features or syntactic variables, as topic and discourse function may influence the use of your variable. In fact, being able to analyse larger chunks of discourse may also be helpful when looking at phonological variables, e.g. if you're interested in stylistic variation. This point highlights the disadvantages of partial transcription: it restricts your analysis as you have to identify potential factors ahead of time.

This is even more the case if you don't transcribe at all and only note how certain variables are realised. For example, in the case of intervocalic (t), you may just listen to a recording and note its pronunciation as either [t], glottal stop, flap or unclear. As a minimum, you should also write down the word in which your variable occurred, the time at which it occurred and who used it. While this is a very time-efficient method, its shortcomings for further analysis are obvious.

2.3 Coding and extracting your data for quantitative analysis

If you have transcribed all of your data, you should now go through the transcripts and code for the variables you're interested in, i.e. you either read your transcripts and mark up those linguistic items you're investigating in a system that makes sense to you, or if you've compiled a searchable corpus, you could just run a search for a particular linguistic item. As noted, software such as ELAN and Praat make it increasingly straightforward to store transcriptions that are still linked to and aligned with the sound recording. This is great because it means you can listen to examples that you find, when your text-based search finds them. This increases your coding's reliability.

Whatever you do, you should end up with data that you should store in some kind of data spreadsheet to facilitate analysis, your next step. This will allow you to observe the distribution of a particular variant more clearly. It will also enable you to see the effect of particular factors on this variable if you run a statistical analysis. Excel is often used for this purpose as it also enables simple statistic analysis and can create graphs (which is very easy – try it, just click on 'insert', go to 'graph' or 'chart', select the type of graph you want and experiment with it a little). There are various ways to put your data into an Excel spreadsheet. If you've already counted up all your tokens and focus on a particular linguistic context, you may just put the information for every single speaker, like in Table 1.2. Put social factors into columns followed by the variables indicating how many tokens of each variant a particular speaker used; e.g. speaker one, a female in her

Table 1.2   Summary data extracted by speaker for (t) variable

Speaker	Sex	Age group	Intervocalic T	Intervocalic glottal stop	Unclear
001	Female	20–30	56	0	2
002	Female	30–40	20	10	1
003	Male	20–30	33	13	0

twenties, used 56 [t] tokens intervocalically, never used a glottal stop in this context and pronounced 2 tokens in a way that were impossible to categorise.

A set up like this will allow you to test for different social and linguistic factors and conduct a statistical analysis, such as a multivariate analysis which allows you to determine the factor contribution to the occurrence of a particular variant. Of course, such a set up wouldn't allow you to investigate possible linguistic factors in much depth using statistics alone as the information is listed per speaker. Alternatively, you may include more information in your spreadsheet and extract information for every single token like in Table 1.3. This will allow you to conduct a much more thorough statistical analysis and investigate a variety of different factors, such as tense, negation, agreement, class, etc., and their influence on the type of token used.

One of the statistical tools commonly used in variationist sociolinguistics is Goldvarb/VARBRUL which calculates the significance of each factor group for the variable (Sankoff et al. 2005). Many linguists prefer to use the R statistical analysis package, which allows researchers with more statistical training to conduct a wider range of tests than Goldvarb does. Goldvarb has one advantage over R in providing a very user-friendly interface and presents results in quite transparent terms. Other statistical packages, such as SPSS, can of course also be used. Alternatively, if you only want a very rough idea of how significant your data is, you could conduct a chi-square test by calculating the test statistic yourself or using one of the many calculators available online.

When writing up your analysis and presenting your data, think about how you want to do this. Tables 1.2 and 1.3 are good ways to organise raw data for statistical analysis, but (usually) *not* for presenting your data in a paper. Put your data into tables and graphs that are visually organised and digested. Don't organise them by informant number but by factors that you want to focus on in your analysis (e.g. age or gender) and their total numbers, percentages or normalised frequencies. Consult a research article of your choice to see how this is done.

2.4 Analysing and interpreting the data

If you are interested in a quantitative analysis of your data, you should definitely conduct a statistical analysis, as this will tell you what factors significantly influence the distribution of your variants, which you can then present in your results and discussion section before developing an argument of what your results may mean. It is beyond the scope of a general introduction like this to teach you how to choose and use appropriate statistical tests in analysing your work – you should seek out specialist guides if this is your interest, for example Paolillo (2001).

Table 1.3 Data extraction by token for existential constructions in Bequia English. (Tokens are coded for a range of unique linguistic and social factors.)

Negation	Tense	Subject	Verb	Agreement	Community	Sex	Recording number	Unique speaker ID code	Line	Token
0	s	i	H	v	M	f	002	2	1808	you know, it HAD some Frangipani trees by the rectory there
0	S	i	H	v	M	f	002	2	1811	Right between f- between the church and the wall it HAD a lot of ant,
0	S	o	H	v	M	f	002	2	1220	That's when you was growing up; HAD a lot of land and I mean that was our staple crop
0	P	i	H	g	L	f	318	>	368	Spelling, all them, dictation, it HAVE more they call me- take me from the work here
0	S	t	B	s	L	f	317	+	515	so, and when I go up there WAS more work
0	P	i	H	l	L	f	317	+	439	because it HAS other thing.
										we were living in what you call bad days.
0	P	t	B	s	P	m	034	H	34	But-but now there IS more light and so on
0	p	t	B	p	P	m	034	H	76	there IS people in Bequia they're very friendly people,
N	P	i	H	v	H	f	004	4	1737	I was making my third child when that Jack Spania did sting me, because it didn't HAVE no road
0	S	i	G	v	H	f	006	6	2142	I see one day a girl come down by the bayside in the harbour, it GOT some old nail in the sea, and that nail run right up in she foot

If your interest is of a qualitative nature (e.g. you want to know how narratives are used to express speaker identities), you will read through your transcripts looking out for anything that strikes you as noteworthy in respect to your research question. Present your results and think about what your results may mean – what the story is behind your results. Then write your discussion or conclusion section and tell your reader how to interpret your results. Since every data set is different, the stories tend to vary as well. We can't tell you how to interpret your own data but you can and should practise interpreting a piece of data before you work on your own (see exercises).

2.5 Writing up your research

When writing up your research you will most likely divide your paper into the following sections: introduction, literature review, methods and tools, which should cover about one third of your paper, and results, discussion, and conclusion, which should cover the remaining two thirds. The sections may overlap to a greater or lesser extent but should all recognisably be present. Consult Swales and Feak (2004) if you want to find out more about conventions of academic writing.

The introduction and literature review sections introduce and motivate your research and provide some needed background information for the study. In your methods section, you should reflect on methods used, questionnaire design, choice of informants, ethical issues and methodological problems. It is extremely important for the readers to know what methods the study is based on, and why you made certain choices as opposed to others. Don't leave all your write-up to the very end – instead, write your introduction and literature review while researching the literature, write the methods section while designing your research tools, etc.

Your results and discussion section(s) present and discuss your results, and in your conclusion section you should try to extrapolate from your study. You should pull all the different strings together here. First summarise your most important findings and relate them to previous arguments. Answer all the questions you raised earlier and provide an explanation for your results while ruling out others. Make sure to present evidence in favour of your interpretation. This is also the place to address objections that other scholars may have towards your research. Be realistic and honest. Most importantly, link your own results and explanations to other research and give an indication of potential future research. Then take a step back and tell the reader what your results mean in the big scheme of things. How do your results, previous research and your explanation go together? What does it all mean? Where does this particular line of research stand now after you've conducted your study?

We started this paper with a question ('how to start?') and we finish with a question ('where are you now?'). Hopefully, in between these two questions we've provided you with enough information to enable you to start finding some answers, and – most importantly – to have fun while doing it!

REFERENCES AND FURTHER READING

American Anthropological Association Code of Ethics (1998) http://www.aaanet.org/committees/ethics/ethcode.htm. Accessed 4 April 2009.

Atkinson, J. Maxwell and John Heritage (1999) Jefferson's transcript notation. In Adam Jaworski and Nikolas Coupland (eds) *The Discourse Reader*. London and New York: Routledge, 158–166.

Boersma, Paul and David Weeninck (2009) Praat: Doing phonetics by computer, version 5.1.20. http://www.fon.hum.uva.nl/praat/. Accessed 6 November 2009.

Bucholtz, Mary (2000) The politics of transcription. *Journal of Pragmatics* 32: 1439–1465.

Cameron, Deborah (2001) *Working with Spoken Discourse*. London: Sage.

De Vaus, David (2002) *Surveys in Social Research*. 5th Ed. London: Routledge.

Dines, Elizabeth R. (1980) Variation in discourse – "and stuff like that." *Language in Society* 9: 13–31.

Eckert, Penelope (1998) Vowels and nail polish: the emergence of linguistic style in the preadolescent heterosexual marketplace. In Nancy Warner et al. (eds) *Proceedings of the 1996 Berkeley Women and Language Conference*. Berkeley: Berkeley Women and Language Group, 183–190.

ELAN: Language archiving technology, version 3.8.0 (2009) http://www.lat-mpi.eu/tools/elan/. Accessed 6 November 2009.

Fry, D. B. (1947) The frequency of occurrence of speech sounds in Southern English. *Archives Néerlandaises de Phonétique Expérimentales* 20: 103–106.

Holmes, Janet and Stephanie Schnurr (2006) 'Doing femininity' at work: more than just relational practice. *Journal of Sociolinguistics* 10: 31–51.

Ito, Rika and Sali Tagliamonte (2003) *Well* weird, *right* dodgy, *very* strange, *really* cool: layering and recycling in English intensifiers. *Language in Society* 32: 257–279.

Johnstone, Barbara (2000) *Qualitative Methods in Sociolinguistics*. New York and Oxford: Oxford University Press.

Kiesling, Scott Fabius (1997) Power and the language of men. In Ulrike Hanna Meinhof and Sally Johnson (eds) *Language and Masculinity*. Oxford: Blackwell, 65–85.

Labov, William (1966) *The Social Stratification of English in New York City*. Washington, DC: Center for Applied Linguistics.

Labov, William (1972) The social motivation of a sound change. In William Labov *Sociolinguistic Patterns*. Philadelphia: University of Pennsylvania Press, 1–42.

Lavandera, Beatriz R. (1978). Where does the sociolinguistic variable stop? *Language in Society* 7: 171–82.

Llamas, Carmen, Louise Mullany and Peter Stockwell (eds) (2007) *The Routledge Companion to Socio-linguistics*. London and New York: Routledge.

Meyerhoff, Miriam and Nancy Niedzielski (2003) The globalisation of vernacular variation. *Journal of Sociolinguistics* 7: 534–555.

Meyerhoff, Miriam (2006) *Introducing Sociolinguistics*. London and New York: Routledge.

Meyerhoff, Miriam and James A. Walker (2007) The persistence of variation in individual grammars: copula absence in 'urban sojourners' and their stay-at-home peers, Bequia (St Vincent and the Grenadines). *Journal of Sociolinguistics* 11: 346–366.

Milroy, Lesley and Matthew Gordon (2003) *Sociolinguistics: Method and Interpretation*. Malden and Oxford: Blackwell.

Milroy, Leslie and James Milroy (1992) Social network and social class: toward an integrated sociolinguistic model. *Language in Society* 21: 1–26.

Nevalainen, Terttu (1999) Making the best of 'bad' data. *Neuphilologische Mitteilungen* 100: 499–533.

Paolillo, John C. (2001) *Analyzing Linguistic Variation: Statistical Models and Methods*. Chicago: Center for the Study of Language and Information.

Preston, Dennis (1985) The Li'l Abner syndrome: written representations of speech. *American Speech* 60: 328–336.

Purnell, Thomas, William Idsardi and John Baugh (1999) Perceptual and phonetic experiments on American English dialect identification. *Journal of Language and Social Psychology* 18: 10–30.

Sankoff David, Sali A. Tagliamonte and Eric Smith (2005) Goldvarb X: a multivariate analysis application. Freeware accessible at http://individual.utoronto.ca/tagliamonte/Goldvarb/GV_index.htm.

Starks, Donna and Zita McRobbie-Utasi (2001) Collecting sociolinguistic data: some typical and some not so typical approaches. *New Zealand Sociology Journal* 16: 79–92.

Swales, John M. and Christine B. Feak (2004) *Academic Writing for Graduate Students, Second Edition: Essential Tasks and Skills*. Ann Arbor: University of Michigan Press.

Tagliamonte, Sali A. (2006) *Analysing Sociolinguistic Variation*. Cambridge: Cambridge University Press.

Trudgill, Peter (1988) Norwich revisited: recent linguistic changes in an English urban dialect. *English World Wide* 9: 33–49.

Walker, James A. (2010) *Variation in Linguistic Systems*. London and New York: Routledge.

Walker, James A. and Miriam Meyerhoff (2006) Zero copula in the Eastern Caribbean: evidence from Bequia. *American Speech* 81: 146–163.

Wolfram, Walt (1993) Identifying and interpreting variables. In Dennis R. Preston et al. (eds) *American Dialect Research*. Amsterdam: John Benjamins, 193–221.

Zhang, Qing (2005) A Chinese yuppie in Beijing: phonological variation and the construction of a new professional identity. *Language in Society* 34: 431–499.

EXERCISES

exercise 1

Questionnaire design

Consider the questionnaire below and note some good and bad things about it. How would you improve it? It was designed with the following question in mind: Does the high use of English in women's magazines in Germany influence the readers' use of English words when speaking German? The questionnaire was originally in German and was distributed only to women. The copy below is a translation.

Questionnaire

> Hello! I am doing a study on linguistic attitudes and the use of the German language amongst the young. Please fill in this questionnaire as honestly as possible. All responses will remain anonymous. Thank you for your time.

1. How old are you? ____
2. Do you sometimes read one of these magazines: Elle, Cosmopolitan, Freundin, Brigitte? If yes, please circle which one(s).

3. Do you use the following words (when speaking German)? Please mark the box which corresponds to your response. Example:

English loanword	Always	Often	Sometimes	Never
Cool		X		
Happy				
Trendy				
Girly				
Loser				
Relax				
Boss				
News				
Okay				
Kids				

4. Please circle all words that fit:

   a) English words are considered to be:
       Trendy / unwelcome / cool / lazy / easy / stupid / other (please specify)
   b) The German language is:
       Distinguished / old / precise / old fashioned / beautiful / pure / other (please specify)
   c) German culture is:
       Important / superficial / rich / superior / old fashioned / diverse / interesting / other (please specify)
   d) American culture is:
       Important / superficial / rich / superior / cool / unwelcome / interesting / omnipresent / crude / other (please specify)

5.   For each statement, please mark the box which best reflects your opinion.

	Strongly agree	Agree	Unsure	Disagree	Strongly disagree
English is the language of the future.					
Borrowing English words into German is harmful to German.					
We should be open to all languages and cultures.					
Welcoming borrowings into German can evolve.					
Magazines should make an effort to avoid borrowings.					
English words make German more modern.					

6.   In your opinion, why do magazines use English borrowings?

_____

_____

_____

If you have any other comments with regard to this questionnaire, please write them on the back of this page. Thank you for your help!

Sampling technique

What sampling technique would you use for the general representation of a speech community, for example of Manchester, England? What sampling technique would you use if you were particularly interested in certain members of a speech community, for example male adolescents from Eastern Europe in Manchester? And what sampling technique would you use for approaches to variation that are of a more qualitative nature or are focusing on language style, for example how male adolescents from Eastern Europe in Manchester express and negotiate masculinity in single and mixed-sex conversations?

exercise 2

Data collection

Group A

You want to investigate the effects of language contact in a large multicultural city where you live. You want to find out about the ways in which people in immigrant communities use certain linguistic features. You will concentrate on a variety of linguistic features to analyse this issue in several immigrant communities. You have four months to collect the data and have been awarded research money that covers your living expenses and initial travel costs. You also have £ 500/$1000 for additional research expenses at your disposal.

Group B

You want to investigate how language is used among residents in a residential home for elderly people. You want to find out how linguistic variation is used to construct and express social identities, you are particularly interested in the networks, groupings and social categories residents are part of and construct for themselves in this particular community. You will concentrate on a variety of linguistic features to analyse this issue. You have four months to collect the data and have been awarded research money that covers your living expenses and initial travel costs. You also have £ 500/$1000 for additional research expenses at your disposal.

Both groups discuss the following questions:

1. What data do you want to collect (activity type, linguistic variables)?
2. What social factors do you want to investigate?
3. How much data do you need from how many speakers? Will you be needing a data grid? If so, design one.
4. How could you gain access to informants and enter the community?
5. What sampling technique(s) will you be using?
6. Will you be recording 'naturally occurring' data or will you be conducting interviews, using word lists, reading passages, question & answer sessions, story telling, map tasks, etc.?

Ethics

Read these excerpts from the code of ethics of the American Anthropological Association (http://www.aaanet.org/committees/ethics/ethcode.htm). Why and under what circumstances may an informed consent form not be appropriate? Discuss.

Anthropological researchers should obtain in advance the informed consent of persons being studied, providing information, owning or controlling access to material being studied, or otherwise be identified as having interests which might be impacted by the research. It is understood that the degree and breadth of informed consent required will depend on the nature of the project and may be affected by requirements of other codes, laws, and ethics of the country or community in which the research is pursued. Further, it is understood that the informed consent process is dynamic and continuous; the process should be initiated in the project design and continue through implementation by way of dialogue and negotiation with those studied. Researchers are responsible for identifying and complying with the various informed consent codes, laws and regulations affecting their projects. Informed consent, for the purposes of this code, does not necessarily imply or require a particular written or signed form. It is the quality of the consent, not the format, that is relevant. [. . .]

Anthropological researchers who have developed close and enduring relationships (i.e., covenantal relationships) with either individual persons providing information or with hosts must adhere to the obligations of openness and informed consent, while carefully and respectfully negotiating the limits of the relationship. While anthropologists may gain personally from their work, they must not exploit individuals, groups, animals, or cultural or biological materials. They should recognize their debt to the societies in which they work and their obligation to reciprocate with people studied in appropriate ways.

Data interpretation

Consider the following transcriptions of Bequia Creole recorded by Miriam Meyerhoff, James Walker and Jack Sidnell in 2003–05 (Walker & Meyerhoff 2006, Meyerhoff & Walker 2007, with thanks to Agata Daleszyńska). [Bequia is an island in the Eastern Caribbean. It is part of St Vincent and the Grenadines.]

Group A

Which features in the extracts would be amenable to quantitative analysis? Identify as many potential variables as you can. State what you believe the important variants are, and why.

Then, choose a variable and try to extract all of its variants into an Excel spreadsheet and code your tokens for three selected factor groups. What kinds of features would you expect to investigate as potential constraints on the variables? How could you imagine making your findings about these variables relevant to linguistic theory?

Group B

What kinds of information do these recordings offer for the sociolinguist who is more interested in qualitative analysis? Where might you go next to find supplementary sources of data?

How might this information inform debates about, and questions in, linguistic theory?

Paget Farm, 007, Male, 73 years old. [Speakers 2 and 3 are teenage interviewers.]

[2]   Do you think that everybody in Bequia speaks the same? Like the- the language, like Paget-Farm, is the same, like Hamilton, like-

[3]   Mt-Pleasant

[2]   Mt-Pleasant, Lower-Bay

[007]   No, everybody have different, like in- in different village, because look at Mt-Pleasant. They entirely has a different speech altogether.

[2]   You remember black people couldn't go up there?

[3]   You could remember those days?

[007]   Yes they use to stone you.

[2]   Yeah, is only now,

[007]   Is only now you know,

[3]   only now yeah, most of them deal with black people now.

[007]   No, uh-huh. Them have uh never love black people, yes they use to call them what? I forget they had a name they use to call uh "Nigger" yeah, say I don't. If you go to a dance

and you hold one of them. They say "let me go I don't- I don't fight with black people let me go!" (laughing)

[2]   They does talk so in truth.

[007]   Yeah, there was a, well they- from what I learned, these people came from uh, Irish, they are Irish people,

[2]   and Portuguese.

[007]   They- according to The-Brief-History-of-Saint-Vincent, they was sent to Barbados as Irish bond slaves

[2]   Ok

[007]   And uh, some broke away from Barbados and live in Dorcetshire-Hill in Saint-Vincent, and then I guess what break away from Dorcetshire-Hill, those, some of what came to Mt-Pleasant. So that is how we get them here.

[2]   So, you- when you go to Saint-Vincent, for example, when you go over there, do people just look at- hear you talking or something and tell you well, "you are Bequia person".

[007]   Well, they would know because, why they would know you from Bequia, is because uh when you go to Saint-Vincent long time ago you use to go in a fishing boat, because every weekend you will go to Saint-Vincent to sell corned fish, well at least to market you fish and then after marketing the fish now, you would uh buy provision, you will, well you had to say is was an- like an exchange. You sell your fish and then you buy what's they selling.

[2]   Ok

[007]   So then they would know you from Bequia, and if you from Canouan, because the people down had a different accent.

[2]   I notice sometimes when you go to Saint-Vincent you don't even have to open your mouth for people to know.

[2]   That you from Bequia

[3]   They believe that- ok, Bequia only have clear people brown skin nice face

[007]   Well if you know families in Bequia like me, if- if I look at you, I could tell you which family you from (laughing)

Mount Pleasant, 303, Male 64 years old. [Speakers 2 and 3 are mother and daughter interviewers.]

[3]   Some people have left Bequia, (inc) what made you stay?

[303]   What made me stay? Because I love it. I born here and I love it. Sixty-four years. I love it still, and still continuing to love.

[3]   Nothing never really happen that made you feel like, you know, going away? Moving away?

[303]   No, not, at one time I had intention, but when I really study what it is.

[2]   Uh-huh.

[303]   I say it don't make sense. To go in the cold to- to punish yourself in the cold and you could live here in the same and nice happy life way you going in the cold to do?

[2]   Yeah.

[303]   If you young, fine, you get a little bit of experience out there of what going on, but in them time who went away stayed away, they never came back.

[2]   Okay.

[303]   My aunt (Wynn), she live a hundred-and-seven years and she ne- once she came back that I know of. My uncle went away before my father born, he live and died, my father died and he ain't know- they ain't know each other.

[303]   Just because of a whipping from my- my grandfather. Wa- wa- was Uncle-O. Put a flogging on him down there and he tell him when he go away he will never come back.

[2]   Huh.

[303]   He never did come back. And he live close to a hundred too.

[2]   Okay.

[303]   All of my aunts (inc) that went away close to a hundred they never-

[2]   So uh is um (inc) a long life span in the family?

[303]   Yes, our family- the [name] family is a widespread, but they intermixing different- maybe [other names] and ever- everything you inter- kinda, like a royal family.

[2]   So you never travel much outside um, the Caribbean (islands)

[303]   Well I round the islands Trinidad, up through the island, up to Guadeloupe, Barbados, but in- in the early stages you do different things for a living. You start out the one you didn't get through, you go the other until I came into the contracting field.

[2]   So uh contracting was you- was your um-

[303]   Carpentry was my-

[2]   What age you start doing that?

[303]   I start doing carp- well we started building scooters first, that was our transport, there was no- no pitch road in Bequia. One little piece been down by, from Mount-Pleasant corner down to Sunny-Carib gate that was the only pitch been in Bequia, first piece and we use to leave every day and down the road there with the scooters and when you get down there police behind you. You had to run. So it was no freedom for we really. Every time you try to do something to- to gain little experience you was tied back, so who got on to learn different to fishing you don't have to be a scholar to be a fisherman. Anybody could be a fisherman.

exercise 6

Data collection

Read the article "Vowels and nail polish: The emergence of linguistic style in the preadolescent heterosexual marketplace" by Penny Eckert (1998) and identify:

a.   data type

b.   sampling technique, and

c.   framework of analysis used in this study.

Why did Eckert use this type of analysis as opposed to others?

Which linguistic and extralinguistic variables does Eckert investigate and why did she choose these?

exercise 7

Working with spontaneous and natural data

Introduction and background

This exercise allows you to explore the methods needed in order to identify, analyse and start to write up a good assignment that focuses on features of naturally occurring speech. It is designed for collaborative work. The optimal size for a group is 2–4. The discussion you have with the other members in your group is expected to play a significant part in enabling you to get the most out of the exercise.

Step 1

Form a group of 2–4.

Step 2

Imagine you are answering the following essay topic. Read the topic and the data quickly. The guided analysis starts in Step 3.

Words like *oh* in spontaneous speech can be viewed in two very different ways. One view is that they are "fillers", that is, they fill pauses or breaks in conversation without adding any meaning. Another view is that they do contribute additional meaning, but this meaning isn't inherent to *oh,* rather it emerges in the dynamics of conversation. Consider the following four examples of the use of *oh* and evaluate the extent to which they seem to be fillers or they seem to add meaning to the conversation.

(1)

Lesley: Did you get my letter?
Mum: Uh, yes, thank you. I've answered it.
Lesley: Can you work it all out?
Mum: Oh yes, yes of course I could.
Lesley: What did you think then?

(2) Andrew and Ian are brothers.
Andrew: Is Mum there?
Ian: Why?
Andrew: I just want to talk to her.
Ian: Not coming home for tea now, lad?
Andrew: Eh?
Ian: You not thinking you're coming home for tea now, lad?
Andrew: Oh no. I just want to tell her something.

(3) Jan and Ann are friends.
Jan: She was upset because she'd waited such a long time. It's beautiful furniture, it really is lovely. It makes that room.
Ann: Is it like yours?
Jan: Oh no, it's far nicer than mine.

(4)

Interviewer: But if you get the go-ahead, are you sure you can fund the development out of your own resources?
Weinstock: Oh yes. There's no difficulty about that.

Step 3

Go back to the question topic. Highlight or extract terms that are central to your task. (These will probably be mostly verbs.)

Step 4

Assign one to two examples to each member of your group. Spend no more than three minutes deciding what you think *oh* is doing in your example(s). You will have to consider not only the turn *oh* is in, but the turn(s) immediately before (and in example 1, the turn after).

Step 5

Get some rough ideas from the group down on paper. "Rough" means it might be a short list of nouns and verbs.

Are there are any shared insights?

Are there major differences in what you conclude about the examples?

Step 6: Going from analysis to write up.

Now you have to think about how to transfer these insights into a well-structured essay. Below you will find a *Process Grid*. Work across the process grid with your group, jotting your ideas for

1. setting the scene (introduction, literature review, methods)
2. presenting the data
3. analysing the data

This should form the basis of an outline or first draft for your essay. Don't forget that it will also need a short conclusion that explicitly and conclusively addresses the essay question.

Setting the scene *Check your answers at Step 3.*	What's the point here? How will you explain the point? Is there relevant literature? What are your methods?	Where can you go to get this information? Jot some ideas here
Presenting the data *Check your answers at Step 4.*	What is the relevant data? Can you talk about *oh* on its own, or do you need to talk about more of the discourse?	Jot some ideas here.
Analysing the data *Check your answers at Step 5.*	What's interesting in your findings? Are there systematic general-isations across the examples? Are there thought-provoking contradictions? How will you explain/justify (a) the generalisations or contradictions, and (b) explain why they are systematic or thought-provoking?	Jot some ideas here.

Segment frequency within a language

In southern British English, an analysis of the frequency
of vowels and consonants in conversation produced the
following totals (after D. B. Fry, 1947).

Consonants		Vowels	
	%		%
n	7.58	ə	10.74
t	6.42	ɪ	8.33
d	5.14	e	2.97
s	4.81	aɪ	1.83
l	3.66	ʌ	1.75
ð	3.56	eɪ	1.71
r	3.51	iː	1.65
m	3.22	əʊ	1.51
k	3.09	a	1.45
w	2.81	ɒ	1.37
z	2.46	ɔː	1.24
v	2.00	uː	1.13
b	1.97	ʊ	0.86
f	1.79	ɑː	0.79
p	1.78	aʊ	0.61
h	1.46	ɜː	0.52
ŋ	1.15	ɪə	0.34
g	1.05	ɪə	0.21
ʃ	0.96	ɔɪ	1.14
j	0.88	ʊə	0.05
ʤ	0.60		
ʧ	0.41		
θ	0.37		
ʒ	0.10		

PART ONE

Identities, Style and Politeness

Editors' Introduction to Part One

THE CONCEPT OF IDENTITY has become an important explanatory framework in sociolinguistics, especially in research related to style and politeness. In both these areas, developments have taken place during the last couple of decades that show a shift from explaining style and politeness using more rigid theoretical frameworks (e.g. Labov's attention-to-speech for style and Brown and Levinson's conception of politeness) to describing these concepts as heavily influenced by local negotiations of speaker identities and to frameworks that incorporate such negotiation. Studies within these latter frameworks often result in more local analyses in line with the postmodern turn (see Coupland 2001 and Schilling-Estes 2003 on the speaker-design approach for style and Watts 2003 for developments in politeness research). In this section of the Reader, we have collected some articles which are particularly useful examples of various modes of analysis in research on style and politeness. The notion of identity is mobilised explicitly or implicitly in many of these articles to explore the complex interrelations between identity and style on the one hand and identity and politeness on the other hand.

Style has always been considered an important dimension of linguistic variation, conditioned by group social characteristics and individual identities and circumstances. This complex relationship between style and other factors creates a methodological and theoretical problem for which different solutions have been proposed. Labov's attention-to-speech approach, Bell's audience-design and the speaker-design approach (Coupland 2001, Schilling-Estes 2003) are usually taught in introductory sociolinguistics classes. Examples of the latter two are included in the Reader. We have not included an example of the attention-to-speech framework as it is such a foundational idea that it has influenced the very concept of the sociolinguistic interview, which often consists of different modes of data elicitation to record different speech styles (see Trudgill, Kerswill & Williams, Haeri, and Schleef & Meyerhoff, all this volume). Recent reformulations of the original framework can be found in Labov 2001.

The first article in this Reader summarises the main concepts of the audience-design framework and reworks one of its important weaknesses: the relationship between responsive and initiative modes of style-shifting, the latter of which Bell aims to explain with the concept of referee design. The concept of identity is also present in this framework and Bell dedicates a good deal of his article to explaining how linguistic features serve as identity markers. Hay, Jannedy and Mendoza-Denton frame their article in the research tradition of audience-design. They investigate the monophthongisation of /ay/ in the speech of Oprah Winfrey. They show that both lexical frequency as well as ethnicity of referee influence the phonetic realisation of this variable, demonstrating the importance of internal linguistic as well as external social factors.

Zhang's article is an example of the speaker-design approach. This approach breaks down the original dichotomy between social and stylistic variation, based on the idea that identity is dynamic and performatively expressed, and that identity projection includes both permanent aspects as well as fleeting aspects of one's identity (see Schilling-Estes 2003 for a more detailed description of this approach). Eckert (1998, in this Reader) is another excellent example of this approach and very nicely exemplifies the emergence of linguistic style in the preadolescent heterosexual marketplace at a school in California.

The two articles on politeness exemplify politeness phenomena in two different cultures and at two different points in the development of the research literature on politeness. Brown and Levinson's (1987) theory of politeness would have been another worthy reading to include here, since so much research is based on their ideas, but we decided not to include this since it is widely discussed in introductory textbooks. Politeness theory accounts for the redressing of affronts to face by face-threatening acts to addressees. It was formulated in the late seventies and has spurred a huge amount of empirical research. Laver's article makes reference to Brown and Levinson's early formulations of politeness theory and in particular relates linguistic routines to negative and positive politeness. This article, along with Laver's 1975 article on phatic communication, is a classic sociolinguistic reading on the important role that linguistic routines play in negotiating social relationships. In his article, Laver argues that linguistic routines are an important resource for polite behaviour as they reduce face threats. These routines are guided by a polite norm and deviation from it implicates an attempt to negotiate the social relationship between conversationalists. This focus on norms and their negotiation is also found in current research on politeness, such as Watts' (2003) work on politeness phenomena.

Ide considers politeness from a different perspective and challenges the validity of politeness theory as proposed by Brown and Levinson for non-Western cultures. She questions the universality of their principles from the perspective of languages with honorifics, in particular Japanese. She argues, for instance, that Brown and Levinson neglect the speaker's use of polite expressions when they are not based on interactional strategies, but instead are based on social convention, an aspect which she labels discernment.

Finally, Watts' 2003 publication, although not included here, represents another very important step in research on politeness. His framework breaks away from limitations of previous models and argues that commonsense notions of politeness and impoliteness, in particular how these notions are discursively constructed, should be the object of study in politeness research. He bases his model on Bourdieu's concept of social practice and argues that (im)polite utterances involve the conversationalists in a struggle for power. Here again, local analyses of language and speakers' negotiations of identity play a very important part, a theme that will be picked up in many subsequent contributions to the Reader, especially in Sections 5 and 6.

REFERENCES

Brown, Penelope and Stephen C. Levinson (1987) *Politeness: Some Universals in Language Usage*. Cambridge: Cambridge University Press.

Coupland, Nikolas (2001) Language, situation, and the relational self: theorizing dialect-style in sociolinguistics. In Penelope Eckert and John R. Rickford (eds) *Style and Sociolinguistic Variation*. Cambridge: Cambridge University Press, 185–210.

Labov, William (2001) The anatomy of style-shifting. In Penelope Eckert and John R. Rickford (eds) *Style and Sociolinguistic Variation*. Philadelphia: Cambridge University Press, 85–108.

Laver, John (1975) Communicative functions of phatic communion. In Adam Kendon, Richard M. Harris and Mary Ritchie Key (eds) *Organization of Behavior in Face-to-Face Interaction*. The Hague: Mouton, 215–37.

Schilling-Estes, Natalie (2003) Investigating stylistic variation. In J. K. Chambers, Peter Trudgill and Natalie Schilling-Estes (eds) *Handbook of Language Variation and Change*. Oxford: Blackwell, 375–401.

Watts, Richard J. (2003) *Politeness*. Cambridge: Cambridge University Press.

FURTHER READING

Bell, Allan (1984) Language style as audience design. *Language in Society* 13: 145–204.

Bell, Allan (1999) Styling the other to define the self: a study in New Zealand identity making. *Journal of Sociolinguistics* 3: 523–41.

Coupland, Nikolas (1980) Style shifting in a Cardiff work setting. *Language in Society* 9: 1–12.

Coupland, Nikolas (1984) Accommodation at work: some phonological data and their implications. *International Journal of the Sociology of Language* 46: 49–70.

Coupland, Nikolas (1985) 'Hark, hark the lark': social motivations for phonological style-shifting. *Language and Communication* 5: 153–72.

Eckert, Penelope and John R. Rickford (2001) (eds) *Style and Sociolinguistic Variation*. Cambridge: Cambridge University Press.

Guendouzi, Jackie (2004) 'She's very slim': talking about body-size in all-female interactions. *Journal of Pragmatics* 36: 1635–653.

Holmes, Janet (1995) *Women, Men and Politeness*. London: Longman.

Mills, Sara (2003) *Gender and Politeness*. Cambridge: Cambridge University Press.

Rickford, John R. and Faye McNair-Knox (1994) Addressee- and topic-influenced style shift. In Douglas Biber and Edward Finegan (eds) *Sociolinguistic Perspectives on Register*. Oxford and New York: Oxford University Press, 235–76.

Schilling-Estes, Natalie (1999) Situated ethnicities: constructing and reconstructing identity in the sociolinguistic interview. *University of Pennsylvania Working Papers in Linguistics* 6: 137–51.

Sifianou, Maria (1993) *Politeness Phenomena in England and Greece: A Cross-cultural Perspective*. Oxford: Oxford University Press.

Ting-Toomey, Stella (ed.) (1994) *The Challenge of Facework: Cross-cultural and Interpersonal Issues*. Albany: State University of New York Press.

Chapter 2

Allan Bell

BACK IN STYLE: REWORKING AUDIENCE DESIGN[1]

1. INTRODUCTION

I TAKE THE SOCIOLINGUIST'S core question about language style to be this:

Why did **this speaker** say it **this way** on **this occasion**?

There are three points to be made about such a catchline: first, the sociolinguist's ultimate interest in examining style is the *why* question – a search for explanations. The search for explanation presupposes a search for – and the existence of – regularities, of patterns. Secondly, the question implies an alternative, a choice – a "*that* way" which could have been chosen instead of a "this way." It locates linguistic style in language difference (see Irvine, 2001). Thirdly, the context of style is a *speaker* – a first person, an I, an ego, an identity or identities – together with the *situation* she or he is in – however we may believe that situation subsists or is defined, either theoretically or specifically.

The audience design framework (Bell 1984) had its genesis twenty-something years ago when I looked for an explanation for the style-shift I was finding in [. . .] the language of radio news in Auckland, New Zealand (Bell 1977). The organization of New Zealand public broadcasting[2] meant that two of the radio stations I was recording originated in the same suite of studios, with the same individual newsreaders heard on both radio networks. It was in effect a natural matched guise situation (Lambert 1967). Station YA was New Zealand's "National Radio," which has a higher status audience than the local community station ZB (see Bell 1991 for detail).

I examined a number of phonological and syntactic variables, including intervocalic /t/ voicing. In NZ English, intervocalic /t/ can be realized as an alveolar voiced flap or

Source: Bell, Allan (2001) Back in style: reworking audience design. In Penelope Eckert and John R. Rickford (eds) *Style and Sociolinguistic Variation*. Cambridge: Cambridge University Press, 139–169.

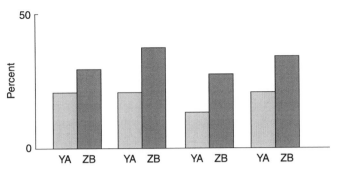

Figure 2.1 Percentage of intervocalic /t/ voicing by four newsreaders on two New Zealand radio stations, YA and ZB (from Bell 1984).

stop instead of as a voiceless stop, making words such as *writer* and *better* sound like *rider* and *bedder*. [. . .] Figure 2.1 shows the percentage of intervocalic /t/ voicing for four newsreaders I recorded on both these stations.

The newsreaders shifted on average 20 [percentage points] in each linguistic environment between stations YA and ZB. Single newsreaders heard on two different stations showed a consistent ability to make considerable style-shifts to suit the audience. These switches between stations were at times made in a very short space of time. At off-peak hours a single newsreader might alternate between YA and ZB news with as little as ten minutes between bulletins on the different stations.

Why then the shifts? There is after all just one individual speaker producing two divergent styles. The institution is the same in both cases. The topic mix of the news is similar (in some cases, even the same scripted news items are read out on both stations). The studio setting is identical. And there is no reason to suppose that the amount of attention paid to speech is being systematically varied. Of all the factors we might suggest as possible influences on these shifts in news language style, only the audience correlated with the shifts evident here.

Looking beyond my study, I began to see that the same regularities which were writ large in my own media-originated data were operating in face-to-face communication. Later I discovered that outside sociolinguistics this idea was not quite new, when in the closing stages of the doctoral work I encountered speech accommodation theory (Giles and Powesland 1975) and benefited from the insights Howard Giles had recently been drawing about style from a social psychological perspective. Later I came to call my approach "audience design." The label was of course not new either – it derived from Sacks, Schegloff, and Jefferson's "recipient design" (1974) by way of Clark (e.g. Clark and Carlson 1982).

2. THE GIST OF AUDIENCE DESIGN

I will summarize what I take to be the main points of the audience design framework [. . .]. At this stage I will not critique the framework, but will flag the points to which I will return for later reworking.[3]

[. . .] [O]ver a dozen years down the track, I find myself still in substantial agreement with what I wrote then – with one main exception, which I shall return to below. [. . .] The gist of audience design can be summarized in the following points.

1: Style is what an individual speaker does with a language in relation to other people

This is the basic tenet of audience design – that style is oriented to people rather than to mechanisms or functions. Style focuses on the person. It is essentially a social thing. It marks inter-personal and inter-group relations. It is interactive – and active. [. . .] [T]his is really a premise rather than a hypothesis. Our view of style is ultimately derived from our view of the nature of personhood. Behind audience design lies a strong, general claim that the character of (intra-speaker) style-shift derives at an underlying level from the nature of (inter-speaker) language differences between people. It is a reflex of inter-speaker variation.

2: Style derives its meaning from the association of linguistic features with particular social groups

The social evaluation of the group is transferred to the linguistic features associated with the group. So style derives from inter-group language variation by way of social evaluation [. . .]. This has been noted at least since Ferguson and Gumperz (1960). Evaluation of a linguistic variable and style-shift of that variable are reciprocal, as Labov (1972) demonstrated. Evaluation is always associated with style-shift, and style-shift with evaluation. These findings must be accounted for in a theory of style.

Stylistic meaning therefore has a normative basis. A particular style is normally associated with a particular group or situation, and therefore carries with it the flavor of those associations (cf. Myers-Scotton's 1993 "markedness model" of inter-lingual code-switching).

[. . .]

3: Speakers design their style primarily for and in response to their audience

This is the heart of audience design. Style shift occurs primarily in response to a change in the speaker's audience. Audience design is generally manifested in a speaker shifting her style to be more like that of the person she is talking to – this is "convergence" in the terms of the Speech/Communication Accommodation Theory developed by Giles and associates (e.g. Giles and Powesland 1975, Coupland et al. 1988). Rickford and McNair-Knox's exemplary study of "Foxy" (1994) provides good supporting socio-linguistic evidence for this assertion.

Response is the primary mode of style-shift (Figure 2.2) Style is a responsive phenomenon, but it is actively so, not passively. [. . .] For someone to speak is to respond and be responded to: "An essential (constitutive) marker of the utterance is its quality of being directed to someone, its *addressivity*" ([Bakhtin] 1986:95).

I regard audience design, then, as part of a dialogic theory of language. [. . .] This is why it is entirely natural that there should be a link between stylistic and inter-speaker differences. Dialogue is the natural instantiation of language. We should no more conceive of language without audience than of language without speaker.

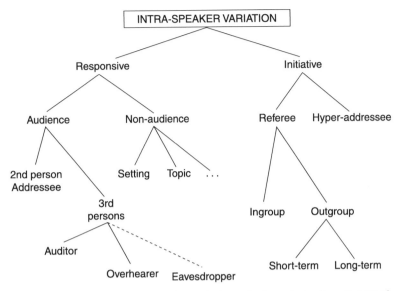

Figure 2.2   Style as response and initiative: audience design and referee design (from Bell 1984).

4: Audience design applies to all codes and levels of a language repertoire, monolingual and multilingual

Audience design does not refer only to style-shift. Within a language, it involves features such as choice of personal pronouns or address terms (Brown and Gilman 1960, Ervin-Tripp 1972), politeness strategies (Brown and Levinson 1987), use of pragmatic particles (Holmes 1995), as well as quantitative style-shift (Coupland 1980, 1984).

Audience design applies to all codes and repertoires within a speech community, including the switch from one complete language to another in bilingual situations (Gal 1979, Dorian 1981). It has long been recognized that the processes which make a monolingual shift styles are the same as those which make a bilingual switch languages (e.g. Gumperz 1967). Any theory of style needs to encompass both monolingual and multilingual repertoires – that is, all the shifts a speaker may make within her linguistic repertoire.

5: Variation on the style dimension within the speech of a single speaker derives from and echoes the variation which exists between speakers on the "social" dimension

This is the Style Axiom (Bell 1984:151). [. . .] The axiom is meant to apply both diachronically and synchronically. That is, it refers both to the historical origins of styles, and to the ongoing basis on which styles may be said to carry social meaning. [. . .]

The Style Axiom encapsulates the now often-noted fact that the same linguistic variables operate simultaneously on both social and stylistic dimensions, so that for one isolated variable it may be difficult to distinguish a "casual salesman from a careful pipefitter," in Labov's well-turned phrase (1972:240). It also reflects the quantitative relationship of the social and stylistic dimensions – that the range of style variation is less than the range of inter-speaker variation (cf. Preston 1991). But this is not just a quantitative relation without independent, causal motivation [. . .]. Social evaluation is the engine which links the two.

Audience design is therefore a strategy by which speakers draw on the range of linguistic resources available in their speech community to respond to different kinds of audiences. [. . .] [Speakers] are very active in exploiting the resources of their speech community, as I shall argue below.

These differences are not just in terms of social class, but also of gender, ethnicity, age, etc. If a linguistic feature or pattern is used differently by speakers of different gender or ethnicity, then it will usually be used differently *to* those people as listeners. We can see this in the morphological and syntactic variables analyzed in Rickford and McNair-Knox (1994), and at the pragmatic level of language in the fact that the same groups both receive and give most compliments and apologies (Holmes 1995).

6: Speakers have a fine-grained ability to design their style for a range of different addressees, as well as for other audience members

These are the classic findings of the accommodation model. At its essence, speech accommodation theory proposed that speakers accommodate their speech style to their hearers in order to win approval (Giles and Powesland 1975). The theory was extensively developed, expanded, and revised during the 1980s (e.g. Thakerar, Giles, and Cheshire 1982, Coupland et al. 1988). [. . .] [A]nd we can compare with Youssef's study (1993) on the role of auditors and overhearers in affecting a speaker's style.

7: Style-shifting according to topic or setting derives its meaning and direction of shift from the underlying association of topics or settings with typical audience members

The hypothesis that shifts according to topic echo shifts according to audience [. . .] [is] the foundation of Fishman's proposal (e.g. 1972) of domains as an integrative concept for style-shift or language switch, and Rickford and McNair-Knox (1994) found some supporting data in their study. The evidence is, however, not clear, nor is it obvious whether the appeal to an audience association is helpful or necessary. However, this kind of association between topic types and audience types has been widely noted including for example by Finegan and Biber (1994, 2001). The common character of the shifts invites a common explanation in terms of either audience or discoursal function.

8: As well as the "responsive" dimension of style, there is the "initiative" dimension (Figure 2.2) where the style-shift itself initiates *a change in the situation rather than* resulting from *such a change*

Sociolinguists have drawn attention to this distinction at least since Blom and Gumperz (1972) coined the terms "situational" and "metaphorical" switching.[4] In situational switching there is a regular association between language and social situation. These situational switches reflect the speech community's norms of what is appropriate speech for certain audiences. Initiative style trades on such regular associations, infusing the flavor of one setting into a different context. Here language becomes an independent variable which itself shapes the situation.

In initiative style-shift, the individual speaker creatively uses language resources often from beyond the immediate speech community, such as distant dialects, or stretches those resources in novel directions. [. . .] [I]t usually draws on existing if distant resources and remakes them – for instance using other dialects, whether social or geographic, other languages, or earlier forms of the user's own language.

The relationship between the responsive and initiative modes of style-shift is, however, one of the principles I will rework below.

9: Initiative style-shifts are in essence "referee design," by which the linguistic features associated with a reference group can be used to express identification with that group

Initiative style-shifts derive their force and their direction of shift from their underlying association with classes of persons or groups. They focus on an often-absent reference group – for example by adopting a non-native accent – rather than the present addressee. Referees are third persons not usually present at an interaction but possessing such salience for a speaker that they influence style even in their absence.

Initiative style-shift is essentially a redefinition by speakers of their own identity in relation to their audience. The baseline from which initiative shifts operate is the style normally designed for a particular kind of addressee. Examples of referee design include the use of non-native dialects in television commercials (Bell 1990, 1992); [. . . and] Rampton's research (1995) on "crossing" – the use of Panjabi, Creole, and Indian English by British youth of other ethnicities [. . .].

Referee design can involve a speaker shifting to identify more strongly with their own ingroup, or to an outgroup with which they wish to identify. It can even involve simultaneous identification with two groups at once [. . .].

[Referee design] is the area where I assess audience design to be in most need of serious rethinking, and I will return to this task below.

10: Style research requires its own designs and methodology

To progress beyond our current level of knowledge, research on style needs to be tailored to that end, not just grafted on to a study with other main aims. The speakers we sample, what we record them saying, and even the kinds of analysis we carry out, are specific to our concern with style rather than, for instance, with dialect differences. I report now on one project which has aimed to investigate style in its own right and test many of the audience design hypotheses.

3. DESIGNING RESEARCH ON STYLE

The focus of this project is on issues of sociolinguistic accommodation, the linguistic presentation of self in response to others, and the effect of gender and ethnicity on these. It examines and seeks to explain the ways speakers talk to each other differently depending on the characteristics of their interlocutors, their own self-presentation, and other factors in the speech situation. Specifically, it tests certain of the hypotheses about style from Bell (1984) and, for example, aims to:

1.   Investigate how speakers vary their style in response to a systematically varied range of addressees.
2.   Make aspects of the informants' identities salient, especially gender and ethnicity, and investigate how these identities are expressed in stylistic choices, particularly in cross-gender and cross-ethnic interviews.
3.   Investigate how speakers vary their style in response to a systematically varied range of topics, from the formal to the informal, and in relation to referee personas (e.g. talking about teachers when discussing education, and about bosses when discussing work).
4.   Elicit the standard Labovian interview "styles" and calibrate these against style-shifts according to audience and topic.

I present some detail on the design of the study because it is an example of how one can specifically design a project on style, and is also of a kind which has not to my knowledge been undertaken before.

3.1 Speaker sample

The language sample consists of three interviews conducted with each of four speakers. A set of four informants aged in their twenties were interviewed in succession by a set of four interviewers (Table 2.1). The informant and interviewer samples were each structured by gender and ethnicity, so that each contained a Maori woman, Maori man, Pakeha woman and Pakeha man.[5] Thus, for example, the Maori man was interviewed first by the Maori male interviewer, then by the Maori woman, and lastly by the Pakeha man. The

Table 2.1   Structure of style project sample: four informants each talk to three different interviewers

Interviewers	Informants			
	MF	MM	PF	PM
MF	1st	2nd	3rd	–
MM	2nd	1st	–	3rd
PF	3rd	–	1st	2nd
PM	–	3rd	2nd	1st

Notes:
Ethnicity: Maori (M); Pakeha (P)
Gender: Female (F); Male (M).

fourth possible combination of interviewers and informants was intentionally excluded (the practicalities of a fourth successive interview with each informant being prohibitive).

While gender and ethnicity were varied, other factors were held as constant as possible:

- Age: all four speakers were in their early to mid twenties.
- Class: all were middle class, had either done and/or were currently undertaking further education, and were employed in or currently training for professional occupations.
- Origins: all were New Zealanders of (at least) several generations' standing.
- Familiarity: all informants and interviewers were strangers to each other.

The demographic and other assessments were all done through a preliminary interview by the project's Research Manager.

In addition, we tried to keep aspects of the setting constant. Interviews were conducted in the informants' own homes. No third parties were present. Interviewers were asked to dress in a neutral fashion (neither too formal nor too untidy), and similarly both to each other and for each of the three interviews they were to conduct.

3.2 Interview design

The attempt to hold factors constant extended to interview design as well as personal characteristics and setting. [. . .] An interview situation was inevitable in order to structure the content in a comparable way across the encounters. So the attempt to elicit maximally informal speech was sacrificed to some extent by the need to ensure comparability across the interviews, e.g. by topic, and even by framing of topic. This is one example of the different methodology needed for style research, and paid dividends in enabling us to compare how different informants presented their opinions and identities in response to the same questions.

Three standardized questionnaires were designed, one for each of the interviews conducted with each informant. Each interview consisted of four components:

1. Free conversation
    e.g. holidays, living in Wellington, danger of death.
2. Set topics
    Work, education, issues of gender and ethnicity.
3. Reading tasks
    e.g. word lists, minimal pairs, Maori place names.
4. Other tasks
    e.g. British/American lexical alternates, use of *Ms.* versus *Miss/Mrs.*

In general there was an initial language-related task to begin the interview, settling the two participants in. Then it proceeded into free conversation (with certain topics offered for discussion by the interviewer), and on to one or more set topics of discussion, concluding with another task. The free conversation was intended to achieve some level of "casual" speech, without expecting to elicit truly "vernacular" talk.

An obvious issue for the study was what rationale could be given to the informants for recording them three times in as many weeks. The justification given was twofold – and genuine: that we had a range of topics to explore with them, too much for a single interview. And in particular, that people say different things to different people, which was why there was to be a series of interviews involving different interviewers.

The first interview was designed as a baseline. [. . .] So Interview 1 contained a reading passage, a word list, and a minimal pairs list [. . .]. The "free conversation" topics in this interview were:

- Danger of death.
- Family history was explored as a means of focusing part of the interview on the informant's identity – particularly their ethnic identity, which in this interview they shared with the interviewer.
- What it was like at school. The telling of childhood experiences is a means of eliciting maximally informal speech [. . .] (cf. Labov 1972, 1984). [. . .]

The first interview contained two set topics: education and work. These were chosen as being the archetypal "formal" topics, as used for instance in Fishman's domain model (1972). The education topic concentrated on the content of the informant's formal schooling and subsequent education. It was intended to contrast with the earlier more casual discussion of school life from the viewpoint of the students. There was a set of questions about teachers, good and bad. This [. . .] bears upon the hypothesis that one talks about the topic of education in a similar style to how one might talk to an educationalist. Talking about the teacher is the closest simulation of this situation in this interview design. Thus the referee associations here were to be with teachers, whereas the reference group of the earlier discussion on school life was to be "other kids." (In practice, of course, the "free" and "set" topics did not divide so neatly.)

A basic principle of the interview design was to make gender salient in the cross-gender interviews, and ethnicity salient in the cross-ethnic interviews. So the set topic for the second interview – the cross-gender combination – was gender, focusing the informants on their own gender identity and its contrast with the interviewer's. Similarly, the primary topic of discussion in the third, cross-ethnic interview was the issue of ethnic relations and identity in New Zealand.

[. . .]

4. SOME FINDINGS

4.1 Discourse particle eh

The pragmatic particle *eh* is a salient sociolinguistic marker in NZ English, as it is also in Canadian English (although the function and prosody associated with the form are not necessarily the same). The main study of New Zealand *eh* is by Meyerhoff (1994) using the Porirua sample of NZ English (Holmes, Bell, and Boyce 1991). Linguistically *eh* is a tag. Its chief discourse function seems to be to invite the interlocutor's participation: [. . .] it conveys a meaning like "you know the kind of thing I mean."

Table 2.2   *eh* index in speech by informants to interviewers

By informants	To interviewers			
	MM	MF	PM	PF
MM	46	26	19	–
MF	2	4	–	0
PM	0	–	0	1
PF	–	0	0	0

Notes:
Ethnicity: Maori (M); Pakeha (P)
Gender: Female (F); Male (M).

I quantify this and other pragmatic features in this study using an index of the number of tokens per amount of speech (Bell and Johnson 1997). The index counts the occurrences of *eh*, divides by the number of words produced by the speaker, then multiplies by a factor of 10,000. This gives a normalized base of tokens per 10,000 words, which is in fact close to the average interview length in this database.

Informants' usage According to both the findings of our previous research and popular stereotype, the discourse particle *eh* is a marker of the English of Maori people, especially men. This pattern is confirmed here (Table 2.2). There is high *eh* usage by the Maori male with indexes of 46, 26, and 19. The Maori woman uses some *eh*, but at a much lower frequency – indexes of 4, 2, and 0. The marker *eh* is all but absent from the speech of the Pakeha informants. [. . .] So *eh* is functioning here mainly as a marker of group identity – foremost of ethnicity (Maori), and secondarily of gender (Maori men). This fits the association between linguistic features and group usage outlined above as point 2 of the summary of audience design.

Further, as hypothesized in points 3 and 6 in that summary, the speakers use different amounts of *eh* with different interlocutors. The Maori man uses *eh* more with the Maori male interviewer (46), less with the Maori woman (26), and least with the Pakeha man (19). This is paralleled by the Maori woman informant, albeit at a much lower level of frequency. [. . .] [This is] the sort of precisely graded style-shift which is predicted by audience design. [. . .]

We can also assess how these findings bear on other audience design hypotheses sketched earlier. The Style Axiom (point 5 above) proposes that the range of style-shift by any one speaker will be less than the range of usage between different speakers. The difference in *eh* usage across these four speakers with all interviewers ranges from an index of 0 for the Pakeha woman to 46 for the Maori man. This range of 46 indeed considerably exceeds the amount of style-shift for any one speaker – the maximum style-shift is 27 (from 46 to 19) by the Maori man.

[. . .]

Interviewers' usage Moving from this comparative orderliness, we now examine the inter-viewers' level of *eh* in the same interviews. Interviewers of course had a very different role in these encounters from the informants. Their job was to encourage the informants to talk, so they provided much less speech. By quantifying their *eh* usage only over the amount of their own speech we can distinguish their usage from that of the informants.

Table 2.3   *eh* index in speech by interviewers to informants

To informants	By interviewers			
	MM	MF	PM	PF
MM	6	28	29	–
MF	10	25	–	5
PM	0	–	0	3
PF	–	35	14	9

Notes:
Ethnicity: Maori (M); Pakeha (P)
Gender: Female (F); Male (M).

Nevertheless their role differentiation needs to be kept in mind as a potential influence on their speech.

In Table 2.3 we see that the lowest usage of *eh* is by the Pakeha female interviewer – but also by the Maori male with indexes of 6, 10, 0! This is against the identity pattern we have been led to expect by the informant analysis. Its explanation seems to lie in the way in which the Maori male interviewer conducted his interviews, producing a minimum of speech himself, but with an easy, comfortable presence that encouraged his interlocutors to talk. His three interviews yielded the lowest ratios of interviewer-to-informant speech out of all twelve interviews. He therefore literally gave himself little chance to use *eh* at all (or any other pragmatic feature).

The highest interviewer usage is by the Maori woman and Pakeha man. The Pakeha female interviewer's usage of some *eh* (5, 3, 9) also contrasts with the Pakeha female informant's total non-usage [. . .].

Probably the clearest pattern in interviewer usage is that the Pakeha male interviewer does a lot of accommodating to his audience. He reciprocates the zero *eh* usage of the Pakeha male informant in his baseline interview. As the demographics of his informant get more distant, he uses more *eh* – an index of 14 to the Pakeha woman, and 29 to the Maori man. We can also note mutual accommodation in his interview with the Maori man, with the Maori man shifting from his high baseline of 46 (Table 2.2) to a much lower *eh* level (19), and the Pakeha male interviewer shifting from a zero base to a rather high usage of 29 (Table 2.3). [. . .] In this case both shift, and they in effect overshoot each other.

The main remaining puzzle is that usage of *eh* to the Pakeha woman is almost as high as to the Maori man, with interviewer indexes in speech to her of 35, 14, and 9 (Table 2.3). This seems to go against what one would expect from audience design: the interviewers are using a feature which is absent from their interlocutor's own speech. It is indeed counter to [the] principle [that people accommodate to features present in their interlocutor's individual or group speaking style], although I think there is an explanation: the Pakeha female informant was a quite hesitant speaker, and I suspect that interviewers wanted to encourage her to talk.

[. . .]

4.2 Maori language usage

The second data set concerns the usage of the Maori language in the context of NZ English. Maori is a minority language in New Zealand, under considerable threat from English. New Zealand is one of the world's most monolingual nations. English is the first language of at least 90 percent of the 3.5 million population – and the only language of 85 percent, most of whom are of British descent. Only a small proportion of Maori people – and still fewer younger Maori – can speak the Maori language fluently (Te Taura Whiri 1996). Maori has therefore followed the typical pattern of an indigenous tongue overwhelmed by an imperial language.

However, the language has gained increasing official recognition over the past decade, and is undergoing a renaissance along with a revival in Maori cultural, social, and political identity and power. Immersion pre-school and school programs aim to produce a new generation of speakers. [. . .]

In this kind of situation, where biculturalism is an important social and political matter, the usage of Maori words and the way in which Maori words are pronounced within the flow of English-language talk, have become salient, culturally and politically charged issues. [. . .] How Maori placenames are pronounced is increasingly an issue in its own right.

[. . .]

Maori placenames Most New Zealand placenames are Maori, and pronunciation according to a Maori or English model is a very obvious indicator of ethnic orientation or sensitivity. The pronunciation of the twenty Maori placenames from the list of English and Maori names read at the beginning of this interview was analyzed to identify whether informants used a pronunciation closer to English or to Maori. [Seven pronunciation features were analyzed.]

In each word the [. . .] sounds were marked 0 for a Maori pronunciation or 1 for an English pronunciation. These were tallied as scores, averaged, and normalized to a five-point scale, with 0 representing purely Maori pronunciation and 4 representing purely English pronunciation (at least for the sounds analyzed). By way of example, some of the possible pronunciations of *Kerikeri* would be coded and scored as in Table 2.4 (there are of course other possible combinations of the variant pronunciations). Table 2.5 shows where the pronunciation of the twenty words fell on the scale for each informant, and the informant's average rating for Maori versus English pronunciation. Against these criteria, the pronunciation of the Maori man was closest to Maori at 0.9 on the 0–4 scale, followed

Table 2.4 Scores for possible pronunciations of *Kerikeri*

Pronunciation	Alignment	Raw score	Normalized score
[kerikeri]	fully Maori	0	0
[kerikeri]	largely Maori	2	1
[keriːkeriː]	midway	4	2
[kʰeriːkʰeriː]	largely anglicized	6	3
[kʰiriːkʰiriː]	fully anglicized	8	4

Table 2.5   Four informants' pronunciations of twenty Maori place names according to Maori or English norms (score 0 = fully Maori; 4 = fully anglicized)

		Informants			
	Score	MM	MF	PM	PF
Fully Maori	0	8	4	0	0
	1	7	8	0	0
	2	3	5	2	0
	3	2	2	5	8
Fully English	4	0	1	13	12
Total place names		20	20	20	20
Mean score (0–4)		0.9	1.4	3.5	3.5

by the Maori woman (1.4). The pronunciations of the Pakeha man and woman were both closest to the English end of the scale (3.5).

[. . .]

5. LANGUAGE AS IDENTITY MARKER

In these analyses, we find encapsulated the essence of how linguistic features operate as identity markers which is the basis of how style *means* in the audience design framework. The choice of a Maori-identified particle [or] a more Maori pronunciation of a placename [. . .] marks ethnic identity.

For the two Maori speakers their pronunciation registers their identification with their own Maori heritage. For the Pakeha speakers, it marks their degree of sensitivity to Maori pronunciation as an important ethnic and cultural matter – remembering that Maori-Pakeha relations were the explicit set topic of discussion in Interview 3. We can compare how the informants understand and present their views on ethnicity at the discourse level with their expression of ethnic identity through specific linguistic features. The Pakeha man showed little overt sympathy with Maori language or culture, either in his discussion of ethnic relations or in his linguistic performance. [. . .]

The Pakeha woman, by contrast, showed awareness [. . .]: We can construe her attempted pronunciations as audience design. She is speaking to a Maori, and therefore tries – within her limited knowledge of Maori language – to accommodate towards native-like pronunciation of Maori words. [. . .]

For all speakers, then, Maori language usage is a means of declaring either their own ethnic identity, or their sensitivity to another's identity. It parallels some speakers' use of Maori words within the conversational sections of the interviews, and the overt expression of opinions on ethnic relations during the set-topic discussion. So we can talk in terms of accommodation or non-accommodation, for the Pakeha speakers, and this fits passably with an audience design approach.

But in what terms do we explain the Maori informants' pronunciations? They are not accommodating to the interviewers through convergence. However, nor are they necessarily intentionally dissociating themselves from the individual interviewer through divergence. The Maori man and the Pakeha male interviewer had an amicable, jointly constructed exchange about the exercise after its completion. The Maori woman, however, passed the comment "I'd like to hear some of the others read these," indicating she recognized the pronunciation alternatives as a site of ethnic distinction. This also is in line with her more confrontational approach to the ethnicity discussion compared with the Maori man. In this interview her delayed and cryptic answers to questions related to Maori language and culture come across as reluctance to discuss these matters with a non-Maori interviewer. [. . .]

What the Maori informants seem to be doing is expressing and affirming their own ethnic identity as Maori, to which divergence from the interviewer is incidental. This can be explained as referee design, specifically what I have called hyper-speaker shift (Bell 1984:201) – a short-term shift towards a heightened form of one's own group's speech. [. . .] This is undoubtedly going on here. But I am no longer sure that it can be considered the exceptional, marked case which I treated it as in 1984. The question is not whether the above description is accurate – it seems to fit the case well – but whether referee design is secondary as implied. This leads me on to my primary modification to the audience design framework as originally proposed.

6. CONCLUSION

6.1 Integrating audience and referee design

To my mind, the greatest problem for the audience design framework as outlined – and indeed the main challenge for any theory of style – is to take account of the dynamic, initiative use of style by individual speakers to express aspects of their identity (points 8 and 9 in the summary of audience design above), while retaining a worthwhile level of generalization. One main critique made of frameworks such as audience design which attempt to systematize style is that they are reductionist. They run the risk of minimizing or discounting the complexity of speakers' moment-by-moment, self-expressive use of language (although one could argue that an approach which is as richly person-oriented as audience design is by definition not reductionist). This is indeed an issue for audience design, but it is equally one that *any* style model will face, because any attempt to discern patterns or regularities in people's style will be open to the same critique.

Individual speakers use style – and other aspects of their language repertoire – to represent their identity or to lay claim to other identities. They may do this in ways and on occasions which are certainly unpredictable before-hand, and sometimes uninterpretable *post hoc*. This is what I have classed as referee design – the linguistic expression of identification with a reference group who is important to the speaker, usually in response to a change in some aspect of the audience. This reference group may be the speaker's own ingroup, as evidenced earlier in analysis of the Maori/English examples.

[. . .]

I share concerns (Finegan and Biber 2001) that the concept of "audience" may be in danger of being overextended to encompass a wide range of imagined or possible reference personas. The strength of audience design as proposed in 1984 is its falsifiability. It is possible for its predictions to be proved wrong. So I remain wary of widening its scope to become a catch-all, while convinced of the need for some extension. It is notable that extensions of the notion of audience as an explanatory concept are often very natural ones. That is, we come across a pattern in our data that puzzles us, and search for an explanation of why it is so. What is the reason that this speaker chose to say it this way on this occasion? That explanation may go beyond strict accommodation to the present audience, but what is very obviously going on in the situation may be the design of talk in relation to some person or group in a way that is a natural extension of the audience approach. Moreover, this is precisely the form of explanation that *any* framework finds itself reaching for when faced by such patterns.

What lies at the base of these debates is our view of the nature of personhood. Such views of course are not a provable hypothesis of sociolinguistics or any other academic discipline. They are a premise, a prime based on our own belief system. My belief is that a person is indeed more than a static bundle of sociological categories – although to say that someone is male, or Pakeha, or middle class does tell us something about that person. [. . .]

But I also believe that a person is more than an ever-shifting kaleidoscope of personas created in and by different situations, with no stable core – although to say that we appear as child to our parents, employee to our boss, partner to our partner does tell us something about the person. We do not recreate ourselves moment by moment out of nothing. We are not a *tabula rasa*. We bring to the present the shapings of our past, of our relationships, of our environment. Yet we are more than the sum of those things.

[. . .]

There are norms for different situations and groups. An analyst wishing to cut loose from all such categorization must provide an explanation for the pervasive if partial regularities which we find in speakers' style choices – just as those who wish to establish generalizations must make allowance for that significant chunk of style which even their best theories refuse to account for. [. . .] There is a sense (*pace* Coupland 2001) in which we are *not* enacting a persona in producing our own native dialect [. . .]. When we talk our vernacular (however we may define that), we are in some sense "being ourselves."

Therefore we need [. . .] a framework which acknowledges that much of our inter-personal linguistic behavior displays a pattern which can be discerned. I call that pattern audience design, and hold that it is largely guided by our response to our audience. We also need a framework which acknowledges that we are continually making creative, dynamic choices on the linguistic representation of our identities, particularly in relation to those others we are interacting with or who are salient to us. This I have called referee design.

I think the basis of such a dynamic view of style is present in my concept of referee design [. . .].

I now tend to think that we have to acknowledge referee design as an ever-present part of individuals' use of language. We are always positioning ourselves in relation to our own ingroup and other groups, and our interlocutors. This was expressed in Bell (1984:184), but was not worked through far enough: "The responsive–initiative distinction is a continuum rather than a dichotomy. Response always has an element of speaker initiative; initiative invariably is in part a response to one's audience." What I now suggest is that these may be two complementary and coexistent dimensions of style, which operate simultaneously in all speech events. Yes, we are designing our talk for our audience. But we are also concurrently designing it in relation to other referee groups, including our own ingroup.

[. . .]

Catering for the dynamic and the referee is not in fact a new proposal. Referee design under another name is the core of Le Page's approach to style, treating every utterance as "an act of identity towards an audience" (1980:13). He formulates it as a general sociolinguistic principle (McEntegart and Le Page 1982:105): "Each individual creates for himself patterns of linguistic behaviour so as to resemble those of the group or groups with which from time to time he wishes to be identified." Similarly, Traugott and Romaine (1985) propose that style should be considered as primarily "strategic." [. . .] What we are now finding in the study of monolingual style-shift, inter-lingual code switching and multilingual language use is a wide recognition of the pervasiveness of both the responsive and the initiative facets of language use. [. . .]

6.2 Integrating quantitative and qualitative analyses

This complementarity of audience and referee has a correlate in the kind of linguistic analysis we do. Audience design will often, though not always, be able to deal in quantification – that is, a speaker's style will be amenable to counting the relative frequency of certain variants. [. . .] It seems to me undeniable that quantitative style-shift can be correlated with differences in audience. It is equally undeniable that this does not exhaust the account we are to give of style – even of that particular variable. Individual tokens of the variable may have heightened significance in the flow of the interaction, or they may cluster together with each other or with other variables in a way which is significant. Referee design will often deal in the qualitative, the one-off, the single salient token which represents an identity. [. . .] [M]y analyses of television commercials (Bell 1990, 1992), where referee design is rife, show how a single token of a salient variable can be enough to stake a stylistic claim.

[. . .]

My analysis above of Maori pronunciation in fact shows on a small scale the combination of quantitative and qualitative approaches. [. . .]

In addition to quantitative and qualitative approaches, however, we will need a third level of analysis – co-occurrence. This level has rather dropped out of sight since Ervin-Tripp's classic paper (1972). Sociolinguists have concentrated on the alternation she identified, focusing on single variables, and ignored the co-occurrence of a range of variables and features in a stretch of talk. The stress on co-occurrence is a hallmark of Biber's approach to style (Finegan and Biber 1994, 2001), but there is no reason why it should not also inform variationist or qualitative approaches to language use. A main issue, however, for such analyses is to ensure that they do not become remote from the individual language features which they bring together, just as quantification of a sociolinguistic variable must ensure it is not entirely removed from the on-line qualitative occurrence of the individual tokens which are being counted.

So my proposal is for a three-layered approach to stylistic analysis of language:

- Quantification of particular stylistic features. This will be partly in standard variationist terms, of relative frequency, of counting actual over potential occurrences. But *absolute* frequency also plays a part – the frequency with which a *variable* occurs, not just the relative frequency of its different variants.
- Qualitative analysis of the individual tokens of a stylistic feature – while recognizing that not all (or even most) individual occurrences will be explicable. Such information illuminates or even alters the interpretation we might offer solely on the basis of quantification [. . .].
- Analysis of the co-occurrence of different features in stretches of language. [. . .]

Co-occurrence analysis concentrates on the patterning of two or more linguistic features in the flow of speech. While qualitative analysis of online talk enables us to see how a single feature is distributed in a stretch of talk, co-occurrence analysis combines the patterns for more than one feature. It builds a picture of where, for instance, certain kinds of features cluster together or are entirely absent. We will seek to interpret these patterns in terms of the identities and relationships which participants are representing at different points of their interaction. Bell and Johnson (1997) develop in more detail this kind of on-line analysis and a means of displaying it for the interviews discussed in the present paper. This analysis reveals for the *eh* variable that the Maori man clusters his tokens of *eh* in stretches of speech where Maori identity is most in focus – discussions of family, Maori culture, and Maori language.

We will seek in the first instance to interpret the patterns we find in relation to audience design. We will expect this to be most evident in the quantitative analysis, but it will also inform the qualitative and the co-occurrent approaches. [. . .] We will then interpret those same patterns in relation to referee design, seeking to understand how the speaker may be positioning herself in relation to different referee groups, including her own ingroup. We will anticipate that this will be most evident in the qualitative analysis. The analysis of co-occurrence is likely to be informed more equally by both audience and referee design.

I believe such an approach can take us a good way to understanding why "this speaker said it this way on this occasion." Nevertheless, I still expect the creativity of individual speakers to leave some things unpredictable, and I for one think that such an element of the mysterious and unfathomable about persons will – and should – remain.

NOTES

1.   This chapter represents my thinking at the time of the workshop where it was presented (1996). I acknowledge the support of the New Zealand Foundation for Research, Science and Technology in funding this study as part of the New Zealand English Programme in the Department of Linguistics, Victoria University of Wellington. I am grateful to the Department for its hospitality over several years. I appreciate the work of Gary Johnson in undertaking and writing up the analyses presented here, and in contributing to the project as a whole (e.g. Bell and Johnson 1997). I also acknowledge the contribution of Nikolas Coupland (e.g. 1996, 2001) to my thinking about style. Lastly, I wish to recognize John Rickford for putting style back on the agenda of North American sociolinguistics, for applying audience design (Rickford and McNair-Knox 1994), and for encouraging me back into style after I had been some years away.

2. This structure has only been demolished in the late 1990s with the sale of Radio New Zealand's commercial stations (such as ZB) into private (foreign) ownership. National Radio remains as a network funded by the levied "broadcasting fee."

3. Again, I have avoided both modification and elaboration of the framework until now, partly cautioned by the example of accommodation theory which has, to my mind, overelaborated itself and so risked both losing touch with its core insights and becoming impractically complex.

4. Blom and Gumperz's definitions and exemplifications of their distinction seem to me, however, after repeated attempts at interpretation, to be inconsistent. Myers-Scotton (1993:52) notes the same problem.

5. Maori are the indigenous Polynesian inhabitants of New Zealand/Aotearoa, and now make up some 15 percent of the population. "Pakeha" is the term for New Zealanders of European (mainly British) origin who colonized the country from the nineteenth century. They make up some 80 percent of the population.

REFERENCES

Bakhtin, Mikhael M. (1986) *Speech Genres and Other Late Essays*. Austin: University of Texas Press.

Bell, Allan (1984) Language style as audience design. *Language in Society*. 13, 2: 145–204.

Bell, Allan (1990) Audience and referee design in New Zealand media language. In Allan Bell and Janet Holmes (eds) *New Zealand Ways of Speaking English*. Bristol: Multilingual Matters and Wellington: Victoria University Press, 165–194.

Bell, Allan (1991) Audience accommodation in the mass media. In Howard Giles, Justine Coupland and Nikolas Coupland (eds) *Contexts of Accommodation: Developments in Applied Sociolinguistics*. Cambridge: Cambridge University Press, 69–102.

Bell, Allan (1992) Hit and miss: Referee design in the dialects of New Zealand television advertisements. *Language and Communication*. 12, 3/4: 327–340.

Bell, Allan and Gary Johnson (1997) Towards a sociolinguistics of style. *University of Pennsylvania Working Papers in Linguistics*. 4, 1: 1–21.

Blom, Jan-Petter and John J. Gumperz (1972) Social meaning in linguistic structure: Code-switching in Norway. In John J. Gumperz and Dell Hymes (eds) *Directions in Sociolinguistics: The Ethnography of Communication*. New York: Holt, Reinhart and Winston, 407–434.

Brown, Penelope and Steven C. Levinson (1987) *Politeness: Some Universals in Language Usage, 2nd ed.* Cambridge: Cambridge University Press.

Brown, Roger and Albert Gilman (1960) The pronouns of power and solidarity. In Thomas A. Sebeok (ed.) *Style in Language*. Cambridge, MA: MIT Press, 253–276.

Clark, Herbert H. and Thomas B. Carlson (1982) Hearers and speech acts. *Language* 58, 2: 332–373.

Coupland, Nikolas (1980) Style-shifting in a Cardiff work-setting. *Language in Society*. 9, 1: 1–12.

Coupland, Nikolas (1984) Accommodation at work: Some phonological data and their implications. *International Journal of the Sociology of Language*. 46: 49–70.

Coupland, Nikolas (1996) Hark, hark the lark: Multiple voicing in DJ talk. In David Graddol, Dick Leith and Joan Swann (eds) *English: History, Diversity and Change*. Milton Keynes: The Open University and London: Routledge, 325–330.

Coupland, Nikolas (2001) Language, situation, and the relational self: Theorizing dialect-style in sociolinguistics. In Penelope Eckert and John R. Rickford (eds) *Style and Sociolinguistic Variation*. Cambridge: Cambridge University Press, 185–210.

Coupland, Nikolas, Justine Coupland, Howard Giles and Karen Henwood (1988) Accommodating the elderly: Invoking and extending a theory. *Language in Society*. 17, 1: 1–41.

Dorian, Nancy C. (1981) *Language Death: The Life Cycle of a Scottish Gaelic Dialect*. Philadelphia: University of Pennsylvania Press.

Ervin-Tripp, Susan M. (1972) On sociolinguistic rules: Alternation and co-occurrence. In John J. Gumperz and Dell Hymes (eds) *Directions in Sociolinguistics: The Ethnography of Communication*. New York: Holt, Reinhart and Winston, 213–250.

Ferguson, Charles A. and John J. Gumperz (eds) (1960) *Linguistic Diversity in South Asia (International Journal of American Linguistics* 26, 3). Bloomington: Indiana University Press.

Finegan, Edward and Douglas Biber (1994) Register and social dialect variation: An integrated approach. In Douglas Biber and Edward Finegan (eds) *Sociolinguistic Perspectives on Register*. Oxford: Oxford University Press, 315–347.

Finegan, Edward and Douglas Biber (2001) Register variation and social dialect variation: The Register Axiom. In Penelope Eckert and John R. Rickford (eds) *Style and Sociolinguistic Variation*. Cambridge: Cambridge University Press, 235–267.

Fishman, Joshua A. (1972) Domains and the relationship between micro- and macrosociolinguistics. In John J. Gumperz and Dell Hymes (eds.) *Directions in Sociolinguistics: The Ethnography of Communication*. New York: Holt, Reinhart and Winston, 235–253.

Gal, Susan (1979) *Language Shift: Social Determinants of Linguistic Change in Bilingual Austria*. New York: Academic Press.

Giles, Howard and Peter F. Powesland (1975) *Speech Style and Social Evaluation*. London: Academic Press.

Gumperz, John J. (1967) On the linguistic markers of bilingual communication. *Journal of Social Issues*. 23, 1: 48–57.

Holmes, Janet (1995) *Women, Men and Politeness*. London: Longman.

Holmes, Janet, Allan Bell and Mary Boyce 1991. *Variation and Change in New Zealand English: A Social Dialect Investigation* (Project report to the Foundation for Research, Science and Technology). Wellington: Victoria University of Wellington, Department of Linguistics.

Irvine, Judith T. (2001) "Style" as distinctiveness: The culture and ideology of linguistic differentiation. In Penelope Eckert and John R. Rickford (eds) *Style and Sociolinguistic Variation*. Cambridge: Cambridge University Press, 21–43.

Labov, William (1972) *Sociolinguistic Patterns*. Philadelphia: University of Pennsylvania Press.

Labov, William (1984) Field methods of the project on linguistic change and variation. In John Baugh and Joel Sherzer (eds.) *Language in Use: Readings in Sociolinguistics*. Englewood Heights, NJ: Prentice-Hall, 28–53.

Lambert, Wallace E. (1967) A social psychology of bilingualism. *Journal of Social Issues*. 23, 2: 91–109.

Le Page, Robert B. 1980. Projection, focussing, diffusion. *York Papers in Linguistics*. 9: 9–31.

McEntegart, Damian and Robert B. Le Page (1982) An appraisal of the statistical techniques used in the sociolinguistic survey of multilingual communities. In Suzanne Romaine (ed.) *Sociolinguistic Variation in Speech Communities*. London: Edward Arnold, 105–124.

Meyerhoff, Miriam (1994) Sounds pretty ethnic, eh?: A pragmatic particle in New Zealand English. *Language in Society*. 23, 3: 367–388.

Myers-Scotton, Carol (1993) *Social Motivations for Code-Switching: Evidence from Africa*. Oxford: Clarendon.

Preston, Dennis R. (1991) Sorting out the variables in sociolinguistic theory. *American Speech*. 66, 1: 33–56.

Rampton, Ben (1995) *Crossing*. London: Longman.

Rickford, John R. and Faye McNair-Knox (1994) Addressee- and topic-influenced style shift: A quantitative sociolinguistic study. In Douglas Biber and Edward Finegan (eds.) *Sociolinguistic Perspectives on Register*. Oxford: Oxford University Press, 235–276.

Sacks, Garvey, Emanuel A. Schegloff and Gail Jefferson (1974) A simplest systematics for the organization of turn-taking in conversation. *Language*. 50: 696–735.

Te Taura Whiri i te Reo Maori/Maori Language Commission (1996) Ae ranei, he taonga tuku iho? National Maori Language Survey 1995: Provisional findings. Wellington: Te Taura Whiri.

Thakerar, Jitendra N., Howard Giles and Jenny Cheshire (1982) Psychological and linguistic parameters of speech accommodation theory. In Colin Fraser and Klaus R. Scherer (eds.) *Advances in the Social Psychology of Language*. Cambridge: Cambridge University Press, 205–255.

Traugott, Elizabeth Closs and Suzanne Romaine (1985) Some questions for the definition of "style" in sociohistorical linguistics. *Folia Linguistica Historica.* 6, 1: 7–39.

Youssef, Valerie (1993) Children's linguistic choices: Audience design and societal norms. *Language in Society.* 22, 2: 257–274.

QUESTIONS

content

1. What is "the heart" of audience design?
2. What is the relationship between individual style variation and inter-group (social) variation?
3. What is meant by "truly 'vernacular' talk"? In what sense is Bell using *vernacular* here?
4. What is the difference between "responsive" and "initiative" style shifting?
5. How did Bell design his experiment to focus on style shifts triggered by changes in audience?
6. Bell says that the distribution of *eh* in Maori males' interviews is "the sort of precisely graded style-shift which is predicted by audience design". Explain how audience design predicts the patterns found.

concept

1. Bell notes that "initiative" shift is common in TV advertisements, e.g. tea adverts featuring speakers with "posh" British accents; adverts for large cars featuring a "West Coast" US accent.

   a. Do you agree with him that this kind of "referee design" expresses identification with the group of speakers who typically use those linguistic features?

   b. Can you think of examples where people put on accents, "initiative" shifts, where identification is **not** intended? What does the shift do then?

2. Bell quotes part of Le Page's "acts of identity" approach to style. In other work, Le Page says that style shifting enables the speaker to resemble the linguistic patterns of a group s/he wishes to identify with from time to time, **with the proviso that s/he has access to those models**. How might the addition of this proviso enrich the understanding of individual style?

3. Consider the following tables. The first one shows the frequencies of two variables in a group of DC Heroes (Batman, Wonderwoman, Superman and Green Lantern) and a group of Marvel Heroes (Spider-man, The Hulk, Silver Fox and Hawkeye). The second one shows the frequencies of the same variables in the speech of Green Lantern and Silver Fox when speaking to their fellow heroes and to the other set of heroes.

   Explain which hero observes the Style Axiom, and which does not.

	Flapping of intervocalic /t/	Raising of short /æ/
DC Heroes (Batman, Wonderwoman, Superman, Green Lantern)	80 %	20 %
Marvel Heroes (Spider-man, The Hulk, Silver Fox, Hawkeye)	60 %	55%

		Flapping of intervocalic /t/	*Raising of short /æ/*
Green Lantern	to other DCs (ingroup)	85 %	7 %
	to Marvels (outgroup)	78 %	16 %
Silver Fox	to other Marvels (ingroup)	53 %	60 %
	to DCs (outgroup)	83 %	18 %

Chapter 3

Jennifer Hay, Stefanie Jannedy, and Norma Mendoza-Denton

OPRAH AND /AY/: LEXICAL FREQUENCY, REFEREE DESIGN, AND STYLE

1. INTRODUCTION

MONOPHTHONGIZATION OF /AY/ TO the long low center nucleus [a:] is an extensively documented feature of both Southern US and African American English (Ash and Myhill 1986, Fasold and Wolfram 1970, Labov 1994). In this paper, we show that this ethnically and socially stratified sociophonetic variable has a stylistic dimension, co-varying with the ethnicity of the referee in the speech of a single speaker. Bell (1984, 1992) argues that nonparticipants such as referees and overhearers can influence speech style. These claims can be difficult to test because of the confounding factor of a usually present audience. From videotaped segments of the *Oprah* show we isolated the influence of the referee (usually an upcoming guest scheduled to appear on the show) by selecting only segments where the speaker (Winfrey) and addressee (general TV/studio audience) were constant.

[. . .]

1.1. Stylistic variation and referee design

We conceive of the sociophonetics of speaking style as going beyond traditional static dichotomies such as formal/casual or read/spontaneous. Speaking style can be seen as individual speakers' creative and proactive deployment of various elements in their repertoire. It is the linguistic implementation, at any given time, of a combination of the many varieties (standard, vernacular, African American English), registers (interview, babytalk, lecture) and degrees of formality at that speaker's disposal.

Source: Hay, Jennifer, Stefanie Jannedy and Norma Mendoza-Denton (1999) Oprah and /ay/: lexical frequency, referee design, and style. In *Proceedings of the 14th International Congress of Phonetic Sciences*, San Francisco, August 1999. (Proceedings on CD-ROM)

Style-shifting has been observed in the speech of Oprah Winfrey, and characterized as a device to appeal to a cross-section of viewers. Analyses in the literature center on topic and lexical choice (Lippi-Green 1997, Luce 1986). Our discussion here will focus on vocalic variation.

Considering stylistic variation within the framework of audience design, Bell (1992) defines referees as "third persons not physically present at an interaction but possessing such salience for the speaker that they influence language choice even in their absence." (1992: 328). For the purposes of this paper, and to disentangle the effects of audience and addressee, we define the referee as an absent party about whom Winfrey is talking. [. . .]

We selected portions of the show in which there was no guest on stage, and Winfrey was facing the camera and addressing the studio and television audience. Thus the audience and addressee were not only identical, but constant across segments. The genre was also constant, generally consisting of the introduction of a guest, or a preannounce-ment of segments scheduled for later in the show. The one element which did vary across these segments, then, was the person that Winfrey was introducing or discussing. We decided to test the hypothesis that the referee was salient, and that, through referee design, Winfrey's variable implementation of /ay/ from [ay] to monophthongized [a:] would signal a shift from her more common usage of General American English (GAE) to African American English (AAE). We hypothesized that Winfrey would adopt more features of AAE when talking about an African American guest, than when the guest was not African American.

2. METHODOLOGY

We extracted 229 words containing /ay/ from monologues from the Oprah Winfrey show, sampling speech as described above from a series of shows that aired during the 1996–97 season. In our analysis, only tokens which were identified as fully mono-phthongized by both auditory and acoustic criteria were treated as instances of monophthongization. All other tokens are regarded as diphthongs.

Two listeners performed an auditory analysis of the data: a token was coded as monophthongized only when both listeners agreed on the classification. To provide acoustic verification of the auditory analysis, the vowel quality was coded based on spectrographic displays: each token in the data set was labeled either as monophthong or as diphthong from wide band spectrograms.

[. . .]

3. RESULTS

3.1. Ethnicity of referee

An AA [African American] referee significantly increases the probability of mono-phthongization (ChiSquare = 18.95, df = 1, p < .001). This statistic is based on 195 tokens – only those tokens in our data set for which there was a clear referee. The distribution is shown in Table 3.1.

Table 3.1   Ethnicity of referee and monophthongization

	Diphthong	Monophthong	Total
AA referee	55	33	88
Non-AA referee	96	11	107
Total	151	44	195

This is strong evidence that ethnicity of the referee plays an important part in influencing sociophonetic speech style. Rickford and McNair-Knox (1994) show that ethnicity of interviewer (addressee) and topic (sometimes overlapping with referee as we have defined it) similarly influence morphosyntactic and sociophonetic variation, with speakers less likely to use AAE variables with a Euro-American interviewer than with an African American one. A related finding was reported by Coupland (1990), who monitored the speech of a Cardiff travel agent, and found that the speaker emphasized affinity with the client by accommodating her speech style in five phonological variables.

Although contextual factors such as ethnicity of referee have been shown to be important in stylistic variation and audience design, our results here represent the first study, to our knowledge, to add instrumentally analyzed sociophonetic data to the findings in this area.

3.2. Lexical frequency

A second factor which facilitates the speaker's monophthongization of /ay/ is lexical frequency. Frequent words are more prone to monophthongization. All items in the corpus were identified as "frequent" (occurring five or more times in our small corpus of Winfrey's speech), or "infrequent" (occurring fewer than five times). Inflectional variants were treated as identical for the purposes of this frequency count. Frequent items are significantly more likely to undergo monophthongization than infrequent items. (ChiSquare $= 6.62$, df $= 1$, p $< .025$). The distribution is shown in Table 3.2, and based on all 229 tokens in our corpus.

3.3. Ethnicity and frequency as predictors of the data

We performed a binomial stepwise regression analysis on those 195 tokens for which both referee and lexical frequency information was available. The regression was performed with the Goldvarb program (Rand and Sankoff 1990). Both ethnicity of referee

Table 3.2   Lexical frequency and monophthongization

	Diphthong	Monophthong	Total
Frequent	105	47	152
Not frequent	66	11	77
Total	171	58	229

and lexical frequency were significant predictors of the variation in our data set. Of these significant factors, ethnicity of referee was the better predictor of monophthongization. An African American referee had the effect of promoting monophthongization, with a probability weight of .688, while a non-African American referee disfavored mono-phthongization at 0.343 (where probability weights greater than .5 (.5–1.0) promote monophthongization and probability weights less than .5 (.5–0) inhibit it).

High lexical frequency (appearing five or more times in the corpus) favored mono-phthongization, (with a probability weight of 0.588), while low lexical frequency (appearing less than five times) inhibited monophthongization (probability weight of 0.350). The entire model, incorporating both lexical frequency and ethnicity of referee, was significant to p <.03. (Input 0.185, log likelihood = −91.218).

4. DISCUSSION

4.1. Monophthongization as a reductive process

Lindblom's model (1990) of hypo- and hyper-speech suggests that speakers will adopt a clear speaking style in conditions under which perception may be difficult. In cases in which the hearer is estimated to have few obstacles to perception, however, features of clear speech will be absent. This prediction, together with the rapidly growing body of evidence that frequency is important for speech perception (Luce 1986, Pierrehumbert et al. 1998 and others) leads us to predict that reductive phenomena should be most prevalent in frequent words.

[. . .]

Word frequency also has an effect on non-reductive processes. Mendoza-Denton (1997) investigated the variable raising of /ɪ/ in the speech of California Chicano English speakers, and found that within this ethnic contact variety, a subset of monomorphemic pronominal words with high frequency led the incidence of raising. Similar results are reported by Houston (1985) in her morphophonological study of the variable (ING), where she finds that of all the grammatical categories, the same high-frequency lexical set exhibits the highest probability and percentage of velar application in all American and British dialects that she investigated (1985: 152–154, 354).

While there has not to our knowledge been any work focussing on the extent to which frequency affects monophthongized /ay/ in AAE, we might not be surprised to discover that this monophthongization in AAE is more extreme in frequent words than in less frequent words.

4.2. Frequent words as the locus of style

One of the questions that arises from Bell's account of audience design and referee design is the process of selection of the lexical items that will carry the work of the variation. Work in the area of grammaticalization (Traugott 1989) has identified lexical frequency as determining possible areas of the language where innovations in meaning can take place. It is in highly frequent words that a speaker finds the crucial combination of a) ease of processing (Jescheniak and Levelt 1994) and b) the repeated opportunity of presentation that would be needed to layer new grammatical or social meaning. In the area of perception of frequent words Boyland (1996) finds that morphosyntactic combinations that co-occur frequently come to be processed and stored as single units, thereby freeing up some cognitive load and making these easy-to-process, highly frequent items candidates for taking up different linguistic functions. [. . .]

Our results regarding the importance of lexical frequency in the monophthongization of /ay/ for a single speaker, combined with the observed relationship between referee and monophthongization in the sociolinguistic modality, support a model where it is highly frequent words which emerge as the best candidates for the display of speaker style.

5. CONCLUSION

This paper demonstrates the influence of referee design, an external social factor, and lexical frequency, an internal linguistic factor, in the variable realization of /ay/ in the speech of Oprah Winfrey.

There remain several sociophonetic and broader sociolinguistic questions that might be followed up in this study. In the sociophonetic realm, one might investigate the interplay of various simultaneous sociophonetic variables in the creation of a particular style. If monophthongization of /ay/ plays a role in signalling affiliation with a particular referee, what might other combinations of sociophonetic variables tell us about additional contextual factors?

Some macro sociolinguistic issues that arise include the relationship between language attitudes and linguistic variation. Winfrey has in the past expressed strong language attitudes disapproving of African American English, and justifying her sentiments based on the documented history of its reception (Lippi-Green 1997). These attitudes were particularly salient during the Ebonics controversy of 1997–98. During one show, Winfrey calls Ebonics the "Ebonic plague." How do we reconcile her negative attitudes toward AAE with her stylistic use in referee design of a feature that has been associated with the AAE-speaking community?

The results presented here do not mean that this speaker's variably monophthongal /ay/ is being used to straightforwardly or even consciously mark membership in the AAE community, nor do we mean to imply that the speaker has the limited choice of only two varieties (GAE and AAE) in her repertoire. Among other possibilities, she could be using /ay/ monophthongization in combination with other features in the production of a more delicately nuanced style that we have only just begun to uncover. What is striking from this data is the relation (without assuming causation) between speaker monophthongization, lexical frequency, and African American addressees in the discourse.

ACKNOWLEDGMENTS

We would like to thank the Mendoza-Dentons for help with transcription, Keith Johnson for technical advice, and Allan Bell for useful discussion at the early stages of this project.

NOTE

1.   The authors are listed in alphabetical order.

REFERENCES

Ash, S. and J. Myhill (1986) Linguistic correlates of inter-ethnic contact. In D. Sankoff (ed.) *Diversity and Diachrony*. Amsterdam and Philadelphia: John Benjamins.

Bell, A. (1984) Language style as audience design. *Language in Society* 13: 145–204.

Bell, A. (1992) Hit and miss: referee design in the dialects of New Zealand television advertisements. *Language and Communication* 12, 3–4: 327–340.

Boyland, J. T. (1996) Morphosyntactic change in progress: a psycholinguistic approach. Ph.D. Dissertation University of California at Berkeley.

Coupland, N. (1980) Style-shifting in a Cardiff work setting. *Language in Society* 9: 1–12.

Fasold, R. and W. Wolfram (1970) Some linguistic features of Negro dialect. In R. Fasold and R. Shuy (eds) *Teaching Standard English in the Inner City*. Washington, D.C.: Center for Applied Linguistics.

Houston, A. (1985) Continuity and change in English morphology: the variable (ING). Ph.D. Dissertation. University of Pennsylvania.

Jescheniak, J.D. and J.M. Levelt (1994) Word frequency effects in speech production: retrieval of syntactic information and phonological form. *Journal of Experimental Psychology: Learning, Memory and Cognition* 20: 824–843.

Labov, W. (1994) *Principles of Linguistic Change: Internal Factors*. London: Blackwell.

Lindblom, B. (1990) Explaining phonetic variation: a sketch of the H & H hypothesis. In W. Hardcastle and A. Marchel (eds) *Speech Production and Speech Modelling*. Dordrecht: Kluwer, 403–409.

Lippi-Green, R. (1997) The real trouble with Black English. In *English with an Accent: Language Ideology and Discrimination in the United States*. London: Routledge.

Luce, P.A. (1986) Neighborhoods of words in the mental lexicon. Ph.D. Dissertation, Indiana University.

Mendoza-Denton, N. (1997) Chicana/Mexicana identity and linguistic variation: an ethnographic and sociolinguistic study of gang affiliation in an urban high school. Ph.D. Dissertation, Stanford University.

Peck, J. (1994) Talk about racism: framing a popular discourse of race on Oprah Winfrey. *Cultural Critique*. Spring 1994.

Pierrehumbert, J., J. Hay and M.E. Beckman (1998) Speech perception, wellformedness & lexical frequency. Paper presented at the 6th Conference on Laboratory Phonology, York, England.

Rand, D. and D. Sankoff (1990) *GoldVarb 2.0: A Variable Rule Application for the Macintosh. CRM-1585*. Montreal: Université de Montréal.

Rickford, J. R. and F. McNair-Knox (1994) Addressee- and topic-influenced style shift: a quantitative sociolinguistic study. In D. Biber and E. Finegan (eds) *Perspectives on Register: Situation Register Variation within Sociolinguistics*. Oxford: Oxford University Press.

Traugott, E. C. (1989) On the rise of epistemic meanings in English: an example of subjectification in semantic change. *Language* 65: 31–55.

QUESTIONS

content

1. Who are the *audience* and who are the *referees* in the Oprah data?
2. Who do the authors think Oprah will use most tokens of monophthong /ay/ with, and why? Does she?
3. What kinds of words do the authors predict will be most subject to monophthongization – frequent or infrequent words? Why?

concept

1. If a monophthongized variant of the /ay/ variable is taken to be a "reductive phenomen[on]", this supposes that Oprah's norm is a diphthong for this variable. Do you think this assumption is warranted? Why?
2. Recent research on frequency effects on variation strongly suggest that we need to differentiate between changes in progress and stable variation, as the two types of variables pattern quite differently with respect to frequency effects. If you had to guess which kind of variable would be more sensitive to frequency effects, which would you pick, and why?

Chapter 4

Qing Zhang

A CHINESE YUPPIE IN BEIJING: PHONOLOGICAL VARIATION AND THE CONSTRUCTION OF A NEW PROFESSIONAL IDENTITY

INTRODUCTION

[. . .]

In this article, I present a quantitative analysis of the use of four phonological variables by two professional groups in Beijing: an emergent group consisting of professionals working in foreign businesses, and an established group of professionals employed in state-owned enterprises. Comparing the linguistic practices of the two groups demonstrates significant intergroup variation in the use of all four variables. I draw on the construct of the linguistic market originally developed in the works of Bourdieu (e.g. [. . .] Bourdieu 1977, 1991) to explain the sharp intergroup variation. Differences between the two groups are shown to be intimately related to the emergence of a transnational Chinese linguistic market in which a cosmopolitan variety of Mandarin Chinese becomes a valuable form of symbolic capital. At the same time, linguistic features are examined as symbolic resources used by the professionals in foreign businesses to give meaning to their new social identity that is not bounded by a territorial matrix.

Several studies have found the construct of the linguistic market a useful tool to account for sociolinguistic variation (Sankoff & Laberge 1978, Haeri 1996, Eckert 2000). A linguistic market is generally defined as a symbolic market, constituted by various social domains within which linguistic exchanges take place. Linguistic products are not equally valued in a linguistic market. The language legitimized by the market sets the norm against which the values of other ways of speaking and varieties are defined (Bourdieu 1977). Those who command the legitimate language possess the linguistic capital, a form of symbolic capital, that may bring them rewards (both material and symbolic) from the market. The power of Bourdieu's linguistic market as an analytical tool for linguistic

Source: Zhang, Qing (2005) A Chinese yuppie in Beijing: phonological variation and the construction of a new professional identity. *Language in Society* 34: 431–466.

practice lies in the nature of the market as part of a larger structured symbolic domain. It draws attention to the social and economic conditions of linguistic production and reproduction, and to the power relations of language users as both producers and consumers of language. [. . .] Bourdieu's conception of the linguistic market is criticized by Woolard 1985 for its overemphasis on the unified nature of the linguistic market, where the only legitimate language is claimed to be the language of the dominant class or standard language (see also Milroy & Milroy 1992). Woolard has proposed alternative linguistic markets that give value to local varieties.

[. . .]

The construct of the linguistic market is especially relevant to examining the relation between linguistic practice and socioeconomic change in the current context of mainland China. [. . .] The rapid restructuring of the economic system and the commodification forces of the market economy have changed the ways in which material and symbolic resources are used and valued in the reconfiguration and construction of (new) social distinctions. Using the construct of linguistic market, I examine the sharp intergroup linguistic variation as integral to broader socioeconomic changes that have brought about weakened state control of access to socioeconomic (including employment) opportunities and allocation of all kinds of resources. The emergence of a new job market brought about by a globalized economy has placed a premium not only on educational credentials and professional expertise but also on linguistic skills. Individuals have become competitors as well as commodities on the job market, where access to desired job opportunities (which may lead to better socioeconomic opportunities) is based on the value of the individual as both a competitor and a commodity. This study examines linguistic variation as constituting the symbolic capital (including educational credentials, professional expertise, and all the components under the rubric of self-presentation, including appearance, dress and manners) that adds value to the individual as a commodity in demand as well as a viable competitor on the market.

While the linguistic market may shed light on the general patterns of variation found, it is inadequate to explain the nuanced social meanings of linguistic variation – that is, why particular linguistic features are favored over others, and how they become resources to distinguish the professionals in foreign businesses from their counterparts in the state sector. To explain the meanings of sociolinguistic variation, I draw on developments in treating sociolinguistic variation as a symbolic resource in the construction of social identity (e.g. Mendoza-Denton 1997, Eckert 2000). Such an approach examines linguistic variation on a par with other symbolic resources used by a new professional group to establish their emergent social identity in Beijing and in a larger, transnational Chinese context. Thus, by examining the interaction between linguistic market and language as symbolic resource in identity construction, the present study of sociolinguistic variation is situated in the broader landscape of urban China, which is undergoing globalization and transition from a former socialist egalitarian society to a socioeconomically more stratified one. [. . .]

OVERVIEW OF THE CURRENT SOCIOECONOMIC SITUATION OF CHINA

China has been undergoing economic reform since the late 1970s. Drastic changes have been taking place in the economic, social, cultural, and ideological arenas. [Relevant to this study are] changes in three aspects [. . .]: (i) increased income disparity that leads to diversified lifestyle choices and emergence of new urban elites; (ii) China's opening up to the global market; and (iii) China's becoming a participant in the transnational Chinese community. [This refers to businesses – mainly from Hong Kong, Taiwan, Macau, Singapore, and Thailand – which make a large contribution to foreign direct investment in mainland China.]

[. . .]

METHODOLOGY AND INFORMANTS

The fieldwork for this study was conducted between 1997 and 1998 in Beijing, China. The primary participants in the study are Chinese yuppies who are top and middle-level managerial professionals working for large, prestigious international businesses in Beijing. They share the three characteristics of the core new elite in the foreign business sector described by Pearson 1997: high income, high educational level, and the prestigious status of their companies. For comparative purposes, a group of managerial-level professionals working for state enterprises was also studied. They all worked for large national corporations and had college-level education. Their monthly salaries, ranging from 1,000 to 4,000 yuan, are much lower than those of the yuppies. Each individual was contacted through "a friend of a friend." The speech data were collected by means of sociolinguistic interviews conducted at the participants' workplaces. Each interview lasted for a minimum of 45 minutes. The interview focused on two general topics: professional experience, and Beijing society and culture [henceforth topic 1 and topic 2]. [. . .] The data used for the quantitative analysis in this study is drawn from interviews with 14 yuppies and 14 state professionals. Members of both groups were born and grew up in Beijing, where they also acquired their primary, secondary, and tertiary (four-year university) education. They had not lived in another region for a continuous period longer than three years. [. . .] Each group had an equal number of women and men. [. . .]

LINGUISTIC VARIABLES AND DATA

As the linguistic variation to be discussed involves Beijing Mandarin and Mainland Standard Mandarin, a brief description of the relation between the two is necessary here. Beijing Mandarin is a variety in the northern Mandarin dialect group. The standard variety of spoken Mandarin in China is called *Pǔtōnghuà*. According to its official definition, it takes "northern Mandarin as its basis, the Beijing Mandarin phonological system as its norm of pronunciation, and exemplary modern *báihuà* ['vernacular'] literary language [as opposed to classical Chinese] as its norm of grammar" (*Xiàndài Hànyǔ Cídiǎn* 1983:890). In the rest of the article, I refer to *Pǔtōnghuà* as Mainland Standard Mandarin (MSM) to distinguish it from other, including non-mainland, Mandarin varieties. While

Beijing Mandarin (BM) and MSM share the same phonemic inventory, it is certainly not the case that all Beijingers speak MSM. Neither is it true that BM and MSM are two monolithic entities. Variation has been found among BM speakers of different age groups, and between urban and suburban speakers (Linguistic Group 1995:7–8, fn.12). In addition, many localisms and phonological features of Beijing Mandarin are not incorporated into MSM. Just as speakers of northern Mandarin may have a hard time understanding speakers whose native varieties are not northern Mandarin (e.g., Yue or Wu varieties), visitors to Beijing often complain that they cannot understand local Beijing speech. The difference between BM and MSM can be described as a continuum. At one end is BM with its various local features. The fewer the local Beijing features or the less they are deployed, the closer the language is to MSM. Like MSM speakers elsewhere, Beijingers speak MSM with varying degrees of a local accent. In Beijing, as in most parts of China, MSM is usually used in radio and television broadcasting (with the exception of some programs that feature local aspects of the city and its people), state bureaucracy, and educational institutions, and as a lingua franca in interactions among participants from various parts of the country. For the purposes of this study, I would like to point out one characteristic of the relation between the spoken standard variety and the written variety. The symbolic dominance of the standard language is established mainly through the written standard variety. The spoken variety, or local varieties of MSM, functions mainly as a lingua franca. Their relationship is further explicated vis-à-vis the construct of the linguistic market in the section where I explain the linguistic variation found between the two professional groups.

Of particular concern here are four phonological variables. All four variables are socially significant in Beijing. In other words, they are recognized by Beijingers as speech features associated with certain social attributes of certain types of personae. As will be explained in detail below, such naturalized linkage between linguistic features and certain social groups or characters is an example of local language ideology at work (Irvine & Gal 2000, Irvine 2001). Specifically, these linguistic features are interpreted as implicating distinctive qualities of three character types in Beijing. In the following discussion, I categorize the linguistic variables into two groups in terms of their association with localness and with specific character types. The first category consists of three [local] variables whose variants are associated with two local personae, *jīng yóuzi* "Beijing smooth operator" and *hútòng chuànzi* "alley saunterer." The second category [i.e. the cosmopolitan variable] involves a tone feature that is not local to Beijing and is associated with a new persona connected by locals with the transnational Chinese mass media.

The local variables

Beijing Mandarin has a unique speech style that encompasses segmental features as well as complex prosodic, lexical, and rhetorical features. [. . .] There is a rich literary tradition of writing in the Beijing vernacular (L. Zhang 1994). As the literary classics have been read and passed on from generation to generation, they have reified a few local characters that have taken on a life of their own and become cultural icons of and for Beijingers (Zhao 1991). The most famous of these are *jīng yóuzi* "Beijing smooth operator" and *hútòng chuànzi* "alley saunterer."

[. . .]

Although no study has pinpointed the exact linguistic features that contribute to the smooth style, I have found that Beijingers identify two features with smoothness. The first is rhotacization of the syllable final, and the second is lenition of retroflex obstruent initials. [Lenition refers to a process by which a strongly articulated (fortis) consonant becomes weakened to its lenis counterpart.] As both features are associated with the "smooth operator" character, I discuss them together as a subgroup of the local variables and refer to them as the "smooth operator" variables.

The "smooth operator" variables

The rhotacization of the syllable final, commonly known among Chinese speakers as *érhuà*, involves the addition of a subsyllabic -ɹ to the final, which causes it to become rhotacized (Chao 1968, Y. Lu 1995). In the following examples, the IPA transcriptions of the non-rhotacized forms are followed by their rhotacized counterparts.

(1)   "here" *zhè* [tʂɤ], *zhèr* [tʂɤɹ]
(2)   "goal" *mùbiāo* [mupiau], *mùbiāor* [mupiauɹ]

[. . .] Rhotacization is not the only feature that contributes to the perception of "heavy r-sounding." Additionally, it involves lenition of the group of retroflex obstruent initials, /ʂ/, /tʂ/, and /tʂʰ/ [which was described as "swallowing sound" by one participant]. In Beijing Mandarin, these retroflex initials sometimes are lenited and realized as the approximant [ɹ] (Chao 1968). Lenition can occur word-medially (in a multisyllabic word) and across word boundaries. It is briefly mentioned by Chao 1968 and Norman 1988, both of whom claim lenition to be a feature of weakly stressed (i.e., neutral tone) syllables. In my data, however, lenition also occurs in stressed (i.e., tonal) syllables. In this article, the retroflex obstruent initials are represented by the fricative (ʂ). The tokens used in the statistical analysis are word-medial occurrences, as shown in the following two examples. In (3), the second syllable of *xuésheng* "student" has neutral tone. In (4), the second syllable of *huāshēng* "peanut" has high level tone.

(3)   "student" *xuésheng* [ɕyɛʂən], *xuéreng* [ɕyɛɹən]
(4)   "peanut" *huəshēng* [huaʂən], *huəreng* [huaɹən]

[. . .]

The "alley saunterer" variable

[. . .]

While the smooth operator character can apply to many types, the alley saunterer calls forth a stereotypical lower-class male image (D. Yang 1994). The essential quality of an alley saunterer is lack of education and ambition, and being limited to the local.[. . .]

The speech feature associated with the alley saunterer image is the interdental realization of the dental sibilants /s/, /ts/, and /tsʰ/ as [θ], [tθ] and [tθʰ], respectively. In this article, they are represented by /ts/, and I refer to this as the "alley saunterer" variable. In the following examples the realizations in MSM are presented first, followed by that illustrating the "alley saunterer" variant:

(5) "alley saunterer" *hútòng chuànzi* [hutʰuŋ tʂʰuantsɿ], *hútòng chuànthi* [hutʰuŋ tʂʰuantθɿ]
(6) "now" *xiànzài'* [ɕiantsai], *xiànthài* [ɕiantθai]

[. . .]

The "cosmopolitan" variable

Variation in the use of the three local variables discussed above indicates differential degrees of local accent which can be located along the BM-MSM continuum. The fourth variable is the realization of a neutral tone as a full tone in a weakly stressed syllable. It differs from the previous three variables in two respects: First, it is suprasegmental in some sense, whereas the other three are purely segmental. Second, the use of a full tone instead of a neutral tone indicates not only using less of the local Beijing accent (moving away from the local dialect) but also moving away from MSM. In recent years (Hong Kong) Cantonese and Taiwan Mandarin have exerted an influence on MSM in both lexicon and phonology (S. Chen 1991). In this respect, new cultural icons brought about by *Gǎngtái* popular culture (e.g., Barmé 1993, Gold 1993) play a pivotal role in the spread of non-mainland Mandarin features. The use of full tone instead of a neutral tone is well known among Chinese mainlanders, particularly northern Mandarin speakers, as evidence of *Gǎngtái*-accented Mandarin. This feature is stereotypically associated with *Gǎngtái* pop music stars and business people. In the rest of the article I refer to this as the "cosmopolitan" variable. In the following examples, the neutral tone realization in the Pinyin and IPA transcriptions is followed by the full tone variant, with the vowel and its tone mark in boldface:

(7) "understand" *míngbai* [miŋpai], *míngbái* [miŋ**p**á**i**]
(8) "student" *xuésheng* [ɕyɛʂəŋ], *xuéshēng* [ɕyɛʂ**ə**ŋ]

In Beijing Mandarin and other northern Mandarin varieties, every stressed syllable has a full tone with a fixed pitch value. In other words, every stressed syllable has one of the four Mandarin tones. When a syllable is weakly stressed, it has neutral tone (Chao 1968). Unlike the four basic tones, a neutral-tone syllable does not have a fixed pitch value. Its pitch is determined by the tone of its preceding syllable (Chao 1968, Norman 1988, Qian 1995). While neutral tone is a common feature of the northern Mandarin dialect group, it is particularly prominent in BM. In contrast, most of the southern varieties, such as Cantonese, Min, and Shanghainese, have very limited use of neutral tone (Chao 1968, Qian 1995). Beijing Mandarin neutral-tone syllables are significantly weaker than those in other northern Mandarin varieties, and they are particularly short in duration and articulated with less intensity (Y. Lu 1995).[. . .]

Table 4.1   Effects of professional group and gender on variation[a]

Variable	Prof. Group		Gender		Topic		Input	Sig.
	Yuppie	State	Female	Male	Topic 1	Topic 2	Input	Sig.
Rhotacization	.246	.733	.346	.644	Not significant		.710	.003
Lenition	.348	.660	.387	.616	.438	.571	.447	.000
Interdental[b]	.332	.664	(1%)	(27%)	.406	.574	.224	.000
Full tone[c]	(21%)	(0%)	.655	.320	.608	.408	.183	.000

[a] Additional factor groups included in the runs: internal constraints.
[b] The VARBRUL results for the interdental realization of /ts/ are for males only.
[c] The VARBRUL results for the full tone realization of a neutral tone are for yuppies only.

DATA ANALYSIS

The data were coded for linguistic and social constraints. Statistical analyses were conducted using GoldVarb 2.0 (Rand & Sankoff 1990), a stepwise multiple regression program designed specifically for linguistic analysis. Both internal and external constraints were analyzed. This article focuses on the effects of the social constraints of professional group, gender, and topic on patterns of variation. Note that a VARBRUL weighting value above 0.5 indicates that a factor favors the occurrence of the variant in question. A value below 0.5 indicates a disfavoring effect.

Two prominent patterns emerged after the initial analysis in which the three social constraints were treated as independent, as shown in Table 4.1. First, there was a sharp contrast between the two professional groups across all four variables. The yuppies used all of the local variants significantly less than the state professionals did. Specifically, the two "smooth operator" variables patterned similarly. The professional group was the most significant factor group, and gender was secondary. The "alley saunterer" variant was almost categorically associated with male speakers, with the state professionals strongly favoring it; only three tokens were produced by two female speakers, both state professionals. The state professionals did not use the "cosmopolitan" full tone variant at all. The second prominent pattern was that women used local variants less than men. In addition to the sharp contrast in terms of professional group and gender, topic – though a significant factor group for all variables except rhotacization – did not have as prominent an effect as the other two factor groups. Full tone was the only variant that demonstrated a robust shift depending on topic: It was used significantly more often by the yuppies in Topic 1 (VARBRUL value = 0.608) when discussing job-related experiences.

Further analyses were carried out to examine the effects of gender and topic within each professional group. The VARBRUL results are presented in Tables 4.2 and 4.3. The two groups showed different patterns of variation with regard to both gender and topic. The results in percentages are presented graphically in Figure 4.1 (gender variation) and Figure 4.2 (topic variation).

Except for the "alley saunterer" variant, which was overwhelmingly favored by male speakers in both groups, gender variation was mild to insignificant in the state group but dramatic among the yuppies. In the former group, differences in the use of rhotacization and full tone were insignificant. Variation was moderate in the use of lenition, with male state professionals slightly favoring it at 0.545 in terms of VARBRUL value, or merely 6%

Table 4.2   Effects of gender and topic in yuppie group

Prof. Group	Variable	Gender		Topic			
		Female	Male	Topic 1	Topic 2	Input	Sig.
Yuppie	Rhotacization	.263	.708	.423	.568	.433	.044
	Lenition	.309	.708	.376	.636	.267	.000
	Interdental	(0%)	(15%)	Not significant		.119	.000
	Full tone	.655	.320	.601	.408	.183	.000

Additional factor groups included in the runs: internal constraints.

Table 4.3   Effects of gender and topic in state professional group

Prof. Group	Variable	Gender		Topic		Input	Sig.
		Female	Male	Topic 1	Topic 2		
State	Rhotacization	Not significant		Not significant		.864	.009
	Lenition	.453	.545	Not significant		.613	.005
	Interdental	(1%)	(40%)	.326	.656	.369	.000
	Full tone	(0%)	(0%)	(0%)	(0%)		

Additional factor groups included in the runs: internal constraints.

more than female speakers. In contrast, across all four variables, female yuppies overwhelmingly favored the non-local variants. Hence, the observation based on the initial analysis that female speakers disfavored the non-local variants (see Table 4.1) is inaccurate. In fact, female speakers in the state group used the two "smooth operator" variants much more often than male yuppies (see Figure 4.1). Women's appearing to be conservative was due primarily to female yuppies' extremely limited use of the local features.

Similar to gender variation, the state group demonstrated slight topic variation, whereas this was again significant in the yuppie group. Only one feature – the "alley

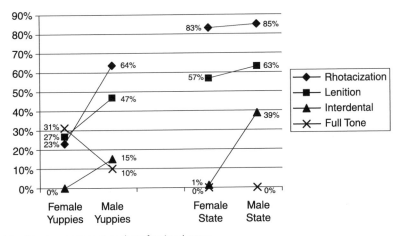

Figure 4.1   Gender variation in each professional group.

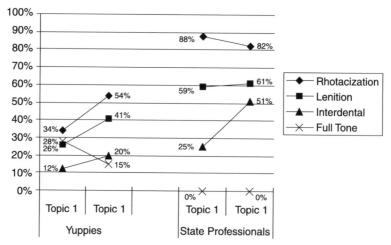

Figure 4.2   Topic variation in each professional group.

saunterer" variant – was used significantly more often in Topic 2 by the state professionals. It is arguable that their lower use of the interdental variant in Topic 1 is related to the stigmatized nature of the "alley saunterer" image and the negative qualities associated with it – fecklessness and lack of education. The same feature did not show a significant topic shift among the (male) yuppies when examined together with internal constraints (preceding segment and tone) (see Table 4.2). However, when topic was examined by itself, the VARBRUL weightings were Topic 1, 0.434; Topic 2, 0.596; significance, 0.0125. In addition, a chi-square test on the frequencies of the interdental variant in the two topics showed that the p value was less than or equal to 0.025, which indicates that the difference is significant. The non-local variants of the other three variables were all used significantly more often when the yuppies discussed their work-related experiences.

The above results demonstrate that gender plays a different role in the two professional groups. I argue that explanations for the differential gender patterns require an examination of the emergence of the new professional group, and specifically of the different career trajectories of the men and women in the foreign businesses. Differences in their career trajectories may contribute to the differential role of language in their careers. Another significant factor lies in the different gender dynamics in the business practices of the two sectors, which may affect patterns of language use among the women and men in state and foreign companies. Broadly put, in the foreign sector, influence from the Western corporate culture may contribute to differences in the types of jobs that men and women tend to hold. During my study, I found women clustered in front-end jobs such as office administration and public relations. It was much easier for me to find male managers than female managers. In the state sector, state feminism, dating from the Maoist period, still to some degree prevents overt gender discrimination in job assignment. In many of my interviews with state managers, I was received by a male secretary. The placement of women in "decorative" positions was relatively less conspicuous in the state sector than in the foreign businesses. Such different gender dynamics may lead to differences in the role of women as symbolic capital of the corporation, and it may further the differential value of standard Mandarin's contributing to the overall symbolic value of women in the two sectors. Detailed analysis and explanations for gender-related variation would require far more space. In the rest of this article, I focus on the variation between the two professional groups.

EXPLANATIONS

The most striking difference between the state professionals and the yuppies lies in their use of the "cosmopolitan" full tone variant. The other three variables show similar though less dramatic patterning, with the state professionals favoring the local variants. As mentioned earlier, the full tone variant is evidence of influence from non-mainland Mandarin varieties. The state professionals thus appear to be less affected by this influence than the yuppies are. One factor directly related to this difference is the extent of contact with non-mainland Mandarin varieties and their speakers. Because of the nature of their work, professionals in foreign businesses have more opportunities to interact with non-mainland Mandarin speakers who use the full tone variant. Hence, their use of the full tone is almost surely related to their greater exposure to this feature. While exposure is a condition for speakers to pick up a linguistic form, however, it does not entail consequent usage; speakers who are exposed to certain linguistic features may or may not use them. Whether or not speakers use an incoming linguistic form and to what extent they use it are further determined by social factors such as power relations, social networks (Milroy 1980, Bortoni-Ricardo 1985), community or group membership (Bucholtz 1996; Eckert 1988, 2000), and social orientation (Labov 1963, Gal 1978). As explained earlier, Chinese mainlanders, especially urbanites, are exposed to non-mainland Mandarin varieties, and Beijingers are familiar with the use of full tone when a neutral tone is expected. Furthermore, Table 4.2 shows that within the yuppie group, there is significant gender variation in the use of full tone. Exposure alone cannot explain why female yuppies use the full tone variant more often than male yuppies, since it can be assumed that they have similar exposure to this feature.

In what follows, I argue that rather than treating the full tone variable in isolation as a marker of "yuppieness," explanations for its variable use should be sought in relation to variation in the three local variables from the perspective of contrast in the styles of the two professional groups. As shown in Figure 4.3, for each variable, the state professionals

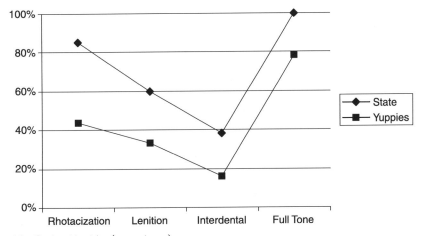

Figure 4.3   Contrast in styles (percentages).

use the local variant more often than the yuppies. Hence, in terms of the degree of localness, the speech style of the state professionals is prominently Beijing whereas that of the yuppies, with the adoption of the full tone, is comparatively cosmopolitan.

In the following analysis of the different patterns of linguistic behavior by yuppies and state professionals, I draw on Bourdieu's (1977, 1991) notion of linguistic market, and I examine linguistic resources as symbolic resources that give meaning to an emergent cosmopolitan identity.

Changing economy, changing markets

While the yuppies' less frequent use of the three local Beijing features might be interpreted as an indication that they speak a more standard variety of MSM, such an interpretation in terms of standardness masks the complexity of their linguistic practice. Their adoption of the "cosmopolitan" full tone variant in addition to their lesser use of local features shows that the linguistic resources they employ are not limited to MSM. [. . .]

The use of the full-tone realization of a neutral tone in Beijing is identified as non-local and non-mainland. Hence the yuppies' adoption of this feature makes their speech not only non-local but also non-mainland. The linguistic difference between the two professional groups cannot simply be described along a linear dimension from vernacular to standard. Rather, the yuppies draw on features from both BM and non-mainland Mandarin varieties to construct a new and non-local variety of Mandarin, and they use that to construct a cosmopolitan yuppie style. In the rest of the article, I refer to this new variety as "cosmopolitan Mandarin."[1] I argue that the yuppies' use of this cosmopolitan variety of Mandarin is related to the interaction between their participation in a newly emergent linguistic market and using the cosmopolitan variety of Mandarin as a symbolic resource to present their yuppie identity.

In contrast to the yuppies' cosmopolitan style, the state professionals' speech is characterized by local Beijing features. Particularly prominent is their greater use of the "smooth operator" features and the categorical use of the neutral tone in unstressed and weakly stressed syllables. As BM is the phonological basis for MSM and these three features are also shared by other northern Mandarin varieties, the state professionals' speech can be described as MSM with a prominent Beijing accent. Furthermore, the lack of significant topic-dependent shift in their use of rhotacization, lenition, and neutral tone (shown in Table 4.3 and Figure 4.2) shows that these features did not play as significant a role in presenting the professional aspect of their identities as they did for the yuppies.

[. . .]

[. . . T]he assumption that intergroup variation reflects professional group difference fails to explain why state professionals do not show significant topic-dependent variation, or why the yuppies use a cosmopolitan variety that does not strictly conform to the norms of MSM. In what follows, I argue that the intergroup variation is the result of the professionals' participation in two different linguistic markets, and of the differences in the symbolic value of MSM and a new cosmopolitan variety of Mandarin on each market. I show that the state professionals participate in a Mainland Standard Mandarin linguistic market while the yuppies participate in a transnational Chinese linguistic market.[2] Although both are supra-local language markets, the symbolic value of Mandarin on each market is different. This difference contributes to the linguistic difference between the two professional groups.

The Mainland Standard Mandarin linguistic market

MSM, the officially designated common medium of communication in China, is used in large national enterprises and other national and government organizations head-quartered in the capital city. National corporations, the bureaucracy, educational institutions, the media, and other cultural institutions constitute the sites of the MSM linguistic market in Beijing. However, the standard linguistic market in China is not exactly the same as what Bourdieu 1977, 1991 describes. He argues that competence in the legitimate language constitutes the most valuable linguistic capital on the standard linguistic market. Possession of this kind of linguistic capital helps one become a viable participant in the standard linguistic market. In the MSM linguistic market, the spoken variety of MSM does not constitute a profitable form of symbolic capital. As several studies have shown, more than four decades since the initiation of the national language standardization campaign, spoken MSM has not become a social index, nor a symbolic asset necessary for access to elite status in mainland China (Guo 1990, Zhu & Chen 1991, Harrell 1993).

Shuō biāozhǔn pǔtōnghuà "speaking STANDARD MSM" – a slogan in the campaign to promote MSM – does not therefore represent a kind of social prestige sought by the majority of mainland Chinese, except for those who work in a very small number of occupations such as broadcasting, journalism, and entertainment, in which standard MSM is mandated. As Zhu & Chen (1991:99) point out, "No great advantages can be gained if one speaks *Putonghua* [MSM] while no harm can be done if one does not." Hence, nearly four decades after the implementation of the language standardization policy, most Chinese on the mainland are content to speak a localized variety of MSM.

While the spoken variety of MSM does not constitute an especially important form of symbolic capital, linguistic hegemony is established through competence in written Standard Chinese. It is required for access to elite status.

[. . .]

BM is the phonological standard for MSM; hence native Beijingers are, in a sense, native speakers of MSM, or more precisely, native speakers of a local variety of MSM. Hence, unlike many speakers of other Chinese varieties, Beijingers do not have to learn spoken MSM at school. As Bourdieu (1984:86) argues, the encouragement of the acquisition of a specific competence can be achieved only when the market promises or guarantees profit for this competence. The Beijing state professionals in the MSM linguistic market are "endowed" with the linguistic capital which is the officially established common medium for communication. As there is not much anticipation of reward for speaking standard MSM, the state professionals do not have to strive to speak MSM without a Beijing accent. Hence, we should not be surprised to find the much higher frequency in their use of the two best-known Beijing features, and little style-shifting.

The transnational Chinese linguistic market

While the professionals in the state economic sector participate in the MSM linguistic market, the yuppies in the international sector are engaged in a different linguistic market. [. . .] China's participation in the transnational Chinese capitalist community and global economy has given rise to a new job market. In this market, the traditionally dominant system of state-controlled job assignment has become obsolete. Individuals become competitors and commodities in the market. Job applicants have to sell themselves. The selling process starts with the job interview, a totally new experience to job seekers when first introduced by foreign companies. Making a good self-presentation at the job interview – packaging and comporting oneself appropriately according to the rules of the game in the new market – has become a crucial practice for anyone who wants to enter the international business sector, a steppingstone to a new cosmopolitan lifestyle.

To become a commodity in demand in the new market, one has to acquire the kinds of symbolic capital that are valued in that market. On the employer's side, specific language skills alongside educational credentials, specialized skills, and other requirements are expected of job seekers. These include the ability to speak Standard Mandarin without a local accent, and proficiency in one or more foreign languages. English is unquestionably the most valued foreign language at present; others include Japanese, German, and French. Very often, requirements of appearance (*wǔguān duānzhèng* "having regular features"), age, and gender also appear in job descriptions.

In consequence, the establishment of the international business sector has given rise to a new linguistic market that creates linguistic values different from those in the MSM linguistic market. In the latter, the BM phonological system is the standard, and spoken MSM is valuable as a lingua franca. In contrast, the ability to speak Mandarin without a local accent has become profit-generating linguistic capital in the new linguistic market. Working for international businesses engages the yuppies in a market in which MSM is only one of the varieties of Mandarin – others include Taiwan Mandarin, Hong Kong Mandarin, Singapore Mandarin, and so on. [. . .]

I call the new linguistic market the "transnational Chinese linguistic market." Yuppies' use of cosmopolitan Mandarin shows that they do not conform to the norms of MSM, which are based on BM. Indeed, the value of cosmopolitan Mandarin extends far beyond facilitating communication. During their interviews, the yuppies all emphasized speaking Mandarin without a local accent as an important aspect of building their professional and corporate image. For them, therefore, the new Mandarin variety is no longer an object of need – a common medium needed for communication – but a resource for distinction (Bourdieu 1984). The yuppies use the cosmopolitan variety to distinguish themselves from those in the MSM linguistic market. Its use not only distinguishes the yuppies from their state counterparts, but also helps create and perpetuate the sanctions of the new linguistic market.

[. . .]

The use of a cosmopolitan variety has the potential to produce symbolic profit and, ultimately, economic profit, whereas failure or inability to use it would be detrimental to one's image as a competent professional. The fact that senior professionals sometimes go so far as assuming the responsibility of norm reinforcement indicates that the yuppies are aware of the sanctions of the market. In the following example, the speaker, David, is a deputy representative of a European bank:

> Working in a foreign business, it's inappropriate to speak to clients with a heavy Beijing accent. Once, I heard my secretary talking to a client on the phone, she said "*téi wǎn la*" ["too late"]. "*téi*" is Beijing vernacular. I had to tell her to get rid of it.

Constructing a Chinese yuppie identity

Although differences in linguistic markets contribute to the significant intergroup variation reported here, the construct of the linguistic market cannot explain the nuanced meanings of variation. The yuppies' use of the cosmopolitan variety of Mandarin is not an isolated demand of the transnational Chinese linguistic market, but one aspect of a whole set of related practices that constitute a new yuppie style and identity. [. . .]

Through their daily engagement in the new linguistic market, which is part of a broader symbolic market, the yuppies gradually develop practices that comprise the yuppie habitus, reflected in the ways they act, speak, shop, and even eat. All these practices give meaning to who they are. As Jenkins 1996, Eckert 2000, and a host of others have argued, the construction of social identity and community is about the making of meaning. In the rest of this section I show that the yuppies extrapolate and appropriate various resources to make their emergent cosmopolitan identity meaningful.

I have repeatedly emphasized that the yuppies see and present themselves as cosmopolitan business professionals. They are using a cosmopolitan variety of Mandarin to carve out a space in the transnational Chinese community and the global business world. Equally important, however, is that the use of this new variety does not uproot them from their local basis, Beijing. In other words, the yuppies do not construct their new social identity by simply disassociating themselves from being Beijingers and packaging themselves as "Hong Kong-Taiwan wannabes." It is true that they have a global orientation, many of them wear foreign brand names, and all speak foreign languages. However, these are only part of the repository of resources from which they draw to forge their yuppie identity. As Giddens 1991 observes, all cosmopolitans are nonetheless contextually situated in space and time. The space that they are carving out is IN and OF Beijing but not limited to Beijing. They are picking and choosing among local as well as non-local resources to make their identity meaningful in a local context. Linguistic features that are socially significant in the local context are employed by the yuppies so that their identity becomes not only meaningful to themselves, but interpretable and meaningful to others around them.

The purpose of the meaning-making process is twofold: (i) to produce agreement among the members, that is, to make the internal similarity meaningful to members; and (ii) to produce distinctions between their group and significant other groups – that is, to make the external difference meaningful to outsiders. This is achieved through the creation of a style – a system of distinction (Bourdieu 1984, Irvine 2001). As a powerful means of self-expression, style helps us articulate who we are and how we are different from others. It defines the group's boundaries against other groups and defines them "more sharply in relation both to its members and all outsiders" (Clarke 1976:182).

To create a distinctive style, individuals draw upon resources that are accessible to them. However, they do not pick up stylistic material in a free-wheeling fashion. The creation of style can be seen as a process of "bricolage" (Lévi-Strauss 1966) in which the "bricoleur" selects from a LIMITED and PREEXISTING set of materials at hand and arranges them into a meaningful ensemble (see, e.g., studies in Hall et al. 1976; Hebdige 1996 [1979]). California Style Collective 1993 examines the linguistic bricolage of adolescent style through phonological variation. Numerous recent sociolinguistic studies, though not adopting the concept of bricolage per se, also demonstrate the appropriation of socially (and culturally) significant linguistic features to give meaning to various social identities and/or communities (Bucholtz 1996, Barrett 1999, Coupland 2001, Wong & Zhang 2001).

The orchestration of a stylistic ensemble based on a limited set of existing resources is crucial because it establishes the basis or common ground for recognition and identification by both group members and outsiders. The linguistic material that the yuppies pick up represents well-known cultural personae. The connection between these linguistic features and their corresponding personae is well established in the public imagination in Beijing. Hence, the use of rhotacization, lenition, and full tone triggers the connection and thus can be easily recognized. In addition, social and symbolic significance is not the only condition that determines what gets picked up. Another important condition is whether there exists a fit, or to use Clarke's (1976) term, "homology," between a potential symbolic resource and the group's ideology or social orientation. Among the three local features, the yuppies use the two "smooth operator" features to a limited extent, as the smoothness and skillfulness in dealing with business is compatible with the persona of a business professional. They eschew the use of the interdental realization of (ts) because there is little homology between the image of an alley saunterer and a yuppie. The locally established meaning of the interdental variant – fecklessness, restriction to the local market, lack of education and ambition – conflicts in every aspect with the cosmopolitan persona that the yuppies are trying to construct. Meanwhile, they adopt the full tone feature – a symbol of the new cultural icons in the transnational Chinese market – to accentuate the cosmopolitan aspect of their identity. The identity of a Chinese yuppie, like social identity in general, is multiplex (Hall 1996, Jenkins 1996). A Chinese yuppie is simultaneously a cosmopolitan, a business professional, a young person, a Chinese, a woman or a man, and a Beijinger. These multiple aspects intersect with each other and consequently affect the ways in which the yuppies select and appropriate symbolic resources. Finally, rather than examining the meaning(s) of each linguistic variable separately, we have to put the variables back into the system of distinction to elucidate our interpretation of the social meanings of linguistic variables. In other words, the social meanings of the features studied are inseparable from one another. It is not the use or non-use of rhotacization, lenition, and full tone that gives specific meaning to any one of these features. What makes them meaningful is the appropriation of the whole ensemble – the cosmopolitan variety of Mandarin, as well as other practices and resources – in the construction of a yuppie style.

CONCLUSION

[. . .] My analysis of the linguistic market on the one hand challenges Bourdieu's original theorization of the linguistic market which (re)produces and maintains the symbolic value of a single standard language. On the other hand, it suggests that in addition to Woolard's (1985) proposal that there are alternative vernacular/local markets where vernacular norms are valued, we should also consider the existence of supra-local or transnational linguistic markets in which a "standard" variety (of a nation-state or a territorially-based community) may not be the "standard" against which values of other varieties are compared and established. As I have discussed earlier, sociolinguistic variation studies need to look beyond the linear dimension of the standard and vernacular in both the description and treatment of variation data. In other words, the less frequent use of some local features may be far more complex than a simple implication of closer proximity to the "standard" variety. Hence, the vernacular/local market is not necessarily the only "alternative" to the standard linguistic market. In addition to the standard linguistic markets of France or the United States and the alternative markets of Belfast or Catalonia, we can discuss transnational linguistic markets that are not tied to a specific place (though they have local sites). In a transnational linguistic market, a territorially based standard may become an element of localness. What is highly valued in such a market may not be a single variety but several "languages of currency," as discussed in Haeri's (1996:166) study of the sociolinguistic market of Cairo, or a kind of hybrid linguistic competence, such as the cosmopolitan Mandarin in this study and English dominant multilingualism in Piller's (2001) recent study of German advertisements. In such cases, it is not so important to determine which variety – for instance, Cairean Arabic, American English, Mainland Standard Mandarin, Taiwan Standard Mandarin, or German – has greater symbolic value than the others, as to pay attention to the SELECTIVE COMBINATION of features from several varieties that gives value to a kind of non-local (which should not be read as "standard" or "nonstandard") linguistic practice, and yet remains distinctive and meaningful in a local context.

[. . .]

NOTES

1. Linguistic features of cosmopolitan Mandarin are not limited to the use of the full tone. Lexical items, such as expressions from Cantonese and Taiwan Mandarin, as well as Mandarin-English code-mixing, can also give Mandarin discourse a non-local cosmopolitan flavor. Orthography, the use of traditional Chinese characters instead of simplified characters, is another resource to add a cosmopolitan character to written Standard Chinese.
2. It should be noted that I do not assume a discrete linguistic division between the two markets. Neither do I assume that the yuppies participate only in the transnational Chinese linguistic market and the state professionals only in the MSM linguistic market. Rather, as language users in general, both groups are engaged in multiple linguistic markets. Working for international companies engages the yuppies primarily in a transnational Chinese linguistic market, and working for state-owned enterprises engages the state professionals primarily in the MSM linguistic market.

REFERENCES

Barrett, Rusty (1999) Indexing polyphonous identity in the speech of African American drag queens. In Mary Bucholtz et al. (eds) *Reinventing Identities: The Gendered Self in Discourse*. New York: Oxford University Press, 313–31.

Bortoni-Ricardo, Stella Maris (1985) *The Urbanization of Rural Dialect Speakers: A Sociolinguistic Study of Brazil*. Cambridge: Cambridge University Press.

Bourdieu, Pierre (1977) The economics of linguistic exchanges. *Social Science Information* 16: 645–68.

Bourdieu, Pierre (1984) *Distinction: A Social Critique of the Judgment of Taste*. Trans. by Richard Nice. Cambridge, MA: Harvard University Press.

Bourdieu, Pierre (1991) *Language and Symbolic Power*. Ed. by John B. Thompson. Trans. by Gino Raymond & Matthew Adamson. Cambridge, MA: Harvard University Press.

Bucholtz, Mary (1996) Geek the girl: language, femininity, and female nerds. In Natasha Warner et al. (eds) *Gender and Belief Systems: Proceedings of the Third Berkeley Conference on Women and Language*. Berkeley: Berkeley Women and Language Group, 119–31.

California Style Collective (1993) Variation and personal/group style. Paper presented at NWAVE-22. Ottawa: University of Ottawa.

Chao, Yuen Ren (1968) *A Grammar of Spoken Chinese*. Berkeley: University of California Press.

Chen, Songlin (1991) Shehui yisu dui yuyan shiyong de yingxiang: Jiu dangqian Min Yue yu re de taolun [Effects of social factors on language use: A discussion on the current fever of Min and Cantonese dialects]. *Yuwen Jianshe* [*Philology Construction*] 1: 32–3.

Clarke, John (1976) Style. In Hall and Jefferson (eds), 175–82.

Coupland, Nikolas (2001) Language, situation, and the relational self: theorizing dialect-style in socio-linguistics. In Penelope Eckert & John R. Rickford (eds) *Style and Sociolinguistic Variation*. Cambridge: Cambridge University Press, 185–210.

Eckert, Penelope (1988) Adolescent social structure and the spread of linguistic change. *Language in Society* 17: 183–207.

——— (2000) *Linguistic Variation as Social Practice: The Linguistic Construction of Identity in Belten High*. Oxford: Blackwell.

Gal, Susan (1978) Peasant men can't get wives: language change and sex roles in a bilingual community. *Language in Society* 7: 1–16.

Gold, Thomas B. (1993) Go with your feelings: Hong Kong and Taiwan popular culture in Greater China. *China Quarterly* 136: 907–25.

Guo, Youpeng (1990) Hubei Sheng Shiyan Shi Putonghua yu fangyan de shiyong diaochao. [A survey of the use of *Putonghua* and dialects in the City of Shiyan, Hubei Province]. *Zhongguo Yuwen* [*Chinese Philology*] 219: 427–32.

Haeri, Niloofar (1996) *The Sociolinguistic Market of Cairo: Gender, Class, and Education*. London & New York: Kegan Paul.

Hall, Stuart (1996) Who needs identity? In Stuart Hall & Paul Du Pay (eds) *Questions of Cultural Identity*. London: Sage, 1–17.

Hall, Stuart and Tony Jefferson (1976) (eds) *Resistance Through Rituals: Youth Subcultures in Post-War Britain*. London: Hutchinson.

Harrell, Stevan (1993) Linguistics and hegemony in China. *International Journal of the Sociology of Language* 103: 97–114.

Hebdige, Dick. (1996 [1979]) *Subculture: The Meaning of Style*. London: Routledge.

Irvine, Judith (2001) Style as distinctiveness: the culture and ideology of linguistic differentiation. In Penelope Eckert & John R. Rickford (eds) *Style and Sociolinguistic Variation*. Cambridge: Cambridge University Press, 21–43.

Jenkins, Richard (1996) *Social Identity*. London & New York: Routledge.

Labov, William (1963) The social motivation of a sound change. *Word* 19: 273–309.

Lévi-Strauss, Claude (1966) *The Savage Mind*. Chicago: University of Chicago Press.

Linguistic Group (1995) *Zhongguo Fangyan Cihui* [*Chinese dialect vocabulary*] (2nd ed.). Beijing: Character Reform Publishing House.

Lu, Yunzhong (1995) *Putonghua de Gingsheng Yu Erhua* [*Neutral tone and rhotacization in Standard Mandarin*]. Beijing: Beijing Commercial Press.

Mendoza-Denton, Norma C. (1997) Chicana/Mexicana identity and linguistic variation: an ethnographic and sociolinguistic study of gang affiliation in an urban high school. Dissertation, Stanford University.

Milroy, Lesley (1980) *Language and Social Networks*. Oxford: Blackwell.

Milroy, Lesley and James Milroy (1992) Social network and social class: toward an integrated sociolinguistic model. *Language in Society* 21: 1–26.

Norman, Jerry (1988) *Chinese*. Cambridge: Cambridge University Press.

Papastergiadis, Nikos (2000) *The Turbulence of Migration: Globalization, Deterritorialization and Hybridity*. Malden, MA: Polity Press.

Pearson, Margaret M. (1997) *China's New Business Elite: The Political Consequences of Economic Reform*. Berkeley: University of California Press.

Piller, Ingrid (2001) Identity constructions in multilingual advertising. *Language in Society* 30: 158–36.

Qian, Nairong (eds.) (1995) *Xiandai Zhongwen Yuyan Xue* [*Modern Chinese linguistics*]. Beijing: Beijing Language Institute Press.

Rand, David and David Sankoff (1990) GoldVarb version 2.0: A variable rule application for the Macintosh. Montréal: Centre de recherches mathématiques, Université de Montréal.

Sankoff, David and Suzanne Laberge (1978) The linguistic market and the statistical explanation of variability. In David Sankoff (ed.) *Linguistic Variation: Models and Methods*. New York: Academic Press, 239–50.

Wong, Andrew and Qing Zhang (2001) The linguistic construction of the *tóngzhì* community. *Journal of Linguistic Anthropology* 10: 248–78.

Woolard, Kathryn A. (1985) Language variation and cultural hegemony. *American Enthnologist* 12: 738–48.

Xiàndài Hàyǔ Cídiǎn [*Modern Chinese Dictionary*] (1983) Beijing: Commercial Press.

Yang, Dongping (1994) *Chengshi Jifeng: Beijing Yu Shanghai De Wenhua Jingshen* [*City wind of season: The cultural spirit of Beijing and Shanghai*]. Beijing: Oriental Press.

Zhang, Lihang (1994) *Beijing Wenxue De Diyu Wenhua Zhi Mei* [*The beauty of the regional culture of Beijing literature*]. Beijing: China Peace Press.

Zhu, Wanjin and Jianmin Chen (1991) Some economic aspects of the language situation in China. *Journal of Asian Pacific Communication* 2: 91–101.

QUESTIONS

1. How did China change during the last few decades and how does this influence the construction of Chinese identities?
2. What could Zhang mean when she writes "The current sociolinguistic reality of China challenges us to go beyond treating identities and communities as territorially based and conceptualizing linguistic variation along the linear dimension of the standard and the vernacular"? [not in excerpt]
3. What variables (and variants) are chosen for analysis? Why these?
4. How do yuppies and state professionals differ and why?
5. How do the yuppies make their emergent cosmopolitan identity meaningful?

content

concept

1. Papastergiadis argues that the "links between individuals and their communities are deterritorialized" (2000: 85). That is, "people now feel they belong to various communities despite the fact that they do not share a common territory with all the other members" (115). Is this of relevance to this article? If so, how?

2. Zhang mentions the process of "bricolage" in which "the 'bricoleur' selects from a limited and pre-existing set of materials at hand and arranges them into a meaningful ensemble." What styles do you recognize in your own life and what features contribute to it?

Chapter 5

John Laver

LINGUISTIC ROUTINES AND POLITENESS IN GREETING AND PARTING

[. . .]

The purpose of this chapter is to discuss the communicative linguistic patterns of the small-scale routine ceremonies of greeting and parting, and to consider the adaptive, 'other than overt' messages exchanged by participants in these marginal phases of conversational interaction by means of which social relationships are negotiated and controlled.

To set the scene for the functional analysis to be proposed, it may be helpful briefly to discuss the rationale for the existence of a *routine* element in the linguistic patterns of conversation. In the sense to be adopted here, routine behavior is *polite* behavior. The linguistic behavior of conversational routines, including greetings and partings, as well as pleas, thanks, excuses, apologies and small-talk, is part of the linguistic repertoire of politeness. The function of such linguistic routines may therefore be illuminated by the type of analysis that Brown and Levinson (1978) have recently applied to politeness phenomena in conversation generally.

A central concept in the work of Brown and Levinson is that of 'face,' a concept derived partly from Goffman (1967). They distinguish two components of face:

> *negative face*: the want of every 'competent adult member' that his actions be unimpeded by others.
> *positive face*: the want of every member that his wants be desirable to at least some others (Brown and Levinson 1978:67).

There are very many aspects of conversational interaction where face, in the above definition, is at risk. It may be the hearer's face that is threatened, or the speaker's; and it may be either the negative or the positive aspect of face that is concerned. But if the

Source: Laver (1981) Linguistic routines and politeness in greeting and parting. In: Florian Coulmas (ed.) *Conversational Routine.* The Hague: Mouton, 289–305.

strategic ends of speakers in conversational interaction are to be achieved, then to cause overt loss of face is usually counter-productive. The risk to face must therefore be minimized, and this is managed by the use of appropriate polite behavior. Brown and Levinson distinguished between 'positive politeness,' which is 'redress directed to the addressee's positive face' (op cit. p. 106), and 'negative politeness,' which is 'redressive action addressed to the addressee's negative face' (op. cit. p. 134).

The greater the degree of risk to face, the more constrained the options of mitigatory polite behavior become. Conversely, we can propose that interactions in which there is least choice open to the speaker of conventionally-appropriate linguistic behavior are interactions containing the highest risk to face. In other words, *maximum risk leads to maximum routine*, and conversely, *maximum routine reflects highest risk.*

An example of a conversational interaction where the linguistic choices open to the speaker are very constrained is one where an introduction is being performed. In many cultures, the conventions of polite society are almost totally prescriptive in this area, both in terms of the phrases expected of the third party performing the introduction, and often even more strongly of the phrases permitted to the two parties being introduced. In less formal circumstances, the constraints are usually less severe, which indicates a link between formality, politeness, risk and face.

A second example of a highly constrained linguistic routine is constituted by church services of baptism, marriage and burial. On such occasions, nearly all the linguistic material is explicitly prescribed by the conventions of the religious denomination concerned.

One might ask in what way is face at risk in these two examples: What do social introductions and life-crisis ceremonies in church have in common that might justify their parallel treatment? In both cases, social identity is in question. In both cases, a specially-qualified mediator is ratifying the social identity of one or more participants.

[. . .]

In particular, both are concerned with changes in relationship: in the process of introduction, the participants change from a non-solidary to a solidary relationship, and in the case of a marriage ceremony, the standing of the married couple changes within the context of their solidary society.

The general principle that is being drawn here, in the choice of these examples of routine linguistic behavior, is that when such routine is observed, it is not unreasonable to suspect that face is potentially at risk, and that the negotiations that are being tacitly conducted are possibly negotiations of social relationship between the participants. This general principle will be taken to underlie the discussion in the main part of this chapter, which will be concerned with three types of routine linguistic behavior found in the greeting and parting phrases of conversation. These three types are formulaic phrases of greeting and parting, such as 'Good morning' and 'Goodbye;' terms of direct address, such as 'Mr Smith,' 'Robert' and 'Bob;' and small-talk, or 'phatic communion,' such as 'Nice day for the time of year.' In the marginal phases of conversation, where the use of such linguistic routines is most dense, participants conduct their social negotiations about respective status and role partly by means of their choices of formulaic phrase, address-term and type of phatic communion.

The strategies of negotiation of status and role in the marginal phases of conversation can profitably be discussed not only in terms of Brown and Levinson's analysis of politeness phenomena, but also within the framework of conversational logic proposed by Grice (1975). In considering the suitability of individual moves in conversation, Grice formulates a 'rough general principle which participants will be expected . . . to observe,' as follows:

> Make your conversational contribution such as is required, at the stage at which it occurs, by the accepted purpose or direction of the talk exchange in which you are engaged. One might label this the COOPERATIVE PRINCIPLE.
>
> On the assumption that some such general principle as this is acceptable, one may perhaps distinguish four categories under one or another of which will fall certain more specific maxims, the following of which will, in general, yield results in accordance with the Cooperative Principle. Echoing Kant, I call these categories Quantity, Quality, Relation, and Manner (Grice 1975:45).

Gricean maxims (which have not failed to attract a degree of criticism) can briefly be characterized in the following way:

> *Quantity*:   Be as informative as necessary
> *Quality*:   Be truthful
> *Relation*:   Be relevant
> *Manner*:   Be clear, concise and unambiguous

Grice formulated these maxims on the specific assumption that the purpose of conversation was a 'maximally effective exchange of information.' As we shall see, when conversation has a different purpose, different maxims need to be postulated.

Grice points out that speakers may well flout, or apparently flout, a given maxim. Given that the hearer is entitled to assume that the speaker is not trying to mislead him, the hearer is faced with a problem:

> How can (the speaker's) saying what he did say be reconciled with the supposition that he is observing the overall Cooperative Principle? This situation is one that characteristically gives rise to a conversational implicature (Grice 1975:49).

The meaning of 'a conversational implicature' can be understood from the following example offered by Grice:

> A is standing by an obviously immobilized car and is approached by B; the following exchange takes place:
> A: "I am out of petrol."
> B: "There is a garage round the corner". (Gloss: B would be infringing the maxim 'Be relevant' unless he thinks, or thinks it possible, that the garage is open, and has petrol to sell; so he implicates that the garage is, or at least may be open, etc.) . . .
> the speaker (thus) implicates that which he must be assumed to believe in order to preserve the assumption that he is observing the maxim of relation (Grice 1975:51).

Brown and Levinson make Grice's concept of conversational implicature into a valuable tool for the analysis of polite behavior:

(Grice's) Maxims define for us the basic set of assumptions underlying every talk exchange. But this does not imply that utterances in general, or even reasonably frequently, must meet these conditions, as critics of Grice have sometimes thought. Indeed, the majority of natural conversations do not proceed in such a brusque fashion at all. The whole thrust of this paper is that one powerful and pervasive motive for *not* talking Maxim-wise is the desire to give some attention to face . . . Politeness is then a major source of deviation from such rational efficiency, and is communicated precisely by that deviation. But even in such departures from the Maxims, they remain in operation at a deeper level. It is only because they are still assumed to be in operation that addressees are forced to do the inferential work that establishes the underlying message and the (polite or other) source of the departure – in short, to find an implicature, i.e. an inference generated by precisely this assumption. Otherwise the polite strategies . . . would simply be heard as mumbo-jumbo. There is a basic assumption in talk that there is underlying method in the madness (Brown and Levinson 1978:100).

Brown and Levinson give a very large number of examples of different politeness strategies in English, Tamil and Tzeltal in their monograph-length article, which is warmly commended to the reader. Two selected examples may give an indication of their general approach. Both examples, by apparently flouting Grice's maxims, carry the conversational implicature that the speaker wishes to signal his desire to attend to aspects of the hearer's face.

The first example concerns positive politeness, which was described above as directed to the addressee's positive face. [. . .] Positive politeness is characterized by an element of exaggeration, with a consequent flouting of the maxim of quality. Brown and Levinson suggest that this

> serves as a marker of the face-redress aspect of positive-politeness expression by indication that even if S can't with total sincerity say "I want your wants," he can at least sincerely indicate "I want your positive face to be satisfied." Thus the element of insincerity in exaggerated expressions of approval or interest ("How absolutely marvellous! I simply can't imagine how you manage to keep your roses so exquisite, Mrs B!") is compensated for by the implication that the speaker really sincerely wants Mrs B's positive face to be enhanced (op. cit. pp. 106–108).

The second example concerns negative politeness. This was described above as directed to the addressee's negative face, or

> his want to have his freedom of action unhindered and his attention unimpeded. It is the heart of respect behaviour . . . Where positive politeness is free-ranging, negative politeness is specific and focused; it performs the function of minimizing the particular imposition that the Face Threatening Action unavoidably effects. When we think of politeness in Western cultures, it is negative-politeness behaviour that springs to mind. In our culture, negative politeness is the most elaborate and the most conventionalized set of linguistic strategies of FTA redress; it is the stuff that fills the etiquette books . . . Its linguistic realizations – conventional indirectnesses, hedges on illocutionary force, polite pessimism (about the

success of requests, etc.), the emphasis on H's relative power – are very familiar
. . . (op. cit. pp. 134–135).

One example that Brown and Levinson cite of a conventionally pessimistic request of this
sort is:

There wouldn't I suppose be any chance of your being able to lend me your car for
just a few minutes, would there? (op. cit. p. 147).

[. . .]

It should be clear from the discussion above that the process of conversation
displays a continual tension between two general communicative needs – the need to
communicate as efficiently as possible and the need to be polite.

[. . .]

The four maxims that Grice based on the effective exchange of information are
strictly applicable only to those parts of conversation that have a definable propositional
content. In the marginal phases of conversation, only the utterances of phatic communion
have any discernible content of this sort. Address-terms and formulaic phrases of greeting
and farewell such as 'Hello' and 'Goodbye' have no such structure, and are therefore not
susceptible of a standard Gricean analysis. We can therefore gain a broader perspective
of conversation if, as well as Grice's four propositionally-relevant maxims, we adopt his
'social' maxim [. . .], which enjoins speakers to 'Be polite.' We can then see the three
phases of conversation – the initial, medial and final phases – as reflecting obedience to a
varying interplay between the propositionally-based and the socially-based maxims. In the
medial phase, where the main business of the interaction is usually achieved, it may be
that the propositionally-relevant maxims exercise their major influence, with social
factors of politeness playing a less dominant part. In the marginal phases, where greeting
and parting are negotiated, social factors will loom largest, with propositional mechanisms being subordinated to a social purpose.

Armed with the notions of conversational implicature, politeness and positive and
negative face, we can now turn to the more detailed analysis of the routine linguistic
behavior that characterizes the marginal phases of conversational interaction.

An important aspect of positive face is the hearer's need for his social identity to be
acceptable to the speaker. A speaker can obey the social maxim 'Be polite,' and attend to
this aspect of the hearer's face, by using linguistic routines that acknowledge his identity
either explicitly or tacitly. The choice of linguistic routine has to be consistent with the
relative social status of the hearer, with the degree of acquaintance that exists between
the speaker and the hearer, and with situational factors such as the degree of formality
imposed by the occasion of conversation or by the special nature of the setting in which
the conversation is taking place. The plan of the remainder of this chapter will be to
discuss the linguistic routines that constitute the polite norm, where the linguistic forms
chosen are consistent with the three factors of social status, degree of acquaintance
and nature of the situation, and then to discuss the implicature signalled by deviations
from the polite norm, for each of three areas. These areas will be, in turn, terms of direct
address, formulaic phrases of greeting and parting, and finally utterances of phatic
communion.

TERMS OF DIRECT ADDRESS

For a detailed analysis of terms of direct address, the reader is referred to two seminal articles, Brown and Ford (1961) and Ervin-Tripp (1969). The analysis presented here is for address in British English, and is based on the flow-chart approach of Ervin-Tripp. The analysis is initial, merely suggesting the rule structure that underlies usage in this area: further empirical work is needed to ratify the suggestions.

Figure 5.1 summarizes the factors that constrain the polite choice of address terms in British English. The suggested network is classificatory, and not a model of some decision process in the speaker's mind. Some options have been omitted. For example, in certain relationships, no term of direct address is used at all. This choice has been left out of this rather simplified diagram.

It may be helpful to comment on some of the details of the diagram, which is based on characteristics of the addressee, who must be at least slightly known to the speaker. The first analytic decision to be taken is represented by Box 1, where the addressee is classified as 'adult' or 'not adult.' The direction of flow of classificatory decisions is indicated by arrows, and a plus sign at the exit to a box signifies a positive classification, a minus sign a negative classification. Thus if the addressee is a child, no further classificatory decisions are necessary, and FN (first name) will be the polite norm.

In Box 2, a 'marked setting' is one where special address-conventions apply, in which addressees gain their relevant identity through their official and not their personal identity. Examples would be a court of law, a formal meeting, or Parliament. Box 9 reflects the social fact that acquaintances of higher rank or greater age are not addressed by FN unless they have specifically encouraged the speaker to do so by an explicit dispensation, with a phrase such as 'Let's not be formal – please call me Robert.' Without dispensation, TLN (title – either occupational, such as Dr. or sex-specific, such as Mr, Mrs, with last name) is the norm.

As with nearly all linguistic routines concerned with the statement of social relationships, address usage is reciprocal between equals and non-reciprocal between participants of unequal status. Thus an office junior may call the manager 'Mr Smith' but receive 'Charles' in return.

To depart from the polite norm is to trigger a conversational implicature. As Ervin-Tripp comments (1969:102), 'When there is agreement about the normal address form to alters of specific statuses, then any deviation is a message.' We can illustrate this briefly with two examples. The first is where an adult addresses a well-acquainted child not with FN as the polite norm prescribes, but with FNLN 'Bobby Smith.' In such circumstances, even though children seem to learn linguistic routines very slowly, the child usually understands the implicature of reproof. The second example is where equals enjoying a growing acquaintance move from TLN to FN, thereby acknowledging the growth of their intimacy.

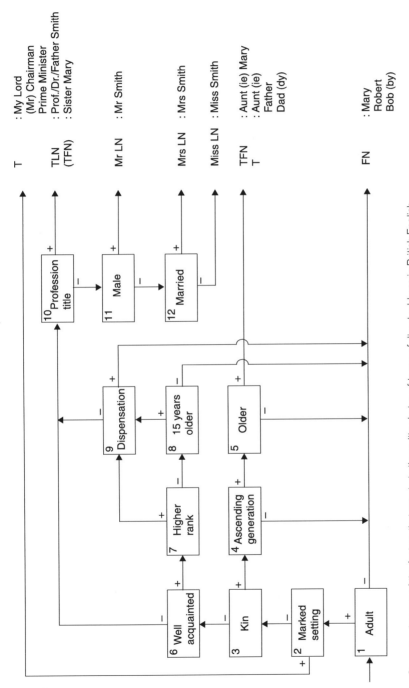

Figure 5.1   Summary diagram of the factors that constrain the polite choice of terms of direct address in British English.

FORMULAIC PHRASES OF GREETING AND PARTING

A similar model can be used to summarize the factors that underlie the polite norm in choice of formulaic terms of greeting and parting. Figure 5.2 shows the network of addressee-characteristics that gives rise to different formulaic usages in British English such as 'Good morning,' 'Morning,' 'Hello,' 'Goodbye,' and 'Bye.' Once again, the analysis is initial, needing further empirical work to amplify the conclusions.

At first sight, the structure of the descriptive model seems simpler than in the case of terms of direct address. But in fact there are some complicating factors, left out of this simplified diagram. One of these is that the choice of formulaic terms often depends almost as much on the characteristics of the speaker as on those of the listener. For example, the formulaic parting phrases 'Cheerio' and 'Cheers' seem to be used almost only by male speakers. 'Hi' and 'Ciao' tend to be used only by young speakers, and 'Wotcher' only by speakers who are both young and male. Factors of social class are also influential, in that particular phrases are not used freely by members of all social classes. 'How do you do' is largely restricted to middle and upper class speakers, and 'How do' and 'Howdy' to working class speakers.

As with terms of direct address, a marked setting constrains the choice of formulaic phrases of greeting and parting to the formal usages 'Good morning/afternoon/evening' and 'Good day/morning/afternoon/evening/night' respectively, together with 'Good-bye.' As phrases of maximum formality and maximum distance, these are also the phrases used to acquaintances of higher rank or greater age who have not offered a dispensation to the speaker to progress to a less formal style.

As a general observation, it is striking that relatives and well-acquainted equals or inferiors are treated with the same informality of formulaic phrase as children. In between the two extremes represented by 'Good morning' and 'Hello,' however, further research is necessary to clarify less obvious usage. The abbreviated phrase 'Morning,' and its equivalents, can certainly be used to superior or older acquaintances who have offered a dispensation, as can the abbreviated 'Bye.' But whether there is a progression of informality from 'Morning' to 'Hello,' and whether 'Goodbye' can also be used legitimately to this category of listener, is not able to be stated with confidence without more evidence. Similarly, the descriptive model offered here does not handle the case of slightly acquainted equals, who have the option of using 'Morning' and its equivalents as well as 'Good morning' etc., but who do not progress to 'Hello' until acquaintance is more established.

Polite usage in this area, as with terms of direct address, is reciprocal between equals and non-reciprocal between participants of unequal status. To depart from the polite norm is to signal by implicature that a change in social relation is being negotiated. To move from 'Good day' to 'Bye' is a large social step; to move from 'Bye' to 'Good day' is an almost irrevocable act of social distancing.

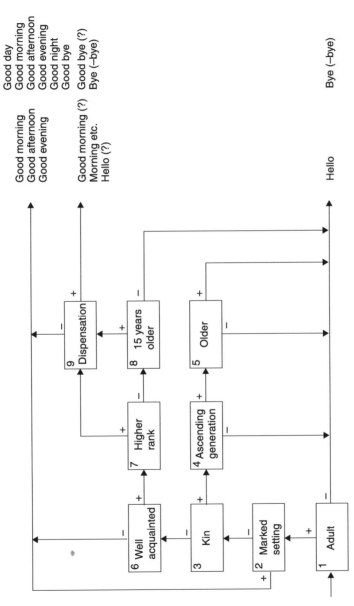

Figure 5.2   Summary diagram of the factors that constrain the polite choice of formulaic phrases of greeting and parting in British English.

UTTERANCES OF PHATIC COMMUNION

The argument that a speaker can signal his perception of the formality of a situation, and of his acquaintance and social relationship with a listener, by his choice of address-term and formulaic phrase of greeting or parting, is reasonably acceptable on the basis of common experience. The argument that similar information can be signalled by a speaker's choice of small-talk, or phatic communion, is perhaps less obvious. The argument is set out in more detail in Laver (1975), and discussion here is limited to a re-analysis, in terms of politeness theory, of some of the data presented in that article.

The small-talk of phatic communion, involving supremely obvious comments about the weather or benevolent admonitions such as 'Take care,' are largely limited to the initial and final phases of conversational interactions, and it will be convenient to treat phatic communion in these two phases separately.

In brief summary, the linguistic routines of phatic communion in the initial phase of conversation seem to have three social functions. The first of these is to defuse 'the potential hostility of silence in situations where speech is conventionally anticipated' (Laver 1975:220). Secondly, it 'has an initiatory function, in that it allows the participants to cooperate in getting the interaction comfortably under way, using emotionally uncontroversial . . . material, and demonstrating by signals of cordiality and tentative social solidarity their mutual acceptance of the possibility of an interaction taking place' (op. cit. p. 221). Thirdly, and most relevantly for present purposes, phatic communion has an exploratory function, 'in that it allows the participants to feel their way towards the working consensus of their interaction' (op. cit. p. 221), partly by revealing their perception of their relative social status. It is this third function which will be discussed here.

The basic position is that a certain pattern of phatic communion constitutes the polite norm, and that the use of this pattern serves as an acknowledgment of the social relationship that exists between the participants. Any deviation from that pattern then triggers the implicature that the speaker is thereby re-negotiating the relationship. The mechanisms of acknowledgment and re-negotiation work in the following way, it is suggested. There are three broad categories of phrases that are typically used as utterances of phatic communion. The first category is made up of phrases about factors common to both speaker and listener, most often about the weather. The syntactic structure of the phrases is typically abbreviated, which helps participants to recognize their phatic communion function. Characteristic phrases are: 'Nice day,' 'What weather,' 'Frost tonight,' 'Nice party,' 'About time the trains were cleaned.' We can call this category the *neutral* category.

The second category is made up of phrases that comment on factors personal to the speaker, which we can call the *self-oriented* category. Phrases in this category would include: 'Hot work, this,' 'I do like a breath of fresh air,' 'My legs weren't made for these hills.' The third category contains phrases that refer to factors specific to the listener, such as 'How's life/business/the wife/the family?,' 'That looks like hard work,' 'Do you come here often?,' which we can call the *other-oriented* category.

The pattern of choice of category that constitutes the polite norm is one where the speakers who are well-acquainted can freely choose any category, but where non-acquainted speakers obey a constraint which depends on relative social status. The neutral category is available to speakers of any social status, but other-oriented phrases are politely available only to speakers of relatively higher status, and self-oriented phrases only to speakers of relatively lower status. Thus, in an encounter between a country gentleman out for a walk and a hedger-and-ditcher clearing nettles from a ditch, polite options include either speaker saying 'Nice day,' the country gentleman saying 'That looks like hard work,' or the hedger-and-ditcher saying 'Hard work, this.'

The effect of violations of the polite norm is often to negotiate a greater solidarity between participants. For the country gentleman to use a self-oriented phrase such as 'I do like a breath of fresh air,' or for the hedger-and-ditcher to use an other-oriented phrase such as 'Out for a breath of fresh air, are you then?' has the effect in both cases of inviting the listener to a momentary solidarity in which the status differential between the two participants, which may be obvious from visible information such as dress, is thereby asserted as irrelevant (Laver 1975:224–225).

Considerations of face in the three categories of phrases are more problematic. Clearly, use of the neutral category threatens no-one's face. But the use of either of the other two categories may concern both positive and negative face. For example, to use an other-oriented phrase such as 'How's the wife?' could be thought to threaten the listener's negative face in that such an enquiry invades his family life; but it also attends to his positive face in an obvious way, as would 'Nice tie,' etc. To use a self-oriented phrase might be thought to threaten one's own negative face, by being revealing about oneself and thus in some sense giving the listener power through information; but it also attends to one's own positive face, in that it takes an opportunity to present onself as potentially interesting to the listener.

Where ceremonial behavior in the initial phase of conversation is often rather brief, the linguistic routines of phatic communion in the closing phase of conversation are often highly elaborate, suggesting a very high degree of risk to face. That participants are vulnerable to threat is clear if we consider the two principal functions that phatic communion serves in the closing phase:

> Firstly, it allows the participants to achieve a cooperative parting, in which any feeling of rejection by the person being left can be assuaged by appropriate reassurance from the person leaving. Secondly, it serves to consolidate the relationship between the two participants, by means of behaviour which emphasizes the enjoyable quality of the encounter, the mutual esteem in which the participants hold each other, the promise of a continuation of the relationship, the assertion of mutual solidarity, and the announcement of a continuing consensus for the shape of encounters in the future (Laver 1975: 231).

We can refer to the two major types of function being served by phatic communion in the closing phase as *mitigation* and *consolidation*. The use of these terms highlights the attention that the participants typically apply to the care of their relationship in this fragile phase: nearly all the actual utterances are examples of self-oriented and other-oriented phrases, and neutral comments seem to be used rather seldom. The polite norm in the closing phase, between participants who do not meet often, seems to be to use at least one mitigatory or consolidatory phrase, together with some appropriate formulaic phrase of parting. To omit such reparatory acts entirely is rare, and triggers a somewhat extreme implicature of rejection.

Mitigatory comments are usually addressed to the negative aspect of face, often setting the reason for terminating the encounter in a compulsion external to the speaker. Typical comments are: 'I'm sorry, I have to go, I have to give a lecture,' 'I'm afraid I must be off, I have to relieve the babysitter.' Such comments attend to the negative face of the speaker. A particularly interesting sub-category of mitigatory comment is where 'deference is expressed to the needs of the listener himself, as the compelling external authority' (Laver 1975:230). Examples of this type of attention to the listener's negative face are 'Well, I musn't keep you,' and 'I guess you have to get on, I'll be going.'

Consolidatory comments are addressed to the positive aspect of face. Esteem for the other participant is implied, in comments such as 'It was nice seeing you,' 'I do enjoy our little talks' and 'How nice to see you again.' Consolidatory caring for the other participant is shown in comments on future welfare, such as 'Hope your cold gets better soon,' benevolent admonitions like 'Watch how you go' and benedictions such as 'God bless' (Laver 1975: 230). Other consolidatory comments mention arrangements for the continuation of the relationship, as in 'See you next Saturday,' or 'Don't be such a stranger, come again soon.' Consolidation in a wider network of common acquaintances also occurs, in comments such as 'Say hello to Anne for me' or 'Remember me to Bob.'

CONCLUSION

This chapter has explored three types of linguistic routines found in the marginal phases of conversations, in the small-scale ritual ceremonies of greeting and parting. It was suggested that a polite norm exists in the choice of such linguistic routines, such that obedience to the norm has the effect of acknowledging the social identity of the listener, in terms of his relative social status, and of the degree of acquaintance between the participants. Violating the polite norm, by using other choices of greeting or parting behavior, carries the conversational implicature of negotiating a change in the relationship between the participants, usually towards greater intimacy or greater distancing. It was also suggested that a fundamental motive for polite behavior of the sort described is to pay attention to the 'face' of either or both of the participants.

Linguistic routines of greeting and parting, far from being relatively meaningless and mechanical social behavior, can thus be understood as extremely important strategies for the negotiation and control of social identity and social relationships between participants in conversation.

REFERENCES

Brown, Penelope and Steven Levinson (1978) Universals in language usage: politeness phenomena. In E. Goody (ed.) *Questions and Politeness*. London etc.: Cambridge University Press, 56–310.

Brown, Roger and Marguerite Ford (1961) Address in American English. *Journal of Abnormal and Social Psychology* 62: 375–85.

Ervin-Tripp, Susan (1969) Sociolinguistics. In Leonard Berkowitz (ed.) *Advances in Experimental Social Psychology*. New York: Academic Press, 93–107.

Goffman, Erving (1967) *Interaction Ritual: Essays on Face to Face Behavior*. Garden City, New York: Anchor Books.

Grice, H. Paul (1963) Logic and conversation. Portion published in Peter Cole and Jerry Morgan (eds) *Syntax and Semantics 3: Speech Acts*. New York: Academic Press, 41–58.

Laver, John (1975) Communicative functions of phatic communion. In Adam Kendon, Richard M. Harris and Mary Ritchie Key (eds) *Organization of Behaviour in Face-to Face Interaction*. The Hague, Paris: Mouton, 215–37.

QUESTIONS

Content

1. What is the link between politeness theory and linguistic routines such as greetings and partings?
2. What is the link between Grice's maxims and linguistic routines such as greetings and partings?
3. When a teacher utters the following sentence: 'Maggie Miller, will you please stop disrupting class.' Does the teacher choose the polite norm? If yes, for what situation? If not, what is the effect and what would have been the polite norm?
4. Are the results for terms of address and formulaic terms of greeting and parting still correct today?
5. What do terms of address, formulaic terms of greeting and parting, and small talk have in common?

Concept

1. The term *Ms* is not included in the chart of terms of address. What does the term *Ms* mean to you? Redraw the chart and include the term in your description.
2. Analyze and compare these four American service encounters in respect to address, greeting, parting, small talk (including categories of neutral, self and other oriented phatic communion). How do speakers orient to positive / negative face needs? What is the polite norm?

1. Clothing store A

S: How are you today Sir?=
C: =Fine (2.0) (puts merchandise on counter)
S: That's good (22.0)
(S scans; then folds merchandise and puts it into a
  bag)
(C is getting his credit card ready)
S: Fifty dollars eighty eight cents (16.0)
(C hands card over, S gets receipt ready and gives
  it C to sign, C signs; S gives card back to C)
S: Here you go=
C: =Thank you (55.0)
(S gets receipt ready and gives receipt and
  merchandise to C)
S: Here you go Sir=
C: =Thank you=
S: =Receipt's in the bag/ Have a good day
C: Bye

2. Clothing store B (older female customer
  talking to younger male server)

S: Hello
C: Can you give me a gift card, dear=
S: =Yeah (2.0) how much did you want it for?
C: Ehm/ Twenty dollars
(S is getting gift card ready) (7.0)
C: Do I (3 syll.) or can I use my debit card?(.)
S: Debit card is fine
C: laughs
(S is still working on gift card) (80.0) (He
  gives it to the customer)
C: Is this mine/ or yours=
S: =This one's yours=
C: =ok (1.0)
S: You're all set
C: ok
S: Have a nice evening
C: (nods and walks away while putting gift
  card into bag)

3. Drugstore
S: Hello. Is that it?=
C: =That's it (1.0)
(S. takes the merchandise and scans it.)
S: Ninety-four
(C. gets his money and hands it to the S)
(S takes the money and types the amount into
   the cash register)
S: Six cents back/ (S hands C the money) /Did
   you need your receipt for this?=
C: =No thanks=
S: =Alright/ Have a nice day=
(C puts merchandise into his backpack)
C: =Thank you/ You too=
S: =Thanks

4. Hardware department in department store
S: Is someone helping you guys?
(addresses wife and husband; she is doing
   the buying)
C: Not really/(.) Well/ I mean/ there was
   somebody here/ but he was like I'll be
   back or something=
S: =Sure (.)
C: He saw me/Have to get outta here while I
   can (laughs)
(S scans merchandise and puts it into a bag)
S: (laughs) I just can't do it anymore/ he's lost
   the will to live (2.0)
S: seven ninety-three (4.0)
(C gives credit card to S)
S: Here's your card back (15.0)
(S gets receipt ready and hands it over to C to
   sign)
S: Sign in the little box here
(C signs; she did not sign in the right place
   and shows receipt to S)
C: Is that a problem?
S: Oh/ that's ok/ that's ok/ don't worry/ just
   pretend
(C signs again)
S: See/ that's good=
C: =ok
(S hands over receipt and bag)
S: There you go=
C: =Thanks=
S: =Have a good one=
C: =You too

Transcription conventions

S server
C customer
    Simultaneous speech
(0.0) Pauses or gaps in tenths of second
(.) Micropause
(2 syll) Uncertain passage of transcription, with
    number of syllables indicated where possible

== Latched utterances
CAPS Relatively loud speech
: Lengthened syllable
? Rising intonation
/ Tone group boundary
- cut off
' stressed syllable

Chapter 6

Sachiko Ide

FORMAL FORMS AND DISCERNMENT: TWO NEGLECTED ASPECTS OF UNIVERSALS OF LINGUISTIC POLITENESS

INTRODUCTION

IN THE PAST FIFTEEN years, universal principles of linguistic politeness have been presented, notably by Lakoff (1973, 1975), Brown and Levinson (1978, 1987) and Leech (1983).

In discussing the problems of judging the grammaticality of a sentence, Lakoff argues the need to consider the context of a sentence. The context has to be analyzed, she claims, in terms of rules people follow in speaking, i.e. rules of pragmatic competence, which consist of the rule of clarity and the rule of politeness. The rule of politeness, in turn, is elaborated into three further 'rules'. They are 'keep aloof', 'give options' and 'show sympathy'.

Basing their claims on 'face' and 'rationality', common properties of human beings, Brown and Levinson posit the universals for one aspect of language use, i.e. linguistic politeness, and they present a framework of strategies for politeness. This consists of five major clusters of strategies with which most polite, deferential or tactful verbal expressions in different cultures and languages can be explained. These clusters are 'without redressive action, baldly', 'positive politeness', 'negative politeness', 'off record', and 'don't do the Face Threatening Act'.[1]

Leech, in attempting to present the overall principles of pragmatics, treated the politeness principle as one of the three principles in interpersonal rhetoric. This politeness principle consists of six maxims: 'tact', 'generosity', 'approbation', 'modesty', 'agreement' and 'sympathy'.

What is common among these pioneering works is that they claim, whether explicitly or not, the universal applicability of their principles of linguistic politeness.

Source: Ide, Sachiko (1989) Formal forms and discernment: two neglected aspects of universals of linguistic politeness. *Multilingua* 8: 223–248.

However, when examined in the light of languages with honorifics, such as Japanese, none of these frameworks appears adequate. The major linguistic devices for politeness in Japanese either fall outside of these frameworks or play a minor part in them. The frameworks thus appear to be the product of the Western academic tradition, since even Brown and Levinson, who dealt with Tzeltal and Tamil besides English, could not avoid an ethnocentric bias toward Western languages and the Western perspective.

In this paper, neglected aspects in the so-called universal principles of linguistic politeness are presented and explained with illustrations. Focusing on Brown and Levinson's framework, which is the most comprehensive of the three, I will point out the deficiencies of their framework. [. . .]

THE DEFINITION OF LINGUISTIC POLITENESS

[. . .]

I define linguistic politeness as the language usage associated with smooth communication, realized 1) through the speaker's use of intentional strategies to allow his or her message to be received favorably by the addressee, and 2) through the speaker's choice of expressions to conform to the expected and/or prescribed norms of speech appropriate to the contextual situation in individual speech communities.

Here, mention must be made of the difference between the terms 'polite' and 'politeness'. The term 'polite' is an adjective like 'deferential' and 'respectful'. It has a positive meaning: 'having or showing good manners, consideration for others, and/or correct social behavior'.[2] Politeness, on the other hand, is the neutral term. Just as 'height' does not refer to the state of being 'high', 'politeness' is not the state of being 'polite'. Therefore, when we talk about linguistic politeness, we refer to a continuum stretching from polite to non-polite (i.e. zero polite, that is, unmarked for politeness) speech.

NEGLECTED ASPECTS

Heretofore neglected aspects will be discussed from two perspectives: language and use.

Language: Formal forms

The point concerning language arises from the fact that Brown and Levinson's framework fails to give a proper account of formal linguistic forms such as honorifics, which are among the major means of expressing linguistic politeness in some languages. In Japanese, polite requests can be expressed even in imperative forms, if honorific verb forms are used.

(1)   # *Kore-o*   *yome*. (The # marks a non-polite sentence.)
         this-ACC   read
         #'Read this.'

(2)   *Kore-o*   *o-yomi-nasai*   **mase***.*
                    read-REF. HONO. AD.HONO.
        'Read this.'

(3)   *Kore-o*   *yoma*   *nai*   *ka.*
                    NEG.   QUES.
        'Won't you read this?'

(4)   *Kore-o*   *o-yomi-**ni-nari***   *mase*   *n*   *ka.*
                    read-REF. HONO.   AD. HONO. NEG.
        'Won't you read this?'

(1) is a simple imperative without honorifics, and thus is not polite. (2) is imperative but referent and addressee honorifics are used. Therefore, it is polite. (3) is made polite by the use of specific strategies: it has been made less imposing by the strategy of its transformation into a negative and interrogative form. (4) is the combination of (2) and (3), and therefore the most polite of these examples.

We have seen in the example sentences that there are two types of device to make an utterance polite: one is the choice of formal forms as in (2), and the other is the use of strategies, as in (3). It is the former device, the choice of formal forms, that is neglected in the framework proposed by Brown and Levinson.

The use of formal forms is not unique to honorific languages. Well known examples would be the choice of the pronoun V (Vous) in contrast to T (Tu) and the choice of the address term TLN (Title plus Last Name) in contrast to FN (First Name) to mark politeness. The contrast of formal vs. non-formal forms is observed in the forms such as 'hello' vs. 'hi', and 'purchase' vs. 'buy' and 'dine' vs. 'eat'. Besides the lexical level, we have formal forms on the discourse levels. Examples are found in courteous speech formulas such as 'thank you', 'excuse me', and 'it's my pleasure'. Using or not using such formal formulas is another example of the contrast of formal vs. non-formal.

Brown and Levinson (1978, 1987) treat some of those formal forms as expressions of negative politeness strategies. However, they should not be categorized as strategies, since there are some fundamental differences between the choice of formal forms and the use of strategies. Formal forms are 1) limited in choice, 2) socio-pragmatically obligatory, 3) grammatically obligatory, and 4) made in accordance with a person who is not necessarily the addressee, the referent or the speaker him/herself.

First, while the use of strategies allows a potentially unlimited number of linguistic expressions, the use of formal forms is a matter of choices among a limited set of forms. It is very often the case that the choice is made between two alternatives.

Choosing a formal form or expression out of limited varieties of formality makes an utterance polite for the following reasons. According to Levinson, formal forms should be explained as conventional implicature (1983: 129ff). Implicature makes an utterance polite by its indirectness. Ide states, 'When formal forms are used, they create a formal atmosphere where participants are kept away from each other, avoiding imposition. Non-imposition is the essence of polite behavior. Thus, to create a formal atmosphere by the use of formal forms is to be polite' (1982: 382).

Second, the choice of formal linguistic forms is obligatory in the light of social conventions.

(5)   #*Sensei-wa kore-o*   *yonda*
      prof.-TOP   read
      #'The professor read this.'

(6)   *Sensei-wa kore-o*   *oyomi-**ni**-**natta**.*
                               REF.HONO. PAST
      'The professor read this.'

In (6), an honorific form is used in referring to the action of a person of higher status, in this case a professor. This is because the social rules of Japanese society require one to be polite to a high status person like a professor. This use of an honorific verb form is the socio-pragmatic equivalent of grammatical concord, and may thus be termed socio-pragmatic concord. Subject-predicate concord is determined by the social rule of the society in which the language is used. In Japanese society (6) is appropriate, but (5) is not. Thus, the concord of honorifics is sociopragmatically obligatory.

Levinson, in discussing honorifics as the linguistic form in which socially deictic information is encoded, distinguishes two honorifics (1983: 90–91), i.e. relational [forms may vary depending on participant role] and absolute [same forms are used *to* a particular individual, often referred to as an "authorized recipient", or *by* a particular individual, an "authorized speaker"]. He further states that the relational variety is the most important. However, it must be remembered that this can only be said with reference to egalitarian societies. In societies where an honorific system is elaborately developed, it is the absolute variety that is basic. One finds evidence for the absolute variety in a diachronic study (Brown and Gilman 1960) and in the description of honorific systems in stratified societies (Geertz 1960, Koshal 1987). In Japan, too, the absolute variety of honorific can still be found. For example, in the Syuri area of Okinawa Prefecture, the address terms for parents and grandparents and the response forms are determined according to the speakers' social class, i.e. *sizoku* (a family of the samurai class) or *heimin* (a commoner) (Sibata 1988: 6). Levinson makes the general claim that the absolute variety is used either by 'authorized speakers' or toward 'authorized recipients' (1983:91). Figure 6.1 illustrates forms of response in Syuri dialect used by authorized speakers speaking to authorized recipients.

The speaker of the Syuri dialect chooses out of the possible repertoire given to the social standing of the speaker's family, a form appropriate for the recipient's family as well as for the relative status (superior or non-superior) of the interactants. This

RECIPIENT \ SPEAKER		SAMURAI CLASS	COMMONER
SAMURAI CLASS	superior		[u :]
	inferior	[o :]	
COMMONER	superior		[o :]
	inferior	[ə̄]	

Figure 6.1   The absolute honorifics in Syuri dialect (response forms).

choice is absolute as the determining factor depends on ascribed social standing. In the same way, the sociopragmatic concord illustrated in (6) is of the absolute variety. In other words, the use of honorific, i.e. formal forms, determined by the social rules of politeness represents the absolute variety, because the recipient of the honorific in (6), the professor, is authorized to receive formal forms as the token of deference according to the social conventions of the society. On the contrary, the use of honorifics and other formal forms which the speaker can manipulatively choose, according to his or her judgment of his or her relation to the addressee or the referent, shows the relational variety. Thus, the absolute variety is obligatory whereas the relational variety is optional.

Third, there are no neutral forms. Levinson states, 'In general, in such languages (South East Asian), it is almost impossible to say anything at all which is not socio-linguistically marked as appropriate for certain kinds of addressees only' (1983: 90). Therefore, the choice of honorific or plain forms is grammatically obligatory. The choices of pronouns (V or T) and address terms (TLN or FN) in some Western languages can be explained in the same way as the choice of honorifics. The speaker is bound to make an obligatory choice between a formal form V or TLN, and a non-formal form T or FN.[3]

Matsumoto (1987) discusses the obligatory choice of honorifics or plain forms of copulas in Japanese, illustrating three variants of 'Today is Saturday', non-FTA utterances. One is expressed in a plain form (*da*), the second is in the addressee honorific (*desu*), and the third is in the super polite addressee honorific (*de gozaimasu*). She states that even in such cases of non-FTA utterances the speaker is required to make an obligatory choice among the variants, with or without honorifics, according to the formality of the setting and the relationship among the participants.

Fourth, the choice of formal forms is made in accordance with the referent and/or the speaker, which makes the use of formal forms distinct from verbal strategies oriented only toward the addressee. Brown and Levinson (1978: 185ff) and Levinson (1983: 90ff) acknowledge the referent honorific in the case of V/T pronoun alternation. (6) is an example of a referent honorific. The humble variety of honorifics, used to humble the speaker, is illustrated in (9) below:

(7) #*Watasi-* ga iku.
     I   SUBJ go
     #'I (will) go.'
(8) *Watasi-ga* iki- **masu**.
                        ADD.HONO.
(9) *Watasi-ga* **mairi-** **masu**.
          go   HUM.HONO.

(8) is a polite utterance compared to (7), but (9) is even more polite. In (9) both a humble form and an addressee honorific are used for a non-FTA utterance.

It is because of these fundamental differences between verbal strategies and formal linguistic forms that we claim here the need to categorize the devices of linguistic politeness into two basic types. The use of formal linguistic forms is controlled by a different behavioral principle from that underlying the verbal strategies treated by Brown and Levinson.

Usage: discernment

The use of formal forms is inherently dependent upon the speaker's observation of the social conventions of the society of which he or she is a member. In a society we behave according to social conventions, one set of which we may call the social rules of politeness. Ide states the social rules of politeness for Japanese: 1) be polite to a person of a higher social position, 2) be polite to a person with power, 3) be polite to an older person, and 4) be polite in a formal setting determined by the factors of participants, occasions, or topics (1982: 366–377). Except for 2) and 4), which could be relative, these social rules are essentially absolute in quality. Honorifics and other formal linguistic forms, in which the relative rank of the speaker, the referent and the addressee are morphologically or lexically encoded, are used so as to comply with such rules of politeness.

The practice of polite behavior according to social conventions is known as *wakimae* in Japanese. To behave according to *wakimae* is to show verbally and non-verbally one's sense of place or role in a given situation according to social conventions. In a stable society, an individual is expected to behave according to the status and the role of various levels ascribed to or acquired by that individual. To acknowledge the delicate status and/or the role differences of the speaker, the addressee and the referent in communication is essential to keep communication smooth and without friction. Thus, to observe *wakimae* by means of language use is an integral part of linguistic politeness.

The closest equivalent term for *wakimae* in English is 'discernment' (Hill et al. 1986: 347–348). The choice of linguistic forms or expressions in which the distinction between the ranks or the roles of the speaker, the referent and the addressee are systematically encoded will be called the discernment aspect of linguistic politeness, which I claim to be one of the neglected aspects in Brown and Levinson's framework.

In contrast to the discernment aspect, 'the aspect of politeness which allows the speaker a considerably active choice, according to the speaker's intention from a relatively wider range of possibilities' is called the 'volitional' aspect (Hill et al. 1986: 348). Both aspects aim to achieve smooth communication, but they are different in that the speaker's focus is placed on the socially prescribed norm in the former and on his/her own intention in the latter.

Whereas Brown and Levinson dealt with face wants, the discernment aspect of linguistic politeness is distinguished by its orientation toward the wants of roles and settings: discernment is oriented mainly toward the wants to acknowledge the ascribed positions or roles of the participants as well as to accommodate to the prescribed norms of the formality of particular settings. The speaker regulates his or her choice of linguistic forms so as to show his or her sense of place. The sense of proper place is determined by what Brown and Levinson termed the weight of power (P), distance (D), and rank (R). The weight is perceived by the speaker against the background of the social norm.

Thus, honorifics are not used to raise the addressee as Brown and Levinson state, but to acknowledge the status difference between the speaker and the referent, who is very often the addressee. Unlike Brown and Levinson, who assumed the equal status of the speaker and the hearer, the speaker of honorifics assumes a status difference. For example, in (6), the subject of the sentence, the professor, takes an honorific form for the predicate which is appropriate for his or her social standing. The speaker thus [orients] to the social conventions, showing the speaker's sense of the referent's status, by using a referent honorific to mark the subject's deferential position. In the case of (9), the speaker [orients] to the formal situation by using both the morphologically encoded form of self-humbling (a humble honorific) and an addressee honorific.[4]

The speakers of honorific languages are bound to make choices among linguistic forms of honorifics or plain forms. Since the choices cover such parts of speech as copulas, verbs, nouns, adjectives, and adverbs, the discernment aspect of linguistic politeness is a matter of constant concern in the use of language. Since there is no neutral form, the speaker of an honorific language has to be sensitive to levels of formality in verbalizing actions or things, just as a native speaker of English, for example, must be sensitive to the countable and non-countable property of things because of a grammatical distinction of property of the singular and plural in English. Hence, the more elaborated the linguistic system of formality, the greater the part the discernment aspect of language use plays in the language. It follows that languages with honorific systems have a strong concern for the discernment aspect of linguistic politeness.

TYPOLOGY OF LINGUISTIC POLITENESS

Two types

Figure 6.2 summarizes the system of two types of linguistic politeness: one is that of discernment, realized mainly by the use of formal linguistic forms, and the other is that of volition, realized mainly by verbal strategies. It is the latter – volition realized through verbal strategies – that Brown and Levinson treat, and the former – discernment realized through formality of linguistic forms – that they neglect, as discussed above.

Discernment and volition are points on a continuum and in most actual language usage one finds that most utterances are neither purely one nor the other, but to some extent a mixture of the two. In example (4), both aspects are used: the honorifics

USE (Speaker's Mode of Speaking)	LANGUAGE (Kinds of Linguistic Device Mainly Used)	EXAMPLE SENTENCES
DISCERNMENT	FORMAL FORMS honorifics pronouns address terms speech levels speech formulas etc.	(2) (6) (8) (9)
		(4)
VOLITION	VERBAL STRATEGIES Seek agreement Joke Question Be pessimistic Minimize the imposition etc.	(3)

Figure 6.2   Two types of linguistic politeness.

represent formal linguistic forms, and the negation and interrogative markers show verbal strategies.

[. . .]

Each language and society is presumed to have at least these two types of linguistic politeness [discernment and volition]. Further, we assume that each culture is different in the relative weight it assigns to them.

[. . .]

PROBLEMS OF BROWN AND LEVINSON'S FRAMEWORK

Categories of strategies

Let us examine Brown and Levinson's framework and discuss the problems in the light of the neglected aspects.

First, their list of four specific strategies shows a mixture of categories. The crucial error is mixing behavior strategies and linguistic strategies. They put behavior strategies such as 'Notice, attend to H', 'Seek agreement', 'Offer, promise', 'Be pessimistic', 'Minimize the imposition', and 'Give deference' in parallel with linguistic strategies such as 'Use in-group identity markers', 'Question, hedge', 'Impersonalize S and H', or 'Nominalize'. The result is confusion in the categorization of expressions. Some linguistic expressions, such as plural personal pronouns 'we' and 'vous', are categorized under the linguistic strategy 'Impersonalize S and H', while they could also be examples for the behavior strategy 'Give deference'.

The confusion could be resolved if they distinguished consistently between behavioral and linguistic strategies and if they allowed some strategies to be categorized under the aspects of formal forms and discernment. For example, 'nominalize' is a linguistic strategy which makes an expression formal. The nominalized expression 'It is my pleasure . . .' is chosen instead of 'It is pleasing . . .', according to Brown and Levinson, as a strategy of negative politeness to maintain the negative faces of the speaker and the hearer. But it yields a more coherent theory if one regards the use of 'It is my pleasure . . .' as the choice of conventional implicature to accommodate to a formal setting. Just like the use of TLN in a formal setting, it is a way of showing discernment.

Using the concepts of formal forms and discernment will allow us room to locate more properly some of the expressions in Brown and Levinson's strategies. For example, honorifics are found under the strategy 'Give deference': the speaker humbles and abases him/herself, or the speaker raises the hearer (Brown and Levinson 1978: 183). However, as mentioned above, the choice of honorifics or non-honorifics is obligatory even for a non-FTA utterance in Japanese. Thus, the primary use is for showing discernment. Brown and Levinson also categorize the use of 'sir' by a lower status person as an instance of the strategy of 'give deference'. However, this is better explained not as the speaker's volitional choice to raise the hearer, which is the manipulative use, but rather as the speaker's observation of conventional rules of politeness to show discernment. Similarly, the choices of second person pronouns and address terms, which are listed as realizations of 'Give deference', and/or 'impersonalize S and H' would be better explained as realizations of discernment through formal forms as argued above.

The use of polite formulas as discussed in etiquette books was outside the scope of Brown and Levinson's work. There is also no mention of speech levels. In defining linguistic politeness, Brown and Levinson state that they are concerned with the perspective 'beyond table manners and etiquette books' (1987: 1). However, we may argue that nobody can deny that to offer greetings, or to use conventional speech formulas in introducing a friend, is a matter of politeness. It is equally a matter of politeness to choose a formal speech level suitable to a formal situational context. These examples are not subject to volitional choice but are to be selected according to discernment. Expanding Brown and Levinson's framework to include the category of formal forms and discernment will open a place for these expressions.

Social variables

Brown and Levinson extensively discuss social variables for the assessment of the seriousness of an FTA (1978: 78–89). These are power (P), distance (D) and rank (R). However, it is not clear how these variables can help a speaker choose an expression or a strategy. It is difficult, for example, to apply these variables to the positive politeness strategy 'Notice, attend to H'. For this kind of strategy of positive politeness, such psychological variables as affinity, affect or intimacy, which are determined by the speaker's psychological attitude rather than social variables, may be relevant. It is mainly in assessing the degree of politeness within the discernment aspect of linguistic politeness that those social variables of power, distance and rank are relevant, because they are themselves conventionally determined by social rules of politeness.

Assumptions

Brown and Levinson's assumption of the universality of face and rationality provides the basis of their framework. Let us examine the concepts from a non-Western perspective.

Face

Brown and Levinson explain face as follows:

Central to our model is a highly abstract notion of 'face' which consists of two specific kinds of desires ('face-wants') attributed by interactants to one another:

the desire to be unimpeded in one's actions (negative face), and the desire (in some respects) to be approved of (positive face). This is the bare bones of a notion of face which (we argue) is universal, but which in any particular society we would expect to be the subject of much cultural elaboration (1987:13).

This notion of face is derived from that of Goffman, which is the key to account for the phenomena of human interaction. Brown and Levinson treat it as though it were the sole notion to account for politeness phenomena: '. . . while the content of face will differ in different cultures, we are assuming that the mutual knowledge of members' public self-image or face and the social necessity to orient oneself to it in interaction, are universal' (1978: 66–67).

To the mind of a non-Westerner, however, what is crucially different is not the content of face but rather the weight of face itself. In a Western society where individualism is assumed to be the basis of all interaction, it is easy to regard face as the key to interaction. On the other hand, in a society where group membership is regarded as the basis for interaction, the role or status defined in a particular situation rather than face is the basis of interaction.

In fact, Brown and Levinson cite Rosaldo (1982) in which speech act theory, the product of the Western perspective, is criticized on the basis of an ethnographical study among the Philippine Illongot.

> Rosaldo (1982) . . . argues that the Illongot do not interpret each others' speech in terms of the expression of sincere feelings and intention, but stress the expectations due to group membership, role structures, and situational constraints (1987: 14–15).

What Rosaldo aptly describes speech as – 'the expressions of group membership, role structures, and situational constraints' – characterizes the content of the discernment aspect.

Though the details of language use among the Illongot must be assumed to be different from those of Japanese, it is surprising to find that Rosaldo's explanation applies to the use of honorifics in Japanese. For a Japanese speaker, to speak with the proper use of honorifics where it is required is to express that the speaker knows his or her expected place in terms of group membership (in-group or out-group), role structures (relative status, power relationship, specific role relationship such as selling and buying), and situational constraints (formal or non-formal settings).

The use of honorifics, thus, is not just the speaker's strategy to humble the speaker and to raise the hearer's status to minimize threat to the hearer, as maintained by Brown and Levinson. Moreover, honorifics are used even for a non-FTA utterance, as evidenced by the use of honorifics as pragmatic concord in example sentence (6). In other words, honorifics are used even where neither the speaker's nor the addressee's 'face' has anything to do with the utterance.

Rationality

Brown and Levinson elaborate their framework by assuming a Model Person (MP), a willful speaker of a native language, who is endowed with two special properties – rationality and face. By rationality they mean 'the availability to our MP of a precisely definable mode of reasoning from ends to the means that will achieve those ends' (1978: 63). It is this rationality, they believe, that makes it possible for the speaker to make an utterance systematically according to his or her intention. They further state, 'It is our belief that only a rational or logical use of strategies provides a unitary explanation of such diverse kinesic, prosodic, and, linguistic usages' (1978: 61).

However, we have seen above that the use of honorifics can be simply socio-pragmatic concord, which operates just as automatically as grammatical concord, independent of the speaker's rational intention. If the framework of linguistic politeness is to restrict its scope to a rational or logical use of the strategies, we will have to exclude not only the use of honorifics but also greetings, speech formulas used for rituals, and many other formal speech elements which are used according to social conventions.

Brown and Levinson are aware of this limitation. 'Note that we shall be attempting here a reduction of some good, solid, Durkheimian social facts – some norms of language usage – to the outcome of the rational choices of individuals' (1978: 64). They justify their assumption of language use based on rationality over language use according to convention thus: 'conventions can themselves be overwhelming reasons for doing things . . . and there can be, and perhaps often are, rational bases for conventions' (1978: 64). However, they fail to explain how rationality operates actively in conventional use. As Brown and Levinson state, there can be rational bases for convention, which must work on a different level from the individual rational action. The logical reasoning must work on the level of the function of society as well as on the level of the individual. For elaborated explanation, further investigation is needed.

To a native speaker of one of the non-Western languages, this framework based on face and rationality makes its authors appear to be looking at supposed universal phenomena of linguistic politeness with only one eye – that is, a Western eye biased by individualism and the Western academic tradition of emphasizing rationality. Linguistic politeness seen through a non-Western eye is the phenomenon associated mainly with proper behavior in a social organization by complying with the social conventions. This, of course, is looking with another single eye.

[. . .]

CONCLUDING REMARKS

For the speaker of an honorific language, linguistic politeness is above all a matter of showing discernment in choosing specific linguistic forms, while for the speaker of a non-honorific language, it is mainly a matter of the volitional use of verbal strategies to maintain the faces of participants. These appear to be entirely distinct systems of language use working in different languages and societies. However, the two aspects are integral to the universals of linguistic politeness, working potentially in almost all languages; the discernment aspect is actually observed in the use of non-honorific languages as much as the volitional aspect is observed in speaking honorific languages.

[. . .]

NOTES

1.   Brown and Levinson presume that some acts intrinsically threaten face. Assuming that all human beings have 'face wants' which consist of two specific kinds of desires, negative face wants and positive face wants, they set up a model of strategies for minimizing the face threatening acts, i.e. FTA (1978: 65).

2. *Longman Dictionary of Contemporary English* 1978.
3. This is the primary use of pronouns and address terms. It is only in manipulative use of this primary usage that a speaker has the liberty of choosing FN instead of TLN. Brown and Levinson (1978: 88–99) deal only with this manipulative use of address terms and pronouns as examples of a verbal strategy of negative politeness, failing to acknowledge the underlying formal requirement of primary usage.
4. The language use according to discernment is observed in the use of expressions at the discourse level as well. An utterance such as *Gokurousama desita* [Thank you for your trouble. FORMULA] is impolite (markedly minus polite), if used by the inferior to the superior, whereas it is expected for the superior to employ it in speaking to the inferior. The rule underlying this usage is the paternal social convention in Japanese society where the role of the superior is to care for the inferior, not vice versa. The inferior's use of the utterance is impolite because the use of the utterance violates discernment of roles of the society. Similarly, if a listener who is not acquainted with the lecturer says *Senseino ohanasi wa omosirokatta desu* [Your (Professor's) lecture was interesting], he or she is condemned as being impolite. Such an utterance is allowed only by those who are of equal or superior status or on familiar terms with the lecturer. Such a usage is taken as impolite because an audience member who is supposed to be in the role of listening and learning should not assume an equal position by making comments to the lecturer. It is a violation of discernment.

REFERENCES

Brown, Penelope and Stephen Levinson (1978) Universals in language usage: politeness phenomena. In Esther Goody (ed.) *Questions and Politeness*. Cambridge: Cambridge University Press, 56–289.

Brown, Penelope and Stephen Levinson (1987) *Politeness: Some Universals in Language Usage*. Cambridge: Cambridge University Press.

Brown, Roger and Albert Gilman (1960) The pronouns of power and solidarity. In Thomas A. Sebeok (ed.) *Style in Language*. Boston: MIT Press, 253–276.

Geertz, Cliford (1960) *The Religion of Java*. Glencoe, Ill.: Free Press.

Hill, Beverly, Sachiko Ide, Shoko Ikuta, Akiko Kawasaki and Tsunao Ogino (1986) Universals of linguistic politeness: quantitative evidence from Japanese and American English. *Journal of Pragmatics* 10: 347–371.

Ide, Sachiko (1982) Japanese sociolinguistics: politeness and women's language. *Lingua* 57: 357–385.

Koshal, Sanyukta (1987) Honorific systems of the Ladakhi language. *Multilingua* 6: 357–385.

Lakoff, Robin (1973) The logic of politeness; or minding your p's and q's. *Papers from the Ninth Regional Meeting of the Chicago Linguistic Society*, 292–305.

Lakoff, Robin (1975) *Language and Woman's Place*. New York: Harper and Row.

Leech, Geoffrey (1983) *Principles of Pragmatics*. London: Longman.

Levinson, Stephen (1983) *Pragmatics*. Cambridge: Cambridge University Press.

Matsumoto, Yoskiko (1987) Politeness and conversational universals – observations from Japanese. Paper presented at the 1987 International Pragmatics Conference. Antwerp, Belgium.

Procter, Paul et al. (eds) (1978) *Longman Dictionary of Contemporary English*. Harlow and London: Longman.

Rosaldo, Michelle (1982) The things we do with words: Illongot speech acts and speech act theory in philosophy. *Language in Society* 11: 203–237.

Sibata, Takesi (1988) *Nihonjin No Keigo* [The honorifics of the Japanese]. *Kokubungaku* 33–15: 6–10.

QUESTIONS

Content

1. What are Brown and Levinson's main claims regarding politeness?
2. What is Ide's main claim concerning formal linguistic forms and what evidence does she provide in support of her argument?
3. What is Ide's main claim concerning discernment and what evidence does she provide in support of her argument?
4. What is the difference between the discernment and the volition type of politeness?
5. What problems does Ide see with Brown and Levinson's framework?

Concept

1. Consider the four excerpts of service encounters in the question section of the previous article. Are there any honorifics used there? Are honorifics used in these service encounters to raise the addressee, or to acknowledge the status difference between speaker and referent, as Ide argues for Japanese honorifics?
2. The discernment aspect of linguistic politeness is mainly oriented, not towards face wants, but wants of roles and settings. Are we dealing with face wants or wants of roles and settings in these excerpts?
3. What other honorifics are there in English?

Perceptions and Language Attitudes

Editors' Introduction to Part Two

IT IS IN RESEARCH about language attitudes, and attitudes to speakers of different languages, that we best see the breadth and scope of sociolinguistics. In this section, the readings range from controlled experiments in the tradition of psycholinguistics (e.g. Purnell et al., Buchstaller) to discussions about the larger geopolitical influences on language use (e.g. Ferguson). Two papers are by Dennis Preston, reflecting his important position both in advancing the systematic, sociolinguistic study of lay attitudes to language and also in promoting sociolinguists' active engagement with the discriminatory impact that people's language attitudes often have on their interactions with others.

The papers in this section are quite tightly linked, and are intended to provide a solid grounding in important theoretical foundations for work on language attitudes, as well as providing collectively a sound model for students who might be interested in conducting such research themselves. Unsurprisingly, research on language attitudes is a popular topic for undergraduate and taught (post-)graduate students: this kind of research allows students to develop a critical awareness of their own and others' attitudes to the language varieties that surround them. They also satisfy many students' desire to feel as though they are undertaking academic research that really "matters" – the real-world implications of language attitudes are obvious to most people. The attitudes triggered by use of a single word or phrase (such as *be like* as a quotative in Buchstaller's article), the accent used when trying to get an interview to view a new home (Chicano, African American or Standard American English, Purnell et al.), the signals that multilingualism sends about an individual's aspirations for interacting in a global and international community (Ferguson), or whether a writer sends subliminal messages about the intelligence and competence of someone whose speech they are reporting through their choice of spelling system (Preston) – these are all very accessible topics for discussion and as inspiration for independent research. Several of the papers cross-reference each other. We hope this increases the coherence of this section.

Preston's overview paper (Language with an attitude) is a good starting point for understanding the scope of the subject area. His paper on testing attitudes to non-standard spellings (eye dialect) shows how this research can be applied to different modalities. Buchstaller's study includes a detailed discussion of how the semantic differentials were chosen for her research (an important, though often neglected, step), and Purnell et al.'s study provides a good illustration of how the results of this kind of research can be analysed. Ferguson's work is valuable for its focus on language use and language attitudes in institutional contexts. He carefully establishes links between the institutional power issues raised by medium choice from face to face interaction in the classroom (a point explored from a different perspective in Heller's article in Section 3 on multilingual schools in Canada), through to supra-national, global interests in language policy such as the World Bank and multinational companies. This paper would be an excellent starting point for further reading in the politics of language policy and planning, e.g. work by Pennycook (2001) and Skutnabb-Kangas (2000).

Preston's 'Language with an attitude' also introduces the thought-provoking methods and results of perceptual dialectology: research that explores people's awareness of different varieties and their association with specific places. Recent trends in sociolinguistics suggest a much greater willingness to see place/locality as a social construct and not a purely geophysical one (see Britain 2010). Perceptual dialectology allows researchers to explore space as a subjective experience, and to ask social questions about where perceived barriers to communication lie and about what kinds of spatial relationships facilitate communication.

Readers may wonder why we have not included more work on language attitudes and language paedagogy, since there is a good deal of practical work being done in this vein by many sociolinguists around the world. As Ferguson's article shows, there are many opportunities for sociolinguists to contribute to societal and political policy making which often has a profound impact on learners' experience in formal education. We decided that practical outlines of materials etc. are best left to courses and readers on applied linguistics, but we acknowledge that many sociolinguists are making outstanding contributions in this area. Language/dialect awareness projects in many parts of the United States are one example (see work by Kirk Hazen, Walt Wolfram, and Da Pidgin Coup in Hawai'i), as is research which incorporates sociolinguistically informed analyses of variation into the fundamental design of reading programmes for early readers who come to schools speaking non-standard language varieties (see recent work in this vein by William Labov). All the groups and individuals named above have excellent web pages outlining their work and providing examples of practical resources, so we refer interested readers to them as a starting point.

REFERENCES

Britain, David (2010) Language and space: the variationist approach. In P. Auer and J. E. Schmidt (eds.), *Language and Space: An International Handbook of Linguistic Variation*. Berlin: Mouton de Gruyter.
Pennycook, Alistair (2001) *Critical Applied Linguistics: A Critical Introduction*. Mahwah, NJ: Erlbaum.
Skutnabb-Kangas, Tove (2000) *Linguistic Genocide in Education, or Worldwide Diversity and Human Rights?* Mahwah: Erlbaum.

FURTHER READING

Clopper, Cynthia and David Pisoni (2007) Free classification of regional dialects of American English. *Journal of Phonetics* 35: 421–438.
Long, Daniel and Dennis R. Preston (eds.) (2002) *Handbook of Perceptual Dialectology II*. Amsterdam: John Benjamins.

Nardy, Aurélie & Stéphanie Barbu (2006) Production and judgment in childhood: the case of liaison in French. In Frans Hinskens (ed.) *Language Variation–European Perspectives: Selected Papers from the Third International Conference on Language Variation in Europe (ICLaVE 3), Amsterdam, June 2005.* Amsterdam and Philadelphia: John Benjamins. 143–152.

Niedzielski, Nancy (1999) The effect of social information on the perception of sociolinguistic variables. *Journal of Language and Social Psychology* 18: 62–85.

Preston, Dennis R. (ed.) (1999) *Handbook of Perceptual Dialectology I.* Amsterdam: John Benjamins.

Rajah-Carrim, Aaliya (2007) Mauritian Creole and language attitudes in the education system of multiethnic and multilingual Mauritius. *Journal of Multilingual and Multicultural Development* 28: 51–71.

Williams, Angie, Peter Garrett and Nikolas Coupland (1996) Perceptual dialectology, folklinguistics, and regional stereotypes: teachers' perceptions of variation in Welsh English. *Multilingua* 15: 171–199.

Chapter 7

Dennis R. Preston

LANGUAGE WITH AN ATTITUDE

1. LANGUAGE AND PEOPLE

IT IS PERHAPS THE least surprising thing imaginable to find that attitudes towards languages and their varieties seem to be tied to attitudes towards groups of people. Some groups are believed to be decent, hard-working, and intelligent (and so is their language or variety); some groups are believed to be laid-back, romantic, and devil-may-care (and so is their language or variety); some groups are believed to be lazy, insolent, and procrastinating (and so is their language or variety); some groups are believed to be hard-nosed, aloof, and unsympathetic (and so is their language or variety), and so on. For the folk mind, such correlations are obvious, reaching down even into the linguistic details of the language or variety itself. Germans are harsh; just listen to their harsh, gutteral consonants. US Southerners are laid-back and lazy; just listen to their lazy, drawled vowels. Lower-status speakers are unintelligent; they don't even understand that two negatives make a positive, and so on. Edwards summarizes this correlation for many social psychologists when he notes that "people's reactions to language varieties reveal much of their perception of the speakers of these varieties" (1982: 20).

Of course, none of this correlation of stereotypes to linguistic facts will do for linguists, who find the structure of language everywhere complex and fully articulated, reflecting, as most present-day linguists would have it, the universal and species-specific human capacity for language.

[. . .]

The apparent difficulty in establishing language-and-people connections was, at first, a great concern to social psychologists. The person-in-the-street might not be so willing to own up to racist, sexist, classist, regionalist, or other prejudicial attitudes.

Source: Preston, Dennis (2003) Language with an attitude. In J. K. Chambers, Peter Trudgill and Natalie Schilling-Estes (eds) *The Handbook of Language Variation and Change*. Oxford: Wiley-Blackwell, 40–66.

Questionnaires, interviews, and scaling techniques (which asked about such characteristics directly) were suspect data-gathering methods since they allowed respondents to disguise their true feelings, either to project a different self-image and/or to give responses they thought the interviewer might most approve of.

An early method used to circumvent such suspected manipulation of attitudes by respondents was the "semantic differential" technique (developed by the psycholinguist Charles Osgood at the University of Illinois, e.g. Osgood et al. 1957) set within a "matched-guise" stimulus presentation. The Canadian social psychologist Wallace Lambert and his colleagues played recordings of the same speaker (to avoid voice quality interference in judgments) in two "guises" (in the earliest case, in French and English to determine attitudinal responses to these two languages in French-speaking Canada, e.g. Lambert et al. 1960). Judges marked scales of opposites such as "fast-slow," "heavy-light," and so on (which did not appear to directly assess language characteristics), and the statistical treatment and interpretation of these ratings set off a frenzy of language attitude studies (most fully developed in the work of Howard Giles and his various associates and provided with both examples and theoretical foundations in Giles and Powesland 1975). Although this work was not without criticism (for its artificiality and other drawbacks, e.g. Agheyisi and Fishman 1970), it set the standard for such studies for quite some time and managed to provide the first important generalization in language attitude studies – that of the "three factor groups." Analyses of large amounts of data seemed to group together paired opposites which pointed to *competence*, *personal integrity*, and *social attractiveness* constructs in the evaluation of speaker voices (summarized in Lambert 1967). A great deal of subsequent research in this mode confirmed that these constructs were very often at work, and, more interestingly, that standard (or "admired accent") speakers were most often judged highest on the *competence* dimension while nonstandard (or regionally and/or ethnically distinct speakers) were rated higher for the *integrity* and *attractiveness* dimensions. Subsequent work has often conflated the two latter categories into one, usually referred to as *solidarity* (e.g. Edwards 1982).

Even early on, however, it became clear that the path from stimulus to group identification to the triggering of attitudes towards the group so identified was not a trouble-free one. In perhaps the earliest study of attitudes towards regional and ethnic varieties in the US, Tucker and Lambert (1969) note that neither northern nor southern European-American judges identified the ethnicity of educated African-American speakers better than chance (scores ranging from 47 percent to 54 percent). If judges misidentify the group membership of the stimulus voice, how can consistent or even valid attitude judgments be collected? Milroy and McClenaghan (1977) note an interesting consistency of ratings of Scottish, Southern Irish, Ulster, and RP (i.e. "Received Pronunciation," the superposed British-English standard pronunciation) varieties even when judges misidentified accents. They comment on this finding as follows:

> It has been widely assumed that an accent acts as a cue identifying a speaker's group membership. Perhaps this identification takes place below the level of conscious awareness. . . . Presumably by hearing similar accents very frequently [one] has learnt to associate them with their reference groups. In other words, accents with which people are familiar may *directly* evoke stereotyped responses without the listener first consciously assigning the speaker to a particular reference group. (1977: 8–9; italics in original)

Irvine (1996) has more recently commented on this transfer of linguistic features to social facts which apparently make the unconscious reactions Milroy and McClenaghan note possible:

> *Iconicity* is a semiotic process that transforms the sign relationship between linguistic features and the social images to which they are linked. Linguistic differences appear to be *iconic* representations of the social contrasts they *index* – as if a linguistic feature somehow depicted or displayed a social group's inherent nature or essence. (1996: 17; italics in original)

In other words, the presumed social attributes of a group are transferred to the linguistic features associated with it (as Irvine notes), and an occurrence of those features may directly trigger recognition of those attributes without being filtered through (conscious) identification of the group (as Milroy and McClenaghan note). Extremes of such iconicity in American English might include "ain't" and multiple negation, both of which apparently trigger negative evaluations with no need for any (specific) group association.

Although this program of social psychological research into language attitudes has been productive, I believe it has left much to be done. If Irvine is correct, there are at least two very large areas left relatively unexplored.

1.   What linguistic features play the biggest role in triggering attitudes?
2.   What beliefs (theories, folk explanations) do people have about language variety, structure, acquisition, and distribution which underlie and support their attitudinal responses and how might we go about finding them out and using them to supplement and even guide future language attitude research?

2. THE LINGUISTIC DETAIL

Perhaps not surprisingly, the study of the relative importance of various specific linguistic features has not been prominent in the work conducted by social psychologists. They have typically used such global stimuli as "languages" or "dialects" (the latter in the broad sense to include class-, gender-, and even age-related varieties), but they have not asked which of the lower-level features of those varieties were most important to the triggering of an attitudinal reaction. Sociolinguists, on the other hand, armed with the knowledge of the delicate variability in performance, have sought to find out whether or not that variation is mirrored in judgments.

[. . .]

In a recent study, Purnell et al. (1999) recorded three versions of the same speaker saying "hello" in Chicano-English (ChE), African-American Vernacular English (AAVE), and Standard American English (SAE).

As Table 7.1 shows, even though they were exposed to only one word, the respondents identified ethnicity far better than chance (at an "Accuracy Index" level of .72, indicating that better than 70 percent of the tokens were correctly identified). The diagonal cells (*a*, *e*, and *i*) should be approximately 33 percent each if the respondents had been 100 percent accurate, and two of the cells (*e* and *i*, at 27 and 29 percent,

Table 7.1 Confusion matrix and summary statistics by dialect

Responses		Stimuli							Row	
		AAVE			ChE			SAE		Total
AAVE	a	923	(15%)	b	280	(5%)	c	196	(3%)	1,399	(23%)
ChE	d	235	(4%)	e	1,607	(27%)	f	41	(1%)	1,883	(31%)
SAE	g	842	(14%)	h	113	(2%)	i	1,763	(29%)	2,718	(45%)

$X^2 = 4,510$; $df = 4$; $p < 0.001$; $AI = 0.72$; percentages = percent of total for that cell.
Source: Purnell et al. (1999)

respectively) are very close to that ideal. Only cell *a* is low (at 15 percent), and cell *g* shows why: 14 percent of the AAE voices were incorrectly recognized as SAE.

Although this one discrepant cell is difficult to account for, the acoustic factors which allowed identification appear to be straightforward. In an analysis of the tokens of "hello" which were presented for identification, it was found that the first vowel (/ɛ/) was significantly fronter (determined by extracting its F2 value) in the AAVE and ChE guises. Additionally, pitch peak was higher for the /hɛ/ syllable in the AAVE guise token only (as was syllable duration). With these minimal acoustic cues, therefore, AAVE and ChE could be distinguished from SAE (on the basis of a fronter or tenser /ɛ/ vowel), and AAVE could be distinguished from ChE (and further from SAE) on the basis of pitch peak and syllable duration. Purnell et al. (1999) also show how dialect identification allows the realization of attitudinal factors in specific action, for the three varieties used in the acoustic experiment were also used in telephone calls to prospective landlords (each of which began with the sentence "Hello, I'm calling about the apartment you have advertised in the paper"). The two non-SAE varieties fared considerably worse in securing appointments; for example, in the Woodside (CA) area; the SAE speaker guise was given an appointment to see housing at roughly the 70 percent level; both AAVE and ChE guises were given appointments only about 30 percent of the time.

It may not be the case, however, that all linguistic markers of social identity have the same force. In an older study, Graff et al. (1983) altered only the formant characteristics of the onset of the /aʊ/ diphthong in an otherwise typically AAVE speaker from Philadelphia (so that the diphthong was altered to /æʊ/). When the sample was played for African-American and European-American judges in Philadelphia, both groups agreed that the speaker was European-American. Apparently, the realization of this diphthong as /æʊ/ is so strongly associated with European-American speakers that it was able to "overwhelm" any other evidence of ethnicity in the sample.

So far these approaches to linguistic detail in attitude study (or to the background information respondents use in making judgments which reflect attitude) have not assumed any level of awareness of the feature in question by the respondents themselves. [. . .] In other work, however, a more direct appeal to respondent consciousness of variation has been made. Modifying a "Self-Evaluation Test" developed in Labov (1966), Trudgill (1972) measured the difference between performance and obviously conscious self-report for a number of variables in Norwich English. A respondent was acquainted with a local variable and asked to make a self-report of his or her use of it. For example, the vowel of "ear" has a prestigious form [ɪə] and a nonprestigious (local) form [ɛː]. Trudgill classified his respondents as speakers of the prestige form if they used more than

Table 7.2 Percentage over- and under-reporters for the "ear" vowel in Norwich

	Total	Male	Female
Over-r	18	12	25
Under-r	36	54	18
Accurate	45	34	57

Source: Trudgill (1972:187)

50 percent of that form in the casual speech portion of their interviews. He then classified as "over-reporters" those respondents who claimed to use [ɪ ə] but, in fact, preferred [ɛ:] in their casual speech. Likewise, he classified as "under-reporters" those who claimed to use [ɛ:] but in fact preferred the prestige form in their casual speech. The remaining respondents were classified as "accurate." His results are shown in Table 7.2.

These data show that men say they use a great deal more of the local (nonprestigious) form than they actually do (and that women say they use more of the prestigious one). From this, Trudgill suggested that some variables have a "covert prestige," an attraction based on working-class, local, non "school-oriented" norms and that such norms were particularly appealing to men. Women, he suggested, were more oriented, perhaps because of power differentials in society, to norms which reflect the "overt prestige" of the wider society. Although his conclusions are far-reaching for general sociolinguistic work and work on gender in particular, here it is simply important to note that his respondents provided interesting attitudinal information based on specific linguistic features and that those responses were made at a conscious level.

Consciousness, however, may mislead assessment of others' performances as well as our own.

[. . .]

In Labov (1966) [. . .] appeal was made to the conscious level in the evaluation of specific linguistic variables in the construction of an "Index of Linguistic Insecurity." Labov asked respondents in his New York City study which of two variants (e.g. [kætʃ] versus [kɛtʃ]) of a number of variables was correct and which they typically used themselves. Each time they noted that one was correct but that they used the other, he added a point to their "insecurity index." Although he was able to show from this that the most insecure group was the lower-middle class (paralleling a distinct linguistic insecurity he had shown earlier in their hypercorrect behavior in performance, see Schilling-Estes 2002), he did not show the degrees of insecurity associated with the specific variables he presented.

In a modification of this approach, Al-Banyan and Preston (1998) presented a number of traditionally nonstandard morphosyntactic and syntactic constructions to undergraduate students at a large, Midwestern US university. In each case, the respondents were asked if they would (1) always use the construction given, (2) use it only formally, (3) use it in ordinary, "on-the-street" interaction, (4) use it only very casually, or (5) never use it. For example, they were asked to evaluate the sentence "The award was given to Bill and I," illustrating the hypercorrect (but historically well-precedented) substitution of the nominative for oblique case in conjoined noun phrases in object position. They supplied the form they would use in the variety of situations

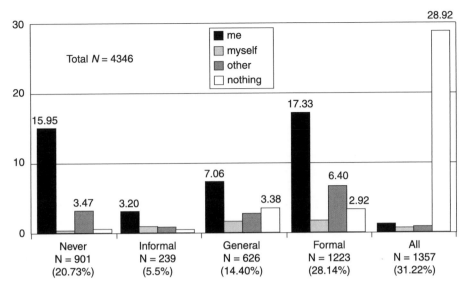

Figure 7.1   Results for ratings of "They gave the award to Bill and I".
Source: Al-Banyan and Preston (1998)

presented [60] them if they did not choose the form given. Their responses were coded according to whether they chose "me," "myself," or "other" as the alternative. Figure 7.1 shows the results for this one grammatical item.

Of the only 21 percent of the respondents who indicated that they would never use this form, the majority (16 percent) indicated that they would use the prescriptively sanctioned "me"; but 28 percent found it the form they would use for "formal" situations, indicating that they would use "me" in less formal contexts. Thirty-one percent (the highest percentage) indicated that it was, for them, the form appropriate for all contexts. If attitudes to "standard" usage are to be measured, such studies as these reveal that a modern standard (for these university students, reflected in the combined "formal" and "always" categories at a level of 59 percent) rather than one which even liberally-minded linguists might agree on needs to be taken into consideration.

Such studies make it clear that language attitudes can be related very specifically to individual linguistic features, but it is equally clear that that relationship is not a simple one. In some cases, precise acoustic features appear to trigger accurate identification (e.g. the frontness or tenseness of the vowel and pitch prominence on the first syllable of "hello" as shown in Purnell, et al. 1999); in others, an acoustic feature appears to be so strongly identified with a group that it can overcome all other surrounding evidence (e.g. the [æ] onset to the /aʊ/ diphthong as a marker of European-American identity in Philadelphia as shown in Graff 1983); in others, the frequency of one variant or another has a powerful effect on social judgments (e.g. r-deletion in New York City as shown in Labov 1966); in still others, there may be a great deal of inaccuracy in both self-report of the use of a specific feature (e.g. for the vowel of "war" as shown in Trudgill 1972) [. . .].

[. . .]

It is hardly surprising [. . .] to find that finely-tuned choices among linguistic features, reflecting the social forces and groups which surround them, play as complex a role in attitudinal formation and perception as they do in language variation itself. In fact, it seems to me that perception, evaluation, and production are intimately connected in language variation and change and that much that might go by the name "sociolinguistics" could as well be known as "language attitude study."

Perhaps some of these differential responses to a variety of linguistic details may operate along a continuum (or several continua) of consciousness or "awareness" (just as language use involves degrees of "monitoring" or "attention to form," e.g. Labov 1972: 208). In Preston (1996a) I review a number of these possibilities for "folk linguistics," suggesting that folk-linguistic facts (i.e. linguistic objects as viewed by nonlinguists) may be subdivided for "awareness" along the following clines.

1.   *Availability*: Folk respondents range in their attention to linguistic features from complete disregard for the frequent discussion of and even preoccupation with them.
2.   *Accuracy:* Folk respondents may accurately, partially accurately, or completely inaccurately represent linguistic facts (and their distribution).
3.   *Detail*: Folk respondents' characterizations may range from *global* (reflecting, for example, only a general awareness of a variety) to *detailed* (in which respondents cite specific details).
4.   *Control*: Folk respondents may have complete, partial or no "imitative" control over linguistic features.

An important fact about these several clines is their relative independence. For example, a respondent who claims only a general awareness of a "foreign accent" may be capable of a completely faithful imitation of some of its characteristics and a completely inaccurate imitation of others. On the other hand, a respondent who is preoccupied with a variety might have no overt information about its linguistic make-up but be capable of performing a native-like imitation of it.

Perhaps the range of so-called language attitude effects ought to be treated in a similar way. That is, attitudinal responses which are based on the respondents' association of a sample voice with a particular social group may be different from ones based on reactions to linguistic caricatures such as *ain't*. Responses which may be based on some sort of cline (e.g. masculine-feminine, degree of "accent") may be different from those based on the recognition of "categorical" features (e.g. correct-incorrect).

3. ATTITUDES AND FOLK PERCEPTIONS

Since linguists know, however, that linguistic details have no value of their own (in spite of the "life" they seem to achieve by virtue of their social associations), it will be important to return to the second of the questions suggested above: what underlying beliefs, presuppositions, stereotypes, and the like lie behind and support the existence of language attitudes? Ultimately, it seems to me, this will require us to give something like an account of a folk theory of language, and in what remains I will try to offer some thoughts in that direction.

In doing language attitude research, perhaps it is important to first determine which varieties of a language are thought to be distinct. For example, where do people believe linguistically distinct places are? That is, what mental maps of regional speech areas do they have? In Preston (1989) I complained that language attitude research did not determine where respondents thought regional voices were from and, worse, did not know if respondents even had a mental construct of a "place" where a voice could be from; that is, their mental maps of regional speech areas might not include one with which a sample voice could be identified.

For example, if one submitted a voice from New England to California judges and the judges agreed that the speaker was "intelligent," "cold," "fast," and so on, researchers could reasonably conclude that Californians judged that voice sample in that way. They should not conclude, however, that that is what Californians believe about New England voices, for a majority of the judges might not have agreed that the voice was from New England. (Perhaps they would have called it a "New York" voice.) More generally, Californians may not even have a concept of "New England" speech. Perhaps the most detailed mental map of regional US speech available to them is one which simply identifies the "Northeast" (whatever their folk name for that region might be).

How can we devise research which avoids this problem? Following the lead of cultural geographers (e.g. Gould and White 1974), we might simply ask respondents to draw maps of where they believe varieties are different. Figures 7.2 and 7.3 are typical examples of such hand-drawn maps from Michiganders.

Although we may profit from an investigation of these individual maps (by, for example, looking at the labels assigned to various regions, as in, e.g. Hartley and Preston 1999), their usefulness for general language attitude studies depends on the degree to which generalizations may be drawn from large numbers of such maps. This may be done by drawing an (approximate) boundary for each salient region from the first map and then "overlaying" each subsequent respondent's map and drawing the "perceptual isoglosses" for each region. A more sophisticated version of this procedure makes use of a digitizing pad which feeds the outlined area of each salient region into a computer so that a more

Figure 7.2   A Michigan respondent's hand-drawn map.

Figure 7.3 Another Michigan hand-drawn map.

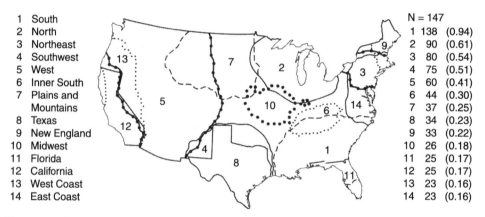

1	South
2	North
3	Northeast
4	Southwest
5	West
6	Inner South
7	Plains and Mountains
8	Texas
9	New England
10	Midwest
11	Florida
12	California
13	West Coast
14	East Coast

N = 147

1	138	(0.94)
2	90	(0.61)
3	80	(0.54)
4	75	(0.51)
5	60	(0.41)
6	44	(0.30)
7	37	(0.25)
8	34	(0.23)
9	33	(0.22)
10	26	(0.18)
11	25	(0.17)
12	25	(0.17)
13	23	(0.16)
14	23	(0.16)

Figure 7.4 Computer-assisted generalizations of hand-drawn maps showing where southeastern Michigan respondents believe speech regions exist in the USA.

precise numeric determination can be made of the "boundary" of each hand-drawn region (Preston and Howe 1987). Figure 7.4 shows a computer-determined map for the mental map of US regional speech areas derived from the hand-drawn maps of 147 southeastern Michigan respondents (from a variety of status and age groups, male and female).

Armed with this "cognitively real" map of the dialect areas of the USA (as seen by Michiganders), we might now approach the study of attitudes towards these regions in a classically social psychological manner. What characteristics would be relevant to an investigation of attitudes to these speech areas? Again, the best method is to go to the respondents themselves. Characteristics for judging were elicited by showing a large number of Michigan respondents a simplified version of Figure 7.4 and asking them to mention any characteristics of the speech of those regions which came to mind. The most frequently mentioned items were selected and arranged into the following pairs.

slow–fast	formal–casual	educated–uneducated
smart–dumb	polite–rude	snobbish–down-to-earth
nasal–not nasal	normal–abnormal	friendly–unfriendly
drawl–no drawl	twang–no twang	bad English–good English

It was important, of course, that the Michigan map was shown to Michigan respondents and that the characteristics elicited were to be used by Michigan judges. Respondents from other areas have different mental maps and might list other characteristics.

The judges (85 young, European-American lifelong southern Michigan residents who were undergraduate students at Michigan State University) were shown a simplified version of Figure 7.4 and given the following instructions:

> This map shows where many people from southern Michigan believe speech differences are in the USA. We will give you a list of descriptive words which local people have told us could be used to describe the speech of these various regions. Please think about twelve of these regions, and check off how each pair of words applies to the speech there.

For example, imagine that we gave you the pair "ugly" and "beautiful"

ugly ___ ___ ___ ___ ___ beautiful
      a   b   c   d   e   f

You would use the scale as follows:

> If you very strongly agree that the speech of a region is "ugly," select "a."
> If you strongly agree that the speech of a region is "ugly," select "b."
> If you agree that the speech of a region is "ugly," select "c."
> If you agree that the speech of a region is "beautiful," select "d."
> If you strongly agree that the speech of a region is "beautiful," select "e."
> If you very strongly agree that the speech of a region is "beautiful," select "f."

The next step in this research is to determine whether or not the number of paired items used in evaluating the regional dialects can be reduced, a procedure normally carried out by means of a factor analysis (which groups together the paired opposites). The results of such an analysis for all areas rated are shown in Table 7.3.[1]

Two groups emerged from this statistical procedure. The first (which I will call "Standard") contains those characteristics which we associate with education and the formal attributes of the society. Note, however, that the last three items in this group ("Formal," "Fast," and "Snobbish") are not necessarily positive traits. Group no. 2 (which I will call "Friendly") contains very different sorts of characteristics (including two which are negative in Group no. 1 but positive here – "Down-to-earth" and "Casual").

These two groups will not surprise those who have looked at any previous studies of language attitudes. As already noted, many researchers have found that the two main dimensions of evaluation for language varieties are most often those of *social status* ("Educated" below) and *group solidarity* ("Friendly" below).

Table 7.3   The two factor groups from the ratings of all areas

Factor group no. 1		Factor group no. 2	
Smart	0.76	Polite	0.74
Educated	0.75	Friendly	0.74
Normal	0.65	Down-to-earth	0.62
Good English	0.63	(Normal)	(0.27)
No drawl	0.62	(Casual)	(0.27)
No twang	0.57		
Casual [formal]	−0.49		
Fast	0.43		
Down-to-earth [snobbish]	−0.32		

Parenthesized factors indicate items which are within the 0.25 to 0.29 range; "−" prefixes indicate negative loadings and should be interpreted as loadings of the opposite value (given in brackets).

A full analysis of the data would go on to consider how each of the regions rated fared with regard to these two groups, but I believe a sample of two particularly important areas (for these respondents and doubtless others) will provide a good insight into the mechanisms at work here.

I have chosen to look at the respondent ratings of areas 1 and 2 from Figure 7.4. The reasons are straightforward. Region 1 is the US "South," and Figure 7.4 shows that it was outlined by 94 percent (138) of the 147 respondents who drew hand-drawn maps. For these southeastern Michigan respondents, it is clearly the most important regional speech area in the USA. The second most frequently rated region (by 90 out of 147 respondents or 61 percent) is the local one, called "North" in Figure 7.4, but perhaps more accurately "North Central" or "Great Lakes." At first, one might be tempted to assert that the local area is always important, but a closer look at Figure 7.2 will show that these southeastern Michigan raters may have something else in mind when they single out their home area; this respondent was not unique among Michigan respondents in identifying Michigan, and only Michigan, as the uniquely "normal" or "correct" speech area in the country.

Table 7.4 shows the means scores for the individual attributes for the North and South. Perhaps the most notable fact is that the rank orders are nearly opposites. "Casual" is lowest-rated for the North but highest for the South. "Drawl" is lowest-rated (meaning "speaks with a drawl") for the South but highest rated (meaning "speaks without a drawl") for the North. In factor group terms, the scores for Group no. 2 (and "−1" loadings, where the opposite value was strongly loaded into a factor group) are the lowest-ranked ones for the North; these same characteristics ("Casual," "Friendly," "Down-to-earth," and "Polite") are the highest-ranked for the South. Similarly, Group no. 1 characteristics are all low-ranked for the South; the same attributes are all highest-ranked for the North.

These scores are not just ordered differently. A series of statistical tests showed that there is a significant difference between the attribute ratings for the North and the South, except for "Nasal" and "Polite." For those attributes in Group no. 1 ("No Drawl," "No Twang," "Fast," "Educated," "Good English," "Smart," and "Normal"), the means scores are all higher for the North. In other words, these Michigan raters consider themselves superior to the South for every attribute of the "Standard" factor group. This is not very surprising, considering well-known folk and popular culture attitudes.

Table 7.4 Means scores of both factor groups for ratings of the "North" and "South"

	Means scores (ordered) South					Means scores (ordered) North		
Factor	Mean	Attribute	Rank		Rank	Factor	Mean	Attribute
–1 & 2	4.66	Casual	1		12.0	–1 & 2	3.53	Casual
2	4.58	Friendly	2		9.5	2	4.00	Friendly
2 & –1	4.54	Down-to-earth	3		6	2 & –1	4.19	Down-to-earth
2	4.20	Polite	4		9.5	2	4.00	Polite
∅	4.09	Not nasal	5		11	∅	3.94	Not nasal
1 & 2	‡3.22	Normal [abnormal]	6		3	1 & 2	4.94	Normal
1	‡3.04	Smart [dumb]	7		4	1	4.53	Smart
1	‡2.96	No twang [twang]	8		2	1	5.07	No twang
1	‡2.86	Good English [bad English]	9		5	1	4.41	Good English
1	‡2.72	Educated [uneducated]	10		8	1	4.09	Educated
1	‡2.42	Fast [slow]	11		7	1	4.12	Fast
1	‡2.22	No drawl [drawl]	12		1	1	5.11	No drawl

* Only significant (0.05) break between any two adjacent means scores; "‡" marks values below 3.5 (which may be interpreted as the opposite polarity – shown in brackets here and in Table 7.3)

For those attributes in Group no. 2 (or –1), the mean score is higher for the South for "Casual," "Friendly," and "Down-to-earth." There is no significant difference for "Polite" (as noted above), and the North leads the South in Group no. 2 attributes only for "Normal," but it is important to note that "Normal" is to be found in both groups. These data suggest that, at least for these 85 young Michiganders, the "Friendly" attributes (excepting only "Polite") are more highly associated with southern speech than with speech from the local area.

[. . .]

Since many of the hand-drawn maps of US dialect areas by Michigan respondents label the local area "standard," "normal" (as in Figure 7.2), "correct," and "good English," there is obviously no dissatisfaction with the local variety as a representative of "correct English." What is the source of the preference for the southern varieties along the "friendly" dimensions? Perhaps a group has a tendency to use up what might be called the "symbolic linguistic capital" of its variety in one way or the other (but not both). Speakers of majority varieties have a tendency to spend the symbolic capital of their variety on a "Standard" dimension. Speakers of minority varieties usually spend their symbolic capital on the "Friendly" dimension.

Perhaps many northerners (here, southeastern Michiganders) have spent all their symbolic linguistic capital on the standardness of local English. As such, it has come to represent the norms of schools, media, and public interaction and has, therefore, become less suitable for interpersonal value. These young Michiganders, therefore, assign an alternate kind of prestige to a variety which they imagine would have more value than theirs for interpersonal and casual interaction, precisely the sorts of dimensions associated with Group no. 2.

Already armed with the information that respondents tend to evaluate language variety along these two dimensions, I took an even more direct approach to eliciting judgments about such variety, again with no recourse to actual voice samples. I asked southeastern Michigan respondents to rate the 50 states (and Washington, DC and New York City) for "correctness." The results are shown in Figure 7.5.

Again, it is clear that the South fares worst. On a one-ten scale (with one being "least correct"), Alabama is the only state which reaches a mean score in the 3.00–3.99 range, and, with the exception of New York City and New Jersey, the surrounding southern states (Texas, Arkansas, Louisiana, Mississippi, Tennessee, and Georgia) are the only other areas rated in the 4.00–4.99 range. In short, the importance of southern speech would appear to lie in its distinctiveness along one particular dimension – it is incorrect English. It is only Michigan which scores in the heady 8.00–8.99 means score range for language "correctness."

What parallel can we find in such work as this to the scores for the attributes in Factor Group no. 2 ("Friendly") already reported? Figure 7.6 shows what Michigan raters have done in a direct assessment of the notion "pleasant" (as was shown above in Figure 7.5 for "correctness"). As Figure 7.6 shows, the South fares very badly again. Alabama (actually tied here by New York City) is the worst-rated area in the USA, and the surrounding southern states are also at the bottom of this ten-point rating scale. One may note, however, that the ratings for the "pleasantness" of the English of southern states are one degree less harsh than those for "correctness." Similarly, there is no "outstanding" (8.00–8.99) rating as there was for "correctness," making Michigan no longer the uniquely best-thought-of area (since it is joined here by Minnesota, Illinois, Colorado, and Washington). In previous work (e.g. Preston 1996b), I have taken this to indicate that

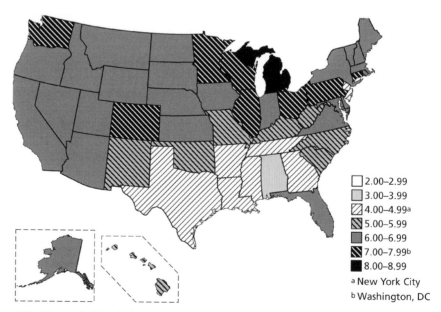

Legend:
- ☐ 2.00–2.99
- ☐ 3.00–3.99
- ▨ 4.00–4.99[a]
- ◼ 5.00–5.99
- ■ 6.00–6.99
- ◼ 7.00–7.99[b]
- ■ 8.00–8.99

[a] New York City
[b] Washington, DC

Figure 7.5 Means of ratings for language "correctness" by Michigan respondents for US English (on a scale of 1–10, where 1 = least, and 10 = most correct).

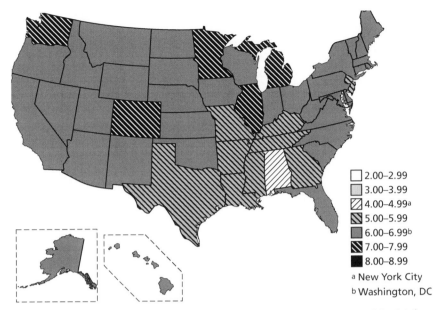

Figure 7.6   Means of ratings for language "pleasantness" by Michigan respondents for US English (on a scale of 1–10, where 1 = least, and 10 = most pleasant).

northern speakers have made symbolic use of their variety as a vehicle for "standardness," "education," and widely-accepted or "mainstream" values.

Then what about US southerners? If northerners (i.e. Michiganders) are committed to their "correctness" but only half-heartedly to the "pleasantness," will southerners (e.g. Alabamians) show an interestingly different pattern of responses? Unfortunately, I have no factor analytic study based on the cognitive maps of southerners, but I can show you how they have responded to the "correct" and "pleasant" tasks already discussed for Michiganders.

Just as one might have suspected, as Figure 7.7 shows, Alabamians are much less invested in language "correctness" (and well they should not be since they are constantly reminded in popular culture and even personal encounters that their language is lacking in this dimension). Imagine the horror of a Michigander in seeing Figure 7.7. Their own "correct" English speaking state scores no better than the fair-to-middling "5" which Alabamians assign to many areas, including their own (showing no break in correctness on a trip from Alabama all the way north to Michigan!).

If Figure 7.8 reminds you of Figure 7.5, you will surely conclude that Alabamians are invested in something, just as Michiganders are, but it is clearly "pleasantness," not "correctness." In this simple task, therefore, I believe to have shown very straight-forwardly the sort of differential investment in local varieties discussed above. In one sense, of course, such studies are "language attitude" studies; in another sense, however, they form important background understandings for the study of attitudes among different social and regional groups. How can we study more detailed aspects language attitudes unless we know that a group is "correctness" investing or "solidarity" investing? And, of course, as I hope to have shown in this entire section, how can we measure language attitudes unless we know something of the cognitive arrangements our

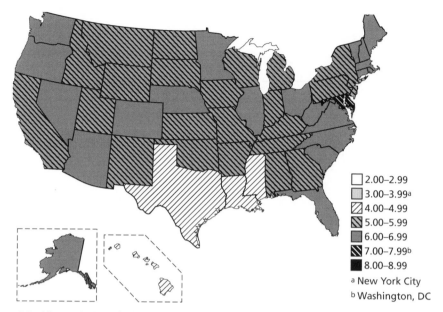

Figure 7.7 Means of ratings for language "correctness" by Alabama respondents for US English (on a scale of 1–10, where 1 = least, and 10 = most correct).

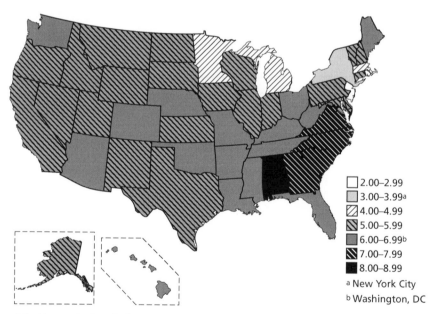

Figure 7.8 Means of ratings for language "pleasantness" by Alabama respondents for US English (on a scale of 1–10, where 1 = least, and 10 = most pleasant).

respondents have made of the terrain we want to explore? Although part of the game belongs to us (the linguistic detail), the real territory (as perhaps in any linguistic work) lies within the cognitive maps (whether of geographic or social facts) of those we study.

4. TOWARD A GENERAL FOLK THEORY

What of the larger promise? How can we go about fashioning a more general folk theory of language, one which surely underlies all attitudinal responses? I believe much of the attitudinal data outlined above, including the mental maps of and attitudinal responses to regional varieties of US English, is dominated by the notions of "correctness" (the more powerful) and "pleasantness." I also believe a great deal of folk belief and language ideology stems from these facts. Speakers of "correct" dialects do not believe they speak dialects, and educational and even legal repercussions arise from personal and institutional devaluing of "incorrect" varieties. On the other hand, speakers of prejudiced-against varieties (like prejudiced groups in general) derive solidarity from their distinct cultural behaviors, in this case, linguistic ones.

In a more direct attempt to get at this underlying fact, although the research tradition is not as long or as active, particularly in the USA, some attitude researchers have collected and analyzed overt folk comment about language (e.g. Labov 1966). When asked how New Yorkers speak, for example, a southern Indiana respondent replied with a little folk poetry (showing that sensitivity to NYC "r" is not an exclusively in-group phenomenon):

> T'ree little boids, sitting on a coib
> Eating doity woims and saying doity woids.

Some comment is more detailed and revealing. The following Michiganders assure the fieldworker (H) that they (just like national newscasters) are speakers of "standard" English:

H: Northern English is standard English?
D: Yeah, yeah.
G: That's right. What you hear around here.
S: Yeah, standard.
D: Because that's what you hear on the TV. If you listen to the newscast of the national news, they sound like we do; they sound sort of Midwestern, like we do.

And, not surprisingly, Michiganders know where English which is not so standard is spoken:

G: Because of TV though I think there's kind of a standard English that's evolving.
D: Yeah.
G: And the kind of thing you hear on TV is something that's broadcast across the country, so most people are aware of that, but there are definite accents in the South.

There are more complex (and rewarding) conversations about social and regional varieties of US English which may be analyzed to show not only relatively static folk belief and attitudes but also how these beliefs and attitudes are used in argument and persuasion. Such investigations are particularly important in showing what deep-seated presuppositions about language are held (e.g. Preston 1994). Many of these conversations (and their parallels and contrasts to professional opinion) are given [in] Niedzielski and Preston (1999). I will provide only one here which I think supports the claim that correctness dominates in US folk perceptions of language but which also allows a slightly deeper look at what sort of theory might allow that domination. H (the fieldworker) has asked D and G (his respondents) if there is any difference in meaning between the words "gift" and "present" (Niedzielski and Preston 1999).[2]

D: Oftentimes a gift is something like you you go to a Tupperware party and they're going to give you a gift, it's – I think it's more impersonal, – than a=
          [
H: Uh huh.
D: =present.
                              [
G: No, there's no difference.
          [
D: No? There's real – yeah there's really no difference.
                                        [
G: There is no difference.
D: That's true. Maybe the way we use it is though.
U: Maybe we could look it up and see what "gift" means.
                    [
D: I mean technically there's no difference.
((They then look up *gift* and *present* in the dictionary.))

Although there are several interesting folk linguistic (and of course discoursal) facts about this short excerpt, the shock for linguists comes in D's remark that there is no difference in the meaning except in "the way we use it." Of course, what other difference could there be? I believe this remark (and many others I have seen in the course of surveying "folk linguistic conversations") points to a folk theory of language in which language itself is somehow external to human cognitive embedding – somewhere "out there." Figure 7.9 illustrates what I have come to believe the essential difference between folk and professional theories to be.

In the linguistic theory, one moves up (and away from) the concrete reality of language as a cognitively embedded fact in the capacities of individual speakers to the social constructions of language similarity. These higher-level constructs are socially real but considerably more abstract than the "real" language, embedded in individual speakers.

In the folk theory, just the opposite is true. A Platonic, extra-cognitive reality is the "real" language, such a thing as English or German or Chinese. Speakers who are directly connected to it speak a fully correct form (the only rule-governed variety), although one may deviate from it comfortably not to sound too "prissy." Go too far, however, and error, dialect, or, quite simply, bad language arises. Since this connection to the rule-governed, exterior "real" language seems a natural (and even easy) one, many folk find it difficult to

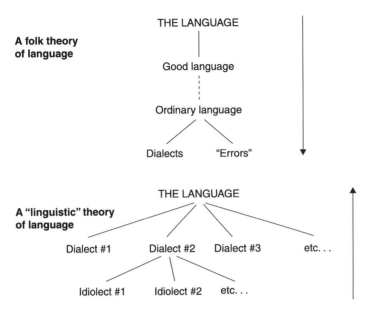

**A folk theory
of language**

THE LANGUAGE

Good language

Ordinary language

Dialects   "Errors"

THE LANGUAGE

**A "linguistic" theory
of language**

Dialect #1   Dialect #2   Dialect #3   etc. . .

Idiolect #1   Idiolect #2   etc. . .

Figure 7.9   Folk and "linguistic" theories of language.

understand why nonstandard speakers, for example, persist in their errors (and often find them simply lazy or recalcitrant).

It is such a theory, I believe, which lies at the root of most evaluations and discriminations of language variety. It is the overwhelming fact against which all language attitude study (at least in US English) must be measured. In short, attitude study, within a linguistic setting, should proceed along both lines of enquiry: what are the linguistic facts of identification and reaction, and what are the underlying constructs which promote and support them? In "correctness," I believe, we have at least some of the answer.

NOTES

1. Although the paired opposites were presented to the respondents with "negative" and "positive" sides randomly distributed, the "positive" poles were all moved to the high (i.e. "6") end of the scale for all the quantitative analyses reported below. I realized after I did this that there might be cultural misunderstandings of what I consider to be the "positive" end. They are "Fast," "Polite," "Down-to-earth," "Educated," "Normal," "Smart," "Casual," "Good English," "Not nasal," "Friendly," "Speaks without a drawl," and "Speaks without a twang." I apologize to readers who disagree with my assignments. That should not detract from the contents of the paper.
2. Since H is not a native speaker, such a question seemed "reasonable."

REFERENCES

Agheyisi, R. and Joshua A. Fishman (1970) Language attitude studies: a review and proposal. *Anthropological Linguistics* 12: 131–57.

Al-Banyan, Ahmed and Dennis R. Preston (1998) What is Standard American English? *Studia Anglica Posnaniensia* 33: 29–46 (Festschrift for Kari Sajavaara).

Edwards, John R. (1982) Language attitudes and their implications among English speakers. In Ellen Bouchard Ryan and Howard Giles (eds) *Attitudes towards Language Variation*. London: Edward Arnold. 20–33.

Giles, Howard and P. F. Powesland (1975) *Speech Style and Social Evaluation*. London: Academic.

Gould, Peter and Rodney White (1974) *Mental Maps*. Harmondsworth, Middx: Penguin.

Graff, David, William Labov and Wendell Harris (1983) Testing listeners' reactions to phonological markers of ethnic identity: a new method for sociolinguistic research. In David Sankoff (ed.) *Diversity and Diachrony*. Amsterdam/Philadelphia: John Benjamins, 45–58.

Hartley, Laura and Dennis R. Preston (1999) The names of US English: valley girl, cowboy, yankee, normal, nasal, and ignorant. In T. Bex and R. J. Watts (eds) *Standard English*. London: Routledge, 207–38.

Irvine, Judith T. (1996) "Style" as distinctiveness: the culture and ideology of linguistic differentiation. Paper presented to the NSF Workshop on "Style," Stanford University, February.

Labov, William (1966) *The Social Stratification of English in New York City*. Arlington, VA: Center for Applied Linguistics.

Labov, William (1972) *Sociolinguistic Patterns*. Philadelphia: The University of Pennsylvania Press.

Lambert, Wallace E. (1967) A social psychology of bilingualism. *Journal of Social Issues* 23: 91–109.

Lambert, Wallace E., R. Hodgson, R. C. Gardner and S. Fillenbaum (1960) Evaluational reactions to spoken languages. *Journal of Abnormal and Social Psychology* 60: 44–51.

Milroy, Lesley and Paul McClenaghan (1977) Stereotyped reactions to four educated accents in Ulster. *Belfast Working Papers in Language and Linguistics* 2: 1–11.

Niedzielski, Nancy and Dennis R. Preston (1999) *Folk Linguistics*. Berlin: Mouton de Gruyter.

Osgood, Charles H., G. J. Suci and P. Tannenbaum (1957) *The Measurement of Meaning*. Urbana: University of Illinois Press.

Preston, Dennis R. (1975) Linguists versus non-linguists and native speakers versus non-native speakers. *Biuletyn Fonograficzny* 16: 5–18.

Preston, Dennis R. (1989) *Perceptual Dialectology*. Dordrecht: Foris.

Preston, Dennis R. (1994) Content-oriented discourse analysis and folk linguistics. *Language Sciences* 16, 2: 285–331.

Preston, Dennis R. (1996a) Whaddayaknow: the modes of folk linguistic awareness. *Language Awareness* 5, 1: 40–74.

Preston, Dennis R. (1996b) Where the worst English is spoken. In Edgar Schneider (ed.) *Focus on the USA*. Amsterdam: John Benjamins, 297–360.

Preston, Dennis R. and George M. Howe (1987) Computerized generalizations of mental dialect maps. In Keith Denning et al. (eds) *Variation in Language: NWAV-XV at Stanford*, Stanford, CA: Department of Linguistics, Stanford University, 361–78.

Purnell, Thomas, William Idsardi, and John Baugh (1999) Perceptual and phonetic experiments on American English dialect identification. *Journal of Language and Social Psychology* (Lesley Milroy and Dennis R. Preston, guest eds, Special Issue: Attitudes, Perception, and Linguistic Features) 18 (March), 189–209.

Schilling-Estes, Natalie (2002) Investigating stylistic variation. In J. K. Chambers, Peter Trudgill and Natalie Schilling-Estes (eds) *The Handbook of Language Variation and Change*. Malden, MA and Oxford: Blackwell, 375–401.

Trudgill, Peter (1972) Sex, covert prestige and linguistic change in the urban British English of Norwich. *Language in Society* 1(2): 179–95.

Tucker, G. Richard and Wallace E. Lambert (1969) White and Negro listeners' reactions to various American-English dialects. *Social Forces* 47: 463–8.

Williams, Frederick, Jack L. Whitehead and Leslie M. Miller (1971) Ethnic stereotyping and judgments of children's speech. *Speech Monographs* 38: 166–70.

QUESTIONS

Content

1. What folklinguistic link between languages and their speakers does Preston propose?
2. Why is it difficult to elicit language attitudes and what methods have been developed to deal with these problems?
3. What are some of the most stable findings of such studies?
4. How does the concept of iconicity help explain some of the explanatory problems of attitude studies?
5. Are all linguistic features equally important in marking social identity?
6. What does Preston mean when he says that the clines of folklinguistic fact are independent?
7. Why is it important to find out about respondents' mental maps?
8. What steps are suggested in preparing an attitude study?
9. Considering Table 7.4, what attributes are used by informants to describe Michigan and southern speech and why are they evaluated like this?
10. How and why do Northerners and Southerners differ when rating all US states for correctness and pleasantness?
11. What is the basis of Preston's folk theory?
12. How can overt folk comments reveal underlying facts about folk beliefs?
13. What should linguists studying language attitudes focus on?

Concept

Bring a map of your country to class with major internal political boundaries indicated. Rate a selection of these areas for pleasantness and correctness. Compare your own map with those of your class mates. How are they similar? How are they different? Can you apply Preston's idea of investment and symbolic capital to your discussion?

Chapter 8

Dennis R. Preston

THE LI'L ABNER SYNDROME:
WRITTEN REPRESENTATIONS OF SPEECH

L INGUISTS, ESPECIALLY SOCIOLINGUISTS, HAVE long been interested
in measuring attitudes to spoken language. There is, however, a dearth of studies
(outside literary analyses) of reader attitudes towards writing which reports speech. The
concern here is with the inaccurate representation of [. . .] status [. . .] which arises from
the use of misspellings in the WRITING OF SPEAKING—a practice common to linguists,
folklorists, sociolinguists, and others who provide written transcripts of spoken language.
The use of alternate spellings in the representation of character in creative writing is not
treated here.

Additionally, this study does not focus on the representation of morphological
variation; such well-motivated (often historically justified) spellings as *clumb* 'climbed'
and *holp* 'helped' are specifically excluded from consideration. The focus here is on
affective responses to such respellings as *gonna*, *wint* 'went', and *sez* in nonliterary
texts.

There are at least three types of respellings to be considered. Such spellings as *gonna*,
jeet 'did you eat', and *snice* 'it's nice' are ALLEGRO SPEECH forms. They attempt to capture
through the use of nonstandard spellings (some more traditional than others) the fact that
the speech is casual, not carefully monitored, relaxed—perhaps slangy. Such forms as
wint 'went', *Hahvuhd* ['Harvard'], and *dis* 'this' are (however phonetically inaccurate or
inconsistent) attempts to capture regional and social features of pronunciation. They
may, without attributing accuracy to them, be called DIALECT RESPELLINGS. Finally,
forms such as *sez* and *wuz* are known as EYE-DIALECT—forms which reflect no phonological difference from their standard counterparts *says* and *was*. These last forms serve
mainly to denigrate the speaker so represented by making him or her appear boorish,
uneducated, rustic, gangsterish, and so on, and it is the claim of this study that nearly ALL
respellings share in this defamation of character.

Source: Preston, Dennis (1985) The Li'l Abner syndrome: written representations of speech. *American Speech*. 60: 328–336.

Though it is justifiable to study the affective response to texts simply for the benefit of understanding more about language attitudes, it is worth pointing out that a good deal of this spelling silliness has crept into respectable academic writing. Folklorists, for example, whose interest in the PURE words of the informant is almost fetishistic, have marred their texts with such spellings in an albeit honest attempt to capture something of the spontaneous and natural character of a live performance (Preston 1982). Linguists' revived interest in conversation has led to transcripts which ignore, justifiably, fine phonetic detail. The interactions reported in such research, however, are often casual, and normal spelling may seem inappropriate. Labov and Fanshel (1977) use such forms as *sorta, jist*, and *t'her* 'to her', and one stretch of speech emerges as "So sh's't'me," which one must assume from the context to mean 'So she says to me'. That sets the stage for some pretty wild respellings.

G'n afternoon sir. W'dju be innerested in subscribing to the Progress Bulletin t'help m'wina trip tuh Cape Kennedy to see the astronauts on the moon shot. You won'haftuh pay til nex'month en you get it ev'ry single day en I guarantee you ril good service. Jus'fer a few short weeks sir, tuh help me win my trip. [Jefferson and Schenkein 1977, 156]

At the far end of this nonsense such antiphonetic horrors as "Wih A one Boat yuh ::: uhlon dohlenko,—" appear (Ryave 1978, 114). Though I can interpret the first part of this to mean 'with, uh, one boat' without too much difficulty, I am still not sure that the rest means 'you hold on; don't let go' (even though the surrounding context makes it clear that dangerous carnival rides are the topic).

Though academic respellings seldom mar intelligibility, they all create a false impression of the speaker, or, worse, they suggest a negative or condescending attitude by the reporter towards his or her informant. On the other hand, perhaps one should not be overconcerned with this practice since it may be argued that, after all, linguists, folklorists, and anthropologists—the most likely readers of such texts—do not share in the general public's status-lowering response to such respellings. However, no one has shown that to be the case; even if it is true, linguists particularly should use caution since others may look to their work as models for data reporting, and relativistic attitudes may not automatically be assumed for nonlinguists and their readers.

The task here, however, will be to show that nonlinguists DO denigrate speakers whose words have been respelled with the apparently innocent respellings called above ALLEGRO FORMS. Since regional and social stereotyping are well known, it would prove little to show that DIALECT RESPELLINGS promote negative character evaluations in readers; additionally, EYE-DIALECT forms are well known caricature-forming devices. If ALLEGRO FORMS can be shown to raise negative responses in ordinary readers, [. . .] there may [. . .] be good public relations reasons to be more careful about respellings which may raise unintended responses. [. . .] [T]he nonlinguists' responses are part of a literate speech community's set of language attitudes and are worthy of study on that basis alone.

The questionnaire in Figure 8.1 was distributed to a number of English composition classes at the State University of New York College at Fredonia in March, 1983.

An analysis of the four speakers' lines will show that the following four combinations of two variables were exploited:

Speaker #1 uses no nonstandard grammar and is assigned no allegro forms.

Speaker #2 uses no nonstandard forms but is represented with two allegro forms (*wanna, gettin'*).

Speaker #3 uses two nonstandard items (*ain't, don't never*) but has nothing respelled.

Speaker #4 uses two nonstandard forms (*ain't* twice) and has two allegro respellings (*givin', gonna*).

The social class labels used in this study were ones which have popular value for all the respondents (principally from western New York and the metropolitan New York City area). The relative rank order is, of course, more important than any ultimate correspondence with a more sociologically responsible set of terms.

Ratings for each of the four speakers [were] sub-divided by respondent age, sex, and ethnic background. Since such a small number of black and Hispanic respondents were sampled, generalizations about their performances are impossible. In the larger white population, males over thirty are excluded from any part of the study since there was only one respondent (who, by the way, marked all four speakers "3" [Middle Class]). The small number of female respondents over thirty is considered separately.

The degree of variance attributable to speaker variables and to sex of respondent for the data collected from whites under thirty was determined by means of a two-way ANOVA (analysis of variance). Only the variables of nonstandardness and allegro respellings in the speakers proved significant. Neither the differences in respondent sex nor the interaction of speaker characteristics and respondent sex was significant. These results permit the pooling of data for all whites under thirty, and the bulk of the remaining comment refers to that group.

The crucial comparisons for the purposes of teasing out just the influences of the allegro speech respellings are those between Speakers #1 and #2 and between Speakers #3 and #4, the sites where the texts differ only in the use of such respellings. An a priori comparison-of-means test was run in conjunction with the ANOVA to study these differences. Recall that the respellings for Speaker #2 did not co-occur with nonstandard

---

The following is a recording of a conversation among young teenagers:
Speaker #1: How did you do on your math test?
Speaker #2: Fair, but I wanna do better next time.
Speaker #3: Why? Ain't your parents giving you your allowance?
Speaker #4: Allowance! Your parents ain't still givin'you money, are they?
Speaker #2: Sure, I've been gettin' five bucks a week for a year.
Speaker #1: You don't want that to stop!
Speaker #3: Mine don't never give me less than ten.
Speaker #4: That's a lot. You ain't gonna beat that.
Many people claim that they can tell the "social class" of a person by listening to him or her speak. Use the following scale to evaluate the above speakers: Lower Class—1; Lower Middle Class—2; Middle Class—3; Upper Middle Class—4; Upper Class—5.
Speaker #1_____
Speaker #2_____
Speaker #3_____
Speaker #4_____
Please provide the following information about yourself; Age_____ Sex M F Home city and state_____ Racial/ethnic background: Black White Hispanic Other.
Would you like to make any comments about how you decided on the ratings you gave?

Figure 8.1 A recorded conversation among young teenagers.

Table 8.1   Comparison of means of respelled and nonrespelled "Speakers"

	t	d.f.
Speaker #1 vs. Speaker #2	4.19*	162
Speaker #3 vs. Speaker #4	1.98**	162
Speakers #1 and #2 vs. Speakers #3 and #4	13.26*	326

* p < .001 (two-tailed test)
** p < .05 (two-tailed test)

items, while those for Speaker #4 did. The results are shown in Table 8.1. The difference between Speaker #1 and Speaker #2 (.57) shows a significance of at least p < .001, which confirms the hypothesis that whatever is being measured by the social class scale is being significantly influenced (lowered) by the introduction of respellings into an otherwise standard performance. Additionally, Speakers #3 and #4 differ by .20, which yields a significance of .05 on a conservative two-tailed test, confirming that, while the difference is statistically significant, the introduction of respellings into texts already negatively evaluated due to nonstandard forms is not so affectively important. This fact corresponds nicely with the socio-linguistic commonplace that grammatical features are more sharply stratified than phonological ones (Wolfram and Fasold 1974, 81). On the other hand, this relatively minor difference should not reassure transcribers who have respelled only nonstandard speakers. If the resultant perceived status is skewed at all by allegro respellings, it is still a misrepresentation, no matter how small. Moreover, this crude study identifies only class lowering as the negative influence of both respellings and nonstandard forms. Perhaps there is an important difference in kind of negative attribution that can be discovered in future work. It is not surprising to see that considerable variance in this study is explained by the contrast between standard and nonstandard forms (t = 13.26)—that is, between Speakers #1 and #2 contrasted with #3 and #4— but that does not do away with the significance of the differences between responses to respelled and non-respelled data. ALLEGRO RESPELLINGS cause lowering of class evaluation in both standard and nonstandard settings.

Though the groups are very small, a few other trends might be noted: (1). Older respondents (+30) rated all speakers with ANY nonstandard or respelled features (#2, #3, #4) lower than younger respondents did and rated the standard, non-respelled speaker (#1) higher. The older respondents' reactions to BOTH deviations from prescriptive norms were stronger. (2). Blacks rated the two speakers with no nonstandard features lower than white respondents did, and they rated the two nonstandard speakers higher. The overall result—a much narrower range—suggests a tendency to avoid stigmatization [. . .] on the basis of language performance facts. Perhaps contrary to this ("perhaps" because we do not know the black respondents' opinion of their own variety), Labov (1966) suggests in several places that those who use stigmatized forms are often better recognizers and harsher evaluators of such usage in others. (3). Female respondents rated the standard, nonrespelled speaker higher than males did, and males rated the speakers with any nonstandardness or respelling less harshly—though, as shown above in the ANOVA, there was no statistically significant difference in the male and female ratings. In terms of earlier research, such differences as these seem to correspond to generalizations about women's greater use of community norms and males' use of nonstandardness for covert prestige (Milroy 1980). Similarly, in every case except for Speaker #4, and especially for Speaker #1, the black female mean is higher than the black male mean, showing a similar trend in that group, though the absence of larger numbers makes even this interpretation risky.

Research with wider ranges of respellings (differentiating, perhaps, between traditional and ad hoc allegro forms) and work with other groups may turn up different response patterns, but it is safe to say, on the basis of this small study, that a pattern of stratification similar to that found in hearers can be isolated in readers. What is strikingly different is that the negative responses are attached to the spellings themselves and not to the pronunciations represented. Totally unwarranted demotions of social status are brought about by honest attempts to imitate in writing something of the impression created by rapid, casual speech.

The respondents, who were invited in the questionnaire to indicate what strategies they used in assigning class labels, were apparently not aware of the difference between nonstandard usage and respellings. One rater who gave #1 a "5" (Upper Class) and #2 a "2" (Lower Middle Class) indicated that her decisions were based solely on "grammar," though, as can be seen above, only respellings differentiated #1 and #2. Another respondent who gave a "4" to #1 and a "3" to #2 indicated that his decisions were based on "sentence structure." More revealingly, perhaps, one informant said that her ratings were based on "the choice of words: wanna, ain't, givin', gettin'." Even a rater who claimed that the task was based on "guesswork" assigned #1, #2, #3, and #4 a "4," "3," "2," and "2," respectively, an almost perfect match to the overall ratings. Perhaps the strongest statement which indicates the failure to separate nonstandard from respelled forms came from the respondent who noted that "ain't and gonna are not words generally used by people in the upper class."

There is some evidence that Speaker #3 might have gained a slightly higher rating from his second sentence—"Mine don't never give me less than ten"—on the basis of economic factors alone. Five respondents noted that they used allowance amount in determining social class. [. . .]

Only a few informants seemed to find the task an unlikely one. One respondent who gave ratings of "3," "3," "2", and "2" said, nevertheless, "I don't feel you can judge a person's social class by just listening to their speech. A well-educated upper-class person may talk so bad at times you may not understand them. Same with the lower class person."

One respondent combined at least two folk-linguistic notions in a single comment: "The sentences which contained more slang terms, I thought were from the lower class because the teenagers would have probably picked this language up from their less educated parents." At least the use of "slang" to mean "nonstandard" and the incorrect (if widespread) notion that teenagers learn a great deal of language behavior from their parents make this an especially interesting folk explanation—an indication of the ethnographic richness of respondent rationale. Another respondent made an interesting separation of class and education: "I think it's hard to judge a person's class by how they speak. Speakers 3 and 4 could have been upper middle class or even upper class but with a bad education. Too many things would determine how someone speaks."

What is clear, however, from all these comments is that NO respondents were apparently ever troubled by the fact that speech was being evaluated from writing. Every rater seemed to believe that he or she had a clear insight into speech from the written representation of it, yet it is certainly likely that the normal production of allegro forms by a speaker who used no nonstandard constructions would not result in the same social class downgrading if the forms were heard rather than seen as allegro respellings. This study shows that writing and speech are as confused as ever for the nonlinguist, but it should help establish a separate existence for a set of attitudes to writing that purports to be speech. Though such attitudes may be productively manipulated by creative writers, the use of respellings by linguists, sociologists, anthropologists, folklorists, psychologists, and others who want authentic reports of spoken language with a minimum of phonetic detail may be seriously questioned.

The ethnography of language in a literate speech community cannot be discovered by reference to talk alone. Whatever the respondent protocols were in reaching the ranking given above, it is clear that more-or-less phonetically accurate respellings of allegro speech forms played some role in the respondents' assignment of social ranks and that those ranks are different from those which would have been assigned on the basis of actual speech.[1]

NOTE

1.   I am especially grateful to Carol G. Preston and to two anonymous members of the Editorial Advisory Committee of *American Speech* who suggested a number of important stylistic and material improvements. I am also grateful to Professor Nancy Boynton of the State University of New York College at Fredonia who gave me important advice on statistics; any errors in math are mine. My special thanks to the composition students and their instructors who participated in this study.

REFERENCES

Jefferson, Gail and Jim Schenkein (1977) Some sequential negotiations in conversation: unexpanded and expanded versions of projected action sequences. *Sociology* 11: 87–103. Rpt. Schenkein, 155–72.

Labov, William (1966) *The Social Stratification of English in New York City*. Washington, D.C.: Center for Applied Linguistics.

Labov, William and David Fanshel (1977) *Therapeutic Discourse*. New York: Academic.

Milroy, Lesley (1980) *Language and Social Networks*. Oxford: Blackwell.

Preston, Dennis R. (1982) Ritin' fowklower daun' rong: folklorists' failures in phonology. *Journal of American Folklore* 95: 304–26.

Ryave, Alan L. (1978) On the achievement of a series of stories. Schenkein, 113–32.

Schenkein, Jim (ed.) (1978) *Studies in the Organization of Conversational Interaction*. New York: Academic.

Wolfram, Walt and Ralph Fasold (1974) *The Study of Social Dialects in American English*. Englewood Cliffs: Prentice-Hall.

QUESTIONS

1.   What is the difference between *eye-dialect, dialect respellings* and *allegro forms*?
2.   What is Preston's rationale for focusing on the contrast between allegro forms and respellings?
3.   What was the most important difference between evaluations of Speakers 1 and 2 and Speakers 3 and 4?
4.   Why does Preston think the results indicate Black informants "avoid stigamatization"? Do you agree?

Content

1. Preston identifies a weakness in his study, namely that a lower ranking for social class is the only measure for appraising negative evaluations. He suggests there are probably others. What would you add, and why?

2. This research was conducted before the use of respellings and allegro forms became widespread in computer-mediated communication and texting. If you were to redo this study, do you think a person's participation in these mediums would be likely to have an effect on the results? In what way?

3. What does Preston mean in his conclusion when he talks about "honest attempts" to imitate rapid and casual speech? Do you think it is helpful to talk about respellings and allegro forms in terms of honest (and misleading) attempts? Explain why you think this.

Chapter 9

Thomas Purnell, William Idsardi, and John Baugh

PERCEPTUAL AND PHONETIC EXPERIMENTS ON AMERICAN ENGLISH DIALECT IDENTIFICATION

[. . .]

Nationally [in the United States], African Americans lag behind Whites in median home value (61%; U.S. Census Bureau, 1995). This disparity may follow from such complex and interrelated issues as lower-paying employment (as indicated by a median family income 58% of White households'), self-segregation, and housing discrimination. Varying levels of influence have been attributed to discrimination in the segregation of neighborhoods, from a prominent role where discrimination accounts for 20% to 30% of segregation (Courant, 1978; Tobin, 1982; Yinger, 1986) to a minor role of no more than 15% (Clark, 1986, 1993; Galster & Keeney, 1988). Myers and Chan (1995) place race as a reliable indicator of discrimination in mortgage lending, accounting for 70% of the gap in rejection rates while controlling for other factors. Regardless of the size of the effect, discrimination is indisputably present in our society and led Congress in 1988 to amend laws protecting against housing discrimination.

Intentional discrimination is fomented when an applicant's race (or gender) is evident to a potential home seller (or employer, etc.). At least two cues to race and gender act as triggers: visual and auditory. These two stimuli influence a minority's success when entering into, and advancing within, the housing market. This chapter examines the linguistic nature of housing discrimination among minority groups, studying the nature of auditory discrimination of racial speech cues. We are particularly interested in the possibility of auditory discrimination in the absence of any visual cues and in determining the existence of micro-linguistic (i.e., phonetic) markers of dialect (Labov, 1972b). Our preliminary findings from four experiments indicate that (a) dialect-based discrimination takes place, (b) ethnic group affiliation is recoverable from speech, (c) very little speech is needed to discriminate between dialects, and (d) some phonetic correlates or markers of dialects are recoverable from a very small amount of speech.

Source: Purnell, Thomas, William Idsardi and John Baugh (1999) Perceptual and phonetic experiments on American English dialect identification. *Journal of Language and Social Psychology* 18: 10–30.

Throughout this chapter we discuss three broad dialects of American English: African American Vernacular English (AAVE), Chicano English (ChE), and Standard American English (SAE). These dialects are chosen because of data availability and the fairly strong ethnic group affiliation tied to the dialects (confirmed in the second experiment described below). [. . .]

We began by asking whether dialect discrimination is possible by using phonetic cues alone, and if it is possible, what cues trigger discrimination. [. . .] [W]e seek to demonstrate that the identity of race (or national origin) is reflected, not only visually but also auditorily in an individual's speech. In addition, we endeavor to establish that listeners hear and positively identify a speaker's dialect with great accuracy. The following experiments reveal the possibility of auditory discrimination and the probability of social discrimination by auditory identification of dialects. [. . .]

EXPERIMENT 1

Baugh's personal experiences while trying to rent an apartment in the San Francisco area provided an impetus and opportunity to study dialect identification and discrimination. This portion of our research addresses the issue of whether housing discrimination is exhibited in the absence of visual cues. Most legal cases appealing to the Fair Housing and the Civil Rights Acts try to establish that the defendant discriminated against the plaintiff because of obvious visual cues. [. . .] [T]his experiment indicates that housing discrimination arises in the absence of these visual cues. In predominantly White geographic locales where discrimination against minorities would potentially be the greatest, the percentage of appointments secured to view housing is less than chance for callers using nonstandard dialects. Projecting this to the population at large, the evidence shows that a member of a minority group is much less likely to get an appointment to see an apartment in these White locales, even when he or she is qualified to purchase or rent in those areas. In these examples, auditory discrimination arises without visual contact.

[. . .]

We are compelled to understand the possibility of auditory discrimination from cases like *HUD v. Ross* (1994). In this suit, Judge Cregar notes the role accent played in the outcome of the case.

> It is undisputed that Magaly Dejesus and Teresa Sanchez are Hispanic. Their distinct Hispanic accents clearly revealed their national origin to Mr. Ross. Although neither filled out a rental application, Mr. Ross did not afford them the opportunity to do so. [. . .] (p. 8)

This example and a few others (e.g., *City of Chicago v. Matchmaker Real Estate Sales Center*, 1992) with respect to Ms. Frazier's "accent") demonstrate that individuals are capable of being held liable because of their auditory assessment of a speaker.

However, not all jurists agree that racial identity is ascertained in the absence of visual prompting.

[. . .]

For our first experiment, the null hypothesis is that there is no significant difference in appointments made by locale by dialect. The test hypothesis entails a relation between the racial and ethnic constituency of a geographic area and the success in establishing an appointment by dialect type. [. . .]

Method

Baugh conducted the telephone interviews in person. Because Baugh (who is African American) grew up in inner-city communities in Philadelphia and Los Angeles, he is personally familiar with AAVE, ChE, and SAE dialects. This use of a tridialectal speaker controls for cross-speaker variation. In this respect, this study differs from other such guise studies as Lambert and Tucker (1972) and Tucker and Lambert (1975), which use different speakers in experiments determining attitudes toward dialects.

Prospective landlords in five distinct locales were identified by classified advertisements in regional newspapers. [. . .] Baugh telephoned the landlords on three separate occasions, randomly using each dialect in different sequences with no less than 30 minutes between calls. Each call began with the phrase, "Hello, I'm calling about the apartment you have advertised in the paper." Different return telephone numbers were used for each dialect, along with different pseudonyms. This procedure of anonymity parallels legally approved practices of testers used by the Department of Housing and Urban Development and similar organizations when suspecting discriminating practices by landlords [. . .].

Results and discussion

The results show a clear pattern of potential discrimination associated with the three dialects by geographic area. Thus, we reject the null hypothesis and accept the experimental hypothesis. Tables 9.1 [and] 9.2 [. . .] show that the percentage of appointments made in each locale corresponds approximately with the ethnic makeup of the geographic area. Tables 9.2 and 9.3 display 1990 census data for percentage of population [. . .] who

Table 9.1   Confirmed appointments to view apartments advertised for rent in different Greater San Francisco geographic areas (in percentages)

Dialect guise	Geographic area				
	East Palo Alto	Oakland	San Francisco	Palo Alto	Woodside
AAVE	79.3	72.0	63.5	48.3	28.7
ChE	61.9	58.3	53.2	31.9	21.8
SAE	57.6	68.7	71.9	63.1	70.1
Total number of calls for each locale	118	211	310	263	87

Note. AAVE = African American Vernacular English; ChE = Chicano English; SAE = Standard American English.

Table 9.2   Population in different Greater San Francisco geographic areas by race and ethnicity (in percentages)

| | Geographic area | | | | |
Population	East Palo Alto	Oakland	San Francisco	Palo Alto	Woodside
African American	42.9	43.9	10.9	2.9	0.3
Hispanic	36.4	13.9	13.9	5.0	3.8
White	31.7	32.5	53.6	84.9	94.7

Source. U.S. Census Bureau (1990).

Table 9.3   Householders in different Greater San Francisco geographic areas by race and ethnicity (in percentages)

| | Geographic area | | | | |
Householder	East Palo Alto	Oakland	San Francisco	Palo Alto	Woodside
African American	47.1	43.2	10.0	2.4	0.2
Hispanic	23.4	9.6	10.1	3.7	1.8
White	34.6	39.7	64.9	88.1	97.0

Source. U.S. Census Bureau (1990).

belong to particular racial and ethnic groups (U.S. Census Bureau, 1990). If the null hypothesis is rejected (i.e., if the positive appointment rate hovered around chance), then we expect a 50% success rate for each cell in Table 9.1. Percentages above and below the 50% mark indicate a variance from chance. By examining all tables, we observe that in the traditionally White areas, Woodside and Palo Alto, the strongest bias is against the non-standard dialects.

[. . .]

[I]n the present experiment, ChE guises not only follow the general trend of AAVE guises but also have the lowest percentage success rate in securing an appointment. This is even true in the geographic areas where the number of Hispanics exceeds the number of African Americans (San Francisco, Palo Alto, and Woodside).

We conclude, given the evidence of this first experiment, that auditory cues constitute stimuli for disparate impact and nonaccidental disparate treatment cases. [. . .] Disparate impact cases involve indirect, and often unintentional, cases of discrimination. Furthermore, there may be reasons for the paucity of civil rights cases in which the burden of proof rests at least indirectly on auditory cues, as compared to the preponderance of cases that involve visual ones. One possibility is that the auditory kinds of discrimination are difficult to monitor. In addition, potential householders may scarcely suspect that they are being discriminated against; the landlord subtly discriminates by informing the minority speaker that there are no vacant apartments. This is supported by a survey reported in Clark (1993), indicating that the primary source of discrimination is the individual landlord. The upshot of variation by neighborhood within a general metropolitan area is that it corroborates evidence that segregation is fairly local (Massey & Hajnal, 1995).

EXPERIMENT 2

Given that Baugh is tridialectal and might favor one dialect over the others as a default dialect, we might wonder whether the guises in the first experiment are representative of the appropriate racial group and not exaggerated stereotypes instead. Following the first experiment, a series of experiments on "ethnic identification" evaluations were conducted. The next experiment is an attempt to understand whether dialect identification is possible at the macro-linguistic or sentential level. In contrast, subsequent experiments explore identification at the micro-linguistic level.

Much is already known about the sentence- and morpheme-level differences between SAE and AAVE, along with the phonemic and lexical alternations (see, e.g., Baugh, 1983; Dillard, 1972; Labov, 1969, 1972a; Wolfram, 1969). Several of these phonological and morphophonemic differences could possibly affect our research. One of the notable characteristics of AAVE that [is] different from SAE is the absence in AAVE of certain sonorants, /r ɪ n/, in syllable coda position. Other sounds, as well, may be absent from AAVE, for example, /-s/ suffixes (plural, third person singular, possessive) and consonants (particularly /t d/) from consonant clusters. AAVE also exhibits final obstruent devoicing and consonant mergers, such as [θ ~ f].

Another important nonstandard dialect in the United States is Chicano English (ChE), which is also part of our investigation. Several studies examine the linguistic differences between ChE and SAE (e.g., González, 1988; Penfield, 1984; Penfield & Orstein-Galicia, 1985; Wald, 1984). Particularly important is the phonetic study of Godinez (1984). Again, we need to pay close attention to the phonological and morphophonemic differences between the dialects. Intonation on utterances of all sizes differs between ChE and SAE. For example, utterances in ChE begin at a higher pitch, although ChE intonations pattern more closely with English than with Spanish. Segmental changes differentiate SAE and ChE, for example, palatal interchange, fricative and affricate devoicing, and labiodental fricatives merging into coronal stops. Like AAVE, ChE modifies certain consonant clusters, especially initial and final clusters involving /s/. Unexpectedly, however, the mean duration of ChE vowels is more closely aligned with SAE vowels than with Spanish vowels.

Stimulus tokens for this experiment were recorded by speakers of the three target dialects. The number of speakers, totaling 20, varied across the racial and ethnic groups. In addition, Baugh recorded tokens in each of the three dialects. Each token consisted of the sentence, "Hello, I'm calling to see about the apartment you have advertised in the paper." The tokens were then randomized for presentation.

In the experimental stage, 421 undergraduate and graduate students at Stanford (382 native speakers of English, 39 nonnative speakers) listened to each token once without response. The students then listened to the tokens a second and a third time, indicating two presumed traits in a forced-choice experiment. The two traits students were asked to evaluate the listeners for were the race/ethnicity and gender of speakers. The possible answers for race and ethnicity were "African American," "Hispanic

American," and "European American." Combined with the two choices of gender, participants selected one of six possible responses for each token.

Given that each token has the possibility of being assigned one of six choices, the null hypothesis is that each guise should be identified correctly 16.6% of the time. We predict instead [. . .] that these guises are identifiable at the same rate as nontridialectal ones.

Results and discussion

The results of this study indicate that participants systematically identified Baugh's guises as being produced by an African American male (i.e., using AAVE), a Latino (i.e., using ChE), or a White male (i.e., using SAE) (see Table 9.4). Thus, we reject the null hypothesis and accept the test hypothesis.

[. . .] These macro-linguistic cues to dialect present an advantage as they are overt indicators of a speaker's ethnic identity. The problem, though, that this study faces is in explaining micro-linguistic, or more subtle, cues.

EXPERIMENT 3

To determine the feasibility of investigating the phonetics of dialects, a second perceptual experiment was conducted in which we tested listeners' ability to recognize dialects at the micro-linguistic, or phonetic, level. The results are intended to contribute to our understanding of the psychological processes enabling phonetic distinctions.

This third experiment deals with two basic issues of dialect production and perception. Dialects differ in their syntactic, morphological, or semantic subcomponents, but our concern is to understand the role played by phonetics and phonology. First, we ask, "How do dialects differ in pronunciation?" and second, "How do listeners identify dialects

Table 9.4   Dialect and racial identification

Dominant dialect/racial identification	Guise or gender	% Correct identification
AAVE/African American	Male	97
	Male	95
	Female	85
	Baugh (AAVE)	84
	Male	77
ChE/Hispanic American	Baugh (ChE)	91
	Male	86
	Female	79
SAE/European American	Male	92
	Female	87
	Baugh (SAE)	86
	Female	86
	Female	83
	Male	81

Note. AAVE = African American Vernacular English; ChE = Chicano English; SAE = Standard American English.

by pronunciation?" Because discrimination may crop up in telephone conversations, this experiment helps us better understand the cognitive role phonetics plays in establishing listeners' beliefs about a speaker's racial identity.

Phonetic features in the speech stream [. . .] are used for speaker and dialect recognition. Whether a given feature is contrastive [i.e. used for distinguishing words] or noncontrastive is a language-particular (and dialect-particular) choice and therefore must be learned. The learning results in shared knowledge about society in general, interlocutors' positions in society, and appropriate discourse norms given the discourse situation (Baugh, 1983). [. . .] One consequence of having to learn the phonetic grammar of a dialect is that individual speakers can control several dialects. Competency in more than one dialect is quite common, especially among speakers of nonstandard varieties. Thus, among speakers of AAVE, the presence or absence of /-s/ suffixes is tied to familiarity and dialect group membership, rather than to racial characteristics of the speaker (Baugh, 1983).

[. . .]

The null hypothesis in this experiment is that there is no difference between the dialects by identification. That is, each dialect should display recognition at the level of chance. Instead, we predict that the phonetic characteristics in a short portion of speech are sufficient to trigger identification across the dialects.

Method

For this experiment, only the word *hello* from Baugh's single-sentence utterances spoken in AAVE, ChE, and SAE were used. The word was extracted from the sentence, "Hello, I'm calling about the apartment you have advertised in the paper." We have several reasons for examining one word. This allowed us to hold external factors to a minimum. Second, it also illustrates how little speech is needed for dialect identification. "Hello" is a self-contained utterance, making perceptual studies more natural. By focusing on one short word, we are able to hold utterance duration well below one second ($\bar{x} = 414$ msec.), making it comparable to other studies (e.g., Walton & Orlikoff, 1994). The word *hello* neutralizes lexical, syntactic, and phonological differences across dialects. In other words, it lacks the environment in which we expect other dialectal variations.

This experiment was conducted during two semesters, Spring and Fall 1997. For this study, we used 50 undergraduates at the University of Delaware (Spring 1997: 30; Fall 1997: 20). All of the participants were Caucasian native speakers of SAE. Ten instances of "hello" repeated twice for each of the three dialects comprised one block of data. These 60 tokens were randomized. Each participant was twice presented with the block of data so that a total of 120 tokens were presented to each participant. During a 2-second pause, participants indicated, for each token, which dialect they believed they heard. The data below are combined from the two iterations of the experiment.

Results and discussion

[. . .]

The results show that, overall, participants are able to successfully identify tokens among the dialects when only hearing the word *hello*.

[. . .]

[W]e have established that listeners are capable of discriminating among dialects and that this discrimination is eased by a low-level identification of the dialects in a short amount of time. What still remains is at least a partial explanation of what phonetic features of the speech stream act as sociolinguistic markers.

EXPERIMENT 4

We performed a variety of acoustic measurements on the same "hello" data used in the perceptual experiment (Experiment 3). In this acoustic experiment we looked for acoustic differences between the dialects to determine cues listeners use to identify dialects. Our answer, from the acoustic measurements, is that at least four acoustic cues are viable for distinguishing at least one dialect from the other two: the frequency of the second formant in the /ɛ/, the location in the word where the pitch reaches a peak, the duration of the first syllable /hɛ/, and the harmonic-to-noise ratio (HNR).

[. . .]

Method

Following other studies (e.g., Klatt & Klatt, 1990; Stevens & Hanson, 1995; Walton & Orlikoff, 1994), we measured each instance of "hello" for several acoustic characteristics. We measured the segment, syllable, and word durations (and ratio of these durations to the duration of the word). [. . .] The 30 tokens (10 for each dialect) were compared on 28 variables by running a three-way analysis of variance (ANOVA) for the different variables.

Results and discussion

[. . .]

[The authors find that how much /ɛ/ is fronted in *hello* is the best cue for working out how people distinguish the three varieties: ChE and AAVE from SAE. The other phonetic features they checked were not significant.].

[. . .]

CONCLUSION

The experiments described in this article link housing opportunities with dialect use. Housing discrimination induced by speech characteristics does take place. Dialects are discriminated by normal listeners. Very little speech is required for dialect identification—a single word suffices. Dialects are discriminated with acoustic phonetic measures. Patterns of perceptual misidentification point to a multiplicity of factors for further study.

Looking back at the experiments as a whole, we should wonder whether the acoustic characteristics of the guises influenced the outcome of the discrimination survey. Consider that in Table 9.1 percentages of appointments made using ChE guises are the lowest in four of five geographic areas. Although we might be led to believe from this result that Hispanic Americans experience more discrimination than African Americans, we could well be misled. In [Experiment 3], however, ChE tokens are identified much better than AAVE tokens. Putting the two observations together, we see a possibility that ChE tokens as produced by Baugh are more salient as exemplars of nonstandard speech than his AAVE tokens, and they are thus less likely to be confused with the SAE tokens.

[. . .]

NOTES

1. What we are suggesting goes beyond what is covered under rules of evidence (Graham, 1987). Rule 901(b)(5) states that voice identification is permissible as evidence to identify the voice. We propose that rules of evidence govern the identification of race by way of a speaker's voice. Thus, if a plaintiff shows that she has a voice representative of a nonstandard dialect and that the defendant can ascertain when any voice possesses characteristics of the dialect under review, then evidence is established in favor of the plaintiff.

2. In fairness to the parties involved, the judge ruled in favor of the defendants because of a preponderance of evidence indicating that Ms. Rancatti had neither acted in a racist fashion nor acted habitually in such manner.

REFERENCES

Baugh, J. (1983) *Black Street Speech: Its History, Structure and Survival*. Austin: University of Texas Press.

City of Chicago v. Matchmaker Real Estate Sales Center, 982 F. 2d 1086 (7th Cir. 1992).

Clark, W. (1986) Residential segregation in American cities: a review and interpretation. *Population Research and Policy Review* 5: 95–127.

Clark, W. (1993) Measuring racial discrimination in the housing market: direct and indirect evidence. *Urban Affairs Quarterly* 28: 641–649.

Courant, P. (1978) Racial prejudice in a search model of the urban housing market. *Journal of Urban Economics* 5: 329–345.

Dillard, J. (1972) *Black English: Its History and Usage in the United States*. New York: Random House.

Galster, G. and W. Keeney (1988) Race, residence, discrimination, and economic opportunity: modeling the nexus of urban racial phenomena. *Urban Affairs Quarterly* 24: 87–117.

Godinez, M. (1984) Chicano English phonology: norms vs. interference. In J. Orstein-Galicia (ed.) *Form and Function in Chicano English*. Rowley, MA: Newbury House, 42–48.

González, G. (1988) Chicano English. In D. Bixler-Márquez and J. Orstein-Galicia (eds) *Chicano Speech in the Bilingual Classroom*. New York: Peter Lang, 71–82.

HUD v. Ross (HUDALJ 01–92–0466–8, July 7, 1994) [On-line]. Available: http::www.hud.gov/alj/pdf/ross.pdf.

Klatt, D. and L. Klatt (1990) Analysis, synthesis, and perception of voice quality variations among female and male talkers. *Journal of the Acoustic Society of America* 87: 820–857.

Labov, W. (1969) Contraction, deletion, and inherent variability of the English copula. *Language* 45: 715–762.

Labov, W. (1972a) *Language in the Inner City: Studies in the Black English Vernacular*. Philadelphia: University of Pennsylvania Press.

Labov, W. (1972b) *Sociolinguistic Patterns*. Philadelphia: University of Pennsylvania Press.

Lambert, W. and G. Tucker (1972) *Bilingual Education of Children: The St. Lambert Experiment*. Rowley, MA: Newbury House.

Massey, D. and Z. Hajnal (1995) The changing geographic structure of Black–White segregation in the United States. *Social Science Quarterly* 76: 527–542.

Myers, S. and T. Chan (1995) Racial discrimination in housing markets: accounting for credit risk. *Social Science Quarterly* 76: 543–561.

Penfield, J. (1984) Prosodic patterns: some hypotheses and findings from fieldwork. In J. Orstein-Galicia (ed.) *Form and Function in Chicano English*. Rowley, MA: Newbury House, 49–59.

Penfield, J. and J. Orstein-Galicia (1985) *Chicano English*. Philadelphia: John Benjamins.

Stevens, K. and H. Hanson (1995) Classification of glottal vibration from acoustic measurements. In O. Fujimura and M. Hirano (eds) *Vocal Fold Physiology: Voice Quality Control*. San Diego, CA: Singular Publishing Group, 147–170.

Tucker, G. and W. Lambert (1975) White and Negro listeners' reactions to various American-English dialects. In J. Dillard (ed.) *Perspectives on Black English*. The Hague, The Netherlands: Mouton, 369–377.

U.S. Census Bureau (1990) Census of population and housing [On-line]. Available: http::govinfo.kerr.orst.edu/stateis.html.

U.S. Census Bureau (1995) Housing in metropolitan areas—Black households [On-line]. Available: http::www.census.gov/apsd/www/statbrief/sb95_5.pdf.

Wald, B. (1984) The status of Chicano English as a dialect of American English. In J. Orstein-Galicia (ed.) *Form and Function in Chicano English*. Rowley, MA: Newbury House, 14–31.

Walton, J. and R. Orlikoff (1994) Speaker race identification from acoustic cues in the vocal signal. *Journal of Speech and Hearing Research* 37: 738–745.

Wolfram, W. (1969) *A Sociolinguistic Description of Detroit Negro Speech*. Washington, DC: Center for Applied Linguistics.

Yinger, J. (1986) Measuring racial discrimination with fair housing audits: caught in the act. *American Economic Review* 76: 881–893.

QUESTIONS

Content

1. What three guises were tested in this study?
2. In Experiment 1,

    a. which guise elicited most appointments to view an apartment overall?
    b. where was an African-American English speaker most likely to get an appointment?
    c. where was a Chicano English speaker most likely to get an appointment?

3. Did Experiment 2 validate the use of the three guises or not?
4. In Experiment 3, why did they choose to focus on the word "Hello"?
5. What part of "Hello" turns out to carry the most information about speaker ethnicity?

Concept

1. If the subjects in Experiment 4 usually identified each guise correctly on the basis of one word, what are the implications of this for future use of the matched guise technique?
2. It is common to use university students as the subjects for linguistic experiments like these. For example, in Experiment 2, the different guises were validated by university students. Do you think university students are a good source on which to base attitudes data? Why (not)?

    Consider also the methods used – do you think forced choice questions were a good way to elicit perceptions?

Chapter 10

Gibson Ferguson

LANGUAGE EDUCATION POLICY AND THE MEDIUM OF INSTRUCTION ISSUE IN POST-COLONIAL AFRICA

IN THIS [READING, WE consider] the medium of instruction, and specifically the role of pupils' home languages in the educational process. On this occasion, however, the focus is on the very different context of the multilingual post-colonial states of Africa, where the choice of instructional medium is the key issue in language planning in education. It is also a highly controversial one, with many academic commentators (e.g. Barrett 1994, Phillipson 1992, Rubagumya 1990, Trappes-Lomax 1990, Williams and Cooke 2002, Stroud 2003, Alidou 2004, Mazrui 2004) calling for the use of English and other former colonial languages to be restricted in favour of a greater role for African languages. This is seen as necessary for (1) promoting the development of indigenous languages, (2) improving the educational performance of pupils, particularly the less able and (3) mitigating the inequalities which are aggravated by the use of official languages of foreign origin over which large sectors of the population have little, or no, control.

This [reading] reviews some of these arguments, but our focus will not so much be on the educational merits of the use of home languages (i.e. local indigenous languages), [. . .] as on the socio-political constraints shaping language education policy. The justification for this selectivity is that advocacy of educationally justifiable policy reforms is more likely in the end to be persuasive if it is borne in mind that policies on instruction media are as much politically as educationally motivated. Indeed, as Tollefson and Tsui (2004b: 2) remark in the introduction to their volume, it is common for the educational case for reform to be trumped by political, social or economic agendas.

[. . .]

We turn first [. . .] to an overview of current policies on media of instruction in sub-Saharan Africa, and to the problems attached to them.

Source: Ferguson, Gibson (2006) *Language Planning and Education*. Edinburgh: Edinburgh University Press, 179–198.

1. CURRENT POLICIES ON MEDIA OF INSTRUCTION: ARTICULATING THE PROBLEM

The tendency in much of anglophone Africa, with a few interesting exceptions,[1] is for education to be conducted through an indigenous language medium[2] for the first three or four years of primary education, with a switch taking place thereafter to exclusively English medium instruction. In Lusophone and Francophone Africa, by contrast, Portuguese and French respectively tend to be the official languages of instruction from the start, though in certain countries (e.g. Mozambique: see Benson 2000) this policy is under review following relatively successful experimentation with bilingual media inclusive of local languages.[3] Table 10.1 summarises the situation in a limited but not unrepresentative range of mainly anglophone countries.

This, of course, is only a portrait of official policies. The actual situation on the ground is a good deal more complicated in that it is very common for teaching in the local language, or some combination of the local indigenous language and the exoglossic official language medium, to continue for some years after the official switch of medium, producing a de facto bilingual medium. One of the principal reasons for this classroom code-switching is simply that teachers find it necessary to make themselves understood by pupils who have only limited proficiency in the official language medium.

1.1 Media of education in lower primary school

There is widespread academic agreement that the mother tongue or a local language well known in the community is, in principle, the most suitable medium for education in the initial years of education. Put briefly, the educational argument is that cognitive development and subject learning is best fostered through teaching in a language the child knows well. Instruction in a language familiar to pupils improves immeasurably the quality of interaction between teacher and pupil. It also narrows the psychological gulf between home and school, integrates the school better into the local community and

Table 10.1   The medium of education at lower primary level in selected African countries

Years	1	2	3	4	5	6	7	8	9	10	11	12	Local language medium
Malawi	▦	▦	▦	▦									Chichewa
Tanzania	▦	▦	▦		▦	▦	▦						Kiswahili
Botswana	▦	▦	▦	▦									Setswana
Burundi	▦	▦	▦										Kirundi
Ghana	▦	▦	▦										various languages
Nigeria	▦	▦	▦										various languages

Key:

▦	Local or indigenous language medium
	Metropolitan language medium

gives recognition to the language and culture the child brings to school with positive effects on the self-esteem of individuals and local communities (see Benson 2002). The work of Cummins (1979, 1984) and others suggests, moreover, that consolidation of the child's L1 facilitates subsequent acquisition of a second language [. . .].

In spite of equivocal early research findings (e.g. Engle 1975), these arguments are increasingly bolstered by empirical evidence. For example, [. . .] Williams (1996) shows that fifth-year primary pupils in Malawi, where the medium until grade 4 is Chichewa, have no worse reading abilities in English than primary five pupils in Zambia, where the official medium is English from grade 1. Moreover, the Malawian pupils show far greater reading ability in their local language, Chichewa, than the Zambian pupils do in their local language, Nyanja.[4]

Given, then, that there is little dispute in academic, if not in policy-making circles, that an indigenous, local language, related to the mother tongue, is the most effective medium of early education, the rest of this paper focuses on the more contentious choice of media at the upper primary and secondary levels of education.

1.2 Media of instruction at upper primary and secondary levels of education

In many African countries, where English is the medium in the upper primary and secondary education cycles, there is little exposure to English outside class, especially in rural areas, and this coupled with poor teaching of the language in primary school often means that pupils arriving at secondary school have insufficient proficiency to learn subject matter presented in English. The most striking and extreme illustration of this derives from Tanzania where Criper and Dodd's 1984 study found that:

> Most pupils leave primary school unable to speak or understand simple English. A selected few enter secondary school but they are so weak in English that they are unable to understand lessons or read textbooks in English. (Criper and Dodd 1984)

Certainly, Tanzania, for country-specific reasons, is an extreme case, but there are indications that similar problems exist in a number of other African countries. Williams and Cooke (2002: 307), for example, report adverse findings on the situation in upper primary schools in Zambia, Zimbabwe, Zanzibar, Mauritius and Namibia.

[. . .]

[I]n Francophone Africa there are few indications that the situation is significantly better, with Alidou (2003: 108), for example, reporting a 25 per cent drop-out rate between grades 4 and 5 in the primary schools of Burkino Faso, Mali and Niger, and continuing underperformance, relative to international levels, of African students on tests administered in French or English.[5]

There is a body of evidence, then, to indicate that in many African countries education is ineffectively delivered, a situation clearly wasteful of financial and human resources. And, while the causes of this underperformance are multiple and various, relatively successful experimentation with bilingual media incorporating local languages (see Benson 2000, 2002; Fafunwa et al. 1989) provides a reasonably plausible basis for believing that the use of foreign language media, unfamiliar to many pupils, is at least one contributory factor. Certainly, this is a guiding assumption of the many applied linguistics academics (e.g. Rubagumya 1990, Trappes-Lomax 1990, Arthur 1994, Williams 1996, Mazrui 2004, etc.) who have argued that English (or French for that matter) should be replaced by an indigenous language medium, which, because it is better understood by pupils, will produce a better quality of classroom interaction and promote higher levels of scholastic attainment.

This proposal is, as we have seen, theoretically and empirically defensible, and is supported, moreover, by some quasi-experimental evidence. For example, Prophet and Dow (1994) in a Botswana study taught a set of science concepts to an experimental group in Setswana and to a control group in English. They then tested understanding of these concepts and found that form one secondary school students taught in Setswana had developed a significantly better understanding of the concepts than those taught in English. In addition, the latter group experienced some difficulty in expressing their ideas in English. At the form three level, however, they found that 'the language of instruction had no real impact on their understanding of the science concepts covered in the lesson' (Prophet and Dow 1994: 214). The Setswana and English groups performed equally well.

Given this kind of evidence, the plausibility of the theoretical arguments, and the weight of academic opinion in favour of reform, it may be wondered why English has not long since been replaced by indigenous languages as the medium of instruction. The answer is that choice of medium is not just an educational matter but also a profoundly political one, and that in Africa the tendency, as mentioned earlier, has been for educational considerations to be subordinated to socio-political ones. We now turn to consider these.

2. CHANGING THE MEDIA OF INSTRUCTION: CONSTRAINTS ON POLICY

The impediments to policy change on the media of instruction are various: some socio-political, some economic, some practical. We turn first to a consideration of the socio-political constraints.

2.1 Socio-political constraints

Historically, one of the more frequent justifications, or explanations, for the retention of former colonial languages as official languages and as media of education is that they are ethnically neutral, and therefore advance rather than retard the cause of nation-building and national unity [. . .]. By contrast, so the argument goes, choosing any one (or more) languages(s) from a range of competing indigenous languages as media of education at upper primary/secondary level would advantage one ethnic group over another and in this way risk political discord or worse.

In some quarters, these arguments are dismissed either as mere self-serving rhetoric, masking the interests of neo-colonialists or those anxious to maintain their privileged position, or as signifying an uncritical attachment to an outmoded European one-nation one-language nationalist ideology. It would be unwise, however, in discussion of a continent troubled, like parts of Europe, by ethnically based conflicts (e.g. in Congo DRC, Ivory

Coast, Sudan, Somalia, Uganda), to dismiss them entirely, despite the germs of truth the criticisms contain. (Outside Africa, after all, for instance in Sri Lanka, there are historical grounds for believing that decisions on media of instruction have played a part in the exacerbation of ethnic tensions.)

A brief example from Zambia may help illustrate the point. Van Binsbergen (1994: 144–5) describes in detail the situation in the western province of Zambia, where in colonial and pre-colonial days the Nkoya, a minority ethnolinguistic group, were sub-jugated and incorporated into a larger Lozi state. Nkoya resentment at Lozi domination persisted into the post-colonial period and they interpreted the lack of official recogni-tion of their language as Lozi oppression.[6] With this history, it is not difficult to imagine the tensions that would arise from the imposition of Silozi as a regional medium of learning, or for that matter the potential for conflict on a national scale occasioned by, say, the imposition of a Silozi medium of instruction on the Bemba. The wider point here is that closer study of the history of the internal politics of regions or subregions, not only in Zambia but elsewhere in Africa, highlights the tensions that could be exacerbated by elevating one indigenous language over another in the educational field.

That said, there are two major considerations to mention, which significantly attenuate the force of the argument from national unity. The first is that while colonial language media may be ethnically neutral, they are far from neutral socio-economically in that they substantially advantage the wealthier, urban class, whose children have easier access to books, satellite television and private English classes [. . .]. Paradoxically, however, it is this very propensity to divide socially and to advantage a small but powerful urban social elite that furnishes a motive for the retention of English medium education, as we shall see.

The second point is that in a minority of African states (e.g. Tanzania, Swaziland, Burundi, Botswana), by reason either of extreme multilingual diversity (Tanzania) or relative linguistic homogeneity (Swaziland), there already exists a widely accepted indigenous national language (e.g. Kiswahili in Tanzania), whose selection as an edu-cational medium of secondary education could in no manner be realistically represented as a potential threat to national unity. Yet even here, in the most socio-linguistically propitious circumstances for reform, English remains the medium of secondary educa-tion. There must, therefore, be some alternative socio-political or economic explanation for the retention of English.

2.1.1 The attractiveness of English

The most important of these, exceeding the national unity factor in explanatory power by far, is the economic power and attractiveness of English. It is a language that is perceived to be, and manifestly functions as, a gatekeeper to educational and employment opportunities, so social advancement. No wonder then that competence in English and English medium education is highly valued by parents, students and the wider public, all of whom see it as a form of 'linguistic capital'.

From a range of countries comes ample evidence of the strong demand for English. In Mozambique, for example, urban employees are willing to spend considerable portions of their small salaries to fund attendance at private English classes, and in many parts of Africa, such as Tanzania, private English-medium schools, principally for children of the political and business elites, are booming (Vavrus 2002: 37; Mafu 2003: 276). [. . .] From South Africa, meanwhile, Broom (2004: 523) reports not just strong parental demand for English but sustained pressure for schools to effect a transition to English medium as early as possible. Where schools do not comply, parents are quite ready to transfer their children to schools where English has been adopted as the medium of instruction.

The attractiveness of English is also partly fuelled by the corresponding unattractiveness – for parents – of education in indigenous language media. In South Africa, these bear historical connotations of oppression and disempowerment, but there is also a feeling, harboured by many parents here and elsewhere in Africa, that education through indigenous languages is dead-end education, there being relatively little reading material in these languages beyond school books and few well-paid employment opportunities accessed by knowledge of them.

Changing such attitudes is clearly an important matter, but also a large-scale language planning undertaking, involving no less than a complete rehabilitation of the status of African languages. This, in turn, would require changes in the economic status of these languages – to incentivise their study; their use in prestigious public domains – to increase their prestige; and an increase in the variety of reading, educational and entertainment material available in the language(s) to enhance their attractiveness, not to mention, as Broom (2004: 524) suggests, 'the development of a culture of literacy and reading in these languages'. It would seem on the face of it, then, that there is no immediate prospect of rapid attitudinal change.

Meanwhile, many of those looking to English to deliver socio-economic advancement will end up disappointed. Many will fail in English, and in countries where only 10 to 20 per cent of children continue to secondary school, many will be excluded from participation in public life and from the modern sector labour market by lack of proficiency in English.

But this does not mean that demand for English is irrational at the individual level, [. . .] the reason being that, while there is no guarantee of individual mobility with English, without it there is the virtual certainty of exclusion from higher education, salaried positions in the modernised sector of the economy, travel abroad and so on. [. . .] The same factors also explain the general reluctance of politicians to embark on a course of action that would restrict access to English or displace it as a secondary school medium, for to do so would be to court considerable public displeasure, or worse.

The wider point here is the familiar one that school reflects society and has limited power of itself to change it. [. . .] Given the present economic order, English in Africa still leads to the more attractive, better paying modern sector jobs, and as long as this situation persists, which is probable given globalisation and the weakness of many African economies, politicians are unlikely to swim against the tide of public opinion by switching the medium away from English.

2.1.2 Vested interests

We come finally to another factor sometimes adduced as a reason for the retention of English medium education: the vested interests of ruling elites (see Myers-Scotton 1990). English, it is argued, helps elites maintain their privileged position by excluding the mass of the population, who have less easy access to the language and to the resources needed to develop a high level of proficiency. It is a mechanism, in short, by which elites are able to reproduce their privilege in the succeeding generation, and one, therefore, they are unlikely to dismantle voluntarily.

The argument has some plausibility, in some countries more than others, but it would probably be a mistake to give it too much prominence, for there are other constraints, in all likelihood more powerful, that are also responsible for the ongoing policy inertia. We turn now to a brief consideration of the more salient of these.

2.2 Economic and practical constraints

Not to be forgotten in any discussion of medium of instruction policies in Africa is the presence of constraining external forces, the nature of whose operation is perhaps most clearly visible in Tanzania, a country where, as noted above, there are relatively few sociolinguistic impediments to an indigenous national language medium. In 1982 there were, in fact, well-founded expectations that the country would shortly move to Kiswahili medium in secondary education, but not long after, in 1984, these hopes were dashed with an official announcement that English would after all be retained.

Relevant to understanding this apparent policy 'u-turn' are two key factors. First, by the early 1980s Tanzania had entered a period of prolonged economic crisis, increasing the country's dependency on external support and undermining, simultaneously, confidence that the country could successfully implement such a far-reaching reform at a time of financial stringency. Second, the then president, Julius Nyerere, mindful perhaps of this economic weakness, was in favour of maintaining English medium instruction to 'guard against parochialism' and to protect the country's international links within and beyond the African continent. He was fearful too, according to Russell (1990: 370), that 'the use of English might die out altogether if it were taught only as a subject'.

Illustrated here is the not unfounded anxiety, felt by governments in other parts of Africa and indeed elsewhere (e.g. Malaysia: see Gill 2004: 144), that a shift away from English medium at secondary level would isolate the country from the international community, limit inward investment from the richer countries of the North and above all, obstruct access to science and technology – thus diminishing economic competitiveness.[7] These fears, one might add, become especially acute where the country in question (e.g. Tanzania) is economically weak and dependent on external donor support.

Nor can one ignore the influence of globalisation. The autonomy of African states as policy-making units is, in common with nation states elsewhere, increasingly constrained by global economic and political forces. Increasing numbers of African academics, writers, politicians, business executives, financiers, civil servants and university students inhabit a 'globalised landscape' (Fardon and Furniss 1994: 16). Electronic forms of communication (email and the Internet) and improved transport increase the permeability of national boundaries to the flow of information and people. The net effect is greater interdependence, which, in turn, strengthens the need and demand for proficiency in international lingua francas, especially English.

Set alongside these external macro forces are impediments of a more practical nature that can conveniently be grouped into three rough categories: (1) linguistic resources, (2) books and learning materials and (3) financial resources and educational infrastructure.

2.2.1 Linguistic resources

One of the more commonly cited, and even more frequently exaggerated, obstacles to the use of African languages as media of instruction is that they lack the requisite level of linguistic resources for performing this function: graphisation, standardisation, codification, scientific and technical terminology and an extensive elaborated vocabulary. Certainly, it is true that many indigenous languages remain understandardised, lacking the developed orthographies and vocabulary that would facilitate their introduction as educational media. It is also true that developing and 'intellectualising' (Liddicoat and Bryant 2002: 10) many languages simultaneously would be a costly undertaking.

That said, considerable progress has been made, especially with regard to national languages. Kiswahili, for example, already possesses the necessary attributes of standardisation, codification and a sufficiently elaborated vocabulary for use as a secondary level medium of instruction, a monolingual dictionary of Kiswahili having been published in 1981 followed in 1990 by a dictionary of scientific terms (Roy-Campbell 2003: 89). [. . .] In South Africa, meanwhile, PanSALB, the main South African language planning agency, has been mandated to elaborate terminology for the nine historically disadvantaged official languages (e.g. Tshivenda, Xitsonga, etc.), which, though partially developed in possessing 'written forms, literary work, dictionaries and terminology lists' (Finlayson and Madiba 2002: 40), require further development in the area of modern terminology.

These instances, and successful corpus planning activity elsewhere on behalf of languages such as Malay[8] – which is now a medium in tertiary education – show that the cultivation/intellectualisation of indigenous African languages is perfectly feasible technically. The greater obstacle, then, is not so much the technical operations of elaboration or standardisation, administratively and logistically complex though these may be (Finlayson and Madiba 2002: 48), as the availability of resources and the political willingness to commit them, which, in turn, hinges on attitudes to these languages.

This leads us to a further point of some importance, which is that it is by no means obvious that corpus planning should always and necessarily precede the implementation of a given language as a medium of instruction. Form tends to follow function, and, as Nadkarni (1984: 154) suggests, if a language is not first put to use in a given function, it is hardly likely to develop the relevant linguistic resources.

[. . .]

2.2.2 Books and learning materials

Another much cited practical obstacle to adopting indigenous language media is the relative dearth of textbook and learning materials in these languages, the only solution for which would be the large-scale production, or translation, of books across a range of curricular subjects, a matter not just of finding suitably qualified authors or translators but also the necessary paper, publishers and distributors. Not impossible, of course, but clearly a costly and time-consuming business. Boyle (1995: 294), for example, points out how the 1984 Hong Kong Educational Commission, which recommended the publication of textbooks in both Chinese and English, seriously underestimated the 'enormity' of the task. And anyone with experience of donor-supported textbook production projects involving, for example, the supply of a single English language textbook to schools throughout a developing country, can testify to the considerable effort and administration required.

Again, this is not to say the provision of textbooks in a new language medium is an insuperable obstacle. Recent developments in desktop publishing technology may help, though, as far as we aware, there is – as yet – no conclusive demonstration of this. It is to say, rather, that implementation of a change of this magnitude, which would additionally involve accustoming teachers to teaching subjects in a language they had not themselves been taught in, would require confidence, commitment and, above all, money – a crucial factor to which we now turn.

2.2.3 Financial resources and educational infrastructure

Central, and critical, in discussions of media of instruction in the context of the resource-weakened education systems found in parts of Africa is the question of financial resources, to which we have already alluded in previous discussion. Here it is useful at the outset to recall the very adverse conditions in which schooling often takes place.

In Malawian and Zambian primary schools, for instance, Williams (1996) depicts the following kind of conditions: large classes of fifty or more pupils and a shortage of desks for pupils to sit at, paralleling a shortage of classrooms with some classes held in the open air as a result. [. . .] In many countries it is not that unusual for the teacher to hold the only copy of a key textbook. From Mozambique, Benson (2002: 307; 2004: 266) also reports adverse conditions: chronic illness among pupils, and frequent school closures due to strikes or teacher absence. Across a swathe of countries teachers are poorly paid and frequently poorly trained, if at all (see Cleghorn and Rollnick 2002: 350 on Kenya), and it is unsurprising, therefore, that the methods employed to teach the second/foreign language often leave much to be desired. Finally, many primary school systems are characterised by high drop-out rates and less than universal enrolment, particularly among girls. Secondary schools, meanwhile, tend to cater to a small, relatively select sector of the age-population.

This somewhat depressing catalogue of problems has not been assembled for its own sake, however, but to make three main points. The first is that ministries of education in sub-Saharan Africa have many problems to cope with and many competing spending priorities. Given the conditions outlined above, and their fundamental task of delivering basic education to the population, it would be unsurprising, even justifiable, if they elected to commit their available financial resources to the improvement of the basic educational infrastructure – books, desks, teacher-training – rather than to a change of instructional medium, necessary though that might also be.

Second, given the scale of spending required to ameliorate school conditions, and given the fact that in many countries as much as 90 per cent of the primary education budget is allocated to recurrent expenditure on teachers' salaries – leaving little over for books, equipment or maintenance – it is likely that a policy directed at changing the medium of instruction, whether at primary or secondary level, would require substantial multilateral or bilateral external donor support. Whether such support will be forth-coming, however, is an uncertain and controversial matter. Mazrui (2004: 45) for example, alleges that the World Bank speaks with a forked tongue on this matter, espousing – on the one hand – a rhetoric supportive of the use of the mother tongue in early primary education but refraining, on the other, from committing resources to the 'linguistic Africanisation of all primary education' because it has, Mazrui (2004: 49) claims, a vested interest in the maintenance of European languages of instruction.

Comparatively little empirical evidence is advanced, however, to support the stronger of these claims. Certainly, there are good grounds for believing that past structural adjustment policies[9] of the IMF-World Bank were not helpful to educational development, and that the World Bank has taken little interest in pushing forward an agenda of 'linguistic Africanisation' beyond the initial stages of primary school. But there are indications that it is prepared to fund experimental programmes using local languages as media in early primary education, the primary bilingual education project in Mozambique (1993–97) being a case in point (Benson 2000: 50).

The third and perhaps most important point is that, given the circumstances described above, we need to question the proposition that a change to an indigenous language medium at upper primary or secondary level would of itself resolve the problems of educational underachievement, whose causes are, in fact, more plausibly [. . .] multiple, [. . .] it seems likely that much-needed improvements in educational quality require not just changes in policy but simultaneous micro-level change in educational practices, in resource provision and the implementation of policy, the two being interdependent. As Cummins (1998) has pointed out [. . .], use of the home language is no educational panacea; bilingual education can be effectively as well as poorly delivered. [. . .] Too great a burden of expectation placed on policy reform, or, indeed, change in any one single factor, is likely, experience suggests, to lead only to disappointment.

2.2.4 The influence of higher education

Talk here of educational infrastructure leads us to a final factor constraining changes in instructional media at secondary level, the influence, namely, of higher education. The reason this is significant is that the different levels of the education system interlock, the output of one level generally constituting the input of another, with lower levels often seen as preparatory in some measure for the level immediately above. The effect is that higher levels of education tend to exert considerable, often undue, influence on curricular provision at the level below. Thus, where English (or some other former colonial language) is the medium at university, as it so often is in post-colonial Africa[10] – especially in science and social science subjects – pressure develops for that language to be employed also as a medium at secondary school. The pressure comes largely from parents and pupils, who harbour aspirations, no matter how unrealistic in practice, of progressing to university; and is evident not just in Africa but beyond. In Hong Kong, for instance, this is one of the factors, along with the economic, that explains parental demand for English medium secondary education, even where many, perhaps most, understand the educational benefits of the mother tongue medium (Tsui 2004: 100).

[. . .]

In Africa, meanwhile, concern that students graduating from nominally English medium secondary schools possess insufficient proficiency to cope with university study in English has prompted the establishment of communication skills units in many uni-versities (e.g. in Kenya), catering mainly to the needs of first year students. It is not unreasonable to suppose, therefore, that abandoning English medium at secondary level would only exacerbate these difficulties. One obvious solution, of course, would be to adopt an indigenous national language medium at university level, but such a course of action would run up against many of the constraints we have already outlined, and more besides.

3. THE MEDIUM OF INSTRUCTION ISSUE AND THE ROLE OF THE APPLIED LINGUIST

[. . .]

[R]adical change in policies on media of instruction beyond early primary schooling is unlikely in the near future. English medium is strongly entrenched, particularly at secondary level, for reasons that have little to do with any educational rationale or merit. The principal implication is that applied linguists might be well advised to complement continued advocacy of policy reform with investigation of measures that might – in the meantime – mitigate some of the adverse effects of the use of foreign language media. Taking this as a cue, we outline very briefly some of the ameliorative measures that might be considered, at the level of both policy and pedagogy. The tentative and programmatic nature of what follows indicates the scope of the research that still needs to be undertaken.

3.1 Ameliorating a difficult situation

3.1.1 Bilingual education

The medium of instruction issue in sub-Saharan Africa is sometimes presented, in political circles at least, as if it were a matter of a binary choice between either English/ French/Portuguese or some indigenous language. But, of course, [. . .] this is not the case at all. Bilingual education, the use of two languages as media of instruction – whether for different subjects or at different times of day (see Jacobsen and Faltis 1990 for a full range of language alternation possibilities) – is an obvious alternative option with merits applied linguists could usefully draw to the attention of policy-makers. [. . .] [I]t may allow the popular demand for English to be reconciled with the continued development of pupils' skills in a language more closely related to their home language, skills that will positively impact on the acquisition of English as a second language. It is a strategy that makes sense, too, in a sociolinguistic environment where speakers are already accus-tomed to using different languages for different purposes. And it accords well with Laitin's (1992) useful 3 ± 1 language 'rationalisation' formula for language-in-education planning, which proposes that – for optimal functioning in a multilingual African society – an individual's language repertoire should include between two and four languages: four if they are members of a linguistic minority and two if their mother tongue happens to be also the national language. The three base languages in the formula are (1) a former colonial language as language of wider communication (LWC), (2) an indigenous national language and (3) a local or regional official language.

This is not to deny that the implementation of a bilingual education strategy will be formidably difficult, or feasible on any other than a gradual, piecemeal basis (see Benson 2002: 313). [. . .]

Nor is it to deny that bilingual education already has an unofficial existence, taking the form of widespread classroom code-switching (CS) by teachers who feel instinctively that it is necessary for pupils to learn through an imperfectly understood foreign language. And, significantly, the evidence suggests (Ferguson 2003, Martin-Jones 1995) that they are right, that CS is a useful resource for mitigating the difficulties of learning through a foreign language. There is a good case, then, for moderating official hostility to CS, for acknowledging its prevalence and, indeed, for incorporating awareness of CS as a resource into teacher education curricula.[11]

3.1.2 Transitioning between media

Remaining at the level of policy, another matter calls out for closer attention: the transition from one language medium to another, a switch that in Africa usually takes place at the end, or in the middle years, of primary education, and one that is typically not as well managed as it might be. Reform efforts here could potentially focus on (1) the timing of the switch, (2) the phasing of the switch or (3) preparation for the switch.

As regards timing, there is a good educational case for delaying the switch to a foreign language medium for one or two years so that in Botswana, for example, English medium would be officially introduced in grade 5 or 6, not 4, and in Tanzania in, say, year 3 of secondary school rather than year 1. The advantages of such delay [are]: it allows more time for the consolidation of vital L1 literacy skills, facilitates subject content learning in the middle years of primary school and enhances the status of indigenous languages. A further benefit is that it may allow more efficient use to be made of the limited numbers of primary school teachers with sufficient English language proficiency to teach effectively through the language, a common problem being (and not just in Africa) that there are too few such individuals to cover many primary grades (see Davies 1999: 70).

Standing in the way of such a reform, however, looms the familiar obstacle of public and political reluctance to embrace any circumscription of the educational role of English. In which case greater weight may need to fall not on timing but on the preparation for, and phasing of, the switch to English medium. Phasing refers to the gradual implementation of the switch of medium over a number of years subject by subject, starting first, as Clegg (1995: 16) suggests, with contextually supportive subjects. The rationale, of course, is that this alleviates some of the stress many pupils suffer when the switch is made more abruptly. Helpful here would be the devolution of some decision-making powers to school level so that headteachers and their staff can decide – in the light of locally available teaching resources – which subjects should make the switch first.

As regards preparation, meanwhile, a variety of potentially helpful measures come to mind. One is the reintroduction of the intensive crash courses of L2 instruction that once immediately preceded the switch of medium – for example in the Tanzania of the late

1960s and early 1970s, where there used to operate a six-week intensive course based around Isaac's textbook *Learning Through Language*. [. . .]

3.1.3 Curriculum innovation

Another potentially helpful measure might be the introduction, or reintroduction rather, from upper primary school onwards of the programmes of extensive reading that were a prominent feature of secondary school syllabuses in East Africa in the 1960s and Malaysia in the 1970s, and which have since been successfully implemented in English medium Hong Kong secondary schools (Hill 1992: 2). Properly implemented (Hill 1992), these can significantly increase exposure to the target language with beneficial effects, the evidence suggests (Day and Bamford 1998; Hill 1992; Krashen 1993), on reading fluency, vocabulary learning and overall proficiency in the second language. [. . .]

3.1.4 Learning materials: quantity and readability

Moving on now to issues of materials, classroom pedagogy and teacher education, we turn first to the crucial matter of L2 learning materials, starting with the simple question of quantity and availability. One of the more robust findings of studies conducted by the World Bank and other agencies (e.g. Fuller 1987, Fuller and Heyneman 1989, Heyneman et al. 1983) into factors associated with school quality is that in situations where there is a shortage of textbooks, as is the case in many African schools, an increase in their quantity, improving the ratio of pupils per textbook, is one of the most effective single inputs towards raising levels of pupil achievement. No medium can be effective without text-books, and it is plainly important, then, that the basic resources are made available.

Quantity, however, will not suffice if the textbooks are not used properly and if they are not readable. The latter point is a particular matter of concern in view of accumulating evidence (see e.g. Chimombo 1989) that many of the books currently in use are linguistically unsuitable because they take little account of the fact that readers are learning through an L2 medium. Peacock (1995: 394), for example, refers to research from a range of countries showing that 'the demands of science texts are often above the level and capacities of the primary school children they are intended for'. He also cites MacDonald's (1990) South African study, which exposed a substantial gap between the language used in science texts and that taught in the English language syllabus up to that same stage both in terms of vocabulary ('from 38 per cent to 55 per cent of the vocabulary used was not taught in the (English) schemes') and previously untaught logical connectives (Peacock 1995: 393).

Clearly, then, there is ample scope for research into the readability of the textbooks used across the curriculum in L2 medium situations, the aim of which would be to generate guidelines for textbook authors and publishers. Such research would need to take account not just of vocabulary and syntax, the usual inputs to traditional readability formulas, but also other factors impinging on comprehensibility: discourse, lay-out, visual support, use of metaphor and analogy, and rate of information unloading, not forgetting important non-textual factors that play a role, specifically the manner in which teachers mediate L2 medium texts (see Martin 1999).

3.1.5 Classroom pedagogy and teacher education

[. . .]

One of the more reliable routes to improved classroom pedagogy [. . .] may lie in revised and improved teacher education [. . .]. [I]n an L2 medium system all teachers, whatever their subject, are condemned to be language teachers with a responsibility to attend to their own as well as pupils' use of the various languages in their repertoires. The implication is clear: components on bilingual education, second language learning theory, L2 language improvement and language awareness could profitably feature on the training curriculum of teachers of, say, biology or geography as well as on that of language arts teachers, particularly at secondary level (see Benson 2004: 215 for further suggestions on teacher training in developing countries). [. . .]

3.2 Concluding remarks

Many of the measures proposed above are not new, and many may well turn out not to be feasible. But this is testimony in itself to the need for further research and experimentation, and at least the preceding discussion may contribute to the elaboration of a fresh research agenda focusing on practice as well as policy. Such an agenda is needed, for much current education is inefficient, wasteful and inimical to development, and, while changes in the medium of instruction policy may resolve some of these problems, there is, as argued earlier, little immediate prospect of radical policy change. Also, while there is a large literature on policy, empirical studies of the processes of L2 medium instruction in Africa, and of how those processes might be made more efficient, are rather less abundant. There still remains, then, much work for applied linguists to do.

NOTES

1. One exception is Zambia, where English functions as the official medium from grade 1 of primary school.
2. Terms used in this [reading] to refer to various different types of language or language variety (e.g. 'mother tongue' or 'indigenous language') are problematic. 'Mother tongue', for example, is unsatisfactory because in Africa many children grow up with bilingualism as their 'mother tongue'. And 'mother tongue education' may be a misnomer because, while the language used at home and in early primary education may bear the same name, they may in fact be quite different varieties. 'Indigenous language', too, is problematic when used to contrast with 'former colonial language', for many Africans do, in fact, speak English, or to an even greater extent Portuguese (see Vilela 2002: 308), as their native, first language, albeit in an Africanised form. That said, as a matter of convenience we shall persist with these terms because they are widely used and seem unlikely in the present context, given this caveat, to provoke serious misunderstanding.
3. There is a long tradition of experimentation with bilingual primary schooling, incorporating local languages as media of instruction, in Francophone countries such as Burkino Faso, Mali and Niger. But even after twenty years of experimentation there have been no moves to extend the use of bilingual media to all mainstream primary schools in the state sector (Alidou 2003: 110).
4. Chichewa and Nyanja are in fact very closely related languages.

5.   Alidou (2003: 106–8) draws on UNESCO research data (UNESCO 2000 *Status and Trends 2000: Assessing Learning Achievement*. Paris: UNESCO).

6.   Having lived in Kaoma (formerly Mankoya), the centre of the Nkoya heartland, from 1977 to 1982, the author can confirm the reality of such tensions.

7.   These very factors feature prominently in the explanation given by the then Malaysian prime minister, Dr Mahathir Mohamed, of the government's 1993 decision to reinstate English as medium of higher education in science, engineering and medical courses after many years of Bahasa Malaysia medium (see Gill 2004: 144).

8.   The Malaysian corpus planning agency, *Dewan Bahasa dan Pustaka*, has played a leading role in elaborating a corpus of scientific and technical terms in Malay (see Chapter 2, Ferguson 2006), greatly facilitating the completion in 1983 of a switch from English to Malay medium instruction in all subjects in public university education (Gill 2004: 142).

9.   The heyday of 'structural adjustment' policies was the 1980s and early 1990s. Imposed by the IMF-World Bank (in part as a remedy for the heavy burden of external debt servicing), they prescribed, among other things, privatisation of state enterprises, liberalisation of capital controls and the reduction of public expenditure, including expenditure on education.

10. The overwhelming dominance of English in published academic writing and the problems of elaborating indigenous national languages have tended to render efforts to dislodge the former colonial language from its role at this level very difficult. In the great majority of African post-colonial states, therefore, the former colonial language remains the medium of education at university.

11. Regrettably, space constraints disallow any more detailed consideration of this important phenomenon. For a review of official attitudes to classroom CS, and of its merits as a pedagogical resource, see Ferguson (2003). For an overview of research on classroom CS, see Martin-Jones (1995).

REFERENCES

Alidou, H. (2003) Language policies and language education language in Francophone Africa: a critique and a call to action. In S. Makoni, G. Smitherman, A. Ball and A. Spears, (eds) *Black Linguistics: Language, Society, and Politics in Africa and the Americas*. London: Routledge, 103–116.

Alidou, H. (2004) Medium of instruction in post-colonial Africa. In J. Tollefson, and A. Tsui, (eds) *Medium of Instruction Policies: Which agenda, whose agenda?* Mahwah, NJ: Lawrence Erlbaum, 195–214.

Arthur, J. (1994) English in Botswana primary classrooms: Functions and constraints. In C. Rubagumya, (ed.) *Teaching and Researching Language in African Classrooms*. Clevedon: Multilingual Matters, 63–78.

Barrett, J. (1994) Why is English still the medium of education in Tanzanian secondary schools? *Language, Culture and Curriculum* 7: 3–28.

Benson, C. (2000) The primary bilingual education experiment in Mozambique, 1993–1997. *International Journal of Bilingual Education and Bilingualism*, 3: 149–166.

Benson, C. (2002) Real and potential benefits of bilingual programmes in developing countries. *International Journal of Bilingual Education and Bilingualism* 5: 303–317.

Benson, C. (2004) Do we expect too much of bilingual teachers? Bilingual teaching in developing countries. *International Journal of Bilingual Education and Bilingualism* 7: 204–221.

Boyle, J. (1995) Hong Kong's educational system: English or Chinese. *Language, Culture and Curriculum*, 8: 291–304.

Broom, Y. (2004) Reading English in multilingual South African primary schools. *International Journal of Bilingual Education and Bilingualism* 7: 506–528.

Chimombo, M. (1989) Readability of subject texts: Implications for ESL teaching in Africa. *English for Specific Purposes* 8: 255–264.

Clegg, J. (1995) Education through the medium of a second language: Time to get serious about results. In British Council *Dunford House Seminar Report 1995*. Manchester: The British Council, 12–19.

Cleghorn, A. and A. Rollnick (2002) The role of English in individual and societal development: A view from African classrooms. *TESOL Quarterly* 36: 347–372.

Criper, C. and W. Dodd (1984) *Report on the Teaching of the English Language and its Use as a Medium in Education in Tanzania*. London: ODA/British Council.

Cummins, J. (1979) Linguistic interdependence and the educational development of bilingual children. *Review of Educational Research* 49: 222–51. Reprinted in C. Baker, and N. Hornberger, (eds) 2001. *An Introductory Reader to the Writings of Jim Cummins*. Clevedon: Multilingual Matters, 63–95.

Cummins, J. (1984) *Bilingualism and Special Education: Issues in assessment and pedagogy*. Clevedon: Multilingual Matters.

Cummins, J. (1998) *Beyond Adversarial Discourse: Searching for common ground in the education of bilingual students*. Presentation to the California State Board of Education, Sacramento, California, February 1998. http://ourworld.compuserve.com/homepages/jwcrawford/cummins.htm) Accessed 18 July 2003.

Davies, A. (1999) *An Introduction to Applied Linguistics*. Edinburgh: Edinburgh University Press.

Day, R. R. and J. Bamford (1998) *Extensive Reading in the Second Language Classroom*. Cambridge: Cambridge University Press.

Engle, P. (1975) The use of vernacular languages in education. *Papers in Applied Linguistics; Bilingual Education Series No 3*. Virginia, Center for Applied Linguistics.

Fafunwa, B., J. Iyabode Macauley and J. Sokoya (eds) (1989) *Education in the Mother Tongue: The primary education research project (1970–78)*. Ibadan, Nigeria: University Press Ltd.

Fardon, R. and G. Furniss (1994) Introduction: Frontiers and boundaries – African languages as political environment. In R. Fardon and G. Furniss (eds) *African Languages, Development and the State*. London: Routledge, 1–29.

Ferguson, G. (2003) Classroom code-switching in post-colonial contexts: functions, attitudes and policies. In S. Makoni and U. Meinhof (eds) *Africa and Applied Linguistics*. *AILA Review* 16, Amsterdam: John Benjamins, 38–51.

Ferguson, G. (2006) *Language Planning and Education*. Edinburgh: Edinburgh University Press.

Finlayson, R. and M. Madiba (2001) The Intellectualisation of the Indigenous Languages of South Africa: Challenges and Prospects. *Current Issues in Language Planning* 3: 40–61.

Fuller, B. (1987) What school factors raise achievement in the Third World? *Review of Educational Research* 57: 255–292.

Fuller, B. and S. Heyneman (1989) Third World school quality: Current collapse, future potential. *Educational Researcher* 18: 12–19.

Gill, S.K. (2004) Medium of instruction policy in higher education in Malaysia: Nationalism versus internationalization. In J. Tollefson and A. Tsui (eds) *Medium of Instruction Policies: Agenda? Whose Agenda?* Mahwah, NJ: Lawrence Erlbaum, 135–152.

Heyneman, S., D. Jamison and X. Montenegro (1983) Textbooks in the Philippines: Evaluation of the Pedagogical Impact of a Nationwide Investment. *Educational Evaluation and Policy Analysis* 6: 139–150.

Hill, D. (1992) *The EPER Guide to Organising Programmes of Extensive Reading*. Edinburgh: Institute for Applied Language Studies, University of Edinburgh.

Jacobsen, R. and C. Faltis (eds) (1990) *Language Distribution Issues in Bilingual Schooling*. Clevedon, Avon: Multilingual Matters.

Krashen S. (1993) *The Power of Reading*. Eaglewood Colorado: Libraries Unlimited.

Laitin, D. (1992) *Language Repertoire and State Construction in Africa*. Cambridge: Cambridge University Press.

Liddicoat, A. and P. Bryant (2002) Intellectualisation: A current issue in language planning. *Current Issues in Language Planning*, 3: 1–4.

Macdonald, C. (1990) *School-based Learning Experiences: A Final Report of the Threshold Project*. Pretoria: Human Sciences Research Council.

Mafu, S. (2003) Postcolonial language planning in Tanzania: What are the difficulties and what is the way out? In C. Mair (ed) *The Politics of English as a World Language*. Amsterdam: Rodopi, 267–278.

Martin, P. (1999) Bilingual Unpacking of Monolingual Texts in Two Primary Classrooms in Brunei Darussalam. *Language and Education* 13: 38–58.

Martin-Jones, M. (1995) Code-switching in the classroom: Two decades of research. In L. Milroy and P. Muysken (eds) *One Speaker, Two Languages: Cross-disciplinary perspectives on code-switching*. Cambridge: Cambridge University Press, 90–111.

Mazrui, Alamin (2004) *English in Africa after the Cold War*. Clevedon: Multilingual Matters.

Myers-Scotton, C. (1990). Elite closure as boundary maintenance: The case of Africa. In B. Weinstein (ed) *Language policy and political development*. Norwood: Ablex, 25–32

Nadkarni, K. (1984) Cultural pluralism as a national resource: Strategies for language education. In C. Kennedy (ed) *Language Planning and Language Education*. London: Allen and Unwin, 151–159.

Peacock, A. (1995) An agenda for research on text material in primary science for second language learners of English in developing countries. *Journal of Multilingual and Multicultural Development* 16: 389–401.

Phillipson, R. (1992) *Linguistic Imperialism*. Oxford: Oxford University Press.

Prophet, R. and J. Dow (1994) Mother tongue language and concept development in science: A Botswana case study. *Language, Culture and Curriculum* 7: 205–217.

Roy-Campbell, Z. (2003) Promoting African languages as conveyors of knowledge in educational institutions. In S. Makoni, G. Smitherman, A. Ball, and A. Spears (eds) *Black Linguistics: Language, society, and politics in Africa and the Americas*. London: Routledge, 83–102.

Rubagumya, C. (ed.) (1990) *Language in Education in Africa: A Tanzanian perspective*. Clevedon, Avon: Multilingual Matters.

Russell, J. (1990) Success as a source of conflict in language planning: The Tanzanian case. *Journal of Multilingual and Multicultural Development* 11: 363–375.

Stroud, C. (2003) Postmodernist perspectives on local languages: African mother-tongue education in times of globalisation. *International Journal of Bilingual Education and Bilingualism* 6: 17–36.

Tollefson, J. and A. Tsui (2004) The centrality of medium-of-instruction policy in socio-political processes. In J. Tollefson and A. Tsui (eds) *Medium of Instruction Policies: Which agenda, whose agenda?* Mahwah, NJ: Lawrence Erlbaum, 1–18.

Trappes-Lomax, H. (1990) Can a foreign language be a national medium? In C. M. Rubagumya (ed.) *Language in Education in Africa: A Tanzanian perspective*. Clevedon, Avon: Multilingual Matters, 94–104.

Tsui, A. (2004) Medium of instruction in Hong Kong: One country, two systems, whose language? In J. Tollefson and A. Tsui (eds) *Medium of Instruction Policies: Which agenda, whose agenda?* Mahwah, NJ: Lawrence Erlbaum, 97–116.

Van Binsbergen, W. (1994) Minority language, ethnicity and the state in two African situations: The Nkoya of Zambia and the Kalanga of Botswana. In R. Fardon and G. Furniss (eds) *African Languages, Development and the State*. London: Routledge, 142–188.

Vavrus, F. (2002) Postcoloniality and English: Exploring language policy and the politics of development in Tanzania. *TESOL Quarterly* 26: 373–397.

Vilela, M. (2002) Reflections on language policy in African countries with Portuguese as an official language. *Current Issues in Language Planning* 3: 306–316.

Williams, E. (1996) Reading in two languages at Year Five in African primary schools. *Applied Linguistics* 17: 182–209.

Williams, E. and J. Cooke (2002) Pathways and labyrinths: Language and education in development. *TESOL Quarterly* 36: 297–322.

QUESTIONS

Content

1. What is the usual medium of instruction for primary (elementary) school instruction in different parts of Africa?
2. How "neutral" are the former colonial languages as mediums for instruction (as is sometimes argued)?
3. What are some of the practical constraints on implementing vernacular language education?
4. What are some of the ways in which applied linguists can contribute to the development of policy and practice?

Concept

1. To what extent do you agree that it's important for early years education to be given in the language(s) used in university teaching? Can you think of examples of places where there are different languages for primary/secondary (elementary and high school) and tertiary education?
2. A newly independent nation state has approached your study group to act as consultants in trying to implement a policy of universal vernacular language education. (If you don't have a regular study group, set one up for this exercise!)

   a. What background information will you want to collect in order to advise them well?
   b. What encouragement and warning will you give them about implementing their policy?

3. Here is a list of several countries where there are many vernacular languages (both indigenous and immigrant) that could be used in education. Choose one of them and do some research to find out:

   a. if the national language(s) and vernacular languages are accepted in education (and at what levels);
   b. if there is a single national language policy (if so, whether it is actually applied throughout the country; if not, what the reasons are for localising the policy).

Nigeria	Philippines	Russia
Papua New Guinea	South Africa	Brazil
China	France	Canada
Australia	India	Spain

Chapter 11

Isabelle Buchstaller[1]

SOCIAL STEREOTYPES, PERSONALITY TRAITS AND REGIONAL PERCEPTION DISPLACED: ATTITUDES TOWARDS THE 'NEW' QUOTATIVES IN THE U.K.[1]

1. INTRODUCTION

[. . .] IT HAS BEEN SHOWN on numerous occasions that attitudinal research can broaden our understanding of how change in the linguistic system is perceived by its very users (i.e. Dailey-O'Cain 2000; Deeringer 2004; Niedzielski 1996, 2002).[2] Importantly for this study, Dailey-O'Cain (2000) has reported on attitudes towards one particularly salient innovative variant, *like*, in its focuser and quotative use, as exemplified in (1) and (2), amongst U.S. American respondents.

1. **I'm like** '*urgh*' you know.
2. I'd see her **like** banging this ehhm calculator to get it on during the exam.

Dailey-O'Cain has found that U.S. respondents associate quotative *be like* (as in 1) mainly with younger speakers and women. It also triggers a range of associations with personality traits, many of which can be subsumed in the category 'social attractiveness', or solidarity traits (cf. Agheyisi and Fishman 1970).

In this article, I will focus on *be like* in its quotative function and on its competitor variant, *go*, as in (3):

3. X: **he goes** 'it will be alright up there because like they won't be going around checking engine number and stuff'
    Y: h ah ah a[ha ha ha
    X: [and **I'm like** 'shit'

[. . .] A number of studies have suggested that *be like* might eventually push out *go* (Bakht-Rofheart 2002; Singler 2001). However, as we lack systematic evidence of *go's*

Source: Buchstaller, Isabelle (2006) Social stereotypes, personality traits and regional perception displaced: attitudes towards the 'new' quotatives in the U.K. *Journal of Sociolinguistics* 10: 362–381.

perceptual load, we cannot make any informed claims about the interplay of *be like* and *go* on the attitudinal level. Do *be like* and *go* bear the same social associations? Are they perceived as being used by the same kind of people? This study fills the gap and investigates the conscious and subconscious attitudes involved in the perception of both quotatives, *be like* and *go*, in the British Isles.

Furthermore, the present article investigates the way in which attitudes towards global linguistic resources pattern and vary across two spatially non-contiguous communities, the U.S. and the British Isles. Subsequent to its first mention in the U.S. (Butters 1982), *be like* has travelled the globe and has been reported in many varieties of English. Variationist research has amply documented its intralinguistic and extralinguistic constraints in various localities. But no research has been done on the perceptual side of this salient case of global language change outside of its starting point, the U.S. Have speakers of other varieties borrowed the social attitudes reported above for U.S. English? Or has *be like* gained new meanings within the specific borrowing socio-geographical context, a scenario that Meyerhoff and Niedzielski (2002) have referred to as 'reallocation of attitudes'? [. . .] In the light of the growing interest in globalization phenomena (Blommaert 2003; Heller 2003; Johnstone 1999; McConnell 1997; Meyerhoff and Niedzielski 2002, 2003; Milroy 2004; Pennycook 2003), this article sets out to investigate perceptual load at the transnational level. Given that socio-psychological information is high context information (von Hippel 1994), that is information that needs a certain amount of interpersonal contact to be transmitted and maintained, we might assume that attitudinal information is not easily transmitted across the Atlantic. Indeed, a comparison with Dailey-O'Cain's (2000) findings as well as other reports from the U.S. literature will show that there has undeniably been a certain amount of reallocation of attitudes. This suggests that the local assignment of perceptions is a complex process whereby social meaning is created and re-created by speakers of the receptor variety.

[. . .]

2. PREVIOUS REPORTS ON ATTITUDES TOWARDS *BE LIKE* AND *GO*

[. . .] Reports from the U.S. suggest that the newcomer quotative *be like* triggers relatively strong attitudes. Blyth, Recktenwald and Wang (1990: 224) inform us that 'in general the respondents found (. . .) the use of *be like* to be indicative of middle-class teenage girls. Typical epithets to describe *be like* were "vacuous", "silly", "airheaded", "California" '. A number of studies report that, irrespective of the linguistic reality, U.S. informants tend to perceive *be like* as a feature of female speech (Dougherty and Strassel 1998; Lange 1986; Romaine and Lange 1991). This squares with Dailey-O'Cain's (2000) findings that, while perception and reality often clash, U.S. English informants attribute *be like* to female speakers. Also, most of her respondents agree in their perception of *be like* as a youth trend.

Apparently, the U.S. American public also has very strong feelings about quotative *go*. Ferrara and Bell (1995) tell us that *go* is clearly and stereotypically associated with lower-class male speech style, a 'blue-collar feature'. Blyth, Recktenwald and Wang (1990: 224) report that 'in general, respondents found the use of *go* to be indicative of uneducated, lower-class males (. . .) Typical epithets to describe the users of *go* were "jocks", "blue-collar", "men like Rocky" '. [. . .] In summary, previous research from the U.S. suggests that *be like* and *go* trigger strong, consistent, and almost diametrically opposite perceptions amongst American respondents.

3. METHOD

Attitudinal data was collected from 89 male and 102 female informants from two age bands, probable *be like* users (ages 15–30, all of whom were students) and probable non-*be like* users (age 31+). In terms of their regional origin, 94 informants are from Scotland, 76 from England and 15 from Wales or Ireland. Six other U.K. informants did not further specify their regional provenance. This paper reports on highly educated speakers only. All have received university education.

In order to get at their covert and overt associations, all informants were asked to complete a matched guise test and a social attitudes questionnaire. I will now discuss the collection procedure for perceptions towards *be like* in some detail. The same procedure was used for *go*.

Ever since Lambert, Giles and Picard's (1960) foundational study, classic matched guise tests have relied on spoken guises that were produced by the same speaker in different varieties. Dailey-O'Cain (2000) has adapted this technique for her purposes. Her guises were spoken by the same speaker in the same variety but differ with respect to the presence or absence of the stimulus: half of her guises contained *be like* and the other didn't. This set-up allowed her to test for attitudes towards one specific linguistic item.

However, one shortcoming of spoken 'global stimuli' (Preston 2002) is that audio-recordings contain a wealth of linguistic features, each of which has the potential to trigger its own associations. For example, spoken guises do not lend themselves to the testing of stereotypes pertaining to the gender of a speaker (Sachs, Lieberman and Erickson 1973). It is also hard if not impossible to use spoken guises in order to test for perceptions concerning the nationality of the speaker using a certain stimulus. [. . .]

In practice, any study investigating the regional associations of a particular linguistic feature runs into the following dilemma: if the matched guise carrier material contains variables that trigger regional associations, the informants might react to these and might therefore be biased in their judgments. But even if it were possible to create a locally neutral spoken carrier guise, informants might still be confused if their regional perceptions towards a particular stimulus (such as *be like*) are not met by the corresponding phonological variants commonly found in the variety they associate the stimulus with.

To get around this problem, the present study attempts to control for sociolinguistic variability by using a modified version of the matched guise test. Following [. . .] Preston [who] demonstrated that 'patterns of stratification similar to that found in hearers can also be isolated in readers' (1985: 334), I chose to use written stimuli. The stimuli are transcriptions of naturally occurring talk-in-interaction produced by a 17-year-old working-class woman from Newcastle. [. . .] Both texts contained 12 turn constructional units of transcribed speech.[3] They included neither non-standard spellings nor non-standard grammar and there were no notations of allegro speech (Preston 1985). [. . .] [T]he texts were prepared so that the presence and absence of *be like* was the only distinguishing factor between them. Both were judged by a jury of British native speakers for regional neutrality and nativeness. Because this study tests informants' attitudes towards one particular linguistic item and therefore relies on informants noticing the stimulus, a high density of stimulus per carrier material was desirable. One text contained three instances of *be like*, the other text contained only quotative *say* (see the appendix; for the significance of the frames, see below).

Importantly, Campbell-Kibler (2005), Nguyen (2004) and Williams, Garrett and Coupland (1999) have shown that topic makes a big difference with respect to how people are [. . .] perceived. [. . .] In order to overcome the problem of finding texts with equivalent content [. . .] this study . . . [swapped] the stimuli tokens between Texts 1 and 2: half of the informants were given a survey in which the tokens of *be like* were in Text 1; the other half were given a survey in which the tokens of *be like* were in Text 2. In the appendix, the slots into which *be like* was placed are marked with frames. Hence, if the results turn out to be significant, the effect cannot have been generated by the content, or by any variable in the surrounding co-text. The trigger can only be the stimulus *be like*. The same texts were used for *go*.[4]

In the questionnaire, the two texts were presented side by side. After reading them carefully, the informants completed a survey which aimed at testing their covert associations with the stimulus. They were asked the following questions: How old do you think each speaker is? (to be chosen from four age brackets). What do you think is the sex/gender of each speaker? (. . .) What do you think is the social class of each speaker? They also had to assess the speaker of Texts 1 and 2 on the basis of a number of personality traits (see below).

Once the respondents had completed the matched guise test, they were given a social attitudes questionnaire. This part of the survey tapped into the respondents' conscious attitudes towards the stimulus. In order to make the informants aware of the item they were to assess, the questionnaire repeated a piece of the text with the stimulus highlighted. The respondents were then asked: Do you associate *be like* with older or younger, (. . .) female or male, (. . .) working-class or middle-class speakers? The final question was: Where do you think *like* comes from? This was aimed at revealing whether the informants had any local associations with the stimulus. Especially with respect to *be like*, which has purportedly been imported from the U.S. (Singler and Woods 2002; Tagliamonte and Hudson 1999), it is of great interest to investigate lay informants' perceptions (Meyerhoff and Niedzielski 2003).

4. RESULTS

I will now briefly discuss the results of the matched guise test for *go*, which will be used as a comparative base for *be like*. Table 11.1 comparatively depicts the scores for the text containing the stimulus (*go*) and the text without it (*not*). Whether or not a speaker uses *go* had very little effect on the covert social perceptions of the speaker. A univariate ANOVA did not yield any significant results for *go*'s association with the social attributes age, gender and class.[5] This finding suggests that British English respondents do not have any strong covert attitudes with respect to *go*'s social patterning. However, Ladegaard (1998) has shown that the responses tapping into overt and covert associations can be very different. And indeed, the results of the social attitudes questionnaire revealed that British respondents do have quite consistent overt stereotypes with respect to the type

Table 11.1   Matched guise test results for *go*'s associations with age, gender, and class (in % frequency, respondent N = 88)

Social category		Guise		F (1, 174)
		go	not	
Age	15–20	21	22	
	21–30	52	33	.551
	31–40	13	28	n.s.
	41+	14	18	
Gender	male	45	42	.001
	female	56	58	n.s.
Class	working	48	61	.722
	middle	51	39	n.s.

Table 11.2   Overt attitudes results for *go* (N = 90)

Social category		%	N
Age	young	76	69
	old	6	5
	Don't know	**18**	**16**
Gender	male	16	14
	female	24	21
	Don't know	**61**	**55**
Class	WC	56	50
	MC	8	7
	Don't know	**37**	**33**

of person who typically uses *go*. Table 11.2 illustrates the distribution of answers given to the question 'Do you associate *go* with. . . .?'

[. . .] [W]hen asked for their overt stereotypes, my respondents widely agree that *go* is a feature of younger people's speech (76%). Only a few responses in this category are 'I don't know' (18%). Also, class triggers quite consistent stereotypes among respondents in the British Isles; most see it as a feature of working-class speech (56% versus 8%).[6] For gender the most frequent answer was 'I don't know' (61%).

As mentioned above, [. . .] the only attitudinal data on *go* to date is anecdotal evidence cited in the literature. A comparison with reports from the U.S. reveals that the perceptual load of *go* on both sides of the Atlantic is similar in some respects and different in others. In both localities, *go* is associated with WC (working-class) speakers. However, other social connotations are quite dissimilar: (i) *go* does not carry any association with male speakers in the U.K.; and (ii) the association of *go* with younger speakers revealed here has not been reported from the U.S.

Let us now move on to the covert attitudes towards the other quotative, *be like*. A univariate ANOVA reveals that whether or not speakers use the feature *be like* had a significant effect on their perceived age (p < .001). British respondents strongly associate *be like* with younger people's speech. On the other hand, amongst my British respondents, the presence or absence of *be like* in a text of transcribed speech does not trigger any associations with respect to the social categories [gender] and class ($p_{gender} = .247$, $p_{class} = .668$, n.s.). The finding that *be like*-use makes one sound younger parallels Dailey-O'Cain's (2000) results for the U.S. But because Dailey-O'Cain (2000) did not test for gender or class, we do not have any comparative data on U.S. respondents' covert attitudes regarding these two social categories.

In fact, the covert associations of my British respondents neatly fits the outcome of distributional studies. Variationist sociolinguistic research has shown that the newcomer quotative *be like* patterns strongly by age in every variety investigated thus far, with the temporal isogloss of *be like*-use (Singler 2001) reportedly rising from around 39 in 1990 (Blyth, Recktenwald and Wang 1990) as the generation of *be like* users grows older (Buchstaller 2006; Tagliamonte and D'Arcy 2004). Reports on *be like*'s distribution with respect to other social variables, such as gender and class, are much less consistent, though, in the U.K. as well as elsewhere (Blyth, Recktenwald and Wang 1990; Buchstaller 2004; Macaulay 2001; Singler 2001; Tagliamonte and Hudson 1999).

Let us now compare the above results from the matched guise test with the respondents' overt attitudes as revealed by the social attitudes questionnaire. British lay respondents have a particularly high consensus on the age of *be like*-users: 93 percent associate *be like* with younger speakers and only six percent said they were unsure. This outcome parallels the results of the matched guise test shown in Table 11.3, where the social trait 'age' came out as highly significant in a between-guise comparison. It also tallies with findings from the U.S.: Dailey-O'Cain (2000) reported that 98 percent of her informants (39 out of 40) associated *be like* with younger speakers.

However, my U.K. respondents remain quite divided about the gender and class affiliation of *be like*. Almost 60 percent of the answers for class and gender were 'I don't know'. The remaining responses were relatively unequivocal. My informants attributed *be like* more to female (34%) and working-class (31%) speakers than to male (7%) and middle-class (11%) speakers. Note in comparison the much clearer

Table 11.3 Matched guise test results for *be like*'s associations with age, gender, and class (in % frequency, N = 101)

Social category		Guise		$F(1, 186)$
		like	not	
Age	15–20	44	17	
	21–30	41	36	30.259***
	31–40	13	30	
	41+	3	17	
Gender	male	47	39	1.347
	female	53	61	n.s.
Class	working	53	51	.184
	middle	47	49	n.s.

* $p < .05$, ** $p < .01$, *** $p < .001$

gender-stereotypes in the U.S.: 80 percent of Dailey-O'Cain's (2000) informants (24/30) associate[d] *be like* with the female speaker (Dailey-O'Cain did not investigate perceptions towards class).

Overall, the stereotypes towards *be like* in the U.K. are relatively similar but not equivalent to the ones reported from the U.S. In both localities, *be like* is clearly associated with younger speakers. But while *be like* is . . . associated with WC women in the British Isles, *be like* is perceived more as feature of MC (middle-class) women in the U.S. Similarly, U.S. and U.K. respondents agree on the socio-economic class but not on the gender and age of *go*-users. Taken together, these findings suggest that the perceptual load of global variables is not necessarily equivalent in different varieties. Attitudinal assignment towards globally transferred linguistic material seems to be a relatively complex process, whereby incoming features are assessed and re-evaluated by speakers from the borrowing variety. During the adoption process, speakers in the U.K. are attaching new and potentially different local social meaning to them. I will come back to this argument below during the discussion of personality traits.

Finally, it is important to note that whereas *be like* and *go* are perceptually in complementary distribution in the U.S. (*be like* being associated with young middle-class women and *go* being associated with lower-class males), U.K. respondents seem to associate *be like* and *go* with speakers of roughly the same social profile. Amongst my British respondents, the two quotatives share an association with young WC and female speakers, and the majority answered 'I don't know' for their gender perceptions. However, the next part of this survey, which taps into the associations of *be like* and *go* with personality traits and regional associations, will yield important perceptual differences between the two.

5. PERSONALITY TRAITS

For the collection of the personality traits, [. . .] 45 undergraduate students from various parts of the British Isles studying at the University of Edinburgh were given the traits Dailey-O'Cain (2000) had used for her U.S. informants. The students were asked which of the traits made sense in a study that tests perceptions with respect to *be like* and *go* in the British Isles and which ones they would supplement. They excluded some of Dailey-O'Cain's traits as not culturally applicable and suggested various other attributes. A pilot study with the questionnaire was run in order to avoid the problem of ambiguous traits [. . .] (Dailey-O'Cain 2000: 73, footnote 13). The final list of traits used in this study reads as follows: *calm — giddy*; *trendy/cool — old-fashioned*; *educated — uneducated*; *annoying — pleasant*; *British — non-British*; *animated — boring*; *intelligent — stupid*; *confident — non-confident*; *extroverted — introverted*; *professional — unambitious*; *glamorous — dull*; *popular — unpopular*.

The personality traits were administered as part of the matched guise test given to the informants identified in the methodology section. The traits were presented on a bi-polar 5-point scale with binary opposite poles (cf. the semantic differential technique originally developed by Osgood, Suci and Tannenbaum 1957). It is important to remember in this context that the methodology used in this study aimed at independence of the stimulus from the carrier-material by swapping the stimuli between the texts (as explained in the methodology section). It is hence impossible that associations with a

Table 11.4   Personality judgments for *go* and *be like*

Trait	$F(1, 176)$
The use of *go* is associated with the speaker seeming *more*:	
introverted	4.257*

Trait	$F(1, 178)$
The use of *be like* is associated with the speaker seeming *more*:	
giddy	26.383***
animated	6.129*
trendy/cool	8.334*
The use of *be like* is associated with the speakers seeming *less*:	
educated	4.152*
ambitious	6.785**
pleasant	13.819***

Note: Means are from 5-point scales. Higher values indicate higher values of the variables.
*$p < .05$, **$p < .01$, ***$p < 001$

particular personality trait – such as friendliness or intelligence – were triggered by the content of the snippet of speech in which the stimulus was embedded.

Table 11.4 shows that my British English informants are very divided in their evaluation of *go*-use. [. . .] [O]nly one trait was chosen at a level of significance: *go*-use seems to be associated with a more introspective person. This confirms the findings reported above from the matched guise test: U.K. respondents seem not to have very strong and unanimous covert attitudes towards *go*. [. . .]

Be like, on the other hand, triggers a number of attitudes amongst my British English informants. Six traits – half of the overall set – achieved significance (p < .05). [. . .] [A]s in Dailey-O'Cain's (2000) study, *be like*-use is associated with positive as well as negative traits. [. . .] [F]or my British English respondents, *be like*-use makes the speaker sound more giddy, animated and trendy. But the speaker of the *be like*-guise is also judged to be less ambitious and less educated. [. . .] The significant negative outcomes for the traits ambitious and educated are interesting given that informal conversation after the survey revealed that the main perceived group of *be like*-users are university students. Hence, *be like* seems to be associated with a certain kind of student: lively, cool, carefree, and with few academic aspirations. Finally, speakers who do not use *be like* were judged to be more pleasant but also (via extrapolation from the positive traits above) more old-fashioned and more boring.

Interestingly, respondents' age did not significantly interact with the association of any of these traits. British informants from different age brackets seem to have similar attitudes towards the feature *be like*. This is an interesting result, as it suggests that the age gap in *be like*-production does not manifest itself in a different perception of the users of the variant. People in the generation of *be like*-users basically have the same perceptions towards other *be like*-users as people in age bands who do not use the variant. Importantly, [. . .] *be like* and *go* trigger very different associations with respect to the perceptions of the personality traits of their users. [. . .]

A comparison of the two personality traits, educated and intelligent, that have been tested in the U.S. and in Britain yields the following results: on both sides of the Atlantic, the presence or absence of *be like* does not give rise to any significant associations with respect to the speaker's intelligence. But for both groups of informants, the use of *be like* is associated with the speakers seeming less educated, though in the U.S. (p < .005) more so than in the U.K. (p < .05). Therefore, in the U.S. and in the U.K., the use of *be like* sparks negative ratings on status traits (such as education and ambition). Importantly, however, Dailey-O'Cain (2000) found that in the U.S. *be like*-use triggers only positive associations with solidarity traits. In contrast, in the U.K., the stimulus prompts positive social attractiveness judgements (trendy, animated) *as well as* negative ones (unpleasant). [. . .] Hence, it seems that the adopters, when borrowing spreading linguistic resources, form their own attitudes about these features, rather than simply taking on second-hand attitudinal load. The following section on spatial associations will lend substance to this claim.

6. REGIONAL AFFILIATION

This section investigates British respondents' perceptions with respect to *go* and *be like*'s geographical source. Quotative *be like* is commonly considered a global phenomenon that spread from its epicentre in the U.S. outward [. . .]. To date, we have no information whether, after the innovation has found its way to the U.K., people in Britain associate *be like* with the U.S., or more specifically with the West. In cases of global borrowing of variables, it is important to investigate whether their original geo-spatial associations travel with them or whether the items become nativized on the perceptual level [cf. Meyerhoff & Niedzielski 2003, and this volume].

Quotative *go* is an entirely different story. Its first attestation [as a quotative] in the OED [is] 1791, [but] up until now, no research has been done on the geo-spatial origins of quotative *go* (Buchstaller 2006). This section seeks to investigate the perceived local provenance of *go*. Do U.K. informants perceive *go* as typically British? [. . .]

In the matched guise test, neither *be like* nor *go* triggered any local associations [. . .]. Note also that the personality trait *British – non-British* did not yield any significant results for *be like* or *go* either. Hence, my British respondents do not seem to harbour any strong covert geo-spatial attitudes towards any of the two new quotatives.

Let us now move on to the overt stereotypes. Table 11.5 depicts the results of the question 'Where do you think *go/be like* comes from?'. As the table reveals, 12 percent of the respondents think that *go* comes from the U.S. Only 4 percent think that it is British. Nine percent offer some other geo-spatial origin (Latin with 3 tokens, Japanese with 1 token). However, 74 percent of the respondents answer that they have no idea or give

Table 11.5 Associations of *go* and *be like* with locality (in % frequency)

	go		*be like*	
	%	N	%	N
U.S.	12	11	37	36
British	4	4	3	3
Other	9	8	4	4
No idea	74	67	56	55

comments which pertain to *go*'s sociolinguistic distribution . . . [which] shows that respondents in the British Isles neither consider *go* overwhelmingly foreign, nor claim its local origin themselves. To them, it seems to be thoroughly embedded within the all-English system and does not trigger any strong local associations.

Let us now move on to *be like*. The finding that *be like* does not trigger any strong covert local associations in the U.K. is surprising, especially given the fact that it has been consistently ascribed to a U.S. English source in the literature (Dailey-O'Cain 2000; Singler and Woods 2002; Tagliamonte and Hudson 1999). This raises the question of whether U.K. informants harbour [geolinguistic] stereotypes that can be tapped into with the social attitudes questionnaire. Table 11.5 [shows] that my respondents have much more of an opinion about the local associations of *be like* than about *go* [. . .] [y]et, more than half of the informants [. . .] do not know where *be like* comes from or give an answer which does not link it to any specific locality. [. . .]

Amongst those informants who have overt attitudes about the geographical provenance of *be like*, an overwhelming majority associate the stimulus with the U.S. (37%). No other national variety achieves such high frequency responses (only 3% British and 4% elsewhere, mainly Australia and the Caribbean). [. . .] Hence, even though we have heard over and over again that *be like* spread from the United States into other varieties, British speakers do not seem to overwhelmingly perceive it that way. *Be like*'s association with the U.S. and more specifically with California – frequently reported from America – does not translate into a strong perceptual trend in the U.K.

7. CONCLUSION

[. . .]

A comparison of the attitudes towards *be like* and *go* on both sides of the Atlantic has shown that we cannot assume that the same perceptual information is associated with global features in different localities. While *be like* is indeed perceived on both sides of the Atlantic as [+young], which, in fact, correlates perfectly with the sociolinguistic reality in both places, respondents in the two localities have differing perceptions concerning its association with gender, personality traits and geo-spatial origin. These findings lead me to conclude that if *be like* has been imported from the U.S., speakers in the British Isles have not simply passively adopted the social attitudes attached to it. Rather, the adoption of global resources is a much more agentive process, whereby travelling features are actively re-evaluated and manipulated on the perceptual level. As linguistic resources are borrowed across the Atlantic, they may lose or gain associations during the process, or; alternatively, already existing percepts may be re-analyzed and re-evaluated. Consequently, for speakers of the borrowing variety, new associations interact with possibly second-hand ones and aspects of existing meaning can become more or less salient during the process.

Overall, these findings seem to suggest that the perceptual load of globally travelling features is a locally specific conglomeration of meaning, which does not simply mirror the attitudinal make-up in the donor variety. It seems, therefore, that attitudes fall into the 'high context' category of social information (Audretsch 2000; Meyerhoff and Niedzielski 2003; von Hippel 1994), and thus are open to reassignment by speakers of the adopting variety. Just as a reallocation of linguistic form is well attested (Britain 2002; Britain and Trudgill 1999; Buchstaller 2006; Trudgill 1986), this study shows a reallocation of attitudes and stereotypes. In this sense, attitudinal information can present an important backdrop to distribution studies in cases of global language trends.

[. . .] Further research in the U.K. should also test to what extent the perceptual load of quotative *be like* reported here overlaps with and cross-influences connotations of *like* as a discourse marker, as in (4):

4. So **like** I don't know that's affected me a lot when it comes to **like** being able to do things **like** um there was one thing I wanted to do.

Finally, it is important to stress two limitations of this study which resulted from the general set-up. Firstly, in order to achieve general comparability with Dailey-O'Cain's (2000) study, the group of informants gathered for this project were all highly educated. Secondly, it would have obviously been advantageous to work with spoken guises. But the nature of the questions this study was asking would have made it impossible to work with natural spoken guises as they would have contained too many variables that were not controlled. The rapid advances in language processing will hopefully make it possible in due time to synthesize a voice which is gender-neutral but nevertheless 'real' sounding enough to be used as a stimulus. By using the same text-to-speech script with or without the stimuli, such an experiment could create guises which are completely controlled for independent variables.

NOTES

1. An earlier draft of this article, entitled 'Putting perception to the reality test' was presented at the NWAVE 32 at the University of Pennsylvania. Thanks especially to Miriam Meyerhoff and Jennifer Dailey-O'Cain for feedback on earlier versions of the paper. Any remaining shortcomings are obviously my own.

2. In fact, social-psychological factors have often been shown to be conditioning variables in the course of language change (cf. research by Eckert 1989, 2000; Labov 1972, 2001; Marshall 2004; Weinreich 1953 [1974]).

3. The classic definition of a turn constructional unit (TCU) is that of a unit of speech up until a point of syntactic, prosodic and pragmatic completion. More recently, however, the concept has been revisited (Ford, Fox, Thompson 1996, 2002; Schegloff 1996; Selting 1996). Consequently, the definition has come to include other features such as prosody, pragmatics, gaze and body posture as well as the context in which it has been uttered.

4. Obviously, the texts given to the informants did not contain frames. Also, every informant was only given one set of surveys. No respondent completed both the *be like* and the *go* questionnaire.

5. Note in this respect that the high ratio of stimulus (3 tokens per 12 TCUs) makes it highly unlikely that this non-significant effect is due to a poverty of the stimulus.

6. However, British respondents are more divided in their attitudes towards class than towards age because a larger number of the respondents selected 'I don't know' (37% versus 18%).

REFERENCES

Agheyisi, Rebecca and Joshua Fishman (1970) Language attitudes: A brief survey of methodological approaches. *Anthropological Linguistics* 12: 137–157.

Audretsch, David (2000) Knowledge, globalization, and regions: An economist's perspective. In John Dunning (ed.) *Regions, Globalization, and the Knowledge-Based Economy*. Oxford: Oxford University Press. 63–81.

Bakht-Rofheart, Maryam (2002) Avoidance of a new standard: Quotative use among Long Island teenagers. Paper presented at NWAVE 31, Stanford University, California.

Blommaert, Jan (2003) Commentary: A sociolinguistics of globalization. *Journal of Sociolinguistics* 7: 607–623.

Blyth, Carl, Sigrid Recktenwald and Jenny Wang (1990). I'm like, 'Say what?!'. A new quotative in American oral narrative. *American Speech* 65: 215–227.

Britain, David (2002) Diffusion, levelling, simplification and reallocation in past tense BE in the English Fens. *Journal of Sociolinguistics* 6: 16–43.

Britain, David and Peter Trudgill (1999) Migration, new-dialect formation and socio-linguistic refunctionalisation: Reallocation as an outcome of dialect contact. *Transactions of the Philological Society* 97: 245–256.

Buchstaller, Isabelle (2002) BE Like USE? BE Goes US? Paper presented at NWAV 31, Stanford University, California.

Buchstaller, Isabelle (2004) The sociolinguistic constraints on the quotative system – British English and U.S. English compared. Unpublished PhD dissertation. Edinburgh: University of Edinburgh.

Buchstaller, Isabelle (2006) Diagnostics of age graded linguistic behaviour: The case of the quotative system. *Journal of Sociolinguistics* 10: 3–30.

Butters, Ronald (1982) Editor's note [on be like 'think']. *American Speech* 57: 149.

Campbell-Kibler, Kathryn (2005) Listener perceptions of sociolinguistic variables: The case of (ING). PhD thesis. Stanford, California: Stanford University.

Dailey-O'Cain, Jennifer (2000) The sociolinguistic distribution and attitudes towards focuser *like* and quotative *like*. *Journal of Sociolinguistics* 4: 60–80.

Deeringer, Michael (2004) The 'be + all' construction: A sociolinguistic perspective. Unpublished manuscript. Stanford, California: Stanford University.

Dougherty, Kevin and Stephanie Strassel (1998) A new look at variation in and perception of American English quotatives. Paper presented at NWAV 27, University of Athens, Georgia.

Eckert, Penelope (1989) *Jocks and Burnouts: Social Categories and Identity in the High School*. New York: Teachers College Press.

Eckert, Penelope (2000) *Linguistic Variation as Social Practice*. Oxford: Blackwell.

Ferrara, Kathleen and Barbara Bell (1995) Sociolinguistic variation and discourse function of constructed dialogue introducers: The case of be + like. *American Speech* 70: 265–290.

Ford, Cecilia, Barbara Fox and Sandra Thompson (1996) Practices in the construction of turns: The 'TCU' revisited. *Pragmatics* 6: 427–454.

Ford, Cecilia, Barbara Fox and Sandra Thompson (2002) Constituency and the grammar of turn increments. In Cecilia Ford, Barbara Fox and Sandra Thompson (eds.) *The Language of Turn and Sequence*. Oxford: Oxford University Press. 14–38.

Heller, Monica (2003) Globalization, the new economy, and the commodification of language and identity. *Journal of Sociolinguistics* 7: 473–492.

Johnstone, Barbara (1999) Uses of Southern-sounding speech by contemporary Texan women. *Journal of Sociolinguistics* 3: 505–522.

Labov, William (1972) *Sociolinguistic Patterns*. Philadelphia, Pennsylvania: University of Pennsylvania Press.

Labov, William (2001) *Principles of Linguistic Change: Social Factors*. Cambridge, Massachusetts: Blackwell.

Ladegaard, Hans (1998) Assessing national stereotypes in language attitude studies: The case of class-consciousness in Denmark. *Journal of Multilingual and Multicultural Development* 19: 182–198.

Lambert, Wallace, Howard Giles and Omer Picard (1960) Evaluational reactions to spoken language. *Journal of Abnormal Social Psychology* 60: 44–51.

Lange, Deborah (1986) Attitudes of teenagers towards sex-marked language. Unpublished manuscript. Georgetown. Washington: Georgetown University, Linguistics Department.

Macaulay, Ronald (2001) You're like 'why not?' The quotative expressions of Glasgow adolescents. *Journal of Sociolinguistics* 5: 3–21.

Marshall, Jonathan (2004) *Language Change and Sociolinguistics: Rethinking Social Networks*. Basingstoke, U.K.: Palgrave Macmillan.

McConnell, Grant (1997) Global scale sociolinguistics. In Florian Coulmas (ed.) *Handbook of Sociolinguistics*. Cambridge, U.K.: Blackwell. 322–357.

Meyerhoff, Miriam and Nancy Niedzielski (2002) Standards, the media, and language change. Paper presented at NWAV 31, Stanford University, California.

Meyerhoff, Miriam and Nancy Niedzielski (2003) The globalisation of vernacular variation. *Journal of Sociolinguistics* 7: 534–555.

Milroy, Leslie (2004) 'The accents of the valiant': Why are some sound changes more accessible than others? Paper presented at the 15th Sociolinguistics Symposium. University of Newcastle upon Tyne, U.K.

Nguyen, Jennifer (2004) Transcription production as linguistic behavior: An investigation of transcriptions as indicative of language attitudes and ideologies. Poster presented at the 15th Sociolinguistics Symposium, Newcastle, U.K., April 1–4. www.ncl.ac.uk/ss15/papers/paper_details.php?id=222.

Niedzielski, Nancy (1996) Acoustic analysis and language attitudes in Detroit. *University of Pennsylvania Working Papers in Linguistics: (N)Waves & Means*. Philadelphia, Pennsylvania: University of Pennsylvania, Department of Linguistics. 73–85.

Niedzielski, Nancy (2002) Attitudes towards Midwestern English. In Daniel Long and Dennis Preston (eds.) *Handbook of Perceptual Dialectology*. Philadelphia, Pennsylvania and Amsterdam, The Netherlands: John Benjamins. 321–328.

Osgood, Charles, George Suci and Percy Tannenbaum (1957) *The Measurement of Meaning*. Urbana, Illinois: University of Illinois Press.

Pennycook, Alastair (2003) Global English, rip slyme, and performativity. *Journal of Sociolinguistics* 7: 513–533.

Preston, Dennis (1985) The Li'l Abner syndrome: Written representations of speech. *American Speech* 60: 328–236.

Preston, Dennis (2002) Language with an attitude. In J.K. Chambers, Peter Trudgill and Natalie Schilling-Estes (eds.) *The Handbook of Language Variation and Change*. Malden, Massachusetts: Blackwell. 40–66.

Romaine, Suzanne and Deborah Lange (1991) The use of *like* as a marker of reported speech and thought: A case of grammaticalization in progress. *American Speech* 66: 227–279.

Sachs, Jacqueline, Phillip Lieberman and Donna Erickson (1973) Anatomical and cultural determinants of male and female speech. In Roger Shuy and Ralph Fasold (eds.) *Language Attitudes: Current Trends and Prospects*. Washington, D.C.: Georgetown University Press. 74–84.

Schegloff, Emanuel (1996) Turn organization: One intersection of grammar and interaction. In Elinor Ochs, Emanuel Schegloff and Sandra Thompson (eds.) *Interaction and Grammar*. Cambridge: Cambridge University Press. 52–133.

Selting, Margret (1996) On the interplay of syntax and prosody in the constitution of turn-constructional units and turns in conversation. *Pragmatics* 6: 358–388.

Singler, John (2001) Why you can't do a VABRUL study of quotatives and what such a study can show us. *University of Pennsylvania Working Papers in Linguistics* 7: 257–278.

Singler, John and Laurie Woods (2002) The use of (be) like quotatives in American and non-American newspapers. Paper presented at the NWAV 32, Stanford University, California.

Tagliamonte, Sali and Alex D'Arcy (2004) *He's like, she's like*: The quotative system in Canadian youth. *Journal of Sociolinguistics* 8: 493–514.

Tagliamonte, Sali and Rachel Hudson (1999) *Be like* et al. beyond America: The quotative system in British and Canadian youth. *Journal of Sociolinguistics* 3: 147–172.

Trudgill, Peter (1986) *Dialects in Contact*. Oxford: Blackwell.

von Hippel, Eric (1994) 'Sticky Information' and the locus of problem solving. *Management Science* 40: 429–439.

Weinreich, Uriel (1953) [1974]. *Languages in Contact: Findings and Problems*. Publications of the Linguistic Circle of New York 1 (New York, 8th repr.). The Hague, The Netherlands: Mouton.

Williams, Angie, Peter Garrett and Nikolas Coupland (1999) Dialect recognition. In Dennis Preston (ed.) *Handbook of Perceptual Dialectology*. Philadelphia, Pennsylvania and Amsterdam, The Netherlands: John Benjamins, 345–359.

APPENDIX

Matched guise texts

Text 1:

A: this man came to my door
             He was like   'Jesus is your friend'
             with a big cross
B: ha ha ha ha
A: he said 'you should come over
             and have a cup of tea over at the church'
             and   I'm like   'oh yes yes'
             I'm too nice to slam the door on anybody
B: you might just say 'get lost'
A: he was like   'do you believe in Jesus'
             and I say 'I've never really thought=
             =about it'
             'you should think about that'

Text 2:

X: this Gipsy woman came up to us
             and says 'do you want us to read your hand'
             and I was but I had no money
             and so   I say   'I've got no money'
             and she was so nice
             usually I walk half a mile away from them
Y: they just ask you to pay
X: no   she just says   'do you want a gipsy
             to read your hand'
             and   I'm saying   'I've got no money'
             and she said 'God bless you' and
             and tottled off

QUESTIONS

Content

1. What groups of speakers are stereotypically associated with use of quotative *go* and quotative *be like*?
2. What method does Buchstaller use to get at:

    a. *overt attitudes*
    b. *covert attitudes?*

3. What social groups are most strongly associated with use of:

    a. *go*
    b. *be like?*

4. What personality traits are most strongly associated with users of:

    a. *go*
    b. *be like?*

Concept

1. Lake Superior State University maintains an annually updated list of words nominated to be banned for over-use or mis-use. You can find their annual lists here: http://www.lssu.edu/banished/

    When do quotative *go* and quotative *be like* first appear? (You'll have to check the poster archive to go back as far as possible.) What can you infer about the progression of *go* and *be like* in the US and the development of attitudes from the LSSU data?
2. Do you agree that "spoken guises do not lend themselves" well to tests of attitudes about gender and nationality/region of the speaker? Do you think there might be ways of getting around the possible problems?
3. Research on silent reading finds that most people hear a voice in their head while reading, and unless the context strongly prompts people to think of another voice, the default voice they hear is reported to be more or less their own. Do you think reading a text for the experiment would have caused Buchstaller's respondents to impose their own accent on the stimulus? If so, how might this have impacted on the results?

Multilingualism and Language Contact

Editors' Introduction to Part Three

MULTILINGUALISM AND LANGUAGE CONTACT are topics of high current interest as they can have immense applied linguistic and political repercussions. They are by no means new phenomena but rather are the usual linguistic situation in most areas of the world, with monolingualism being the exception. What is new, however, is the steady increase in language contact situations through migration and a rise in cultural contact, including commercial, scientific and technological advances or dependence. While increased linguistic contact can of course be stable, it frequently results in language death, shift, or, at the personal level, monolingualism. This happens for a variety of reasons which, unfortunately, often include trends to suppress multilingualism at the political or personal level. The articles assembled here address some of the issues involved in multilingualism and language contact, and they do so on various planes of analysis ranging from more global, domain analyses (e.g. Choi) to analyses at the micro interactional level (e.g. Rampton).

Choi revisits the patterns of bilingualism between Guarani and Spanish in Paraguay, which was the subject of an extremely important early paper on domain-based code-switching by Joan Rubin. She documents an increase in the use of Spanish and bilingual use and a decrease in the use of Guarani, the "smaller" language. A similar trend of language shift is found by Kulick and Stroud in their article on code-switching in Gapun (Papua New Guinea). In this case, it is the language Taiap that is losing ground to the more widely used Tok Pisin. They argue that code-switching in Gapun is a vehicle for the ongoing demise of the village vernacular.

The next two articles move us away from the contact of languages to contact of dialects. Blom and Gumperz' classic article on code-switching in Hemnes, Norway, where Ranamål (the local dialect) and Bokmål (one of the Norwegian standards) are spoken, suggests that the local dialect is maintained because it has social value as a signal of distinctiveness and of a speaker's identification with others of local descent, while locals regard the standard as the language of nonlocal activities, such as education and power on the national scene. This article is important because it develops the idea that social meaning can be attributed to particular varieties, it emphasises the importance of local cultural knowledge and social meaning in explaining language use, and also lays out a distinction between metaphorical and situational code-switching.

While Blom and Gumperz investigate dialect contact at the level of the varieties in question and focus on social explanations, Britain investigates actual linguistic features of the varieties in contact and, while also entertaining social factors, explains his data using mostly linguistic factors. In his study of koineisation in a dialect contact situation in the Fens of eastern England, he finds that the koineisation process, which started over 300 years ago, is not yet complete for some variables, while for others a stable form seems to have appeared over 200 years ago.

Similarly to Blom and Gumperz, Heller explores how speakers understand and evaluate different varieties, in this case in multilingual schools in Canada. However, she presents her findings from a different angle and within a different tradition of analysis; that of languages as a resource. Her article is a very fine example of a micro analysis of language use in order to explore larger social categories. Heller shows that bilingual education is not only about language learning and maintenance, but also about constructing the value of the varieties in a community repertoire – in this case English, standard French and the local French vernacular. It is about negotiating and defining who can use what code and in what context, i.e. what "legitimate language" is in a bilingual classroom. By exploring these issues within the classroom, it is possible to develop an idea of whose interests are favoured, whose interests are marginalised and the role bilingual education plays in the welfare of minority groups.

In his article on language crossing, Rampton expands on the available research on code-switching by describing innovative verbal practices among pupils in London. Apart from describing language crossing, this article has more general implications for research on code-switching, for example for Blom and Gumperz' notion of metaphorical code-switching and the emergence of "new plural ethnicities".

Finally, Meyerhoff and Niedzielski's article explores some general principles of globalisation and, based on a study of New Zealanders' attitudes to linguistic variants, suggests that the concept of globalisation with localisation is an important one for variationists. It is a concept that is relevant to all studies in this section as the global and the local have been of direct or indirect importance in all studies discussed here. We hope that we have shown in this section the variety of methodological and explanatory frameworks that can be mobilised to explore the issues of multilingualism and language contact, ranging from domain-based usage studies at the macro level; to code-switching, social meaning, and the role of linguistic factors in dialect emergence; to micro investigations of language use and ideological questions.

FURTHER READING

Chambers, J.K. (2002) Dynamics of dialect convergence. *Journal of Sociolinguistics* 6: 117–130.

Cutler, Cecilia (1999) Yorkville crossing: a case study of hip hop and the language of a white middle class teenager in New York City. *Journal of Sociolinguistics* 3: 428–442.

Dorian, Nancy (1981) *Language Death: The Life Cycle of a Scottish Gaelic Dialect.* Philadelphia: University of Pennsylvania Press.

Dorian, Nancy (ed.) (1989) *Investigating Obsolescence: Studies in Language Contraction and Death.* Cambridge: CUP.

Edwards, John R. (1995) *Multilingualism.* London: Penguin.

Edwards, Viv (2004) *Multilingualism in the English-Speaking World.* Oxford: Blackwell.

Ferguson, Charles A. (1959) Diglossia. *Word* 15: 325–340.

Fishman, Joshua (1972) Domains and the relationship between micro- and macro- sociolinguistics. In: J.J. Gumperz and D. Hymes (eds.): *Directions in sociolinguistics*. New York: Holt, Rinehart and Winston, 435–453.

Gal, Susan (1978) Peasant men can't get wives: language change and sex roles in a bilingual community. *Language in Society* 7: 1–16.

Grosjean, François (1982) *Life with Two Languages*. Cambridge, MA: Harvard University Press.

Haugen, Einar (1950) The analysis of linguistic borrowing. *Language* 26: 210–231.

Hinskens, Frans, Jeffrey L. Kallen and Johan Taeldeman (2000) Merging and drifting apart: convergence and divergence of dialects across political borders. *International Journal of the Sociology of Language* 145: 1–28.

Holm, John (1989) *Pidgins and Creoles*. Cambridge: Cambridge University Press.

LePage, Robert B. and Andrée Tabouret-Keller (1985) *Acts of Identity: Creole-Based Approaches to Language and Ethnicity*. Cambridge: Cambridge University Press.

Lippi-Green, Rosina (1994) Accent, standard language ideology and discriminatory pretext in the courts. *Language in Society* 23: 163–198.

Matras, Yaron (2009) *Language Contact*. Cambridge: Cambridge University Press.

Myers-Scotton, Carol (2002) *Contact Linguistics*. Oxford: Oxford University Press.

Myers-Scotton, Carol (2006) *Multiple Voices: An Introduction to Bilingualism*. London: Blackwell.

Rickford, John R. (1987) *Dimensions of a Creole Continuum: History, Texts, and Linguistic Analysis of Guyanese Creole*. Stanford, CA: Stanford University Press.

Romaine, Suzanne (1995) *Bilingualism*. Oxford: Blackwell.

Thomason, Sarah G. (2001) *Language Contact*. Edinburgh: Edinburgh Uiversity Press.

Wei, Li (2000) (ed.) *The Bilingualism Reader*. London: Routledge.

Chapter 12

Jinny K. Choi

BILINGUALISM IN PARAGUAY:
FORTY YEARS AFTER RUBIN'S STUDY

INTRODUCTION

PARAGUAY, A GEOGRAPHICALLY AND demographically small country, is
situated in the centre of South America. It occupies an area of 157,046 square miles
(407,752 square kilometres) with a total population of 5,206,101 (Paraguay, 2003).
Despite its diminutive size, Paraguay presents a rich and interesting cultural and linguistic
panorama. According to the latest national census of 2002, 59.2% of the total population
prefers to speak Guaraní at home and in 35.7% of the homes the predominant language is
Spanish (Paraguay, 2003). Some 56.7% of the country's population resides in urban areas
and 43.3% belongs to the rural sector. Spanish is the preferred home language for 54.7%
of those who reside in the cities, while in the rural areas Guaraní is the predominant
language in 82.7% of the homes.

[. . .] Joan Rubin's 1968 publication made the world aware of the interesting
linguistic situation in Paraguay, which had been virtually unknown outside the country
until then. This renowned work examined sociolinguistic issues related to Paraguay's
complicated linguistic situation within a well established theoretical and methodological
framework. Rubin determined the social variables and the causal factors in the selection
of languages by examining data acquired in a field study from 1960 to 1961 in a rural area
(Itapuamí) and in the rural–urban area of Luque. The analysis pointed out that the use
of the two languages was related to the rural/urban dichotomy which, according to the
author, is of primary importance in determining language use. Guaraní is associated with
that which is informal, intimate and less serious. Spanish, on the other hand, is the
language of prestige and formality, with social, economic and educational value. In
addition, the author affirmed that bilingual efficiency was increasing in Luque, especially
from Guaraní monolingualism to Spanish–Guaraní bilingualism (Rubin, 1968: 116).

Source: Choi, Jinny K. (2005) Bilingualism in Paraguay: forty years after Rubin's study. *Journal of Multilingual and Multicultural Development* 26: 233–248.

[. . .] Corvalán (1985) critiques the general objectives of Paraguay's formal education of the 1970s and 1980s as follows: [. . .]

> With respect to language planning for primary education, the document decrees that 'One will value and communicate with confidence in the national languages and develop the basic skills of listening, speaking, reading, and writing in the Spanish language; listening and speaking in the Guaraní language'. Tacitly, it is relegating Guaraní – one of the national languages – to an inferior status to that of Spanish in the educational process and what is even more serious is that we are confining it to a process of stagnation and impoverishment. (Corvalán, 1985: 98–99)

[. . .]

Gynan (1998) studies language attitudes whose results confirm as well as disclaim some observations made by de Granda (1988) and Rubin (1968). The author states that there is clearly an ambivalent attitude towards Guaraní, which is consistent with Rubin's findings. [. . .] This author reports that the pride associated with Guaraní is more ethnolinguistic and the pride towards Spanish is related to its 'utilitarian' use (Gynan 1998: 55). Gynan's 2001 study constitutes a thorough and up-to-date presentation of the sociolinguistic and language planning issues of Paraguay. Upon examining the census and demographic data, Gynan predicts the vitality of the Guaraní language in the future, despite a notable growth in the number of monolingual Spanish speakers and a stable growth of Spanish–Guaraní bilingualism (Gynan 2001: 106–107). On the other hand, Solé's analyses of Paraguayan bilingualism, based on language census and survey sample from the urban sector, assert the continual growth of Spanish monolingualism in Asunción and urban areas (Solé 1991, 1996).

Studies by Choi are research projects dedicated to examining the complexity of the phenomenon of the two languages in contact from both historical and sociolinguistic perspectives (Choi 1998a, 1998b, 2000, 2001). Furthermore, the author examines the attitudes of secondary school students in Asunción regarding their two official languages and language use. She finds inconsistency between attitude and use in that the use of Guaraní does not reflect a positive attitude toward and opinion of the native language on the part of the participants (Choi 2003). The same author also examines the effects of the efforts toward the promotion of Guaraní and the significant events in language planning during the last decade of the 20th century (Choi 2004). She compares data from 1990 and 2000 and asserts measurable advances in the use of Guaraní as well as its decrease in some domains among younger generations in urban areas.

The current study hopes to take yet another step toward a more complete knowledge of the linguistic reality of Paraguay. The main objectives of the study are to offer an overview of the use of the two languages and to examine the linguistic changes that have occurred in four decades, and the motivations behind such changes based on a comparison of the data obtained by Rubin in 1960–1961 and data from 2000–2001. Moreover, the results from this comparison will provide a means for examining the directionality of bilingualism in Paraguay.

HISTORICAL BACKGROUND

In most parts of Latin America a visible division and social marginalisation occur between the indigenous populations and the rest of society. These indigenous peoples, who are dominated politically, and the dominant group, are yet to find a solution to the socio-cultural problem that results from this segregation. From the first encounter between these groups emerge the beginnings of stratification, with the lowest levels occupied by the natives. However, in Paraguay, a rapid process of *mestizaje*, or racial mixture, occurred with the union of European men and native women. This cultural fusion was the result of various factors such as: the absence of white women, the geographic situation of Paraguay which hindered communication with other population centres that had greater contact with Spain, and the poor economic conditions resulting from the lack of gold and precious stones (Benítez 1985; Cardozo 1985; Velázquez 1970). In this way, '*se origina un sistema diferenciado de estratificación basado principalmente en la lengua*' (a differentiated stratification system based mainly on language originates) (Corvalán 1981: 50). *Mestizos*, that is, people of mixed race, in Paraguay grow up in a bilingual environment. As de Granda (1988) asserts, Paraguay is a bilingual, monocultural nation, different from other Latin American countries in which a clear linguistic as well as cultural segregation can be observed. Nevertheless, within this bilingual context, there are two very distinct linguistic domains for Spanish and Guaraní. The use of Guaraní is limited to familiar and informal environments, while Spanish is the language of governmental, administrative and educational activities. Guaraní is a symbol of national identity, whereas Spanish is the key to social and economic advancement.

These two languages have played significant roles in different stages of the history of Paraguay. The Jesuits made an important contribution to Paraguayan bilingualism. The use of Guaraní and Spanish was common in *reducciones*, Jesuit mission villages. From their arrival to Paraguay in 1587, the Jesuits, instead of imposing the teaching of Spanish to the natives, encouraged them to read and write in their mother tongue (Castañeda Delgado 1991; Massare de Kostianovsky 1995; Merino & Newson 1994). Thus Guaraní became the language of daily communication and religious rituals.

The government of the first president José Gaspar Rodríguez de Francia (1814–1840) resulted not only in political isolation, but it also created obstacles to the sociopolitical, cultural and educational development of the new nation. During his dictatorship the majority of the Spanish-speaking elite, as well as anyone who was against his regime and authority, were expelled, imprisoned or killed (Cardozo 1985; Cooney 1983). As stated by Gynan (2001: 81), 'Francia's policies definitely strengthened Guaraní while weakening the Spanish-speaking sector . . .'. Under his regime, Paraguay was totally isolated from the rest of the world. All sociopolitical and cultural relations, as well as commercial exchanges with other countries, were completely cut off (Chávez 1991; Cooney 1983). The majority of Paraguayans were able to read and write thanks to his mandatory and free-of-charge educational system at the elementary level. Nevertheless, closing of higher education institutions and lack of books and newspapers due to complete cut-off of contact with the world brought negative impacts to this developing nation (Benítez 1985; Cardozo 1985; Cooney 1983). The next dictator, Carlos Antonio López, restructured the educational system, pursuing higher education, but his interest was always in promoting Spanish (Benítez 1985). Despite his academic concern, a study shows that 'under Carlos Antonio López, schooling worsened. By 1862, the year of his death, there were 25,500 children enrolled in schools out of a population of 800,000, but illiteracy was greater than in 1840' (Warren 1949: 183, cited in Gynan 2001: 82). During his regime, exterior relations were highlighted and foreign influence was promoted, especially that of Europe and Argentina (Benítez 1985). The bloodiest war in the history of Paraguay, the War of the Triple Alliance (1865–1970), led by Carlos Antonio López's son and successor, Francisco Solano López, left the country in a devastating state: economic disaster, loss of territory and the death of many people, especially of men, resulting in a massive decrease in the number of Spanish-speakers (Mendoza 1968). It was during this war and the Chaco War (1932–1935) that Guaraní recovered its status as a national symbol (Centurión 1970). However, the use of Guaraní *no llega a adquirir popularidad o prestigio* (does not achieve popularity or prestige) (Corvalán 1981: 48), especially in the urban regions of the country.

For a long time Guaraní was considered to be the cause of intellectual dullness and poor academic performance. Further, it was considered an impediment to learning 'proper' Spanish (Corvalán 1981, 1985; Rubin 1968). Intellectual achievement was measured by proficiency and fluency in Spanish. Spanish was Paraguay's only official language until 1992, the year in which Guaraní was granted official status by the National Constitution. Likewise, in that same year, the teaching of both official languages was approved for the educational curriculum across the entire country (Paraguay 1993). This *Plan Nacional de Educación Bilingüe de Mantenimiento* is the result of several decades of effort towards better language and educational planning, after having implemented the *Plan de Enseñanza Media* of 1971 and the Transitional Bilingual Education Program initiated in 1983 (Corvalán 1999). The last three decades of the 20th century have been the most crucial period in the history of the Guaraní language. A language that was spoken only in familial and informal circles is now an academic language, taught and learned in all formal educational institutions. It is hoped that the efforts and political decisions directed towards the expansion, enrichment and maintenance of Guaraní will help to change the negative image of the native language and will promote its unfettered use in all linguistic domains.

METHODOLOGY

Rubin's questionnaire (1968) was used as the model for designing the survey for the present study[1] that was conducted in the years 2000–2001. The questionnaire includes questions that ask for personal information (e.g. age, studies completed, place of residence, etc.) and a series of questions pertaining to linguistic use. A total of 71 residents of the city of Luque participated in the current study. The results of the self-reported questionnaire data are compared with the data collected by Rubin in 1960–1961 from 66 residents of the same city. The only information available on Rubin's participants is that they were bilinguals (1968: 101). All of the participants, 34 men and 37 females, from the 2000–2001 study have been residents of this city for at least 15 consecutive years. They reported being linguistically proficient in both languages. The age of the participants ranges from 18 to 59 and the mean age is 33.3.

Luque is located approximately 10 miles (16 km) from Asunción, Paraguay's capital city. Rubin chose this site precisely because of its intermediate location between the rural areas and the capital in order to observe transitional linguistic features. According to the author, approximately 25% of the population commuted to the capital daily in 1960–1961 (Rubin 1968). Currently the degree of contact with the capital is much higher due to improved methods of transportation and communication, as well as the availability and quality of educational and job opportunities in the capital city. Many residents of Luque commute daily to Asunción for a host of reasons which include work, school, social functions or simply to go shopping. In addition, the International Airport is located in Luque. In the decade of the 1990s, a 'shopping' (as it is called in Asunción) was constructed near the entrance to Luque which is now one of the four largest upscale shopping malls in the country. Currently the atmosphere that prevails in Luque could be considered that of a suburb of Asunción.

DATA AND ANALYSIS

As can be observed in the following tables, in four decades a dramatic change has taken place in the city of Luque with respect to language use. The results are provided in both numbers and percentages to facilitate the overall comparison between the results of the two sets of data. Similarly, Chi-square results are presented in order to allow for a more accurate statistical analysis.

[. . .]

For centuries, Guaraní has been the language associated with the family circle. However, according to our data, it appears that a language shift, or the loss of Guaraní, has taken place in the family domain. While these results show a significant reduction in the use of Guaraní, an increase in preference for the use of both languages can be observed in the case of interactions with family members (Table 12.1). The use of Spanish has also increased in all cases, except in interactions with children (from 58.6% to 50.8%). [. . .] While there is currently an effort to revive Guaraní through extension of its use in formal and public domains, as has been mentioned previously, it is accompanied by a loss of the same in informal and family contexts (Table 12.2). These data signal notable changes in the choice of languages used in interactions with those outside the family circle. According to the statistical analyses, the differences are significant, except in two cases, interactions with the doctor and with friends in Asunción.

[. . .]

DISCUSSION

Rubin had predicted an increase in bilingualism in Luque (1968: 116). The results of the current study appear to support, to a certain degree, the author's predictions. With respect to the linguistic changes that have occurred in Luque over the past 40 years, one of the most noteworthy points is the trend toward the use of both languages. Likewise, along with this advance of bilingualism, the loss of Guaraní and the increase in the use of Spanish can be observed in almost all of the situations and types of interactions examined in this study. There are only two areas where significant changes did not take place,

Table 12.1   What language would you use ____ ?

Year	Spanish	Guaraní	Both	Total
1. With your spouse				
1960–1961	10 (18.9%)	16 (30.2%)	27 (50.9%)	53 (100%)
2000–2001	20 (32.8%)	6 (9.8%)	35 (57.4%)	61 (100%)
schicell = 15.1292	df = 2	$p = 0.000^*$		
2. With your spouse in front of your children				
1960–1961	22 (44%)	14 (28%)	14 (28%)	50 (100%)
2000–2001	28 (47.5%)	2 (3.4%)	29 (49.2%)	59 (100%)
schicell = 22.9514	df = 2	$p = 0.000^*$		
3. With your children				
1960–1961	34 (58.6%)	6 (10.4%)	18 (31%)	58 (100%)
2000–2001	31 (50.8%)	2 (3.3%)	28 (45.9%)	61 (100%)
schicell = 7.73516	df = 2	$p = 0.020^*$		
4. With your parents				
1960–1961	10 (15.4%)	37 (56.9%)	18 (27.7%)	65 (100%)
2000–2001	13 (18.6%)	28 (40%)	29 (41.4%)	70 (100%)
schicell = 8.49992	df = 2	$p = 0.014^*$		
5. With your grandparents				
1960	6 (11.8%)	39 (76.4%)	6 (11.8%)	51 (100%)
2000	8 (12.7%)	33 (52.4%)	22 (34.9%)	63 (100%)
schicell = 36.3143	df = 2	$p = 1.302E{-}8^*$		
6. With your siblings				
1960–1961	10 (16.7%)	29 (48.3%)	21 (35%)	60 (100%)
2000–2001	21 (29.6%)	17 (23.9%)	33 (46.5%)	71 (100%)
schicell = 19.0878	df = 2	$p = 0.000^*$		
7. With the housekeeper				
1960–1961	3 (16.7%)	9 (50%)	6 (33.3%)	18 (100%)
2000–2001	13 (23.6%)	11 (20%)	31 (56.4%)	55 (100%)
schicell = 110.505	df = 2	$p = 0^*$		

* $p < 0.05$.

namely, interactions with the doctor and interactions with friends in Asunción. We have also seen one case of a reverse trend, that is, in interaction with teachers; here results indicate a decrease in the exclusive use of Spanish (from 87.9% to 59.4%) and greater bilingual use (from 12.1% to 37.5%) and greater use of Guaraní (from 0% to 3.1%) in academic contexts. While this result represents a favourable change towards bilingualism, the loss of Guaraní in almost all domains does not appear to be a positive indicator for the maintenance of the native language. In contrast to the 1970s, when there were efforts to identify the Guaraní language as a national symbol, currently there are numerous efforts targeted towards expanding the sociocultural contexts in which Guaraní is used with the goal of maintaining the language and national bilingualism.

Rubin considered four variables that influenced the choice of language in Paraguay: the location of the interaction, the formality or informality of the situation, the degree of intimacy between the interlocutors and the degree of seriousness of the interaction. According to the author, the location of the interaction is the most important variable for

Table 12.2   What language would you use ____?

Year	Spanish	Guaraní	Both	Total
8. With your boss				
1960–1961	16 (51.6%)	8 (25.8%)	7 (22.6%)	31 (100%)
2000–2001	46 (71.9%)	3 (4.7%)	15 (23.4%)	64 (100%)
schicell = 51.4898	df = 2	$p = 6.593 \times 10^{-12*}$		
9. With your friends in the neighbourhood/on the streets of Luque[2]				
1960–1961	8 (27.6%)	12 (41.4%)	9 (31%)	29 (100%)
2000–2001	19 (26.8%)	15 (21.1%)	37 (52.1%)	71 (100%)
schicell = 79.0374	df = 2	$p = 0^*$		
10. With your friends in downtown Asunción/on the streets of Asunción				
1960–1961	29 (50%)	6 (10.3%)	23 (39.7%)	58 (100%)
2000–2001	40 (56.3%)	3 (4.2%)	28 (39.4%)	71 (100%)
schicell = 3.61122	df = 2	$p = 0.164$		
11. With your neighbours				
1960–1961	11 (17.5%)	32 (50.8%)	20 (31.7%)	63 (100%)
2000–2001	12 (16.9%)	13 (18.3%)	46 (64.8%)	71 (100%)
schicell = 38.3967	df = 2	$p = 4.594 \times 10^{-9*}$		
12. At el Mercado (Market)				
1960–1961	3 (5.6%)	35 (64.8%)	16 (29.6%)	54 (100%)
2000–2001	12 (17.4%)	21 (30.4%)	36 (52.2%)	69 (100%)
schicell = 47.1805	df = 2	$p = 5.687E\text{-}11^*$		
13. With schoolteachers[3]				
1960–1961	58 (87.9%)	0 (0%)	8 (12.1%)	66 (100%)
2000–2001	38 (59.4%)	2 (3.1%)	24 (37.5%)	64 (100%)
schicell = 22.4296	df = 2	$p = 0.000^*$		
14. With the doctor				
1960–1961	56 (86.2%)	1 (1.5%)	8 (12.3%)	65 (100%)
2000–2001	60 (84.5%)	1 (1.4%)	10 (14.1%)	71 (100%)
schicell = 0.39563	df = 2	$p = 0.820$		
15. With the *curandero* (witchdoctor)				
1960–1961	0 (0%)	43 (89.6%)	5 (10.4%)	48 (100%)
2000–2001	8 (13.1%)	20 (32.8%)	33 (54.1%)	61 (100%)
schicell = 57.2894	df = 2	$p = 3.629E\text{-}13^*$		
16. With the priest				
1960–1961	29 (50.9%)	12 (21%)	16 (28.1%)	57 (100%)
2000–2001	55 (78.6%)	3 (4.3%)	12 (17.1%)	70 (100%)
schicell = 24.7054	df = 2	$p = 0.000^*$		

* $p < 0.05$.

predicting language choice in Paraguay, and she states that 'when in Asunción (even though the highest number of bilinguals in the country live here) people of Luque feel they should speak Spanish because they consider it the only language of Asunción' (Rubin 1968: 104). The clearest example of the contrast between language use in Luque and Asunción can be seen in the answers to the questions 'with your friends in the neighbourhood (Luque)' and 'with your friends in downtown Asunción'. In comparing

Table 12.3   What language would you use ___?

Year	Spanish	Guaraní	Both	Total
17. When you are angry				
1960–1961	9 (16.1%)	30 (53.6%)	17 (30.3%)	56 (100%)
2000–2001	21 (30%)	16 (22.9%)	33 (47.1%)	70 (100%)
schicell = 30.0985	df = 2	$p = 0.000^*$		
18. To tell a joke				
1960–1961	2 (3.2%)	38 (61.3%)	22 (35.5%)	62 (100%)
2000–2001	10 (14.3%)	18 (25.7%)	42 (60%)	70 (100%)
schicell = 51.8754	df = 2	$p = 5.437 \times 10^{-12*}$		
19. To say intimate things				
1960–1961	12 (20.7%)	30 (51.7%)	16 (27.6%)	58 (100%)
2000–2001	49 (69%)	3 (4.2%)	19 (26.8%)	71 (100%)
schicell = 118.462	df = 2	$p = 0^*$		

* $p < 0.05$.

these two situations, greater use of Spanish occurs in Asunción, but the case of Asunción did not show a statistically significant change ($p = 0.164$) in four decades; only a minimal increase can be seen in the use of Spanish (50% to 56.3%) and a decrease in the use of Guaraní, from 10.3% to 4.2%. On the other hand, in Luque there was a notable displacement of Guaraní (41.4% to 21.1%) and an increase from 31% to 52.1% in the use of both languages, a statistically significant change ($p = 0$).

One of the public places in Asunción where interactions in Guaraní take place most commonly is El Mercado 4, the largest open market in the city. This market attracts vendors, merchants and clientele from all over the country. Here, all types of merchandise as well as local and imported products can be found. Many of the vendors in the market come from the rural areas and for most of them their native language is Guaraní. Despite the tradition of using Guaraní to carry out interactions in the market, the displacement of Guaraní is also evident here; the data revealed a decrease of 34.4% [points] in the use of Guaraní (from 64.8% to 30.4%), and a trend towards the use of Spanish and of the two languages that show an increase of 11.8% [points] (from 5.6% to 17.4%) and of 22.6% [points] (from 29.6% to 52.2%), respectively.

The second factor in language use is the formality or the informality of the situation. In formal situations, such as interactions with the doctor, with the boss, with teachers and with the priest, Spanish is required. The data from 2000 to 2001 show an even greater use of Spanish in formal interactions, especially with the boss (51.6% in 1960–1961 and 71.9% in 2000–2001) and with the priest (50.9% in 1960–1961 and 78.6% in 2000–2001). Language use in informal situations, specifically in intimate and less serious interactions, is discussed in the following section.

Guaraní is considered the language of intimacy. Rubin (1968: 106–107) states that 'for most Paraguayans, Guaraní is the language of intimacy indicating solidarity of identity with the addressee . . .'. However, according to the data from the current study, there is a loss in the use of Guaraní in intimate interactions with the family. In the following interactions there was a significant decrease in the use of Guaraní: 20.4% [points] in interactions with a spouse, 24.6% [points] with a spouse in front of children, 7.1%

[points] with children, 16.9% [points] with parents, 24% [points] with grandparents, 24.4% [points] with siblings and 30% [points] with the housekeeper (Table 12.1). This is a disturbing finding, as the loss of the language in informal and family domains also occurred in the final stage of language shift in other bilingual communities (Baker 1985; Dorian 1994; Garzon 1992; Hornberger 1988; King 1997, 1999). Moreover, an important factor for language maintenance is 'the intergenerational language transmission' (Fishman 1991). Not only keeping the language in the family domain, but also teaching it to their children is a crucial issue (Hinton 1994; Hornberger 1998; Krauss 1992, 1996).

Guaraní was used to express humorous or less serious remarks, and because of this, jokes were told in Guaraní (Rubin, 1968). According to the data from 1960–1961, 3.2% of the respondents told jokes in Spanish, 61.3% in Guaraní and 35.5% in both languages. In light of the findings of the current study, one could not assert that only Guaraní is associated with things that are less serious: 14.3% of the respondents tell jokes in Spanish, 25.7% in Guaraní and 60% in both languages.

The linguistic changes that have occurred in the city of Luque are due to several factors. The urbanisation of Luque is inevitable, given that this city is located close to the capital and the ease and accessibility of public transportation facilitate travel between the two cities. Travel from Luque to Asunción occurs daily and frequently, just as if the trips were taking place within the same city. And, of course, the foreign influence and urbanisation that can be seen in Asunción directly affect Luque's cultural and linguistic situation. Spanish maintains its international status and continues to be the symbol of urbanisation and social advancement.

In addition, according to the census figures from the period between 1962 and 2002, the urban population has increased while a corresponding decrease has been observed in the rural population [. . .]. This change in population distribution by areas, especially the increase in the urban population (from 35.8% of the total population of the country in 1962 to 56.7% in 2002), may also reflect the increase in the population that prefers the use of Spanish. With all of the demographic and cultural progress that has occurred in the country in general and in the areas surrounding the capital, the increase in the use of Spanish is not surprising in the least. It is true that the native language has advanced in several linguistic domains, but without a doubt, Spanish continues to be the language of the majority of administrative, sociocultural and educational functions as well as the language of the press (newspapers, magazines, literature, etc.) and the communication media (television, internet, etc.).

CONCLUSIONS

In the preceding pages we have examined the linguistic changes that occurred in Luque during the final decades of the last century. The following points summarise the results of a comparison of Rubin's data from 1960 to 1961 with those from the current study carried out in the years 2000–2001.

(1)   A decrease in the use of Guaraní in almost all linguistic domains, familiar as well as formal, can be observed.

(2)   The only exception is in the academic arena, in which Spanish is no longer the only language of instruction; bilingual use is being promoted and there have been

minimal but measurable advances in the use of the Guaraní language with teachers, thanks to the new educational curriculum under which courses in Guaraní and bilingual education programmes have been introduced.

(3) Two of the variables considered by Rubin, location and formality, can be applied to the current linguistic situation. The remaining two, the degree of intimacy and seriousness, are not applicable. There has been a measurable displacement in the use of Guaraní in intimate interactions within the family and in informal contexts.

(4) The results of the current analysis support the predictions of Rubin with respect to the increase in bilingual efficiency in Luque, but we have also observed an increase in the use of Spanish in the majority of the interactions examined.

At the beginning of this third millennium, an increase in bilingual use and a growing preference for the use of Spanish in the urban regions of the country have been noted. The question that remains is whether this bilingual situation or the use of the two languages in the interactions that were examined in this study will continue. The reality is that modernisation and foreign influence continue to flourish and with these sociocultural advances, language change will be more inclined toward the extended use of Spanish and an increase in its domains, particularly in the urban sector of the country. Gynan (2001) predicts increased vitality of Guaraní and a continual growth of Guaraní monolingualism in the rural areas. On the other hand, the urban sector seems to be progressively more bilingual and Spanish speaking, as predicted by Rubin (1968) and Solé (1991, 1996) and confirmed in the present study. Consequently, these different tendencies may cause an increasingly clear and marked division in the linguistic distribution that characterises the urban and rural communities in Paraguay, forcing them in opposite directions with respect to the Spanish/Guaraní linguistic dichotomy.

NOTES

1. Some of the questions on the questionnaire were ambiguous. For example, questions such as 'What language would you use when you are angry?', 'What language would you use to tell a joke?', that do not indicate with whom the person is angry or to whom the joke is being told. The answer could vary depending on the identity of the interlocutor being communicated with. Similarly, the question 'What language would you use with your spouse in front of your children?' could have several interpretations. One could choose Guaraní if their children have difficulty understanding the language and he/she does not want them to understand what is being discussed with the spouse. Alternatively, one could intentionally use Spanish in the presence of his/her children as it is the academic language and the language of prestige. The latter was Rubin's interpretation. With respect to the questions 'What language would you use with your parents?' and 'What language would you use with your grandparents?', there is a possibility that with one parent or grandparent one would speak in one language and with another parent or grandparent in a different language. Despite shortcomings in Rubin's questionnaire, the majority of the questions was utilised in the current study for the purposes of comparison and in order to be able to examine language change.

2. There were some changes to questions 9 and 10 in the current study. Rubin's questions were 'What language would you use to speak with your friends on the streets of Luque?' and 'What language would you use with your friends on the streets of Asunción?', while the questions for this study were 'What language would you use with your friends in the neighborhood (Luque)?' and 'What language would you use with your friends in downtown Asunción?'

3.   The exclusive use of Spanish in the 1960s was due to the enormous pressure that was exerted on both students and teachers to use Spanish in schools (Rubin 1968). Since the 1980s, this situation slowly began to change with the introduction of the Guaraní language as a subject in the academic curriculum and even more so with the implementation of bilingual education programmes in the institutions of formal education. As a result of these changes, in the current context, the question 'What language would you use with teachers?' is ambiguous due to the fact that there are Guaraní classes with instructors that teach those classes, in addition to the majority of classes taught in Spanish. Regardless, the trend towards bilingual use in the academic domain is a positive sign of the revival of the native language.

REFERENCES

Baker, C. (1985) *Aspects of Bilingualism in Wales*. Clevedon: Multilingual Matters.

Benítez, L.G. (1985) *Historia del Paraguay. Epoca colonial*. Asunción: Comuneros.

Cardozo, E. (1985) *Apuntes de historia cultural del Paraguay*. Asunción: Biblioteca de Estudios Paraguayos.

Castañeda Delgado, P. (1991) La iglesia y la corona ante la nueva realidad lingüística en Indias. In *I Simposio de Filología Iberoamericana*. Zaragoza: Libros Pórticos, 29–42.

Centurión, C.R. (1970) *Breve reseña histórica de la Guerra del Chaco*. Asunción: Gráfico.

Chávez, J.C. (1991) *Compendio de historia paraguaya*. Asunción: Imprenta Salesiana.

Choi, J.K. (1998a) Languages in contact: a morphosyntactic analysis of Paraguayan Spanish from a historical and sociolinguistic perspective. Dissertation, Georgetown University.

Choi, J.K. (1998b) Sobre los orígenes de la doble negación en el español del Paraguay. *Hispanic Linguistics* 10: 236–250.

Choi, J.K. (2000) [-Person] direct object drop: the genetic cause of a syntactic feature in Paraguayan Spanish. *Hispania* 83: 531–543.

Choi, J.K. (2001) The genesis of *Voy en el mercado*: the preposition *en* with directional verbs. *Word, the Journal of International Linguistic Association* 52: 181–196.

Choi, J.K. (2003) Language attitudes and the future of bilingualism: the case of Paraguay. *International Journal of Bilingual Education and Bilingualism* 6: 81–94.

Choi, J.K. (2004) La planificación lingüística y la revaloración del guaraní en el Paraguay: comparación, evaluación e implicación. *Language Problems and Language Planning* 28: 241–259.

Cooney, J.W. (1983) Repression to reform: education in the Republic of Paraguay, 1811–1850. *History of Education Quarterly* 23: 413–428.

Corvalán, G. (1981) *Paraguay: nación bilingüe*. Asunción: Centro Paraguayo de Estudios Sociológicos.

Corvalán, G. (1985) *Estado del arte del bilingüismo en América Latina*. Asunción: Centro Paraguayo de Estudios Sociológicos.

Corvalán, G. (1999) Políticas lingüísticas, integración y educación en el Paraguay. *Ñemity: Revista bilingüe de cultura* 37: 18–24.

De Granda, G. (1988) *Sociedad, historia y lengua del Paraguay*. Bogotá: Instituto Caro y Cuervo.

Dorian, N. (1994) Purism vs. compromise in language revitalization and language revival. *Language in Society* 23: 479–494.

Fishman, J. (1991) *Reversing Language Shift: Theoretical and Empirical Foundations of Assistance to Threatened Languages*. Philadelphia: Multilingual Matters.

Garzon, S. (1992) The process of language death in a Mayan community in southern Mexico. *International Journal of the Sociology of Language* 93: 53–66.

Gynan, S.N. (1998) Attitudinal dimensions of Guaraní–Spanish bilingualism in Paraguay. *Southwest Journal of Linguistics* 17: 35–57.

Gynan, S.N. (2001) Language planning and policy in Paraguay. *Current Issues in Language Planning* 2: 53–118.

Hinton, L. (1994) *Flutes of Fire: Essays on California Indian Languages*. Berkeley: Heyday.

Hornberger, N.H. (1988) *Bilingual Education and Language Maintenance: A Southern Peruvian Quechua Case*. Dordrecht: Foris.

Hornberger, N.H. (1998) Language policy, language education, and language rights: indigenous, immigrant, and international perspectives. *Language in Society* 27: 439–458.

King, K.A. (1997) Language revitalization in the Andes: Quichua use, instruction, and identity in Saraguro, Ecuador. Dissertation, University of Pennsylvania.

King, K.A. (1999) Inspecting the unexpected: language status and corpus shifts as aspects of Quichua language revitalization. *Language Problems and Language Planning* 23: 109–132.

Krauss, M. (1992) The world's languages in crisis. *Language* 68: 6–10.

Krauss, M. (1996) Status of Native American language endangerment. In G. Cantoni (ed.) *Stabilizing Indigenous Languages*. Flagstaff, AZ: Northern Arizona University, 16–21.

Massare de Kostianovsky, O. (1995) Historia y evolución en la población en el Paraguay. In D. Rivarola and G. Heisecke (eds) *Población, urbanización y recursos humanos en el Paraguay*. Asunción: Centro Paraguayo de Estudios Sociológicos, 209–234.

Mendoza, R. (1968) Desarrollo y evolución de la población paraguaya. *Revista Paraguaya de Sociología* 12: 5–14.

Merino, O. and L.A. Newson (1994) Jesuit missions in Spanish America: the aftermath of the expulsion. *Revista de Historia de América* 118: 7–32.

Paraguay (2003) *Dirección general de estadística, encuestas y censos 2002*. Asunción: Dirección General de Estadística, Encuestas y Censos.

Rubin, J. (1968) *National Bilingualism in Paraguay*. The Hague: Mouton.

Solé, Y.R. (1991) The Guaraní–Spanish situation. *Georgetown Journal of Languages and Linguistics* 2: 297–348.

Solé, Y.R. (1996) Language, affect and nationalism in Paraguay. In A. Roca and J.B. Jensen (eds) *Spanish in Contact. Issues in Bilingualism*. Somerville: Cascadilla, 93–111.

Velázquez, R.E. (1970) *Breve historia de la cultura en el Paraguay*. Asunción: Gráficos.

QUESTIONS

Content

1. What attitudes towards Guaraní are there among the Paraguayan population and what factors play a role in the relatively strong position of Guaraní?
2. Read through the data tables. What language shift trends (to Guaraní, Spanish, or bilingual language use) can you identify in (1) the family circle, (2) formal contexts (doctor, boss, priest), (3) informal contexts (friends in neighbourhood, neighbours, witchdoctor), (4) the school context, (5) in Asunción (friends in Asunción and the market), (6) emotionally-loaded situations?
3. What factors influence the choice of language?

Concept

1. Choi uses self-reported questionnaire data. What are the advantages and disadvantages of this method?
2. Compare Choi's results with an apparent time study of language shift conducted by Susan Gal in a small Austrian town near the Hungarian border where Hungarian (H) and German (G) are spoken. How are her results similar or different from Choi's and, if different, what reasons may there be?

Table 12.4   Language choice patterns in Oberwart, Austria

Speaker	Age	1	2	3	4	5	6	7
A	64	H	H	H	H	H	H	H
B	64	H	H	H	H	G/H	G/H	G
C	62	H	H	H	H	G/H	G/H	G
D	61	H	H	H	H	G/H	H	G
E	40	H	H	H	G/H	G	G	G
F	52	H	H	G/H	H	G	G	G
G	27	H	H	G/H	G	G	G	G
H	25	H	G/H	G/H	G	G	G	G
I	17	H	G/H	G	G	G	–	G
J	15	H	G/H	G	G	G	–	G

1 to God
2 to grandparents' generation
3 to parents' generation
4 friends and age-mate neighbours
5 children and their generation
6 Bilingual government officials
7 Doctors

Adapted from Gal, Susan (1978). Peasant men can't get wives: language change and sex roles in a bilingual community. *Language in Society* 7: 1–16.

Chapter 13

Don Kulick and Christopher Stroud

CODE-SWITCHING IN GAPUN: SOCIAL AND LINGUISTIC ASPECTS OF LANGUAGE USE IN A LANGUAGE SHIFTING COMMUNITY

INTRODUCTION

TOK PISIN HAS BY now spread to most areas of Papua New Guinea, and is today unarguably the nation's most important language in terms of communicative expediency. Exactly how the spread and consolidation of Tok Pisin has affected communication patterns and language in PNG is, however, a fairly unresearched question. With the exception of Laycock's (1966) article on Tok Pisin and Abelam, and G. Sankoff's early work on code-switching in Buang (1971), little attention has been paid to the kinds of impact that Tok Pisin has had on the PNG vernaculars. Only recently has the realization that Tok Pisin is in fact affecting the vernaculars led to several articles which discuss lexical and structural incorporations from Tok Pisin into these languages (Chowning 1983; Ross 1984; Holzknecht n.d.). In addition, there are increasing anecdotal and published accounts that Tok Pisin is affecting certain groups so profoundly that they currently are in the process of abandoning their village vernaculars entirely (Kulick 1987; Colburn 1985; Nekitel 1985; Hooley 1987, Bradshaw 1978; Dutton 1978; Lithgow 1973; Wurm 1983; Mühlhäusler 1979; Foley 1987; Haiman 1979).

This paper will be concerned with how Tok Pisin and a village vernacular interact in such a situation of language shift. We will focus on the speech patterns of a small (population 90–110), rural village called Gapun. Gapun is located about 10 miles inland from the northern coast of PNG, roughly midway between the Sepik and Ramu rivers. The vernacular language spoken in the village is a Papuan language, seemingly an isolate, called Taiap by the villagers. The Taiap language is spoken only in Gapun, but it is now being replaced by Tok Pisin, in the sense that children are no longer learning it. No village child under 10 actively commands the village vernacular; they all speak only Tok Pisin.

Source: Kulick, Don and Christopher Stroud (1990) Code-switching in Gapun: social and linguistic aspects of language use in a language shifting community. In John W.M. Verhaar (ed.) *Melanesian Pidgin and Tok Pisin*. Amsterdam and Philadelphia: John Benjamins, 205–234.

Aspects of the relationship between the socialization of these children and language shift have been presented elsewhere (Kulick 1987). What we specifically wish to exemplify and discuss here are some of the ways in which Tok Pisin and Taiap actually are used by the villagers in day to day communication.

One of the most striking characteristics of language use in Gapun is the villagers' predilection for code-switching, which we define here in the standard way to mean the alternate use of two or more languages within a single stretch of discourse, an utterance or a constituent. Unlike some communities described in the literature (e.g. Bentahila 1983; Poplack 1984), in Gapun, no stigma is attached to language mixing, and villagers make extensive use of both inter- and intrasentential code-switching. When asked why they "change languages" as much as they do, the villagers remark dryly, "if Tok Pisin comes to your mouth you use Tok Pisin. If Taiap comes to your mouth you use Taiap". Older men do occasionally complain loudly that younger children do not command the vernacular, but no one is ever chastized for code-switching. Indeed, as we shall see below, code-switching between Tok Pisin and the vernacular has become an essential part of the villagers' linguistic repertoire.

In what follows, we will begin by outlining the general sociolinguistic situation in the village. Thereafter, code-switching in Gapun will be examined from three different points of view. First, we will give examples of the kinds of code-switching that occur there, linking the code-switching to social and discourse contexts in which it occurs. This is followed by a brief discussion of how the Tok Pisin-vernacular intersentential code-switching in Gapun is structured linguistically.

[. . .]

SOCIOLINGUISTIC DATA

Like the small language groups discussed in Sankoff 1977, adult villagers in Gapun are now, and traditionally have been, multilingual. Table 13.1 summarizes the language capabilities of the villagers.[1]

It is clear from Table 13.1 that older men in Gapun speak two or more vernaculars, in addition to Tok Pisin. The majority of these men also has receptive competence in one or more additional vernacular languages. The reasons for this extreme multilingualism lie largely in the fact that Tok Pisin only established itself as a lingua franca in the lower Sepik area during and after WWII. Before this, Gapun villagers needed to know the vernaculars spoken in other villages, since few non-Gapuners ever learned Taiap.

In generation II, men's active competence in vernacular languages has, with three exceptions, been reduced to the point where most men only actively command their own vernacular and Tok Pisin. These men almost all have passive competence in one or more vernaculars, but note that this competence is for the most part in the Kopar language. Adjora is absent from the communicative repertoire of several men, and geographically distant languages like Watam have disappeared completely. Interestingly, women in this generation are generally more actively multilingual than their husbands, a fact that certainly is a reflection of the role that Tok Pisin played in its early stages of incorporation in the village. It is well known that because Tok Pisin traditionally has been learned by men during periods of contracted labour, women have tended to learn it later and have in

Table 13.1   Languages known by villagers living in Gapun in 1987

Men			Women		
Age	Languages spoken	Understood	Age	Languages spoken	Understood
			Generation I		
65	T, A, K, TP	B	60+	T	A, K, TP
60+	T, A, K, TP	B, W			
60	T, A, K, TP	W			
55+	T, A, K, B, TP	W			
55+	T, K, W, TP	A, M			
50	T, K, TP	A, B			
			Generation II		
48	T, A, TP	K	43	A, TP	T, K
47	T, A, K, TP	W	43	T, A, K, TP	
42	T, TP	K, A	40	T, A, K, TP	
40	T, TP	K, A	38	T, A, K, TP	
40	T, TP	K, A	37	T, A, K	TP
40	T, A, K, TP		35	T, A, K, TP	
37	T, TP	K	35	T, P, TP	
37	T, TP	K, A	34	T, TP	K, A
36	T, TP	K, A, P	33	T, TP	K, A
34	Bu, TP	T	33	P, TP	T
34	T, TP	K	32	T, TP	K, A
30	T, TP	K	28	K, TP	T
26	Bu, TP	T	27	T, K, TP	
25	T, TP	K, A			
			Generation III		
23	T, TP	K	22	T, TP	K
22	T, TP	K, A	20	T, TP	
19	T, TP	K	19	T, K, TP	
18	T, K, TP	A	19	T, TP	K
16	T, TP	K	18	T, TP	K
14	T, TP	K	18	T, A, TP	K
14	T, TP	K	16	T, TP	K
14	TP	T	16	T, TP	K
14	T, TP	K	16	T, TP	K
14	T, TP	K	14	T, TP	K, A
13	T, TP	K	13	T, TP	K
12	TP	T	13	T, TP	K
12	T, TP	K	12	T, TP	K, A
10	T, TP		12	T, TP	K
10	T, TP	K	10	TP	T
			10		T, TP
			Generation IV		
9	TP	T	9	TP	T, A
9	TP	T	9	TP	T, K
8	TP	T	8	TP	T
8	TP	T	8	TP	T
8	TP	T	8	TP	T
7	TP		7	TP	T, A

Table 13.1 continued

Men			Women		
Age	Languages spoken	Understood	Age	Languages spoken	Understood
5	TP		7	TP	T
5	TP		6	TP	T
4	TP		6	TP	T
4	TP		4	TP	
3	TP	?	4	TP	T
2	TP	?	4	TP	?
1	TP		4	TP	?
1	TP		3	TP	
			2	TP	?
			2	TP	

Note: Men and women in generations I and II who do not actively speak Taiap are inmarried from other communities
Key: T = Taiap
A = Adjora
K = Kopar
Bu = Buna
M = Murik
TP = Tok Pisin
W = Watam
B = Bien/Angoram
P = Pankin/Aion

some cases even been reported to be "actively hindered" from learning it (Herdt 1981:334). In their communication with neighbouring villagers then, women continued to be dependent on vernacular languages long after men had already begun to use Tok Pisin in these contexts.

It is the following generation in which women shift away from vernacular multilingualism to bilingualism in Tok Pisin and Taiap, and passive competence in another vernacular (Kopar). Note then that women in general are lagging behind men in their language shift, a pattern which is the reverse of what often is found in language shift situations in Europe (Dorian 1981; Gal 1979; cf Hill and Hill 1977). Although it is not evident in Table 13.1, this is even the case in the latest generation of children – here a number of girls aged 8–9 who do not command the vernacular actively at least use certain formulaic Taiap phrases and responses in play and, occasionally, in interactions with adults. No boy under 10 does this.

It thus appears that Tok Pisin has entered the linguistic repertoire of the Gapun villagers first at the expense of other village vernaculars, and ultimately at the expense of the villagers' own vernacular. This situation constitutes empirical evidence against Laycock's (1979:87) suggestion that the expansion of Tok Pisin has not significantly altered the number of languages which Papua New Guinean villagers learn. Clearly, Gapun villagers are less multilingual now than they were before they had access to Tok Pisin. In fact, the current trend in the village is towards monolingualism in Tok Pisin. No child under the age of 10 actively commands Taiap, and we have observed that some of the youngest children in the village under the age of 8 do not even possess a passive knowledge of the vernacular.

LANGUAGE USE IN THE VILLAGE

Given the fact that all villagers except children are at least bilingual, it is perhaps not too surprising to learn that in village conversations Tok Pisin and Taiap are used in constant interplay. The situation in the village is so fluid that no domain, speech genre or topic is generally dominated by any one language; with the single significant exception of religion.[2] The single most important factor influencing the villagers' language choice is their conversational partner. Talk in Gapun, as in other Papua New Guinean communities (Goldman 1983; articles in Brenneis and Myers 1984) is basically an activity stressing or ultimately resulting in consensus and agreement. Silence is considered by the villagers to be an ominous indication of displeasure or anger, and they are anxious to avoid long silences in the company of others. Because of its consensual nature, talk in most social situations is carefully monitored by all present, and the topics and opinions that one converses about with others are all finely adjusted to suit the general mood and opinions of those within hearing range. Accommodation of this type often extends to choice of language. Villagers in Gapun are keen to accommodate others linguistically, and those who know other vernacular languages frequently use them, in stretches at least, when talking to men or women from neighbouring villages. Code-switching of this type was traditionally both necessary (since few outsiders spoke Gapun's vernacular) and prestigious: the senior men proudly note that in knowing a lot of languages they are still following the custom of their mythical founding ancestor, Kambedagam, who was, in distinction to the mythical founding ancestors of other nearby villages, multilingual.

Ways in which vernacular multilingualism interacts with Tok Pisin can be seen in the following example. Speaker A is a Gapun Big man, seated in his men's house. He has just heard a visiting man from Singrin (a nearby Kopar-speaking village) call into the men's house for two men to leave the men's house and follow him somewhere. As one man gets up to leave, A asks which other man the Singrin man wants.[3]

(1) A: *Mbɨ mɛnandi?* A: Who else?
  B: *Em ia. Soŋor ia.* B: Him. Songor.
  A: *Ej. Ah. Aria. Mi* A: Ej. Ah. OK.
   maŋgawna. Yu go You go. You go
   pastaim. Ndɨkawɔ then. Put that
   amana. thing here.

Even though the Singrin man spoke in Tok Pisin when he summoned the two men from A's men's house, A asks his question in the Singrin language. Another Gapun man answers A in Tok Pisin, pointing to the other man, Songor, who had been summoned. A then adresses Songor in the Singrin language (*Mi maŋgawna*). Songor does not speak this language, and in addressing him in it, A is probably using language choice as a subtle way of exerting dominance over the Singrin man. Thus although ostensibly addressing Songor, A is actually giving permission to the Singrin man to take Songor away from his men's house for a few minutes. Having told Songor to go in the Singrin vernacular, A then repeats his utterance in Tok Pisin, thereby emphasizing it (see below examples (11), (12), (13)). Finally, A tells Songor to leave his basket while he goes. A says this in Songor's vernacular, Adjora, which is as different from the Taiap and Singrin languages as French is from Greek and Russian.

Speaker accommodation of this type is also used by the villagers when they talk to children, and this is one reason why language shift is occurring in Gapun. In the following example, Angara and her husband Masambe are questioning their six year old daughter Jari about whether their youngest child, Basama (26 months) really had fallen into a well a few days earlier, as they had heard.

(2) Angara: *Ŋayarkɛ ani . . . ɔtitɛk awinəni? Basama.*

A: Is it true that what's her name . . . fell into the water? Basama.

Jari: *Mm*

J: Mm

Angara: *Ah?*

A: Ah?

Jari: *Mm*

J: Mm

Angara: *Anakŋan ɔrɔmni?*

A: When?

Masambe: *Ani kukuwɔkrɛ ɔtitɛk? (pause) Ah?*

M: Who took her (to the well) so that she could fall? (pause) Ah?

Jari: (softly) *Ndamor kisim em igo wantaim na em i pundaun long wulwara.*

J: (softly) Ndamor took her with us and she fell into the well.

Masambe: *Husat i kisim em igo?*

M: Who took her?

Jari: *Ndamor.*

J: Ndamor.

Masambe: *Ndamor kisim em igo na husat i wok long lukluk istap long en . . .*

M: Ndamor took her and who was watching her . . .

Here Jari's father accommodates her by switching to Tok Pisin once Jari has begun in that language. The rest of his interrogation is carried out in Tok Pisin.

Another way in which Taiap and Tok Pisin are mixed together in Gapun is that villagers routinely incorporate elements from one language into the other within one and the same utterance. Certain words, especially nouns denoting everyday items such as betel nut, sago, fire, basket, coconut, water and so on, are likely to be named in the vernacular, even if the rest of the utterance is in Tok Pisin.

(3) *Painim wanem samting long sapwar bilong mi?!*
'What are you looking for in my basket?!'

(4) *Igo kisim airŋa tin bilong mi i kam*
'Go get my lime-tin and bring it'

Most common objects like these also have equivalents in Tok Pisin, however, and these are sometimes used, even in a vernacular utterance.

(5) *ŋa basket-nɨ prukaku wakarɛ*
'I'm not working on a basket'

Tok Pisin verbs are very frequently incorporated into vernacular utterances and are inflected according to Taiap patterns.

(6) *njɛ   aŋgɔ   rausim -tu-ku-n*
    dog   this   get rid-IMPER-3SG:FEM:U-2SG:A
    'Get rid of this dog!'

(7) *ŋɨ Pɔtɔ-rɛ   ɔ-kɨ-nɛt-a,*
    he Wongan-LOC   go-IRR-3SG:MASC:A-CONJ,
    hatwok-kɨ-nɛt
    hard work-IRR-3SG: MASC:SUBJ
    'He will go to Wongan and work hard'

Very rarely, vernacular verbal morphology will be suffixed to a Tok Pisin verb in a Tok Pisin utterance.

(8) *yu   kaikai-api,   bai   mipela   go*
    2SG   eat-COMPLETED   FUT   1PL   go
    'When you've finished eating, we'll go'

    In the recent literature on code-switching, questions have been raised about whether to classify nouns and verbs like those in examples (3)–(7) as code-switches or loan words or nonce borrowings (Poplack 1984; Sankoff, Poplack, Vanniarajan 1985). [. . .] For now we simply wish to point out that no matter how they are classified, these types of nouns and verbs are often linked to longer switches into the villagers' other language(s), a phenomenon that Clyne (1967) has called triggering (see also Bentahila 1983). This is exemplified below:

(9) *Tapunana nimeŋɔ. Tapunana tupela de. Na Tapu ino stap.*
    Sande em karim, Mande em indai olgeta.
    'For Tapu thus. For Tapu two days. And Tapu didn't live. Sunday she gave birth, Monday she died.'

In this example, the speaker is referring to a magic staff that was consulted when a young woman named Tapu was ill late in her pregnancy. The staff foretold that she would die in two days, and she did. In recounting this, the speaker switches from the vernacular, choosing the Tok Pisin words *tupela de* 'two days' instead of the equally common vernacular equivalent *arɔ sɛnɛ* (lit. 'days two'). Having switched to Tok Pisin to say 'two days', the speaker completes his utterance in that language. Although we agree with those researchers who regard it as fruitless to search for explanations for every code-switch in a text, we think that a possible interpretation of (9) is that the Tok Pisin NP *tupela de* acts as a trigger for the speaker to continue in Tok Pisin.

    Another kind of triggering distinguished by Clyne is anticipational triggering, where a switch is made before the speaker actually reaches the particular item which motivates the switch.

(10) *Sakeyi anire sokoi baim-tukun? Mangan i kam baim brus bilong mi!*
    'Who did Sake buy tobacco from? (Hey people from) Mangan, come buy my tobacco!'

Here the speaker uses a Tok Pisin verb *baim* 'to buy' inflected with vernacular endings. This particular verb, however, is almost never used in this way; the vernacular equivalent *m.ɔsɛtukun* is very common and would normally be used here. Again, we would suggest that it is possible in this case that the speaker anticipated her call in Tok Pisin to people from Mangan (a distant village with a vernacular unknown to any Gapun villager) to buy her tobacco, and that this influenced her lexical choice of the Tok Pisin verb *baim* over the Taiap equivalent.

STYLISTIC FUNCTIONS OF CODE-SWITCHING

A major reason why code-switching in Gapun is so prevalent is because of the many pragmatic uses to which it lends itself. The villagers themselves never talk about or reflect upon their code-switching as such, and to ask them directly why they switch languages invariably evokes the kind of response noted [earlier in the article]. As Gumperz (1982:65) has observed, however,

> in bilingual situations the participants' awareness of alternative communicative conventions becomes a resource, which can be built on to lend subtlety to what is said.

Thus while the Gapun villagers do not verbalize their reasons for or reactions to code-switching, our own observations of their speech and of their evaluations of the speech of others strongly indicate that they are keenly aware that code-switching has rhetorical power. Skillful code-switching in Gapun can greatly increase the drama in a story or argument, and rhetorical points are frequently scored in both the vernacular and Tok Pisin. Emphasis can be achieved through code-switching and irony can be underlined.

Demonstrating this point empirically poses certain problems, because it is not possible to construct an exhaustive typology of code-switching functions. Like other conversational strategies, the meanings carried by code-switches are negotiated in the actual, culturally specific context in which they occur; and this means that code-switches can be neither predicted nor can any one type of code-switch (e.g. repetition) be assigned a particular context-free function. When we now turn to how villagers use code-switching rhetorically therefore, it is important to keep in mind that we are generalizing from analyzed texts and from 15 months of intensive observation of the villagers' speech patterns. We are not illustrating rules, but are rather highlighting tendencies.

An extremely common use of code-switching in the village involves repetition, where a speaker says something in one language and then repeats the same thing in the other language. This type of repetition often serves to emphasize a command or serve as a warning.

(11) mother to daughter, who is playing with a baby:
    Ɔrɛtukun. Earŋgarana. Ɔrɛtukun. LUSIM EM! Ɛnɛ nda tawairunak
    'Let her alone. She better not cry.
    Let her alone. LET HER ALONE!
    I'm gonna thump you now.'

(12) *Kisim buai bilong mi ikam. Harim ah? *
    Kisim buai bilong mi ikam. ŊAŊAN MINJIKƐ KUKUWE! KAKAT!
    'Bring my betel nut. Do you hear?
    Bring my betel nut. BRING MY BETEL NUT! HURRY UP!'

Note that emphatic code-switching of this nature can occur either to or from the vernacular; i.e. it is not the case that Tok Pisin, say, has more threatening connotations than Taiap. The emphasis, or in these cases, the threat, is embedded in the *fact* of the code-switch, not in the direction of the switch.

Another use of this type of repetition is to emphatically agree with a previous speaker. In using two languages in this way, emphatic agreement can be stretched out to considerable lengths, as is evident in (13).

(13) A: *i no gutpela*   A: that's not good
      B: *ɛŋɡon wakarɛ*   B: it's not good
      C: *rabis*   C: rubbish
      D: *supwaspwa ŋayar*   D: really bad
      E: *tru ia*   E: that's true

In addition to its emphatic function, however, repetition of the same utterance in two languages is quite often used simply for the sake of repetition. Gapun villagers do not share common Western notions that repetition is unnecessary or tiresome, and the three marked speech genres most common in the village — oratory in the men's house; the *kros*, where women and sometimes men sit in their houses and hurl long monologues of abuse at people who have offended them in some way; and *stori*, where people sit informally and tell jokes, gossip and talk about experiences that they or others have had in the bush or the village — all require that speakers repeat themselves and the speech of others again and again. In fact, much of the villagers' talk is devoted to repeating things that they and others have just said. While such repetitions often do serve emphatic functions, as shown above, the habit of repetition is carried over to non-emphatic contexts, and speakers frequently repeat quite banal comments in both languages.

(14) *Mi bai go nau. Ŋa nda ɔkinɛtana.*
      'I'm going to go now. I'm going to go now.

(15) *Ambuli pitiŋar yuwɔn aŋgi ŋarɛ atɔwuk . . . ɡawrɔŋan itnɨ puŋɡɔkawukŋan em i stap long as bilong ɡawrɔ ɨa.*
      'Ambuli your bush-knife is down at my place . . . it's standing by the trunk of the *ɡawrɔ* (a kind of tree) It's by the trunk of the *ɡawrɔ*.

Both (14) and (15) were uttered quietly, almost mumbled, in informal contexts. The switches were not accompanied by any sort of verbal emphasis or pause, nor did they evoke any response or reaction from those who heard them.

In addition to repetition, code-switching in Gapun can also be employed to hotly deny or contradict what a speaker experiences as an accusation.

(16) A: *minijikɛ ana? Ŋanan minijikɛ ana?!*   A: where's the betel nut?
                                                    Where's my betel nut?!

      B: *mi no save long minijikɛ bilong yu!*   B: I don't know about your betel nut!

(17) A: *Yu save mekim ol kainkain pasin. Mi les.*   A: You're always doing bad things. I'm
                                                          sick of it.

      B: *Mai! Yu tɔwɛr awtak!*   B: Enough! You shut up!

Yet another use of code-switching is to create and highlight dramatic contrasts.

(18) A: *Yu, ɛnɛ ambinənɨ ŋa ɛnɛ kut ainda? Wasɔnɛtəŋa mbɔta, nɔŋɔr kiwɔk, ŋa kakun, nau mi*
      stap nau.
      Mi nogat sik moa. Nau mi stap olgeta, mi winim taim. Ŋa ɛnɛ kut inda.
      B: *Yu hap indai ia.*
      A: *Ŋa wasɔnɛtəŋa!*
      A: You, now how is it I'm alive? Dying, I went and the woman took me and I ate
      (some enchanted herbs), now I'm alive now. I'm not sick anymore.
      Now I'm completely alright. I'm beating Time. I'm alive now
      B: You almost died
      A: I died!

In the above example, A code-switches to add drama to his "death", contrasting the fact
that he died (in the vernacular) with his recovery (in Tok Pisin). A also code-switches to
emphatically summarize and complete his story (. . . *mi winim taim. Ŋa ɛnɛ kut inda*).
Note how speaker B (a Gapun man) switches to Tok Pisin to signal emphatic agreement
with A (cf. example (13)), and how A answers him in the vernacular in order to
contradict him and stress that he had not merely "almost" died, he had *died*.

The type of dramatic contrasts seen in the example above are especially common in
kros-es, or shouting matches, where irony, sarcasm and scandalous accusations all fly
copiously and freely. In (19), a woman is screaming loudly at her younger sister because
the sister's baby started crying at night and the sister was off somewhere and not around
to quiet it.

(19) *Yu tatukun ɔrɔm?! Aŋqwarkɛ ɔrɔm?! Yu lukim ol bikpela man islip pinis?! Yu hanwas yuwɔn*
      daramnikɛ wuk?! Yu lukim taim tu ah?! Haumas tru yu tokim mi pastaim. Wanem taim?
      Apinun yet ah?! Ah?! Ol man i stap long ples? Ol i toktok i stap ah?! Babasak indɛ mbɔr
      bibiknɨ prukar ɛkrukuk. Yu pik ia. Harim ah? Yu wanpela pik meri stret.
      You see the time?! Is it time to be out?! You see all the Big-men sleeping?! You got
      a watch?! You see the time?! What time is it, tell me then. What time is it?! It's still
      afternoon, ah?! Ah?! Is everyone still out around the village? They're all out
      talking?! Idiot, you're out prowling like a pig. You're a pig. Do you hear? You're a
      real pig-woman.

Dramatic contrasts on the intrasentential level are also achieved through code-switching.
Utterances expressing hypotheticality or consequences (if/when X, then Y) tend to
evoke code-switching.

(20) *Nɛknɨ kɔkɨr kukuukutak desela hed bilong yu bai bruk tupela hap.*
      'You bring your head up this step that head of yours is gonna get split in two'

(21) *ŋɨ ɛŋgɔn kuta, John ɔmɨnŋanɛtrɛ em desela sik i kamap.*
      'He was alright, then when John got married this sickness came'

We will discuss this type of intrasentential switching below [. . .].

The final ways to be exemplified here in which villagers code-switch in order to
achieve particular discursive affects are in rendering quotations (22), and in interrupting
a speaker, changing the topic or gaining the floor (23), (24).

(22) *ŋi̱/Murimatɔmi̱n Aɡrana nandɛni̱kɛ namnəŋgen: "yu save lainim ol pikinini long poisen ia?"*
    Did he/Muri's husband say to Angrana: "You teach the kids about sorcery?"

(23) A: *Ol stilman. Nogat wanpela ɡutpela pasin i save stap long bel bilong ol. Stil tasol i pulap.*
        Wanpela bilong ol i kam [bai mi tokim em stret. .
    B: [*Yu nam tatukun? Kem ŋan barani̱ mbɔta* . . .
    A: Thieves. There's not one good quality in them. They're full of thievery. If one
        of them comes, [I'm really going to tell him. .
    B: [Have you heard? Kem went to his garden and . . .

(24) *ŋayi nandɛ namri̱nɛt – pasim maus bilong yupela na harim mi.*
    'I'll tell you this – shut your mouths and listen to me.'

Once again we want to stress that the functions which we have exemplified above are
by no means exhaustive. They merely represent some of the most common ways in which
Gapun villagers employ code-switching in their day-to-day conversations with one
another. The value of this kind of functional description, we believe, lies partly in its
ethnographic interest (the fact that the villagers code-switch repetitively as heavily as they
do indicates for example that repetition is perceived as a significant element in discourse.
This in turn leads the ethnographer to explore the implications of such repetition in social
terms such as the importance that villagers place on consensus), and partly in its
comparative character. It is interesting that the pragmatic uses to which code-switching in
Gapun is put are extremely similar to those of other, totally unrelated communities, e.g.
the Arab-French bilinguals in Morocco (Bentahila 1983) or the three communities
discussed in Gumperz 1982. This type of relative uniformity suggests the existence
of pragmatic universals of code-switching, similar perhaps to the kind of politeness
universals described by Brown and Levinson (1987).

GRAMMATICAL CONSTRAINTS ON CODE-SWITCHING

[. . .]

What we will do now is exemplify the kinds of code-switches that appear in one 90
minute recording of a village meeting held in Gapun in mid-1986. The analyzed text
contained 178 unambiguous code-switches.

[. . .]

We will begin with code-switches which occur intrasententially. Table 13.2 displays
the distribution of the intrasentential code-switches occurring in the speech of the
villagers in this analyzed text.

It is evident in Table 13.2 that the vast majority (29 = 77%) of intrasentential code-
switches in the villagers' speech occurs in one of three ways: between a main and
subordinate clause (S+COMP S), after a complementizer and before a subordinate clause
(COMP+S) (both these categories are included under one heading S+COMP in Table 13.2),
or between two clauses that stand in a coordinate relationship (S1+S2).

[. . .]

Table 13.2   Intrasentential code-switches

	N	%
S + COMP	17	41
$S_1 + S_2$	12	29
X + S	8	20
NP + VP	2	5
V + NP	1	2.5
N + MOD	1	2.5
Total	41	100

We noted above [. . .] that nouns from both languages and verbs from Taiap are extremely frequently incorporated into the other language in the villagers' speech. We have not treated those elements as code-switches except when they clearly were not integrated morphologically or syntactically into the host language.

[. . .]

The great bulk of all code-switching in Gapun occurs between sentences (77% vs 23%). Table 13.3 displays the intersentential code-switches in the analyzed text. These were classified according to the pragmatic characteristics discussed [in the section on stylistic functions of code-switching].

The villagers of Gapun clearly have a preference for pragmatically oriented intersentential code-switching, which indicates that code-switching in Gapun is indeed perceived by them to be largely a rhetorical device which can be used to achieve some pragmatic effect. That this rhetorical, intersentential type of code-switching dominates in the village is probably a byproduct of the role that speech is understood to have in the community. We have already mentioned several times that talk in Gapun is essentially an activity which stresses consensus. Repeating what other speakers have said, or expanding and elaborating their comments is an effective way of underscoring consensus. It has also been noted that the most important and frequently engaged in speech genres in the village – oratory, the *kros*, and *stori* – all require that speakers command particular types of rhetorical skills. It appears that in Gapun, code-switching has been adopted as a way of demonstrating those skills. So agreement becomes more emphatic, denials become harsher, sarcasm more cutting, stories more dramatic and oratories more effective when code-switching is used. Code-switching in Gapun has thus become what

Table 13.3   Intersentential code-switches

	N	%
expansion	59	43
repetition	43	31
emphatic (dis)agreement	17	13
change topic, gain floor	12	9
interjection	3	2
quotation	3	2
Total	137	100

Poplack (1980:614–15) refers to as a discrete discourse mode[4] which all bilingual villagers have recourse to and can draw upon whenever they wish to achieve particular stylistic and rhetorical effects.

[. . .]

But Gapun is now experiencing language shift, and there is clearly a link between the present predominance of the code-switching discourse mode and the fact that Taiap is losing ground to Tok Pisin. Gapun code-switching patterns could be represented on a continuum, stretching from the village elders, who code-switch often, to villagers between 35 or 40 and 8, who code-switch frequently, to children younger than 10, who do not code-switch at all (or very rarely, using only formulaic phrases) because they are not bilingual. Faced with such a continuum, it is hard not to conclude that code-switching in Gapun is a vehicle for the ongoing demise of the village vernacular.

NOTES

1.   This table is based on what Kulick knows to be the language competences of the villagers, on the basis of self-reports and 15 months of intensive observation of their language behavior.

2.   Our own observations and the villagers' self-reports confirm that every aspect of religion – mass, private prayer, talking about religion – is verbalized exclusively in Tok Pisin.

3.   Utterances in vernacular languages and their translations are underlined. Tok Pisin utterances and their translations are not. Furthermore, the following abbreviations are used in the morpheme-by-morpheme glosses.

HAB = Habitual
SUB = Subordinating marker
CONJ = Conjunction
ERG = Ergative
U = Undergoer argument/object of transitive verb
A = Actor argument/subject of transitive verb
S = Subject of intransitive verb
POSS = Possessive
LOC = Locative
INF = Infinitive marker
REL = Relative marker
FUT = Future
PRED = Predicate marker
EMP = Emphatic
IRR = Irrealis
INTENT = Intentive marker

4.   In Poplack's article, this term is used to denote only "generalized use of intrasentential code-switching", since she wishes to argue that a code-switching mode of discourse emanates "from a single code-switching grammar composed of overlapping sectors of L1 and L2". Leaving aside that question entirely, we see no reason why a code-switching mode of discourse should not be postulated even for communities like Gapun, where speakers tend to switch intersententially but where they nevertheless switch very frequently, and where the community's linguistic repertoire would be perceived by speakers to be immeasurably poorer without recourse to code-switching.

REFERENCES

Bentahila, A. (1983) Motivations for code-switching among Arab-French bilinguals in Morocco. *Language and Communication* 3: 233–243.

Bradshaw, J. (1978) Multilingualism and language mixture among the Numbami. *Kivung* 11(1): 26–49.

Brown, P. and S. Levinson (1987) *Politeness: Some Universals in Language Usage*. Cambridge: Cambridge University Press.

Chowning, A. (1983) Interaction between Pidgin and three West New Britain languages. *Pacific Linguistics* A-65: 191–206.

Clyne, M. (1967) *Transference and Triggering*. The Hague: Martinus Nijhoff.

Colburn, M. (1985) Ogea sociolinguistic survey. Mimeo.

Dutton, T. (1978) The 'Melanesian Problem' and language change and disappearance in southeastern Papua New Guinea. Mimeo.

Foley, W. (1987) *The Papuan Languages of New Guinea*. Cambridge: Cambridge University Press.

Gal, S. (1979) *Language Shift*. New York: Academic Press.

Goldman, L. (1983) *Talk Never Dies: the Language of Huli Disputes*. London: Tavistock.

Gumperz, J. (1982) *Discourse Strategies*. Cambridge: Cambridge University Press.

Haiman, J. (1979) Hua: a Papuan language of New Guinea. In: Shopen (ed.) (1979).

Herdt, G. (1981) *Guardians of the Flutes*. New York: McGraw-Hill.

Hill, J. and R. Hill. (1977) Language death and relexification in Tlaxcalan Nahuatl. *International Journal of the Sociology of Language* 12: 55–67.

Holzknecht, S. (n.d.) Tok Pisin influences in Austronesian languages in the Upper Markham and Ramu valleys. Mimeo.

Hooley, B. (1987) Death or life: the prognosis for central Buang. In: Laycock and Winter (eds) (1987): 275–85.

Kulick, D. (1987) Language shift and language socialization in Gapun: a report of fieldwork in progress. *Language and Linguistics in Melanesia* 16: 125–151.

Laycock, D. (1966) Papuans and Pidgin: aspects of bilingualism in New Guinea. *Te Reo* 9: 44–51.

Laycock, D. and W. Winter (eds) (1978) *A World of Languages. Papers Presented to Professor S.A. Wurm on his 65th Birthday*. Canberra: The Australian National University [*Pacific Linguistics* C-100].

Lithgow, D. (1973) Language change on Woodlark island. *Oceania* 44(2): 101–108.

Mühlhäusler, P. (1979) *Growth and Structure of the Lexicon in New Guinea Pidgin*. Canberra: The Australian National University [*Pacific Linguistics* C-52].

Nekitel, O. (1985) *Sociolinguistic Aspects of Abu'*. Unpublished thesis, Australian National University.

Poplack, S. (1984) Constrasting patterns of code-switching in two communities. In Warkentyne (ed.) (1984).

Poplack, S. (1980) Sometimes I'll start a sentence in English y termino en español: toward a typology of code-switching. *Linguistics* 18: 581–618.

Ross, M. (1984) Current use and expansion of Tok Pisin: effects of Tok Pisin on some vernacular languages. In: Wurm and Mühlhäusler (eds) (1984): 539–556.

Sankoff, D., S. Poplack and S. Vanniarajan (1985) The case of the nonce loan in Tamil. Paper presented at the XIV Conference on New Ways of Analyzing Variation.

Sankoff, G. (1980) [1977] Multilingualism in Papua New Guinea. In G. Sankoff (1980).

Sankoff, G. (1980) [1971] Language use in multilingual societies. Some alternative approaches. In G. Sankoff (1980).

Sankoff, G. (1980) *The Social Life of Language*. Pennsylvania: University of Pennsylvania Press.

Shopen, T. (ed.) (1979) *Languages and their Status*. Massachusetts: Winthrop Publishers.

Warkentyne, H.J. (1984) *Methods V: Papers from the V International Conference on Methods in Dialectology*. Victoria: University of Victoria.

Wurm, S. (1983) Grammatical decay in Papuan languages. Mimeo.

Wurm, S. and P. Mühlhäusler (eds) (1984) *Handbook of Tok Pisin (New Guinea Pidgin)*. Canberra: The Australian National University [*Pacific Linguistics* C-70].

QUESTIONS

1. When did Tok Pisin enter the village community? Who introduced it and why?
2. What are the current language trends with regard to Tok Pisin in the village?
3. What factors influence language choice in the village?
4. What kind of code-switches occur in the community?
5. What are the stylistic functions of code-switching?
6. What grammatical constraints are there on code-switching and what conclusions do Kulick and Stroud draw in regard to the status of code-switching in Gapun?

Create a list of the different functions of code-switching Kulick and Stroud mention. How do these functions relate to the concepts of situational and metaphorical code-switching? Are all cases covered by these terms? Do we need more categories?

Chapter 14

Jan-Peter Blom and John J. Gumperz

SOCIAL MEANING IN LINGUISTIC STRUCTURE: CODE-SWITCHING IN NORWAY

THIS STUDY OF THE meaning of linguistic choice in a Norwegian community exemplifies what is meant by an integrated sociolinguistic approach. Ethnography and linguistics both are drawn upon, technically and conceptually; but more than that, the outcome is an understanding of social constraints and linguistic rules as parts of a single communicative system. The conceptual framework for the social analysis here leans on the work of Leach (1954) and Barth (1966) and Goffman (1964).

[. . .]

Given a particular aggregate of people engaged in regular face-to-face interaction, and given some knowledge of the speakers' linguistic repertoire (Gumperz 1964b), we wish to relate the structure of that repertoire to the verbal behavior of members of the community in particular situations.

Data on verbal interaction derives from approximately two months' field work in Hemnesberget, a small commercial and industrial town of about 1300 inhabitants in the center of the Rana Fjord, close to the Arctic Circle in northern Norway. The settlement owes its existence to the growth of local trade and industry following the abolition of government-sanctioned trade monopolies covering most of northern Norway in 1858. Since the Middle Ages, these monopolies had kept the area's economy dependent upon a small elite of merchant and landholding families with connections to southern Norway, separated by great differences in wealth, culture, and education from the tenant farmers, fishermen, estate laborers, and servants who formed the bulk of the populace. Apart from a few shop owners and government officials, present-day Hemnesberget residents are mostly descendants of these latter groups. They have been attracted to the town

Source: Blom, Jan-Peter and John Gumperz (1972) Social meaning in linguistic structure: codeswitching in Norway. In John Gumperz and Dell Hymes (eds) *Directions in Sociolinguistics*. New York: Holt, Rinehart and Winston, 407–434.

from the surroundings by new economic opportunities there, while a hundred years of relatively free economic development have splintered the old ruling circles. Many of this former elite have moved away, and the remainder no longer forms a visible social group in the region.

Present inhabitants of Hemnesberget earn their livelihood mainly as craftsmen in family workshops or in the somewhat larger boat-building and lumber-processing plants, all of which are locally owned.

[. . .]

While at the beginning of the century Hemnesberget was the most important communications and commercial center in the area, it has been eclipsed in recent years by government-sponsored economic development which has turned the town of Mo i Rana, at the mouth of Rana Fjord, into Norway's major iron- and steel-producing center. The region of Mo has grown from about 1000 inhabitants in 1920 to almost 9000 in 1960, largely through immigration from the region of Trøndelag and southern Norway. It now boasts several modern department stores, hotels, restaurants, and cinemas. The railroad from Trondheim in the south through Mo and on north to Bodø was completed shortly after World War II, and the road system is steadily improving. All these new communication arteries, however, now bypass Hemnesberget, which has all but lost its importance as a communication link for both land and sea traffic.

[. . .]

THE COMMUNITY LINGUISTIC REPERTOIRE

Most residents of Hemnesberget are native speakers of Ranamål (R), one of a series of dialects which segment northern Norway into linguistic regions roughly corresponding to other cultural and ecological divisions (Christiansen 1962). As elsewhere in Norway, where local independence and distinctness of folk culture are highly valued, the dialect enjoys great prestige. A person's native speech is regarded as an integral part of his family background, a sign of his local identity. By identifying himself as a dialect speaker both at home and abroad, a member symbolizes pride in his community and in the distinctness of its contribution to society at large.

Formal education, however, is always carried on in the standard, the language of official transactions, religion, and the mass media. Norwegian law sanctions two standard languages: Bokmål (formally called Riksmål) and Nynorsk (formerly Landsmål), of which only Bokmål (B) is current in northern Norway.

Education is universal and, allowing for certain individual differences in fluency, all speakers of Ranamål also control the standard. Both Bokmål and Ranamål, therefore, form part of what we may call the community linguistic repertoire (Gumperz 1964b), the totality of linguistic resources which speakers may employ in significant social interaction. In their everyday interaction, they select among the two as the situation demands. Members view this alternation as a shift between two distinct entities, which are never mixed. A person speaks either one or the other.

The fact that the two varieties are perceived as distinct, however, does not necessarily mean that their separateness is marked by significant linguistic differences. Pairs such as Hindi and Urdu, Serbian and Croatian, Thai and Laotian, and many others which are regarded as separate languages by their speakers are known to be grammatically almost identical. The native's view of language distinctions must thus be validated by empiricial linguistic investigation.

We began our analysis by employing standard linguistic elicitation procedures. A series of informants selected for their fluency in the dialect were interviewed in our office and were asked to produce single words, sentences, and short texts, first in the dialect and then in the standard, for taping or phonetic recording by the linguist. These elicitation sessions yielded a series of dialect features which are essentially identical to those described by Norwegian dialectologists (Christiansen 1962).

The vowel system distinguishes three tongue heights

- high: front unrounded i, front rounded y, central rounded u, back rounded o
- mid: front unrounded e, front rounded ö, back rounded å
- low: front unrounded æ, front rounded ø, back a.

Consonants occur either singly or as geminates. Vowels are phonetically short before geminates, consonant clusters, and palatalized consonants. There are two series of consonants: unmarked and palatalized. Unmarked consonants include

- stops p, b, t, d, k, g
- spirants f, v, s, š, j, ç
- nasals m, n, ŋ
- trill r, lateral l, and retroflex flap ḷ.

The palatal series contains tj, dj, nj, and lj. On the phonetic level, a set of cacuminal or retroflex allophones occur for the sequences rs [ʂ], rd [ḍ], rt [ṭ], and rn [ɳ].

The local pronunciation of the standard differs from the "pure" dialect as follows: Bokmål does not have the phonemic distinction between the palatalized and non-palatalized series of consonants. Only nonpalatalized consonants occur. In addition, it does not distinguish between mid front rounded /ö/ and low front rounded /ø/; only the former occurs. On the purely phonetic level, dialect allophones of the phonemes /æ/ and /a/ are considerably lower and more retracted than their standard equivalents. The dialect furthermore has a dark allophone [ɬ] of /l/ where the standard has clear [l]. The cacuminal or retroflex allophones of /s/, /d/, /t/, and /n/, and the flap /ḷ/, however, which are commonly regarded as dialect features, are used in both varieties, although they tend to disappear in highly formal Bokmål.

Morphological peculiarities of the dialect include the masculine plural indefinite suffix -æ and the definite suffix -an, e.g., (R) hæstæ (horses), hæstan (the horses), contrasting with (B) hester and hestene. In verb inflection the dialect lacks the infinitive suffix -e and the present suffix -er of regular verbs. Further differences in past tense and past participle markers and in the assignment of individual words to strong or weak inflectional classes serve to set off almost every dialect verb from its standard Norwegian equivalent.

Here are some examples of common regular and irregular verbs and their standard equivalents:

Infinitive		Present		Past		Past Participle			
(R)	*(B)*	*(R)*	*(B)*	*(R)*	*(B)*	*(R)*	*(B)*		
finj		*finne*	*finj*	*finner*	*fanj*	*fant*	*fønje*	*funnet*	(find)
vara or *va*		*være*	*e*	*ær*	*va*	*var*	*vøre*	*vært*	(be)
jær	*jøre*	*jær*	*jør*	*jol*	*jøre*	*jort*	*jort*	(do)
læs	*lese*	*læs*	*leser*	*læst*	*leste*	*læst*	*lest*	(read)

Other important dialect features appear in pronouns, common adverbs of time, place, and manner, conjunctions, and other grammatically significant function words. Here is a list of some of the most common distinctive forms of personal pronouns and possessive pronouns:

(B)	*(R)*	
jæjj	*og*	(I)
mæjj	*meg*	(me)
dæjj	*deg*	(you)
hann	*hanj*	(he)

(B)	*(R)*	
hunn	*ho*	(she)
hanns	*hanjs*	(his)
hennes	*hinjers*	(hers)
dere	*dåkk*	(you)(plural)
di	*dæmm**	(theirs)

* Sometimes also *di* and *deres*.

[. . .]

These data constitute empirical evidence to support the view of the dialect as a distinct linguistic entity.

[. . .]

RANAMÅL AND BOKMÅL AS CODES IN A REPERTOIRE

[. . .]

[To illustrate the differences between Ranamål and Bokmål] in a sentence pair like *hanj bor på nilsen's paŋšonat* and its Bokmål equivalent *hann bor pa nilsen's paŋsonat* "He lives in Nilsen's pensionat," only the realizations of /a/, /ɬ/, and /nj/ which appear in our list of dialect characteristics differ. In other relevant respects the two utterances are identical. Furthermore, even in the case of these dialect characteristics, speakers do not alternate between two clearly distinguishable articulation points; rather, the shift takes the form of a displacement along a scale in which palatalized consonants show at least three degrees of palatalization, strong [nj], weak [nʲ], and zero [n] and /a/ and /æ/ each show three degrees of retraction and lowering.

While a switch from Norwegian to English implies a shift between two distinct structural wholes, the Bokmål-Ranamål alternation, in phonology at least, seems more similar to conditions described by Labov (1966b) for New York speech. A speaker's standard and dialect performance can be accounted for by a single phonetic system.

[. . .]

The effect of structural similarities on speakers' perception of speech differences is somewhat counterbalanced by the fact that choice among these variables is always restricted by sociolinguistic selection constraints [also referred to as co-occurrence rules] such that if, for instance, a person selects a standard morphological variant in one part of an utterance, this first choice also implies selection of pronunciation variables tending toward the standard end of the scale.

[. . .]

The most reasonable assumption is that the linguistic separateness between the dialect and the standard, i.e., the maintenance of distinct alternates for common inflectional morphemes and function, is conditioned by social factors.

Some idea of how this came about can be obtained by considering the conditions under which the two varieties are learned. The dialect is acquired in most homes and in the sphere of domestic and friendship relations. As a result, it has acquired the flavor of these locally based relationships. However, dialect speakers learn the standard in school and in church, at a time when they are also introduced to national Norwegian values. It has therefore become associated with such pan-Norwegian activity systems.

Since the adult population has equal access to both sets of variants, however, the developmental argument does not provide sufficient explanation for the maintenance of distinctness. Immigrants to urban centers around the world, e.g., frequently give up their languages after a generation if social conditions are favorable to language shift. The hypothesis suggests itself, therefore, that given the initial acquisition patterns, the dialect and the standard remain separate because of the cultural identities they communicate and the social values implied therein. It is this aspect of the problem that we intend to explore in the remaining sections of the article.

[. . .]

Effective communication requires that speakers and audiences agree both on the meaning of words and on the social import or values attached to choice of expression. Our discussions will be confined to the latter. We will use the term *social significance*, or *social meaning*, to refer to the social value implied when an utterance is used in a certain context.

In general, the assignment of value to particular objects or acts is as arbitrary as the referential naming of objects. Just as a particular term may refer to a round object in one group and a square object in another, so also the value of actions or utterances may vary. Thus the same term may indicate geographical distinctions in one community and symbolize social stratification elsewhere. Social meanings differ from referential meanings in the way in which they are coded. Whereas reference is coded largely through words, social meaning can attach not only to acoustic signs but also to settings, to items of background knowledge, as well as to particular word sequences. In Hemnes, e.g., values attached to a person's family background or to his reputation as a fisherman are important in understanding what he says and influence the selection of responses to his actions.

[. . .]

LOCAL ORGANIZATION AND VALUES

[. . .] The majority of those who claim local descent show a strong sense of local identification. To be a *hæmnesværing* "Hemnes resident" in their view is like belonging to a team characterized by commonalty of descent. [. . .] The dialect is an important marker of their common culture.

[. . .]

The meaning attached to local descent and dialect use—to being part of the "local team"—is clearly seen when we consider those members of the community who dissociate themselves from this "team." Traditionally, in northern Norway the local community of equals was separated from the landowning commercial and administrative elite by a wide gulf of social and judicial inequality. Since the latter were the introducers and users of standard Norwegian, the standard form was—and to some extent still is—associated with this inequality of status. Many of the functions of the former elite have now been incorporated into the local social system. Individuals who fill these functions, however, continue to be largely of nonlocal descent. Although they may pay lip service to locally accepted rules of etiquette and use the dialect on occasion, their experience elsewhere in Norway, where differences in education, influence, and prestige are much more pronounced, leads them to associate the dialect with lack of education and sophistication. Therefore, they show a clear preference for the standard.

Such attitudes are unacceptable to locals, who view lack of respect for and refusal to speak the dialect as an expression of social distance and contempt for the "local team" and its community spirit. It is not surprising, therefore, that their loyalty to the dialect is thereby reaffirmed. For a local resident to employ (B) forms with other local residents is in their view to *snakk fint* or to *snakk jalat* – "to put on airs."

[. . .]

CONTEXTUAL CONSTRAINTS

[. . .] There is by no means a simple one-to-one relationship between specific speech varieties and specific social identities. Apart from the fact that values attached to language usage vary with social background, the same individual need not be absolutely consistent in all his actions. He may wish to appear as a member of the local team on some occasions, while identifying with middle-class values on others. In order to determine the social significance of any one utterance, we need additional information about the contextual clues by which natives arrive at correct interpretations of social meaning.

[. . .]

We will use the term *setting* to indicate the way in which natives classify their ecological environment into distinct locales [e.g. the home, workshops and plants, the school, etc.].

[. . .]

A closer specification of social constraints is possible if we concentrate on activities carried on by particular constellations of personnel, gathered in particular settings during a particular span of time [e.g. class sessions as opposed to meetings in the school]. We will use the term *social situation* to refer to these. [. . .]

Thus alternative social definitions of the situation may occur within the same setting, depending on the opportunities and constraints on interaction offered by a shift in personnel and/or object of the interaction. Such definitions always manifest themselves in what we would prefer to call a *social event*. Events center around one or at the most a limited range of topics and are distinguishable because of their sequential structure. They are marked by stereotyped and thus recognizable opening and closing routines. The distinction between situation and event can be clarified if we consider the behavior of Hemnes residents who are sometimes seen in the community office, first transacting their business in an officially correct manner, and then turning to one of the clerks and asking him to step aside for a private chat. The norms which apply to the two kinds of interaction differ; the break between the two is clearly marked. Therefore, they constitute two distinct social events, although the personnel and the locale remain the same.

The terms setting, social situation, and social event as used here can be considered three successively more complex stages in the speaker's processing of contextual information. [. . .] To demonstrate how these factors influence language usage in Hemnesberget, we turn now to some examples drawn from participant observation.

The fact that the dialect reflects local values suggests that it symbolizes relationships based on shared identities with local culture. Casual observations and recording of free speech among locals in homes, workshops, and the various public meeting places where such relationships are assumed do indeed show that only the dialect is used there. However, statuses defined with respect to the superimposed national Norwegian system elicit the standard. Examples of·these are church services, presentation of text material in school, reports, and announcements—but not necessarily informal public appeals or political speeches—at public meetings. Similarly, meetings with tourists or other strangers elicit the standard at least until the participants' identity becomes more clearly known.

SITUATIONAL AND METAPHORICAL SWITCHING

When within the same setting the participants' definition of the social event changes, this change may be signaled among others by linguistic clues. On one occasion, when we, as outsiders, stepped up to a group of locals engaged in conversation, our arrival caused a significant alteration in the casual posture of the group. Hands were removed from pockets and looks changed. Predictably, our remarks elicited a code switch marked simultaneously by a change in channel cues (i.e., sentence speed, ryhthm, more hesitation pauses, etc.) and by a shift from (R) to (B) grammar. Similarly, teachers report that while formal lectures—where interruptions are not encouraged—are delivered in (B), the speakers will shift to (R) when they want to encourage open and free discussion among students. Each of these examples involves clear changes in the participants' definition of each other's rights and obligation. We will use the term *situational switching* to refer to this kind of a language shift.

The notion of situational switching assumes a direct relationship between language and the social situation. The linguistic forms employed are critical features of the event in the sense that any violation of selection rules changes members' perception of the event. A person who uses the standard where only the dialect is appropriate violates commonly accepted norms. His action may terminate the conversation or bring about other social sanctions. To be sure, language choice is never completely determined; sociolinguistic variables must be investigated empirically. Furthermore, situations differ in the amount of freedom of choice allowed to speakers. Ritual events, like the well-known Vedic ceremonies of South Asia, constitute extreme examples of determination, where every care is taken to avoid even the slightest change in pronunciation or rhythm lest the effectiveness of the ceremony be destroyed. [. . .]

In Hemnesberget, as our example will show later on, speakers are given a relatively wide choice in vocabulary and some choice in syntax. Selection rules affect mainly the variables discussed previously. Values of these variables are sociolinguistically determined in the sense that when, on the one hand, we speak of someone giving a classroom lecture or performing a Lutheran church service or talking to a tourist, we can safely assume that he is using (B) grammatical forms. On the other hand, two locals having a heart-to-heart talk will presumably speak in (R). If instead they are found speaking in (B), we conclude either that they do not identify with the values of the local team or that they are not having a heart-to-heart talk.

In contrast with those instances where choice of variables is narrowly constrained by social norms, there are others in which participants are given considerably more latitude. Thus official community affairs are largely defined as nonlocal and hence the standard is appropriate. But since many individuals who carry out the relevant activities all know each other as fellow locals, they often interject casual statements in the dialect into their formal discussions. In the course of a morning spent at the community administration office, we noticed that clerks used both standard and dialect phrases, depending on whether they were talking about official affairs or not. Likewise, when residents step up to a clerk's desk, greeting and inquiries about family affairs tend to be exchanged in the dialect, while the business part of the transaction is carried on in the standard.

In neither of these cases is there any significant change in definition of participants' mutual rights and obligations. The posture of speakers and channel clues of their speech remain the same. The language switch here relates to particular kinds of topics or subject matters rather than to change in social situation. Characteristically, the situations in question allow for the enactment of two or more different relationships among the same set of individuals. The choice of either (R) or (B) alludes to these relationships and thus generates meanings which are quite similar to those conveyed by the alternation between *ty* or *vy* in the examples from Russian literature cited by Friedrich (1972). We will use the term *metaphorical switching* for this phenomenon.

The semantic effect of metaphorical switching depends on the existence of regular relationships between variables and social situations of the type just discussed. The context in which one of a set of alternates is regularly used becomes part of its meaning, so that when this form is then employed in a context where it is not normal, it brings in some of the flavor of this original setting. Thus a phrase like "April is the cruelest month" is regarded as poetic because of its association with T. S. Eliot's poetry. When used in natural conversation, it gives that conversation some of the flavor of this poetry. Similarly, when (R) phrases are inserted metaphorically into a (B) conversation, this may, depending on the circumstances, add a special social meaning of confidentiality or privateness to the conversation.

The case of the local who, after finishing his business in the community office, turns to a clerk and asks him to step aside for a private chat further illustrates the contrast between metaphorical and role switching. By their constant alternation between the standard and the dialect during their business transaction, they alluded to the dual relationship which exists between them. The event was terminated when the local asked the clerk in the dialect whether he had time to step aside to talk about private affairs, suggesting in effect that they shift to a purely personal, local relationship. The clerk looked around and said, "Yes, we are not too busy." The two then stepped aside, although remaining in the same room, and their subsequent private discussion was appropriately carried on entirely in the dialect.

THE EXPERIMENT

Our discussion of verbal behavior so far has relied largely on deductive reasoning supported by unstructured ethnographic observation. Additional tests of our hypothesis are based on controlled text elicitation. We have stated that gatherings among friends and kin implying shared local identities must be carried on in the dialect. If we are correct in our hypothesis, then individuals involved in such friendly gatherings should not change speech variety regardless of whether they talk about local, national, or official matters.

In order to test this, we asked local acquaintances whom we knew to be part of the network of local relationships to arrange a friendly gathering at which refreshments were to be served and to allow us to record the proceedings as samples of dialect speech. Two such gatherings were recorded, one in the living room of our local hosts, and the other in the home of an acquaintance. The fact that arrangements for the meeting were made by local people means that the groups were self-recruited. Participants in the first group included two sisters and a brother and their respective spouses. One of the men was a shopkeeper, one of the few in this category who claims local descent; his brothers-in-law were employed as craftsmen. All three men are quite literate compared to workmen elsewhere in the world and well read in public affairs. They are active in local politics and experienced in formal committee work. The second group included three craftsmen, friends and neighbors who worked in the same plant, and their wives. One of these had served as a sailor on a Norwegian merchant vessel for several years and spoke English. Participants were all quite familiar with standard Norwegian, and our recorded conversations contain several passages where the standard was used in quoting nonlocal speech or in statements directed at us.

Methodologically, self-recruitment of groups is important for two reasons. It ensures that groups are defined by locally recognized relationships and enables the investigator to predict the norms relevant to their interaction. Furthermore, the fact that participants have preexisting obligations toward each other means that, given the situation, they are likely to respond to such obligations in spite of the presence of strangers. Our tape recording and our visual observations give clear evidence that this in fact was what occurred.

Our strategy was to introduce discussion likely to mobilize obligations internal to the group, thus engaging members in discussion among themselves. This proved to be relatively easy to do. When a point had been discussed for some time, we would attempt to change the subject by injecting new questions or comments. In doing this, we did not, of course, expect that our own interjections would predictably affect the speakers' choice of codes. Participants were always free to reinterpret our comments in any way they wished. Nevertheless, the greater the range of topics covered, the greater was the likelihood of language shift.

As a rule, our comments were followed by a few introductory exchanges directed at us. These were marked by relatively slow sentence speeds, many hesitation pauses, and visual clues indicating that people were addressing us. Linguistically, we noted some switching to the standard in such exchanges. After a brief period of this, if the topic was interesting, internal discussion began and arguments that referred to persons, places, and events we could not possibly be expected to have any knowledge about developed. The transition to internal discussion was marked by an increase in sentence speed and lack of hesitation pauses and similar clues. The tape recorder was run continously during the gatherings, and after some time participants became quite oblivious to its presence.

Only those passages which were clearly recognizable as internal discussion were used in the analysis; all others were eliminated. The texts obtained in this way consist of stretches of free discussion on diverse topics. The following passages show that our hypothesis about the lack of connection between code switching and change in topic was confirmed.

Group I

Topic: Chitchat about local events

GUNNAR: *ja de va ein så kåmm idag—ein så kåmm me mælka—så så hanj de va så varmt inj på mo i går—ja, sa eg, de va no içe vent anjæ dåkk må no ha meir enn di anjrann bestanjdi.*

Yes, there was one who came today—one who came with milk—so he said it was so warm in Mo yesterday. Yes, I said, there is nothing else to be expected, you people must always have more than anybody else.

Topic: Industrial planning

ALF: *her kunj ha vore eit par sånn mellomstore bedreftæ på ein førtifæmti manu so ha besæftigæ denna fålke detta så ha gådd ledi amm vinjtærn.*

There might have been here some medium-size plants employing forty to fifty men which then could offer work to those who have nothing to do in winter.

Topic: Governmental affairs

OSCAR: *vi jekk inj før denn forste injstilijingæ ifrå šeikommitenn.*
"We supported the first proposal made by the Schei Committee."

Item 1 deals with a local topic in a somewhat humorous way; items 2 and 3 concern planning and formal governmental affairs. All these passages are clearly in the dialect. Of the phonological variables, [nj] and [lj] show the highest degree of palatalization and [a] and [æ] the highest degree of retraction throughout. Morphophonemic dialect markers are (R) *ein* "one," *så* "who," *içce* "not," *dåkk* "you," *meir* "more," *her* "here," *jekk* "went," *ifrå* "from." Even lexical borrowings from the standard such as *injstiljing* "proposal" and *bedreftæ* "plants" are clearly in dialect phonology and morphology. We find one single instance of what seems to be a standard form: (B) *mellom/* (R) *imelja* "middle." But this only occurs as part of the borrowed compound *mellomstore* "medium-size." In several hours of conversation with both groups, marked by many changes in topic, we have found a number of lexical borrowings but not a clear instance of phonological or grammatical switching, in spite of the fact that all informants clearly know standard grammar.

While our hypothesis suggests that switching is constrained in those situations which allow only local relationships to be enacted, it also leads us to predict that whenever local and nonlocal relationships are relevant to the same situation, topical variation may elicit code switching. To test this, we selected members of a formerly quite active local peer group. For the last few years these individuals had all been at universities in Oslo, Bergen, and Trondheim. They returned home in the summer either for vacation or to take up local employment. In conventional interview sessions, all participants claimed to be pure dialect speakers and professed local attitudes about dialect use. They thus regarded themselves as members of the local "team." As fellow students, however, they also shared statuses that are identified with pan-Norwegian values and associated with the standard. Our assumption then is that if topical stimuli are introduced which elicit these values, switching may result.

Three gatherings were arranged in the home of one of our informants. Refreshments were again served. Elicitation strategies were similar to those employed with the first two groups, and similar ranges of topics were covered. The examples cited here show that our hypothesis was again confirmed.

Group II

Topic: Chitchat about drinking habits

BERIT: *ja, ja, mæn vi bjynjt anjer veien du—vi bjynjt i barnelošen—så vi har de unjajort.*
Yes, yes, we started the other way, we started in the children's antialcoholic league. So we have finished all that.

Topic: Industrial development

BERIT: *jo da viss di bare fikk de te lønn seg—så e i værtfall prisnivåe hær i Rana skrudd høger enn de e vanligvis anner stann i lanne.*

Yes, if they could only manage to make it profitable—so in any case the prices tend to be higher here in Rana than is common in other places in the country.

Topic: Informal statement about university regulations

OLA: *mænn no ha dæmm læmpæ pa de.*
But now they have relaxed that.

Topic: Authoritative statement about university regulations

OLA: *de voel du mellom en faemm saeks.*
You choose that from among five or six.

Comparison of Berit's and Ola's first statement with their second statements shows considerable shifting in each case. Thus Berit's second utterance has such unpalatalized forms as *anner* (vs. *anjer*), and raised and less retracted [a] in *da*. She also uses standard variables (B) *fikk*/(R) *fekk*, (B) *viss*/(R) *vess*, (B) *værtfall*/(R) *kvart fall*, (B) *hær*/ (R) *her*, etc. Ola's second statement is characterized by (B) *mellom*/(R) *imelja* and (B) *en*/(R) *ein*. Similarly, his [æ] in *fæmm* and *sæks* is raised and fronted. In neither case is the shift to the standard complete—after all the situation never lost its informality. Berit's statement still contains dialect words like (R) *lønn*/(B) *lønne* "to be profitable"; (R) *stann*/(B) *steder* "places"; and Ola has (R) *væl*/(B) *velger* "to choose." What we see then is a breakdown of co-occurrence rules, an erosion of the linguistic boundary between Ranamål and Bokmål. The tendency is to switch toward standard phonology while preserving some morpho-phonemic and lexical dialect features of (R). Features retained in this manner are largely those which also occur in other local dialects and to some extent also in Nynorsk. They have thus gained some acceptance as proper dialect forms. Those characteristics which locals refer to as broad speech, i.e., those that are known as local peculiarities, tend to be eliminated.

It must be noted as well that Berit and Ola also differ in their pronunciation of the phonological variables. Ola's normal pronunciation shows the strong palatalization of consonant and extreme vowel retraction characteristic of most residents. Berit's normal pronunciation has medium palatalization and medium retraction. Both, however, switch in the same direction, in response to similar situational and topical clues, and this agreement on the rules of stylistic manipulation is clearly more important in this case than the mere articulatory difference in Berit's and Ola's speech.

The social character of the style switch was clearly revealed when the tape-recorded conversations were played back to other Hemnes residents. One person who had been working with us as a linguistic informant at first refused to believe that the conversations were recorded locally. When he recognized the voices of the participants, he showed clear signs of disapproval. Apparently, he viewed the violation of co-occurrence rules as a sign of what is derogatorily called *knot* "artificial speech" in colloquial Norwegian. Some of the participants showed similar reactions when they heard themselves on tape. They promised to refrain from switching during future discussion sessions. Our analysis of these later sessions, however, revealed that when an argument required that the speaker validate his status as an intellectual, he would again tend to use standard forms in the manner shown by Berit and Ola. Code selection rules thus seem to be akin to grammatical rules. Both operate below the level of consciousness and may be independent of the speaker's overt intentions.

Additional information about usage patterns in group III was provided through a fortunate accident. One of our sessions with this group was interrupted by a [. . .] [local youth with a cognitive disability], who has the habit of appearing in people's homes to solicit assistance for his various schemes. Here are some examples of remarks addressed to him by Berit and Solveig, of all the members of the group the most prone to use standard forms. Her normal pronunciation shows the least amount of consonant palatalization. She is socially more marginal to Hemnes than other members of the group.

Group III

Topic: Talking to a [. . .] local youth

BERIT: *e de du så vikarier førr hanj no.*
    Are you a stand-in for him now?
SOLVEIG: *hanj kanj jo jett gåte, haj kanj no va me.*
    He is good at word games, he should participate.

Both Berit and Solveig's pronunication in these examples becomes identical with the ordinary speech of Ola and of the members of group I. The extreme palatalization of [nj] and the lowering of [a] is not normal for them; they clearly are talking down in this case. Their stylistic range, as well as their facility in switching, seem to be greater than those of the others.

In comparing the behavior of the first two groups with that of group III, we find two different kinds of language-usage patterns. All three groups speak both the dialect and the standard. Groups I and II, however, show only situational switching. When members talk to each other, differences of formality or informality to topic are reflected only in the lexicon. Pronunciation and morphology do not change. Those groups shift to (B) phonology and grammar only when remarks are addressed directly to us who count as outsiders or in indirect quotes of such matters as government rules, on officials' statements, etc. In such instances of situation switching, therefore, Ranamål and Bokmål are kept separate throughout by strict co-occurrence restrictions. In group III, however, deviation from the dialect results both from metaphorical and situation switching. Metaphorical switching, furthermore, involves a breakdown of the co-occurrence restrictions characteristic of situational shifts.

The dialect usage of locals, on the one hand, corresponds to their view that the two varieties are distinct, and to their insistence on maintaining the strict separation of local and nonlocal values. For the students, on the other hand, the distinction between dialect and standard is not so sharp. Although they display the same general attitudes about the dialect as the team of locals, their behavior shows a range of variation rather than an alternation between distinct systems. It reflects a de facto recognition of their own nonlocal identification.

A fourth conversational group further illustrates the internal speech diversity in the community. The principal speakers here are two men, A and B, and C, who is A's wife. All come from families who tend to dissociate themselves from the egalitarian value system of the local team. Their normal style of speech was Bokmål for remarks directed at us as well as for in-group speech. Only in a few instances when A began telling local anecdotes did he lapse into Ranamål. (R) forms were introduced as metaphorical switches into what were basically (B) utterances to provide local color, indicate humor, etc., in somewhat the same way that speakers in group III had used (B) forms in (R) utterances.

In the course of the evening A and C's teen-age daughter joined the conversation. She expressed attitudes toward the dialect which are quite similar to those of the students in group III and thus are somewhat different from those of her parents. The few samples we have of her speech show (R) phonology similar to that of Berit and Solveig in group III.

Although the picture of language usage derived from the four groups seems at first highly complex, it becomes less so when viewed in relation to speakers' attitudes, interactional norms, and local values. All Hemnes residents have the same repertoire. Their linguistic competence includes control of both (R) and (B) rules. They vary in the way in which they use these rules. Expressed attitudes toward (R) and (B) do not provide an explanation for these differences in speech behavior. The most reasonable explanation of the ways in which these groups differ seems to be that the dual system of local values, differences in individual background, and the various social situations in which members find themselves, operate to affect their interpretation of the social meaning of the variables they employ.

[. . .]

REFERENCES

Barth, Fredrik (1966) *Models of Social Organization*. Royal Anthropological Institute of Great Britain and Ireland. Occasional Papers. London.

Christiansen, Hallfried (1962) *Målet i Rana*. Oslo: Institut for Sociologi, Universitetet i Oslo.

Friedrich, Paul (1972) Social context and semantic feature: the Russian pronominal usage. In John Gumperz and Dell Hymes (eds) *Directions in Sociolinguistics: The Ethnography of Communication*. New York: Holt, Rinehart and Winston, 270–300.

Goffman, Erving (1964) The neglected situation. In John J Gumperz and Dell Hymes (eds) *The Ethnography of Communication. American Anthropologist* 66, 6, pt. II: 133–137.

Gumperz, John J. (1964) Linguistic and social interaction in two communities. In John J Gumperz and Dell Hymes (eds) *The Ethnography of Communication. American Anthropologist* 66, 6, pt. II: 137–154.

Labov, William (1966) *The Social Stratification of English in New York City*. Center for Applied Linguistics, Washington, DC.

Leach, Edmund (1954) *Political Systems of Highland Burma*. Cambridge, Mass.: Harvard University Press.

QUESTIONS

Content

1. What is the linguistic situation in Hemnesberget?
2. What evidence do Blom and Gumperz provide in support of their view of dialect features as variables within a single grammatical system?
3. What factors influence selection patterns of the two varieties and how did these patterns come about?
4. What does the term social meaning refer to and how does it relate to Ranamål and Bokmål?
5. What is the social structure like in Hemnesberget and how does it relate to language use?
6. What contextual constraints influence language use?
7. What are situational and metaphorical code-switching?
8. What type of code-switching occurs in groups I and II of the experiment?
9. What type of code-switching occurs in group III of the experiment?

Concept

Do you often hear people code-switch? What languages are used? What social meaning do these languages and code-switching activities have to you? What social meaning might they have to the conversationalists themselves?

Chapter 15

David Britain

DIALECT CONTACT, FOCUSING AND PHONOLOGICAL RULE COMPLEXITY: THE KOINEISATION OF FENLAND ENGLISH

1. INTRODUCTION

RESEARCH ON KOINEISATION, THE linguistic processes provoked by dialect contact, has been busying sociolinguists for quite a considerable period of time. Back in 1959, Ferguson suggested that the precursor of modern Arabic was a koine resulting from contact between speakers of diverse Arabic dialects. Blanc (1968) proposed a parallel origin for Israeli Hebrew. There have been an increasing number of studies which have, for example, considered koineisation as the key process leading both to the emergence of overseas Hindi and Bhojpuri-based varieties spoken by indented labourers and their descendants in Fiji (Siegel 1987), Mauritius (Domingue 1971), South Africa (Mesthrie 1991) and Trinidad (Mohan 1978, Bhatia 1988), as well as to the development of post-colonial English varieties in North America and Australasia (Bernard 1969, Dillard 1975, Trudgill 1985, 1986).

Trudgill's (1986) book *Dialects in Contact*, an account of the role linguistic accommodation plays in new dialect formation, as well as an analysis of koine development in a number of contact scenarios around the world, has triggered more recent research on the topic, particularly on new town dialects (Kerswill 1994a, 1994b, 1996; Kerswill and Williams 1992; Simpson, forthcoming), and the dialects of newly settled reclaimed areas (Britain 1991, 1997; Scholtmeijer 1990, 1992). We now have a much fuller understanding of the likely *outcomes* of koineisation, namely simplification (the increase in grammatical regularity and decrease in formal complexity); levelling (the eradication of marked variants in the dialect mix); reallocation (the refunctionalisation of input variants); and the creation of interdialect (linguistically intermediate) forms.

We know much less, however, about the intermediate stages of the koineisation process itself. This is because, as Kerswill quite rightly states (1994a:70–71), most

Source: Britain, David (1997) Dialect contact, focusing and phonological rule complexity: the koineisation of Fenland English. *Penn Working Papers in Linguistics: A Selection of Papers from NWAVE 25*, 4: 141–169.

research on dialect contact has consisted of 'post-hoc observation of completed changes, for the most part three or more generations after the migration took place'. He has been one of the few, in his research on the new dialect of Milton Keynes in southern England, to concentrate on the *process* of koine formation, as spoken through the mouths of young children of that city.

In this article, I look at koineisation in a dialect contact scenario which began over 300 years ago, in the Fens of eastern England. A comparison of a range of data sources, from Ellis (1889) right through to a recently collected corpus (Britain 1991), demonstrates that the koineisation process, for some variables at least, is barely complete, yet for others appears to have led to the emergence of a stable form over 200 years ago. Despite the long period of time over which koineisation has been underway, therefore, we are still able to see the crystallisation of some dialect features in progress, and hence begin to assess the constraints on new dialect development. Why, then, do some linguistic forms focus quickly, while others do so much more slowly? We will look to social, but particularly linguistic explanations in our attempt to answer this question. In the next section, I will discuss the rather special nature of the dialect contact in the Fenland speech community, as well as evidence that it is a koineised variety. In Section 3, I briefly describe the data sources used in the analysis. The following two sections present evidence of two variables, one which has been koineised for at least 200 years, another which is still focusing today. Section 6 attempts to address why there is such a time difference in the emergence of the koineised forms. We finally conclude in Section 7.

Figure 15.1 The location of the Fens.

2. DIALECT CONTACT IN THE FENS

The Fens (see Figure 15.1) are a low-lying area of eastern England situated about 75 miles directly north of London, and 50 miles east of Norwich. Compared with the rest of southern England it is a rather sparsely populated region, many parts of which have a population density less than a fifth of that of England as a whole. The area has a rather unique geomorphological and demographic history. [. . .] In the early 17th century, the northern coastline lay up to 12 miles further south than at present. Most of the Fenland population at that time lived on a few islands of higher ground and in small communities on this northern coastline. The southern two-thirds of the Fenland consisted of undrained marshland which was subject to tidal flooding in summer and more continuous flooding in winter, and was hence too unstable for permanent settlement. The overall livelihood of many small Fenland communities was directly related to the success of efforts to hold the water back. Even the northern coastline settlements, the most stable and relatively heavily populated, witnessed major flooding in 1439, 1550, 1570, 1607 and 1613 (Darby 1974).

The mid-17th century proved to be a major turning point in the history of the Fens when Dutch engineers were commissioned to begin work on Fenland drainage. Much of the major work was completed by the late 17th century, but in some areas drainage and reclamation were not complete until the early part of the 20th century. A previously barely passable marshland evolved into fertile arable land. The impact of the reclamation on the Fenland's demographic structure was considerable. Subsequent to drainage, the Fens saw quite rapid demographic growth, particularly in those central Fenland areas which had previously been less accessible and most susceptible to flooding. The influx came from both east (Norfolk) and west (Peterborough and Lincolnshire), though the demographic evidence suggests that relatively few came from further afield than the surrounding counties (see Britain 1997:19–20 for more detail about demographic growth and settler origins). The mixture of varieties brought into the Fens in the late 17th and 18th centuries suggests a dialect contact scenario similar to that seen much later in the polderlands of the Netherlands (Scholtmeijer 1990, 1992).

The lack of intercommunication between eastern and western sides of the Fens before reclamation is reflected in the fact that the Fens today are the site of one of the most important dialect transition zones in British English. Probably the two most often cited isoglosses are the /ʊ – ʌ/ ('cup', 'butter') and the /a – aː/ ('castle', 'last') boundaries, which run north-east to south-west through the Fenland (Orton and Tilling 1969). In addition, at a more local level, the area acts as an important boundary between East Anglian and Midland dialects. Following reclamation, however, the distinct eastern and western varieties spoken by the in-migrants of the 17th and 18th centuries would be subject to the processes of koineisation discussed in Section 1 above. An analysis both of the Survey of English Dialects data for this area (Orton and Tilling 1969) and of my own 81-speaker corpus of data collected in the late 1980s uncovered a number of examples, demonstrating not only that the variety spoken in the Fens straddles a major transition zone, but that it is also in many ways typical of the koineised linguistic varieties described by Trudgill (1986). Some of the transitions include:

- The presence or absence of /h/: absent to the west, present to the east.

- The realisation of /au/: [ɛ:] to the west, [ɛu] to the east.
- The realisation of vowels in unstressed syllables: past tense '-ed' forms and '-ing' forms are realised with [ɪ] to the west, but [ə] to the east.

As far as koineisation is concerned, we can observe, firstly, the *levelling* of marked features from the immigrant varieties. Absent from the central Fenland variety, but typical of dialects to the east are:

- The preservation of a 'nose' [nɒuz] / 'knows' [nʌuz] distinction.
- The presence of 'do' conjunctions, as in 'don't stroke the cat do he'll bite you', where, as Trudgill (1995) explains, the conjunction derives from the grammaticisation of a shortened form of 'because if you do'.
- The absence of third person present tense -*s* (Trudgill 1974: 96).

Present in northern and western varieties, but not usual in the central Fens are:

- [ɛ] forms of /ei/ in words such as 'take' and 'make'.
- The use of 'while' meaning 'until': 'don't come while four o'clock'.

In addition, we can see examples of the *reallocation* of input variants to serve new social or contextual functions (see Trudgill 1986), or in the cases described below, new lexical or allophonic positions:

- The reallocation of north-western and south-eastern forms of Middle English in words such as 'bath' and 'plant' into lexical sets matching neither input variety. Whereas varieties to the north-west of the Fens would have a short [a] vowel in these words, and south-eastern varieties would consistently have a longer (although in this region still quite front) [a:], in the central Fens speakers use [a] in some words and [a:] in others, though it is often the case that each interdialect speaker has a different lexical set in each class.
- The central Fenland has an allophonic distribution of /ai/ similar to that found in Canada and many parts of the northern US. Centralised [əi] onsets are found before voiceless consonants and open ones [ɑi] before voiced consonants, /ə/ and morpheme boundaries. This distribution, I have claimed (Britain 1997), is the result of the reallocation of western open onsets of /ai/ and eastern central onsets to different phonological environments in the central Fenland.

Finally it has interdialect features, features which are phonetically intermediate forms of the input variants:

- It has, for example, an intermediate [ɣ] for /ʌ/: the varieties to the north and west have [ʊ], and to the east and south [ʌ].

Like many varieties subject to koineisation, Fenland English was once considered by folk linguists to be relatively standard-like, presumably since the levelling process had eradicated marked regional features present in neighbouring or immigrant dialects (cf. Read 1933, Bernard 1969, Dillard 1975, Gordon 1983, Trudgill 1986). Ellis cites the data gatherer from the central Fenland town of Wisbech, a Mr Little, who claimed that the town had "very little dialect proper" (1889:253) and that "the fen country generally is the home of pure speech, by which I mean, of language but little differing from the ordinary literary English" (1889:254). Similar sentiments were expressed by Miller and Skertchly (1878).

All of the above features differentiate east from west, emphasising both the role the undrained Fens played in hindering east-west communication, and the quite radical linguistic differences which existed (and still exist) to either side.[1]

For the rest of this paper, I wish to look in more detail at two of these koineised features: the reallocated [əi]-[ɑi] forms of /ai/ and the interdialectal [ɤ] form of /ʌ/. As we will see, despite the fact that both involve ongoing changes that were underway in English long before Fenland draining, all evidence suggests that the dialect contact which followed reclamation focused one new dialect form very quickly, while the other was much slower in crystallising a distinct koineised form. I firstly present the evidence which demonstrates this differential rate of focusing, and secondly ask why we should expect such a difference. In doing so, I draw parallels between variable rates of focusing of new dialects in contact situations on the one hand, with the variable acquisition of second dialects on the other (Payne 1980, Chambers 1992, Kerswill 1996).

3. SOURCES OF DATA

In order to assess the extent to which Fenland Raising and interdialectal [ɤ] have focused in the central Fens, we are able to draw upon a number of sources, some written, others in the form of oral recordings, some traditional dialectological, others analysed within a more modern variationist framework. They give us a picture, albeit patchy in the case of the earlier and traditional data sources, of the past 170 years of Fenland English. By comparing the development of /ai/ and /ʌ/ in these data sets we will be able to chart the progress of koineisation in this variety.

The earliest source we have at our disposal is Ellis (1889). This is a dialect survey of the traditional type, based on information from over 1100 locations in Great Britain. Data in the form of spontaneous transcriptions of reading passages and word lists was sent to Ellis by a combination of trained dialect enthusiasts (such as Thomas Hallam) or interested locals. The reliability of the data is therefore open to considerable question, but in some locations (luckily including the Fenland for some variable features) Hallam was sent to check the validity of the local data collectors' work and investigate some features more thoroughly.

Secondly we have the data from the Fenland localities set out in the Basic Materials of the Survey of English Dialects [SED] (Orton and Tilling 1969), a traditional dialectological survey of 311 largely rural localities, two of which, Outwell in Norfolk and Warboys in Cambridgeshire, are in the central Fenland. The SED data from these sites can be compared with localities surveyed to the east of the Fens, such as Little Downham in Cambridgeshire, and to the west, such as Crowland in Lincolnshire.

Finally we have 3 corpora of contemporary recordings. Between 1987 and 1990, I collected a corpus of recordings of 81 working class Fenlanders of two broad age groups: old (45–66) and young (16–30) (Britain 1991). Most recordings consist of 60 to 90 minutes of informal conversation with second-order network links across the Fens,

Figure 15.2 Principal Fenland urban centres and other locations mentioned in the text.

from Spalding and Warboys in the west to West Winch and Soham in the east (see Figure 15.2). In addition to my own data, I was fortunate enough to find two corpora which I could analyse in the same way as my own recordings. The King's Lynn corpus, housed in that town's local library, was recorded as part of a Manpower Services Commission Local History Project carried out in the mid-1980s. All of the 10 speakers were over 55 years old and most in their 70s. The Chatteris corpus in the town's museum is a collection of 11 individual recordings made over a number of years between 1974 and 1985 by the curator. Ten of these recordings are of working class residents of Chatteris. Most were at least 70 years old. The other recording was of a former Olympic ice-skater, also in his 70s, from Outwell, near Wisbech (see Figure 15.2).

4. 'FENLAND RAISING' OF /ai/

In most instances, /ai/ derives from Middle English ī. Its historical development is linked to a large-scale set of phonological changes commonly known as the Great Vowel Shift (GVS). The GVS is believed to have begun sometime in the 15th century (Wells

1982: 184) and possibly completed in the south-east of England by around 1600 (1982: 185), although in some parts of the UK, such as the north-east, the GVS has not completed to this day. As part of the GVS, ME ī and ū became diphthongs and subsequently the onsets of these diphthongised forms became gradually more open and central before reaching the more advanced contemporary forms (Lass 1987, Wells 1982).

In the central Fens, speakers of all age groups consistently retain an allophonic distinction similar to Canadian Raising: centralised [əi] onsets before voiceless consonants, and open onsets, [ɑi], or even open monophthongs, [ɑ:], before voiced consonants, /ə/ and morpheme boundaries. In varieties spoken to the west of the Fens we find open onsets in all environments, whereas to the east centralised onsets are found in most environments. Figures 15.3, 15.4 and 15.5 show the realisations of /ai/ according to following segment found in the speech of three speakers from my corpus: typical central (Emneth: see Figure 15.2), eastern (Wayhead) and western (Peterborough) speakers respectively.[2] Bearing in mind the demographic history of the Fens, and the phonological naturalness of such allophony, I have argued (Britain 1997) that the 'Fenland Raising' demonstrated here by the Emneth speaker, but typical throughout the central Fens, is a dialect contact phenomenon, a reallocation of western open onsets and eastern raised onsets to different phonological environments.

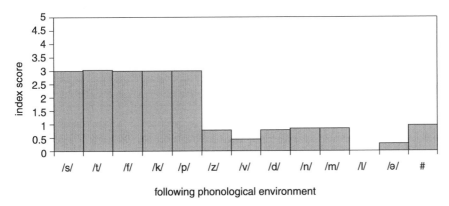

Figure 15.3   Onsets of /ai/ used by a speaker from Emneth in the central Fens.

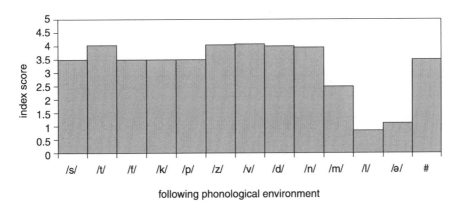

Figure 15.4   Onsets of /ai/ used by a speaker from Wayhead in the eastern Fens.

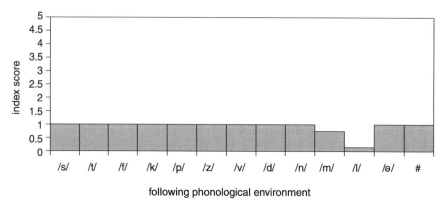

Figure 15.5   Onsets of /ai/ used by a speaker from Peterborough in the western Fens.

We have good evidence to suggest that 'Fenland Raising' has been present in the central Fens for almost 200 years. In Ellis (1889) there is little evidence to enable us to judge the progress of /ai/ which was not one of the sounds Ellis was particularly interested in. There is no reliable data from the central Fenland town of Wisbech, for example.

However, an allophonic split is found in the central Fenland community of Wryde near Thorney, where Hallam reports [nəit] but [tɑim] (Ellis 1889: 254).

In the Survey of English Dialects data, the central Fenland locations of Warboys (informants born between 1883 and 1889) and Outwell (born between 1874 and 1889) show the allophonic distinction, with [ʌɣ – ʌi] in 'night' and 'ice', and [ɑi – ɒi] in 'time' and 'sky'. Locations to the east and west do not show such an allophonic distinction.

The Chatteris Museum data from the Chatteris men and the Outwell ice-skater, born in the early years of the 20th century, also shows very clear allophony. Compare their realisations in Figure 15.6, with those found in the eastern Fenland King's Lynn corpus, where the use of centralised forms is not limited simply to before voiceless consonants.

My own data from the central Fens shows very little age grading, with /ai/ allophony present in the speech of young and old alike. Figure 15.7 shows the index scores for four speakers. Harry, the oldest, was born in 1922, Wayne, the youngest, in 1972.

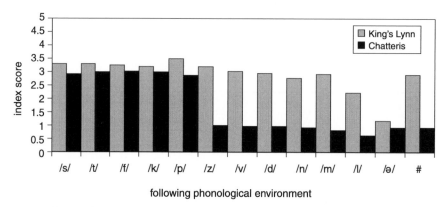

Figure 15.6   Onsets of /ai/ used in the King's Lynn and Chatteris corpora.

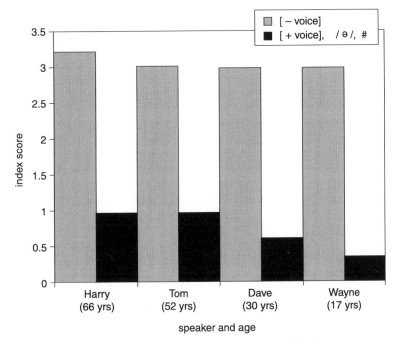

Figure 15.7   Onsets of /ai/ used by four central Fenland speakers from Wisbech.

The apparent time data clearly show that there has been little change in the status of Fenland Raising between the oldest and youngest generations. If anything, the distinction has become greater as monophthongal forms become more prevalent before voiced consonants, /ə/ and morpheme boundaries.

5. INTERDIALECTAL [ɣ] FORMS OF /ʌ/

The origins of present-day /ʌ/ in Southern British English are complex. The largest source of this lexical set is Middle English ŭ occurring in words such as 'butcher', 'cushion', 'luck' and 'up'. Around London in the 16th century, certain but not all of the words in this class underwent unrounding and lowering (and more recently fronting) from [ʊ] to [ʌ] (and in some varieties, such as Cockney, [a]). In addition, a few /ʌ/ class words have their origins in ME ō such as 'blood' and 'flood', and others ('among', ME ang/ong, for example) have alternative sources. Furthermore, a number of borrowings have joined the /ʌ/ class: bungalow, yuppie (see Britain, in preparation).

The changes which led to the development of /ʌ/ from ME ŭ and ō were resisted in vernacular varieties of Northern England which retain [ʊ] in ME ŭ and have either [ʊ] or [u:] in the ME ō set and [ɒ] or [ʊ] in 'among', for example. Borrowings with [ʌ] in southern varieties typically have [ʊ] in the north, hence [bʊŋgələʊ] and [jʊpi:]. The dialect transition between the northern /ʊ/ area and the southern area with both /ʊ/ and /ʌ/ straddles the Fens (see, for example, Chambers and Trudgill 1980:128).

The contact between northern and southern forms which arose following re-clamation could potentially have had a number of linguistic outcomes. One possibility would be a lexically determined reallocation of northern and southern forms in the new intermediate dialect. This is what appears to have developed in the case of the /a – aː/ transition in words such as 'plant' and 'after' discussed earlier in this article. Alternatively, since the change to /ʌ/ is an innovation, we could perhaps have expected the southern, possibly more prestigious form to 'win' the dialect conflict and lead to the further gradual diffusion of /ʌ/ north- and westwards. Neither of these possibilities appears to have materialised. Instead, the data suggests that a phonetically intermediate form between [ʌ] and [ʊ], namely [ɤ], has emerged as the norm in the central Fenland.

Unlike in the case of /ai/, however, the evidence suggests that this interdialectal form in the central Fenland has only very recently focused from a broad and diffuse range of variants [ʊ – ʏ – ɤ – ɐ – ʌ – ɐ] used by speakers across the speech community. Furthermore, the interdialectal form has only focused among the young living in and around the central Fenland town of Wisbech, and not in other central Fenland locations, which remain largely diffuse.[3] Our real time data sources demonstrate the long term diffuseness of the realisations of /ʌ/, as well as the more recent interdialect focusing.

Ellis considers the /ʊ – ʌ/ split to be one of the more important dialect distinctions in his research (1889:15–17) and his data provides evidence of thorough and detailed analysis of realisations in towns and villages along the isogloss. We therefore have quantitatively *more*, and, because of the checking and rechecking of data sources by his main fieldworker Hallam, *better* information about this variable than any other in the area under investigation. He notes that the town of Wisbech is mixed with interdialectal forms [ʊ – ɤ – ʌ – ɜ] used by young and old: he cites forms from a 13 year old boy and a 39 year old man as well as older residents of the town. Other central Fenland locations that he labels 'mixed' or 'transitional' include: north Cambridgeshire (1889:249), March (252) and Chatteris (253).

Despite the impression one might gain from looking at some published maps derived from its data, the Survey of English Dialects (Orton and Tilling 1969) also provides evidence both of the existence of interdialectal forms, and the unfocused nature of those interdialectal realisations. Whereas the 'northern'-type SED locations of Crowland and Lutton have [ʊ] in words such as 'money', 'thunder' and 'guzzle', realisations such as [ɤ – ʌ] are cited for the central location of Outwell and [ʊ – ʏ – ɐ – ʌ] for the central eastern village of Little Downham. Chambers and Trudgill (1980) reanalyse the SED data, and demonstrate the transitional nature of this dialect 'boundary'. They categorise different lects in the Fens (and other parts of Eastern England and the Midlands) as having either 'fudged' forms (phonetically intermediate) or 'mixed' forms (the variable use of both the ingredient forms).

The data from the Chatteris and King's Lynn archives further illustrate the un-focused nature of the interdialect form. The results of the analysis of these corpora are in Figures 15.8, 15.9 and 15.10.

Finally, my own data corpus, collected in the late 1980s, demonstrates the gradual focusing of the central intermediate variant [ɤ] in and around Wisbech. Figure 15.11 shows the relationship between age and variant use for the four speakers whose consistent use of 'Fenland Raising' we saw earlier. It is only among the younger two speakers, particularly Wayne, that the [ɤ] form has focused. Older speakers and those outside Wisbech and its suburbs remain diffuse. Figure 15.12, for example, shows the variant scores of four speakers from other parts of the central Fenland.

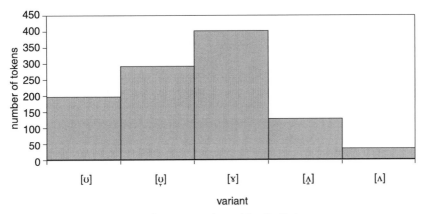

Figure 15.8   Realisations of /ʌ/ in the Chatteris speakers of the Chatteris corpus.

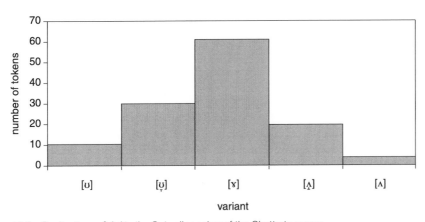

Figure 15.9   Realisations of /ʌ/ in the Outwell speaker of the Chatteris corpus.

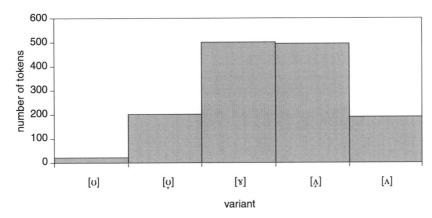

Figure 15.10   Realisations of /ʌ/ in the King's Lynn corpus.

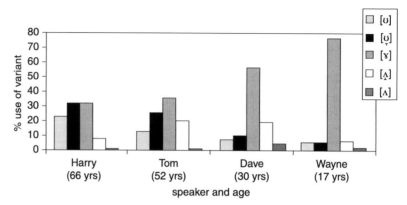

Figure 15.11   The use of /ʌ/ by four central Fenland speakers from Wisbech.

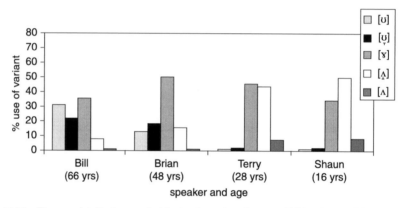

Figure 15.12   The use of /ʌ/ by four central Fenland speakers from non-Wisbech central Fenland locations.

6. NEW DIALECT ACQUISITION: EXPLAINING VARIABLE RATES OF FOCUSING

The question which the remainder of this article attempts to address is why certain forms (in this case 'Fenland Raising') focus more quickly during the koineisation process than others (interdialectal [ɤ], for instance). In trying to answer the question, we can draw on both social-psychological and linguistic explanations (Trudgill 1986, Chambers 1992, Kerswill 1996). Firstly we can look to the salience of the forms. Fenland Raising is a 'marker' (Labov 1972), with speakers across the Fens showing great awareness of regional and social variation of /ai/. It was regularly mentioned as locally significant – many informants in my own sample claimed to be able to spot Wisbech speakers by their use of /ai/ (but weren't able to accurately pinpoint what it was about /ai/ that distinguished Wisbech from elsewhere) (see Britain 1997). /ʌ/, on the other hand was a very unsalient sound altogether. Nobody in my survey mentioned it as being a feature which showed regional variation, despite the huge phonetic difference in the range of variants used in the Fens. Trudgill (1986: 51) has noted a lack of saliency of this feature more generally in East Anglia, and Ellis made a similar discovery over a century before. [. . .] It is possible, therefore, that the salience of Fenland Raising supports and is itself enhanced by its use as a local identity marker in the central Fens, distinguishing the area from both east and west. /ʌ/, on the other hand, lacks salience and is not used in this way. However, the evidence of focusing of an interdialectal form among youngsters in Wisbech for whom /ʌ/ is still unsalient suggests we need to look elsewhere for a full explanation.

In addition to social reasons, linguists have also sought linguistic explanations for variable rates of dialect acquisition (Payne 1975, 1980, Trudgill 1986, Chambers 1992, Kerswill 1996). Payne's (1975, 1980) pioneering research on the acquisition of Philadelphia English by in-migrants found, for example, that while the in-migrants rather successfully acquired the fronting of the onsets of /u:/ and /ʌʊ/ and the raising of the onset of /ɔi/, none accurately acquired the tensing and raising of /æ/. In a synthesis and extension of the work on second dialect acquisition, Chambers (1992: 682–687) accounts for this finding in terms of rule complexity. He claims that in second dialect acquisition scenarios, simple phonological rules progress faster than more complex ones.

In Philadelphia, Payne's results demonstrate that the successfully acquired forms were all relatively straightforward, categorical phonetic changes, whereas the rule governing the tensing and raising of short /æ/ is extremely complex (Payne 1975, Chambers 1992, Labov 1989). Chambers provides further examples from his own research of Canadian children acquiring the southern British English of Oxfordshire. He finds that while they are relatively successful at devoicing /t/—a simple rule—they are much less successful at acquiring 'vowel backing', i.e., the /a – ɑ:/ split of southern England.

I would like to claim that we can look to the same sociolinguistic principle, that simple rules progress faster than complex ones, to explain why Fenland Raising focused more quickly in the Fens than interdialectal [ʁ]. First we must justify our application of the principles of second dialect acquisition suggested on the basis of speakers' relatively short-term contact with the target variety, to new dialect focusing where the contact is ultimately much longer term. Both second dialect acquisition and new dialect focusing, of course, involve dialect contact. However, in the case of the latter the focusing is being conducted not only by adults, but also by children acquiring their first variety. Roberts and Labov (1995) report that children native to Philadelphia are mostly successful in acquiring the very complex, lexically diffused /æ/ tensing/raising rule. There are, however, some important factors in new dialect formation, particularly of the sort witnessed in the Fens, which make the koineisation process in such conditions rather more complex than in the acquisition of varieties where a clear target dialect is predominant.

Robert Le Page, in whose work with Andrée Tabouret-Keller the notions of 'focused' and 'diffuse' in their sociolinguistic sense originate (Le Page 1978, Le Page and Tabouret-Keller 1985), claims that our choice of socio-linguistic variants represents an act of identity. The individual, he maintains, 'creates for himself the patterns of his linguistic behaviour so as to resemble those of the group or groups with which from time to time he wishes to be identified' (Le Page and Tabouret-Keller 1985: 181). Our ability to do so is constrained by the extent to which we can identify those groups, have adequate access to them and the ability to analyse their linguistic behaviour, have sufficient motivation to join those groups, gain feedback from them, and have the ability to modify our behaviour to become more like that of the target group.

Initially, in a new dialect scenario such as that in the Fens, or in other such settings where there was no (or only a very small) native population speaking the same language, these target groups to which one may focus either do not exist, because new groups have yet to form in the new speech community, or are absent, because the in-migrant groups left them behind, usually permanently, in their original speech communities. Such new dialect communities must therefore create the groups and develop afresh the stronger network ties (L. Milroy 1980, J. Milroy 1992) which can act as focal points. I have discussed elsewhere (Britain 1997) some of the potential motivations for joining such groups. The ability of the koineising dialect speakers to analyse the linguistic behaviour of their peers must be constrained by the wide mixture of varieties under contact, and feedback from other speakers, although accommodatory, is likely to be linguistically distinct and diffuse. Children in such scenarios are in a position of having to focus a new norm from a diffuse target variety spoken in a speech community only beginning to develop new social groupings, identities and distinctions. The fact that this process in the sparsely populated Fens began well before education was universal (no school environment, therefore, to encourage the development of wider peer group norms) further impedes focused koine development. In such an environment, principles of second dialect acquisition and those of new dialect formation seem comparable, notwithstanding the time differences involved.

Fenland Raising, as we saw earlier, and despite the inhibiting factors outlined above, focused quite quickly in the Fens. If, as our evidence suggests, it was present in the area around 1800, then it must have focused towards the time at which most of the major reclamation work was nearing completion. It is, moreover, a *relatively* simple rule, the allocation of raised onsets to a position of phonetic naturalness before voiceless consonants in the same syllable, and open onsets to positions before voiced consonants, morpheme boundaries and schwa.

Interdialectal [ɤ], on the other hand, is only now being focused by the youngest speakers in one urban centre of the central Fens. The reasons for this are, I suggest, at least in part due to a number of linguistic factors which combine to make the focusing of one variant extremely complex:

- The complexity of the /ʊ – ʌ/ split: there is little phonological conditioning of this split, and even where there are tendencies, there are always exceptions. For example:

  - Many of the /ʊ/ class words have preceding bilabials/labiodentals (e.g. bush, full, put, woman, pudding, bosom), yet there are many exceptions (buck, fund, pump, won, punch, bucket).
  - Many of the /ʊ/ class are followed by /ʃ/ or /l/ (e.g. bush, push, wool, full), but again there are exceptions (rush, gush, lush, dull, gull, hull).
  - If the vowel precedes /g/ or /dʒ/, it is usually /ʌ/ (e.g. mug, bug, rug, budge, fudge, sludge); the principal exception is 'sugar'.

- The proximity of the area with no /ʌ/: the north-west of the Fens is linguistically 'northern' in English terms, having /ʊ/ in both 'pus' and 'puss', for example. Because this is a rural area, school catchment and travel-to-work areas are large and it is possible for some speakers from areas with southern variants to go to school or work in places with no /ʌ/ and vice versa. Any movement beyond the locality will involve contact with speakers with different proportions of the different variants.

- The presence of variants of /ʌ/ – which overlap with those of the /ʊ/ class: even those speakers who have /ʌ/ (in some phonemic sense, though not necessarily matching RP or other more southern varieties of English English) may well in some situations have variants of /ʌ/ realised as [ʊ], while on other occasions having [ʌ] or [ɤ] or some other variant *in the same word*.
- The wide phonetic range of variants present in the community: as mentioned previously, variants noted in my data range from [ʊ] to [ɐ].
- The presence of ongoing change in /ʌ/ in neighbouring regions: /ʌ/ continues to open and front in southern British English – Cockney has reached [a]. Speakers are therefore exposed to variants which continue to phonetically diverge.
- The lack of phonological or lexical conditioning of variant choice: initial analyses suggest that there is little or no significant phonological or lexical conditioning of the variants in the /ʌ/ class in this speech community.

Together, these have severely inhibited the focusing of one particular variant, the intermediate [ɤ], such that it is only recently that one has emerged. Why it has emerged now is puzzling. One possibility is that it is linked to a change underway in southern British English which is unrounding and beginning to lower the vowel in /ʊ/ class words. However, Laver (1995), in a small pilot study, found that this change was being led by a considerable margin by middle class girls in the sample of secondary school children he studied, whereas my Fenland sample comprises only working class speakers. [. . .]

7. CONCLUSION

We have been able to track koineisation-in-progress in the Fens, despite the fact that the original contact began over 300 years ago. Some linguistic norms of the new variety crystallised quite quickly. We have seen evidence, for example, of Fenland Raising in even our very early dialectological sources. Other features such as interdialectal [ɤ] are only now showing evidence that a focused norm has evolved.

[. . .]

More detailed investigations of a range of different speech communities in the *process* of focusing new linguistic norms at all levels are clearly required if we are to *explain* the outcomes of contact and koineisation. A more fruitful and extensive dialogue with other areas of language contact research (e.g., pidginisation and language death) will doubtless move this endeavour forward. The constraints on the phonological focusing of Fenland English provide one small clue as to the direction in which we must look.

NOTES

1. More recent changes, however, have come largely from the south, from London, including /l/ vocalisation, labio-dental approximant [ʋ] forms of /r/, and the merger of /f/ and /θ/, and non-initial /ð/ and /v/.
2. Index scores: 0 = [ɑː], 1 = [ɑi], 2 = [ʌi], 3 = [əi], 4 = [ɤi], 5 = [ɒi].
3. The search for phonological and lexical constraints on variant choice is still underway [. . .] but so far no significant tendencies have been found.

REFERENCES

Bernard, J. R. (1969) On the uniformity of spoken Australian English. *Orbis* 18: 63–73.

Bhatia, T. (1988) Trinidad Hindi: its genesis and general profile. In R. K. Barz and J. Siegel (eds) (1988) *Language Transplanted: The Development of Overseas Hindi*. Wiesbaden: Otto Harrassowitz, 179–196.

Blanc, H. (1968) The Israeli koine as an emergent national standard. In J. Fishman, J. Das Gupta and C. Ferguson (eds) *Language Problems in Developing Nations*. New York: Wiley, 237–251.

Britain, D. (1991) Dialect and space: a geolinguistic study of speech variables in the Fens. PhD. dissertation. University of Essex, Colchester.

Britain, D (1997) Dialect contact and phonological reallocation: 'Canadian Raising' in the English Fens. *Language in Society* 26: 15–46.

Chambers, J. K. (1992) Dialect acquisition. *Language* 68: 673–705.

Chambers, J. K. and P. J. Trudgill (1980) *Dialectology*. Cambridge: Cambridge University Press.

Darby, H. (1974) *The Medieval Fenland*. Newton Abbott: David and Charles.

Dillard, J. (1975) General introduction: Perspectives on Black English. In J. Dillard (ed.) *Perspectives on Black English*, 9–32.

Domingue, N. (1971) Bhojpuri and Creole in Mauritius. PhD Dissertation. University of Texas, Austin.

Ellis, A. (1889) *On Early English Pronunciation: Part V*. London: Truebner and Co.

Gordon, E. (1983) New Zealand English pronunciation: an investigation into some early written records. *Te Reo* 26: 29–42.

Kerswill, P. (1994a) Babel in Buckinghamshire? Pre-school children acquiring accent features in the New Town of Milton Keynes. In G. Melchers and N-L. Johannesson (eds) *Non-Standard Varieties of Language*. Stockholm: Almqvist & Wiksell, 64–83.

Kerswill, P. (1994b) *Dialects Converging: Rural Speech in Urban Norway*. Oxford: Clarendon Press.

Kerswill, P. (1996) Children, adolescents and language change. *Language Variation and Change* 8: 177–202.

Kerswill, P. and A. Williams (1992) Some principles of dialect contact: evidence from the New Town of Milton Keynes. In I. Philippaki-Warburton and R. Ingham (eds) *Working Papers 1992*. Reading: Department of Linguistic Science, University of Reading, 68–90.

Labov, William (1972) *Sociolinguistic Patterns*. Philadelphia: The University of Pennsylvania Press.

Labov, W. (1989) Exact description of the speech community: short *a* in Philadelphia. In R. Fasold and D. Schiffrin (eds) *Language Change and Variation*. Amsterdam: John Benjamins, 1–57.

Lass, R. (1987) *The Shape of English: Structure and History*. London: Dent.

Laver, M. (1995) A study into the use of the variable (ʊ) among pupils from different schools in Hampshire and Suffolk. Unpublished research project, University of Essex, Colchester.

Le Page, R. B. (1978) Projection, focusing, diffusion. *Society for Caribbean Linguistics Occasional Papers* 9: 9–32.

Le Page, R. B. and A. Tabouret-Keller (1985) *Acts of Identity: Creole-Based Approaches to Language and Ethnicity*. Cambridge: Cambridge University Press.

Mesthrie, R. (1991) *Language in Indenture: A Sociolinguistic History of Bhojpuri-Hindi in South Africa*. London: Routledge.

Miller, S. H. and S. B. J. Skertchly (1878) *The Fenland: Past and Present*. Wisbech.

Milroy, J. (1992) *Linguistic Variation and Change*. Oxford: Blackwell.

Milroy, L. (1980) *Language and Social Networks*. Oxford: Blackwell.

Mohan, P. (1978) Trinidad Bhojpuri: a morphological study. PhD dissertation. University of Michigan.

Orton, H. and P. M. Tilling (1969) *Survey of English Dialects: Volume 3: East Midlands and East Anglia*. Leeds: Edward Arnold.

Payne, A. (1975) The reorganisation of linguistic rules: a preliminary report. *Pennsylvania Working Papers on Linguistic Change and Variation* 1: 1–35.

Payne, A. (1980) Factors controlling the acquisition of the Philadelphia dialect by out-of-state children. In W. Labov (ed.) *Locating Language in Time and Space*. New York: Academic Press, 143–178.

Read, A. (1933) British recognition of American speech in the 18th century. *Dialect Notes* 6: 313–334.

Roberts, J. and W. Labov (1995) Learning to talk Philadelphian: acquisition of short *a* by pre-school children. *Language Variation and Change* 7: 101–112.

Scholtmeijer, H. (1990) De uitspraak van het Nederlands in de IJsselmeerpolders. *Leuvense Bijdragen* 79: 385–425.

Scholtmeijer, H. (1992) *Het Nederlands van de IJsselmeerpolders*. Kampen: Mondiss.

Siegel, J. (1987) *Language Contact in a Plantation Environment: A Sociolinguistic History of Fiji*. Cambridge: Cambridge University Press.

Simpson, S. (forthcoming) Dialect contact in Telford new town. Unpublished research project. University of Essex, Colchester.

Trudgill, P. J. (1974) *The Social Differentiation of English in Norwich*. Cambridge: Cambridge University Press.

Trudgill, P. J. (1986) *Dialects in Contact*. Oxford: Basil Blackwell.

Trudgill, P. J. (1985) New dialect formation and the analysis of colonial dialects: the case of Canadian Raising. In H. J. Warkentyne (ed.) *Papers from the 5th International Conference on Methods in Dialectology*. Victoria: University of Victoria, 34–45.

Trudgill, P. J. (1995) Grammaticalization and social structure: nonstandard conjunction-formation in East Anglian English. In F. Palmer, (ed.) *Grammar and Semantics*. Cambridge: Cambridge University Press, 135–147.

Wells, J. C. (1982) *Accents of English 1: An Introduction*. Cambridge: Cambridge University Press.

QUESTIONS

1. What is koineisation and what is its outcome?
2. How have demographic changes influenced language in the Fens?
3. What does Britain conclude for Fenland raising and for interdialectal [ɣ] forms of /ʌ/?
4. Why do certain forms (in this case 'Fenland Raising') focus more quickly during the koineisation process than others (interdialectal [ɣ], for instance)?

Content

Why might the [ɣ] variant have emerged and what group may lead this change in the future?

Concept

Chapter 16

Monica Heller

LEGITIMATE LANGUAGE IN A MULTILINGUAL SCHOOL

INTRODUCTION

[. . .]

Ever since the Canadian federal government symbolically invested in French-English bilingualism as a counterbalance to Quebec francophone nationalism, aspiring politicians must be considered bilingual in order to have any legitimacy as leaders on the national stage. But while some people, like Pierre Trudeau or Brian Mulroney, had to be so bilingual as to constitute walking matched-guise tests, others, like Mulroney's short-lived successor, Kim Campbell, only had to have a passable knowledge of French in order to be taken seriously (Campbell's rise and fall may have been meteoric, but it wasn't her French that was her downfall). The reason for this is that Trudeau and Mulroney are from Quebec, the source of the menace to the federal government, whereas Campbell is from British Columbia, far from the fray.

In Canadian political life, and in most other aspects of our life as well, there are complex sets of expectations regarding bilingual proficiency, which depend greatly on your position in Canadian society and which have an impact on the extent to which people are prepared to listen to you and to believe what you say. We use these judgments constantly in daily life, and it is no surprise that the legitimacy of a candidate's quest for power should repose, at least in part, on his or her ability to manipulate the codes of authority, that is, French and English, in ways that are consonant with other aspects of who that candidate is. Who we are constrains to whom we can speak, under what circumstances, and, most important for my purposes here, *how*.

This, of course, is the essence of Bourdieu's concept of "legitimate language," which he formulates thus:

Source: Heller, Monica (2001) Legitimate language in a multilingual school. In Monica Heller and Marilyn Martin-Jones (eds) *Voices of Authority: Education and Linguistic Difference.* Westport: Ablex, 381–402.

[W]e can state the characteristics which legitimate discourse must fulfill, the tacit presuppositions of its efficacy: it is uttered by a legitimate speaker, i.e. by the appropriate person, as opposed to the impostor (religious language/priest, poetry/poet, etc.); it is uttered in a legitimate situation, i.e. on the appropriate market (as opposed to insane discourse, e.g. a surrealist poem read in the Stock Exchange) and addressed to legitimate receivers; it is formulated in the legitimate phonological and syntactic forms (what linguists call grammaticalness), except when transgressing these norms is part of the legitimate definition of the legitimate producer (Bourdieu 1977, 650)

The key elements of legitimate language (or discourse) from Bourdieu's perspective include being a legitimate speaker, addressing legitimate interlocutors, under specific social conditions, in language that respects specific conventions of form. While 'Bourdieu's notion of form seems restricted to things like phonology and syntax, I want to enlarge it here to include language *choice*. I also want to consider how examining language *use*, that is, the deployment of language forms in social interaction, reveals the relationship among the different dimensions of legitimate language.

My purpose here is to use this concept of legitimate language to examine some important aspects of the role of language in bilingual (or multilingual) educational contexts. First, I want to explore how specific kinds of language practices are legitimized (and for whom and under what circumstances). Second, I want to take a look at how legitimizing those practices helps advance or marginalize the interests of different groups in such contexts, groups that are distinguished from each other in terms of their actual linguistic repertoires and in terms of the linguistic repertoires people think they should have. Finally, I want to examine what this tells us about the development of relations of power among such groups through the process of bilingual or multilingual education.

In other words, I want to argue that certain language practices and language forms are considered legitimate in educational settings while others are not. Generally, these "others" are not utterly suppressed (although I suppose they may be) but instead form an object of more-or-less painful, more-or-less serious struggle. Our job is to understand why some language is legitimate and some is not, and what that means for the participants in the setting. Of course, much of this problem the way I have stated it holds for any kind of linguistically variable setting; my interest here, however, is limited to the kinds of bilingualism and multilingualism that increasingly characterize educational settings in Europe and North America.

I have become interested in this issue over many years of watching the ways in which the manipulation of French and English is used in Canada to advance the interests of francophones and anglophones occupying a variety of social positions. I have become concerned with the ways these processes unfold in education, an institutional context of great political and social significance especially for francophones, who have invested in it nothing less than the mission of preserving French language and culture in a society dominated by English-speakers.

In order to explore these issues here I will draw on my experience in French-language minority education in Ontario, Canada's largest province and one in which English, although by no means the only language spoken, is still clearly the dominant one. The context in which I work does not correspond to most orthodox definitions of "bilingual education," in that it is actually *monolingual* education, but a monolingual education that takes place in a bilingual and frequently multilingual context and that in fact aims at achieving individual bilingualism through institutional monolingualism (cf. Heller 1994a).

My discussion is based on the ethnographic work in a French-language high school in the Toronto area and will focus on data collected from the fall of 1991 to the spring of 1993. Here I will call the school École secondaire Samuel de Champlain, or simply Champlain. (Samuel de Champlain was one of the major figures in the seventeenth-century French colonization of North America.) However, before turning to an examination of the legitimization and contestation of language practices at Champlain, I will first briefly describe the nature of Franco-Ontarian education and provide some background regarding this particular school.

FRANCO-ONTARIAN SCHOOLS AND CULTURAL DIVERSITY

[. . .] Francophones have fought long and hard for the right to have schools in which French is the language of instruction. [. . .] The rate of assimilation of francophones outside Quebec, especially since World War II, has remained fairly high. [. . .]

The Franco-Ontarian school system is principally designed to maintain the French language and culture in Ontario, to resist the crushing domination of English. But the nature of francophone militancy since the 1960s has raised some paradoxes regarding this mission. First, the principal purpose of political mobilization has been to facilitate francophone access, as francophones, to mainstream provincial, national, and international political and economic processes. Of course, these processes unfold mainly in English. Thus francophone resistance to English has nothing to do with rejecting it, with building an alternative francophone world, but instead is about creating a francophone space from which to more easily enter the anglophone world [i.e. enable francophones to speak English and take part in Ontarian, mostly anglophone, society]. This has worked best for middle-class francophones who are now in their forties and fifties, who participated in the early struggles of the 1960s and 1970s, and many of whom now occupy jobs made necessary by successful mobilization, for example, teaching or other professional or paraprofessional positions in newly created French-language educational institutions; civil service positions in governments that have accepted, since Trudeau in the 1960s, the ideology of bilingualism and of francophone minority rights; or administrative positions in francophone lobbying or cultural organizations (cf. Welch 1988; Frenette and Gauthier 1990).

Most of the teachers and many of the parents at Champlain have lived these experiences, occupy these positions, and see the world in this way. For them, the resolution of the paradox lies in the principle that francophones can only successfully enter the modern world as equals if they can fall back on institutions that are monolingual and belong to them. They focus on the struggle of francophones, seen as a unified group with a common history, turned outward against but simultaneously in collaboration with the anglophone majority, seen also as a unified and undifferentiated group.

Some students in the school also take this position, mainly those who grew up in Quebec (this is especially strong since many of these students are in Ontario, as it were, against their will, dragged there because of a parent's employment or search for employment or by family break-ups and other traumas). But many students in the school live a different reality, one in which English is part of their everyday world. French-language schools attract assimilated francophones and middle-class anglophones no less interested in the valuable resource of bilingualism than are middle-class francophones; there are therefore students in those schools whose English is much better than their French. As immigration to Canada, particularly to Toronto, has increased over the past 10 or 15 years, many others have come from places where French is a majority language or a prestigious second language (Poles, Iranians, Vietnamese, Somalis, etc.); they are not used to having to struggle against the stigmatization of French (indeed, many look down on the "inferior" variety of French that they are surprised to encounter in Canada). Many of these students are coping with the realities of having immigrated to what is, in the end, an English-dominated city; they are much less worried about losing their French than they are about learning English. Finally, the very success of francophone mobilization has transformed and widened the gulf between the new professional and public sector elite and the working class. This diversity raises the second paradox, which pits real heterogeneity and inequality against the imagined uniformity that supposedly underlies francophone solidarity and legitimates the existence of French-language minority schools.

Most Franco-Ontarian schools have no choice but to accept such a wide range of students; in some cases, there are legal rights to access, and in many cases there is a strong feeling of moral obligation, but in any case the schools need the numbers. Thus schools that legitimate their separate existence on the grounds of a uniform and distinct cultural reality and set of needs and on the grounds that only autonomous institutions can provide egalitarian access to social mobility, in fact serve an increasingly diversified and stratified clientele.

LANGUAGE PRACTICES AT L'ÉCOLE CHAMPLAIN

With these issues in mind, two years ago I undertook an ethnographic study of l'École Champlain. It is a small school, with about 400 students from grade 7 through to the end of high school (roughly ages 12 to 18). In 1992–1993, the major groups of students (accounting for about half the school population) included French Canadians (mainly from Quebec, Ontario, and New Brunswick), Toronto-born children of mixed marriages or anglophone background, and (mainly ethnic Somali) students from Somalia, Ethiopia, and Djibouti (most of whom had arrived within the previous three years). There were also significant numbers of francophone Europeans, Iranians, Lebanese, and Haitians, as well as many other groups. Some of these students had been in the Franco-Ontarian school system since elementary school (indeed, some had known each other since kindergarten); some went to immersion schools; many others were schooled elsewhere before moving to Toronto. The class backgrounds of the students were quite varied, although many of the francophones with long roots in Canada (Franco-Ontarians, Québecois, and Acadiens) were of working-class background, and most of the English-dominant students were middle class. My sense is that many of the Somali students were members of their country's elite. The school structure, consistent with that of the rest of the Ontario system, is stratified by what are known as "levels of difficulty"; in other words, the system is streamed. The levels that are important for my purpose here are the university-preparatory "advanced" level, and the vocational training-oriented "general" level. Most of the working-class French-Canadians and most of the Somalis and Haitians found themselves in the lower levels at the time to which I refer here.

In the course of this study, I have been asking two questions, both focusing on the role of language in the processes central to the school's mandate and legitimacy. The first has to do with the link between the forms of language valued at school, the linguistic repertoires of the students, and the verbal performances that are evaluated as part of the process of achieving school success. The second has to do with the role of language in the construction of cultural identity, in the context of the school's investment in *la francitude*. In other words, I am interested in the ways in which what the students can offer as verbal performance in the classroom is evaluated in academic as well as in cultural terms by the representatives of school authority. I am also interested in the ways in which the students themselves construct their cultural identity on the basis of their experiences at school and elsewhere. The questions are linked because they both speak to a central concern of minority education, the question of *whom* that education is for. Who has a right to be in this school? Whose needs are to be considered paramount? Whose interests are to be served?

In order to examine how these questions are linked in practice, I will use the lens of the concept of legitimate language to explore two specific aspects of communicative processes at Champlain: language choice and turn-taking in the classroom. Language choice is primarily a question of form, of the *how* of speaking (as opposed to the "who" or the "under what circumstances"). Turn-taking is a question both of "how" and of "who," a question of legitimate users of the legitimate forms using those forms as they should. Turn-taking is one of the aspects of language use that show how different dimensions of legitimate language interact. Both turn-taking and language choice are central to the norms that allow us to understand the ideological content of life at school and that we can use to explore to whom they apply and under what conditions.

[. . .]

LANGUAGE CHOICE

At Champlain, as at any other Franco-Ontarian school, language choice is a highly charged domain. Obviously, the use of French is considered extremely important, both by representatives of school authority and by many parents. At the same time, it is generally held to be true that many students actually prefer to speak English. Indeed, this belief has held in every Franco-Ontarian school in which I have ever set foot and is reflected in official discourse in any number of ways. One that stands out is the amount of time and money devoted by the Ontario Ministry of Education and many school boards to analyzing the extent to which French is actually spoken in French-language minority schools and to developing strategies to promote the use of French in those schools (Heller 1994b). Underlying all these preoccupations is a concept of bilingualism as a pair of fully developed monolingualisms, as distinct from a unified form of competence drawing from a range of language varieties.

Consequently, at Champlain, as at many other schools, teachers work on the creation of institutional monolingualism as a component of this idea of bilingualism and therefore spend a fair amount of time exhorting or imploring, in shouts and in whispers, "*Parlez français!*" I argued earlier that this use of French in school is an essential element of the school's legitimacy and of the ability of the school's supporters to advance their interests through the school. If students do not speak French at school, there are no grounds to claim a distinct set of resources and a distinctive credential of value in the middle-class symbolic and material marketplaces. Of course, the students' relatively infrequent free choice of French also legitimizes the maintenance of a state of panic; we *must* strengthen our schools if we are not to lose our children—children who, we can demonstrate by a stroll through the corridors, are in severe danger of assimilation.

Students are thus surrounded by manifestations of the school's (and by extension, parents') will that they speak French. The use of French becomes a symbol of the acceptance of school authority. Significantly, English then becomes available as a means of contesting that authority (and only English, as the symbol of the dominant society whose hegemony Franco-Ontarian schools exist to resist). I have seen students calmly answer a teacher's question in English, provoking anger, acquiescing by repeating themselves in French. I have heard them argue that the French-only rule doesn't apply until the bell rings, carving out an autonomous space for themselves in the temporal organization of the school day. Most of the students who consistently use English on the floor of public, institutional discourse in fact end up leaving the school.

Students from outside Canada who speak no English learn the powerful significance of English very quickly. For example, Mohamud, a Somali boy newly arrived in Canada, spent most of his first semester struggling against his placement in the general-level Français course. Every day, he argued against the teacher's choice of pedagogical content, interrupted her, failed to turn in his homework, came to class late, and in other ways displayed his anger and resistance. All of the talk between the teacher, Lise, and Mohamud surrounding this process was in French (and indeed Mohamud was proud of his skills in that language), while discussions between Mohamud and other Somalis in the classroom took place in Somali. However, one day the running disputes between Mohamud and Lise came to a head, and Lise decided she had to send Mohamud to the school office for discipline. Mohamud's last rejoinder to Lise was suddenly in English, as he stormed out of the class, slamming the door behind him.

While in many ways the school tries to suppress the use of English, school staff members also often recognize it as a reality in the lives of many of their students. While this is rarely acted on in advanced-level Français classes, presumably because of the importance of these classes in fulfilling goals related to the prevailing ideology of institutional monolingualism, it may be acted on with varying frequency in general-level Français classes and in other subject areas, where teachers are more often confronted with various kinds of contradictions between values accorded to French and English and have less invested in maintaining classroom monolingualism. When such teachers encounter communication difficulties or when they need to refer to students' outside experience to make a point, they generally assume that they should do so with reference to English. In one advanced-level science class, for instance, the teacher dictated notes on natural fibers, instructing the students where and how to list materials such as wool, silk, cotton, and linen (Extract 1). Students are most likely to have run into these items at home or in stores, buying clothes, and therefore might be expected to be more familiar with the English than the French forms:

Extract 1

à côté de coton et lin on n'a pas du tout (xxx) produit naturel le lin <u>linen</u> *en anglais okay donc ajouter le lin dans votre liste de fibres naturels le lin* <u>linen</u> *en anglais* (next to cotton and linen we have absolutely no (xxx) natural product "*le lin*" <u>linen</u> in English okay so add linen to your list of natural fibres "*le lin*" <u>linen</u> in English)

The discourse surrounding language choice in the classroom thus supposes a fundamental opposition between French and English and also is built on the expectation that those two languages form the totality of the linguistic repertoires of the student body. That reality, as we have seen, has changed, and students speak in fact many other languages. Teachers' tendency to explain things with reference to English can be mystifying to the many new students who speak no English. Lise once engaged a Somali student in the conversation shown in Extract 2.

Extract 2

Student: *qu'est-ce que ça veut dire "indice"?* (what does "*indice*" mean?)
Lise: *indice (pause) mon Dieu comment est-ce qu'on traduit "indice"?* index *en anglais (xxx) une façon une façon de (xxx)* ("*indice*" [pause] my God how do you translate "*indice*" "index" in English [xxx] a way a way to [xxx])

Lise recognized that a translation to English was not going to help, and so found a way to paraphrase.

At the moment, though, only one other language, Somali, is really spoken by sufficient numbers of students to make a difference (although there have occasionally been pockets of Farsi-speakers here and there in the school). The preference for Somali-speakers to use their language among themselves even in the classroom, while at one level rather unsurprising, does create dilemmas for the teachers. Many of them understand that speaking Somali is as important to those students as speaking French is for them, and yet to countenance use of that language while suppressing the use of English by other students seems unjust. Lise faced this problem in her general-level Français class, populated as it was by students of French Canadian origin who preferred to speak English (the forbidden language) and Somalis, who always talked to each other in Somali.

One student remarked on a similar dilemma in the English as a Second Language class, the student population of which was made up of Somalis and newly arrived French Canadians. This student, a francophone from Quebec, asked the teacher why she allowed the Somalis to speak Somali to each other when she continually asked the francophones to stop speaking French. Well, she replied, it's their (the Somalis') mother tongue. The francophone protested that French was *his* mother tongue. Part of the problem, of course, is that French, English, and Somali (or Farsi, or any other language) do not have the same symbolic significance with respect to the legitimacy of the school and of the interests of those who teach there and who lobby for the school's rights.

French is the language of the school, English the loved and hated, respected and feared language of the dominant society (while often also the students' mother tongue). Other languages have no part to play in this script and instead introduce a new dynamic for which Franco-Ontarian education has been largely unprepared, the problem of internal relations of power. Focused intently on internal solidarity, Franco-Ontarian education lacks the means to attend to this question. Because little attention has been devoted to this problem, it has to be dealt with on a case-by-case basis; each teacher has to decide what she or he wants to do about students speaking other languages in the classroom, for instance. The strong province-wide convention symbolized by the eternal cry of "*Parlez français!*" has as its subtext "Don't speak English"; it is in the province's classrooms that people have to work out the relationship between French and languages other than English.

At least as much attention is devoted to the form of French to be used as is devoted to assuring the language's presence in the school. One salient characteristic of Canadian francophone political mobilization has been the development of a Canadian standard French, which establishes a new terrain of legitimate language, distinct both from the old imperialist-imposed standard of European French and the still-stigmatized Canadian French vernaculars. This process does not radically alter the basic notion of what it means to be a francophone in Canada; it accepts the idea that a standard variety is necessary and reinforces the notion that the only good kind of bilingualism is one in which people speak multiple monolingual linguistic varieties. The new standard is as harsh in its judgments of interference from English as was the old one. The major difference lies in who has control of the definition of legitimate form, and here the purpose is clearly to place that control in the hands of the new, educated, and mobilized elite (and more particularly in the hands of professionals of language: language planners and terminologists, translators and teachers). Schools are important sites for the construction of this standard and for its deployment in gatekeeping and credentialing.

In Champlain's classrooms, one sees reflections of these processes. In classes where French is taught as a subject matter, particularly in advanced-level classes, care is taken to teach this standard form. *Anglicismes* are identified as such and corrected, whether in texts or in the stream of speech. In one advanced-level French class, for example, the exchange shown in Extract 3 took place.

Extract 3

Teacher: *pourquoi lit-on?* (why do we read?)
Student: *pour relaxer* (to relax)
Teacher: *pour se détendre, "relaxer" c'est anglais* (to "*se détendre*" [relax], "relaxer" is
English)

In a course on French for business purposes, a section of the textbook (written and published in Quebec) was devoted to *anglicismes*, and the presentation both in the text and in class assumed knowledge both of English and of the "erroneous" forms in question. Teachers also take pains to substitute standard variants for forms that spring from Canadian vernaculars (such as *vue* [movie] instead of *film; à cause que* [because] instead of *parce que*; and so on). (Competing European regional forms, such as the distinctive Swiss and Belgian numeral system, are also corrected, but with greater tolerance.) Even distinctively Canadian pronunciation is muted, internationalized. The effect is to value the verbal displays of students who come from middle- or upper-class well-educated backgrounds, especially those who grew up in areas where French is a majority language. Students in one class consistently explained the success of one of their peers with the comment, "Well, of course, he's from France." It also permits the relative success of students who have learned their French mainly at school and who can produce good academic French, although their skills at using French in social interaction may be weak. Finally, it devalues any number of authentic but regional vernaculars and any form that too strongly betrays the speaker as a second-language learner of French.

[. . .]

I take the examples I have just given as evidence of three sorts of contradictions:

1. contradictions between an emphasis on the development of some form of standard monolingual-variety French as a hallmark of the school and the concrete possibility that one can at least graduate from Champlain without actually mastering that French;

2. contradictions between the construction of a French Canadian identity and the valuing, on the one hand, of European French and the devaluing, on the other, of Canadian French vernaculars; and

3. contradictions between Somali and Haitian students' valuing of European French and inability to speak English, and their placement in general-level classes oriented toward Canadian French vernacular and contact-variety speakers.

At Champlain, legitimate language is French. This is unambiguously true for written work and for public and official discourse. In classroom interaction, French is preferred and English dispreferred, and hence any use of English must be seen as a direct contestation of the legitimacy of French and by extension of the teacher's authority. It is not clear yet how the school feels about the language of its own minorities. Further, only Canadian and European standard forms of French are accepted; consistent production of anything else has consequences for streaming and for marks and even for teachers' assessment of whether a student belongs in this school at all.

As long as this definition of legitimacy is accepted in the classroom in direct, public interactions with the teacher, other forms of language can be tolerated. Students can speak English in whispered asides to each other; if called upon to place their utterances on the common, public floor, they typically rephrase what they have to say in French or deny having said anything at all. They can speak English in the hallways to each other, but not to a teacher or even to a visitor. They can speak Somali, they can speak Arabic, they can speak Farsi, they can speak Haitian Creole; they can codeswitch and play with language as much as they like, as long as it is to each other and not on the school's official floor. To do otherwise is to risk conferring the status of impostor on either the school or the student speaker.

TURN-TAKING, LEGITIMATE LANGUAGE, AND LEGITIMATE SPEAKER-HEARERS

A brief examination of turn-taking in the classroom provides another way to look at the construction of legitimate language. I will focus on the significance of two models of turn-taking that compete in Champlain's classrooms. The first is a model of sequential turn-taking on a unified floor. It is the one that best typifies our expectations of what classrooms are like: Each person takes the floor in turn, and everyone participates in the same conversation. Usually, but not necessarily, the teacher selects the speakers. This is the model that Champlain teachers use, a model that structures the public, official, on-record, French floor of classroom talk. The competing floor is multivocal and non-sequential. Many people can talk at once or may overlap. This is the typical form of off-the-record talk, which usually takes place in a language other than French and over which the teacher exerts no control. As long as the two are kept separate, there is little problem; it is clear which format has official sanction. Occasionally, however, the two collide. This happens most clearly in classrooms with significant numbers of Somali students, who appear to favor this format, and was inadvertently reinforced in at least one classroom.

In the general-level Français class, a great deal of emphasis is placed on oral language skills. Lise, the teacher, took this up by trying to give students greater control of talk, even rearranging chairs and desks into a circle or a U-shape instead of keeping them in rows. However, she inevitably ended up frustrated at what appeared to be the students' inability to stick to a topic and to listen to each other. Instead of the sequentiality and unified floor that she had hoped to map onto group discussion, what she got was lots of people talking more or less at the same time, on floors that shifted both in terms of topic and in terms of participants. In the end, she always put the students back into their rows, and over time she felt obliged to define explicit codes of conduct and to introduce more teacher-oriented transmission-type teaching than she felt intellectually comfortable with.

For Lise, the theme of the semester eventually became the theme of "*le respect.*" In many ways, the reason has to do with Mohamud's explicit challenges to her authority. But through various interactional episodes, including these challenges and Lise's and other students' responses to them, we can see the outlines of the relative importance and interplay of the various dimensions of legitimacy.

In one episode, Lise organized student presentations. She began by circulating an evaluation sheet. Extract 5 gives the exchange that followed.

Extract 5

Lise: *on vous laisse deux minutes pour vous préparer puis après ça on commence* (you have two minutes to prepare yourselves and after that we start)
Leila: *d'accord* (okay)
Abdul: *Leila et Abdi*
Lise: *Zahra (xxx) feuille Abdul tu lui as donné à à* (Zahra [xxx] sheet Abdul you gave it to to)
Abdul: *oh e (speaks in Somali)*
Lise: *(xxx) aujourd'hui vous parlez en Français* ([xxx] today you speak French)
Abdul: *d'accord je vais parler Français* (okay I'll speak French)
Lise: *okay alors on écoute Leila et Abdi* (okay so we listen to Leila and Abdi)
Student: *chut* (shh)
Student: shut up (shut up)
Lise: *okay on recommence quand on fait une présentation orale ou un exposé on s'attend vraiment à ce que à ce que les gens écoutent* . . . (okay we start again when we do an oral presentation and exposé we really expect people to listen . . .)

The episode goes on in this vein for another few minutes, but this extract is sufficient to show how Lise uses her position to take the floor and uses the floor to make explicit what will count as legitimate language (French, not Somali) and to reinforce the conventions of turn-taking. She defines the situation as a "*présentation orale,*" and she states that in such a situation the speakers speak and everyone else listens. She does not let the episode begin until that has been established.

Lise has privileged use of interruptions and self-selections when she is not in fact the designated speaker and addressee, because she is the teacher (and so she is always a legitimate speaker or hearer). She uses this position to make other communicative conventions clear.

Among the conventions she defined, one says that no foul language is allowed [. . .].

[. . .]

Another convention that Lise makes explicit is that students call other students by their first names [. . .] and that students stick to the subject as defined by the teacher.

[. . .]

At another moment, Lise asks the students to put their desks in a U-shape and organizes a discussion on the meaning of the word "*respect*." The episode is too long to reproduce here; for my purposes there are two essential elements. The first is Lise's statement that respect means listening quietly when someone else talks *("lorsqu'(il y a) une personne qui parle tu dois apprendre à te taire"* [when (there is) someone talking you have to learn to be silent]). The second is the form that the discussion takes; throughout Lise attempts to exert control by selecting speakers and by enforcing precisely what she wants to teach, namely, that others should listen when one person has the floor. In fact, however, there are often numerous discussions going on at once, and student talk often overlaps. (Sometimes such overlapping talk might be characterized as collaborative, in that there is a shared topic and mutual addressing of turns; at other times, speakers are ignored, and competing topics with different sets of interlocutors are opened up simultaneously with someone else's ongoing talk. This last happens more when some students take the floor than others, and I take this to be an index of the legitimacy of the speakers.)

The importance of the interplay of different aspects of legitimacy is revealed in another episode (Extract 9) a few days later. Here, Mohamud's challenge to Lise has been taken up. Lise has decided that if Mohamud is unhappy with what she is doing in class, then she will briefly turn the class over to him. He has decided to do what is for him a more credible activity than group discussions and pen-and-paper exercises, namely, a good old-fashioned *dictée*. He follows this with a lecture on the relations between men and women in Somalia. Throughout this episode, however, Mohamud has trouble acting and being taken seriously in the teacher role. First, he breaks the "no foul language" rule [. . .] then, the other students start giving him a hard time, interrupting him, complaining about the comprehensibility of his speech and asking questions [. . .]. Anne, one of the French Canadian students, mocks his intonation.

[. . .]

Mohamud is not allowed to do what Lise does (admittedly not always successfully) in terms of using the floor to establish control; he is not a legitimate speaker. He may partly disqualify himself by using foul language, but likely he is prevented by other students from taking on a role he does not rightly have a claim to simply because he is, like them, a student. Interestingly, however, the challenges to Mohamud are phrased not in terms of his status but in terms of his mastery of the legitimate forms of language (we can't understand you, you have an accent, you talk too fast).

This examination of turn-taking in Lise's Français général class shows us how important the conventions of legitimate form are (speak polite French). But it also shows that form is not everything; form must be used appropriately (in a unified floor by designated speakers). In the end, this dimension of language use is nothing less than "*respect*." But there is more: Being a designated speaker is not the same as being a legitimate speaker. Mohamud is a designated speaker, but he does not get the "*respect*" that Lise does. Lise often can take the floor despite not being a designated speaker, because her authority as a teacher is invested in that kind of control over turns at talk (hers and everyone else's). (This is also why Mohamud's contestation is so effective; it aims directly at the legitimacy of Lise's control over turns at talk and over topics.)

The turn-taking conventions of the classroom reinforce the teachers' control of the situation, including therefore their ability to define and maintain the definition of legitimate language. Through controlling the shape of classroom talk, they can control its form, and they can also control who count as legitimate speakers and hearers. Finally, the external shape of talk, its deployment in interaction, may be as important as its structure, its internal form. Possessing the legitimate variety may not get you anywhere if you cannot or do not use it according to the rules of the game. Looking at turn-taking allows us to see who the legitimate speakers are of what legitimate forms and how they use those forms to regulate both access to knowledge and displays of knowledge.

CONCLUSION

At Champlain, the processes of interaction in the classroom, as I have presented them here, reveal some profound contradictions that, in the end, serve the interests of some participants better than they serve others. While the value of French and of specific varieties of French, as well as of francophone identity, is clear, there is no simple correlation between possessing those varieties and identities and doing well at school or being seen as a central player there. Some students speak and write standard French, identify themselves as francophones, and do well. But others can do fairly well despite not fully mastering standard French or identifying themselves as francophones. These students have North American mainstream class-based knowledge about how to do school, including knowledge of how to use language, which appears at least as important as their knowledge of certain linguistic structures. (Also, the school needs to maintain a certain level of enrollment, and the presence of English-dominant students is part of the basis of the justification for francophone militancy.) In addition, some students who identify themselves as francophones but who speak the vernacular do poorly, in part because the stigmatization of their linguistic skills overrides their authenticity. Further, other students (notably the Somalis) encounter difficulties because their lack of knowledge of the school's expectations of how to use language overrides their mastery of linguistic structures. Legitimacy is thus both more and less than mastery of the forms of standard French, although it is always defined with reference to standard French. It is also knowing when and how to use them and being a member of a group with the right to use them or not to use them, depending on the circumstances.

Underlying these facts is the fundamental contradiction of a school made for people who speak French and English and aspire to professional careers that finds itself faced with many other kinds of students. In the end, the school serves the interests of the bilingual, francophone politically mobilized middle class that fought so hard for its creation and, ironically, also the interest of anglophones who have managed to acquire academic French. These are the two groups for whom French-English bilingualism is important and for whom the school represents a crucial source of valued linguistic capital. In the struggle, the cultural dimensions of Franco-Ontarian education are marginalized and folklorified, icons of a reality long gone and perhaps always an invention. New participants fight for a way into this game, but find frequently that they have to learn more than just French in order to be allowed to play.

[. . .]

The analysis of bilingual classroom discourse [. . .] becomes a window onto the opportunities and obstacles that bilingual education presents to different kinds of students, as well as a glimpse at the strategies teachers and students use to deal with them. By understanding what constitutes legitimate language in a bilingual classroom, we can see whose interests are favored and whose are marginalized and how bilingual education contributes to the welfare of minority groups.

REFERENCES

Bourdieu, P. (1977) The economics of linguistic exchanges. *Social Science Information* 16: 645–668.

Frenette, N. and L. Gauthier (1990) Luttes idéologiques et cultures institutionnelles en éducation minoritaire: le cas de l'Ontario français. *Revue Éducation Canadienne et Internationale* 19: 16–31.

Heller, M. (1994a) *Crosswords: Language, Education and Ethnicity in French Ontario.* Berlin, N.Y.: Mouton de Gruyter.

Heller, M. (1994b) La sociolinguistique et l'éducation franco-ontarienne. *Sociologie et Sociétés* 26: 155–166.

Welch, D. (1988) The social construction of Franco-Ontarian interests towards French-language schooling. Unpublished Ph.D. thesis, Graduate Department of Education, University of Toronto.

QUESTIONS

Content

1. What is Heller trying to show in this article?
2. What is the main purpose of the Franco-Ontarian school system and what (two) paradoxes has it raised?
3. What are the major groups of students at the school?
4. What are Heller's main research questions and what communicative processes does she explore to answer them?
5. What is the linguistic repertoire of the student body and what is it perceived to be?
6. What do English and French symbolize in the classroom?
7. How does the concept of legitimate language relate to the form of French used in class?
8. Who is a legitimate speaker and what is legitimate language in respect to turn-taking?
9. For whom does the school represent a crucial source of valued linguistic capital and why?

Consider what a graduating student at Champlain (presumably a native speaker of Canadian French) had to say, in fractured French, in the yearbook next to his picture:

> *"Je m'exkuze pour leuh kalité de lengue, mais kum vous savé tousse, la frensaix ne fue jammait une çujais dent lakel je sui d'ouwer"* (Excuse the quality of my language, but as you all know, French was never a subject in which I am gifted)

1.   What is 'French' for this student?
2.   What is the legitimate language for this student and how does the student position himself in this note?

Chapter 17

Ben Rampton

LANGUAGE CROSSING AND THE REDEFINITION OF REALITY

[. . .]

LANGUAGE CROSSING: A PRELIMINARY DEFINITION

The term 'language crossing' (or 'code-crossing') refers to the use of a language which isn't generally thought to 'belong' to the speaker. Language crossing involves a sense of movement across quite sharply felt social or ethnic boundaries, and it raises issues of legitimacy that participants need to reckon with in the course of their encounter. In line with this, in the adolescent friendship groups where I studied it (Rampton 1995a), crossing either occasioned, or was occasioned by, moments and activities in which the constraints of ordinary social order were relaxed and normal social relations couldn't be taken for granted.

SOME EXAMPLES

The examples of crossing that follow come from a research project which used the methodologies of ethnographic and interactional sociolinguistics to examine four closely interrelated dimensions of socio-cultural organisation: language, seen both as a central element in social action and as a form of knowledge differentially distributed across individuals and groups; the 'interaction order' mapped out by Erving Goffman; institutional organisation, encompassing domains, networks, activity types, social roles and normative expectations; and social knowledge specifically as this relates to race and ethnicity. Two years of fieldwork focused on one neighbourhood of the South Midlands

Source: Rampton, Ben (1998) Language crossing and the redefinition of reality. In Peter Auer (ed.) Code-switching in Conversation: Language, Interaction and Identity. London and New York: Routledge, 290–317.

of England, with twenty-three 11 to 13 year olds of Indian, Pakistani, African Caribbean and Anglo descent in 1984, and approximately sixty-four 14 to 16 year olds in 1987. Methods of data-collection included radio-microphone recording, participant observation, interviewing, and retrospective participant commentary on extracts of recorded interaction. The analysis was based on about 68 incidents of Panjabi crossing, about 160 exchanges involving stylised Asian English, and more than 250 episodes where a Creole influence was clearly detectable, and three significantly different contexts for language crossing were identified: interaction with adults, interaction with peers, and performance art.

Here is the first example: [. . .]

Participants: Ray (13 years old, male, of Anglo/African-Caribbean descent; wearing radio-mike), Ian (12, male, Anglo descent), Hanif (12, male, Bangladeshi descent), others.

Setting: 1984. Coming out of lessons into the playground at break. Ian and Ray are best friends. Stevie Wonder is a singer whose song 'I just called to say I love you' was very famous. Ray has a bad foot (see line 17).[1]

```
      RAY         IA:N:
      HANIF       (      )
      IAN         ((from afar)) RAY THE COO:L RAY THE COO:L
      HANIF       yeh Stevie Wonder YAAA ((laughs loudly))
 5    RAY                              [it's worser than that
      IAN         ((singing)):     [I just called to say
      HANIF       ha (let's) sing (him) a song
      IAN         I hate you
      HANIF       ((loud laughs))
10    ANON        ((coming up)) () are you running for the school (.)
      RAY         huh
      ANON        are [you running for the school=
      RAY             [no
      ANON        = [I am
15    IAN            [he couldn't run for th- he couldn't [run for the school
      RAY                                        [SHUT UP=
      RAY         =I couldn- I don wan- [I can't run anyway
      HANIF                             [right we're wasting our [time=
      IAN                                                       [I did=
20    HANIF       = [come on (we're) wasting our time=
      IAN           [you come last ()
      HANIF       = [[mʌmʌmʌ:]
      ANON          [I came second
      IAN         ((singing)) I just called to say [I got      ] a big=
25    RAY                                          [I hate you]
      IAN         =[lʊlla:]
                  ((Panjabi for 'willy'))
      HANIF AND        ((loud laughter))
      OTHERS
```

RAY   ((continuing Ian's song)) so's Ian Hinks (1.5)
       ((Ray laughs)) no you haven't you got a tiny one (.)
30   you've only got (a arse)

In this extract, Ian directs some Panjabi abuse at his good friend Ray, and among other things, the formulaic use of song helps to ensure that it is understood as ritual and jocular, not personal and serious (cf. Labov 1972; Goodwin and Goodwin 1987). When he starts out in lines 6 and 8, he seems to be identifying himself with the first person expressed in the song, but when he repeats it in lines 24 and 26, it looks as though he's putting the words in Ray's mouth rather than claiming the 'I' for himself – certainly, Ray's retaliation in line 28 suggests that it's him that has been attributed the item in Panjabi, not Ian. Whatever, Ian comes off best in their brief exchange of ritual abuse: Ian's [lʊlla:] upstages Ray's effort to preempt him in line 25; it is Ian who wins an enthusiastic response from third parties in line 27; and in lines 29 and 30, Ray evidently judges his own immediate retort (line 28) as itself rather weak.

[. . .]

The last example of crossing [. . .] relates to a breach of conduct, though here the putative offender is a younger pupil and the language used is a variety I've called stylised Asian English. [. . .]

Participants and setting: At the start of the school year, Mohan (15 years, male, Indian descent, wearing radio-microphone), Jagdish (15, male, Indian descent) and Sukhbir (15, male, Indian descent) are in the bicycle sheds looking at bicycles at the start of the new academic year. Some new pupils run past them.

SUKH   STOP RUNNING AROUND YOU GAYS (.)
SUKH   [((laughs))
MOH   [*EH (.) THIS IS NOT MIDD(LE SCHOOL)* no more (1.0)
        ([aɪ   dɪs   ɪz nɛtʰ mɪd   nəʊ mɔ:])
        ˌthis is a reˌspective (2.0) (school)
        ([dɪs ɪz ə ɹəspektɪv])
5 MOH   school (.) yes (.) took the words out my mouth (4.5)

In this extract, Mohan was claiming that the norms of conduct appropriate to secondary pupils during breaktime had been broken, and here, Goffman's account of remedial interchanges (1971: 95–187) helps to explain the way that stylised Asian English figured in the episode. Goffman argues that two kinds of issue arise when infractions occur. One of these is 'substantive', relating to practical matters such as the offender making amends and the offended showing that they are not going to accept the way they have been treated. The other kind of issue is ritual, which in contrast is concerned with the way in which participants display their more general respect and regard for social norms and personal preserves (Goffman 1971: 95–98, 100, 116) – here the concern is with 'indicating a relationship, not compensating a loss' (1971: 118).

In line 1, the initial noticing of the infraction was announced by a normal vernacular English 'prime' – an attempt to get the (putative) offender to provide a remedy which they might do by desisting, apologising and/or giving an explanation (Goffman

1971: 154ff., 109–114). Propositionally, the utterance in line 3 only reminded the (disappearing) addressee that old rules of conduct no longer applied, but the switch to stylised Asian English made a symbolic proclamation about the transgression's relation to a wider social order. In switching away from his normal voice to Stylised Asian English, Mohan aligned the offence with a more general social type, so that the offending act was now cast as a symptom. Stylised Asian English was stereotypically associated with limited linguistic and cultural competence (Rampton 1995a: chs 2.3, 3 and 6) and the switch implicitly explained the transgression by imputing diminished control and responsibility to the offender. In doing so, it achieved the same effect as a sanction: 'the significance of . . . rewards and penalties is not meant to lie in their intrinsic worth but in what they proclaim about the [actor's] moral status . . . and [their] compliance with or deviation from rules in general' (Goffman 1971: 95, 98).

CROSSING: THE DEFINITION ELABORATED

Two things seem to run through [. . .] these examples (as well as many more). First, the speakers moved outside the language varieties they normally used, and they briefly adopted codes which they didn't have full and easy access to. Admittedly, there were important differences in the extent to which they incorporated these other varieties into their habitual speech. But acts of this kind were frequently commented on (with varying degrees of both enthusiasm and disapproval), and constraints on the use of both Creole and stylised Asian English were evident in the fact that white and Panjabi youngsters generally avoided Creole in the company of black peers, while white and black peers hardly ever used stylised Asian English to target Panjabis.

Second, these appropriations occurred in moments and activities when 'the world of daily life known in common with others and with others taken for granted' (Garfinkel 1984: 35) was problematised or partially suspended. These interruptions to the routine flow of normal social order took a wide range of different forms, and varied very considerably in their scale and duration (see Rampton 1995a for comprehensive exemplification). Crossing occurred:

- in the vicinity of interactional breaches, delicts and transgressions [. . .];
- in ritual abuse, which works by suspending considerations of truth and falsity (cf. Labov 1972; Goodwin and Goodwin 1987; [. . .]);
- in open states of talk, self-talk and response cries, which constitute time away from the full demands of respectful interpersonal conduct (Goffman 1981: 81, 85, 99; [. . .]);
- at the boundaries of interactional enclosure, when the roles and identities for ensuing interaction were still relatively indeterminate (Goffman 1971: ch. 7; Laver 1975, 1981; Rampton 1995a: ch. 3.3);
- in games, where there was an agreed relaxation of routine interaction's rules and constraints (Turner 1982: 56; Sutton-Smith 1982; Rampton 1995a: chs 6.7, 7.2);
- in the context of performance art (cf. Gilroy 1987: 210–216; Rampton 1995a: Part III);
- and in cross-sex interaction, which in a setting where everyday recreation was single-sex and where many parents discouraged unmonitored contact between

adolescent girls and boys, itself seemed special, unusually vested with both risk and promise (Shuman 1993: 146; Rampton 1995a: chs 7.7, 10.8).

We can summarise this relationship with moments and events in which the hold of routine assumptions about social reality was temporarily loosened by saying that crossing was intricately connected with what Turner calls 'liminality' and the 'liminoid'.

These two points support each other and permit at least two inferences. First, the intimate association with liminality meant that crossing never actually claimed that the speaker was 'really' black or Asian – it didn't finally imply that the crosser could move unproblematically in and out of the friends' heritage language in any new kind of open bicultural code-switching. Second, crossing's location in the liminoid margins of interactional and institutional space implied that in the social structures which were dominant and which adolescents finally treated as *normal*, the boundaries round ethnicity were relatively fixed.

Even so, these boundaries weren't inviolable, and quite plainly, adolescents didn't submit reverentially to absolutist ideas about ethnicity being fixed at birth or during the early years of socialisation. Language crossing cannot be seen as a runaway deconstruction of ethnicity, emptying it of all meaning, but its influence wasn't left unquestioned, invisibly and incontrovertibly pervading common sense. Crossing was an established interactional practice that foregrounded inherited ethnicity itself, and in doing so, it at least partially destabilised it. In Bourdieu's terms, crossing can be seen as a form of 'heretical discourse' which broke the doxic authority of the idea that ethnically, you are what you're born and brought up (1977: 168–70; 1990: 129). As such, crossing warrants close attention in sociological discussion of the emergence of 'new ethnicities of the margins', multiracial ethnicities 'predicated on difference and diversity' (Hall 1988). [. . .]

CROSSING'S RELEVANCE TO RESEARCH ON CODE-SWITCHING

[. . .] As the previous section tried to make plain, language crossing seemed to be poised at the juncture of two competing notions of group belonging. On the one hand, crossing was a significant practice in the negotiation of an emergent sense of multiracial youth community. But at the same time, this sense of multiracial adolescent community was itself fragile, set around by ethnic absolutism, a powerful common sense in which Creole was Caribbean and Panjabi Panjabi, and it seemed to be this tension that generated the feeling of anomaly in language crossing, pressing it into the liminal margins of everyday interactional practice.

Interpreted in this way, language crossing represents a cultural dynamic that merits rather more attention in code-switching research than it has perhaps hitherto received.

In the past, studies of code-switching have generally tended to focus on the conduct of groups in which the use of two or more languages is a routine expectation, either because people have grown up with a multilingual inheritance, or because they have moved into areas or institutions where the use of additional languages is an unremarked necessity (e.g. Blom and Gumperz 1972; Gal 1989; Duran 1981; Grosjean 1983; Auer 1988; Romaine 1988; cf. Woolard 1988: 69–70). Because of this emphasis on languages which are unexceptional within the in-group, code-switching research has often provided a rather restricted notion of ethnic processes, tending to focus only on variation in the salience and cultural contents of ethnic categories, not on ethnic *recategorisation*, on the exploration or adoption of alternative or competing ethnicities. In a great deal of code-switching research (as indeed in a lot of research on intercultural communication), participants are seen as having a rather limited choice: (a) they can maintain and/or embrace and cultivate the ethnicity they have inherited, or (b) they can de-emphasise or abandon it, so that ethnicity drops from the repertoire of identities available and meaningful to them. The study of language crossing throws light on a further option: exploring other people's ethnicities, embracing them and/or creating new ones (cf. Rampton 1995a: ch. 11.6; 1995b).

Although it isn't a major thematic interest in code-switching research, there is in fact a growing number of studies which suggest that this third kind of inter-ethnic process is very far from rare. Hewitt's (1986) study of white Creole users in south London was an important precedent for my own research, and in cultural studies and anthropology, it has also now been followed by Jones (1988) and Back (1996). Elsewhere, broadly comparable accounts of the intricate sociolinguistics of social and/or ethnic redefinition have been produced by the Hills on Nahuatl and Spanish in Mexico (Hill and Hill 1986; Hill and Coombs 1982), by Heller on French and English in Canada (1988, 1992), by Woolard on Castilian and Catalan in Catalonia (1988, 1989), and by Cheshire and Moser on English and French in Switzerland (1994) (see also Haarmann 1989; Eastman and Stein 1993).

[. . .]

[Rampton continues his discussion of language crossing and makes the following points:]

1. By focusing overwhelmingly on bilingual ingroups, research has traditionally tended to neglect the emergence of new plural ethnicities, built in an *acceptance* of old ones (Hall 1988).

2. To gain any purchase on the exploration and/or renegotiation of reality – in my research, a reality of race stratification and division – full recognition needs to be given to Gumperz's notion of metaphorical code-switching, though this needs some further clarification, perhaps most profitably by being drawn into close association with Bakhtin's notion of double-voicing (1984: 181–204).

3. For the same reason, it would be helpful if code-switching research relaxed its commitment to discovering coherence and systematicity in code-switching, and attended more closely to incongruity and contradiction. In the process, a clearer view would emerge of the (not infrequent) local occasions when code alternation no longer functions adequately as a contextualisation cue and instead becomes part of the 'main action', an object of explicit political dispute (cf. Goffman 1974: ch. 7; Hewitt 1986: 169, 181).

4. To respond adequately to all three of these points, the notion of conversation used in code-switching research needs to be a very broad one, and it is also essential to attend to the representations of code-switching and language difference in artful performance and the public media.

[. . .]

NOTES

1.   In the ensuing extracts, transcription conventions are as follows:

[ ]	IPA phonetic transcription (1989 revision)
'	high stress
ˌ	low stress
,	low rise
:	lengthening
[	overlapping turns
=	two utterances closely connected without a noticeable overlap, or different parts of the single speaker's turn
(·)	pause of less than one second
—	break-off/unfinished word
(1.5)	approximate length of pause in seconds
p	piano/quietly
pp	very quietly
f	forte/loudly
ff	very loudly
CAPITALS	loud
(())	'stage directions', or comments
()	speech inaudible
(text)	speech hard to discern, analyst's guess
italics	instance of crossing of central interest in discussion
	Names have been altered.

BIBLIOGRAPHY

Back, L. (1996) *New Ethnicities and Urban Culture*. London: UCL Press.

Bakhtin, M. (1984) *Problems in Dostoevsky's Poetics*. Minneapolis: University of Minnesota Press.

Cheshire, J. and L.-M. Moser (1994) English as a cultural symbol: the case of advertisements in French-speaking Switzerland. *Journal of Multilingual and Multicultural Development* 15/6: 451–469.

Eastman, C. and R. Stein (1993) Language display: authenticating claims to social identity. *Journal of Multilingual and Multicultural Development* 14: 187–202.

Garfinkel, H. (1984) [1967] *Studies in Ethnomethodology*. Oxford: Polity Press.

Gilroy, P. (1987) *There Ain't no Black in the Union Jack*. London: Hutchinson.

Goffman, E. (1971) *Relations in Public*. London: Allen Lane.

Goffman, E. (1974) *Frame Analysis*. Harmondsworth: Penguin.

Goffman, E. (1981) *Forms of Talk*. Oxford: Blackwell.

Goodwin, M. and C. Goodwin (1987) Children's arguing. In S. Philips, S. Steele and C. Tanz (eds) *Language, Gender and Sex in Comparative Perspective*. Cambridge: Cambridge University Press: 200–248.

Haarmann, H. (1989) *Symbolic Values of Foreign Language Use*. Berlin: Mouton de Gruyter.

Hall, S. (1988) New ethnicities. *ICA Documents* 7: 27–31.

Heller, M. (1992) The politics of code-switching and language choice. *Journal of Multilingual and Multicultural Development* 13: 123–142.

Hewitt, R. (1986) *White Talk Black Talk*. Cambridge: Cambridge University Press.

Hill, J. and D. Coombs (1982) The vernacular remodelling of national and international languages. *Applied Linguistics* 3: 224–234.

Hill, J. and Hill, K. (1986) *Speaking Mexicano: The Dynamics of Syncretic Language in Central Mexico*. Tucson: University of Arizona Press.

Jones, S. (1988) *Black Culture White Youth*. Basingstoke: Macmillan.

Labov, W. (1972) *Language in the Inner City*. Oxford: Blackwell.

Laver, J. (1975) Communicative functions of phatic communion. In A. Kendon, R. Harris and M. R. Key (eds) *Organisation of Behaviour in Face-to-Face Interaction*. The Hague: Mouton, 215–238.

Rampton, B. (1995a) *Crossing: Language and Ethnicity among Adolescents*. London: Longman.

Rampton, B. (1995b) Language crossing and the problematisation of ethnicity and socialisation. *Pragmatics* 5/4: 485–514.

Shuman, A. (1993) "Get outa my face": Entitlement and authoritative discourse. In J. Hill and J. Irvine (eds) *Responsibility and Evidence in Oral Discourse*. Cambridge: Cambridge University Press, 135–160.

Sutton-Smith, B. (1982) A performance theory of peer relations. In K. Borman (ed.) *The Social Life of Children in a Changing Society*. Norwood, NJ: Ablex, 65–77.

Turner, V. (1982) Liminal to liminoid in play, flow and ritual. In *From Ritual to Theatre: The Human Seriousness of Play*. New York: PAJ, 20–60.

Woolard, K. (1988) Code-switching and comedy in Catalonia. In M. Heller (ed.) *Code-Switching: Anthropological and Sociolinguistic Perspectives*. The Hague: Mouton de Gruyter, 53–76.

Woolard, K. (1989) *Double Talk*. Stanford, Calif.: Stanford University Press.

QUESTIONS

Content

1. What is language crossing?
2. Where does language crossing occur in examples 1 and 2 and why is it language crossing?
3. Generally speaking, when does crossing occur and why is it worth studying?

Concept

1. The language crossing example below involves Creole. What happens in the excerpt below? What is Creole / Black English doing here and why is this an example of language crossing?

Participants: Asif (15, male, Pakistani descent, wearing the radio-microphone), Alan (15, male, Anglo descent), Ms Jameson (25+, female, Anglo descent), and in the background, Mr Chambers (25+, male, Anglo descent).

Setting: 1987. Asif and Alan are in detention for Ms Jameson, who was herself a little late for it. She is explaining why she didn't arrive on time, and now she wants to go and fetch her lunch.

```
      MS J     I had to go and see the headmaster
      ASIF     why
      MS J     (    ) (.) none of your business
      ALAN     a- about us (     )
  5   MS J     ((p)) no I'll be [back
      ASIF                      [((f)) hey how can you see the=
               =headmaster when he was in dinner (.)
      MS J     ((quietly)) that's precisely why I didn't see him
      ASIF     what (.)
 10   MS J     I'll be back in a second with my lunch [()
      ASIF                                            [((ff)) NO [[]=
```

=((f)) dat's sad man (.) (I'll b)=
=I [had to miss my play right I've gotta go
ALAN   [(with mine   )
15   (2.5) ((Ms J must now have left the room))
ASIF   ((Creole influenced)) ((f)) *l:unch* (.) you don't need no=
                      ([l::ʌnʧ)
=lunch [*not'n* grow anyway ((laughs))
         ([natʔn gɹəʊ])
ALAN   [((laughs))
ASIF   have you eat your lunch Alan

Chapter 18

Miriam Meyerhoff and Nancy Niedzielski

THE GLOBALISATION OF VERNACULAR VARIATION

1. INTRODUCTION

THE SPREAD OF SOME innovative forms in New Zealand English – specifically, the use of a flap for intervocalic (t) such that /bɛtə/ is realised as /bɛɾə/, glottal replacement or debuccalisation of word-final (t) such that /bʌt/ is realised as /bʌʔ/, the shift from use of *lorry* to *truck, bonnet* to *hood, zed* to *zee*, the use of *No way* as an emphatic negator, and the quasi-lexical variable of the new quotative *be like* (as in, *And I'm like 'Excuse me, can I help you?'*) – have all been attributed to the influence of external varieties of English. In the sociolinguistics literature, it has been argued that the glottal stop in place of word-final (t) continues to reflect the role of southern British English as a benchmark for New Zealand English, but for most of the variables just mentioned, the source of influence has generally been attributed to U.S. culture and U.S. English. Just as the perceived influence of U.S. English on other (inarguably different) languages such as French has met with mixed feelings in France, the perceived influences of U.S. language and culture are met with mixed feelings in New Zealand. Responses generally fall into one of two camps: an embracing of potential, or regrets and outright hostility, and the result is a societal tension that is exploited in some of New Zealand's best contemporary comedy. (Bauman 1998: 1 discusses the way 'globalisation' is more generally becoming something of a shibboleth.)

The responses are, therefore, familiar ones. They tap into and overlap with more general discourses and arguments about the advantages and disadvantages of 'globalisation' circulating at this point (Klein 2000). The similarity is that language is seen as a commodity and like other commodities, particularly manufacturing and entertainment, it is seen to be falling under the globalising sway of U.S. culture and norms. In these discourses, U.S. English is discursively constructed as a 'category killer', that is, a

Source: Meyerhoff, Miriam and Nancy Niedzielski (2003) The globalisation of vernacular variation. *Journal of Sociolinguistics* 7: 534–555.

competitor that enters a market, 'with so much buying power that they almost instantly kill the smaller competitors' (Klein 2000: 134).

Of course, this argumentation is not always explicit, but even when it is only implicitly present in the analysis of ongoing variation and change, it seems to us that we have a responsibility to ask ourselves how much we are committed to extending the theoretical baggage of globalisation theory into variationist sociolinguistics, or whether we are interested only in superficial similarities between apparently transnational linguistic phenomena and the global spread of other commodities or ideas.

This paper considers how variationist sociolinguistics might connect with theories about globalisation, and it will use the situation of ongoing changes documented in New Zealand English as the basis for this exploration. Since previous analyses of these changes have laid the ground for drawing superficial parallels between language and other commodities, it seems to us appropriate to use them as the basis for exploring the potential for deeper, interdisciplinary connections with globalisation theory.

[. . .]

2. INTERDISCIPLINARY CONNECTIONS AND TYPES OF KNOWLEDGE

In this section we will argue that sociolinguists studying variation and change ought to be motivated to look more closely at globalisation theory on both empirical and theoretical grounds. Empirically, it is clear that, at least superficially, the linguistic variables we are concerned with do seem to involve diffusion from a major economic and/or cultural centre to a smaller, less influential centre. [. . .] This tradition, which is of course heavily influenced by Pierre Bourdieu's notions of symbolic capital, has, as far as we are aware, the longest tradition among francophone sociolinguists. It was spelt out for English-speaking sociolinguists in Sankoff and Laberge (1978), but Labov's ([1963] 1972) analysis of the social function of centralised variants of /ai/ and /au/ on Martha's Vineyard relies fundamentally on the idea of linguistic variants serving as social capital.

[. . .]

Perhaps a stronger, and more general, theoretical motivation for variationists to look at globalisation theory is the fact that, in general, we have hypothesised that the constraints on the spread of linguistic innovations are essentially the same as those that constrain the spread of other innovations. A good example of this can be seen in Trudgill's (1983) work using the Gravity Model, drawn from sociology. He found that this model provided a good account of the manner in which linguistic innovations often 'jump' from one large population centre to another, rather than dispersing in a wave-like pattern emanating from a central starting point. (This model was supported independently in Callary 1975.) So the Gravity Model provides a satisfying symmetry between the behaviour of linguistic variants and trends in the transmission and spread of innovations in other domains, including technology and knowledge (Audretsch 2000: 68–69).

Similarly, Lesley and Jim Milroy's use of social networks in their analysis of the sociolinguistic stratification of variables (J. Milroy and L. Milroy 1978: L. Milroy 1980) shows that some of the principles and constraints operating on the distribution of innovative variants at a very local level in a speech community are similar to those that constrain the transmission of other social (including epidemiological) innovations through networks (Rogers 1995; Valente 1995). Labov's (2001) work confirms that in both Philadelphia and Belfast social networks are a significant factor in the diffusion of linguistic innovations, though he notes that the effect of social networks is not consistent across all subgroups of speakers (see especially Labov 2001: 331–333).

Social networks are also an important factor in the study of globalisation. Some time ago, economists identified a paradox associated with globalisation, namely that it goes hand in hand with increased localisation (or regionalisation). First elaborated in Markusen (1996), the paradox can be summed up as 'sticky places in slippery space' (Storper 2000 and Dunning 2000 develop the sticky places metaphor further).

[. . .]

Moreover, it seems clear from research in other social sciences that there is a qualitative difference in what kinds of innovation get diffused across slippery space or in sticky places. Economists' studies of global markets and global trends show that the kind of very local face-to-face networks that the Milroys, Cheshire (1982), Nichols (1983), and Eckert (2000) have highlighted as pivotal for the transmission of language change are also vital for the transmission of other knowledge-based innovations. For example, Audretsch (2000: 73) shows that innovations in high tech do not spread simply because there is a critical mass of interested individuals in close physical proximity (this is reported to be true even somewhere like Silicon Valley). On the contrary, they find that innovations are spread only if there is face-to-face, quality contact between individuals.

Building on Markusen's notion of sticky places in slippery space, Von Hipple (1994) distinguishes between 'high-context', 'uncertain' or 'sticky' knowledge, and simple information. High-context knowledge is transmitted via face-to-face interaction and through frequent and repeated contact between individuals. Audretsch paraphrases this (helpfully, we think) as 'tacit knowledge'. The insight from this research is that the simple information of an innovation may pass from Point A to Point B easily and without a lot of personal contact, but only fairly superficial aspects of the innovation are transferred in this way. Economists find that in order for the tacit or high-context knowledge that includes the social *meaning* of an innovation to be transferred, there needs to be highly local contact between individuals.

The importance of the parallels between these independent findings and the findings in studies of variation and change is that they support our fundamental hypothesis that linguistic behaviour is constrained by the same principles that constrain other social behaviour. As we begin to look a bit beyond changes that are strictly local, limits on the supra-local transfer of *quality* information which have been identified when there is no face-to-face contact, will re-emerge as an important consideration.

3. WHAT IS GLOBALISATION?

[. . .]

[The authors introduce two definitions of globalisation: Levitt's (1983) definition, which is more outcome-oriented and McGrew's definition below.]

Where Levitt's definition emphasises an end state, McGrew characterises globalisation principally as a process:

> Globalisation . . . describes the process by which events, decisions, and activities in one part of the world come to have significant consequences for individuals and communities in quite distant parts of the globe. . . . [T]he concept therefore has a spatial connotation. On the other hand it also implies an intensification on the levels of interaction, interconnectedness or interdependence . . . alongside the [spatial] stretching goes a deepening of the . . . processes. (McGrew 1992: 23)

Certainly, a process-oriented notion of globalisation resonates better with the emphasis sociolinguistics currently places on the emergence of the meaning of variables through conversational negotiations than with Levitt's outcome-oriented one. We will return to McGrew's process-based definition of globalisation in our discussion of the sociolinguistic variables that follows, and simultaneously introduce some comments on the limitations to the terms in which globalisation is framed in economics and business studies.

4. DETAILS OF THE VARIABLES IN NEW ZEALAND ENGLISH

The four variables in New Zealand English which are the subject of this paper can be grouped into two classes (Table 18.1). One class is lexical or quasi-lexical variables and another class is phonetic variables. We turn to the lexical variables first.

4.1 Lexical variables

Lexical pairs. The full set of lexical pairs is given in Table 18.2. In these pairs, both words have the same denotational meaning, but in each case, the variant on the left is considered more conservative (and is often the variant which also occurs in conservative southern British English) and the variant on the right is found in U.S. (or North American) English. For each variant, you can find at least some native speakers of New Zealand English who report that they use that form. The innovative forms that are reported as being used most often by New Zealanders are *truck* (now almost categorical), *movies, can* (for food), *pants* (as in trousers) and *hood* (of a car).

Table 18.1   Variables in New Zealand English analysed as reflecting the influence of international varieties of English

Variable	Innovative variant(s)	Source?
Lexical pairs	*hood, pants, gas, cookie, movies, truck*	U.S. English (Bayard 1989; Meyerhoff 1993)
Quotative verb	*be like*	U.S. English
Intervocalic (t)	alveolar flap, [ɾ]	U.S. English (Holmes 1995b)
Word-final (t)	glottal stop, [ʔ]	Southern British English (Bayard 1990; Holmes 1995b)

Table 18.2 Full list of lexical pairs variables (Table 18.1) with frequencies of reported use in 1989 in sample of 60 working class New Zealanders (from Meyerhoff 1993; numbers do not always equal 100 because of alternate options offered)

Conservative variant	Innovative variant	Frequency of conservative/innovative variants
torch	flashlight	97/2
biscuit	cookie	95/0
petrol	gas	88/7
jersey	sweater	86/4
lift	elevator	85/10
serviette	napkin	83/11
bonnet (car)	hood	76/24
tin (food)	can	76/24
pictures	movies	53/37
trousers	pants	46/41
lorry	truck	3/97

Bayard (1989) suggested that the inroads being made by the U.S. English variants reflected the increasing influence that U.S. culture was having on New Zealand culture. Meyerhoff's (1993) subsequent examination of the distribution of these forms in a working class community north of Wellington concurred. The frequency with which people reported using innovative forms increased among the youngest speakers and was (generally) lowest in the oldest speakers. When this data was first presented (Meyerhoff 1991), an explicit link was made between the ongoing linguistic changes and the adoption of other aspects of U.S. popular culture. Bayard also cited the use of *No way* as an emphatic negator as evidence of U.S. English colonising New Zealand English. More recently, the use of *be like* as a verb of quotation has been informally identified as evidence of U.S. English exerting an influence on New Zealand English norms.

Quotative be like. *Be like* is a particularly vigorous and regionally promiscuous variable. In work on the use of *be like* in Glasgow, Scotland and York, England, Macaulay (2001) and Tagliamonte and Hudson (1999) hypothesise that the quotative has spread from U.S. English. This hypothesis is actually stated more clearly in Tagliamonte and Hudson's work; Macaulay is less committed, and at times overtly queries the U.S. link (2001: 17). In the end, Macaulay seems to suggest that the media has been the vector of transmission (as Bayard and Meyerhoff did for the lexical pairs in New Zealand English). If this is correct, it raises a host of significant questions (which have a tendency to recur in sociolinguistics). We have seen here that there is evidence to assume that the transmission of linguistic innovations is unexceptional. Yet we have also reviewed interdisciplinary research which supports the importance of face-to-face networks for the transmission of high context, tacit knowledge about innovations, and this would seem to rule out the mass media as a significant factor in the transmission of detailed sociolinguistic variation. Resolving this apparent conundrum lies beyond the scope of this article, but it is addressed in Meyerhoff and Niedzielski (2002).

4.2 Phonetic variables: (t)

Both of the phonetic variables discussed for New Zealand English affect the realisation of (t). Holmes (1994, 1995a, b) has documented two apparent changes in progress occurring simultaneously in New Zealand English. The relevant data is summarised in Table 18.3. The first change affects the intervocalic realisation of the alveolar stop. Holmes' data shows that the (t) in, for example, 'sort of' and 'butter', is realised as an alveolar flap 65 percent of the time in the speech of New Zealanders under the age of 30 and 50 percent of the time in the speech of New Zealanders over 40.

The second change affects (t) word-finally. In words like 'let' and phrases like 'get lost' or 'hot dog', Holmes reports that coda (t) is realised as a glottal stop 25 percent of the time by speakers under 30 and 16 percent of the time by speakers over 40. As researchers did with the lexical variables, Holmes attributes these innovations directly to borrowings from external varieties of English. She notes that both British and U.S. English are socially and economically more dominant varieties than New Zealand English is, and concludes that they therefore constitute prestige targets for at least some members of the New Zealand speech community. From southern British English New Zealanders take the glottal variant in coda position; from U.S./North American English, they take the flapped intervocalic variant.

5. ISSUES WITH THE PREVIOUS ANALYSES OF VARIATION IN NEW ZEALAND ENGLISH

In the case of some lexical variables, it may appear to be clear that the ultimate source of an innovation is some external variety of English. In the case of others (and perhaps especially for phonetic variables), the source may be less clear for a number of reasons, including independent, cross-linguistic parallel developments. In this section, we offer some issues that arise from the analyses offered for variation and change in New Zealand English that have just been reviewed and which we feel have larger implications for theoretical treatments of, and the empirical study of, variation.

5.1 A conceptual issue

Let us consider first a conceptual problem we have with the claim that New Zealanders simultaneously see British and U.S. English as targets with vernacular prestige. The problem here is not with the notion that speakers might hold multiple varieties in high esteem (indeed, the distinction between covert and overt prestige was an attempt to explicitly address this). The problem here is the notion of British and U.S. English being

Table 18.3   Summary of (t) variables in New Zealand English from Holmes (1995b: 59, 63)[1]

	18–30 year olds	40–55 year olds
(t)-flapping: /t/ V_V →/ɾ/	65%	50%
(-t) glottal: /t/ _#→ /ʔ/	25%	16%

simultaneously targets for a set of speakers, since Standard U.S. and Standard British English are widely perceived as standing in direct opposition to each other, representing mutually exclusive targets. (This is, of course, a folk perception. As Trudgill and Hannah 2002 show, there are many similarities between the Standard varieties in the U.S. and Britain.) We would suggest that the idea that New Zealanders might be simultaneously trying to sound more British and more American paints a picture of psychological insecurity which doesn't fit well with other facts of language change in New Zealand English. Even if New Zealanders *are* trying to sound more American and/or more British by using these consonantal and lexical variants, this somehow has to be reconciled with the fact that this gesture is embedded in an entire vowel system that is increasingly distinctive from any other variety of English (including other Southern Hemisphere varieties). Moreover, since the ongoing changes in the vowel system occur cumulatively far more frequently than the variables under discussion, this seems to us to compound the problems associated with saying that U.S. and British English are 'targets'.

We can see several reasons why it is tempting to characterise the situation in terms of external targets. Firstly, the quantitative analysis of variation generally assumes that variation is targeted (i.e. motivated by a desire to sound like some prototypical speaker of an ingroup or outgroup). Secondly, and related to the first, it immediately offers a causal motivation for the phenomenon under investigation. These two reasons may have played a role in the previous analyses of New Zealand English variables. However, we would suggest that another, very local, reason may also have played a part in encouraging New Zealand sociolinguists to represent the variation in terms of external, prestige targets. This is sensitivity to what is known in New Zealand as 'cultural cringe'.

Cultural cringe refers to a particular colonial mindset from which many New Zealanders would actively want to distance themselves today. It is a term used informally to refer to attitudes or statements that deprecate or belittle local achievements or mores, while discursively constructing some external alternative as aesthetically, morally or pragmatically 'better'. Crucially, the alternatives are presented as being better solely because they are associated with a prestigious external reference group. Historically, Britain held a special position as the principal benchmark against which New Zealanders were measured, perhaps especially in the arts and high culture, while in the sciences, both Britain and the U.S. held a privileged place. The 'cringe' arises when a comparison is made between indigenous New Zealand standards and achievements and comparable achievements in Britain or the United States, and the local ones are *a priori* seen as being worse. So, for example, any overseas degree from Britain or the U.S. was perceived as better than any New Zealand degree. Success at home in the arts didn't count for as much as success in Britain did. The high culture and arts of indigenous New Zealanders, Maori or Pakeha, were not studied as closely or venerated as significant achievements as much as were the schools of music and architecture, and the painting styles of the 'old country'. In short, the term is a vernacular expression summing up aspects common to many contexts of colonialism.

Times change, of course, and though one can find vestiges of cultural cringe in many walks of New Zealand life, it is clear that how New Zealanders define themselves (and, of course, many different definitions have been and are being forged) is less and less likely to be in terms of an apologetic comparison with overseas norms and aesthetics. Indeed, in some circles there is a heightened sensitivity to anything that seems to resemble the old, colonial mindset of looking for external aesthetic or behavioural models. This is perhaps particularly true because of the ambiguity inherent in the negotiation of post-colonial identities. There is both a temporal sense of post-coloniality and a social and political sense of post-coloniality; developments that are post-colonial only in the temporal sense can be perceived as being in competition with and distractions from the second, change-oriented enterprise (cf. Kavoori 1998 who talks about the 'ambivalence' of the term 'post-colonial').

There may be something to be learnt from the way in which New Zealand socio-linguists have attributed changes in progress to speakers' adoption of both U.S. and British English as linguistic targets, and also from the absence of a critical evaluation of the socio-psychological paradox involved in claiming both as targets. We suggest that, ironically, previous analysts may have been ready to make this jump because, without even realising it, they have been reacting with their own heightened sensitivity to the possibility that changes in the language might reflect a new stage of neo-colonialism. That is, as soon as any data is found that even superficially supports the possibility that New Zealanders are looking beyond homegrown models for behaviour, they have felt a need to raise the alarm in their analyses. We think, for instance, that there was an underlying and unspoken fear that if New Zealanders were adopting a glottal variant of coda (t), this might indicate that they had not quite managed to shake off a tendency to see British English as normative. Furthermore, there may have been a (again, underlying) fear that variants similar to U.S. norms indicated that New Zealanders were simply swapping the colonising influence of one supra-regional English-speaking powerhouse for another. In other words, more reflexes of cultural cringe, just when some people had thought New Zealand was growing out of that.

Whether or not we want to attribute a fear of renewed manifestations of cultural cringe to the analysis of this variation in New Zealand English as being due to New Zealanders' orientation to external targets, the conceptual grounds for our critique of the analysis still need to be addressed. In addition, there appear to be some issues arising from the methods used to arrive at this conclusion. Since we believe these apply generally to the future study of the globalisation of variables, we will turn to them in more detail now.

5.2 Some methodological issues

The methodological issues associated with the analysis of all four variables come down to a paucity of necessary data. If meaningful headway is to be made in evaluating the possibility that there is globalisation of variation, we need to reaffirm norms for good practice. These will ensure that when we talk about a variable in New Zealand English as having been adopted from U.S. English, it is clear that we are in fact looking at the same variable in both places. We take our lead in this case from Rickford and McNair-Knox (1994) and Temple and Tagliamonte (2001). Both of these studies provide good examples of the kind of basic linguistic groundwork that must be a methodological prerequisite for comparisons between varieties. Rickford and McNair-Knox, for instance, establish that when they compare the same variable in the speech of an African-American teenager with Black and White addressees, they really are comparing frequencies of the same variable in both contexts. They do this by first carefully verifying that the same linguistic constraints operate on, for example, copula deletion with both addressees, and moreover that the ranking of groups and factors within groups stays essentially the same in the two contexts under comparison. It seems that we may reasonably expect standards similar to these to be met when comparisons between dialects are made.

For instance, at the moment, it is not known whether the same linguistic constraints operate on word-final (t) in British English and New Zealand English, or whether the same linguistic constraints operate on intervocalic (t) in U.S. English and New Zealand English. Strassel's (1997) work on (t)-flapping in U.S. English shows that the flapping rule applies variably even there. That is, in formal speech, *Vto* sequences (e.g. *veto, motto*) are flapped 42 percent of the time and non post-tonic *VtV* sequences (e.g. *responsibility, relatively*) are flapped 73 percent of the time. We would like to see similar data on the linguistic constraints on flapping in New Zealand English, but this is data that Holmes' studies do not provide. (The same kinds of reservations about inter-variety comparison of word-final (t) can also be held, except with this variable we have even less information on the linguistic constraints in British English than Strassel provides us with on flapping in U.S. English.) If indeed the constraints on flapping are the same as in U.S. English, and if the constraints are ranked similarly in New Zealand English, this would considerably strengthen the argument that New Zealanders have adopted or targeted the flapping variable found in U.S. English. However, in the absence of such data, accounts should perhaps be stated in more qualified terms.

Macaulay (2001) notes that the question of comparability between varieties is also an issue with the analysis of *be like*. The formal and functional uses of *be like* in British English do not seem to directly parallel its uses in U.S. English. He concludes, therefore, that although it is likely that the variable originated in U.S. English, it has clearly been reanalysed and indigenised by speakers in Glasgow. Indeed, ongoing work by Buchstaller (2002) on quotatives in British and U.S. English indicates that the formal and functional differences between *be like* in U.S. English and British English are as marked as the similarities are.

The important point here, especially with regard to the general extension of aspects of globalisation theory to the study of language variation, is that we may ultimately want to distinguish between cases where language variation involves the transfer of high context knowledge, and others where the knowledge is localised in the same way that knowledge about innovations is localised in other domains. In our case, it means that we may want our descriptions of variation to distinguish clearly between cases where the details of the social and linguistic 'meaning' of a variable are manifested in the nature and ranking of the constraints operating on the variable, and cases where different linguistic codes share only a superficial similarity in the form of a variable, but the constraints on the variable have been (re)created in, say, different communities of practice. This distinction may be important not simply because it provides more empirical detail, but also because it provides the basis for further theoretical developments. It may help us better understand how the transmission of linguistic innovations across non-proximate (slippery) space resembles, or is autonomous of, other forms of globalisation.

The second methodological issue we have concerns the typological unmarkedness of some of the variants under scrutiny. The influence of U.S. and British English is asserted as if that is the only possible source of the innovation, when, in at least some cases, the possibility of independent, parallel development cannot be ruled out. This is particularly germane if the variables do not seem to share fundamentally similar constraints. If the constraints are appreciably different (and it remains to be determined how different 'appreciably' is), we think that good linguistic practice should include an evaluation of whether the variants are cross-linguistically marked or unmarked. If they are highly unmarked, we would argue that a case needs to be made that rules out the possibility of superficial, though independent, convergence of the two varieties. For example, /t/ is often flapped intervocalically cross-linguistically, and /t/ is often subject to debuccalisation in coda position cross-linguistically (Harris and Kaye 1990). Given the phonetic naturalness of (t)-flapping and debuccalisation, a thorough examination of the possible global transmission of the (t) variables ought to show compelling reasons for assuming that they arise in New Zealand English as a consequence of the hegemonic influence of global varieties of English.

The same general point about relative markedness can be made for nonphonological variables too. Cross-linguistically, there are numerous attestations of verbs or adverbs meaning 'like' or 'similar' grammaticalising as ways of introducing quotations. Several papers in Güldemann and von Roncador (2002) show this, and Meyerhoff and Niedzielski (1998) provide a small survey of cross-linguistic parallels in the functions of 'like'. Given this, arguments about the transfer of *be like* as a quotative verb from U.S. English to other varieties of English ideally should take into consideration, and then rule out, the possibility of independent, parallel developments.

Of course, as studies of linguistic variation have shown, linguistic and social factors may interact. The replacement of syllable- or word-final (t) with a glottal stop is typologically so unremarkable that it occurs in U.S. English as well as British English, but no-one has suggested that the U.S. models for this variant are the target for New Zealanders. Likewise, some varieties of British English realise intervocalic /t/ in a manner that is perceptually very similar to a flap (e.g. glottal reinforcement of /t/ in Newcastle), but again, there is no suggestion that this is the model for New Zealanders' intervocalic flapping.

A final methodological issue is that it is asserted that speakers are targeting external varieties of English for all these variables without establishing how much these variants sound American or British to the average New Zealander. Meyerhoff (1993) acknow-ledged that this was a problem for her analysis, and noted that it stopped her from providing an adequate account of why some lexical pairs seem to shift to the innovative form and others do not (compare the frequencies for *cookie* and *can*). In other words, we have no way of evaluating the extent to which these variables have been nativised or transformed in a new speech community.

If, for example, New Zealanders do perceive forms like [bɛɾə] or variants like *flashlight* to be American then that would strengthen the claim that this variation is a consequence of the increasing global influence and spread of U.S. English. However, if the forms are perceived to be no more or less Kiwi than [bɛtə] or *torch* then we may want to think not so much in terms of the globalisation of U.S. English as in terms of a more vernacular variety of New Zealand English. For our purposes, *vernacular* is used in its original sense: that variety which is used by speakers in their most unself-conscious states (Labov 1972). As such, these forms are not part of a more self-conscious alignment with a non-New Zealand identity, but rather, they are part of the variety a speaker may use in those very contexts when one is least mindful of one's speech.

Recasting things this way does not change the fact that a variant may indeed have originated in U.S. English – and along with the arguments posited above regarding markedness, such origins suggest a means for such forms appearing in the vernacular –

but it shifts our theoretical focus. Instead of approaching the globalisation of linguistic variation with the sole focus on the end-states (as in Levitt's definition of globalisation), we gain a picture of globalisation that also emphasises the processes involved, specifically those that shift a form from one that signals a given non-local identity, to one that signals a more local one. This moves us more to McGrew's notion of globalisation which emphasised the spatial and the qualitative expansion of an innovation.

A further attraction of seeing changes in New Zealand English as part of the globalisation of a vernacular base is that it allows us to link changes taking place simultaneously in the apparent category killer, U.S. English. This shift to a focus on a global vernacular base allows us to talk about the apparent influence of external reference groups on U.S. English, as evidenced, for example, in the use of *wee* (as in 'little'), or *wank(er)*. At present, external influences on the linguistic heavyweight(s) like U.S. English are ignored. However, variationists might like to consider the possibility that all of these changes can be understood as facets of one underlying phenomenon. If we conceive of changes occurring across all varieties of English in terms of a broadening of the set of forms available to English speakers in the most informal (and therefore local) context, this avoids the (we think, highly problematic) claim that Americans are in any way trying to sound Scots (with *wee*) or British/Australasian (with *wank(er)*).

We have undertaken some preliminary work exploring New Zealanders' attitudes to the competing lexical pairs. This forms part of a larger exercise in evaluating the limits of the effects of the media on sociolinguistic variation (Meyerhoff and Niedzielski 2002). A web-based questionnaire was administered as a pilot study in September/October 2002. After working through several example and training sentences, respondents were asked to evaluate the typical 'New Zealand-ness' or 'Kiwi-ness' of 41 sentences. The lexical pairs were only one set of variables tested in the sentences. The test included a number of distractor sentences as well. Only responses from people who indicated that they have lived in New Zealand since childhood are reported here. The numbers of respondents are small, but the pilot revealed some interesting factors we will need to control for the full study.[2] Though we must necessarily be cautious then in interpreting the results, they do provide us with some helpful indicative trends.

The results from the pilot generally support our suspicion that some lexical variants have been localised by New Zealanders. That is, some innovative variants are perceived to be just as typical of New Zealand speech as their more long-standing equivalent. On the other hand, other lexical items seem to remain clearly indexed to some external (U.S. or British) norm and these are perceived as being in opposition to native New Zealand variants.

Example 1 illustrates the kind of question posed to the respondents, and shows the six-point scale on which they were asked to evaluate the typical 'New Zealand-ness' of the sentence: *not at all New Zealand* scored 1 point; *absolutely New Zealand* scored 6 points. Scores for each variant were averaged.

Example 1: Sample question and possible responses in attitudes survey

He got sick of waiting for the lift, so he walked up instead.

- Not at all New Zealand.
- Little bit.

- Entirely.
- Somewhat.
- Very.
- Absolutely New Zealand.

Table 18.4 shows that for some words, there was very high agreement between respondents as to whether they were *absolutely, very* or *not at all New Zealand*. This agreement was measured by ranking all variables according to the standard deviation of responses. There was a clear break between words where the standard deviation for the whole sample was less than 1.3, and words where the standard deviation was greater.

Words like *jersey* (s.d. = 1.06), *lift* (s.d. = 1.07), *biscuit* (s.d. = 1.2) and *cookie* (s.d. = 1.26) are those on which there is high agreement, that is, there is considerable consistency across individuals on the relative New Zealand-ness of the item. The next words, *petrol* (s.d. = 1.48), *torch* (s.d. = 1.53), *pictures* (s.d. = 1.56), *sweater* (s.d. = 1.57), *trousers* (s.d. = 1.64), *tin* (s.d. = 1.65), and *serviette* and *gas* (s.d. = 1.69) are words on which there is moderate consistency in attitudes across individuals. The remainder (s.d. 1.7 < 2.2), can be considered words on which there is low consistency of attitudes across individuals. In order, these are: *pants, can, lorry, napkin, elevator, truck, flashlight, movies, hood* and *bonnet*. Note that, as we might expect (but is not necessarily the case), two sets of lexical pairs are represented here by both variants: *lorry* and *truck*, and *hood* and *bonnet*. Perceptions about *hood* and *bonnet* show the highest incongruencies between individuals, and the same person may rank a sentence carrying one variant as being equally (a) typical of New Zealand English as a sentence carrying the other variant.

These preliminary findings indicate that within the superset of lexical pairs, there are clearly distinct subsets: some variants are spreading, yet are widely perceived to be exotic, and some variants are spreading, but appear to be nativising, or to be being reinterpreted as local [the broadening of the vernacular base]. Variants that are widely and relatively uniformly perceived to be exotic might well have rather different histories and paths of diffusion within the speech community than ones that are quickly reanalysed, and which, instead of being seen as borrowings, are perceived to be home-grown variants. If this proves to be true, then we may, in turn, be able to enrich our analysis of the global hegemony of some varieties of English with the facts of idiosyncratic changes, such as front vowel raising, that characterise New Zealand English today and which seem to be such clear declarations of independent (and, in all senses, post-colonial) identities.

Let us be quite clear, however, that this is not to deny that hegemony may still be an issue. Werbner (1997) criticises (quite rightly, we think) 'diasporic intellectuals' whose

Table 18.4 Attitudes towards variable lexical items in New Zealand English: variants with most consistent responses (N = 21)

Lexical item	Most frequent response	Average of all responses	Consistency of attitudes*
lift	Absolutely New Zealand	Very New Zealand	High
jersey	Very New Zealand	Very New Zealand	High
biscuit	Very New Zealand	Very New Zealand	High
cookie	Not at all New Zealand	A little bit New Zealand	High

* As measured by standard deviation < 1.3

stance of relativism celebrates post-colonial hybridity, while trivialising the politics of ongoing exploitation and oppression. Nor do we understand or argue that localisation is necessarily a form of subversion and protest. Klein (2000) does a good job of critiquing the way social and economic hegemony are bundled together with the globalisation of markets; however, in celebrating as subversive the way groups like Australia's *Buga-Up* (the group that ironically defaces billboard advertising) co-opt global trends and global marketing campaigns, we think that she fails to see that such a celebration of individualism can also be construed as a manifestation of the hegemony of American cultural values (we are reminded of Cameron's 2000 critique of the export of American norms for politeness in service encounters). For this reason, it is important that the study of variation strike a balance between finding a space for speakers' attitudes and perceptions while not privileging these perceptions at the expense of macro-level critiques of power.

Many cultural critics (e.g. Kraidy 2002; Parameswaran 2002; Shome 1996; Werbner 1997) would argue that this creative co-optation constitutes only the chimera of resistance and is not to be celebrated. Kavoori (1998) is right, we think, to draw our attention to how closely the (economic, ethnic and class) interests of globalisation and post-colonialism are entwined, though he is probably unduly pessimistic about the ability of post-colonial theory to critique this (Parameswaran 2002: 288; Shome 1998). For instance, Parameswaran's critique focuses attention on the role of the mass media, arguing that they are 'key sites' where the related ideologies of globalisation and post-colonialism are 'repeatedly manufactured and distributed' (2002: 312). We take it that the role of the sociolinguist in all of this is to illuminate the extent to which speakers' patterns of language variation and use reify or challenge the interests of globalisation and post-colonialism, and thereby contribute to the mapping of the diffuse workings of power (Kraidy 2002: 334).

NOTES

1. Holmes reports that differences for both variables are significant at $p < 0.001$, but only gives percentage figures. Note percentages reported for middle-class speakers in Table 18.3 (Holmes 1995b: 63) differ slightly from those discussed in the text (1995b: 61). I have used the figures from Table 18.3.

2. For example, some respondents indicated that the relative inacceptability of a sentence might be due to the choice of preposition used, a variable not under consideration, or the choice of tense-aspect marking in the verb phrase.

REFERENCES

Audretsch, David B. (2000) Knowledge, globalisation, and regions: an economist's perspective. In John H. Dunning (ed.) *Regions, Globalisation, and the Knowledge-Based Economy*. Oxford: Oxford University Press, 63–81.

Bauman, Zygmunt (1998) *Globalisation: The Human Consequences*. Cambridge: Polity Press.

Bayard, Donn (1989) 'Me say that? No way!': The social correlates of American lexical diffusion in New Zealand English. *Te Reo* 32: 17–60.

Bayard, Donn (1990) Minder, Mork and Mindy? (-t) glottalisation and post-vocalic (-r) in younger New Zealand English speakers. In Allan Bell and Janet Holmes (eds) *New Zealand Ways of Speaking English*. Wellington: Victoria University Press, 149–164.

Buchstaller, Isabelle (2002) BE like U.S. English? BE goes U.S. English? Paper presented at New Ways of Analyzing Variation 31, Stanford University, California.

Callary, Robert E. (1975) Phonological change and the development of an urban dialect in Illinois. *Language in Society* 4: 155–169.

Cameron, Deborah (2000) *Good to Talk: Living and Working in a Communication Culture*. London: Sage.

Cheshire, Jenny (1982) *Variation in an English Dialect: A Sociolinguistic Study*. Cambridge: Cambridge University Press.

Dunning, John H. (2000) Regions, globalisation, and the knowledge economy: the issues stated. In John H. Dunning (ed.) *Regions, Globalisation, and the Knowledge-Based Economy*. Oxford: Oxford University Press, 7–41.

Eckert, Penelope (2000) *Linguistic Variation as Social Practice*. Oxford: Blackwell.

Güldemann, Thomas and Manfred von Roncador (2002) *Reported Discourse: A Meeting Ground for Different Linguistic Domains* (Typological Studies in Language). Amsterdam, The Netherlands and Philadelphia, Pennsylvania: John Benjamins.

Harris, John and Jonathan Kaye (1990) A tale of two cities: London glottaling and New York City tapping. *The Linguistic Review* 7: 251–274.

Holmes, Janet (1994) New Zealand flappers: an analysis of T voicing in New Zealand English. *English World-Wide* 15: 195–224.

Holmes, Janet (1995a) Glottal stops in New Zealand English: an analysis of variants of word-final /t/. *Linguistics* 33: 433–463.

Holmes, Janet (1995b) Two for /t/: Flapping and glottal stops in New Zealand English. *Te Reo* 38: 53–72.

Kavoori, Anandam P. (1998) Getting past the latest 'post': assessing the term 'post-colonial'. *Critical Studies in Mass Communication* 15: 195–202.

Klein, Naomi (2000) *No Logo: No Space, No Choice, No Jobs*. London: Flamingo.

Kraidy, Marwan M. (2002) Hybridity in cultural globalisation. *Communication Theory* 12: 316–339.

Labov, William [1963] (1972) *Sociolinguistic Patterns*. Philadelphia, Pennsylvania: University of Pennsylvania Press.

Labov, William (2001) *Principles of Linguistic Change: Social Factors*. Oxford: Blackwell.

Levitt, Theodore (1983) The globalisation of markets. In Robert Z. Aliber and Reid W. Click (eds) *Readings in International Business: A Decision Approach*. Cambridge, Massachusetts/London: The MIT Press, 249–266.

Macaulay, Ronald (2001) You're like 'why not?' The quotative expressions of Glasgow adolescents. *Journal of Sociolinguistics* 5: 3–21.

McGrew, Anthony G. (1992) Conceptualizing global politics. In Anthony G. McGrew and Paul G. Lewis (eds) *Global Politics: Globalisation and the Nation State*. Cambridge: Polity Press, 1–28.

Markusen, Anne (1996) Sticky places in slippery space: a typology of industrial districts. *Economic Geography* 72: 293–313.

Meyerhoff, Miriam (1991) Not just Ninja Turtles – lexical shift in working class New Zealand English. Paper presented at the Ninth New Zealand Linguistics Conference, Canterbury University, Christchurch, New Zealand.

Meyerhoff, Miriam (1993) Lexical shift in working class New Zealand English. *English World-Wide* 14: 231–248.

Meyerhoff, Miriam and Nancy Niedzielski (1998) The syntax and semantics of *olsem* in Bislama. In Matthew Pearson (ed.) *Recent Papers in Austronesian Linguistics. UCLA Occasional Papers in Linguistics 21*. Los Angeles: UCLA Department of Linguistics, 235–243.

Meyerhoff, Miriam and Nancy Niedzielski (2002) Standards, the media and language change. Paper presented at New Ways of Analyzing Variation 31, Stanford University, California.

Milroy, James and Lesley Milroy (1978) Belfast: change and variation in an urban vernacular. In Peter Trudgill (ed.) *Sociolinguistic Patterns in British English*. London: Edward Arnold, 19–36.

Milroy, Lesley (1980) *Language and Social Networks*. Oxford: Blackwell.

Nichols, Patricia C. (1983) Linguistic options and choices for Black women in the rural South. In Barrie Thorne, Cheris Kramarae and Nancy Henley (eds) *Language Gender and Society*. Cambridge, Massachusetts: Newbury House, 54–68.

Parameswaran, Radhika (2002) Local culture in global media: Excavating colonial and material discourses in *National Geographic*. *Communication Theory* 12: 287–315.

Rickford, John and Faye McNair-Knox (1994) Addressee- and topic-influenced style shift. In Douglas Biber and Edward Finegan (eds) *Sociolinguistic Perspectives on Register*. Oxford and New York: Oxford University Press, 235–276.

Rogers, Everett M. (1995) *The Diffusion of Innovations*. New York: Free Press.

Sankoff, David and Suzanne Laberge (1978) The linguistic market and the statistical explanation of variability. In David Sankoff (ed.) *Linguistic Variation: Models and Methods*. New York: Academic Press, 239–250.

Shome, Raka (1996) Post-colonial interventions in the rhetorical canon: an 'other' view. *Communication Theory* 6: 40–59.

Shome, Raka (1998) Caught in the term 'post-colonial': why the 'post-colonial' still matters. *Critical Studies in Mass Communication* 15: 203–212.

Storper, Michael (2000) Globalisation and knowledge flows: an industrial geographer's perspective. In John H. Dunning (ed.) *Regions, Globalisation, and the Knowledge-Based Economy*. Oxford: Oxford University Press, 42–62.

Strassel, Stephanie M. (1997) Variation in American English flapping. In Claude Paradis, Diane Vincent, Denise Deshaies and Marty Laforest (eds) *Papers in Sociolinguistics: NWAV-26 à l'Université Laval*. Quebec: Editions nota bene, 125–135.

Tagliamonte, Sali and Rachel Hudson (1999) *Be like* et al. beyond America: the quotative system in British and Canadian youth. *Journal of Sociolinguistics* 3: 147–172.

Temple, Rosalind and Sali Tagliamonte (2001) New ways of analyzing t/d deletion: evidence from British English. Paper presented at New Ways of Analyzing Variation 30, North Carolina State University, North Carolina.

Trudgill, Peter (1983) *On Dialect: Social and Geographical Perspectives*. Oxford: Oxford University Press.

Trudgill, Peter and Jean Hannah (2002) *International English: A Guide to the Varieties of Standard English*. London: Arnold.

Valente, Thomas W. (1995) *Network Models of the Diffusion of Innovations*. Cresskill, New Jersey: Hampton Press.

Von Hipple, E. (1994) Sticky information and the locus of problem solving: Implications for innovation. *Management Science* 40: 429–439.

Werbner, Pnina (1997) Introductions: The dialectics of cultural hybridity. In Pnina Werbner and Tariq Modood (eds) *Debating Cultural Hybridity: Multi-cultural Identities and the Politics of Anti-racism*. London: Zed Books, 1–26.

QUESTIONS

Content

1. According to Meyerhoff and Niedzielski, why should variationists look at globalisation?
2. What is the difference between Levitt's and McGrew's definition of globalisation, particularly when applied to the study of sociolinguistic variables?
3. What conceptual and methodological issues/problems are there with previous analyses of variation in New Zealand English?
4. What does the perception test of the localness of lexical pairs show and what may these results mean for the diffusion of linguistic variables?

Concept

Meyerhoff and Niedzielski show how the perceived localness of lexical pairs can be tested. Why is this important and how can this be done for phonetic variables?

PART FOUR

Variation and Change

Editors' Introduction to Part Four

MANY OF THE ARTICLES in different sections of this Reader deal, in one way or another, with language variation. For a lot of sociolinguists, an important reason for studying variation is that the patterns of variation we find in a community of speakers at a particular time may provide evidence about the diffusion and uptake of changes taking place in language over a larger period of time. The papers in this section all have language variation at their core, and we have chosen them because they are particularly good examples of the intimate connections between the study of variation and language change.

The first paper has sometimes been credited with starting the field of sociolinguistics off. Labov's study of language variation on the island of Martha's Vineyard is one of the most cited papers in linguistics, but it is not nearly so often brought into juxtaposition with other studies working in the framework it founded. The paper is a substantial piece of work — it is reproduced here in its entirety — and in its entirety, it remains an important work, strongly suggesting a programmatic development Labov may have envisaged for the field of sociolinguistics.

Readers with only a minimal linguistics background may struggle somewhat with the lengthy section on how he determined how many variants to divide the attested forms he collected into. They may also find the long discussion of linguistic constraints challenging reading. The later discussion of how social factors correlate with the degree of raising in the (ay) and (aw) diphthongs can be read and appreciated without necessarily having worked through the more technical earlier sections. Having said that, aspiring sociolinguists should find it instructive to consider the connections he draws between formal descriptions of linguistic forms, the careful layering of historical dialectology data and synchronic variation, and the relative weighting of linguistic and social constraints. The basic principles in this article and a methodology that involves different modes of observation, and different age groups of speakers, continue to inform the field of sociolinguistics today.

One of Labov's major points in the Martha's Vineyard study was to demonstrate the non-random nature of what had hitherto been dismissed as "free variation", i.e. without any underlying rhyme or reason. With this study, Labov provided an alternate vision: one where a lot of linguistic puzzles could be addressed more satisfactorily if, in addition to the more familiar linguistic factors, social and attitudinal factors were considered as possible influences on people's language behaviour.

One of the methodological innovations introduced in this paper (and expanded on in Labov's subsequent work in New York City, Labov 2006) is the sampling of speakers of different ages within a speech community. By assuming that speakers in different age cohorts preserve the dominant linguistic norms of their speech community when they were growing up (and were fixing their grammar and phonology), sociolinguists can study changes *as they take place*, rather than having to wait until they have gone to (near) completion as historical linguists do. This sampling of different age groups has become known as studying change in *apparent time*. Apparent time studies complement real time studies, when a linguist compares records (written or recorded) of how people spoke at one time and records of how people spoke at a later time. Tagliamonte & Ito's paper provides an excellent model of how apparent time studies have continued to develop, maintaining a clear link between historical and synchronic data, and also providing readers with a valuable indication of some of the recurring patterns typical of many variables studied in urban dialectology studies. In particular, the role women within a particular age group may play in leading changes in progress.

Sankoff & Blondeau's paper addresses the reliability of the assumptions underlying apparent time, drawing on both apparent time data and real time data to study the change from a uvular "r" to an apical "r" in Montreal French. We have heavily excerpted this paper for the Reader in order to highlight this aspect of S&B's research. In the original, there is considerable detail on the historical context of the sound changes affecting /r/ in Montreal, personal data on speakers' backgrounds and use of /r/ in discourse, as well as much careful documentation of the reasoning and methods behind the comparison of different sub-samples of speakers at different times. Readers who are seriously engaged with the notion of apparent time should refer to the original, which like Labov's study provides a comprehensive model of how sociolinguistic studies of variation and change are inter-connected with other fields of linguistics and the social sciences.

Similarly, Trudgill's article considers the extent to which predictions based on apparent time data have been borne out in real time. He returns to the Norwich community he had described in detail a decade earlier, and finds several distinct profiles for the changes he had documented in the 1970s. He considers the possible impact that social and demographic changes in the area may have had on the trajectory of the different variables. Changes in people's attitudes to local and extra-local variants appear to have occurred over time, and Trudgill attempts to systematise these in terms of who the principal agents of change are and whether the variable is mainly dependent on linguistic or non-linguistic constraints. Some of these ideas foreshadow recent work on new dialect formation by both Trudgill (2004) and Labov (2007).

Cameron's article is also heavily excerpted from the original, where three linguistic variables in Puerto Rican Spanish are examined, parallels (or the lack of them) with variables in a number of other languages are also reviewed, and there is a good deal more discussion of sociological research on the interaction patterns among children. Cameron's concern is to explore the details of variation in different age cohorts of younger speakers, pre-teens and adolescents. This is in order to explore in more detail *how* and *why* gender differences in language might emerge during this crucial developmental period. In doing so, Cameron asks challenging questions about how the empirical patterns, e.g. in T&I, emerge. Cameron's paper (particularly in its entirety), would provide a helpful and thought-provoking link between variationist approaches to gender differences in language and the more ethnographically informed approaches which feature more prominently in Section 6 of this Reader, as would S&B's full-length discussions about individual speakers' life histories and their sociolinguistic profile.

REFERENCES

Labov, William (2006) *The Social Stratification of English in New York City*, 2nd ed. Cambridge: Cambridge University Press.

Labov, William (2007) Transmission and diffusion. *Language* 83: 344–387.

Trudgill, Peter (2004) *New-Dialect Formation: The Inevitability of Colonial Englishes*. Edinburgh: Edinburgh University Press.

FURTHER READING

Blake, Renée and Meredith Josey (2003) The /ay/ diphthong in a Martha's Vineyard community. *Language in Society* 32: 451–485.

Chambers, Jack K. and Peter Trudgill (1999) *Dialectology*. Cambridge: Cambridge University Press.

Chambers, J.K., Peter Trudgill and Natalie Schilling-Estes (2003) (eds) *Handbook of Language Variation and Change*. Oxford: Blackwell.

Cukor-Avila, Patricia and Guy Bailey (2001) The effects of the race of the interviewer on sociolinguistic fieldwork. *Journal of Sociolinguistics* 5: 254–270.

Eckert, Penelope and John R. Rickford (2001) (eds) *Style and Sociolinguistic Variation*. Cambridge: Cambridge University Press.

Meyerhoff, Miriam (2001) Dynamics of differentiation: on social psychology and cases of language variation. In Nikolas Coupland, Christopher Candlin and Srikant Sarang (eds) *Sociolinguistics and Social Theory*. London: Longman, 61–87.

Schilling-Estes, Natalie (2003). Investigating stylistic variation. In J.K. Chambers, Peter Trudgill and Natalie Schilling-Estes (eds) *Handbook of Language Variation and Change*. Oxford: Blackwell, 375–401.

Smith, Jennifer (2001) '*Ye ø na hear that kind o' things*': negative do in Buckie'. *English World-Wide* 21: 231–259.

Tagliamonte Sali and Jennifer Smith (2003) 'Either it isn't or it's not': neg/aux contraction in British dialects. *English World-Wide* 23: 251–282.

Weinreich, Uriel, William Labov and Marvin Herzog (1968) Empirical foundations for a theory of language change. In W. P. Lehmann and Y. Malkeil (eds) *Directions for Historical Linguistics: A Symposium*. Austin: University of Texas Press, 95–188.

Chapter 19

William Labov

THE SOCIAL MOTIVATION OF A SOUND CHANGE

THE WORK WHICH IS reported in this chapter concerns the direct observation of a sound change in the context of the community life from which it stems.[1] The change is a shift in the phonetic position of the first elements of the diphthongs /ay/ and /aw/, and the community is the island of Martha's Vineyard, Massachusetts. By studying the frequency and distribution of phonetic variants of /ay/ and /aw/ in the several regions, age levels, occupational and ethnic groups within the island, it will be possible to reconstruct the recent history of this sound change; by correlating the complex linguistic pattern with parallel differences in social structure, it will be possible to isolate the social factors which bear directly upon the linguistic process. It is hoped that the results of this procedure will contribute to our general understanding of the mechanism of linguistic change.

The problem of explaining language change seems to resolve itself into three separate problems: the origin of linguistic variations; the spread and propagation of linguistic changes; and the regularity of linguistic change. The model which underlies this three-way division requires as a starting point a variation in one or several words in the speech of one or two individuals.[2] These variations may be induced by the processes of assimilation or differentiation, by analogy, borrowing, fusion, contamination, random variation, or any number of processes in which the language system interacts with the physiological or psychological characteristics of the individual. Most such variations occur only once, and are extinguished as quickly as they arise. However, a few recur, and, in a second stage, they may be imitated more or less widely, and may spread to the point where the new forms are in contrast with the older forms along a wide front. Finally, at some later stage, one or the other of the two forms usually triumphs, and regularity is achieved.

Whereas for the first stage we are often overwhelmed with an excess of possible explanations, we have quite the reverse situation in attempting to account for the

Reprinted from: Labov, William (1972) The social motivation of a sound change. In William Labov *Sociolinguistic Patterns*. Philadelphia: University of Pennsylvania Press, 1–42.

propagation and regularity of linguistic changes. A number of earlier theories which proposed general psychological, physiological or even climatic determinants have been discarded for some time.[3] The contribution of internal, structural forces to the effective spread of linguistic changes, as outlined by Martinet (1955),[4] must naturally be of primary concern to any linguist who is investigating these processes of propagation and regularization. However, an account of structural pressures can hardly tell the whole story. Not all changes are highly structured, and no change takes place in a social vacuum. Even the most systematic chain shift occurs with a specificity of time and place that demands an explanation.

Widely divergent ideas appear to exist as to what comprises an explanation of the mechanism of change. The usual diachronic procedure, as followed in palaeontology or geology, is to explore the mechanism of change between states by searching for data on intermediate states. It follows that we come closer and closer to an accurate depiction of the mechanism of change as the interval between the two states we are studying becomes smaller and smaller. This is certainly the method followed by such historical linguists as Jespersen, Kökeritz, and Wyld, and it is the motivation behind their extensive searches for historical detail. On the other hand, a viewpoint which favors the abstract manipulation of data from widely separated states has been propounded by M. Halle (1962); explicit defense of a similar attitude may be found in H. Pilch's (1955) study of the vowel systems of Shakespeare, Noah Webster, and present-day America. Neither Halle nor Pilch distinguishes the three aspects of change outlined above.

It would seem that the historical approach is more appropriate to an empirical science concerned with change, even over a narrow time span, as this approach leads to statements which are increasingly subject to confirmation or disconfirmation. At the same time, such a close view of historical change makes us increasingly skeptical of the value of limitations on the kinds of data which may be considered: as, for instance, that the linguist explains linguistic events only by other linguistic events. One would expect that the application of structural linguistics to diachronic problems would lead to the enrichment of the data, rather than the impoverishment of it.[5]

The point of view of the present study is that one cannot understand the development of a language change apart from the social life of the community in which it occurs. Or to put it another way, social pressures are continually operating upon language, not from some remote point in the past, but as an immanent social force acting in the living present.

Sturtevant (1947:74–84) has outlined a concise theory of the spread and consolidation of language changes which consistently views this process in its social dimension. One sentence in particular will serve as an excellent theme for this investigation:

> Before a phoneme can spread from word to word . . . it is necessary that one of the two rivals shall acquire some sort of prestige.[6]

It is hoped that the study of the particular case under discussion will lend support to this general view of the role of social interaction in linguistic change.

THE ISLAND OF MARTHA'S VINEYARD

The island of Martha's Vineyard, Dukes County, Massachusetts, was chosen as a laboratory for an initial investigation of social patterns in linguistic change.[7] Martha's Vineyard has the advantage of being a self-contained unit, separated from the mainland by a good three miles of the Atlantic Ocean. At the same time, the Vineyard has enough social and geographic complexity to provide ample room for differentiation of linguistic behavior. We are also fortunate in having the records of the *Linguistic Atlas of New England* (henceforth abbreviated LANE) as a background for the investigation.[8] It is over thirty years since Guy Lowman visited Martha's Vineyard; his interviews with four members of the old families of the island give us a firm base from which to proceed, and a time depth of one full generation which adds considerably to the solidity of the conclusions which can be drawn.

Figure 19.1 shows the general outlines of Martha's Vineyard, and Table 19.1 gives the population figures from the 1960 Census. The island is divided into two parts by an informal, but universally used distinction between *up-island* and *down-island*. *Down-island* is the region of the three small towns where almost three-fourths of the permanent population live. *Up-island* is strictly rural, with a few villages, farms, isolated summer homes, salt ponds and marshes, and a large central area of uninhabited pine barrens.

As we travel up-island from Vineyard Haven, we come first to the town of West Tisbury, which contains some of the most beautiful farms and fields of the island, now largely untilled and ungrazed. At Chilmark, the ground rises to a series of rolling hills which look out to the Atlantic on one side, and to Vineyard Sound on the other. Chilmark's salt pond is permanently open to the Sound through a narrow channel, and so serves as a permanent harbor for the dozen fishermen who still operate from the docks of the village of Menemsha in Chilmark. Finally, at the southwest corner of the island, there is the promontory of Gay Head, and the houses of the 103 Indians who represent the original inhabitants of Martha's Vineyard.

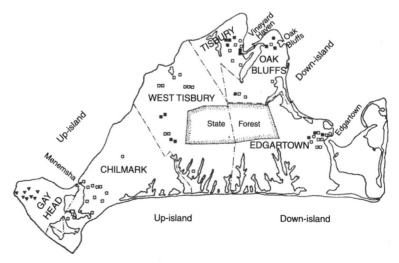

Figure 19.1 Location of the 69 informants on Martha's Vineyard. Ethnic origin is indicated as follows: ☐ English, ■ Portuguese, ▼ Indian. Symbols placed side by side indicate members of the same family.

Table 19.1   Population of Martha's Vineyard

Down-island [*towns*]	*3,846*
Edgartown	1,118
Oak Bluffs	1,027
Vineyard Haven	1,701
Up-island [*rural*]	*1,717*
Edgartown	256
Oak Bluffs	292
Tisbury	468
West Tisbury	360
Chilmark	238
Gay Head	103
Total	*5,563*

Source: From U.S. Bureau of the Census, *U.S. Census of Population: 1960. Number of Inhabitants. Massachusetts.* Final Report PC(1)–23A (Washington, D.C.: GPO, 1962), Table 7, p. 23–11.

The 6,000 native Vineyarders fall into four ethnic groups which are essentially endogamous. First, there are the descendants of the old families of English stock, who first settled the island in the 17th and 18th centuries: the Mayhews, Nortons, Hancocks, Allens, Tiltons, Vincents, Wests, Pooles—all closely related after ten generations of intermarriage. Secondly, there is a large group of Portuguese descent, immigrants from the Azores, Madeira, and the Cape Verde Islands. There are Portuguese all along the southeastern New England coast, but the Vineyard has the largest percentage of any Massachusetts county. In 1960, 11 percent of the population was of first- or second-generation Portuguese origin; with the third- and fourth-generation Portuguese, the total would probably come close to 20 percent.[9]

The third ethnic group is the Indian remnant at Gay Head. The fourth is the miscellaneous group of various origins: English, French Canadian, Irish, German, Polish. Though the sum total of this residual group is almost 15 percent, it is not a coherent social force, and we will not consider it further in this paper.[10]

Another group which will not be considered directly is the very large number of summer residents, some 42,000, who flood the island in June and July of every year. This tide of *summer people* has had relatively little direct influence on the speech of the Vineyard, although the constant pressure from this direction, and the growing dependence of the island upon a vacation economy, has had powerful indirect effects upon the language changes which we will consider.

The Vineyard is best known to linguists as an important relic area of American English: an island of *r*-pronouncers in a sea of *r*-lessness. With a 320-year history of continuous settlement, and a long record of resistance to Boston ways and manners, the island has preserved many archaic traits which were probably typical of southeastern New England before 1800. The most striking feature, still strongly entrenched, is the retention of final and preconsonantal /r/.[11] New England short /o/ is still well represented among the older speakers. Exploratory studies of the Vineyard in 1961 showed that most of the special traits of the island speech shown on the LANE maps may still be found among traditional speakers from 50 to 95 years old.

Lexical survivals of 17th-century English are even clearer indications of the archaic nature of the Vineyard tradition. We find *bannock*, for a fried cake of corn meal, *studdled* for 'dirty, roiled' water, in addition to such items as *tempest* and *buttry* listed in the LANE. Perhaps the most dramatic evidence of the fact that the Vineyard represents an underlying stratum is the presence of *belly-gut*, for a face-down sled ride. In LANE records, this form is shown on the Vineyard and in western New England; in the intervening area, it has been overlaid by three successive layers—*belly-bump, belly-flop*, and currently, no word at all.[12]

As interesting as the structure of Martha's Vineyard English may be, it is not the purpose here to contrast one static system with another. We would like to understand the internal structure of Vineyard English, including the systematic differences which now exist and the changes now taking place within the island. For this purpose, we will select for study a linguistic feature with the widest possible range of variation and the most complex pattern of distribution characteristic of Martha's Vineyard.

SELECTION OF THE LINGUISTIC VARIABLE

It would be appropriate to ask at this point what are the most useful properties of a linguistic variable to serve as the focus for the study of a speech community. First, we want an item that is frequent, which occurs so often in the course of undirected natural conversation that its behavior can be charted from unstructured contexts and brief interviews. Secondly, it should be structural: the more the item is integrated into a larger system of functioning units, the greater will be the intrinsic linguistic interest of our study. Third, the distribution of the feature should be highly stratified: that is, our preliminary explorations should suggest an asymmetric distribution over a wide range of age levels or other ordered strata of society.

There are a few contradictory criteria, which pull us in different directions. On the one hand, we would like the feature to be salient, for us as well as for the speaker, in order to study the direct relations of social attitudes and language behavior. But on the other hand, we value immunity from conscious distortion, which greatly simplifies the problem of reliability of the data.[13]

In the exploratory interviews conducted on the Vineyard in 1961, many structural changes were noted that were plainly parallel to changes taking place on the mainland under the influence of the standard southeast New England pattern. Changes in phonemic inventory were found: New England short /o/ is rapidly disappearing; the two low back vowels, /ɑ/ and /ɔ/ are merging. Important changes in phonemic distribution are occurring: the /or ~ɔr/ distinction is disappearing: initial /hw/ is giving way to /h/.[14] Shifts in structured lexical systems, all in the direction of regional standards, can be traced. Archaic syntactic features are disappearing. Yet as interesting as these changes may be, there is no reason to think that their distribution will follow a pattern peculiar to the Vineyard.

In the case of postvocalic /r/, however, we do have a linguistic variable defined by the geographical limits of the island, which follows a social pattern idiosyncratic to Martha's Vineyard. In some island areas, retroflexion is increasing, and in others, decreasing; as we will note later, the social implications of this fact can not be missed. The variations in /r/ are frequent, salient, and involve far-reaching structural consequences for the entire vowel system.

However, the preliminary exploration of the Vineyard indicated that another variable might be even more interesting: differences in the height of the first element of the diphthongs /ay/ and /aw/. Instead of the common southeast New England standard [aɪ] and [aʊ], one frequently hears on Martha's Vineyard [ɐɪ] and [ɐʊ], or even [əɪ] and [əʊ]. This feature of centralized diphthongs[15] is salient for the linguist, but not for most speakers; it is apparently quite immune to conscious distortion, as the native Vineyarders are not aware of it, nor are they able to control it consciously. As far as structure is concerned, we cannot neglect the structural parallelism of /ay/ and /aw/; on the other hand, these diphthongs are marked by great structural freedom in the range of allophones permitted by the system. These are strictly subphonemic differences. Since there are no other up-gliding diphthongs with either low or central first elements in this system, it is not likely that continued raising, or even fronting or backing, would result in confusion with any other phoneme.

The property of this feature of centralization which makes it appear exceptionally attractive, even on first glance, is the indication of a complex and subtle pattern of stratification. This very complexity proves to be rewarding: for when the centralizing tendency is charted in the habits of many speakers, and the influence of the phonetic, prosodic, and stylistic environment is accounted for, there remains a large area of variation. Instead of calling this "free" or "sporadic" variation, and abandoning the field, we will pursue the matter further, using every available clue to discover the pattern which governs the distribution of centralized diphthongs.

The problem becomes all the more significant when it becomes apparent that the present trend on Martha's Vineyard runs counter to the long-range movement of these diphthongs over the past two hundred years. And while this sound change is not likely to become a phonemic change in the foreseeable future, it operates in an area where far-reaching phonemic shifts have taken place in the past. It is, in effect, the unstable residue of the Great Vowel Shift.

THE HISTORY OF CENTRALIZED DIPHTHONGS

It seems generally agreed that the fist element of the diphthong /ay/ was a mid-central vowel in 16th- and 17th-century English (Jespersen 1927:234; Kökeritz 1953:216).[16] We may assume that when Thomas Mayhew first took possession of his newly purchased property of Martha's Vineyard in 1642, he brought with him the pronunciation [əɪ] in *right, pride, wine* and *wife*. The later history of this vowel in America indicates that [əɪ] continued to be the favored form well into the 19th century.[17]

When we examine the records of the LANE, we find that centralized /ay/ was a healthy survivor in the speech of the Atlas informants.[18] We find it scattered throughout the rural areas of New England, and strongly entrenched in the Genesee Valley of western New York. It had disappeared completely from the Midland, but was quite regular—before voiceless consonants—in both the Upper and Lower South. This differential effect of voiceless and voiced following consonants was only a directing influence in the North, but stood as a regular phonetic rule in the South. On Martha's Vineyard, as on neighboring Nantucket and Cape Cod, centralized /ay/ was frequently recorded.

The history of /aw/ differs from that of /ay/ more than our general expectations of symmetry would lead us to predict. There is reason to believe that in England the lowering of /aw/ was considerably in advance of /ay/, and it is not likely that the same Thomas Mayhew used [əu] in *house* and *out* (Jespersen 1927:235–36; Kökeritz 1953: 144–49; Wyld 1920:230–31). The American evidence of the late 18th and 19th centuries, as summed up by Krapp (1925 2:192–96), points to [oʊ] as the conservative, cultured form, giving way to [aʊ] or [ɑʊ], with the rural New England form as [æʊ] or [ɛʊ]. The Linguistic Atlas records show only a hint of parallelism of /ay/ and /aw/ (Kurath and McDavid 1951: Maps 28–29). We find [əʊ] mainly in eastern Virginia, before voiceless consonants, with some small representation in upstate New York, but the principal New England form of [aʊ] stood out against a background of rural and recessive [æʊ]. Martha's Vineyard shows very little centralization of /aw/ in the LANE maps.

This brief review indicates that the isolated position of /aw/ has facilitated phonetic variation on a truly impressive scale. The first element has ranged from [ɪ] to [ɑ], from [ɛ] to [o] all within the same general structural system. Perhaps one reason why /ay/ has not shown a similar range of variation is the existence of another upgliding diphthong, /ɔy/.[19] In any case, as the stage is set for our present view of Martha's Vineyard diphthongs, /ay/ is well centralized, but /aw/ is not. It may be too strong a statement to say that this represents the phonetic heritage of the seventeenth-century Yankee settlers of the island, but we may venture to say that we have no evidence of any intervening events which disturbed the original pattern.

As we begin the systematic study of this centralization pattern, we will refer to the linguistic variables (ay) and (aw) instead of the phonemes /ay/ and /aw/. Where the subphonemic differences in the position of the nucleus of /ay/ and /aw/ are considered to be in *free variation*, and linguistically insignificant, the variants of (ay) and (aw) show significant differences in their distribution and carry sociolinguistic information. In this case (but not always), the variables (ay) and (aw) represent the same phonetic substance as the invariant categories /ay/ and /aw/; the parentheses indicate a different approach to the analysis of variation. Whereas // means that internal variation is to be disregarded as insignificant, ( ) indicates that this variation is the prime focus of study.

THE INVESTIGATION OF (ay) AND (aw)

The summer visitor to Martha's Vineyard gets only a fleeting impression of the native speech pattern. Seven out of every eight human beings on the island are visitors like himself. But for the Vineyarder, there is no effect of dilution. For him, summer visitors have very little status on the island and their ephemeral nature is convincingly demonstrated in the first week in September of every year, when they disappear even more quickly than the insect population of the summer months. The normal native speech of Martha's Vineyard can then be heard as the dominant sound in public places. A knock on any up-island door will no longer produce a Back Bay stockbroker, but the rightful owner in possession once again. As a rural up-islander he is very likely to use a high degree of centralization of (ay) and (aw); but in the small town areas of down-island one may also hear this feature, particularly in words such as *right, white, twice, life, wife, like,* but not so much in *while, time, line, I, my, try*. Similarly, one may hear in the streets of Vineyard Haven centralized forms in *out, house, doubt,* but not so much in *now, how, or around.*

In order to study this feature systematically, it was necessary to devise an interview schedule which would provide many examples of (ay) and (aw) in casual speech, emotionally colored speech, careful speech, and reading style. The first of these diphthongs is more than twice as frequent as the second, but even so, several devices were required to increase the concentration of occurrences of both.

1. A lexical questionnaire, using the regional markers shown as most significant in the maps of the LANE, supplemented with recent observations, and concentrating on the following words containing (ay) and (aw):

spider	rareripe	iodine	dying out
sliding	swipe	quinine	flattening out
		scrimy	dowdy
white bread	nigh		outhouse
white of egg	pie	frying pan	backhouse
nightcrawler	sty	fry pan	crouch
lightning bug	firefly		mow
Italian	shiretown		rowen

2. Questions concerning value judgments, exploring the social orientation of the respondent, were so phrased as to elicit answers containing (ay) and (aw) forms.[20] Answers to such questions often gave a rich harvest of diphthongal forms, with contrasting uses of emotionally stressed and unstressed variants.
3. A special reading, used mainly in the high school, was offered ostensibly as a test of the ability to read a story naturally.[21] Since these readings gave the most exact comparisons between speakers, they were utilized for the spectrographic measurements discussed below.

In addition to the formal interview, observations were made in a great many casual situations: on the streets of Vineyard Haven and Edgartown, in diners, restaurants, bars, stores, docks, and many places where the general sound of public conversation could be noted, if not effectively recorded. But these notations only served as a supplementary check on the tape-recorded interviews. The basic information was gathered in the course of 69 interviews with native island speakers made in three periods: August 1961, late September-October 1961, January 1962. These 69 interviews provide the basis for the discussion to follow.

The 69 speakers, somewhat more than 1 percent of the population, represent a judgment sample of the community of native residents, and the groups which are important in the social life and value systems of the island. The sampling is proportional to area rather than population: 40 are up-islanders, and only 29 are from down-island, though over 70 percent of the people live down-island. The most important occupational groups are represented: 14 in fishing, 8 in farming, 6 in construction, 19 in service trades, 3 professionals, 5 housewives, 14 students. The three main ethnic groups are represented: 42 of English descent, 16 Portuguese, and 9 Indian.

The locations of the 69 informants are shown on Figure 19.1, coded by ethnic group. It may be understood that a large proportion of those engaged in fishing are to be found in Chilmark; the farmers are well inland, mainly in West Tisbury; the service trades are heavily concentrated in Edgartown and Vineyard Haven. Of Guy Lowman's four LANE informants, one was in Chilmark, one in West Tisbury, and two in Edgartown.

As a result of these 69 interviews, we have about 3,500 instances of (ay) and 1,500 instances of (aw) as the basic data for this study.

SCALES OF MEASUREMENT

An important step was to construct a reliable, inter-subjective index to the degree of centralization. In the original transcriptions of the tape-recorded interviews a six-point scale of height of the first element was used, ranging from the standard New England form [aɪ] to the fully centralized [əɪ].[22] Such a transcription was intended to push the distinctions noted to the limits of auditory discrimination. This corresponded to the practice of the LANE, in which the same number of degrees of height can be symbolized. However, it was recognized that such fine distinctions could probably only be reproduced consistently by individuals who had attained a high degree of convergence, and then over a very short time span.

Independent instrumental measurements were used to reduce the scale by objective criteria, and to give a certain degree of objective validity to the entire system of transcription.

Acoustic spectrograms were made of 80 instances of (ay) as spoken and recorded by seven different Vineyarders.[23] A study of the assembled formant patterns indicated that one particular moment might be best suited for measuring the degree of height of the first element of the diphthong. This is shown in Figure 19.2, as the point where the first formant reaches a maximum. Measurements of the first and second formant positions at this point seemed to correspond well to the formant measurements for steady state vowels [a] to [ə] in Peterson and Barney's (1952) vowel studies.[24]

The 80 measurements were then plotted on a bi-logarithmic scale, with abscissa and ordinate corresponding to first and second formants. The original impressionistic transcriptions were then entered for each measurement, and the result examined for clear separation of impressionistic levels. On the whole, the stratification was good: the impressionistic ratings with more open first elements showed higher first formant and lower second formant readings. However, the separation of grades 2 from 3, and 4 from 5, was not as clear as the others. A reduced four-step scale was then established, and the resulting correlation shown in Figure 19.3, and the table below.[25]

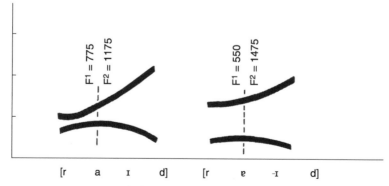

Figure 19.2 Measurement of typical (ay) diphthongs at first formant maximum.

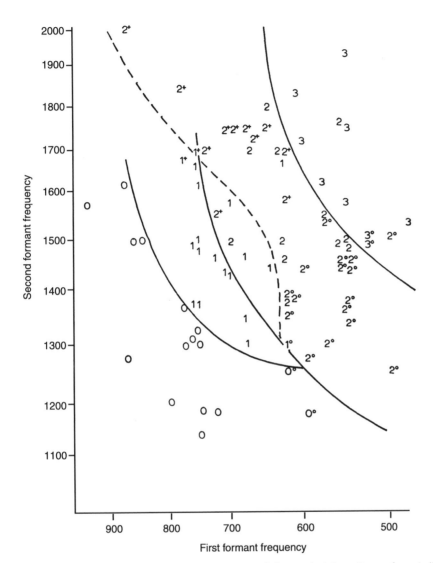

Figure 19.3 Correlation of instrumental measurement and impressionistic ratings of centralization. Nos. 0–3: Scale II equivalents of impressionistic ratings of height of first elements of 86 (ay) diphthongs, assigned before spectrographic measurement. Seven different Martha's Vineyard speakers, males aged 14–60, are represented. ° identifies speaker EP, age 31; + identifies speaker GW, age 15.

	Scale I	Scale II
1	[a] ————————————— 0	
2	[aˑ]	
3	[ɐˑ]	1
4	[ɐ]	
5	[ɐˑ]	2
6	[ə] ————————————— 3	

Figure 19.3 shows the values for Scale II mapped on the bi-logarithmic scale. This is a satisfactory result, with good separation of the four grades of centralization. We have also obtained some justification for the use of the first formant maximum in measuring spectrograms, rather than the second formant minimum. Since the lines separating the four grades parallel the second-formant axis more than the first-formant axis, we have a graphic demonstration that our phonetic impressions are more sensitive to shifts in the first formant than the second.

When this display was originally planned, there was some question as to whether it would be possible to map many different speakers on the same graph. We know that there are significant differences in individual frames of formant reference. Small children, for instance, appear to have vowel triangles organized at considerably higher frequencies than adults. The seven speakers whose readings are displayed in Fig. 19.3 are all male; four are high school students, aged 14 to 15. But the other three are adults, from 30 to 60 years old, with widely different voice qualities.

Ideally, if we were studying the acoustic nature of the (ay) and (aw) diphthongs, we would want a more uniform group of speakers. Secondly, we would ask for better and more uniform recording conditions: one recording was outdoors, two were in living rooms, four in an empty conference room. However, since the object of the testing was to lend objective confirmation to an impressionistic scale of discrimination, it is only realistic to use a range of recordings as varied as the body of material on which the entire study is based. Absence of separation of the four grades in Figure 19.3 might then have indicated only defects in instrumental technique, but a positive result can hardly be derived from such a bias.

It is interesting to note that measurements from no one speaker are distributed over more than half of Figure 19.3, and some speakers are sharply limited to a narrow sector—still occupying portions of all the grades of centralization. For instance, the highly centralized speaker EP, aged 31, accounts for all of the readings in the lower right portion marked with a ° sign: 0°, 2°, etc. He shows no readings higher than 650 or 1500 cps. On the other hand, speaker GW, aged 15, also highly centralized, accounts for the upper left portion; his readings, marked with a + sign, are all higher than 625 or 1550 cps. Again, speaker GM, aged 15, is limited to a belt from lower left to upper right, filling the space between the two just mentioned. Despite the differences in vowel placement, these seven speakers utilize the same dimension to produce the effect of centralized or open vowels: widely separated formants for centralized vowels, adjacent formants for open vowels. The opposition, though not distinctive, is clearly seen as ranging from compact to (relatively) noncompact.

This display then indicates for us that the reduced impressionistic scale shows good stratification in terms of physical parameters, and we may proceed to employ such ratings with some confidence in their validity.

THE LINGUISTIC ENVIRONMENT

We can now plot the distribution of centralized forms for each speaker. This is done for each of the 69 interviews on a chart such as is shown in Figure 19.4. We find that these charts fall into three basic types:

a.   uncentralized norms: all words, or almost all, fall into Grade 0, with at most only a few Grade 1's in favored words such as *right* and *out*.

b.   centralized norms: most words with Grade 2, and only a few Grade 1's for unfavored forms, such as *time* and *cow*.

c.   phonetic conditioning: the influence of the phonetic environment is reflected in a range of values from Grades 0 to 2. Figure 19.4 is an example of this type.

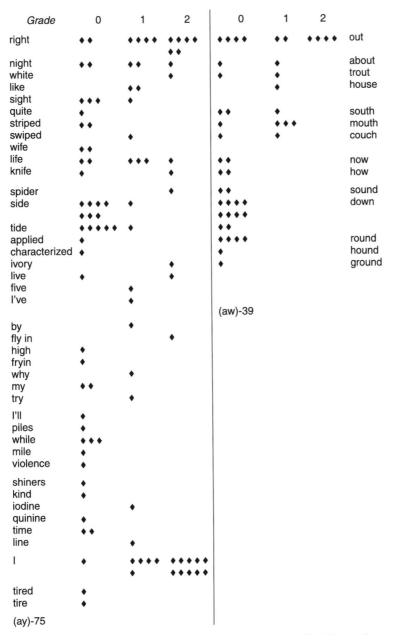

Figure 19.4   Phonetic determination of centralization. Centralization chart for North Tisbury fisherman GB.

Such phonetic conditioning is reminiscent of the phonetic regularity found in the southern United States. (Shewmake 1927). But on Martha's Vineyard, the distribution is more complex, and nowhere codified with the precision to be found in the South. Before proceeding to chart the various social factors which influence this feature, we should consider the influence of the linguistic environment, and primarily phonetic conditioning.

Segmental environment

The influence of the *following consonant* may be indicated by tabulating five general articulatory dimensions:

Not favoring centralization		*Favoring centralization*
(*a*) sonorants	zero final	obstruents
(*b*) nasals		orals
(*c*) voiced		voiceless
(*d*) velars	labials	apicals
(*e*) fricatives		stops

If we apply these oppositions in the order given, from (*a*) to (*e*), we arrive at a consonant series from most favoring to least favorable to centralization, which seems to conform quite well to the facts:

$$/t, s; p, f; d, v, z; k, \theta, ð: ø: l, r; n: m/^{26}$$

The *preceding consonant* follows a rather different pattern, almost the reverse, and has considerably less effect. The most favoring initial consonants in centralized syllables are /h, l, r, w, m, n/, with the glottal stop allophone of zero heading the list. Thus the most favored words are *right, wife, night, light, nice, life, house, out.*

Prosodic factors

Stress regularly increases the degree of centralization for speakers with type (b) and type (c) charts. This is not at all an obvious rule, for the speech of many metropolitan areas shows the opposite tendency: one may note an occasional centralized diphthong in rapid reduced forms, but the same word under full stress is completely uncentralized. This corresponds to the difference between a centralized occurrence and a centralized norm.

A typical case of centralization under stress occurs in this excerpt from a story told by a North Tisbury fisherman:

> Why I could do anything with this dog. I used to drop a [naɪf] or my handkerchief or something, and I'd walk pretty near a quarter of a mile, and I'd stop and I'd turn to the dog: "You go get that! Where'd I lose that [nɐɪf]!"

Stylistic influence

While we find that most urban speakers have a variety of shifting styles of speech, and that interviews under varying conditions will produce varying counts of phonological features, this is not the case with most Vineyarders. The majority are essentially single-style speakers. Sometimes the conversation will take a livelier tone, or a more formal aspect, but the percentage of centralized forms is not significantly affected. Changes in centralization are apparently aspects of a pattern which develops over longer periods of time.[27]

Lexical considerations

A few special words are given greater centralization than their phonetic form or prosodic position would usually account for. An example is *sliding*, meaning coasting with a small sled. It may be that confusion with an alternant form *sledding* is responsible, or that words which originate in childhood, and are seldom spelled, are more prone to centralization.

Distribution by age and time

The overall degree of centralization for each speaker is expressed by the mean of the numerical values of the variants multiplied by 100. Thus for Figure 19.4, the values are (ay)-75 and (aw)-39. We can then find the values of the variable for any group of persons by averaging the values for the members of the group.

We may first wish to see if centralization varies with the age level of the speaker. Table 19.2 indicates that it does. Centralization of (ay) and (aw) appear to show a regular increase in successive age levels, reaching a peak in the 31 to 45 group. We must now consider the reasons for assessing this pattern as evidence for an historical change in the linguistic development of Martha's Vineyard. Is this an example of sound change, or is it merely evidence for a regular change in speaking patterns which is correlated with age?

At this point it is necessary to consider the general question as to whether sound change can be directly observed. The well-known statement of Bloomfield (1933:347) seems to contradict this possibility:

> The process of linguistic change has never been directly observed; we shall see that such observation, with our present facilities, is inconceivable.

Table 19.2   Centralization of (ay) and (aw) by age level

Age	(ay)	(aw)
75–	25	22
61–75	35	37
46–60	62	44
31–45	81	88
14–30	37	46

When this opinion is viewed in the light of Bloomfield's entire discussion of phonetic change, it appears to be strongly motivated by arguments for the absolute regularity of sound change. Bloomfield wishes to show that such change is quite autonomous, "a gradual favoring of some non-distinctive variants and a disfavoring of others," and quite distinct from the normal fluctuation of non-distinctive forms, "at all times highly variable." Yet since direct observations will always pick up this normal fluctuation, "even the most accurate phonetic record of a language at any one time could not tell us which phonemes were changing" (p. 365). The changes we do observe are likely to be the effects of borrowing and analogic change.

Hockett (1958:439), while recognizing the possibility of divergent views, has further refined the doctrine of imperceptible changes as a basic mechanism of linguistic change. Movements of the center of the normal distribution of random variations are, for all practical purposes, not subject to direct observation, while the cruder forms of change which are observed must be due to minor mechanisms. Weinreich (1959) has pointed out the theoretical limitations of this position;[28] here we may profitably examine the result of applying such neo-grammarian thinking to empirical observations.

The prototype of close studies of sound change in a single community is Gauchat's (1905) investigation of the patois of Charmey, in French-speaking Switzerland. Gauchat observed and tabulated differences in six phonological features in the speech of three generations: speakers over 60 years old, those between 30 and 60, and those under 30 (see Chs. 7 and 9 [of Labov 1972]). Hermann returned to the scene in 1929, one generation later, to investigate four of these features: his results confirmed the interpretation of Gauchat's data as evidence for historical change, since three of the four had advanced considerably in the same direction. Yet Hermann (1929) also showed that real time depth is essential for an accurate view, since the fourth feature had not changed since 1903, and was apparently subject to a number of conflicting influences.

The neo-grammarian viewpoint is that such observable shifts are the results of a series of borrowings, imitations, and random variations.[29] These complicated explanations could be applied without contradiction to the present observations on Martha's Vineyard. But we need not make the gratuitous assumption that sound change is something else again, an ineluctable process of drift which is beyond the scope of empirical studies. Here I would like to suggest that the mixed pattern of uneven phonetic conditioning, shifting frequencies of usage in various age levels, areas, and social groups, as we have observed it on Martha's Vineyard, is the process of linguistic change in the simplest form which deserves the name. Below this level, at the point of individual variation, we have events which are sublinguistic in significance. At the first stage of change, where linguistic changes originate, we may observe many sporadic side-effects of articulatory processes which have no linguistic meaning: no socially determined significance is attached to them, either in the differentiation of morphemes, or in expressive function. Only when social meaning is assigned to such variations will they be imitated and begin to play a role in the language. Regularity is then to be found in the end result of the process, as Sturtevant (1947:78–81) has argued, and not in the beginning.[30]

If we now accept the evidence we have on hand as adequate in quantity, reliable, and valid, we must still decide if this particular case is an example of a change in community habits of speech. Two aspects of the question seem to make a good case for a positive answer.

First, the records of the LANE show only moderate centralization of (ay) for the four informants of 1933, aged 56 to 82. It is impossible to calibrate the Lowman transcription against our present scale, especially since his data put more stress on short utterances with stressed, elicited forms. But if we take the LANE symbol [ɐ] as equivalent to our present [ɐ] of Grade 2, it appears that these speakers had centralized norms for (ay) averaging about 86, as high as the highest point reached in our sample for age level 60 to 90, but only half as high as the highest point for age level 30 to 60. If we weigh their performance against a matched group of present-day speakers, we may conclude that there has been an intervening drop of centralization before the present rise.

Secondly, the question of (aw) is conclusive. The LANE informants had an average rating of 06 for (aw): that is, for all practical purposes, zero. The record shows a steady rise in centralization of (aw)—which we have seen to be a completely new phenomenon in Martha's Vineyard English—reaching values of well over 100 for most old family, up-island speakers, and going as high as 211 in one case. No postulated change in speaking habits with age could account for this rise.

The fact that the amount of centralization for the very old, and the very young speakers, is at a minimum, shows that the effect of age cannot be discounted entirely, and it may indeed be a secondary factor in this distribution over age levels.

POSSIBLE EXPLANATIONS FOR A RISE IN CENTRALIZATION

So far, our discussion of centralization, the dependent variable under study, has been merely descriptive. As we turn to the problem of explanation, we are faced with the question of what independent variables to examine. Certainly the structural parallelism of (ay) and (aw) is significant here.[31] Let us assume for the moment that centralization declined to a low point in the late 1930s, and then, after the war, began to rise. At this point we find that a rising first element of (ay) carries the first element of (aw) with it. Such a change in direction would seem to give us a plausible explanation for the parallelism being called into play at this time, rather than the assumption that it suddenly began to operate after a three-hundred-year hiatus.

There remains the prior question, that of explaining (or giving a larger context for) the general rise of centralization on the island. Why should Martha's Vineyard turn its back on the history of the English language? I believe that we can find a specific explanation if we study the detailed configuration of this sound change against the social forces which affect the life of the island most deeply.

If we choose a purely psychological explanation, or one based only on phonological paradigms, we have as much as said that social variables such as occupation, income, education, social aspirations, attitudes, are beside the point. We could only prove such a claim by cross-tabulating the independent social variables, one at a time, with the degree of centralization, and showing that any greater-than-chance correlations are spurious.

However, our first attempts reveal some striking social correlations which are not easily explained away. Table 19.3 shows us the geographical bias of centralization, favoring rural up-island against small-town down-island areas. Table 19.4 shows the occupational biases, with fishermen at the top and farmers at the bottom. If we add to this the data of Table 19.5, showing the distribution by ethnic groups, we find ourselves embarrassed with too many explanations. Are these social variables connected in any

Table 19.3   Geographical distribution of centralization

	(ay)	(aw)
Down-island	35	33
Edgartown	48	55
Oak Bluffs	33	10
Vineyard Haven	24	33
Up-island	61	66
Oak Bluffs	71	99
N. Tisbury	35	13
West Tisbury	51	51
Chilmark	100	81
Gay Head	51	81

Table 19.4   Centralization by occupational groups

	(ay)	(aw)
Fishermen	100	79
Farmers	32	22
Others	41	57

Table 19.5   Centralization by ethnic groups

Age level	English (ay)	(aw)	Portuguese (ay)	(aw)	Indian (ay)	(aw)
Over 60	36	34	26	26	32	40
46 to 60	85	63	37	59	71	100
31 to 45	108	109	73	83	80	133
Under 30	35	31	34	52	47	88
All ages	67	60	42	54	56	90

demonstrable way with the linguistic change? Are they truly independent from one another, or are some of the correlations spurious, the result of some dependence on a larger factor which is logically prior to these? If such a larger pattern exists, we must ask how it originated, and in what way it is connected with the linguistic events. A simple-minded bookkeeping approach will not answer such questions. We will have to gain some insight into the social structure of the island, and the pressures which motivate the social changes of present-day Martha's Vineyard.

THE INTERACTION OF LINGUISTIC AND SOCIAL PATTERNS[32]

To understand Martha's Vineyard, we must first realize that this is a very beautiful place, and a very desirable place to live. But it is not an easy place to earn the kind of living which agrees well with the achievement orientation of modern American society. The

1960 Census shows that it is the poorest of all Massachusetts counties: it has the lowest average income, the highest number of poor people, and the smallest number of rich people.[33] The Vineyard has the highest rate of unemployment: 8.3 percent as against 4.2 percent for the state, and it also has the highest rate of seasonal employment. One might think that life on the island is nevertheless easier: perhaps the cost of living is lower. Nothing could be further from the truth: the high cost of ferrying is carried over to a higher price for most consumer goods. As a result, there are more married women with young children working than in any other county: 27.4 percent as against 17.3 percent for the state as a whole.

The reason for this economic pressure, and the resulting dependence on the tourist trade, is not hard to find. There is no industry on Martha's Vineyard. The island reached its peak in the great days of the whaling industry; for a time, commercial fishing in the local waters buoyed up the economy, but the run of fish is no longer what it used to be. Large-scale fishing is now out of New Bedford on the Grand Banks. Farming and dairying have declined sharply because of the ferry rate, which raises the cost of fertilizer but lowers the profit on milk.

The 1960 Census shows us that the island's labor force of 2,000 souls is heavily occupied with service trades. Only 4 percent are in manufacturing, one-seventh of the state average. Five percent are in agriculture, 2.5 percent in fishing, and 17 percent in construction; these percentages are five, ten, and three times as high as those for the state as a whole.[34]

These economic pressures must be clearly delineated in order to assess the heavy psychological pressures operating on the Vineyarders of old family stock. Increasing dependence on the summer trade acts as a threat to their personal independence. The more far-seeing Vineyarders can envisage the day when they and their kind will be expropriated as surely as the Indians before them. They understand that the vacation business cannot help but unbalance the economy, which produces far too little for the summer trade, but far too much for the winter. Yet it is very hard for the Vineyarder not to reach for the dollar that is lying on the table, as much as he may disapprove of it. We have already noted that many Vineyarders move out of their own homes to make room for summer people.

Those who feel that they truly own this island, the descendants of the old families, have a hard time holding on. Summer people, who have earned big money in big cities, are buying up the island. As one Chilmarker said, "You can cross the island from one end to the other without stepping on anything but *No Trespassing* signs." The entire northwest shore has fallen to the outsiders. In Edgartown, the entire row of spacious white houses on the waterfront has capitulated to high prices, with only one exception, and the descendants of the whaling captains who built them have retreated to the hills and hollows of the interior.

This gradual transition to dependence on, and outright ownership by the summer people has produced reactions varying from a fiercely defensive contempt for outsiders to enthusiastic plans for furthering the tourist economy. A study of the data shows that high centralization of (ay) and (aw) is closely correlated with expressions of strong resistance to the incursions of the summer people.

The greatest resistance to these outsiders is felt in the rural up-island areas, and especially in Chilmark, the only place where fishing is still a major part of the economy.[35] Chilmarkers are the most different, independent, the most stubborn defenders of their own way of living. In order to assess the changing orientation of island groups towards the old family tradition, I included in my interview a battery of questions dealing with the semantics of the word *Yankee*. One question read: "Where on the island would a typical old Yankee be most apt to live?" By far the most common answer was "Chilmark." Chilmarkers were named most often as examples of "typical old Yankees."

Chilmarkers pride themselves on their differences from mainlanders:

> You people who come down here to Martha's Vineyard don't understand the background of the old families of the island . . . strictly a maritime background and tradition . . . and what we're interested in, the rest of America, this part over here across the water that belongs to you and we don't have anything to do with, has forgotten all about . . .
>
> I think perhaps we use entirely different . . . type of English language . . . think differently here on the island . . . it's almost a separate language within the English language.

To a large extent, this last statement is wishful thinking. Much of the language difference depended upon whaling terms which are now obsolete. It is not unnatural, then, to find phonetic differences becoming stronger and stronger as the group fights to maintain its identity. We have mentioned earlier that the degrees of retroflexion in final and preconsonantal /r/ have social significance: at Chilmark, retroflexion is at its strongest, and is steadily increasing among the younger boys.

In Table 19.3, we note that centralization is higher up-island than down-island, and highest of all in Chilmark. In Table 19.4, we note that of all occupational groups, fishermen show the highest centralization. Our total number of cases is too small to allow extensive cross-tabulations, but if we take the group of Chilmark fishermen in the middle age level, from 30 to 60, we find that these five informants have average indexes of 148 for (ay) and 118 for (aw), higher than any other social group which we might select on the island. Conversely, let us list the six speakers with the highest degree of centralization in order of (ay)—that is, the upper 10 percent:

	(ay)	(aw)
Chilmark fisherman, age 60	170	111
Chilmark fisherman, age 31	165	211
Chilmark fisherman, age 55	150	124
Edgartown fisherman, age 61	143	107
Chilmark fisherman, age 33	133	79
Edgartown fisherman, age 52	131	131

It should be noted here that the two Edgartown fishermen listed are brothers, the last descendants of the old families to maintain their position on the Edgartown waterfront in the face of the incroachment of summer people.

We have now established within reason that the strong upturn in centralization began up-island, among Chilmark fishermen, under the same influence which produced parallel results among the few Edgartown residents who shared their social orientation.

Table 19.5 shows the developments by age level for each of the three main ethnic groups. All of the examples we have used so far deal with the English group of old family descent; in Chilmark, this is the only group of any size. Let us continue to follow the development of this group through the succeeding age levels, and examine the interaction of social and linguistic patterns.

We see that centralization reaches a peak in the age level from 30 to 45, and that centralization of (aw) has reached or surpassed (ay) at this point. This age group has been under heavier stress than any other; the men have grown up in a declining economy, after making a more or less deliberate choice to remain on the island rather than leave it. Most of them have been in the armed forces during World War II or in the Korean conflict. Many have been to college, for the English-descent group has a strong bent towards higher education. At some point, each of these men elected to make a smaller living on Martha's Vineyard, while many of their contemporaries left to gain more money or more recognition elsewhere.

Severe strains are created in those who are pulled in both directions; the traditional orientation of Martha's Vineyard has long been inward and possessive, yet the pull of modern achievement-oriented America is even greater for some.

> I think actually it's a very hard thing to make that decision . . . It comes to you later, that you should have made it before. I have another son—Richard—is an aeronautical engineer. He really loves the island. And when he decided to be an aeronautical engineer we discussed it—at length—and I told him at that time: you just can't live on Martha's Vineyard . . . He works at Grumman, but he comes home every chance he gets and stays just as long as he can.

The speaker is a woman of 55, a descendant of the Mayhew family, who left business school in Boston, and returned to the island to become a real estate agent. Her son made the opposite choice; but another family, of long standing in Chilmark, had this to report about their son:

> . . . we had an idea that he'd go away to school, but he really didn't want to go away . . . When he was at Chauncey Hall, they tried to get him to go to M.I.T.; but he said no, he didn't want to go anywhere where he had to learn to do something that he couldn't come back to this island.

We can learn a great deal about centralization by studying such histories of particular families. The two speakers who head the list of centralized speakers on the previous page are father and son. The father, a Chilmark lobsterman, is a thoughtful, well-read man with a passionate concern with the history of the whaling industry; he is perhaps the most eloquent spokesman for the older Vineyard tradition, and the author of the quotation on p. 29. His son is a college graduate who tried city life, didn't care for it, came back to the island and built up several successful commercial enterprises on the Chilmark docks. He shows a high (ay) at 211, considerably more centralized than anyone else I have heard at Chilmark. One evening, as I was having dinner at his parents' house, the conversation turned to speech in general, without any specific reference to (ay) or (aw). His mother remarked, "You know, E. didn't always speak that way . . . it's only since he came back from college. I guess he wanted to be more like the men on the docks . . ."

Here we see a clear case of hypercorrection at work, and from other evidence as well, it is reasonable to assume that this is a very regular force in implementing the phonetic trend we are studying.

When we come to high-school students, we must realize that many of the young people from the old-family group do *not* intend to remain on the island, and this is reflected in the lower average index of Table 19.5. Comparatively few of the sons of the English-descent group will be earning their living on the Vineyard in the next 20 years. In a series of interviews in Martha's Vineyard Regional High School, it was possible to compare speaking habits very closely by means of the standard reading, "After the high winds . . ." A marked contrast was observed between those who plan to leave the island and those who do not. The latter show strong centralization, while the former show little, if any. To highlight this point, we may take four 15-year-old students: the two down-islanders who intend to leave for careers in business and finance show little or no centralization; the two up-islanders who hope to go to college and return to make their living on the island show considerable centralization.[36]

The indexes speak for themselves:

Down-island, leaving	Up-island, staying
(ay)(aw)	(ay)(aw)
00–40	90–100
00–00	113–119

One of the down-islanders, from Edgartown, has fallen very much under the influence of the upper-class Bostonian summer visitors. He has lost all constriction in postvocalic /r/, and has a fronted low center vowel as well in such words as [ka:], 'car'.

CENTRALIZATION AMONG OTHER ETHNIC GROUPS

We can now turn to the special position of the Portuguese and Indian ethnic groups, and see if the same approach can account for the distribution of centralized forms among them.

The most common view of the early Portuguese immigration is that the settlers came from an island with a very similar economy, shared the Yankee virtues of thrift and industry, and fitted into the island life almost perfectly. The Azoreans who came first seemed to have a strong inclination for farming and fishing, rather than factory work; in the Vineyard's rather diffuse economy, there was little concentration of the Portuguese into the kinds of industrial pockets we find on the mainland.[37] Even among the tough-minded Chilmarkers, we find a certain grudging acknowledgment of the Yankee-like orientation of the Portuguese:

> . . . they worked, that's why they were respected. Nobody ever particularly inter-fered with 'em. You hear somebody make a remark about the dumb Portagee or something, but actually I think they've been pretty well respected because they mind their own business pretty well. They didn't ask for anything.

It took some time, however, for the Portuguese-descent group to make its way into the main stream of island life. Intermarriage of Portuguese and Yankee stock occurs, but it is rare. Second-generation Portuguese certainly do not feel at home in every situation: as some Vineyarders put it, these Portuguese have "a defensive attitude." A member of the English group will as a rule speak his mind freely, condemning the summer people and his neighbors with equal frankness. But the second-generation Portuguese never criticizes the summer people in the interview situation, and he is extremely wary of criticizing anyone. When the word *Yankee* is introduced, he shifts uneasily in his chair, and refuses to make any comment at all.

While the speech of the Portuguese second generation is free of any detectable Portuguese influence,[38] it is also lacking the special Vineyard flavor. If we examine the Portuguese age groups over 45 in Table 19.5, which contain a large proportion of second-generation speakers, we find little or no centralization.

This is not the case with third-and fourth-generation Portuguese speakers. In this group, we find centralization very much on the increase, particularly with (aw). In Table 19.5, we see that the age group from 31 to 45 has a very high degree of centralization. This age level contains a great many third-generation Portuguese. It is the first Portuguese group which has entered the main stream of island life, occupying positions as merchants, municipal officers, and many other places of secondary leadership. These speakers consider themselves natives of the island, and in response to the term *Yankee*, they either include themselves, or make fun of the whole idea.

In the youngest age level, the Portuguese-descent group shows a very regular use of centralization, whether second or third or fourth generation, and their average centralization index in the table is, at this point, higher than the English group.

One might think that centralization might be on the way to becoming a marker of the ethnic Portuguese on the island, if such a trend continues. But this possibility runs counter to the strongly democratic nature of present-day Vineyard society. Among high-school students, for example, there appear to be no social barriers between the ethnic groups, in clubs, at dances, and between friends. This situation is especially shocking to some former mainlanders, who would like to draw a color line against some of the children with Cape Verde backgrounds. But despite a few such counter-currents, the unifying, protective nature of Vineyard society shields the island native from the kind of reality which is practiced on the outside.[39]

The reason that the youngest Portuguese group shows higher centralization is that a larger percentage identify themselves with the island and the island way of life, than is the case among the English-descent group. Whereas almost all of the English group leave the island to go to college, and few return, almost all of the Portuguese group remain. As a result, they are gradually supplanting the English group in the economic life of the island.

It is fair enough to say that the main problem of the Portuguese group has not been to resist the incursions of the summer people but rather to assert their status as native Vineyarders. Their chief obstacle has not been the outsiders, but rather the resistance to full recognition from the English-descent group. With full participation in native status has come full use of the special characteristics of Martha's Vineyard English, including centralized diphthongs.

The Indian descent group is relatively small and homogeneous. The hundred citizens of Gay Head are united in a few closely related families. One would think that these survivors of the aboriginal Wampanoag Indians would have had little trouble in asserting their native status. On the contrary, a long tradition of denigration of the Indian has served, for over a hundred years, to rob him of the dignity which should accompany this feat of survival. The issue revolves around the fact that the declining Indian community has necessarily intermarried with outsiders over the past ten generations. The logic of American society dictated that these outsiders should be black. Thus as early as 1764, the Yankee officials of the Vineyard claimed that only one quarter of the Indians were "of pure blood."[40] In 1870, the Governor of Massachusetts took away the reservation status of Gay Head, on the ground that they really weren't Indians at all, and handed them over to the political ministrations of Chilmark.

For many decades, the Indians were literally second-class citizens, and the resentment dating from this period is not entirely gone. On the other hand, we find that a number of Vineyarders, of both English and Portuguese descent, regard the Indians with a mixture of sarcasm and scepticism:

> . . . show me a Gay Head Indian and I'll like to see one.

The Indian people are aware of this situation, as shown in this quotation from one of the Indian informants, a woman of 69:

> These island folks, they don't want to mix at all, up this end. . . . They don't like to give the Indian his name, here on the island. I'll tell you that. They like to be dirty with some of their talk.

Despite the great shift in Vineyard ideology over the past three generations, the Indians still feel blocked, geographically and socially, by the Chilmarkers, "up this end." Their attitude toward the Chilmarkers is ambiguous: on the one hand, they resent the Chilmarkers' possessive attitude toward the island, and the traditional hard-fisted, stiff-necked Yankee line. Their reaction to the word *Yankee* is sarcastic and hostile.[41] But their main complaint is that they deserve equal status, and whether they will admit it or not, they would like to be just like the Chilmarkers in many ways.

As far as centralization is concerned, Table 19.5 indicates that the Indians follow close behind the Chilmarkers. At the same time, they show a greater relative increase of centralization of (aw), similar to the Portuguese development, especially among the young people. Here there are signs of an additional phonetic feature, shared by both Portuguese and Indians: a backed form of (aw), which may be written [ʌʊ]. It is characteristic of five speakers in the sample, all under 30, all fairly low in socio-economic status. Whether it represents a general trend cannot be determined at this point.

We may note that there has been a revival of Indian culture in the form of pageants staged for the tourist trade, beadwork, and other Indian crafts, and with these a revived emphasis on tribal organization. The younger Indians acknowledge that this revival was commercially motivated in its beginnings, but they claim that it is now more than that, and that Indian culture would survive if the vacationers disappeared entirely. The Indian language has been dead for several generations, however, and the ritual formulas must be learned from a book. The Indians are truly traditional speakers of English, and their claim to native status must be expressed in that language.

THE SOCIAL MEANING OF CENTRALIZATION

From the information we now have at hand, there readily emerges the outline of a unifying pattern which expresses the social significance of the centralized diphthongs.

It is apparent that the immediate meaning of this phonetic feature is 'Vineyarder.' When a man says [rɐɪt] or [hɐʊs], he is unconsciously establishing the fact that he belongs to the island: that he is one of the natives to whom the island really belongs. In this respect, centralization is not different from any of the other sub-phonemic features of other regions which are noted for their local dialect. The problem is, why did this feature develop in such a complicated pattern on the Vineyard, and why is it becoming stronger in the younger age levels?

The answer appears to be that different groups have had to respond to different challenges to their native status. And in the past two generations, the challenges have become much sharper through severe economic and social pressures.

The old-family group of English descent has been subjected to pressure from the outside: its members are struggling to maintain their independent position in the face of a long-range decline in the economy and the steady encroachment of the summer people. The member of the tradition-oriented community naturally looks to past generations for his values: these past generations form a reference group for him.[42] The great figures of the past are continually referred to, and those who have died only a few years ago have already assumed heroic stature. "If you could only have been here a few years ago and talked to *N*. He could have told you so many things!"

The sudden increase in centralization began among the Chilmark fishermen, the most close-knit group on the island, the most independent, the group which is most stubbornly opposed to the incursions of the summer people. There is an inherently dramatic character to the fisherman's situation, and a great capacity for self-dramatization in the fisherman himself, which makes him an ideal candidate to initiate new styles in speech. In the early morning, the curtain rises: a solitary figure appears upon the scene. For the course of an entire day, this single actor holds the stage. Then at last, the boat docks; the curtain descends. The play is over, yet the reviews will be read and reread for generations to come.

> I can remember as a boy, when I first started going to sea with my father, he said to me: remember two things. Always treat the ocean with respect, and remember you only have to make one mistake, never to come back.

Centralized speech forms are then a part of the dramatized island character which the Chilmarker assumes, in which he imitates a similar but weaker tendency in the older generation.

For younger members of the English-descent group, we can view the mechanism in greater detail. For them, the old-timers and the up-islanders in particular serve as a reference group. They recognize that the Chilmark fishermen are independent, skillful with many kinds of tools and equipment, quick-spoken, courageous, and physically strong. Most importantly, they carry with them the ever-present conviction that the island belongs to them. If someone intends to stay on the island, this model will be ever present to his mind. If he intends to leave, he will adopt a mainland reference group, and the influence of the old-timers will be considerably less. The differential effect in the degree of centralization used is a direct result of this opposition of values.

The Portuguese group is not faced with a dilemma of going or staying. The main challenge to which this group has responded is from the English group, which has certainly served as a reference group for the Portuguese until very recent times. As the number of Portuguese in prominent positions grows, it is no longer urgent to minimize the effects of being Portuguese, but rather to assert one's identity as an islander.

The Gay Head developments are dictated by the antinomy of values which reigns there. On the one hand, the Indian group resents any bar to full participation in the island life, and the Indians have plainly adopted many of the same values as the Chilmarkers. But on the other hand, they would like to insist as well on their Indian identity. Unfortunately, they no longer have linguistic resources for this purpose, and whether they like it or not, they will follow the Chilmark lead.

The role of the Chilmarker, or "old-time typical Yankee", has declined as the reference group which governs the meaning of "islander" has shifted away from that which governs "Yankee." Even among the Chilmarkers, the more far-sighted members of the community recognize that the term *Yankee* no longer fits the island. Whereas this word may still be a rallying cry in some parts of New England, it has outlived its usefulness on Martha's Vineyard. In emphasizing descent status rather than native status, *Yankee* summons up invidious distinctions which are no longer good currency on the island.

> People don't make so much about it as they used to when I was young. People would make that statement: "I'm a Yankee! I'm a Yankee!" But now you very seldom—mostly, read it in print.[43]

In summary, we can then say that the meaning of centralization, judging from the context in which it occurs, is positive orientation towards Martha's Vineyard. If we now overlook age level, occupation, ethnic group, geography, and study the relationship of centralization to this one independent variable, we can confirm or reject this conclusion. An examination of the total interview for each informant allows us to place him in one of three categories: positive—expresses definitely positive feelings towards Martha's Vineyard; neutral—expresses neither positive nor negative feelings towards Martha's Vineyard; negative—indicates desire to live elsewhere. When these three groups are rated for mean centralization indexes, we obtain the striking result of Table 19.6.

The fact that this table shows us the sharpest example of stratification we have yet seen, indicates that we have come reasonably close to a valid explanation of the social distribution of centralized diphthongs.

Table 19.6   Centralization and orientation towards Martha's Vineyard

Persons		(ay)	(aw)
40	Positive	63	62
19	Neutral	32	42
6	Negative	09	08

THE INTERSECTION OF SOCIAL AND LINGUISTIC STRUCTURES

The following abstract scheme may serve to summarize the argument which has been advanced so far to explain the spread and propagation of this particular linguistic change.

1. A language feature used by a group A is marked by contrast with another standard dialect.
2. Group A is adopted as a reference group by group B, and the feature is adopted and exaggerated as a sign of social identity in response to pressure from outside forces.
3. Hypercorrection under increased pressure, in combination with the force of structural symmetry, leads to a generalization of the feature in other linguistic units of group B.
4. A new norm is established as the process of generalization levels off.
5. The new norm is adopted by neighboring and succeeding groups for whom group B serves as a reference group.

There remains a gap in the logic of the explanation: in what way do social pressures and social attitudes come to bear upon linguistic structures? So far we have assembled a convincing series of correlations: yet we still need to propose a rational mechanism by which the deep-seated elements of structure enter such correlations.

It has been noted that centralized diphthongs are not salient in the consciousness of Vineyard speakers. They can hardly therefore be the direct objects of social affect. The key to the problem may lie in the fact that centralization is only one of many phonological features which show the same general distribution, though none may be as striking or as well stratified as (ay) and (aw). There are no less than 14 phonological variables which follow the general rule that the higher, or more constricted variants are characteristic of the up-island, "native" speakers, while the lower, more open variants are characteristic of down-island speakers under mainland influence.[44] We can reasonably assume that this "close-mouthed" articulatory style is the object of social affect. It may well be that social evaluation interacts with linguistic structures at this point, through the constriction of several dimensions of phonological space. Particular linguistic variables would then be variously affected by the overall tendency towards a favored articulatory posture, under the influence of the social forces which we have been studying. Evidence for such an hypothesis must come from the study of many comparable developments, in a variety of English dialects and other languages. It is enough to note here that it is a plausible mechanism for sociolinguistic interaction which is compatible with the evidence which has been gathered in this investigation.

LIMITATIONS OF THIS STUDY

We noted earlier that one limitation of this study stems from the fact that the variable selected is not salient. This limitation, coupled with the small size of the Vineyard population, made it impractical to explore thoroughly the subjective response of native speakers to centralized diphthongs. Other shortcomings of the technique used on Martha's Vineyard may be seen in the sampling method, which was far from rigorous.[45]

The statements made about developments through various age levels among the Portuguese and Indians are based on an inadequate number of cases. The sample is particularly weak in the down-island area, especially in Oak Bluffs, and the picture of down-island trends is correspondingly weaker than up-island developments. Finally, it may be noted that the interviewing technique was not as firmly controlled as it might have been: a number of changes in the interview structure were made as the study progressed.

With these reservations, we can say that the findings give good confirmation of the main theme of the study: the correlation of social patterns with the distributional pattern of one linguistic variable.[46] The reliability of the index used was tested in several cases where the same informant was interviewed twice, with good results.[47] Indexes for reading style did not diverge sharply from other portions of the interview. The validity of the scale of measurement was well established by instrumental methods, and the validity of the whole seems to be reinforced by the unitary nature of the final interpretation.

The techniques developed on Martha's Vineyard were later refined and applied to a much more complex situation in the urban core of New York City. Here multiple-style speakers are the rule, not the exception; instead of three ethnic groups we have a great many; mobility and change are far more rapid; and the population is huge. Here the sampling requirements must be far more rigid; and the techniques used to assess the social meaning of linguistic cues must be more subtle and complex. Yet the basic approach, of isolating the socially significant variables, and correlating them with the patterns of general social forces, was the same as that which was used on Martha's Vineyard. We can expect that these methods will give us further insight into the mechanism of linguistic change.

NOTES

1. First published in *Word*, 19: 273–309 (1963). An abbreviated version was given at the 37th Annual Meeting of the Linguistic Society of America in New York City on December 29, 1962.
2. See Sturtevant 1947: Ch. 8: "Why are Phonetic Laws Regular?"
3. A number of these theories are reviewed in Sommerfelt 1930.
4. The empirical confirmation of many of Martinet's ideas to be found in Moulton's investigation of Swiss German dialects has provided strong motivation for some of the interpretations in the present essay. In particular, see Moulton 1962.
5. For a parallel criticism of restrictions on the data imposed by Bloomfieldian linguistics, see W. P. Diver's review of W. P. Lehmann's *Historical Linguistics*, in *Word*, 19:100–105 (1963).
6. See also H. Hoenigswald's remarks in "Are There Universals of Linguistic Change?" in Greenberg, ed., 1963, fn. 8: "Sound changes can apparently not be entirely predicted from internal systemic stresses and strains, nor can they be explained as the effect of scatter around a target or norm; they have direction and are in that sense specific, much like other happenings in history."
7. For further details on the social and economic background of Martha's Vineyard, see my 1962 Columbia University Master's Essay, "The Social History of a Sound Change on the Island of Martha's Vineyard, Massachusetts," written under the direction of Professor Uriel Weinreich.
8. Kurath et al. 1941. Background information on the informants is to be found in Kurath 1939.
9. From U.S. Bureau of the Census, *U.S. Census of Population: 1960. General Social and Economic Character-istics. Massachusetts.* Final Report PC(1)—23c (Washington, D.C.: Government Printing Office, 1962), Table 89, p. 23–260.

10. There is a sizeable number of retired mainlanders living on the Vineyard as year-round residents. While they are included in the population total, they do not form a part of the social fabric we are considering, and none of the informants is drawn from this group.

11. On the LANE maps, we find that Guy Lowman regularly recorded the up-island /r/ as [ɚ] in [wɛɪɚ, haɚd, baɚn], and down-island /r/ as [ə.] in the same positions. Essentially the same pattern is to be found among the older speakers today, though not with the regularity that Lowman noted. It is possible that this treatment of /r/ was in fact intended as a broad transcription, for the LANE was much more concerned with vowels than consonants.

12. See Kurath 1949, Fig. 162. *Belly-flop* (and the corresponding lexical item in other regions) has generally shifted for the younger generation to denote a flat dive into the water. Coasting is now a less important sport, and its terminology is appropriately impoverished. The lexical data derived from my own study of Martha's Vineyard is analyzed in detail in W. Labov, "The Recent History of Some Dialect Markers in Martha's Vineyard, Massachusetts," in Davis 1972.

13. Many ingenious devices are needed to detect and eliminate deceit on the part of metropolitan informants, whether intended or not. On Martha's Vineyard, this is much less of a problem, but the effects of the interview situation are evident in the careful style of some informants.

14. The disappearance of New England short /o/ follows the pattern described in Avis (1961). Exploratory interviews at other points in southeastern New England (Woods Hole, Falmouth, New Bedford, Fall River, Providence, Stonington) indicate that the loss of the /or~ɔr/ and /hw~w~/ distinctions is parallel to that on Martha's Vineyard.

15. The terms *centralized diphthongs, centralization*, and *degree of centralization* will be used throughout this study to refer to the various forms of the diphthongs /ay/ and /aw/ with first elements higher than [a]. It is not intended that the terms themselves should imply any process or direction of change, except when used with explicit statements to that effect.

16. Among recent historical linguists, H. C. Wyld (1920:223–25) is a notable exception in positing a front first element in the transition of M.E. *i:* to Mod. E. /ay/, relying on occasional spellings with *ey* and *ei*, but without considering the many other indications of central position.

17. Abundant evidence is given in Krapp 1925(2):186–91.

18. The best view of the distribution of /ay/ may be had from Maps 26–27 in Kurath and McDavid 1951. Centralized diphthongs are well known as a feature of Canadian English, where the effect of the voiceless-voiced consonant environment is quite regular.

19. The possibility of phonemic confusion with /ɔy/ apparently became a reality in the 17th and 18th centuries, in both England and America, when both diphthongs had central first elements.

20. "When we speak of the *right* to *life*, liberty and the pursuit of happiness, what does *right* mean? . . . Is it in *writing*? . . . If a man is successful at a job he doesn't *like*, would you still say he was a successful man?" These questions were generally successful in eliciting the informant's versions of the italicized words.

21. This 200-word reading is constructed as a story told by a teenage Vineyard boy, of the day he found out his father wasn't always right. An excerpt will show the technique involved: "After the high winds last Thursday, we went down to the mooring to see how the boat was making out . . . My father started to pump out the bottom, and he told me to find out if the outboard would start. I found out all right. I gave her a couple of real hard pulls but it was no dice. 'Let me try her,' my father said. 'Not on your life,' I told him. 'I've got my pride.' "

22. The interviews were recorded at 3¾ inches per second on a Butoba MT-5, using a Butoba MD-21 dynamic microphone. A tape recording of the standard reading, "After the high winds . . ." read by five of the speakers whose formant measurements appear on Figure 19.3, and other examples of centralized diphthongs used by Vineyard speakers in natural conversation, may be obtained from the writer, Department of Linguistics, University of Pennsylvania, Philadelphia, Pa. 19104.

23. Spectrograms were made on the Kay Sonograph, using both wide and narrow bands. Seven of these, showing 15 instances of /ai/ and /au/, are reproduced in the master's essay cited above.

24. The degree of overlap shown in Figure 19.3 seems roughly comparable to Peterson and Barney's results.

25. A parallel problem of condensing a finely graded impressionistic scale is discussed in Gauchat et al. 1925: ix. A seven-level transcription of the mid vowels was reduced to five levels, but without the instrumental justification presented here.

26. (ay) and (aw) are rare before /b, g, ŋ, č, j/; /t/ includes [ʔ]. The non-distinctive [ʔ] variant of zero onset also favors centralization heavily, as in the 1 forms of Figure 19.3.

27. One small stylistic influence which appeared was in the standard reading. Those with centralized norms, whose charts were of type b and c, had slightly higher indexes of centralization for reading than for conversation. The opposite effect was noted for those with uncentralized norms.

28. "It is hard to feel comfortable with a theory which holds that the great changes of the past were of one kind, theoretically mysterious and interesting, whereas everything that is observable today is of another kind, transparent and (by implication) of scant theoretical interest."

29. Such arguments were indeed advanced in some detail to explain Gauchat's results, by P. G. Goidanich, "Saggio critico sullo studio de L. Gauchat," *Archivio Glottologico Italiano* 20:60–71 (1926) [cited by Sommerfelt 1930]. As implausible as Goidanich's arguments seem, they are quite consistent with Bloomfield's position cited above.

30. See Hoenigswald 1963 for further considerations which support this view.

31. We might wish to construct a rule here which would, in essence, convert [+compact] to [−compact], simpler by one feature than a rule which would merely convert [aɪ] to a centralized form. While such a statement is satisfying in its simplicity and neatness, it should be clear from the following discussion that it would explain only a small part of the mechanism of linguistic change.

32. The information given in the following discussion of social patterns on Martha's Vineyard was derived in part from conversations with the 69 informants. Even more significant, perhaps, was information gained from discussions with community leaders who were in a position to view these patterns as a whole. I am particularly indebted to Mr. Benjamin Morton, head of the Chamber of Commerce, Mr. Henry Beetle Hough, editor of the *Vineyard Gazette*, and Mr. Charles Davis, superintendent of the Martha's Vineyard Regional High School. Among my informants, I am especially grateful to Mr. Donald Poole of Chilmark, Mr. Benjamin Mayhew, selectman of Chilmark, and Mr. Albert Prada, town clerk of Edgartown.

33. Table 36 of the 1960 census report PC(1)—23c, cited above in fn. 9, shows some striking contrasts among Massachusetts counties. The median family income for the Vineyard is $4,745, as against $6,272 for the state as a whole. Barnstable County (Cape Cod) and Nantucket are also dependent on a vacation economy, yet they show median incomes of $5,386 and $5,373. The most agricultural county in Massachusetts, Franklin, shows a median of $5,455. The state as a whole has only 12.4 percent of families with incomes under $3,000; the Vineyard has 23 percent. The state has 17.0 percent with incomes over $10,000; the Vineyard has only 6.6 percent.

34. See Table 82 of the 1960 census report, as in fn. 33.

35. Despite the low number of Vineyarders listed as fishermen by occupation in the Census, a much larger number of islanders rely upon part-time fishing to supplement their income. In particular, harvesting bay scallops in the salt ponds is a prized source of revenue in the summer months. A great deal of local legislation is designed to protect the professional fishermen from the great number of part-time scallopers taking in too large a share. Much discussion and considerable bitterness develops as a result of this conflict of interest, in which the truly professional Chilmarkers are, psychologically at least, on top.

36. On the question of leaving the island, one of these boys said: ". . . I can't see myself off island somewhere . . . I like it a lot here, like my father goes lobstering. That's quite a bit of fun . . . as long as I get enough money to live and enjoy myself. I was figuring on . . . going into oceanography because you'd be outdoors: it wouldn't be office work."

37. In many ways, the Vineyard seems to be more democratic than the mainland. I have heard on the

mainland strong expressions of hostility between Portuguese groups from the Azores and those from the Cape Verde Islands, but never on Martha's Vineyard.

38. On the other hand, I have heard a strong Portuguese accent from a second-generation Portuguese man, about 40 years old, who was raised on a farm near Taunton, Mass.

39. In several cases, Vineyard youngsters have received rather severe shocks on leaving the island for the armed services or for work in an area where caste restrictions were in force. One boy was put into a black regiment on entering the service, though action from Vineyard leaders had him transferred soon afterwards.

40. A very rich vein of information on this score may be tapped from Richard L. Pease's *Report of the commissioner appointed to complete the examination . . . of all boundary lines . . . at Gay Head* (Boston, 1871). Pease was acting essentially as the hatchet man for the Governor of Massachusetts, to whom he was reporting.

41. "Where they come from—down south somewhere? . . . Lot of 'em come from Jerusalem, you know . . ."

42. In the technical sense developed by R. Merton, *Social Theory and Social Structure* (Glencoe, Ill., 1957).

43. The speaker is one of the Mayhews, a retired Chilmark fisherman, who has as much claim to be a "typical old Yankee" as any person on Martha's Vineyard.

44. In the following list of the variables in question, the up-island form is given first. PHONEMIC INVENTORY: /o/~/ou/ in *road, toad, boat, whole* . . . PHONEMIC DISTRIBUTION: /ɛ/ only before intersyllabic /r/ instead of both /ɛ/ and /æ/; /r/~/ə/ in postvocalic position. PHONEMIC INCIDENCE: /ɪ~ɛ/ in *get, forget, when, anyway, can* . . .; /ɛ~æ/ in *have, had, that*; /ʌ~ɑ/ in *got*. PHONETIC REALIZATION; [ɐɪ~aɪ] and [ɐʊ~aʊ]: [r~ɚ]; [ɪr~ər] in *work, person* . . .; [ə~ʌ] in *furrow, hurry* . . .; [oɐʊ ~oʊ] in *go, no* . . .; [ii~ɪi] and [uu~ʊu]; [ɪᵊ~ɪ] and [ɛᵊ~ɛ].

45. The problem of sampling technique for linguistic variables is a difficult one at the moment. While we are sure that linguistic behavior is more general than the behavior usually traced by survey methods, we do not know how much more general it is, nor can we estimate easily how far we may relax the sampling requirements, if at all.

46. In addition to the positive correlations discussed above, the explanation given is reinforced by certain negative results of alternate explanations. The educational level of the informants is not correlated significantly with degree of centralization. The distribution of substandard or archaic grammar does not correspond to the distribution of centralized forms.

47. For example, two interviews with Ernest Mayhew, Chilmark fisherman, age 83, showed these results: first interview, (ay)-67, (aw)-58; second interview, (ay)-59, (aw)-40. The count for (aw) is based on about one-third as many items as for (ay).

REFERENCES

Avis, W. (1961) The New England short 'o': a recessive phoneme. *Language* 37: 544–558.

Bloomfield, L. (1933) *Language*. New York: Henry Holt.

Greenberg, J.H. (ed.) (1963) *Universals of Language*. Cambridge, Mass.: MIT Press.

Halle, M. (1962) Phonology in generative grammar. *Word* 18: 67–72.

Hermann, M.E. (1929) Lautveränderungen in der Individualsprache einer Mundart. *Nachrichten der Gesellschaft der Wissenschaften zu Göttingen, Philosophisch-historische Klasse.* 11: 195–214.

Hockett, C.F. (1958) *A Course in Modern Linguistics*. New York: Macmillan.

Jespersen, O. (1927) *A Modern English Grammar on Historical Principles I*. London: George Allen.

Kökeritz, H. (1953) *Shakespeare's Pronunciation*. New Haven: Yale University Press.

Kurath, H. (1949) *A Word Geography of the Eastern United States*. Ann Arbor: University of Michigan Press.

Kurath, H. et al. (1941) *Linguistic Atlas of New England*. Providence, R.I.: American Council of Learned Societies.

Kurath, H. and R. McDavid (1951) *The Pronunciation of English in the Atlantic States*. Ann Arbor: University of Michigan Press.

Martinet, A. (1955) *Economie des changements phonétiques*. Berne: Francke.

Moulton, W.G. (1962) Dialect geography and the concept of phonological space. *Word* 18: 23–32.

Pilch, H. (1955) The rise of the American vowel pattern. *Word* 11: 57–63.

Shewmake, E.F. (1927) *English Pronunciation in Virginia*. Davidson, N.C.

Sturtevant, E. (1947) *An Introduction to Linguistic Science*. New Haven: Yale University Press.

Weinreich, U. (1959) Review of Hockett, *Modern Linguistics. Romance Philology*. 13: 329–339.

Wyld, H.C. (1920) *A History of Modern Colloquial English*. Oxford: Basil Blackwell.

QUESTIONS

Content

1. Give one linguistic and one social reason why Labov selects (ay) and (aw) as the variables for his investigation.
2. What was the traditional realisation (pronunciation) of (ay) and (aw) on Martha's Vineyard before Labov did his research?
3. Which groups of speakers on Martha's Vineyard are considered protoypical "islanders", and why?
4. How does Labov unify the results for ethnicity, occupation and region in his account of centralisation?

Concept

1. Labov concludes that a general " 'close-mouthed' articulatory style is the object of social affect" on Martha's Vineyard.

   a. Do you agree that styles, and not individual variables, are what people orient to? Why?

   b. What are the methodological implications of your answer? How should it shape the way you collect data?

2. Labov notes that ideally we would check inferences of change in progress by returning to the community at a later date and sampling again. Describe in detail the kind(s) of pattern(s) you would expect to find, if you went back to Martha's Vineyard, and replicated his study.

Chapter 20

Rika Ito and Sali Tagliamonte

WELL WEIRD, *RIGHT* DODGY, *VERY* STRANGE, *REALLY* COOL: LAYERING AND RECYCLING IN ENGLISH INTENSIFIERS[*]

INTRODUCTION

THE MOST RAPID AND the most interesting semantic developments in linguistic change are said to occur with intensifiers (Quirk et al. 1985:590; Peters 1994:269). . . . What is an intensifier? There are two types – intensives and downtoners (e.g. Stoffel 1901, Quirk et al. 1985). In this article, we restrict ourselves to those of the first type, in part because they are more frequent (Mustanoja 1960:316), but also because, we believe, they are more interesting. [. . .] These are adverbs that scale a quality up (Bolinger 1972:17), as in (1) and (2):

(1)   Maximizers:

    a.   But during the week it was **absolutely** dead. (YRK/d/F/20)[1]
    b.   I mean the chocolate making is **completely** different. (YRK/2/M/62)

(2)   Boosters:

    a.   York's actually a **really** really good University. (YRK/%/M/17)
    b.   They're **very** nice, and **very** catholic [laughs]. (YRK/R/F/41)
    c.   That most people would think, that's **dead** naff. (YRK/H/M/24)
    d.   Yeah it's **well** weird. (YRK/1/F/34)

Two key characteristics of intensifiers are (i) versatility and color, which Bolinger (1972:18) refers to as the result of "fevered invention"; and (ii) their capacity for rapid change and the recycling of different forms, . . . "The process is always going on, so that new words are in constant requisition . . ." (Stoffel 1901:2).

Source: Ito, Rika and Sali Tagliamonte (2003) *Well* weird, *right* dodgy, *very* strange, *really* cool: layering and recycling in English intensifiers. *Language in Society* 32: 257–279.

How does this "fevered invention" amid the vigorous ebb and slow of "constant requisition" happen? The next section summarizes the diachronic development of intensifiers at earlier stages of English. It reveals that competition among intensifiers has been common from as far back as Old English.

HISTORICAL TRAJECTORY

[. . .] [A]ccording to Mustanoja (1960:319–27), *swiþe*, which originally meant simply 'strong', came to mean 'extremely' or 'very', and it became the most popular intensifier in Old and Early Middle English. . . . After the mid-13th century, however, its popularity shifted to other intensifying adverbs, such as *well*, *full*, and *right*. . . .

A summary of the historical trajectory of these changes is shown in Table 20.1.

[. . .] [T]here are also regional differences in the choice of intensifiers from early on. For example, in the South and South Midlands of England, *well* became the most common intensifier after the middle of the 13th century. . . . By the mid-14th century, *well* gives way to *full* and *right*. In contrast, in the North and the North Midlands, *full* is the prevailing intensifier from mid-13th century. Not until a century later does it gradually spread over the rest of the country (Mustanoja 1960:319). Ongoing renewal of popular intensifiers continues in the 15th century [. . .].

Along with these rather dramatic shifts from one century to another, at least from the mid-18th century intensifiers become particularly associated with women. For example, Lord Chesterfield (c. 1694–1773) [. . .] reports having heard a woman describe a very small gold snuff-box as "*vastly* pretty, because it is so *vastly* little" (cited in Jespersen 1922:249–50).

[. . .] Stoffel goes so far as to suggest not only that women use these expressions frequently, that they actually DEVELOPED the intensive use of the innovation. His explanation is that "ladies are notoriously fond of hyperbole" (Stoffel 1901:101); yet he also attributes this preference to children, and what he refers to as "ladies' men" (102).

[. . .]

Table 20.1 Summary of the shift in popularity of intensifiers in English (abstracted from Mustanoja 1960:319–28)

Old English	Middle English	Early Modern English	Modern English						
	12th c.	13th c.	14th c.	15th c.	16th c.	17th c.	18th c.	19th c.	20th c.
swiþe: ——————————→									
well: ———→									
full: 2nd to *swiþe* — 1250 —————→									
right: ——→									
very: —————————————→									
really: —————————→									

Perhaps surprisingly, given the association with women, the use of intensifiers is also associated with colloquial usage and nonstandard varieties. Stoffel observes that they are "exceedingly numerous" in "vulgar parlance and in the dialects" (1901:122). Later, Fries (1940:204–5) divides a cohort of intensifiers used in American English into "Standard" as opposed to "Vulgar" forms, with *very* attributed to "Standard" English and a whole host of others – including *pretty, real* and *so* – relegated to "Vulgar" English.

Finally, the use of intensifiers is said to signal ingroup membership, again subject to changing norms.

[. . .]

Given this backdrop, it is not at all surprising to find in spoken data hearty variability in the use of intensifiers (see 1–2), even in the same speaker in the same stretch of discourse, as in (3), undoubtedly reflecting the coexistence of older and newer layers in the process of change.

(3) a. Apparently I gave him a **right** dirty look and he was going out with somebody at the time and I gave him a **really** dirty look (YRK/O/F/30)

   b. It was **very** unusual . . . It was **real** unusual. (YRK/c/F/70)

   c. . . . and one of them feel down . . . one **dead** expensive plate, **really** expensive. (YRK/H/N/24)

Thus, another important question is: What are the linguistic mechanisms through which this rapid and colorful recyling of forms happens? According to some commentators, this phenomenon reflects one of the general processes of grammaticalization, namely "delexicalization" (Sinclair 1992; Partington 1993: 183). Delexicalization is defined as "the reduction of the independent lexical content of a word, or group of words, so that it comes to fulfil a particular function" (Partington 1993: 183). In the case of intensifiers, a given word starts out as a lexical item with semantic context; often it is a word that comments on speakers' assessments of truth conditions or vouches for the sincerity of their words. Partington refers to this as MODAL use (1993:181).

Partington (1993: 182) observes that this modal-to-intensifier shift is not only a diachronic but also a synchronic phenomenon. While *really* in (4a, b) maintains its modal use reading, when it is used as sentence adverb, in sub-modifying position, as in (4c), the item is far more likely to be perceived as intensifying:

(4) a. **Really**, I could hear her thinking.

   b. Aw, don't rub it in. Ah feel awfu'. I do **really**.

   c. When the horsetail is **really** hot, wrap it up . . . (All cited in Partington 1993: 182)

This scenario of dramatic and multifaceted variation and change presents an interesting area of study. First, because of the relatively rapid rate of change and ongoing attestations of variability, the distribution of intensifiers in apparent time may shed light on the mechanisms of the delexicalization process. Second, because the development of intensifiers is particularly sensitive to factors such as sex (Stoffel 1901; Jespersen 1922) and group membership (Stoffel 1901, Peters 1994), extralinguistic distribution patterns can be used to track the interrelationship between linguistic and social factors in language change. This leads us to a set of plausible hypotheses that can be tested:

(a)   Correlation of intensifiers with particular linguistic contexts can be related with their degree of delexicalization, as discussed by Partington (1993) (and Mustanoja 1960).
(b)   Correlation of intensifiers with social factors can be taken to tap into the social evaluation of the particular intensifier within the community.
(c)   Through the examination of (a) and (b), we may be able to track the inter-relationship between linguistic and social factors in language change.

DATA AND METHODS

We now systematically examine variable usage of intensification in a socially and generationally stratified corpus from the indigenous population of a single community, the city of York in the northeast of England. [. . .] York has retained a somewhat conservative character while at the same time representing a relatively standard northern variety of British English (Tagliamonte 1998). [. . .] For this study, we used a sub-sample of 48 speakers from the corpus, stratified by age and sex, as outlined in Table 20.2.

Circumscribing the variable context

One of the problems in dealing with intensifiers in an accountable, quantitative way is that of circumscribing the variable context. It is an easy task to find the intensifiers them-selves, but difficult, if not impossible, to find where they could have occurred but did not. . . .

In a large-scale study of the collocation of adverbs of degree in contemporary written British and American English,[2] Bäcklund (1973:279) discovered that the vast majority of intensifiers – 72% – were used with adjectival heads, as they were earlier in (1), (2), and (3). Using this as a baseline, our analysis is restricted to adjectival heads, and of these, only in constructions that could possibly be modified by intensifiers. This enables us to approach the use of intensifiers and their lexical forms with a consistent denominator: all adjectives. Thus, a token with adjective *hard*, as in (5a), is included, but not with adverb *hard*, as in (5b). . . .

(5)   a.   It's **really** hard making any money out of it. (YRK/h/F/26)

Table 20.2   Sub-sample of the York English corpus (Tagliamonte 1998)

	Male	Female	Total
17–34	8	8	16
35–65	8	8	16
66+	8	8	16
Total	24	24	48

     b.   I worked ø hard at my A-levels. (YRK /d/F/20)

Contexts that do not permit intensifiers are also excluded. Thus, a token such as (6a), in which the speaker talks about a KIND of teacher and not a DEGREE of scariness, is not included. Similarly, (6b) is excluded because the degree of newness is irrelevant:

(6)   a.   [interviewer] You didn't have any really scary teachers. [008] Oh- God yeah. Tell me. Every school's got a *scary* one. We used to have one. (YRK/h/F/26)

         b.   The circuit Churches have done this twenties to thirties group so you know we're involved in that, which is good. So that's once a month we can get out and meet *new* friends and that so. (YRK/O/F/31)

Sentence constructions that do not permit intensifier use (e.g. comparatives/superlatives and other constructions [. . .] were also excluded, as were constructions involving the lexical items *too* and *so* when their function was other than intensification. [. . .]

Finally, our analysis focuses on affirmative tokens alone.

[. . .]

The variable context thus defined provides a consistent vantage point from which we can track the social evaluation and spread of individual lexical items, as well as ensuring that this analysis can be replicated elsewhere. We now test for the contribution of effects of age, sex, and educational level, as well as internal factors implicated in the expansion to different types of adjectival heads and different types of predication. By using multivariate analyses and the comparative method, we will assess the direction of effect, significance, and relative importance of these factors in apparent time.

RESULTS

Distributional analysis

[. . .] Out of 4,019 adjectival heads, 24% [N = 950] were intensified. When speaker age is taken into account, we observe an interesting pattern in apparent time. Figure 20.1 shows that the frequency of intensification is gradually increasing from oldest to the youngest speakers.

However, an important consideration is to determine WHICH intensifiers are being used. Table 20.3 shows the frequency of intensifiers according to lexical items that occurred 10 times or more.[3]

[. . .] Thirty-eight percent of all the intensifiers used in York are the lexical item *very*. Interestingly, *very* has been used as an intensifier in English since the 15th century (Mustanoja 1960:327), so it has been holding its own for about 500 years.

However, notice the intensifier *really*. This intensifier vies for the highest frequency position; it occurs 30% of the time in our data. The intensifier use of *really* is first attested in the *OED* in 1658, but in research by Peters 1994 it does not appear until the early 18th century. It is much less frequent than *very* in Bäcklund's (1973) study of contemporary written American and British English. More recently, Labov (1985:44) observes that *really* is "one of the most frequent markers of intensity in colloquial conversation" in

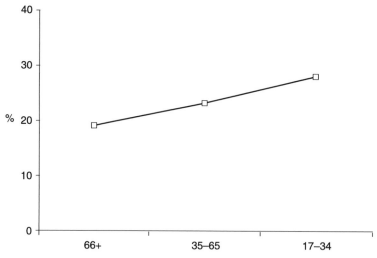

Figure 20.1   Overall distribution of intensification by age.

Table 20.3   Frequency of intensifiers by lexical item (N ≥ 10)

Lexical identity	%	N
very	38.3	364
really	30.2	287
so	10.1	96
absolutely	3.2	30
pretty	3.2	30
too	2.8	27
that	2.7	26
right	1.6	15
totally	1.4	13
completely	1.2	11
bloody	1.2	11
All other items	4.1	40
Total		950

American English. In British English, *really* has not received much attention, but it is reported to be the most common premodifier of adjectives among teenagers in London (Stenström 1999). [. . .]

A full 69% of all the intensifiers in this corpus are *very* and *really*. The remaining 30% comprise a wide range of different intensifiers. Most can be pin-pointed to specific historical periods. Use of intensifier *so* goes back to Old English (Mustanoja 1960:324), as in (7). Examples of *right*, one of the most popular intensifiers in Middle English, are given in (8). *Pretty* [. . .] is first attested in 1565 in *OED*, and Stoffel observes that its use for expressing a high degree is "contemporary usage" (1901:153).[4] The well-known British intensifier *bloody* (9) has been in "colloquial use from the Restoration (1660–) to c. 1750" (*OED* vol. 1, 933). These widely varying dates of origin reveal tremendous differences in time depth for the origins of these intensifiers.

(7)   ʒif he us ʒeunnan wile, þæt we hine **swa** godne gretan moton. (Beowulf 347, cited
      in *OED*, vol. 9, 345)
      ["If he will grant to us that we might address him, **so** good/great a man"]

(8)   a.   He was nat **right** fat. (Ch. CT A Prol. 288, cited by Mustanoja 1960:323)
      b.   I think in my father's days, they was brought up **right** strict weren't they?
           (YRK/k/F/87)

(9)   a.   Not without he will promise to be **bloody** drunk. (1676 ETHEREGE *Man of
           Mode* I. i. (1684), cited in *OED* vol. 1, 933)
      b.   What's it like living here, is it alright? [059] Yeah, **bloody** freezing in winter!
           (YRK/*/ F/23)

[. . .] Most of these intensifiers are used by all age groups in the city of York. Thus, the
layering of old and relatively new forms appears to be a community-wide phenomenon.
    We now turn to an analysis of the two main forms – *really* and *very* – treating the
three main age groups of the community as cohorts, as in Figure 20.2.
    Here we observe a dramatic pattern in apparent time. *Very* is the most frequently
used intensifier for speakers over 35, but it is declining rapidly among the under-35-year-
olds. In contrast, *really* is hardly ever used among the over-35-year-olds but is increasing
in the youngest age group. This reveals a rapidly changing situation in this community.
Moreover, the locus of the changeover appears to be between the middle-aged and
youngest generations.
    [. . .] How can it be that the lexical item *really*, which is found in letters of the early
18th century, appears here to be suddenly expanding among the under-35-year-olds in
the community? The linguistic processes that enable the delexicalization of words that
become intensifiers do not just happen overnight. As we outlined earlier with the case
of *very* in (5), this occurs through a step-by-step process. [. . .] [W]hat we would like to
consider now is whether we can tap into the stages by which delexicalization happens in

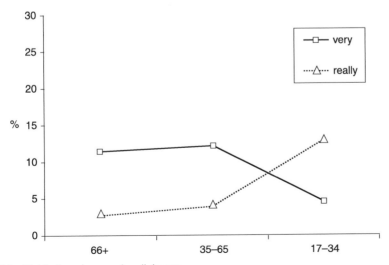

Figure 20.2   Distribution of *very* and *really* by age.

the linguistic system. If it is happening in our data, we should be able to see it in the distributional differences between the generations in York.

One way to do this is to examine collocation patterns. Partington (1993:183) argues that there is a direct correlation between delexicalization and collocational behavior: The more delexicalized an intensifier is, the more widely it collocates.[5] [. . .] For example, *awfully* is more advanced in terms of delexicalization because it collocates with modifiers having positive connotations (e.g. *good*, *nice*, and *glad*) as well as with those having negative ones (e.g. *cruel* and *bad*), whereas *terribly* shows a slight degree of preference for negative items. Thus, [Partington] concludes that "*terribly* has gone a little less far along the road of delexicalisation" (1993:184). [. . .] *Badly* (15b) easily collocates with adjectives having negative connotation, . . . [and] seems to be restricted to use with adjectives derived from verbs with negative connotation (e.g. *burned* and *injured*), although it also goes with *wrong* [. . .]. Thus, *badly* would be a "less grammaticalized" intensifier. In contrast, *very* is highly delexicalized because it combines "very widely indeed and is also the intensifier with the least independent lexical content" (Partington 1993:183).

We can test this by systematically classifying the different adjectival heads and examining the expansion of *really* over *very* across them in apparent time. In order to do this, we operationalized the model provided by Dixon 1977, which divides adjectives into eight groups [. . .]: Dimension (e.g. *big*, *large*, *little*, *small*, *long*, *short*, *wide*, *narrow*, *thick*); Physical property (e.g. *hard*, *soft*, *heavy*, *light*, *rough*, *smooth*, *hot*, *sweet*); Color (e.g. *black*, *white*, *red*); Human propensity (e.g. *jealous*, *happy*, *kind*, *clever*, *generous*, *gay*, *rude*); Age (e.g. *new*, *young*, *old*); Value (e.g. *good*, *bad*, *proper*, *perfect*, *excellent*, *delicious*, *poor*); Speed (e.g. *fast*, *quick*, *slow*); Position (e.g. *right*, *left*, *near*, *far*).

[. . .]

Figures 20.3, 20.4, and 20.5 depict the distribution of *really* and *very* according to these categories for each age group respectively: the oldest generation, the middle generation, and the youngest generation.

In Figure 20.3, the oldest generation, we observe that *really* hardly ever occurs. The most frequent intensifier and the most widespread through all categories is *very*. We note, however, that the contexts where *really* occurs are the categories that are among the most common in the data: value, human propensity, dimension, and physical property.

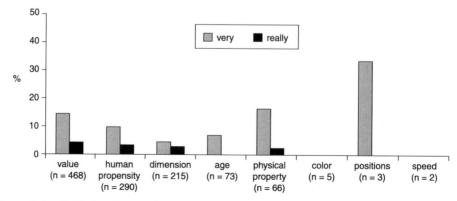

Figure 20.3   Distribution of *very* and *really* by type of the modified adjectives (66+).

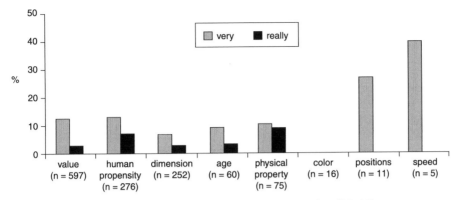

Figure 20.4 Distribution of *very* and *really* by type of the modified adjectives (35–65).

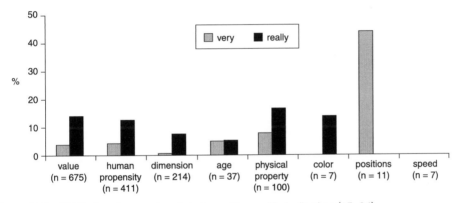

Figure 20.5 Distribution of *very* and *really* by type of the modified adjectives (17–34).

Figure 20.4 represents the middle generation. Here, each of these same categories now has even greater use of *really*. However, its expansion in adjectives of physical property, as in (10), is greatest.

(10) a. So I mean even in winter it's **really** really COLD. (YRK/w/F/48)
 b. It's quite surprising um, how—how—how **really** TIGHT a community it is in its own way. (YRK/s/M/50)

In addition, another category, age, now has use of *really* where it did not have any before.

(11) It was a **really** OLD building, and they wanted to build a new one. (YRK/#/M/37)

Although the middle generation does not exhibit much greater frequency of *really* overall (3% for oldest generation and 4.2% for the middle generation, see Figure 20.2), by comparing Figure 20.3 and Figure 20.4 we can now see that it has spread into additional adjectival types among this cohort.

Finally, Figure 20.5 shows that among the youngest generation, there is an exponential increase in use of *really* across nearly all categories. Moreover, there is spread to an additional category, color. In at least four [contexts] (value, human propensity, dimension, and physical property), use of *really* is double that of *very*. In other words, in the middle generation we observe spread of the form, but only in the youngest generation is there spread along with a leap in frequency. Thus, the spread (or diffusion) of an intensifier pre-dates an overall increase in use. [. . .]

Another way to tap into the gradual delexicalization of intensifiers is to examine their patterning according to function (Mustanoja 1960:326–27). As described earlier, the last stage in the development of intensifier *very* is when it comes to modify predicate adjectives. Extrapolating from these observations, use of intensifiers with predicate adjectives could be taken as evidence for a later stage in the delexicalization process. Higher frequency of use with predicate adjectives over other contexts might reflect an even later development. We can test for this by examining the distribution of intensifiers according to whether they occurred with attributive adjectives (12) or with predicative adjectives (13):

(12) *Attributive:*
But we'd been out in some **very** bad weather. (YRK/L/M/86) [. . .]

(13) *Predicative:*
Oh you were **really** terrified. (YRK/v/F/79) [. . .]

Figures 20.6 and 20.7 show the distribution of *really* and *very* according to this distinction for each age group. These figures consistently show that intensifiers occur far more frequently with predicate adjectives than with attributive adjectives. Moreover, this is consistent for all age groups. Thus, both *really* and *very* are well advanced: Both are used with predicate adjectives, and further, they are both used more frequently in this context than with attributive adjectives. This is not surprising, however, because both have been used in intensifier function for several hundred years – 500 years for *very*, nearly 300 years for *really*.

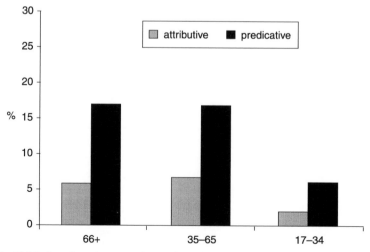

Figure 20.6   Distribution of *very* by age and type of predication.

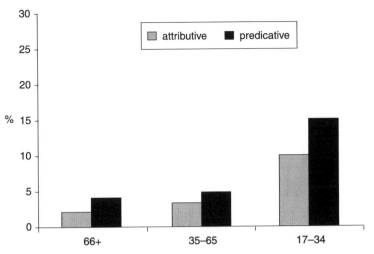

Figure 20.7   Distribution of *really* by age and type of predication.

However, we can also see that the degree of difference between the two adverb types is far greater with *very* than with *really*. Moreover, notice that this is true only among the oldest generation. In the younger generation, for *really*, the effect appears to be as robust as for all the generations with *very*. In other words, the point at which *really* parallels *very* in terms of the operation of this constraint is precisely in the generation where *really* not only expands in function, but also increases in frequency.

In sum, the results from Figures 20.3–20.7 provide two pieces of evidence to support the fact that *very* and *really* represent different degrees of grammaticalization. *Very* is further advanced. First, it collocates more widely [. . .]; second, it has a stronger differentiation between predicate and attribute adjectives across all generations.

Another bit of evidence for positing a different degree of grammaticalization between these two intensifiers is with respect to the difference in their multifunctionality. The prime function of *very* in contemporary English is as intensifier, not with its original meaning 'true' [. . .].[6] Indeed, we examined ten randomly chosen speakers' use of *very* with frequencies ranging from seven tokens to more than forty tokens per person, and we could not find even a single example of *very* with this reading. Subjecting *really* to the same test, however, revealed that it still retains its modal meaning 'truly' [. . .][7]:

[. . .]

Moreover, *really* as modal is far more frequent among the oldest generation than the youngest in our data. In order to show this, the two oldest speakers and the two most frequent users of *really* from the youngest generation were chosen. Table 20.4 shows the distribution of *really* as intensifier and as modal by these four speakers. The oldest male speaker (91 years of age) had only one token of *real*, and it was an intensifier, but all of his *really* tokens had the modal reading. All of the *really* tokens of the oldest female speaker (87 years old) were modal. In contrast, the frequency of *really* as intensifier among the youngest generation is far greater (over 50%).

In sum, our contrastive analysis of *very* and *really* has revealed a number of important internal factors that condition their appearance. However, how significant are they? [. . .]

Table 20.4   Distribution of *really* as intensifier and as emphasizer by four selected speakers

Speaker	Intensifier		Modal		
	%	N	%	N	Total N
91 yr. man	12.5	1	87.5	7	8
87 yr. woman	0	0	100	4	4
24 yr. man	51.1	45	48.9	43	88
26 yr. woman	54.8	17	45.2	14	31

MULTIVARIATE ANALYSIS

In the next section, we subject the incoming intensifier *really* to an analysis that treats both the internal and external factors simultaneously. In addition, because the generations in this community are highly differentiated according to intensifier use and patterning (Figure 20.2), we also divide the data by age group. This enables us to test the influence of the internal factor[s] at different points in apparent time. Table 20.5 shows the results.

[. . .] Higher numbers can be interpreted as favoring *really*, whereas lower ones disfavor it. The higher the number, the greater the contribution of that factor to the use of *really*. The factors for which the numbers are enclosed in square brackets were considered in the analysis but were found not to be significant [. . .].

The internal factor tested in this analysis is SYNTACTIC FUNCTION. Although predicative adjectives consistently favor *really*, notice that this factor reaches statistical significance only in the youngest generation.

The external factors, EDUCATION and SEX, are also involved. Education exerts a consistent statistically significant effect. In both the middle-aged and the youngest

Table 20.5   Three multivariate analyses of the contribution of factors to the probability of *really* in contemporary British English

Input	Old .030			Middle .027			Young .124		
	Weight	%	Ns/Cell	Weight	%	Ns/Cell	Weight	%	Ns/Cell
SYNTACTIC FUNCTION									
Predicative	[.56]	4	541	[.53]	5	731	.54	15	943
Attributive	[.45]	2	613	[.47]	3	614	.44	10	577
Range							*10*		
EDUCATION									
Secondary & beyond	n/a			.60	3	429	.55	15	1049
Up to secondary				.44	3	732	.40	8	471
Range				*16*			*15*		
SEX									
Female	[.51]	3	804	.66	6	732	[.52]	14	880
Male	[.48]	3	350	.31	2	613	[.48]	11	640
Range				*35*					

generation, higher education leads to greater use of *really*.[8] The effect of sex is highly contrastive. In the middle generation it is the most significant factor influencing the use of *really*, with a range of 35 (which is double that of education). In the oldest and youngest speakers, there is no effect at all. The factor weights hover near .50.

This leads to a further observation. Note that although education is selected as statistically significant in the middle-aged speakers, the proportional results show no difference (3% each). In the youngest generation, although there is a slight effect of sex in the percentages (14% for females and 11% for males), it is not selected as statistically significant. Thus, if we had considered only percentage data, we might think that education is not important in the middle generation, yet the multiple regression confirms that it is. Further, we might think that sex is relevant in the middle and youngest generations; once again, the multiple regression confirms that it is not – it is only significant in the middle generation. [. . .]

Let us now examine the interface between education and sex among the middle-aged and the youngest generations in order to see what is underlying these results. [. . .] [By looking at how sex and education interact], we can understand better why sex was not selected as significant for *really* among the youngest generation in the multivariate analysis in Table 20.5. Whereas women led the change to *really* in the middle-aged generation, the dramatic increase in the use of *really* cannot simply be attributed to women continuing to lead the change in the youngest generation because the educated males are implicated equally, if not more so.

DISCUSSION

Our results confirm that use of intensifiers is constantly changing in terms not only of frequency but also of lexical preference.[9] In this community, two intensifiers in particular are used the majority of the time – *very* and *really*. However, this is changing very rapidly among the current population. [. . .] We have also discovered an overriding constraint such that intensifiers are preferred with predicative adjectives, and this is true regardless of the intensifier. This constraint may be linked to expansion in function and increased frequency, because it becomes statistically significant for *really* only among the youngest generation. [. . .]

We have also provided contemporary evidence to support the belief that women lead in the change from one intensifier to another. Moreover, we can pinpoint exactly where: at the point when the newcomer expands in function. In our data, this is in the middle-aged generation. This is the only cohort where sex is selected as statistically significant, and the one where we observe the strongest constraint on the use of the intensifier.

The effect of speaker sex, however, is not as simple as has been reported previously for intensifier use. We cannot merely attribute their use to women's preference for hyperbole, nor can intensifiers be associated entirely with non-standard or vulgar language, since in this study more educated speakers (male or female) favor their use. In fact, the younger educated males are just as likely to use *really* as the women. [. . .]

In addition, all the results reported here confirm that intensifiers represent an excellent site to view grammatical layering in synchronic data. Indeed, intensifiers that have been attested from as early as Old English are still part of the repertoire in this variety of modern English.[10] Thus, it appears that old intensifiers do not fade away; they stick around for a very long time. This extraordinary continuity is consistent with extensive research in the grammaticalization literature, where the perpetuity of old forms and meanings has been traced back over a millennium and more (e.g. Traugott & Heine 1991; Bybee et al. 1994). [. . .]

Finally, and perhaps most provocatively, we have discovered a tremendous generation gap in York English: Use of the intensifier *very* is a mark of being over 35, while favoring *really* should clearly mark one as much younger. But are these trends particular to York alone, or to the UK more generally? Do different communities have different "layers" of intensifiers? To what extent do communities in Britain differ from Anglophone ones in North America and elsewhere? The findings reported here open up the possibility for further investigation. Indeed, we would suggest that systematic comparative studies of intensifiers in English may be a particularly choice means to track the varying rates of grammatical change across dialects, as well as to tap into current trends in contemporary English.

NOTES

* The second author gratefully acknowledges the generous support of the Economic and Social Research Council of the United Kingdom (ESRC) for research grant R00028287. The trajectory *well > right > very > really* reflects the actually historical trajectory of intensifier development in English. Although we discuss only *very* and *really* at length, owing to their high frequency all four are members of the intensifier cohort in York English.

1. The information in parentheses refers to the community York (YRK) and speaker identification, i.e. speaker code, sex, and age.

2. Bäcklund's materials comprise several issues of two British newspapers and one American magazine, representing "educated English." In addition, the corpus comprises eight novels and three plays written by British authors and three novels written by American authors (Bäcklund 1973:10–11).

3. Lexical items *too* and *that* are treated as intensifiers by Bolinger 1972 and Bäcklund 1973, although not by others (e.g. Stoffel 1901, Quirk et al. 1985).

4. Stoffel (1901:148) notes that *pretty* expresses "moderate degree" as well as in the sense of *very*. He further notes that "in contemporary usage it would seem that the adverb *pretty* is especially in favour where, by litotes, a high degree is expressed by an adverb which originally denotes a moderate degree only" (Stoffel 1901:153). Thus, we decided not to exclude this lexical item.

5. Of course, in other areas of grammaticalization, narrowing of collocation patterns is also possible, particularly in cases where items that are disappearing leave residue, e.g. *to* in *today*. We owe this observation to one of the reviewers of this manuscript.

6. Interestingly, one of the original meanings of *real/really* is "true", paralleling the case of *very* (*OED* vol. 8, 201).

7. *Really* in final position, [. . .], is said to have a "softening or cajoling effect" (Stenström 1987:72, cited in Macaulay 1995:127). In Macaulay's Scots data, this type of *really* is much more frequent in the lower-class interviews than in the middle-class interviews. Macaulay interprets such correlations as the projection of middle-class attempts to convey authoritativeness (Macaulay 1995). In the York data, we did not explore such differences with respect to intensifier use; however, in a study of dual form adverbs, we discuss correlations of *-ly* and zero adverbs with class and education (see Tagliamonte & Ito 2002).

8. Unfortunately, the effect of education could not be tested among the oldest generation because all of the speakers in our sub-sample in this age bracket had been educated only to minimal school-leaving age.

9. Whether this is an indication of increase in intensification in the English language more generally, or simply a reflection of age-grading and/or style difference remains an important question for further investigation.

10. The long-term layering and recycling found in this analysis is frequently evident from personal observations from the York community. For example, the second author's son's eight-year old friend remarked one night in York in mid-2001 about ice cream: *It's **well** good* — yet *well* as an intensifier was supposed to have died out by the mid-14th century. Interestingly, a revival of *well* has recently been reported for London teenagers (Stenström 2000).

REFERENCES

Bäcklund, Ulf (1973). *The Collocation of Adverbs of Degree in English*. Uppsala: Almqvist & Wiksell.

Bolinger, Dwight (1972). *Degree Words*. The Hague & Paris: Mouton.

Bybee, Joan L.; Perkins, Revere D.; & Pagliuca, William (1994). *The Evolution of Grammar: Tense, Aspect, and Modality in the Languages of the World*. Chicago: University of Chicago Press.

Dixon, R. M. W. (1977). Where have all the adjectives gone? *Studies in Language* 1(1):19–80.

Fries, Charles Carpenter (1940). *American English Grammar*. New York: Appleton, Century, Crofts.

Jespersen, Otto H. (1922). *Language: Its Nature, Development, and Origin*. London: George Allen & Unwin.

Labov, William (1985). Intensity. In Deborah Schiffrin (ed.), *Meaning, Form and Use in Context: Linguistic Applications*, 43–70. Washington, DC: Georgetown University Press.

Macaulay, Ronald K. S. (1995). The adverbs of authority. *English World-Wide* 16(1):37–60.

Mustanoja, Tauno F. (1960). *A Middle English Syntax*. Helsinki: Société Néophilologique.

Partington, Alan (1993). Corpus evidence of language change: the case of intensifiers. In Mona Baker et al. (eds.), *Text and Technology: In Honour of John Sinclair*, 177–92. Amsterdam & Philadelphia: John Benjamins.

Peters, Hans (1994). Degree adverbs in early modern English. In Dieter Kastovsky (ed.), *Studies in Early Modern English*, 269–88. Berlin & New York: Walter de Gruyter.

Quirk, Randolph; Greenbaum, Sidney; Leech, Geoffrey; & Svartvik, Jan (1985). *A Comprehensive Grammar of the English Language*. New York: Longman.

Sinclair, John (1992). Trust the text: the implications are daunting. In M. Davies & L. Ravelli (eds.), *Trust the Text: The Implications are Daunting*, 5–19. (Advances in Systemic Linguistics: Recent Theory and Practice.) London: Pinter.

Stenström, Anna-Brita (1999). He was really gormless – She's bloody crap: girls, boys and intensifiers. In Hide Hasselgård & Signe Okesfjell (eds.), *Out of Corpora: Studies in Honour of Stig Johansson*, 69–78. Amsterdam & Atlanta: Rodopi.

Stoffel, Cornelis (1901). *Intensives and Down-toners*. Heidelberg: Carl Winter.

Tagliamonte, Sali A. (1998). *Was/were* variation across the generations: view from the city of York. *Language Variation and Change* 10(2):153–91.

Tagliamonte, Sali A. & Ito, Rika (2002). Think *really different*: continuity and specialization in the English adverbs. *Journal of Sociolinguistics* 6(2):236–66.

Traugott, Elizabeth Closs, & Heine, Bernd (1991). Introduction. In E. C. Traugott & B. Heine (eds.), *Approaches to Grammaticalization: Focus on Theoretical and Methodological Issues*, 2–14. Amsterdam & Philadelphia: John Benjamins.

QUESTIONS

Content

1. Explain what it means for a lexical item to be "recycled".
2. Why do Ito & Tagliamonte argue intensifiers offer a particularly informative study of language change? Do you agree?
3. What is the difference between *attributive* and *predicative* adjectives?

   a. Why do Ito & Tagliamonte suggest that use of an intensifier with predicative adjectives indicates a greater degree of grammaticalization?

Concept

1. Stoffel associates use of intensifiers at the turn of the 20th century with "ladies", "ladies' men" and "children". What do you think is the generalization underlying this apparently disparate group of speakers? What (if anything) do you think they have in common?
2. Consider the examples of intra-speaker variation in example (3). Ito & Tagliamonte are concerned with a quantitative study in their corpus over apparent time, but these examples suggest a qualitative approach might be possible. What do you notice about the direction of the switches in each example?
3. Find another study that considers both speakers' sex and speakers' level of education as social variables. What association is there between sex and education in that study, and how does it differ from or resemble the pattern discussed by Ito & Tagliamonte?

Chapter 21

Gillian Sankoff and Hélène Blondeau

LANGUAGE CHANGE ACROSS THE LIFESPAN: /r/ IN MONTREAL FRENCH*

1. INTRODUCTION

[. . .] Weinreich, Labov, and Herzog (1968) demonstrated that change necessarily involves diffusion. They showed that language change implies variation (though not the reverse), and that as an innovation diffuses through the speech community, the social structure of that community conditions its path. Subsequent research has not, however, directly addressed the question of the articulation between language change in the historical sense and language change as experienced by individual speakers. We take this as our central concern in analyzing a phonological change in Montreal French—the community shift in the pronunciation of /r/—on the basis of data collected in 1971 and 1984. We address three major goals in our exploration of the problem. First, we look at the two major types of longitudinal research: trend and panel studies, and evaluate the relative contribution of each. Second, we assess the extent to which predictions based on an apparent-time interpretation of our 1971 age distribution represent a change in progress that has continued, as measured against real time longitudinal data. Third, we reconsider the role of the critical period in language acquisition as it relates to language change.

[. . .]

The current article . . . examines a change in progress in the pronunciation of /r/ in Montreal French [. . .]. Before proceeding to the Montreal case, it is important to explain how the three specific goals of our article fit into the larger project of understanding the relationship between historical change and individual speakers.

Though most sociolinguistic studies over the past forty years have necessarily been synchronic, making use of the present to explain the past (Labov 1975), there are now a

Source: Sankoff, Gillian and Hélène Blondeau (2007) Language change across the lifespan: /r/ in Montreal French. *Language* 83: 560–588.

number of longitudinal research projects that have produced valuable results. These projects, designed mainly as TREND STUDIES, in which communities that had been studied a decade or more previously were resampled, include Brink & Lund 1979, Cedergren 1988, Trudgill 1988, Thibault & Daveluy 1989, Ashby 2001, Blake & Josey 2003, and Josey 2004. A second type of longitudinal study is the PANEL STUDY, in which the same individuals are followed across time. In general, the considerable logistical problems and consequent expense involved in such research have precluded large-scale panel follow-ups; several researchers, however, have carried out such studies, usually with rather smaller samples (e.g. Baugh 1995, Cukor-Avila 2002, Hernandez-Compoy 2003, Nahkola & Saanilahti 2004). Some studies have included both trend and panel components (Paunonen 1996, Blondeau 2001, de Paiva & Duarte 2003, Naro & Scherre 2002, Zilles 2005). Trend studies clearly constitute the best use of resources if the object is to track language change in progress. However, the combination of trend and panel research is essential for the interpretation of change, especially as regards the relationship of change to individual grammars (see also Blondeau 2006 on this point). Both types of longitudinal sociolinguistic research are crucial in building more informed models of the role of individual speakers, over their lifetimes, in language change.

Stability of the grammars of individuals after initial language acquisition is the premise that underlies the concept of APPARENT TIME, introduced by Labov in his early studies of Martha's Vineyard (1963) and New York City (1966) [. . .]. In both cases, he used observations made at earlier periods to verify that, by and large, the speech of older people tends to reflect the state of the language when they acquired it. Table 21.1 represents Labov's review of the logical possibilities for interpretation of two different patterns that might be observed in a synchronic study. When use of a particular variant is plotted against speaker age, we may see either a flat pattern or a regular increasing or decreasing slope with age.[1]

If a synchronic study shows no age differentiation (the 'flat' pattern), we can infer either that no change is occurring—both individual speakers and the community as a whole are stable (interpretation #1), or that all the speakers in the community are changing together at the same rate—both older and younger speakers are at the same stage in a change affecting them equally (interpretation #4). By contrast, a regular slope with age may mean that generation after generation, individuals change as they get older, yet the community remains stable over time. According to this interpretation (#2, AGE GRADING), as each cohort of speakers ages, it steadily increases its use of one variant of the variable. Labov (1964) provides an example of this in analyzing stages that children go through in the acquisition of standard English. Alternately, individuals may retain their childhood patterns, with each age cohort of speakers registering an increasing

Table 21.1   Patterns of change in the individual and the community (adapted from Labov 1994:83)

Synchronic pattern	Interpretation	Individual	Community
flat	1. Stability	stability	stability
regular slope with age	2. Age grading	change	stability
regular slope with age	3. Generational change (= apparent-time interpretation)	stability	change
flat	4. Communal change	change	change

use of the variant upon entering the community. This is the classic apparent-time interpretation (#3) of change in progress.[2]

Judicious use of the apparent-time interpretation of age-graded variability has been a hallmark of sociolinguistic research for the past thirty years. However, given the largely synchronic nature of most studies, it has not been possible to verify models of the locus of change with respect to individual speakers. Sankoff (2005, 2006) suggested a distinction between two separate patterns involving speaker change in a situation where we observe a regular slope correlated with speaker age. In the first or classic case, we can use the term age grading in the traditional sense, assuming a generational pattern that is cyclic or repeats as a function of cultural dictates of what is appropriate to speakers of a given age. But another possibility is 'lifespan change,' in which 'individual speakers change over their lifespans in the direction of a change in progress in the rest of the community' (Sankoff 2005:1011). Such a pattern would be historical (rather than cyclic) in character. Labov's (1994) discussion of Cedergren's (1988) restudy of (ch) variation in Panamanian Spanish demonstrates that the age distribution includes both an apparent-time and an age-grading component. It leaves open, however, the question of whether the age grading observable from the restudy is a matter of age-appropriate frequencies that would be cyclical in character, or a change in which individuals over their lifespans are swept along with historical language change in the wider community. The model put forward in Table 21.2 represents the addition of a lifespan-change component distinct from the traditional concept of age grading in that it does not necessarily imply cyclicity. We explore the extent to which such a model is justified empirically in the present case.

Last, we are interested in how the change is experienced by individual speakers past puberty, and in the relationship of our study to the critical period. The current literature modeling language change tends to locate it within the scope of first language acquisition (e.g. Lightfoot 1999), although [this] is more a tacit assumption in the field than a much researched topic. In a recent treatment of the relationship between brain development and individual phonological systems, Anderson and Lightfoot argue that puberty poses an important limit:

> In the early years of life, the brain develops vast numbers of new synapses, peaking at about 2 years of age. Over the next several years, neurons die and synapses wither, resulting in a specifically limited organization. Neuron death levels out at around age 7, while overall synaptic organization is determined by around the age of puberty. If we assume that the role of experience is to shape and mold this

Table 21.2   Addition of a pattern reflecting lifespan change that accompanies change at the level of the community

Synchronic pattern	Interpretation	Individual	Community
flat	1. Stability	stable	stable
regular slope with age	2a. Age grading	change	stable
regular slope with age	2b. Lifespan change	change	change
regular slope with age	3. Generational change (= apparent-time interpretation)	stable	change
flat	4. Communal change	change	change

specific organization, then whatever is in place by puberty is what we are 'stuck
with'. (2002:209; scare quotes in the original)

Analyzing speakers age fifteen and above across the thirteen-year interval between 1971
and 1984, we verify how labile individuals are in later life, and how our results relate to
what is known about the critical period.

2. /r/ IN MONTREAL FRENCH

[. . .] [R]hotics may have at least three places of articulation ('dental/alveolar; postalveo-
lar/retroflex; and uvular'), and [. . .] 'manner of articulation . . . is at least as variable,
[including] trills, fricatives, approximants, taps/flaps, and vowels' (Wiese 2001:11). As in
numerous other languages, Québécois French includes many of these variants. [. . .] At
the end of the nineteenth century, apical [r] was still the norm in the Province of Quebec
[. . .] (Morin 2002:51). As of the mid-twentieth century, however, there was a clear
geographical split. Vinay's survey of 1947–1950 confirmed that Western Quebec,
including Montreal, was characterized by the traditional apical [r], tapped or trilled
(Vinay 1950). [. . .] A dorsal [R] (velar fricative or uvular trill) was typical of the eastern
part of the province, a zone comprising all points east of Trois Rivières including Quebec
City (Vinay 1950).[3] Canonical /r/ as [r] or [R], then, depends largely on the region.
Though in the course of change in Montreal many speakers vary between the two, we
observe only minimal phonetic conditioning between these variants for the variable
speakers (Sankoff & Blondeau 2007). But a number of other variants occur in rapid
speech . . . [which do] not involve tongue contact with either the alveolar ridge or the
velar/uvular region, [so] they were not considered to represent consonantal targets
and were therefore not included in [our] quantitative analysis. [. . .] Between 1950 and
1970, canonical /r/ in Montreal began to change, with the dorsal [R] making strong
inroads. The conclusion that by 1970, [r] was in 'rapid regression' (Santerre 1978) was
confirmed in an apparent-time calculation by Clermont and Cedergren (1979), hence-
forward C&C, who found that the innovative [R] was increasingly common among
speakers below age thirty-five. [. . .] A multiple regression with rate of [R] use as
the dependent variable show[ed] that 'the single most important factor . . . was the
speakers' age, followed by social class membership, sex, and educational level of
attainment' (Cedergren 1988:49).

[. . .]

In the current article, we use an expanded panel, and also make trend comparisons of
speakers sampled in 1971 and 1984, allowing us to document both real-time change in
the speech community as well as the trajectories of /r/ pronunciation of a number of
individual speakers who were followed across that time span. We focus on the social
factors that differentiate speakers in terms of their use of the two canonical variants, [r]
and [R]. The phonological factors that partially condition the alternation between these
variants are dealt with in Sankoff & Blondeau 2007, where we also consider stylistic
factors, which prove to be almost without influence on the alternation.

3. DESIGN AND METHODOLOGY OF THE CURRENT STUDY

It is widely acknowledged that the most reliable method for studying language change in a community is that of the trend study (Trudgill 1988, Labov 1994). In the ideal case, the follow-up study would resample the community, using the same sampling criteria as the first (de Paiva & Duarte 2003, Zilles 2005). In our case, the 1984 survey was designed mainly as a panel study (Thibault & Vincent 1990); however, the twelve new younger speakers who were added (see below) were used as a nucleus in designing matched subsamples that allow us to make trend comparisons. The logic of these comparisons, involving selected subsamples of thirty-two speakers each (see Figure 21.1), is explained in §§3.1–3.4.

The 1971 sociolinguistic study of Montreal consisted of a random sample of 120 speakers, stratified by age, sex, and social class (Sankoff & Sankoff 1973). In 1984, Thibault and Vincent succeeded in relocating and reinterviewing sixty of the original interviewees, making this the largest and most representative panel study in socio-linguistics. Since the youngest speakers of 1971 were by then twenty-eight years old, they added twelve new speakers between age fifteen and twenty-five, again stratified according to sex and socioeconomic level. To examine change across individual lifespans, we could have studied all sixty of the reinterviewed subjects, [. . .] [but we] weighted our sub-samples toward speakers under forty, who would be most reliably resampled.

In order to be able to construct matched subsamples of different speakers, we set up a sampling stratification scheme that would allow us to resample from the pool of available speakers according to age, sex, and social class. The largest subsamples we could create, given the constraints described above, consisted of thirty-two individuals each [. . .]. To represent a range of social classes, we divided the population into three groups according to their scores on the LINGUISTIC MARKET (LM) index.[4]

3.1 The panel subsample

Constructing a subsample for the panel of speakers to be followed between 1971 and 1984 necessarily involved selecting from among the sixty original speakers who were reinterviewed in 1984.

[. . .]

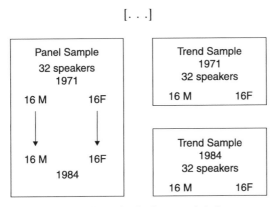

Figure 21.1   Design of the trend and panel samples for the current study.

3.2 The trend subsamples

The subsample from 1971 that would be used as a basis for trend comparisons had to be selected from among the sixty speakers who were NOT reinterviewed in 1984. From this pool of speakers, using the same criteria outlined above, we selected thirty-two individuals, stratified by age, sex, and social class as shown in Table 21.3. [. . .]

The trend subsample for 1984 had to be selected as if we had returned to the speech community and taken a new sample according to the criteria of 1971. [. . .]

3.3 Data coding and analysis

For each speaker in each year, our goal was to code approximately one hundred tokens, beginning about ten minutes into the interview (usually starting at the fifth page of the transcript) and continuing to code each /r/ that occurred. . . . Two coders listened to each tape and noted codes on separate spreadsheets, after which the number of instances of [R] and [r] were noted and the percentage calculated as [R]/([R] + [r]) [. . .]. This procedure is illustrated in Table 21.4, which provides the codings of Hélène Blondeau and Sarah Moretti for Bernard L. (087'71). [. . .]

We then ran a chi-square test on the 2 × 2 table highlighted on the left, and if the difference between the two coders was not significant at the 0.05 level, as in this case, we usually considered the value for that speaker in that year to be the mean of the two codings.[5] . . . [T]he results given in this article represent the analysis of approximately 12,400 tokens, or approximately 115 per speaker sample.

3.4 The logic of comparisons

We selected our panel and trend subsamples from the 120 speakers of 1971 using the same criteria of age, sex, and social class as described above. Drawing two separate

Table 21.3 Composition of 1971 trend subsample by age, sex, and social class (scores on Linguistic Market index divided into 3 groups, corresponding to Working Class, Lower Middle Class, and Upper Middle Class)

Social class	WC (LM ≤ 22)		LMC (LM 22–59)		UMC (LM 60+)		
Age	M	F	M	F	M	F	TOTAL
15–23	2	2	3	2	2	2	13
23–39	2	2	2	2	2	2	12
40 plus	1	1	1	1	1	2	7
Total	5	5	6	5	5	6	32

Table 21.4 Codings for Bernard L. in 1971 by Hélène Blondeau and Sarah Moretti

Coder	[R]	[r]	Vocalized	Deleted	Retroflex	Indistinct	Total	[R]/([R] + [r])
Blondeau	39	44	29	16	2	7	137	47.0%
Moretti	30	28	23	35	4	13	133	51.7%

stratified subsamples from the same community, we would hope to derive the same results. In analyzing the data, we thus first compare the two 1971 subsamples to see whether indeed their behavior is matched in the way we would expect. . . . Next, we look at the panel as a group and examine the extent to which these individuals did or did not change. Finally, the panel's behavior is set in the context of the real-time change as revealed by comparing the two trend samples.

4. THE SITUATION IN 1971

The linguistic situation in 1971 with respect to the major variants of /r/ in Montreal was well documented (Clermont & Cedergren [C&C] 1979, Santerre 1978, Tousignant 1987a, Sankoff, Blondeau & Charity [SBC] 2001). C&C demonstrated that speakers of higher socioeconomic status and younger speakers were most likely to use a higher proportion of the innovative [R] variant.

[. . .]

In selecting our subsamples, we made sure to represent three age groups of speakers, but for analytical purposes, we divide each subsample into sixteen younger and sixteen older speakers [. . .]. In both [the trend study and the panel study samples], speakers age twenty-four and under show means of [R] usage considerably higher than speakers twenty-five and older. The mean [R] percentages for older speakers in the two samples are seven percentage points apart (41.3% for the panel sample and 34.3% for the trend sample), whereas the younger speakers' means are within five percentage points of each other (63.8% for the panel sample and 68.5% for the trend sample). Grouping younger and older speakers together in each subsample, the means are only one percentage point apart (52.5% for the panel and 51.4% for the trend sample). This result allows us to proceed with confidence in studying change over time.

5. CHANGE ACROSS THE LIFESPAN: THE PANEL SPEAKERS OVER TIME

An initial look at the panel as a group can be obtained by considering the group means for the 1984 panel speakers: the thirty-two individuals of the 1971 panel sample, all thirteen years older [. . .].

[. . .] [T]hese speakers have increased their use of [R] over the period. The younger speakers' group mean was 63.8% in 1971; these same people show a mean of 77.8% in 1984, an increase of more than ten percentage points. Perhaps more surprising, given the widespread acceptance of the idea that adults' linguistic systems are relatively stable, is the increase of almost ten percentage points, from 41.3% to 50.8%, for the older group. The means, however, give a misleading picture of the sample members as a homogeneous group. As we discovered in examining the smaller panel sample across the twenty-four-year span from 1971 to 1995 (SBC), the increase is far from uniform when we look at individuals. To separate the speakers into those who were stable and those who changed, we did a chi-square test comparing each speaker's total apical and dorsal /r/ tokens in their 1971 and 1984 samples. Ten of the thirty-two speakers were designated as having

Table 21.5   The 20 stable speakers who remained categorical or near-categorical users of one of the two variants across the study, 1971–1984

Range type	Range of [R]	Trajectory type	No. of speakers	Mean LM	Mean age 1971	Sex ratio F:M
categorical or near-categorical [R]	85–100%	stable	10	39.1	16.9	8:2
categorical or near-categorical [r]	0–17%	stable	10	29.0	30.3	3:7

changed significantly over the period, nine in the expected direction. The tenth speaker, Christine Q. (004), appears to be a counterexample, since her change was in the opposite direction, from 92% to 87% [R]. [. . .] [S]ince she remains in the near-categorical range of Table 21.5, we treated her as one of those speakers who remained stably in that category across time.

We consider first in Table 21.5 a comparison between the speakers who were stable over time: the ten (including Christine Q.) who maintained near-categorical [R], the innovative variant, and the ten who maintained near-categorical [r], the traditional Montreal variant. The two groups have very different social profiles: the group we label 'early adopters' of the innovative form are much younger (just a little more than half the age of the speakers who retain the traditional form) and have a higher mean social-class index on the linguistic market scale. More striking is the very disproportionate sex ratio: drawn from a pool of sixteen male and sixteen female speakers, eight of ten early adopters are female; and seven of ten traditionalists are male, a statistically significant difference.[6] Gender difference is then a third variable, in addition to age and social class, that is important in determining which speakers are early adopters of the innovative form.

The twelve remaining speakers were those whose behavior was more variable. Mid-range speakers are defined as those whose use of [R] fell between 17% and 84% at either period. The mid-range speakers stand out in Figure 21.2, which plots the percentage of [R] for each of the panel speakers in both 1971 (filled diamonds) and 1984 (hollow squares). The overall increase of 12.3 percentage points is clearly not attributable to most speakers having slightly increased their use of the innovative variant. Rather, the increase is due to nine of the thirty-two individual speakers having made a fairly dramatic shift between 1971 and 1984. The trajectories of these nine individuals are designated by arrows connecting their 1971 with their 1984 data points.

At the bottom of the graph, we see two groups of the 1971 speakers in the ellipses: a tight cluster of seven individuals under age thirty, none of whom uses more than 10% [R], and another group of five speakers between the ages of thirty-five and fifty, and who range between 0 and 17%. Ten of these twelve people form the stable group of Table 21.5 in their use of the conservative form. Their 1984 values are displayed in the two dotted ellipses to the right of each of the 1971 groups. Two of them, however, Lysiane B. (007) and Alain L. (104), make substantial changes, abandoning the virtually categorical conservative pattern they displayed in 1971. [. . .]

A majority of mid-range speakers in 1971 (seven out of ten) had moved to the categorical or near-categorical use of innovative [R] by 1984. They are people we call 'later adopters' of the innovative variant. Five of the seven are young; five of the seven are male. As a group, we would characterize their behavior as catching up with their peers, the early adopters. The next three people [. . .] are those mid-range speakers who were stable, somewhat older, behaving more as we had expected older individuals to behave. [. . .] [Last] are the two individuals who moved from virtually categorical use of [r] to dominant use of [R], occupying the upper part of the variable range. Lysiane B. (007) is a case of exceptional upward social mobility, a twenty-four-year-old factory worker when we met her in 1971, a businesswoman in 1984, and when last interviewed in 1995, a successful realtor. [. . .] As far as Alain L. (104) is concerned, we were quite surprised that a man of forty-five would have shown such a remarkable change by the time he was fifty-eight. A car salesman, Alain was interviewed in 1984 at the car dealership where he worked, and much of the talk focused on questions of language and of taste. To attribute his relatively high level of [R] to formality, however, is probably too hasty. We have been unable to show stylistically conditioned variation for any speaker other than the professional actor André L. (065) [. . .] (SBC, Sankoff & Blondeau 2007).

Table 21.5 and Figure 21.2 show clearly that the mid-range use of both variants is not stable. Not only do most speakers cluster at the top or the bottom of the range, but mid-range speakers also tend very strongly to become categorical over time.

[. . .] Looked at in terms of the critical age, the evidence from this panel is that twenty-three of the thirty-two speakers (72%) showed stability over the period of their post-fifteen-year-old lives that we examined; the other nine (28%) increased their use of the innovative form significantly. Perhaps a more telling comparison is to look at the pool of speakers who had not yet adopted the innovative form in 1971. Of the twenty-two speakers who might have changed toward the innovative form, nine, or 41%, did so.

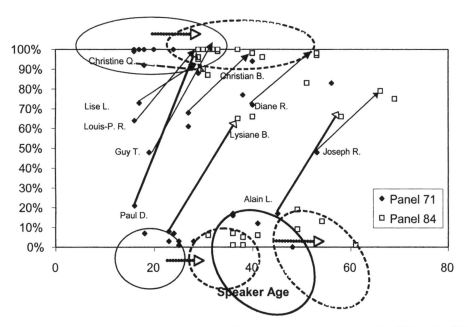

Figure 21.2 Individual percentages of [R]/([R] + [r]) for the 32 panel speakers for 1971 and 1984. Trajectories plotted for all speakers who showed a significant difference between the two years.

We might now ask: is 41% a lot, or a little [. . .]? Are the speakers who make this adult transition the leaders of the change in the community? In the next section, in which we present the results of the trend study, we put these questions into the community perspective.

6. CHANGE IN THE COMMUNITY: THE EVIDENCE OF TREND COMPARISONS

We noted in §3.2 [. . .] that the 1984 trend sample was quite similar to the 1971 trend sample [. . .] [but] there is an unequal number of 'younger' and 'older' speakers. For this reason, we pay most attention to the comparison of younger to younger, and older to older, in tracing the trends between 1971 and 1984.

[. . .] [T]he jump from 68% [R] in 1971 to 92.5% in 1984 among speakers under twenty appears to represent a real-time change in the community. Perhaps even more significantly, the twenty-five-to-fifty-six-year-old trend subsample in 1984 [. . .] shows an even greater increase: from 34.3% in 1971 to 74.9% in 1984. Adults of working age in the Montreal community in 1971 were quite likely to be predominant users of [r], but this was no longer the case in 1984. These trend comparisons clearly indicate that change was vigorous in the community in the 1970s and 1980s.

The trend study, representing a real-time reassessment of the community after a thirteen-year interval, is the basis for assessing real-time change. As such, the community mean indicates a massive shift toward the replacement of [r] by [R] during this period. Although the mean increase of panel speakers seemed to indicate progress toward the incoming form, the trend study confirms that at the community level, the rate of change is much greater, as is evident from the comparisons in Table 21.7.

Table 21.6   Mean social characteristics and mean [R] %, 1971 and 1984 trend subsamples

Trend subsamples	Age range	Mean age	Mean lm	% [R]
16 younger 1971	15–24	18.8	44.5	68.5%
11 younger 1984	15–24	17.9	60.9	92.5%
16 older 1971	25–61	39.2	32.6	34.3%
21 older 1984	25–61	38.6	40.3	74.9%

Table 21.7   Comparison of trend and panel subsamples over time

	Mean [R], younger speakers		Mean [R], older speakers	
	Panel, same speakers	Two separate trend samples	Panel, same speakers	Two separate trend samples
1984	77.8%	92.5%	50.7%	74.9%
1971	63.8%	68.5%	41.3%	34.3%
mean increase	14.0	24.5	9.4	40.6

Our examination of panel speakers as a group across time confirmed that such group means may give a misleading picture of what is going on. The examination of individual speakers led us to infer that the change is being implemented by people who alter their pronunciation quite rapidly, rather than a steady, incremental raising of levels across individual lifespans. An examination of the individual speakers in the two trend samples further illuminates these initial inferences, as can be seen in Figure 21.3.

Figure 21.3 indicates that the real-time change reflected in the community means of Table 21.6 is a product of a very different distribution of speakers in 1971 and 1984. Seven speakers under age thirty-five in 1971 (filled diamonds inside the dotted rectangle at the lower left) were predominant users of the conservative [r]; and only six were in the near-categorical [R] range on the upper left. By 1984, only one speaker under age thirty-five was a predominant user of the conservative form, and with one mid-range exception, all of the other younger speakers were clustered within the near-categorical [R] range. Among those over thirty-five, we see that in 1971, no speaker showed more than 50% [R]; most were clustered at the bottom of the figure in the categorical [r] range. In contrast, by 1984 there were six majority users of [R] among those older than thirty-five.

The panel study showed that early adopters remained stable across the 1971–1984 period. Once having adopted innovative [R], they continued as categorical or near-categorical users of this form. By the time they got to be age thirty-five and older, these early adopters were joined by a number of later adopters, who caught up with the change in later life. But whereas many younger speakers in 1971 were still majority users of the conservative form, this was no longer the case in 1984.

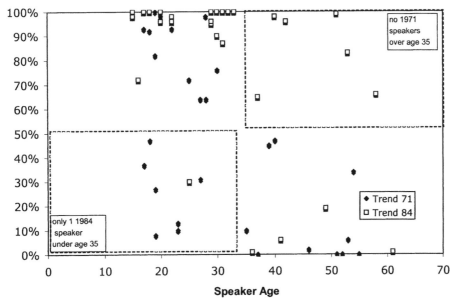

Figure 21.3   Individual percentages of [R]/([R] + [r]) for the 32 trend speakers for 1971 and for the 32 different trend speakers for 1984.

7. THE PROCESS OF CHANGE

[. . .]

7.2 Resolved and unresolved questions

By the evidence reviewed in the preceding section, two possible trajectories can be ruled out as underlying the implementation of this change in the Montreal speech community: (i) the change does NOT proceed mainly by speakers slowly increasing their use of [R] across their lifetimes, and (ii) the change does NOT proceed by successive cohorts of new members entering the speech community bearing a slightly higher value of [R] usage than their older peers. Rather, the inevitable conclusion is that change in the community is a result of individual speakers, especially younger speakers, being added to the pool of majority-users or categorical users of [R].

What is the process by which new speakers get added to the pool? We saw that both in 1971 and even more in 1984, many speakers in the fifteen-to-nineteen age range were already categorical [R] users when they first entered our study. One important question that we can try to answer on the basis of indirect evidence is: did these young speakers acquire categorical [R] usage as part of their initial language acquisition as young children, or did they join the pool of [R] users sometime between first language acquisition in early childhood and the age of fifteen? Given the fact that almost everyone over the age of thirty-five in 1971 was a categorical user of [r], we would have to assume that input from parents of virtually all children in 1971 was categorical [r]. By 1984, the situation would have changed somewhat. Some adolescents born between 1965 and 1970 would have had parents born after 1945 who themselves were predominant users of [R]. Nevertheless, it seems that the majority of our [R] users whose parents were native Montrealers would have heard the [r] variant as their primary input in first language acquisition. They would thus have differentiated themselves from their parents in later childhood or early adolescence.

Indeed, we have some direct evidence on this point. Almost all of the interviews with adolescents were carried out in the family home. Often a parent was present, and often those parents participated to some extent in the interview, being called on by their sons or daughters, for example, to supply information about where their grandparents came from. In some of these cases, we were fortunate to be able to establish the /r/ pattern of the parent. In sixteen of the thirty-one interviews carried out with young people between fifteen and twenty (including all 1971 and 1984 interviews), parents were present, usually the mother. Although we had much smaller samples of these parents' speech, we found no cases where the parent appeared to be anything but an apical [r] user.

We must conclude that a child with two parents who are categorical users of [r] would have [r] as an initial target form. It follows that in 1971 and to a large extent also in 1984, most people who arrived at age fifteen or sixteen as categorical users of [R] were speakers who had actually switched in childhood or early adolescence.

[. . .]

The norm is clearly one of relative stability after adolescence, however, as we saw from the fact that a majority of panel members did not change so radically. Our conclusion is that most of those speakers observed to be categorical users of [R] in late adolescence in fact made the switch earlier in life. Although it is possible that some children were influenced by older siblings who had already adopted the innovative form, the fact remains that there is a fairly sharp break between speakers older and younger than thirty-five in the 1971 data. So while it is possible that some younger siblings of early adopters may have acquired the innovation as part of their L1 acquisition, the older siblings themselves must have gone through the switch process.

In considering the source of the innovation and how it spread initially, it is important to look at both geographic and socio/stylistic considerations. C&C pointed out that [. . .] once the change was in progress in Montreal, it was acceptable and even appropriate for younger speakers to retain the pronunciation of their parents in cases where the parents were from [R]-pronouncing regions.[7]

It is clear that we are dealing here with a change from above (the change has a source outside the community; early adopters are more likely to be female and of a higher socioeconomic status). [. . .]

By 1984, the mid-range speakers we examined still did not behave consciously as if the [R] variant held any particular cachet—for most of them, in the upper range of variable usage, it had become the unmarked variant. By contrast, for some younger speakers, [r] seemed to have taken on meanings of being old-fashioned, having the ring of one's grandparents, of one's teachers, of the clergy. Some younger speakers used it for comic effect. [. . .]

A further mystery concerns the nature of the allophonic variation both between the two allophones in competition, and between them and the other variants of /r/ (SBC, Tousignant 1987a, C&C, Sankoff & Blondeau 2007). For variable speakers, there is a strong tendency to retain [r] in onsets, the most salient position, whereas the innovative [R] seems to appear first in codas in which /r/ is in any case subject to lenition and deletion. It would seem that a high-prestige pronunciation ought to occur first in the most salient position, but in listening to the speech of our variable speakers, it is almost as if [R] creeps in through the back door, where the least attention is being paid. [. . .]

The issues of allophonic variation and of stylistic significance may help to shed further light on the implementation of the change, but it is too late to be able to study the situation of L1 acquisition in families where children ended up with a different allophone from that of their parents. Nevertheless, we think that there are two important facts that need to be underlined here: (i) apical [r] must have been the target and the first acquired form in L1 acquisition for the vast majority of teenagers and young adults in Montreal in 1971 who were early adopters of dorsal [R], given the input they would have had from their parents; and (ii) all of the mid-range speakers under age thirty in 1971 had become categorical or near-categorical users of [R] by 1984. In tracing their trajectories as late adopters, it is reasonable to infer that their early-adopting peers had traced the same trajectory earlier in their lives. Figure 21.4 sketches the trajectories we envisage for the early adopters, after the pattern of those we observed.

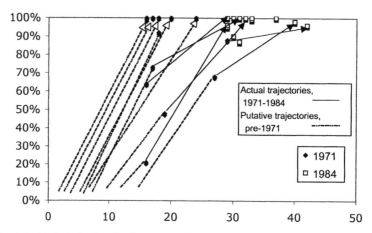

Figure 21.4 Actual trajectories for all mid-range speakers under age 30 in 1971, and putative trajectories for earlier stages.

7.3 Montreal [r] → [R] in a wider perspective

[. . .]

THE IMPLICATIONS OF MONTREAL [r] → [R]. Our study has three major implications that are relevant for other research on change in progress, and for the relationship of change in the community to change across individual lifespans.

(i) **Trend vs. panel comparisons in the assessment of change in progress.** Our study has provided clear evidence for an important methodological principle in longitudinal research: in order to verify inferences about apparent time drawn from synchronic studies, the most important tool is a carefully designed trend study. [. . .]

(ii) **Implications for the use of the apparent-time construct.** [. . .] Our findings [. . .] motivate our proposal to add a new category labeled LONGITUDINAL CHANGE (Sankoff 2005) to the model of the relationship between generational change and age grading. This concept differs from age grading (which generally involves cyclicity), as discussed in § 1.

In our research reported here, the trend study was invaluable in establishing both the direction and the rate of change. However, in most cases where we are interested in assessing change in progress, we do not have the luxury of a trend study. In such cases, we want to know how much we can rely on apparent-time inferences. Here the findings of the panel study must be considered. Insofar as the movement among panel speakers was decidedly directional . . . [t]he conclusion is inescapable: to the extent that older speakers change in the direction of change in progress in their adult lives, apparent time UNDERESTIMATES the rate of change. A major implication of our study for other research that relies on inferences from systematic synchronic-age distributions is that apparent-time calculations correctly identify the direction of change, but may under-estimate the rate of change, a conclusion also reached by Boberg (2004) [. . .].[8]

We concur with Bailey et al. 1991, Bailey 2002, and Tillery & Bailey 2003 that earlier worries about the validity of apparent time in identifying change in progress have proven to be exaggerated.

(iii) **Implications for the relevance of the critical period to language change.** Expecting relative stability in later life, we were surprised to see such a substantial minority of speakers making major changes in their pronunciation. [. . .] Seven of the ten mid-range speakers increased significantly [. . .] moving to the categorical/near-categorical range of use of dorsal [R]. They included all of those speakers under age thirty in the original study. This and other evidence led us to conclude that most of the majority users of [R] in the 1970s and 1980s had changed their pronunciation at some time later than the period of initial L1 acquisition.

This evidence should not be interpreted as a blow against the reality of the critical period, but as an indication of the necessity for greater attention to be focused on the degree and kind of lability that occurs in later life. [. . .]

Our results require us to rethink the relationship between L1 and later language acquisition, and between acquisition and change. [. . .] [I]n a study of caregivers' speech to children in a Scottish community where a local phonetic variant of the diphthong (au) is in variation with a standard variant, Smith and colleagues (2007) have shown that caregivers who use the local variant almost exclusively in their general spontaneous speech nevertheless use the standard at very high rates to young children, especially in contexts of teaching and discipline.

(4)   It's r[u:]nd the wrong way, no turn it r[ʌʉ]nd!
            (Caregiver to child in Buckie, Scotland; from Smith et al. 2007:70.)

. . . [T]his study points to social differentiation in usage patterns during L1 acquisition of a type that may well have an impact on language change.

A further question involves how to model what is going on for speakers who show a dramatic range in their trajectories over only thirteen years. Should we view these people as having restructured their phonologies? [. . .] [O]ur results lead us to believe that adults' abstract phonological systems at age thirty, or forty, or fifty are different from what they were in childhood or at puberty.[9] Change is dramatic in childhood, but it does not stop there. To understand the dynamics of change in the speech community, we must follow language across the lifespan.

NOTES

*   We thank the National Science Foundation for funding this research (Language Change Across the Lifespan, Grant BCS-0132463 to Gillian Sankoff). This joint research was begun when Hélène Blondeau held a postdoctoral fellowship from the Fonds pour la Formation de Chercheurs et l'Aide à la Recherche, Gouvernement du Québec, at the University of Pennsylvania in 1999–2001. We gratefully acknowledge the invaluable contributions of David Sankoff and Henrietta Cedergren in codesigning and implementing (along with the first author) the original Montreal study in 1971; of Pierrette Thibault and Diane Vincent in carrying out the 1984 follow-up study; and of Diane Vincent, Marty Laforest, and Guylaine Martel in undertaking the 1995 follow-up. We are especially grateful to Pierrette Thibault for her help in making materials of many kinds available for our present research, often at short notice, and thank her and Bill Labov for discussion of theoretical and methodological issues, as well as questions of substance. For their assistance in coding and verification of the data, we thank Anne Charity, Alice Goffman, Daniel Alejandro Gonzales, Sarah Moretti, and Sergio Romero. Michael Friesner and Damien Hall not only helped with final coding and verification,

but also made many useful suggestions on an earlier version of the manuscript. We thank Malcah Yaeger-Dror for checking data on some of the speakers whose vowels she analyzed in the 1971 and 1984 corpora and for helpful comments on the manuscript. We also thank Miriam Meyerhoff, Kirk Hazen, Brian Joseph, and two anonymous referees for many constructive comments.

1. Other age-related patterns might of course be possible, but would not be of interest in making temporal inferences.

2. Figure 1, which is discussed in further detail below, serves as an example of these two possible interpretations. According to the apparent-time interpretation, the curve represents a change in progress in which [R] is replacing [r] in the community; according to an age-grading interpretation, young speakers currently using [R] would progressively replace it with [r] as they age.

3. There is no generally agreed upon date as to when Eastern Québec may have adopted dorsal [R]. Noting /r/ variability over several centuries on both sides of the Atlantic, Morin proposes a possible scenario for the eventual establishment of dorsal [R] as the norm in Québec City and elsewhere in Eastern Québec. On this view, apical [r], brought by colonists in the 1600s, would have been established earliest, but dorsal [R] might have been dominant among colonists settling in the capital (Québec City) during the second century of colonization (between 1700 and 1760, when French administration ended). Rivard's 1928 [1901] remarks about dorsal [R] being the result of laziness or childhood habits may attest to its already having been quite well established in Eastern Québec by that time. Morin (2002:51) notes that in the *Atlas linguistique de l'est du Canada*, all the data points from the Eastern Québec region of Nicolet, Rivard's original home, were registered as dorsal [R] in the 1951 survey.

4. Having discovered that the six-point socioeconomic index of Thibault and Vincent (1990) and the linguistic market index devised by D. Sankoff and Laberge (1978), on which scores between 0 and 100 were assigned to every speaker in 1971, were highly correlated ($r = .71$), we decided to use the more highly gradated LM index in choosing our subsample. In selecting the speakers, we cut the scale in such a way as to represent approximately one-third of the speakers in each group, which are labeled (as a heuristic) in Tables 3–6 as UMC (Upper Middle Class), LMC (Lower Middle Class), and WC (Working Class). The UMC group certainly also includes a number of Upper Class speakers; and the WC group includes many members of the underclass—people who in 1971 were unemployed, some of whom were illiterate, had a year or less of formal schooling, and had lived their entire lives on welfare.

5. In this particular case, Alice Goffman had also coded the same recording and her result was 49% [R]. Gillian Sankoff had occasion to listen to that tape again later in the coding procedure, and reconciled the three codings. The data point finally entered for Bernard L. in 1971 was in fact not the mean of all three, but the figure of 47% [R] originally arrived at by Hélène Blondeau.

6. The significance level of $p < 0.05$ was calculated by Fisher's exact test.

7. In documenting consonantal changes in the mid-Rhine region of Germany over a thirty-year period, Bellman and colleagues (1999) found a number of changes moving in the direction of Hochdeutsch, but the towns where change was occurring were those that bordered on areas that already had these features. The actual prestige of the Hochdeutsch forms would presumably have been uniform throughout the region, but the effect of prestige was found only on the boundary, that is, with speakers who had contact with those who already used the prestige form. In our sample, Yannick C. (126), a younger speaker (seventeen years old in 1984), was typical of his generation with 100% [R]. One early influence on his speech, however, may have been the fifteen months he spent with his family in Quebec City at the age of seven when he was in first grade.

8. According to Boberg, 'the behavior of older speakers in late adoption contributes to the speed with which an innovative feature replaces an obsolescent feature in the community as a whole. In this sense, late adoption accelerates rather than retards changes in progress' (2004:258). Contrasting the two phonological variables he studied with numerous lexical variables, Boberg's judicious assessment was that late acquisition by adults was 'most characteristic of lexical variation' (ibid, p. 250), rather than phonological variation as we have seen here.

9. Adult phonology is probably also influenced by literacy. See for example Labov 1964 and Treiman et al. 2002.

REFERENCES

Anderson, Stephen and David Lightfoot (2002) *The Language Organ: Linguistics as Cognitive Physiology*. Cambridge: Cambridge University Press.

Ashby, William J. (2001) Un nouveau regard sur la chute du *ne* en français parlé tourangeau: s'agit-il d'un changement en cours? *French Language Studies* 11: 1–22.

Bailey, Guy (2002) Real and apparent time. In J.K. Chambers, Peter Trudgill and Natalie Schilling-Estes (eds) *The Handbook of Language Variation and Change*. Oxford: Blackwell, 312–332.

Bailey, Guy, Tom Wikle, Jan Tillery and Lori Sand (1991) The apparent time construct. *Language Variation and Change* 3: 241–264.

Baugh, John (1995) Dimensions of a theory of econolinguistics. In Gregory R. Guy, Crawford Feagin, Deborah Schiffrin and John Baugh (eds) *Towards a Social Science of Language: Papers in Honor of William Labov. Vol. 1: Variation and Change in Language and Society*. Amsterdam: John Benjamins, 397–419.

Bellmann, Günter, Joachim Herrgen and Jürgen Erich Schmidt (1999) *Mittelrheinischer Sprachatlas, Band 4: Konsonantismus (Dialektalität. Konsonanten des westgermanischen Bezugssystems. Sproßkonsonanten)*. Tübingen: Niemeyer.

Blake, Renee and Meredith Josey (2003) The /ay/ diphthong in a Martha's Vineyard community: what can we say 40 years after Labov? *Language in Society* 32: 451–485.

Blondeau, Hélène (2001) Real-time changes in the paradigm of personal pronouns in Montreal French. *Journal of Sociolinguistics* 5: 453–474.

Blondeau, Hélène (2006) Panel studies and language variation. In Keith Brown (ed.) *Encyclopedia of Languages and Linguistics*, 2nd edn., vol. 9. Oxford: Elsevier, 150–154.

Boberg, Charles (2004) Real and apparent time in language change: late adoption of changes in Montreal English. *American Speech* 79: 250–269.

Brink, Lars and Jørn Lund (1975) *Dansk Rigsmål I–II: Lydudviklingen siden 1840 med særligt henblink på sociolekterne i København*. [Standard Danish I–II: The phonetic development since 1840 with special regard to the sociolects in Copenhagen.] Copenhagen: Gyldendal.

Cedergren, Henrietta (1988) The spread of language change: verifying inferences of linguistic diffusion. In Peter H. Lowenberg (ed.) *Language Spread and Language Policy: Issues, Implications, and Case Studies* (Georgetown University Round Table on Languages and Linguistics 1987). Washington, DC: Georgetown University Press, 45–60.

Clermont, Jean and Henrietta Cedergren (1979) Les 'R' de ma mere sont perdus dans l'air. In Pierrette Thibault (ed.) *Le Français Parlé: Etudes Sociolinguistiques*. Edmonton, AB: Linguistic Research, 13–28.

Cukor-Avila, Patricia (2002) *She say, she go, she be like*: verbs of quotation over time in African American Vernacular English. *American Speech* 77: 3–31.

de Paiva, Maria and Maria Eugenia Duarte (2003) *Mudança Lingüística em Tempo Real*. Rio de Janeiro: Capa.

Hernandez-Campoy, Juan Manuel (2003) Complementary approaches to the diffusion of standard features in a local community. In David Britain and Jenny Cheshire (eds) *Social Dialectology: In Honour of Peter Trudgill*. Amsterdam: John Benjamins, 23–37.

Josey, Meredith (2004) A sociolinguistic study of phonetic variation and change on the island of Martha's Vineyard. New York: New York University dissertation.

Labov, William (1963) The social motivation of a sound change. *Word* 19: 273–309. [Revised as Ch. 1 in *Sociolinguistic Patterns*. Philadelphia: University of Pennsylvania Press, 1973.]

Labov, William (1964) Stages in the acquisition of standard English. In Roger Shuy (ed.) *Social Dialects and Language Learning*. Champaign, IL: National Council of Teachers of English, 77–103. [Reprinted in H. B. Allen and Gary Underwood (eds) (1971) *Readings in American Dialectology*. New York: Appleton-Century-Crofts, 473–498].

Labov, William (1966) *The Social Stratification of English in New York City*. Washington, DC: Center for Applied Linguistics. [2nd edn., Cambridge: Cambridge University Press, 2006.]

Labov, William (1975) On the use of the present to explain the past. In L. Heilmann (ed.) *Proceedings of the 11th International Congress of Linguists*. Bologna: Il Mulino, 825–851. [Reprinted in Adam Makkai, Valerie Becker Makkai and Luigi Heilman (eds) (1977) *Linguistics at the Crossroads*. Padova: Liviana, 226–261.]

Labov, William (1994) *Principles of Linguistic Change, Vol. 1: Internal factors*. Oxford: Blackwell.

Lightfoot, David W. (1999) *The Development of Language: Acquisition, Change, and Evolution*. Oxford: Blackwell.

Morin, Yves-Charles (2002) Les premiers immigrants et la prononciation du français au Québec. *Revue Québécoise de Linguistique* 31: 39–78.

Nahkola, Kari and Maria Saanilahti (2004) Mapping language changes in real time: a panel study on Finnish. *Language Variation and Change* 16: 75–92.

Naro, Anthony and Maria Marta Pereira Scherre (2002) The individual and the community in real-time linguistic change: social dimensions. Paper presented at New Ways of Analyzing Variation (NWAV) 31, Stanford, CA, October 13.

Paunonen, Heikki (1996) Language change in apparent time and in real time. *Samspel & Variation: Sparkliga studier tillägnade Bengt Nordberg pa 60-arsdagen*. Uppsala: Uppsala Universitet, Institut för Nordiska Sprak, 375–386.

Rivard, Adjutor (1928) [1901]. *Manuel de la Parole*. 2nd edn. Quebec: Garneau.

Sankoff, David and Suzanne Laberge (1978) The linguistic market and the statistical explanation of variability. In David Sankoff (ed.) *Linguistic Variation: Models and Methods*. New York: Academic Press, 239–250.

Sankoff, David and Gillian Sankoff (1973) Sample survey methods and computer-assisted analysis in the study of grammatical variation. In Regna Darnell (ed.) *Canadian Languages in their Social Context*. Edmonton, AB: Linguistic Research, 7–64.

Sankoff, Gillian (2005) Cross-sectional and longitudinal studies in sociolinguistics. In Ulrich Ammon, Norbert Dittmar, Klaus J. Mattheier and Peter Trudgill (eds) *An International Handbook of the Science of Language and Society*, vol. 2. Berlin: Mouton de Gruyter, 1003–1013.

Sankoff, Gillian (2006) Age: apparent time and real time. In Keith Brown (ed.) *Elsevier Encyclopedia of Language and Linguistics*. Oxford: Elsevier, 110–116.

Sankoff, Gillian and Hélène Blondeau (2007) Instability of the [r] ~ [R] alternation in Montreal French: the conditioning of a sound change in progress. In Hans van de Velde and Roeland van Hout (eds) (to appear) *'r-atics 2* (Special issue of *Études & Travaux*).

Santerre, Laurent (1978) Les /R/ montréalais en régression rapide. *Protée* 2: 117–130.

Smith, Jennifer, Mercedes Durham and Liane Fortune (2007) 'Mam, my trousers is fa'in doon!': community, caregiver, and child in the acquisition of variation in a Scottish dialect. *Language Variation and Change* 19: 63–99.

Thibault, Pierrette and Michelle Daveluy (1989) Quelques traces du passage du temps dans le parler des Montréalais, 1971–1984. *Language Variation and Change* 1: 19–45.

Thibault, Pierrette and Diane Vincent (1990) *Un corpus de français parlé. Montréal 84: historique, méthodes et perspectives de recherche*. Sainte-Foy, Quebec: Département de langues et linguistique, Université Laval.

Tousignant, Claude (1987) *La Variation Sociolinguistique: Modèle Québécois et Méthode d'Analyse*. Montreal: Presses de l'Université du Québec.

Treiman, Rebecca, Judy Bowey and Derrick Bourassa (2002) Segmentation of spoken words into syllables by English-speaking children as compared to adults. *Journal of Experimental Child Psychology* 83: 213–238.

Trudgill, Peter (1988) Norwich revisited: recent linguistic changes in an English urban dialect. *English World-Wide* 9: 33–49.

van de Velde, Hans and Roeland van Hout (eds) (2001) *'r-atics: Sociolinguistic, Phonetic and Phonological Characteristics of /r/* (Special issue of *Études & Travaux* 4).

Vinay, Jean-Paul (1950) Bout de la langue ou fond de la gorge? *French Review* 23: 489–498.

Weinreich, Uriel, William Labov and Marvin Herzog (1968) Empirical foundations for a theory of language change. In Winfred Lehmann and Yakov Malkiel (eds) *Directions for Historical Linguistics*. Austin: University of Texas Press, 97–195.

Wiese, Richard (2001) The unity and variation of (German) /r/. In van de Velde and van Hout, 11–26.

Zilles, Ana Maria S. (2005) The development of a new pronoun: the linguistic and social embedding of *a gente* in Brazilian Portuguese. *Language Variation and Change* 17: 19–53.

QUESTIONS

Content

1. Describe the different methods for sampling a community if you are undertaking a *panel study* and a *trend study*.
2. What is the notion of *apparent time*? Describe the underlying assumptions as well as the method(s) associated with it.
3. What does it mean for a person's behaviour to be *labile* or show *lability*?
4. What is the innovative variant of the (r) variable in Montreal French?

   a. What region is it traditionally associated with?
   b. Using the data from the trend study, find out what percentage of the younger speakers use this variant, and what percentage of the older speakers use it.

5. Explain why S&B conclude that "change does NOT proceed mainly by speakers slowly increasing their use of [R] across their lifetimes".

Concept

1. How do the different methods inform our understanding of the relationship between variation and change?

   a. What profiles of language change might you find in a trend study?
   b. What profiles of language change might you find in a panel study?

2. Sankoff & Blondeau conclude that "change in the community is a result of individual speakers ... being added to the pool of majority-users ... of [R]". What are the implications of this for theories of language acquisition?
3. Find at least one other study that deals with language variation and change over the lifespan. To what extent do those findings concur with S&B's conclusion for the Montreal data?

Chapter 22

Peter Trudgill

NORWICH REVISITED: RECENT LINGUISTIC CHANGES IN AN ENGLISH URBAN DIALECT

IN 1968 I CARRIED out what can by now probably be referred to as a traditional sociolinguistic urban dialect survey, employing Labovian methodology, in the English city of Norwich (see Trudgill, 1974). The data obtained was employed, amongst other things, to investigate and make claims about ongoing phonetic and phonological changes in Norwich English. Analysis showed that some of the phonological variables which were investigated appeared to be involved in different forms of social differentiation but to be stable chronologically and not involved in linguistic change. Other variables, on the other hand, did seem to be involved in linguistic change, with some variants in the process of being wholly or partially replaced by others. In many cases it was possible to locate the social class and/or sex group which was the focus of a particular linguistic change (see Trudgill, 1981).

This investigation of linguistic change in the Norwich data was based on the so-called *apparent-time* methodology (Labov, 1966). In the apparent time approach, the speech of older informants is compared with that of younger informants, and, subject to certain safeguards, differences between the speech of older and younger subjects are interpreted as representing linguistic changes, with younger speakers tending to favour newer forms and older speakers tending to favour older forms. The safeguards referred to normally involve comparisons with older records such as those compiled by traditional dialect-ologists, where these are available, to guard against the possibility that some differences may be due to age-grading. There are cases where differences between older and younger speakers are repeated in every generation, and we need to guard against this eventuality wherever possible when using the apparent-time methodology. Obviously, there are many advantages to using the apparent-time methodology as opposed to studying linguistic change in real time, the most obvious of which is that one can study results immediately rather than waiting for 20 years or so to see what happens. There are also, however, some obvious pitfalls, one of which is that one cannot predict with absolute

Source: Trudgill, Peter (1988) Norwich revisited: recent linguistic changes in an English urban dialect. *English World-Wide* 9: 33–49.

certainty which of a number of apparent ongoing changes are going to continue to be successful and which not. One cannot be entirely sure whether one is dealing with a genuine and long-term linguistic change, or with a temporary, possibly fashionable, but ultimately irrelevant fluctuation in usage. In this paper we contrast changes in apparent time, as portrayed in Trudgill (1974), with changes in real time, as these emerge from a more recent follow-up study of the same city, and discuss some of the lessons which emerge.

Typical of the stable variables investigated in the 1968 Norwich survey was (ng). This variable deals with the pronunciation of the -ing suffix in items such as *walking*, *running*, *Reading*, etc. and has two variants, the velar nasal and the alveolar nasal. Indices for this variable were computed in such a way that consistent use of [n] would give a score of 100, while consistent use of the velar nasal would give a score of 0. It emerged from the study that this particular variable was not involved in any ongoing change. [. . .] [W]e can note that variables not involved in change do not demonstrate an even distribution across age-groups, as might have been supposed, but rather a curvilinear age-graded pattern of the sort that we see in Figure 22.1. Other stable variables of this type from the 1968 survey which have this pattern include (h), which deals with the presence or absence of /h/ in the lexical set of *hammer*, *house* etc.; and (a:), which covers the degree of fronting or backing of the vowel of *cart*, *last*, *dance*. Both of these variables correlated with social class, with [h], for instance, being more typical of higher class speakers, and [a:] more typical of lower class speakers. [. . .] Variables of this type thus give the lie to claims that variation is always due to ongoing change.

A Norwich variable typical of the other type, namely those involved in change in the 1968 survey, was (e). This refers to the degree of centralisation of the vowel /ɛ/ before

Figure 22.1   Variable (ng) by age-group and style – 1968 sample.

CS = Casual Speech
FS = Formal Speech
RPS = Reading Passage
WLS = Word List

/ɪ/ [, as in *healthy*]. There are three major variants to this variable: [ɛ], [ɜ], and [ʌ]. Scores were calculated in such a way that consistent use of RP-type [ɛ] would give an index of 0, while consistent use of the most extreme local pronunciation [ʌ] would give a score of 200 (see Chambers and Trudgill, 1980, for a discussion of this methodology). As Figure 22.2 demonstrates, [. . .] this variable contrasts markedly with (ng) in its patterning, and indeed appears to be involved in a rapid change in progress. [. . .] [W]e can note here a very steep slope of the graph upwards from the middle aged speakers to the younger speakers from right to left across the graph indicating a very sharp rise in the use of centralised variants on the part of these younger speakers. [. . .]

In 1983, I returned to Norwich to carry out a follow-up study in the city and to check on the progress of those linguistic variables which had been involved in linguistic change, as well as to investigate more recent developments. I assumed that the 15-year gap would be sufficient for a study of linguistic change in real time, and for predictions arising from the earlier study to be confirmed or disconfirmed. [. . .]

There appear to be in principle two different approaches that one could adopt in returning to the site of one's original research in order to carry out a real-time study, as I have done. First, one could seek out one's original informants and re-interview them to investigate whether, how and to what extent their language had changed. [. . .] There are some obvious difficulties with this approach, particularly the death and other forms of unavailability of some of the informants. The other approach is to return to the field-work site and to interview younger informants who were not born or too young to be included in the original sample. This latter was the course of action that was adopted on my return to Norwich. I believe that this decision has been vindicated. We know of course that the speech of even socially and geographically non-mobile adults does change during the course of their lifetimes. However, [. . .] these changes are in most cases rather small. Most of the more dramatic changes that have recently occurred in the Norwich speech community have not affected at all the speech of those who did not have the

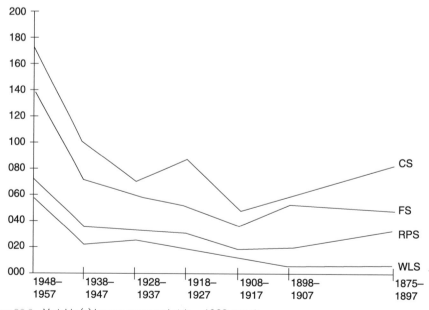

Figure 22.2   Variable (e) by age-group and style – 1968 sample.

features in question by the time they were adults. It is only by studying the speech of the next generation along, it turns out, that we obtain a true picture of the full range of linguistic changes. Ideally, however, the two approaches should be combined [*Eds: see Sankoff & Blondeau 2007*]. In this way we would achieve a better understanding of the relative importance of children, adolescents and adults in the production of different types of linguistic change.

The original Norwich sample consisted of 60 informants who were born between 1875 and 1958 who were thus in 1968 aged between 10 and 93 [. . .]. The sample was a random sample [. . .]. In 1983 I investigated the speech of 17 additional informants, selected on a quota-sample basis to conform to the social class profile of the earlier sample. These informants were born between 1958 and 1973, and were thus at the time aged between 10 and 25. Fifteen extra year-groups were thus added to the sample in line with the fifteen-year gap which had elapsed between the two periods of field-work. There is, then, an overall age-range, in the two samples combined, of 98 years.

Some obvious methodological problems presented themselves in the planning of the 1983 field-work. The biggest problem was perhaps myself. In 1968 I had been a 24-year-old student only recently removed from my native Norwich speech community. In 1983 I was nearly 40 years old and had been away from the speech community for various extended periods of time over a period of 20 years and my speech had clearly changed. In order, therefore, to secure as far as possible comparability of the two data sets, the decision was taken to employ as an interviewer a person younger than myself who had never left the Norwich speech community.

[. . .]

[Likewise], the reading passage which had been employed during the original field-work, and which had been written in a colloquial style designed to provoke relatively informal reading styles, was also now outdated in its content and language. It referred to shops in Norwich which no longer exist, for example, and contained vocabulary typical of the 1960s, such as "the latest gear". However, once again, the decision was taken to retain the reading passage as it stood in order to achieve comparability. This decision does not seem to have caused any difficulties.

We can note that the 1983 work produced some interesting non-phonological findings. For instance, it is clear that a considerable amount of lexical attrition has taken place in the local dialect of younger speakers. [. . .]

Secondly, questions on varieties of language showed that a clear change in linguistic attitudes and awareness has also taken place. To simplify somewhat, we can say that the 1968 middle-class informants tended to make a distinction between the urban dialect of Norwich and the rural Norfolk dialect, and to regard the Norwich dialect as unpleasant and the Norfolk dialect as "nice" or at least "quaint". The working-class informants, on the other hand, tended to have more favourable attitudes towards Norwich speech, and to look down on Norfolk dialect as having unfavourable country yokel connotations. The members of the 1983 sample failed to make such a distinction between the urban and rural dialects, which reflects the reality of [. . .] considerable suburbanisation of the villages surrounding Norwich. They were also altogether more positive about local speech forms. [. . .] On the other hand, there was also a much greater awareness than there had been in 1968 of the way in which outsiders regard local speech forms. This is most probably to be ascribed to increased geographical mobility, and to a very heavy increase in immigration to Norwich, particularly from the Home Counties, in the past 15 years. There was, for example, a definite recognition that people from outside the East Anglian region tended to regard all East Anglians, rural and urban, as "sounding like farmers". We are thus presented with the interesting paradox of an improved self-image as far as Norwich dialect is concerned combined with an increase in defensiveness with respect to the attitudes of outsiders, particularly Londoners. It is possible that these attitudinal factors have been involved in the development of at least one linguistic change, that involving /θ/ and /ð/ (see below). [. . .]

As far as phonetic and phonological change is concerned, a number of changes continue, trends that were already apparent in 1968. For example, the use of the vowel /e:/ in the lexical set of *gate* and *face*, which was vestigial in 1968, has now disappeared from the speech of these 10 to 25-year-olds, although it can still be heard in the speech of older people. We can therefore predict its total disappearance and replacement by the newer form /æi/ in the next 20 years or so. [. . .] [T]he merger of the vowels of *beer* and *bear* as /ɛ:/ is now complete, with all speakers except those from the UMC failing to make this distinction. On the other hand, the merger between the originally distinct lexical sets of *moan* and *mown*, which in the 1968 sample was confined to a small number of middle-class speakers, is now beginning to expand, and a number of speakers from other social class groups are now beginning variably to adopt this feature. There has also been an increase in the use of variants of /ai/ as in *nice* with a back rounded onset [ɑi]. All these phenomena confirm the 1968 apparent-time findings.

However, we are also presented with some interesting phonetic and phonological cases where certain weaknesses in the apparent-time methodology could be argued to have been revealed. For example, there is at least one feature which we can see in retrospect was involved in 1968 in the beginnings of a linguistic change but which was not perceived or treated as such. This is the change in pronunciation of the consonant /r/. The original pronunciation of this consonant in Norwich English was as a post-alveolar approximate. Now, to an astonishing degree, the younger generation has changed over to employing a labio-dental approximant [ʋ]. Figure 22.3 demonstrates the percentages

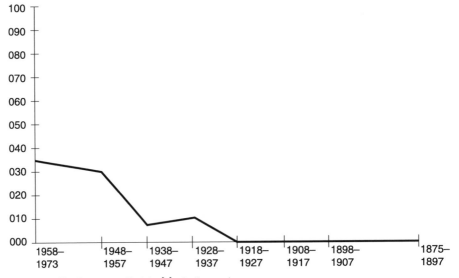

Figure 22.3   % informants with /r/ = [ʋ] – both samples.

of each of the age groups investigated in the two surveys who have the newer labio-dental pronunciation. In fact, this change in Norwich pronunciation is strikingly apparent even to the casual observer. This feature was already present in Norwich English in 1968, as Figure 22.3 shows. The sample of informants was, however, not large enough to throw up very many speakers who had this feature. [. . .] However, rather than cite this phenomenon as an example of an inherent weakness in the apparent-time methodology as such, I prefer to ascribe the failure to spot this particular linguistic change in progress to the smallish sample size and/or to the lack of perspicacity on the part of the investigator. Note that this is one feature that would not have been thrown up by a follow-up approach which relied only on recontacting previous informants: no speakers in Norwich appear to have changed their pronunciation of /r/ in this direction in the course of their lifetimes.

In other cases changes have taken place in Norwich English which were not predicted on the basis of the 1968 apparent-time study simply because there was no trace of them in the data. One example of this type is provided by a phonetic change which has affected the vowel /u:/ of the lexical set of *moan, road, rose*. In Trudgill (1974) I described this phonetically as being typically [ʊu], contrasting with the vowel of *mown, rowed, rows* which was [ʌu]. Now, as we have seen, there is an increasing tendency for these two vowels, under the influence of RP and the neighbouring dialects, to merge, as the corresponding front vowels /e:/ as in *made* and /æi/ as in *maid* already for the most part have. With /u:/ and /ʌu/ the merger remains a minority option. However, the actual realisation of /u:/ in the speech of the majority who retain the distinction is clearly changing. In the speech of the 10 to 25-year-olds in the new sample there is a very clear, readily audible tendency for the first element of the diphthong to be fronted towards [ə], giving pronunciations such as *toad* [təud]. This vowel has long been typical of neighbouring towns to the south of Norwich, such as Lowestoft, but was totally unknown in Norwich in 1968. [. . .] The change is occurring in such a way that realisations of /u:/ are moving closer phonetically to /ʉ:/, hence the confusion. If we in the future note a corresponding fronting of /ʉ:/, of which there is actually no sign as yet, we will therefore be sure that we have observed a push-chain in progress. This, then, is a change which appears to have started in the speech of Norwich speakers born between 1958 and 1960. It is of course unusual to be able to date the inception of a change so narrowly. It is also a change which current research shows to be spreading into the speech of some adults who formerly had the older pronunciation.

A further and more dramatic example of this type is portrayed in Figure 22.4. Here again we have a change not predicted in 1968, not because of any inadequacies in the sample size or on the part of the investigator, but because at that time there was no sign of it whatsoever. [. . .] Of course, we do not necessarily mean to suggest that there were no speakers at all who had this feature in their speech in Norwich in 1968. If our sample had been absolutely massive we might have uncovered a few individuals who had this feature. However, if we had, it is likely that we would have regarded it as an individual idiosyncrasy [. . .]. The change in question is the merger of /θ/ with /f/ together with the non-word-initial merger of /ð/ with /v/ (/ð/ is always found word-initially in items such as *this, those*, etc.). Not a single speaker in the 1968 sample showed even one instance of this phenomenon. In other words, our random sample suggested that nobody born between 1875 and 1958 has this feature in their speech. But, of people born between 1959 and 1973, as many as 70% have it: 41% have the merger variably; and 29% have a total merger, i.e. /θ/ has been totally lost from their consonantal inventories, while

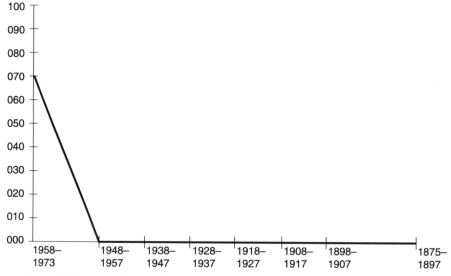

Figure 22.4   % informants with loss of /θ/ and /ð/.

/ð/ is now confined to word-initial position. This is a very surprising phenomenon and one which is not particularly easy to explain. We can note that the loss of interdental fricatives is unsurprising as a linguistic change, these consonants being marked, acquired late by children, and relatively rare in the world's languages. We can also note that it has long been well-known as a feature of the English of London. And we can observe that Norwich is not the only area of southern and central England to be affected by this change: reports and observations suggest that this merger is spreading very rapidly indeed out from London in all directions. What is surprising, however, is the extreme rapidity of this change. Some observers have been inclined to ascribe it to the influence of television programmes that have Cockney heroes popular with young people. This of course fails to explain why it is this feature of London English and no other that has been adopted, and in any case cannot be correct, for if it were we would expect all areas of the country to be affected simultaneously. This is not in fact what is happening. In spite of the rapidity of the change, we are nevertheless able to detect geographical patterning, with areas close to London being affected before areas further away [. . .]. The sheer speed of the change, however, may be due to a softening-up process produced by the engendering of favourable attitudes through television programmes, as well as to the salience of this feature (Trudgill, 1986) and the naturalness of the change. This is a further example of a change which would not have been revealed by the recontact methodology: current observations suggest that no speaker has lost this contrast in post-adolescent years.

In other cases, we find a reverse kind of phenomenon. That is, we observe that some changes which we would have predicted from the 1968 data to be ongoing appear to have stopped or to be continuing in rather complicated and unpredictable ways. For example, we note in the 1983 data a small continuing increase in the use of the glottal-stop realisation of intervocalic and word-final /t/. The variable (t) deals with the realisation of /t/ in items such as *bet* and *better* as [t], [tʔ] or [ʔ]. Scores are calculated in such a way as to give speakers who consistently use [ʔ] an index of 200, and speakers who consistently employ the RP variant [t] a score of 0. Figure 22.5 thus shows a small increase in

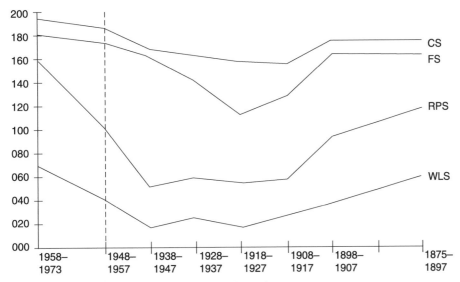

Figure 22.5   Variable (t) by age-group and style – both samples.

glottal-stop usage in casual styles, but it is also apparent that there has actually been a more dramatic increase, if we look at the rise of lines from right to left across the graph, in more formal styles. One reason for this must be that very little increase in glottal-stop usage in casual styles was possible simply because younger speakers were already employing close to 100% anyway. But the increase in formal styles tallies very well with a strong casual impression shared by many older people that younger people in many parts of Britain today no longer feel [ʔ] to be a stigmatised feature to be avoided in certain situations, as older people do. This graph thus provides an interesting example of the way in which a change, having gone almost to completion in casual speech, continues to spread from style to style. We can take this as a vivid example of the way in which linguistic innovations spread not only from person to person, area to area, class to class, and linguistic environment to linguistic environment, but also from contextual style to contextual style. Here is confirmation that most linguistic changes begin in unmonitored, vernacular informal styles and only later spread to more formal varieties of speech. [. . .]

The exception, a further somewhat complex example of change, is provided by the variable (e). As we saw above, the variable (e) was a very clear example, probably the clearest example of all in the 1968 data, of a variable involved in linguistic change. This is apparent in Figure 22.2 from the very steep rise between the scores obtained by those born in 1938 and those born in 1958. The 1983 data, however, shows somewhat surprisingly that this change appears to have halted, except again that the change does continue in the two more formal styles – see Figure 22.6. That is, reading-passage style and word-list style are beginning, as it were, to catch up with the more informal styles. [. . .] What has happened is that centralisation of /ɛ/ in this environment has now gone so far that tokens of /ɛ/ are now identical with, and presumably therefore are capable of being perceived as, tokens of /ʌ/. That is, total merger of /ɛ/ with /ʌ/ before /l/ has been achieved, so that, for example, *hell* and *hull* are now identical. Notice, however, that for the time being the total merger has been achieved only in informal speech. This is evidence that some phonological changes such as mergers proceed in a stylistically

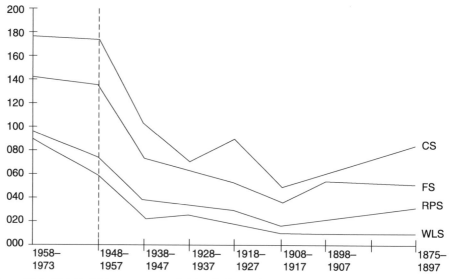

Figure 22.6   Variable (e) by age-group and style – both samples.

gradual way. Exactly *why* the phonological merger means the halting of a phonetic change in progress is not entirely clear, but it seems that a change involving /ɛ/ before /l/ is not carrying over to become a change to /ʌ/ before /l/ once surface identity has been achieved. [. . .]

If we can summarise the findings from our study of linguistic change in real time and the comparison with the earlier apparent-time study, we note that we can differentiate between the changes we have investigated on three different parameters. First, two of the changes studied have been extremely rapid. In the case of the loss of /θ/ and /ð/ we can ascribe this rapidity to multiple causation, with both linguistic and attitudinal factors being involved. The relatively rapid change involving the phonetics of /r/ is less easy to account for, but it is clear that it involves yet another stage in the weakening of the pronunciation of this consonant which, in addition to loss in non-prevocalic position, has also experienced in the last several centuries a progression of changes in the south of England as follows: [r] > [ɾ] > [ɹ] > [ɻ >[ˈɰ] > [ʋ]. The other changes studied have on the other hand been progressing much more slowly, and represent consolidation of existing trends. Secondly, it is probable that some of the changes we have dealt with are to be regarded principally as cases of the geographical diffusion of innovations into the Norwich speech community from outside: the loss of /eː/ is a case in point. Other changes appear to be internal to the system, such as the centralisation of /ɛ/ before /ɪ/ and, probably, the fronting of /uː/. Yet others, such as the loss of /θ/ and the development of [ʋ], are more problematical to categorise and may, as we have seen, come into both categories. Thirdly, some of the changes we have observed appear to be due entirely or mainly to developments in the speech of children, while others seem instead or as well to influence the speech of post-adolescents and adults. However, as Table 22.1 shows, as ever it is more complicated than that.

It is hoped that continuing research in real time in the Norwich speech community will be able to shed further light on these issues. The apparent-time methodology is an excellent sociolinguistic tool for investigating linguistic changes in progress, but,

Table 22.1 Variables involved in linguistic change

	Rapid	Children	Adults	Internal	External
/eː/ in *face*	−	−	+	?	+
beer/bear	−	+	?	+	−
moan/mown	−	−	+	?	+
/r/=[ʋ]	+	+	−	?	+
[ʔ]	−	+	?	?	+
/ɛl/	+	+	?	+	−
/f/>/θ/	+	+	−	?	+

especially provided that one can find something else interesting to do in the meantime, the study of linguistic change in real time is in many ways an even more informative experience.

REFERENCES

Chambers, J.K. & Trudgill, P. 1980. *Dialectology*. Cambridge: Cambridge University Press.
Labov, W. 1966. *The Social Stratification of English in New York City*. Washington, DC: Center for Applied Linguistics.
Trudgill, P. 1974. *The Social Differentiation of English in Norwich*. Cambridge: Cambridge University Press.
Trudgill, P. 1986. *Dialects in Contact*. Oxford: Basil Blackwell.

QUESTIONS

1. Why did Trudgill decide to get a younger interviewer to do the second set of interviews in 1983?
2. Have local attitudes towards Norwich English improved or worsened in the time between studies? How does Trudgill suggest this showed up in the results?
3. Which variant of (t) gets the highest index score?
4. Which phonetic variables documented in the 1970s:

    a. continued in the 1980s?
    b. disappeared?
    c. accelerated?
    d. emerged unexpectedly?

Concept

1. Sankoff & Blondeau discuss different methods for undertaking a real time restudy of a community and they distinguish between *trend* and *panel* studies. Which kind of study did Trudgill do?

2. Explain how mass media (especially TV) might be able to soften people up and speed the progress of a change.

    What would be the underlying process that allows mass media models, like TV, to interact with individual speakers in different speech communities to produce the geographical patterning of (th) as [f]?

3. Trudgill claims that the progress of the (e) variable provides evidence that some sound changes proceed gradually and through different styles. How strong is his evidence?

    The methods Trudgill used align what he means by 'style' with Labov's approach based on attention to speech. Would it be possible to reconcile the facts for (e) with other approaches to style, particularly an audience design one?

Chapter 23

Richard Cameron[*]

AGING AND GENDERING

INTRODUCTION, HYPOTHESIS, AND PREDICTION

IN THEIR INFLUENTIAL REVIEW of research into the interactions of language and gender,[1] Eckert & McConnell-Ginet (1992:468) observe that "sex differences in variation emerge even in communities where the sexes are not systematically separated the way socioeconomic or racial groups are." This observation is similar to an earlier claim by Trudgill (1974:95) that "geographical, ethnic group, and social-class varieties are, at least partly, the result of social DISTANCE, while sex varieties are the result of social DIFFERENCE."

It may be true that females and males are not separated from one another as are socioeconomic or ethnic groups, [. . .] [n]onetheless, a persistent finding across multiple societies is this: Females and males, both as children and as adults, will segregate or separate themselves or will be segregated or separated to varying degrees. In other words, females and males are formed into or will form same-gender groups. Such segregation or separation results in distance.

The tendency to prefer same-gender affiliations emerges early in life, around age 3 or 4 (Harkness & Super 1985, La Freniere et al. 1984, Maccoby 1988). The segregation peaks in early adolescence or middle childhood, followed by a relative lessening of segregation in the teenage years (Hartrup 1983, Larson & Richards 1991, Thorne 1993). [. . .]

However, gender segregation continues beyond childhood as a characteristic of the adult workplace[2] (Maccoby 1998:227; Petersen & Morgan 1995; Wright 1997:318–70), is a characteristic of formal and informal club membership (Perren et al. 2003, Popielarz 1999), and appears to persist into late-life friendships (Jerrome 1981, 1992; Jerrome & Wenger 1999; Matthews 1986; Rawlins 1992).

Source: Cameron, Richard (2005) Aging and gendering. *Language in Society* 34: 23–61.

[. . .] Whatever the reasons [for same-sex affiliation], and there are multiple reasons, one factor does emerge sporadically across the literature. This is age segregation: [. . .] ". . . where age separation is present, gender separation is more likely to occur" (Thorne 1993:51).

These findings have clear implications for quantitative dialect research. [. . .] If females and males tend to separate or be separated from one another in peer groups, their spoken cross-gender interactions will not be as frequent as their interactions with members of the same sex. If less frequent, in line with Bloomfield, one could predict "important differences" (1933: 46). [. . .]

This implication does not seem controversial. Eckert & McConnell-Ginet note, "People tend to develop and regulate their linguistic repertoire through contact with language used by those they speak with regularly" (1992:468). More to the point is Weinreich's forceful statement on the effects of contact: "Contact breeds imitation and imitation breeds linguistic convergence. Linguistic divergence results from secession, estrangement, loosening of contact" (1953: viii).

However, gender segregation [is rarely complete] in that gender segregation is mixed with gender intimacy. [. . .] Also, the degree of gender segregation appears to fluctuate across the lifespan [. . .], in tandem with the fluctuations of age segregation.

How could variationists respond to this implication? Notice that we speak here of differences in degree of same-gender affiliations not as absolutes, but as statistical tendencies that are characteristic of groups.[3] In addition, these differences are hypothesized to wax and wane in degree. Therefore, degrees of difference between groups are of more interest than is the actual frequency, index, or probability values that groups provide for sociolinguistic variables. However, such values are necessary in order to identify the degrees of difference.

[We may state this] as a working hypothesis consisting of three sets of propositions:

(A)   The degree of difference in frequency, index, or probability values for sociolinguistic variables between female and male speakers will wax and wane across the lifespan.

(B)   When sex segregation or separation is greatest, the degree of quantitative difference will be the greatest. This will occur when age segregation or separation is also strongly practiced or enforced.

(C)   When sex segregation or separation is smallest, the degree of quantitative difference will be the smallest. This will occur when age segregation or separation occurs to a lesser extent.

Implicit in this [. . .] are the following assumptions. First, the speakers will be members of the same dialect community.[4] Second, the effects of gender segregation, as seen in degree of quantitative difference, will be contemporaneous with the gender segregation. In other words, the effects of gender segregation on speech will occur at the same time that gender segregation is occurring. [. . .]

This assumption is close to the concept of CONVERGENCE within Accommodation Theory (Beebe & Giles 1984: 8; Meyerhoff 1998), but it differs in the following points. I will further assume that the quantitative effects of convergence among same-gender groups entail socially situated probability matching (Labov 1994: 580–83). This probability matching may result from conscious monitoring and intentional though variable performance (Schilling-Estes 1998). However, not all convergence need be motivated by conscious and intentional identity display or alignment. [Convergence] may also result from inter-speaker and intra-speaker priming or perseveration,[5] [. . .] [priming and perseveration effects] occur in the absence of speaker intention or control even as they require awareness[6] and exposure, [and] may result in long-term effects. [. . .]

This working hypothesis may be supported if and only if the frequency, index, or probability values for individual speakers' use of sociolinguistic variables actually can change across the lifespan beyond the early years of language acquisition. Two studies indicate that such change may occur. These include Baugh's (1996) real-time study of four African American males, and the research of Sankoff et al. (2001) into postcritical period change among adult speakers of Montreal French, both male and female. In the absence of real-time, long-term studies of individuals across the lifespan, our hypothesis could be tested if we may infer the behavior of individuals throughout their lifetimes by studying groups of individuals classified by chronological age and gender, as is done in Apparent Time studies of language change.

Support for the hypothesis would have at least the following characteristics.

- Among children prior to the teen years, we should find the greatest degree of difference between females and males. This is in keeping with the general finding that the tendency to prefer same-gender affiliations emerges early in life around age 3 or 4 and peaks in early adolescence or middle childhood.[7]
- This degree of difference should decrease somewhat during the teen years. This is in keeping with the general finding that gender segregation lessens somewhat, relative to earlier childhood, during the teen years. However, gender segregation is still quite pronounced among many teenagers. As such, support for the hypothesis would emerge if it is the case that teens, relative to middle age groups, show a greater degree of difference between females and males.
- At subsequent stages of the lifespan, we could expect a further decrease in the degree of difference. In particular, during the years of active work life, say from 20 to 60 or 65, we would expect less gender segregation because the workplace, though subject to varying degrees of gender segregation across differing occupations (Petersen & Morgan 1995), shows less age segregation than occurs during the childhood years, when schooling enforces age separation. In effect, the workplace and the working years of adulthood provide, relative to school, more multi-age environments for interaction.[8]
- Beyond the active working years, say 65 and higher, we could expect that quantitative differences between males and females would expand relative to the middle-aged groups. One does not find as much research that clearly documents the daily interaction and friendship patterns of the elderly in ways that researchers have done for children. However, some research demonstrates a preference for same-gender friends and affiliations in late life and indicates that these friendships, not work relationships, become sites of increased spoken interaction (Jerrome & Wenger 1999, Matthews 1986). [. . .] [W]e should find that quantitative differences between males and females expand relative to the middle-aged groups.

These predictions amount to an irregular U-shaped pattern of gender divergences across the lifespan. The greatest degree of difference will be in early childhood, the teenage years, and the post-workplace years of later life. The least degree of difference will occur in the middle years of participation in the workplace. [. . .]

Aside from the implications for variationist sociolinguistics, the hypothesis developed here could have implications for the Dual Culture model of gendered discourse styles (Maltz & Borker 1982, Tannen 1994). This model, however, is much criticized (Thorne 1993:89–109). [. . .] I have attempted to respond to Thorne's arguments by intersecting gender and age with age differences providing a series of contexts across the lifespan. [. . . This is consistent with the idea that] the range of social experiences and constructions of gender identity cannot be categorized adequately into a strict binary division that a Dual Culture model may assume . . . [and the idea that] . . . gender as a social category of experience, action, and opportunity is not clearly isolable from other social categories [. . .].[9]

[. . .]

In the research presented here, I will initially explore the predictions of the gender and age segregation hypothesis by identifying patterned degrees of difference between female and male speakers of Puerto Rican Spanish across the lifespan, using an Apparent Time type of data organization. I will do this by focusing on [. . .] intervocalic (d) [. . .]. [Next], I will return to Puerto Rican Spanish to consider the variable of the fronting of subject noun phrases in *wh*-questions (Lizardi 1993). Like a few other variables, this involves a loss or recession of form, rule, or constraint (Chambers & Trudgill 1980:94). [. . .] Some patterns of differences between females and males are clearly tied to the type of variable involved or to its status as a new and vigorous change in progress. Given these findings, I will argue that, just as other categories of social membership mediate gender expression, so does language mediate gender expression. In other words, we will see that language enables gender expression while simultaneously constraining it, a concept in line with Giddens's (1984:172–74) revision of Durkheim's social facts as involving both "constraint" and "enablement."

THE COMMUNITY

The Puerto Rican data come from fieldwork which I carried out in San Juan during 1989 (Cameron 2000). [I report on data from] 30 males and 32 females. [. . .] [T]he youngest speaker was 5 years old, and the oldest was 84. As shown in Table 23.1, 29 of those interviewed were children, either preteens or teenagers. The remaining 33 were adults

Table 23.1   Number of speakers by age and gender

Age	Male	Female	Total
Preteen	7	9	16
Teen	8	5	13
20s/30s	7	8	15
40s/50s	5	4	9
60s–>85	3	6	9

beyond the teen years. [. . .] I intend the use of chronological age here as a loose indicator of life stage, not as a statement on biological or cognitive aspects of aging. For potential problems with this method of speaker organization, see Eckert (1997:155) and Arber & Ginn (1991:2–4).

INTERVOCALIC (D)

Intervocalic (d) in Spanish is frequently cited as a straightforward illustration of allophonic variation. Goldsmith writes that /d/ and other voiced stops in Spanish "are predictably stops or spirants, depending on phonological context" (1990:70). If intervocalic, stops become spirantized into fricatives. Elsewhere, they retain their stop status. Variationists, however, have noted that the variable of intervocalic (d) has two or possibly three variants. [. . .]

Like Ma & Herasimchuk (1975), I have been able to detect only two variants of intervocalic (d): a voiced fricative or spirantized variant of [d], close to [ð], and the deleted or null form which I represent as [0]. [. . .] In pursuit of identifying where variation was possible, I have excluded certain intervocalic contexts. These include contexts where the following vowel is stressed, as in such words as *ciudad* 'city,' *madera* 'wood,' or *me quedé* 'I stayed.' Also, some English borrowings appeared not to exhibit variation, including *sliding doors* and *videocassette*. A small set of words in Spanish also exhibited no noticeable variation and were thus excluded: *SIDA* (Spanish acronym for 'AIDS'), *radio*, and *alrededor* 'around.' In these words, the intervocalic (d) was never deleted. In contrast, the vernacular form *bofetá* from *bofetada* 'slap' was also invariant, never being produced as *bofetada*. [. . .] I included the words *todo* 'all' and *nada* 'nothing,' which may show three variants, two of which involve deletion. For instance, *todo* may be expressed as [toðoo], [to:] with a long vowel due to coalescence, or [to] with no extra length noticeable. Both [to:] and [to] counted as cases of deletion.

[. . .] In total, 2,227 tokens of intervocalic (d) were analyzed. Turning to Table 23.2, we find both frequency and Varbrul weights.[10] The weights were derived for the spirantized variant [ð] of the variable.

To derive the degree of difference between females and males, we subtract the male Varbrul weight from the female. Thus, the degree of difference between females and males in the preteen group is 20 points; among the teens, it is 51 points; and so forth. If we plot these degrees of difference on a graph, we find the pattern of degree of difference between the genders across the lifespan that is depicted in Figure 23.1.

A few points immediately become clear. First, across the five age groups, we find a consistent and repeated favoring of the spirantized variant [ð] by the female speakers. Second, with respect to frequency data, the null variant is not dramatically high. Third, the greatest degree of difference is found in the teen years. This is followed by a sharp decrease in the middle years, with the dip being lowest between ages of 40 and 59. After this, the degree of difference between females and males in the oldest group increases until it is more than, but close in value to, the degree of difference found in the preteens. This pattern of waxing and waning is found also by using the frequency data. [We] find strikingly similar zigzagging patterns across the lifespan [for two other variables, word-final (s) and direct quotation strategies – discussed in detail in the original, *Eds*].

[. . .]

Table 23.2   Intervocalic (d) by age and gender (frequencies, weights, degrees of difference)

Group		[ð]	[0]	Total	Ivarb weight for [ð]	Degree of point difference
Preteen girl	N	138	62	200	.46	**20**
	%	69	31			
Preteen boy	N	48	52	100	.26	
	%	48	52			
Teen girl	N	91	9	100	.79	**51**
	%	91	9			
Teen boy	N	100	100	200	.28	
	%	50	50			
20/30 female	N	317	60	377	.67	**22**
	%	84	16			
20/30 male	N	237	113	350	.45	
	%	68	32			
40/50 female	N	145	55	200	.50	**14**
	%	72	28			
40/50 male	N	149	101	250	.36	
	%	60	40			
60 + female	N	252	48	300	.67	**28**
	%	84	16			
60 + male	N	93	57	150	.39	
	%	62	38			
Total	N	1570	657	2227		
	%	70	30			

Input Prob.73 Log Likelihood: – 1265.108 Total Chi-Square: .000
Chi-Square/Cell: .000

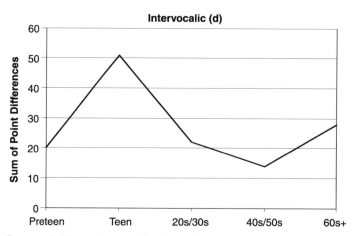

Figure 23.1   Degrees of difference between females and males across the lifespan for intervocalic (d).

A RETURN TO THE HYPOTHESIS AND SOME QUESTIONS

[. . .] I now return to the hypothesis with the following observations. Overall, the hypothesis is partially supported and partially rejected [. . .]. Examining each subproposition, I can say the following:

(A)   The degree of difference in frequency, index, or probability values for sociolinguistic variables between female and male speakers will wax and wane across the lifespan. *(A) is supported by the zigzagging pattern of differences between the groups across the lifespan for each of the three variables.*

(B)   When sex segregation or separation is greatest, the degree of quantitative difference will be the greatest. This will occur when age segregation or separation is also strongly practiced or enforced. *(B) is rejected for the preteens but accepted for teenagers and for the oldest group. Recall that the oldest group shows an increased degree of difference, relative to middle age groups.*

(C)   When sex segregation or separation is smallest, the degree of quantitative difference will be the smallest. This will occur when age segregation or separation occurs to a lesser extent. *(C) is supported by the relative decrease in degree of difference between the genders in the middle years.*

At this point, we can ask additional interrelated questions which our explorations of the hypothesis and the data make possible. I will first ask questions that we can answer within the framework of the hypothesis as formulated. Then, we will turn to questions that push us beyond the hypothesis and the data.

Questions answerable within the framework of the hypothesis include the following three:

(i)   Why do teenagers, relative to the middle age group, show a greater degree of difference between females and males for their values for the sociolinguistic variables?

(ii)   Why do the middle age groups overall show the least degree of difference between females and males for their values for the sociolinguistic variables?

(iii)   Why does the degree of difference between females and males increase in the oldest group relative to the middle age groups?

Questions that go beyond the hypothesis include the following:

(i)   Why is the degree of difference smaller between preteen females and males, contrary to expectation, than between female and male teenagers?

(ii)   Why does the degree of difference between females and males increase among the teenagers relative to the preteens? Also, for [the (d) variable], the degree of difference between females and males is highest overall among the teenagers. Why is this so? [. . .]

(iii)   Would these zigzagging patterns show up in the same way in variables at different stages of change? [. . .]

SOME ANSWERS TO SOME QUESTIONS

The three questions in the first set are directly answerable within the framework of the hypothesis. On the assumption that age and gender segregation are more strongly practiced or enforced during the teenage years and during the post-workplace years, the greater degree of difference between females and males in these groups, relative to the middle age groups, follows from this separation. During the working years of the middle age groups, age separation and, consequently, gender separation are relaxed. Thus, the reduction in degree of difference stems from increased cross-age and cross-gender interaction. With increased cross-gender interaction comes convergence between female and male speakers. This convergence, in quantitative terms, is revealed in the decreased degree of difference between females and males of the middle age groups.

Any exploration of the second set of questions falls outside the predictions made by the original working hypothesis. Therefore, my answers will, of necessity, be speculative. I begin with the small degree of difference between the preteen girls and boys, contrary to my prediction. First, note that although the degree of difference is relatively small, statistical gender differences among these children do emerge. [. . .] However, research by Roberts 1996 on preschool children demonstrates that, early on, children do not directly acquire the gendered patterns of variation that characterize later age groups. [. . .] The children must acquire these behaviors and, like all acquisition, this occurs in stages. Yet such acquisition is not the only type of acquisition that is occurring for preteens. As Guy & Boyd 1990 and Kerswill 1996 also illustrate, children are simultaneously busy acquiring internal grammatical constraints on variation, the acquisition of which may be constrained by critical-period issues in ways that the acquisition of gender constraints on variation are not. Apart from grammatical constraints, children may also be acquiring the social meanings associated with sociolinguistic variables. [. . .] Hence, young children, unlike all other age groups, are engaged in the simultaneous acquisition of multiple types of constraints on variation, one of which is gender. [. . .] [T]he smaller degree of difference between boys and girls, relative to other age groups, could be interpreted as a function of their stage in the acquisition of gendered variation.

Next, we turn to the question of why the degree of difference between girls and boys expands as we go from preteens to teenagers. One may initially identify this expanding degree of difference as a function of continuing acquisition of gendered variation. This is true, yet incomplete because it fails to answer why the increase is so sharp [. . .]. Thorne has observed that as children leave the preteen period and become teenagers, the process of transition is "uneven and fluctuating, the focus of negotiation and occasional conflict" (1993:154). Moreover, as children become teenagers, they will increasingly engage in what Thorne calls "borderwork" or "interaction based on and even strengthening – gender boundaries" (p. 64). The frequency of such interaction, which goes to the strengthening of gender boundaries, would increase if such gender boundaries were important [cf. Eckert 1989]. [. . .] [A]s pointed out by Larson & Richards (1991:295), gender segregation decreases in the teen years, thereby providing more opportunities for borderwork.

Now, as Thorne also proposed, among preteens on the playground, such borderwork can often "carry extra perceptual weight because they are marked by conflict, intense emotions, and the expression of forbidden desires" (1993:85). One element of human behavior that could contribute "extra perceptual weight" is extra variation or, more precisely, an extra degree of difference in patterns of variation, which Speech Accommodation theorists would call "divergence" (Beebe & Giles 1984:8). The extra perceptual weight and the presence of divergence may be inferred from the fact that the widest degree of statistically marked gender differentiation is found among the teens.

In addition, it seems reasonable to assume that incidents of borderwork, like other social interactions, may have both frontstage and backstage dimensions. Here I borrow from Goffman's (1959:112) original use of the term "backstage." Frontstage borderwork would include those moments when cross-gender interaction actually occurs. Backstage borderwork would occur when individuals discuss and rehearse, with friends, their experiences of crossing the gender divide. Given that discussions and rehearsals with friends, at this point, usually means friends of the same gender, [. . .] the backstage discussions of borderwork would seem, of necessity, to involve both convergence among same-gender friends and constructed moments of divergence in which the original borderwork is recalled or reconstructed. [. . .]

In brief summary, I suggest that the increased degree of difference between teenage female and male speakers here is a consequence of the following factors. They are entering a final stage of language acquisition, part of which involves fine-tuning the acquistion of gendered variation. As they do, they also engage more frequently in the perceptually heightened acts of borderwork and backstage discussions of borderwork at a point in life when gender identity acquires an acute importance. [. . .] [T]eenagers straightforwardly illustrate one of the generally accepted propositions about gender that we stated earlier. Gender, as a social category of experience, action, and opportunity, is not clearly isolable from other social categories. [A review of a range of different sociolinguistic variables suggests that the manner, relevance and salience of gender differences are mediated not solely by other social categories but also by the specific linguistic variables available to speakers.] [. . .]

The ideas put forth here may lead to an inference, the content of which I would like to identify and then modify. In order for extra perceptual weight to be assigned, speakers must have linguistic objects onto which perception can latch. [. . .] In variationist terms, [. . .] [t]hese would have to be [. . .] either stereotypes or markers where both types of variables show sensitivity to both stylistic and social stratification (Cameron 2000:260; Labov 1994:78). Indicators which do not show clear (or any) stylistic patterning, would be excluded from this type of social construction. Nonetheless, it is factually wrong to assert that only markers or stereotypes are drawn on for social constructions.[11]

[. . .] I propose that [. . .] some aspects of the [social constructions of gender] involve variables that are below the level of consciousness and are not subject to style shifting, [therefore] not all variationist construction of gender is conscious, nor clearly a function of intention, nor clearly subject to overt speaker control.

[. . .] Chang et al. suggest that the priming or perserveration effects may result in implicit learning, which they identify as the "incidental learning of complex, abstract relations during the performance of a task" (2000: 200). The complex and abstract relations relevant to our purpose here would involve a matching of frequency or probabilities of variants of sociolinguistic variables relative to a socially situated task. The task is the construction and display of gender identity or affiliation during same-gender interactions in which friendship is also constructed and negotiated. In short, individuals will acquire patterns of covariation between variant frequency or probability, and gender construction and friendship construction. Such covariation learning is one type of implicit learning identified by Seger (1994: 174), and, like other types of implicit learning, the learner need not be conscious of the content of covariation, even though the resulting behavior is systematic. Therefore, it follows that indicators may be used for social constructions of gender because they show systematic covariation even in the absence of speaker's awareness.

[. . .]

ANOTHER PATTERN, ANOTHER TYPE OF VARIABLE

Labov anticipates an important qualification of the monotonic age function of changes in progress. He writes: "In chapter 14 . . . it will become apparent that monotonic age functions are in fact impossible, and that every change must show a decline among younger speakers to some extent" (2001: 311). A handful of changes, at times identified as a loss or recession of form, rule, or constraint, support Labov's point here.

[. . .]

Lizardi (1993) investigates the variable position of expressed pronominal and lexical noun phrase subjects within questions introduced by Spanish *wh*-questions. Specifically, the alternation is between preverbal and postverbal subject positions when the *wh*-question word is an argument of the verb. Thus, in a question like *¿Qué tú dijiste?* 'What did you say?', the subject pronoun *tú* occurs preverbally even though [this results in two preverbal arguments]. [. . .] Lizardi is able to trace a change across the generations. The change emerges as a decreasing frequency of postverbal expressed subject noun phrases and an increasing frequency of preverbal and null expressed subject noun phrases within the frame of *wh*-questions. Overall, for speakers under age 50, Lizardi (1993: 80) reports a frequency of postverbal subjects in *wh*-questions of 10%. For speakers over age 50, this frequency is 28%. [. . .] Among the group 3–18 years of age, there is no difference [between female and male speakers] at all. Among the group 19–35, one finds 2 points of difference. Among the group 36–49, females and males are separated by 3 points of difference. But in the oldest group, 50 and higher, females and males show 17 points of difference. Thus, we find not only a decline among young speakers of postverbal subject placement, but across the lifespan we also find a parallel loss of the degree of difference between female and male speakers for this sociolinguistic variable.

Similar patterns are reported in two different studies, Clarke 1990 and Milroy & Milroy 1978. Clarke provides data that indicate the ongoing loss of monophthongal (o) in the English of St. John's, Newfoundland. She gives data for four age groups: 15–19, 20–34, 35–54, and 55 and higher (1990: 115). A comparison of the degree of difference between males and females in the oldest age group with that in the youngest shows that, whereas 22 frequency points separate the females and males in the oldest group, among the teenagers we find but 2 frequency points separating the sexes. The Milroys present data from a study of Belfast English focusing on the progressive loss of the dentality of (t) either in word-initial clusters with [r], as in *train*, or elsewhere in words but close to [r], as in *water*. They depict a degree of difference between female and male speakers in two age groups: 42–55 and 18–25 (1978: 36). Within the older group, the frequency difference between females and males for the recession of dentality of (t) is approximately 40 points. Within the younger group, there is no difference. Like that of Lizardi, the work of Clarke and of the Milroys points to communities in which an older group of females and males distinguished themselves through sociolinguistic variation in ways not accessible to the females and males of the younger generations.

These studies, then, clearly contradict the finding of a teenage peak in degree of difference between females and males. Unlike the other studies I have reviewed, the variables here are rather straightforwardly characterized as involving a loss of form, rule, or constraint in which the loss has come to a close, ending in stability. At the point of stability, we find very little, if any, degree of difference between females and males, even as a slight degree of variation remains.

It is worth pointing out one contrast between the acquired stability of these losses of form, rule, or constraint and such stable sociolinguistic variables as intervocalic (d) and word-final (s) in Puerto Rican Spanish. These losses result in an absence or a massive reduction of options for speakers. If no options exist for the speakers, no gender can be constructed. Stable variables, which show no sign of change across apparent time, provide options for speakers.

Given that gender differences were once expressed through these variables, we find more evidence to support our previous generalization that the manner, relevance, and salience of gender expression is mediated not solely by other social categories but also by the linguistic means available to speakers in their communities. Moreover, as the linguistic means change over time, the linguistic means taken up or available for gender expression will change as well. [. . .]

[. . .]

CONCLUSION

Variationist approaches to gender identity have been criticized in social constructionist terms for disregarding the situated, socially constructed, and fluid nature of gender expression, as well as for taking difference between male and female speakers as primary (Ehrlich 1997). However, by focusing on degrees of difference between males and females at different stages of life, I have revealed striking, systematic zigzagging in degree of gender differences across the lifespan. Where a social constructionist approach would focus on situations as contexts, I have taken different stages of life, loosely indicated by chronological age, as contexts. The zigzagging patterns suggest that gender expression is fluid not only within the situated, co-constructed, and bounded moments of talk-in-interaction, but also across different life stages and, in the case of diachronic change, across lifetimes. Hence, gendering and aging may be said to co-articulate, even as they co-constrain. But it is not enough to say that gender and age mutually influence each other. Among the many influences that may be cited, I would add here the effects of gender segregation as it is mediated by language acquisition, borderwork between the genders, and access to or participation in the multi-age workplace. Moreover, gender segregation may be either mediated or nullified by the types of sociolinguistic variables that are drawn upon in the multifaceted act of gender construction. In effect, we may say that although language enables gender expression, it simultaneously constrains it, a concept in line with Giddens's (1984: 172–74) restatement of Durkheim's "social facts" as involving both "constraint" and "enablement." This last point, indeed, may be made only by a variationist study that does attend to issues of gender difference and differences of linguistic form.

NOTES

*   I want to send very special *muchísimas gracias* to Miriam Meyerhoff and William Labov for critical, insightful, and engaged readings of an earlier version of this research. Over the past two years, I have presented portions of this research at various conferences. In these contexts, on more than one occasion, Greg Guy, Gillian Sankoff, and Shahrzad Mahootian have provided both critical and supportive comments. I admire and love all these people. Finally, I thank Jane Hill and the two reviewers whose very useful comments called for clarification and qualification. I appreciate their attention very much. None of these individuals is responsible for shortcomings in the research. I hope any shortcomings here will stimulate long-term research elsewhere. *Besos a Diana González-Cameron, mi esposa.*

1.   I use the term "gender" here as shorthand for what Bucholtz (2000: 80) terms "social gender" to underscore the difference among grammatical gender, biological sex, and the social behaviors that result from and contribute to social constructions of gender identity or identities. Entwistle 1998 provides an accessible overview and critique of the distinction between "sex" and "gender." For another useful critique of this terminology and accompanying assumptions, see Maccoby (1988: 755). See Harding (1998: 8–20) for a related discussion of "essentialism" versus "constructionism."

2.   Gender segregation also characterizes research into gender, at least language-oriented research. In such important and useful collections as Bergvall et al. 1996, Bucholtz et al. 1999, or Hall & Bucholtz 1995, the authors and editors are either exclusively or predominantly female. See also Benor et al. 2002.

3.   Because the objects of investigation are groups and because the scope is macrosociological, we cannot say anything direct about specific individuals per se. This does not mean, of course, that individuals or subgroups cannot diverge from typical patterns of the larger group's behavior, as Thorne 1993 amply shows. Also see Chambers (1995:84–91) on interlopers and insiders, and Cameron (2000:274–75) on the divergent stylistic patterning of quotation strategies for adults and children in the Spanish of San Juan, Puerto Rico.

4.   I recognize the ambiguity and controversy in the term "dialect community." See Santa Ana & Parodi 1998 for an excellent treatment.

5.   Researchers use a variety of terms to refer to statistically identifiable patterns of repetition. These terms include "priming," "persistence," "perseverance," "perseveration," or "birds of a feather" effect (Pereira Scherre & Naro 1991). I alternate between "priming" and "perseveration" as a reflex of the field. I intend them both to refer to patterned repetition. See Cameron & Flores Ferrán 2004 for more discussion relevant to variation.

6.   The degree and nature of the awareness required for implicit learning is subject to debate. The debate covers both definitions of what counts as awareness, the amount required for different tasks, and whether implicit learning may be conceived of as automatic, in cognitive science's sense of not being subject to intentionality and control. If automatic, or automatic to a degree, it may be the case that implicit learning is subject to influence from other, more explicit processes of learning or cognition. See Seger (1994: 174–79) for these issues.

7.   Actually, if we had a sufficient number of talkative and tape-recorded preteen children from the ages of 3 to 12, we could roughly predict a peak around the age of 10 or 11, relative to the youngest children. One reviewer of this research correctly pointed out that linguistic differences between a child of 5 and one of 11 may dwarf those between an adult of 25 and one of 45. I agree. However,

I do not have data from a sufficient number of preteen children to tease out this particular pattern, if the pattern is to be teased out. Therefore, I make a general and gross prediction about the preteens. Among the preteen Puerto Rican children I have studied and on whom I report on in this article, these are the ages represented:

Age	Female	Male
5	1	–
6	–	1
8	1	1
9	2	2
10	2	–
11	3	3
Total	9	7

The 5-year-old girl and 6-year-old boy were interviewed in a small group with 8- and 9-year-olds. These groups were either boys only or girls only. One 10-year-old girl and one 11-year-old girl were interviewed individually. The 11-year-old was interviewed in her home with the intermittent presence of her younger sister, who was not directly recorded. The other 11-year-old children were interviewed in groups of three children at a time. Future researchers may specifically target this age group in larger numbers to see if the predicted differences emerge.

8. Owing to the macro-sociological nature of this assertion, individual and group divergences, as well as cultural divergences, are not addressed. See note 4 for similar point. Thus, the generalizability of the claim about the multi-age workplace and working stage of life, relative to school, can and should be questioned and tested. Both reviewers of this research noted that certain professions are simultaneously age- and gender-segregated, such as professional athletics or stock exchange work. No professional athletes or stock exchange workers are included in the Puerto Rican sample. Nonetheless, the hypothesis as formulated permits yet another prediction here. Professional athletes and stock exchange workers will differ more from members of the opposite sex than will working individuals of the same age group who work in environments that are less age- and gender-segregated. The reviewers also noted that Thorne's question (1993:108) about "which boys or girls, where, when, and under what circumstances" applies to this period of life as well. I agree. Indeed, Thorne's question may be applied to any social group, however the group is defined. I discuss the relevance of Thorne's question in a subsequent portion of the article, where I use this particular question as an organizing principle of the research presented here.

9. A third point, perhaps an entailment of the second, could be added here. Deborah Cameron (1998:947) identifies this as "the progressive abandonment in feminist scholarship of the assumption that 'women' and 'men' can be treated as internally homogenous groups." If the experiences and constructions of being "women" and "men" vary across micro-sociological contexts of emergent talk-in-interaction and macro-sociological contexts of country, class, ethnicity, or age, then it follows that "women" and "men" cannot be treated as internally homogenous. Related to this is the suggestion that differences within groups of females or differences within groups of males may actually dwarf differences between females and males (Eckert 1989:254; Ostermann 2003; Nichols 1983:59).

10. Varbrul is a form of logistic regression used for multivariate analysis (Paolillo 2002). I have chosen to use Varbrul here for various reasons. First, in previous research (Cameron 2000, 1998) I used the TVARB version of Varbrul for the analysis of word-final (s) and the direct quotation strategies. It was in Cameron (2000:281–82), on the basis of TVARB, that I initially discovered the zigzagging pattern of divergences between females and males for word-final (s) and the quotations, though I then had no

basis for accounting for it. Hence the current work. Upon investigating intervocalic (d), I assumed that further comparison would be best if the basis for comparison were also Varbrul data. Second, the IVARB version of Varbrul permits elimination of factor groups through the Step-Up and Step-Down program. During the Varbrul analysis of intervocalic (d), I submitted a set of six independent factor groups: the intersections of (1) age and gender, (2) upper/lower class and gender, (3) adult occupation and gender, (4) children's public/private school and gender, and then (5) adult occupation only, and (6) children's public/private school only. The Step Up program selected the factor groups (1) age/gender and (3) adult occupation/gender as significant. The Step Down program threw out all other factor groups. However, upon running Varbrul again, it became apparent that the factor groups (1) age/gender and (3) adult occupation/gender overlapped to some extent. Adults include the age groups 20/30, 40/50, and 60 and higher. Thus, I ran Varbrul on intervocalic (d) with factor group (1) age/gender only. One reviewer of this research has questioned the use of Varbrul here because Varbrul assumes independence of factor groups. However, the point of this research is the lack of independence between age and gender. The assumption of independence in Varbrul is between independent factor groups, however they are defined. Thus, if age and gender were coded within the Varbrul analysis as separate independent factor groups, one would expect interaction. Vogt defines interaction as an effect that occurs "when independent variables not only have separate effects but also have combined effects on a dependent variable" (1993:122). By combining age with gender into one factor group, I avoid interaction, a strategy common to Varbrul analysis (Paolillo 2002:89). And recall, Varbrul selected the combined factor group (1) age/gender as significant. I did not investigate internal linguistic nor stylistic constraints on intervocalic (d), as I have done for word-final (s) and direct quotation strategies, because the object of interest is the social patterning.

11. The three Puerto Rican variables discussed here, intervocalic (d), word-final (s), and direct quotation strategies, are all markers. The direct quotation strategies, however, are not clearly markers for the entire San Juan community; the data suggest indicator status for adults but marker status for children (Cameron 2000:274–75). For stylistic information on intervocalic (d), see Cedergren (1973:100).

REFERENCES

Arber, Sara and Jay Ginn (1991) *Gender and Later Life: A Sociological Analysis of Resources and Constraints*. London: Sage.

Baugh, John (1996) Dimensions of a theory of econolinguistics. In Gregory Guy et al. (eds) *Towards a Social Science of Language: Papers in Honor of William Labov: Volume 1: Variation and Change in Language and Society*. Philadelphia: John Benjamins, 397–419.

Beebe, Leslie and Howard Giles (1984) Speech-accommodation theories: a discussion in terms of second-language acquisition. *International Journal of the Sociology of Language* 46: 5–32.

Benor, Sarah, Mary Rose, Devyani Sharma, Julie Sweetland and Qing Zhang (2002) (eds) *Gendered Practices in Language*. Stanford: CSLI.

Bergvall, Victoria L., Janet M. Bing and Alice F. Freed (eds) (1996) *Rethinking Language and Gender Research: Theory and Practice*. Harlow: Longman.

Bloomfield, Leonard (1933) *Language*. Chicago: University of Chicago Press.

Bucholtz, Mary (2000) Gender. *Journal of Linguistic Anthropology* 9: 80–83.

Cameron, Deborah (1998) Gender, language, and discourse: a review essay. *Signs: Journal of Women in Culture and Society* 23: 945–973.

Cameron, Richard (2000) Language change or changing selves?: direct quotation strategies in the Spanish of San Juan, Puerto Rico. *Diachronica* 17: 249–292.

Cameron, Richard and Nydia Flores Ferrán (2004) Perseveration of subject expression across regional dialects of Spanish. *Spanish in Context* 1: 41–65.

Chambers, J. K. (1995) *Sociolinguistic Theory*. Oxford: Blackwell.

Chambers, J.K. and Peter Trudgill (1980). *Dialectology*. Cambridge: Cambridge University Press.

Eckert, Penelope (1997) Age as a sociolinguistic variable. In Florian Coulmas (ed) *Handbook of Socio-linguistics*. Oxford: Blackwell, 151–167.

Eckert, Penelope and Sally McConnell-Ginet (1992) Think practically and look locally: language and gender as community-based practice. *Annual Review of Anthropology* 21: 461–490.

Entwistle, Joanne (1998) Sex/gender. In Chris Jenks (ed.) *Core Sociological Dichotomies*. London: Sage, 151–165.

Giddens, Anthony (1984) *The Constitution of Society*. Berkeley: University of California Press.

Gilbert, Dennis (1998) *The American Class Structure in an Age of Growing Inequality*. 5th ed. Belmont, CA: Wadsworth.

Goldsmith, John (1990) *Autosegmental and Metrical Phonology*. Oxford: Basil Blackwell.

Guy, Gregory and Sally Boyd (1990) The development of a morphological class. *Language Variation and Change* 2: 1–18.

Hall, Kira, Mary Bucholtz (eds) (1995) *Gender Articulated: Language and the Socially Constructed Self*. New York: Routledge.

Harding, Jennifer (1998) *Sex Acts: Practices of Femininity and Masculinity*. London: Sage.

Harkness, Sara and Charles Super (1985) The cultural context of gender segregation in children's peer groups. *Child Development* 56: 219–224.

Hartrup, Willard (1983) Peer relations. In Paul Mussen and E. Mavis Heatherington (eds) *Handbook of Child Psychology, Volume 4: Socialization, Personality, and Social Development*. New York: Wiley, 103–196.

Jerrome, Dorothy (1981) The significance of friendship for women in later life. *Ageing and Society* 1: 175–197.

Jerrome, Dorothy (1992) *Good Company: An Anthropological Study of Old People in Groups*. Edinburgh: Edinburgh University Press.

Jerrome, Dorothy and G. Clare Wenger (1999) Stability and change in late-life friendships. *Ageing and Society* 19: 661–676.

Kerswill, Paul (1996) Children, adolescents, and language change. *Language Variation and Change* 8: 177–202.

Labov, William (1994) *Principles of Linguistic Change: Volume 1: Internal factors*. Malden, MA: Blackwell.

La Freniere, Peter, F.F. Strayer and Roger Gauthier (1984) The emergence of same-sex preferences among preschool peers. *Child Development* 55: 1958–1965.

Larson, Reed and Maryse Richards (1991) Daily companionship in late childhood and early adolescence: changing developmental contexts. *Child Development* 62: 284–300.

Laumann, Edward (1966) *Prestige and Association in an Urban Community*. Indianapolis: Bobbs-Merrill.

Lizardi, Carmen M. (1993) Subject position in Puerto Rican WH-questions: syntactic, sociolinguistic, and discourse factors. Dissertation, Cornell University.

Ma, Roxana and Eleanor Herasimchuk (1975) The linguistic dimensions of a bilingual neighborhood. In Joshua Fishman et al. (eds) *Bilingualism in the Barrio*, 2nd ed. Bloomington: Indiana University Press, 347–479.

Maccoby, Eleanor (1988) Gender as a social category. *Developmental Psychology* 24: 755–765.

Maccoby, Eleanor (1998) *The Two Sexes: Growing up Apart, Coming Together*. Cambridge, MA: Harvard University Press.

Maltz, Daniel and Ruth Borker (1982) A cultural approach to male-female miscommunication. In John Gumperz (ed.) *Language and Social Identity*. Cambridge: Cambridge University Press, 196–216.

Matthews, Sarah (1986) *Friendships Through the Life Course*. London: Sage.

Meyerhoff, Miriam (1998) Accommodating your data: the use and misuse of accommodation theory in sociolinguistics. *Language and Communication* 18: 205–225.

Milroy, James and Lesley Milroy (1992) Social network and social class: toward an integrated sociolinguistic model. *Language in Society* 21: 1–26.

Nichols, Patricia (1983) Linguistic options and choices for Black Women in the rural South. In Barrie Thorne et al. (eds) *Language, Gender, and Society*. Rowley, MA: Newbury, 54–68.

Ostermann, Ana Cristina (2003) Communities of practice at work: gender, facework and the power of *habitus* at an all-female police station and a feminist crisis intervention center in Brazil. *Discourse and Society* 14: 473–505.

Paolillo, John (2002) *Analyzing Linguistic Variation: Statistical Models and Methods*. Stanford: CSLI.

Pereira Scherre, María and Anthony Naro (1991) Marking in discourse: "birds of a feather". *Language Variation and Change* 3: 23–32.

Perren, Kim, Sara Arber and Kate Davidson (2003) Men's organisational affiliations in later life: the influence of social class and marital status on informal group membership. *Ageing and Society* 23: 69–82.

Petersen, Trond and Laurie Morgan (1995) Separate and unequal: occupation-establishment sex segregation and the gender wage gap. *American Journal of Sociology* 101: 329–365.

Popielarz, Pamela (1999) (In) Voluntary association: a multilevel analysis of gender segregation in voluntary organizations. *Gender and Society* 13: 234–250.

Rawlins, William (1992) *Friendship Matters: Communication, Dialectics, and the Life Course*. New York: Aldine de Gruyter.

Roberts, Julie (1997) Hitting a moving target: acquisition of sound change in progress by Philadelphia children. *Language Variation and Change* 9: 249–266.

Sankoff, Gillian, Hélène Blondeau and Anne Charity (2001) Individual roles in a real-time change: Montreal (r > R) 1947–1995. In Hans Van de Velde and Roeland van Hout (eds) *R-atics: Sociolinguistic, Phonetic, and Phonological Characteristics of /r/*. Brussels: Études et Travaux, 141–157.

Santa Ana, Otto and Claudia Parodi (1998) Modeling the speech community: configuration and variable types in the Mexican Spanish setting. *Language in Society* 27: 23–51.

Schilling-Estes, Natalie (1998) Investigating 'self-conscious' speech: the performance register in Ocracoke English. *Language in Society* 27: 53–83.

Seger, Carol (1994) Implicit learning. *Psychological Bulletin* 115: 163–196.

Tannen, Deborah (1994) *Gender and Discourse*. Oxford: Oxford University Press.

Thorne, Barrie (1993) *Gender Play: Girls and Boys in School*. New Brunswick, NJ: Rutgers University Press.

Trudgill, Peter (1972) Sex, covert prestige and linguistic change in the urban British English of Norwich. *Language in Society* 1: 179–195.

Trudgill, Peter (1974) *Sociolinguistics: An Introduction*. Harmondsworth: Penguin.

Vogt, Paul (1993) *Dictionary of Statistics and Methodology: A Nontechnical Guide for the Social Sciences*. Newbury Park, CA: Sage.

Weinreich, Uriel (1953) *Languages in Contact: Findings and Problems*. The Hague: Mouton.

Wright, Erik O. (1997) *Class Counts: Comparative Studies in Class Analysis*. New York: Cambridge University Press.

QUESTIONS

1. At what time(s) of life does Cameron predict there will be the greatest gender differences in the use of linguistic variables?

    a. Why does he expect the differences to be greatest then?

2. To what extent are Cameron's hypotheses supported by

    a. the (d) variable in Puerto Rican Spanish?
    b. the *wh*-question variable in Puerto Rican Spanish?

3. What does Cameron suggest is the crucial difference between the (d) and *wh* variables?

    a. What does this imply for theories about how and when gendered differences will emerge in language?

1. The profile of gender differences across the lifespan for (d) in Puerto Rican Spanish is roughly *U*-shaped. This is similar to the profile for a stable linguistic variable in an individual speaker (see discussions in Cheshire 1987, Downes 1995, Holmes 2001, Meyerhoff 2006 if you aren't familiar with this).
    Can you think of any reason why they might be similar?

2. If Cameron is right and gender segregation is key to the emergence of gender differentiation, what implications might this have for

    a. how we analyse and interpret markers of ethnicity or class?
    b. how we organise our data into different age cohorts (the apparent time hypothesis)?

3. Cameron notes that gender segregation is often less extreme among teenagers compared to younger children. In your experience is this generally true, or does it depend on the kind of activity teenagers are involved in?
    If so, how might this have an impact on the kinds of sociolinguistic questions we might ask or the methodologies we might use to explore those questions?

Social Class, Networks and Communities of Practice

Editors' Introduction to Part Five

THERE ARE NUMEROUS WAYS of grouping and analysing speakers, and it is probably safe to say that at least some sociolinguist, somewhere, has tried every one of them. If they haven't, it will come. In this section of the Reader, we have collected some articles which are particularly useful exemplars of some of the most influential modes of analysis. The notion of a *speech community,* central to Labov's work and a lot of work in social dialectology, is unpacked and problematised in various ways by all the papers in this section.

Milroy & Milroy are well-known in the development of the field of sociolinguistics for introducing the notion of social networks to the analysis of variation and change. The paper here reviews some of the reasons why, for their work in the city of Belfast, networks seemed a more illuminating approach, capturing the crucial dynamics of interaction among Belfast speakers better for them than a class-based model of a speech community. They are at pains to emphasise the complementary nature of social network and social class analyses of communities, and indeed, suggest ways of conceptualising social class that focus on people's life modes more than their location in a scale of occupations or incomes. This approach to analysing class has a tradition going back at least as far as Max Weber's analyses of social class in the early 20thC (Hughes et al. 2003). However, in foregrounding individuals' activities and patterns of association, their aspirations and opportunities, it also provides a useful starting point for appraising and evaluating the other articles in this section.

Kerswill & Williams follow closely M&M's suggested approach and apply this to their fieldwork in older towns and the so-called "New Towns" in Britain (New Towns were created after the Second World War with substantial government support in specific regions). The New Towns involved significant immigration from other parts of the UK, but they were by no means the only areas where there was lots of movement of people in the second half of the 20thC. K&W conclude that the degree of mobility within a community is an additional important factor (over and above class and social networks) in understanding the progression of some sound changes.

Mobility is also a factor in Nevalainen's article on variation in the historical record of English. Nevalainen has led by example in (as she puts it) "making the best of bad data" – showing that many of the patterns observed by sociolinguists in modern studies of variation can be perceived in historical, written corpora of English, and the principles associated with the diffusion of changes are supported by the historical record as well. It is interesting to reflect on the differences in the ways Nevalainen feels it is appropriate to divide up the Early Modern English speech community she is working with. In particular, it might be useful to consider her point that women fall outside the class structure/social networks that the men in her corpus can be divided into. In considering this, it should become apparent that how we define social class or network is contingent on the time and place of the communities we are studying (reinforcing a point made in M&M, and consistent with Weber's emphasis on subjective experience as a basis for class).

Eckert's short paper has already become a classic, and much-beloved by readers from a wide range of backgrounds. Eckert's work has, over decades, integrated the analysis of sound changes that are moving through wider collectivities (let's call them speech communities, for ease of reference) with the analysis of how innovative and conservative tokens are used in intimate and daily interaction. She demonstrates this through use of detailed ethnographic data that draws on a suite of different social behaviour (from the way the kids she's studying sound when they talk, to the way they place their hands on their hips, or interfere with each other's conversations and games). This means the level of social structure that Eckert starts from is one where friendship groupings matter most. Sociolinguists have come to talk about analyses like this as being highly "local", or having "local meaning". In other words, where networks link large numbers of people more or less directly, the communities that Eckert is interested in are defined in terms of kids' activities and face-to-face interactions. Because shared participation in linguistic and other social routines is central to defining membership in such groups, they are called "communities of practice". Eckert examines the phonetic details of different girls' speech in the context of the larger discourses and practices that speech is embedded in.

This approach has been extremely influential in recent years; Eckert's success in combining qualitative analysis with quantitative data has changed the kinds of questions sociolinguists ask about the nature of variation, particularly the nature of correlational relationships, and how individuals' ascription of meaning to isolated uses of an innovative form eventually becomes linked at a collective level and comes to typify the speech of groups of speakers.

Holmes & Schnurr's paper follows nicely from this, offering a more systematic use of discourse analysis to problematise the notion of "femininity" in workplace interactions. Workplaces are also defined very much in terms of local interaction patterns – people come together regularly to fulfil clearly defined tasks, often directed at achieving joint goals (in fact, the notion of the community of practice originated in analyses of how people learn roles in different kinds of workplaces, Lave & Wenger 1991). The conclusion that there are multiple ways of indexing femininities is not unique to H&S; however, their discussion is backed up by a unique and extraordinarily rich corpus of recordings made in many different workplaces. Readers may find it novel or counter-intuitive to think of men as enacting femininities. In this respect, H&S's paper is a good link to many of the papers in Section 6, in particular Barrett's discussion of how gendered and ethnicised ways of speaking are deployed by African-American drag queens.

REFERENCES

Hughes, John A., Wes W. Sharrock and Peter J. Martin (2003) *Understanding Classical Sociology: Marx, Weber, Durkheim, 2nd ed.* London: Sage Publications.

Lave, Jean and Etienne Wenger (1991) *Situated Learning: Legitimate Peripheral Participation.* Cambridge: Cambridge University Press.

FURTHER READING

Bucholtz, Mary (1999) 'Why be normal?': language and identity practices in a community of nerd girls. *Language in Society* 28: 203–223.

Cheshire, Jenny (2000) The telling or the tale? narratives and gender in adolescent friendship networks. *Journal of Sociolinguistics* 4: 234–262.

Cheshire, Jenny (2005) Syntactic variation and beyond: gender and social class variation in the use of discourse-new markers. *Journal of Sociolinguistics* 9: 479–508.

Dodsworth, Robin (2005) Attribute networking: a technique for modelling social perceptions. *Journal of Sociolinguistics* 9: 225–253.

Eckert, Penelope (2000) *Linguistic Variation as Social Practice.* Oxford: Blackwell.

Eckert, Penelope (1989) The whole woman: sex and gender differences in variation. *Language Variation and Change* 1: 245–267.

Holmes, Janet and Meredith Marra (2004) Relational practise in the workplace: women's talk or gendered discourse. *Language in Society* 33: 377–98.

Milroy, Lesley (1982). Social network and linguistic focusing. In Suzanne Romaine (ed.) *Sociolinguistic Variation in Speech Communities.* London: Arnold, 141–152.

Milroy, James and Lesley Milroy (2001) The social categories of race and class: language ideology and sociolinguistics. In Nikolas Coupland et al. (eds) *Sociolinguistics and Social Theory.* London: Longman, 235–60.

Vann, Robert (1998) Aspects of Spanish deictic expressions in Barcelona: a quantitative examination. *Language Variation and Change* 10: 263–288.

Chapter 24

Lesley Milroy and James Milroy

SOCIAL NETWORK AND SOCIAL CLASS: TOWARD AN INTEGRATED SOCIOLINGUISTIC MODEL

ONE OF THE MOST important contributions of Labov's quantitative paradigm has been to allow us to examine systematically and accountably the relationship between language variation and speaker variables such as sex, ethnicity, social network, and – most importantly perhaps – social class. Language variation in large and linguistically heterogeneous cities as well as in smaller communities has been revealed not as chaotic but as socially regular, and Labov and others have shown how investigating this socially patterned variation can illuminate mechanisms of linguistic change. In this article, we focus on the variables of social class and social network, both of which have appeared in some form in a large number of sociolinguistic studies of variation and change. Our principal interest lies not in the complex sociological issues associated with class and network, some of which we discuss here, but in understanding the role of class and network in patterns of linguistic variation and mechanisms of linguistic change.

Social class is fundamentally a concept designed to elucidate large-scale social, political, and economic structures and processes, whereas social network relates to the community and interpersonal level of social organization. Beginning with Bott in 1958 (revised in 1971), a number of British anthropologists developed network-analytic procedures because they were dissatisfied with what they saw as an overreliance on highly abstract social, political, and economic frameworks in accounting for forms of behavior of individuals. Personal social networks were generally seen as contextualized within this broader framework, which was bracketed off to allow attention to be concentrated on developing less abstract modes of analysis capable of accounting for the variable behavior of individuals more immediately. However, it is important to remember that such bracketing off is wholly methodological and does not reflect an ontological reality; no one claims that personal social network structure is independent of the broader social framework that constantly constrains individual behavior. While acknowledging these

Source: Milroy, Leslie and James Milroy (1992) Social network and social class: toward an integrated sociolinguistic model. *Language in Society* 21: 1–26.

constraints, a fundamental postulate of network analysts is that individuals create personal communities that provide them with a meaningful framework for solving the problems of their day-to-day existence (Mitchell 1986:74).

Our own work in Belfast has concentrated chiefly on detailed empirical analysis of linguistic and social variation at this interpersonal and community level, and in this article we want to propose a means of integrating research at this level with research that relates language variation to social class. Like the British sociologist Anthony Giddens, who insisted that "the study of day to day life is integral to the reproduction of institutional practices" (1984:282), we prefer to view the so-called micro- and macrolevels of analysis, to which network and class respectively may be thought to correspond, as embodying complementary rather than conflicting perspectives.

A different question, however, is the adequacy of the conceptualization of class that is current in much contemporary sociolinguistics, several scholars having remarked that the social theory implicitly adopted by sociolinguists is in need of explicit formulation and critique. "Sociolinguists have often borrowed social concepts in an ad hoc and unreflecting fashion, not usually considering critically the implicit theoretical frameworks that are imported wholesale along with such convenient constructs as three-, four- or nine-sector scalings of socioeconomic status" (Woolard 1985:738).

What Woolard is criticizing here is the procedure whereby a particular social class model is imported as an initial ad hoc means of organizing data, not because of its theoretical suitability, but for the purely pragmatic reason that it has been widely used in sociological surveys and so is readily operationalizable. Thus, although many impressively consistent patterns of variation have emerged from urban sociolinguistic work, an adequate social framework within which to interpret their results is still lacking. In attempting now to develop such a framework, it seems best to start with the rich sociolinguistic evidence that has been gathered over the last 25 years, only then looking for a social theory that can account for it coherently. Working in this order will allow principled decisions to be made about the kind of framework required.

We do not claim yet to have found the ideal social class model; in this article, we do no more than try to integrate existing findings and suggest the *kind* of model that seems to be required. A number of sociolinguists have remarked that the conception of social class underlying Labov's work in New York City and Philadelphia is not particularly appropriate (Rickford 1986; Sankoff, Cedergren, Kemp, Thibault, & Vincent 1989). His key sociolinguistic notion of *speech community* emphasizes shared norms of evaluation throughout the community, where speakers are said to agree on the evaluation of these very linguistic norms that symbolize the divisions between them. This sociolinguistic model seems to reflect a consensus view of society of the type associated with the sociologist Talcott Parsons, whereby the community is envisaged as fundamentally cohesive and self-regulating. Yet, the vitality and persistence of nonstandard vernacular communities uncovered by many researchers (including Labov) are more readily interpretable as evidence of conflict and sharp divisions in society than as evidence of consensus.

Although we certainly need to assume some kind of consensus to account for data such as the cross-class agreement on the phonolexical rules for raising and tensing of (a) in Philadelphia (Labov 1981), scholars such as Rickford (1986), working on Guyanese creole, have concluded that conflict models of social class have been unduly neglected by sociolinguists. Indeed, support for a conflict model of society is provided by Labov's own recent work in Philadelphia, where he found progressive segregation and linguistic differentiation between black and white networks (Labov & Harris 1986). Furthermore, a conflict model is essential if we are to account for the phenomenon of linguistic change, with which some kind of social conflict is generally associated. Labov himself has acknowledged that "a thorough-going structural-functional approach to language could be applied only if linguistic systems did not undergo internal change and development" (Labov 1986:283).

Although acknowledging that the question here is one of the relative weight given to conflict and consensus perspectives, rather than an absolute opposition between the two (cf. Giddens 1989:705), we suggest that a social class model based on conflict, division, and inequality best accounts for many of the patterns of language variation uncovered by the detailed work of sociolinguists, generally on phonological or morphological variables. The Marxist notion of the linguistic market has been used in urban sociolinguistics (see Sankoff et al., 1989, for a recent example), the general contention being that language represents a form of social and cultural capital that is convertible into economic capital. Dittmar, Schlobinski, and Wachs (1988) provided a particularly useful exposition of the linguistic market concept in relation to their analysis of Berlin vernacular. However, Woolard (1985) suggested that standard/vernacular opposition emerging from so much research needs to be discussed in terms of *alternative* linguistic markets. This is contrary to Bourdieu's (1977, 1984) view of a single dominant linguistic market where the rule of the legitimate language is merely suspended, its domination temporarily absent, when the vernacular is used.

Our own work as well as that of others supports Woolard's analysis. Just as there is strong institutional pressure to use varieties approximating to the standard in formal situations, effective sanctions are in force in nonstandard domains also. For example, in Belfast, New York City, and (no doubt) elsewhere young men are ridiculed by their peers if they use middle-class forms. Woolard suggested that much recent sociolinguistic work that has concentrated on competing social values using contrastive status/solidarity concepts (or something similar) offers a particularly promising bridge between socio-linguistic and social theory (see Brown & Levinson 1987, for a discussion of such work). A framework that emphasizes competing social values rather than consensus offers a plausible interpretation of the mass of variable linguistic and social detail from inner-city Belfast reported in Milroy and Milroy (1978), L. Milroy (1987a), J. Milroy (1981), and elsewhere. The phonological structure of Belfast vernacular can be coherently described only if it is analyzed as an internally consistent (but systematically variable) vernacular, rather than an unsuccessful approximation to middle-class Belfast or standard English varieties (for a discussion see J. Milroy 1992, Ch. 3). We interpreted close-knit social networks as mechanisms enabling speakers to maintain such vernacular codes, which themselves constitute an actively constructed, symbolic opposition to dominant, legitimized codes.

An analysis in these terms takes us part of the way, but it does not account for wider social structures, and so it needs to be supplemented by an appropriate social class model. The success, persistence, and precise form of the symbolic opposition enacted by small-scale networks will depend not upon community-internal linguistic or interactional factors, but upon the relation of the resisting group to the national economy and to like groups in other cities or states (see Gal 1988). The level of integration of any given group into the wider society is likely to be inversely related to the extent to which it maintains a distinctive vernacular. This is why the outcome in terms of language survival or shift in Belfast may be different from that in Paris or Copenhagen; in Catalonia different from Gascony. It will be constrained by variations in political, economic, and social structures that are specific to these different localities. Furthermore, close study of networks and the language patterns associated with them can give us some idea of the mechanisms that give rise to correlations between language and class.

So far, we have tried to outline some general prerequisites for an integrated and socially coherent sociolinguistic theory, constructed to take account of well-established linguistically detailed findings of urban vernacular research. In the following sections, we summarize the chief principles underlying a network analysis of language variation, looking first at close-knit communities and then at more loose-knit types of network structure of a kind generally associated with mobile individuals. We argue that the structure and social function of what might be described as both "strong" and "weak" network types need to be considered in order to integrate a network model with a sociolinguistically plausible and socially adequate model of class.

NETWORK STRUCTURE IN CLOSE-KNIT COMMUNITIES

A social network may be seen as a boundless web of ties that reaches out through a whole society, linking people to one another, however remotely. But for practical reasons the analyst studies social networks as "anchored" to individuals, and interest has most often focused on relatively strong first-order network ties – that is, those persons with whom *ego* directly and regularly interacts. This principle of anchorage effectively limits the field of study, generally to something between 30 and 50 individuals, although it is assumed that second-order ties to whom ego is linked through others are also influential (see Milroy 1987a).

Two types of personal network characteristics are generally distinguished by anthropologists: *structural*, which pertains to the shape and pattern of the network, and *interactional*, which pertains to the content of the ties. Both structural and interactional characteristics are important in constraining social action. Investigators from several disciplines who have developed formal methods of analyzing the properties of networks have tended to concentrate on structural properties such as density, whereas social investigators who want to account for the observable behavior of individuals tend to give equal weight to interactional features such as the multiplexity, history, durability, frequency, and intensity of ties (see, e.g., Cochran, Larner, Riley, Gunnarsson, & Henderson 1990; Surra 1988). Some important structural and interactional features are conveniently listed by Mitchell (1986).

Our analysis of the relationship between language variation and personal network structure in three Belfast inner-city communities attempted to demonstrate that a close-knit, territorially based network functions as a conservative force, resisting pressures for change originating from outside the network. By close-knit we mean relatively dense and multiplex, these two concepts being of critical importance in a comparative analysis of social networks. In a maximally dense and multiplex network, everyone would know everyone else (density), and the actors would know one another in a range of capacities (multiplexity). Close-knit networks, which vary in the extent to which they approximate to an idealized maximally dense and multiplex network, have the capacity to maintain and even enforce local conventions and norms – including linguistic norms – and can provide a means of opposing dominant institutional values and standardized linguistic norms. Their capacity to do this, however, seems to be dependent on their territorial restriction to specific neighborhoods, the day-to-day behavior of individuals being less constrained by geographically dispersed networks. Network analysis thus offers a basis for understanding the community-level mechanisms that underlie processes of language maintenance, and the persistence over centuries of stigmatized linguistic forms and low-status vernaculars in the face of powerful national policies of diffusing and imposing standard languages is indeed remarkable.

Apart from its theoretical value, a network approach has been found useful in providing a suitable methodology for studying ethnic or other subgroups in the population in situations where a social class model (particularly one that focuses on consensus) is less practical. Quite apart from any theoretical problems, an initial approach in terms of class is difficult if subgroups are distributed unequally with respect to class. A network approach is more feasible with groups who are economically marginal, or powerless, or resident in homogeneous and territorially well-defined neighborhoods. Moreover, a strong sense of ethnicity or of local identity often creates and maintains localized cultural and linguistic norms and value systems that are presented and perceived as sharply opposed to the mainstream values of outsiders. Approaching such communities initially in network rather than class terms can allow the researcher to get a grip on the relation between linguistic variability and social structure. Examples of sociolinguistic applications of network analysis are: Schmidt (1985: Australian aboriginal adolescents), Bortoni-Ricardo (1985: rural immigrants to a Brazilian city), Gal (1979: bilingual peasant workers), Lippi-Green (1989: an Alpine rural community in Austria), V. Edwards (1986: British black adolescents in the Midlands), and W. Edwards (1990: black Detroit speakers). Labov and his colleagues in their Philadelphia neighborhood studies also used the network concept at the fieldwork stage (Labov & Harris 1986). So there is little disagreement on the practical usefulness of a network-based methodology.

[. . .]

The type of close-knit community most easily conceptualized in network terms is likely to be a product of modern city life rather than a residue of an earlier type of social organization. Such groups are important in providing a focal point for stigmatized urban vernaculars and other nonlegitimized linguistic norms, and so need to be accounted for in any sociolinguistic theory. That is why some form of network analysis that examines the relationship between the individual and the primary group is so important. But the observable indicators of *network strength*, a measure of integration into a close-knit group, will vary in kind with community organization. For example, membership in a religious group might be irrelevant in a contemporary northern English coal-mining community, but highly relevant in an English Midlands black community (Edward 1986).

[. . .]

STRONG AND WEAK NETWORK TIES

One important corollary to the link between language maintenance and a close-knit network structure is that outside innovation and influence will be associated with the weakening of such a structure. This accounts for our finding in inner-city Belfast that speakers whose ties to the localized network are weakest are those who approximate least closely to vernacular norms. Such speakers are most exposed to external, often standard-izing, pressures (Milroy & Milroy 1985). There is, however, a general methodological problem associated with network analysis. Although it can be readily operationalized to study speakers whose networks are of a relatively close-knit type, it cannot so readily handle socially and geographically mobile speakers whose personal network ties are not predominantly dense or multiplex. So we cannot easily demonstrate the effects of weak ties by the quantitative methods that are used to demonstrate the effects of strong ties, as in inner-city Belfast, for example. Fortunately, however, a large amount of linguistic evidence is available that enables us to follow the sociolinguistic implications of the line of reasoning developed by Granovetter (1973, 1982) in his examination of the social function of weak network links. Granovetter argued that although strong ties (of the sort associated with close-knit networks) facilitate local cohesion, they lead to overall social fragmentation. This seems to be the kind of interclass and intercommunity fragmentation that we described in Belfast and that Labov pointed to in Philadelphia with respect to black and white groups. However, Granovetter argued that it is the (often numerous) weak ties *between* relatively close-knit groups through which innovation and influence flow and that lead to an overall social cohesion capable of balancing the fragmentation and conflict associated with strong ties. It is important here to keep in mind Granovetter's insistence on the paradox that weak ties can be described as strong in that they "provide links to a community beyond the immediate social circle, information about education and employment opportunities . . . and access to diverse ideas and perspectives" (Cochran 1990: 289). Persons who contract mainly strong, localized, and often kin-based ties are denied parallel access to these resources, and, as we have noted, strong ties of this kind can be norm-enforcing and oppressive.

Following Granovetter's closely argued article, we have proposed not only that groups linked internally mainly by relatively weak ties are susceptible to innovation, but also that innovations between groups are generally transmitted by means of weak rather than strong network ties (e.g., through casual acquaintances rather than kin, close friends, or workmates). Weak ties are, of course, likely to be much more numerous than strong ties. This argument runs somewhat counter to the general assumption that diffusion of linguistic change is encouraged by relatively open channels of communication and dis-couraged by boundaries or weaknesses in lines of communication. However, as we argued in some detail (Milroy & Milroy 1985), there are many well-known patterns of change that are difficult to explain in this apparently common-sense way. Some of these involve large-scale and long-term changes over considerable distances, as discussed by Trudgill (1983, 1986). Examples are the spread of uvular [r] across national boundaries to affect many northern European cities, the spread of certain London features to Norwich, and the appearance of similar developments in unrelated or distantly related languages (e.g., *preaspiration* of voiceless stops in Icelandic and Scottish Gaelic). It is very hard to see how the relevant populations in such cases could be linked by strong ties. Other examples are at a more detailed community level, such as the social configuration of the spread of [a] backing from protestant East Belfast into the Clonard – a West Belfast Catholic community. This spread, which we look at in a little detail, needs to be described within a wider historical, social, and linguistic context.

We studied the variables (a) and (e) very intensively both in the inner-city communities of Clonard, Hammer, and Ballymacarrett and in the slightly higher status communities of Andersonstown and Braniel. We also established a broad social class distribution by means of a doorstep survey carried out on randomly sampled households in Belfast (J. Milroy 1991, 1992; L. Milroy 1987b:82). The vowel /a/ (as in *man, grass*) shows variation across a wide phonetic continuum between long, backed, rounded realizations and shorter front and front-raised realizations. The vowel /e/ (as in *went, question*) varies between long, mid realizations and short, lower realizations (see J. Milroy 1981, for an analysis of the phonological complexities). Realizations of both variables are strongly affected by sex, network structure, and social class of the speaker. The extensive quantitative analysis reported in detail elsewhere (most relevantly for this argument: J. Milroy 1992; L. Milroy 1987a; Milroy & Milroy 1985) shows that raised, lengthened variants of /e/ are associated principally with women and middle-class speakers, and backed variants of /a/ with men and working-class speakers.

It is clear from the historical and dialectological data presented by Patterson (1860), Staples (1898), Williams (1903), and Gregg (1972) that /a/ backing and /e/ raising are both relatively recent phenomena in Belfast but are characteristic of modern Scots and originate in the Ulster-Scots-speaking dialect area of Down and Antrim (as distinct from the Mid- and West-Ulster non-Scots hinterland). As Figure 24.1 shows, East Belfast adjoins the Ulster-Scots region of North Down, whereas West Belfast points southwest down the Lagan Valley, the speech of which is Mid-Ulster, with less Scots influence. Furthermore, immigration to West Belfast is recent and is largely from a Mid- and West-Ulster hinterland. Present-day sociolinguistic evidence suggests that the incoming variants of (e) and (a) are diffusing from east to west of the city; scores for /a/ backing are higher for East Belfast working-class men than for any other group studied, whereas East Belfast working-class women use the low, conservative variants of (e) less than any other inner-city group. The higher status Andersonstown and Braniel speakers exhibit a similar pattern of sex differentiation but, as one might predict from the information presented so far, use the incoming variants of (e) more frequently, and the incoming variants of (a) less frequently, than inner-city speakers.

In summary (and this general distribution is confirmed by a doorstep survey), raised variants of (e) are in the inner-city associated particularly with women (and, we might add, with careful speech styles). They are also associated generally with slightly more prestigious outer-city speech. Incoming variants of (a) show an almost perfectly converse pattern of social distribution, being associated with male, vernacular inner-city speech. Taking this evidence together with the historical and geographical data outlined earlier, we note that although incoming variants of both vowels appear to have originated in the same hinterland Scots dialect, each has assumed a diametrically opposed *social* value in its relatively new urban setting.

The relationship between speaker choice of variant and individual network structure adds a further complexity to this pattern, and it is the overall relationship among social class, sex, and network structures of speaker that is of particular relevance here. Extensive statistical analysis of the relationship between language variation and social

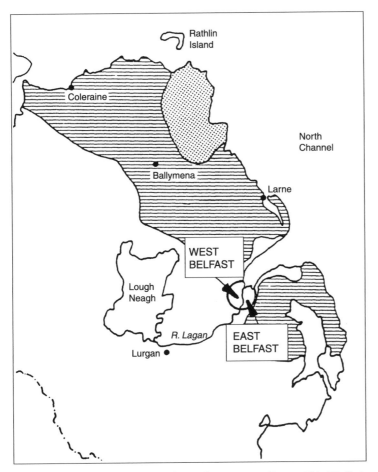

Figure 24.1   Map showing the Ulster Scots area (shaded) in relation to East and West Belfast.

network has shown that whereas choice of variant correlates with network structure among some inner-city subgroups, these sociolinguistic patterns are quite different for each vowel. Although (a) is generally sensitive to network structure, choice of variant is *more closely correlated* with network structure for women than for men; this is despite the fact that women (like middle-class speakers generally) use incoming backed variants much *less frequently* than men. The converse is true of (e); whereas men use incoming raised variants much less than women, the correlation between choice of variant and network structure is higher for men. We argued on the basis of these data that (e) functions particularly clearly for men and (a) for women as a network marker and noted that in each case *it is the group for whom the vowel has less significance as a network marker that seems to be leading the linguistic change*. The complex relationship among class and sex of speaker, network structure, and language use is summarized in Table 24.1, and the data upon which this discussion is based are reported in Milroy and Milroy (1985), L. Milroy (1987a), and J. Milroy (1992).

We are now in a position to relate these patterns to the general argument outlined earlier, namely that a close-knit network functions as a conservative force, resisting pressures for change originating from outside the network. Those whose ties are weakest

Table 24.1 Contrasting patterns of distribution of two vowels involved in change, according to social class and sex of speaker, relative frequency of innovatory variants, and level of correlation with network strength

Change led by	High correlation with network strength
(a) Males (working-class variant)	Females
(e) Females (middle-class variant)	Males

approximate least closely to vernacular norms and are most exposed to external pressures for change. The analysis presented here suggests that the vernacular speakers associated most strongly with the innovation are in each case those for whom the vowel functions least prominently as a network marker. It is as if a strong relationship between the network structure of a given group and choice of phonetic realization of a particular vowel disqualifies that group from fulfilling the role of innovators with respect to that vowel. Conversely, the weakening of the language/network relationship with respect to a group of speakers may be a necessary precondition of that group fulfilling the role of linguistic innovators.

These observations provide further evidence to support the contention that a weakening of network links is implicated in social processes of linguistic change. Furthermore, some innovations seem to have crossed the sectarian boundary in working-class Belfast to produce an intercommunity consensus on norms among the generation of speakers who were most rigidly segregated from each other. The problem of explaining how a linguistic change such as (a) backing could possibly diffuse under such conditions dissolves if we accept Granovetter's principle that it is the multiple weak ties of casual interaction (example for these speakers might be ties contracted in shops and social security offices) through which innovation is routinely transmitted rather than strong neighborhood ties of close association.

[. . .]

THEORETICAL IMPLICATIONS OF A WEAK-TIES MODEL

Speakers whose ties to a localized network are weakest, who approximate least closely to the norms of their local community, and who are most exposed to external pressures are frequently found in the middle-class or upper-working-class areas of cities. However, in the previous section we allude to the practical difficulties in carrying out empirical investigations of loose knit network structures, which characterize residents of Andersonstown and Braniel. Others have encountered the same problems, for example, in the prosperous Berlin suburb of Zehlendorf (Labrie 1988; see also L. Milroy 1987b:198). But as many people (particularly city dwellers, as Wirth suggested) contract weak ties, we need to take such ties into account in our description of sociolinguistic structure. And despite the empirical difficulties in handling weak ties, an extension of network analysis that focuses on the properties provides a crucial link with more abstract social theories of class. It is clear that class-specific network structures are not arbitrarily constituted but emerge from large-scale social and economic processes that themselves give rise to (for example) the social and residential mobility associated with loose-knit networks.

The relationship between the variables of class and network have been considered in some depth by Fischer (1982) in San Francisco and by Cochran et al. (1990) in Germany, Sweden, Wales, and the United States. Investigators have generally emphasized the effects of education and affluence in affording access to a socially and geographically wider range of contacts and in enhancing the ability to maintain those contacts. Generally speaking, middle-class networks (consisting largely of weak ties in Granovetter's sense) are larger, less kin- and territory-oriented and perceived as more supportive. Mewett (1982) examined the relationship between class and network from a different perspective, arguing that *class* differences in small communities begin to emerge over time as the proportion of *multiplex* relationships declines. Observations such as this suggest a route for constructing a two-level sociolinguistic theory, linking small-scale structures such as networks, in which individuals are embedded and act purposively in their daily lives, with larger scale and more abstract social structures (classes) that determine relationships of power at the institutional level.

From the point of view of the sociolinguist, it is smaller scale close-knit networks that renew and maintain local systems of norms and values within which discourse processes of the kind analyzed by Gumperz (1982) are understood and enacted. And it is network structures that link the interactional level with the political and economic, where diverse local responses of linguistic groups are constructed "to material and cultural domination" (Gal 1988). We need such a dual level of analysis if we are to understand the frequently negative self-evaluations of speakers of urban vernaculars, who nevertheless continue to use them in their daily lives. In this section, we use the weak-tie concept to link systematically a network and a class-based analysis.

We have argued that weak ties *between* groups regularly provide bridges through which information and influence flow and are more likely than strong ties, which are by definition concentrated *within* groups, to fulfil this function. Thus, whereas strong ties give rise to a *local* cohesion of the kind described in inner-city Belfast, they lead, as we have noted, to overall fragmentation. Indeed, it is this potential for explaining both patterns – local stability and cohesion versus overall fragmentation and conflict – that allows us to relate a network analysis to a model of social structure at the macro-level. This is an important point, as some of the comments made in recent years about network models in sociolinguistics by, for example, Labov (1986) and Guy (1988) assume that their application is limited to strong ties in close-knit communities; and indeed they have been used chiefly in such communities (but see Bortoni-Ricardo 1985). Guy's remark that network is a microsociological concept, whereas class is macroscopic, seems reasonable if we limit network analysis to close-knit networks. But an analysis that takes into account the function of weak ties allows us not only to link the two levels in a principled way, but to develop a clearer idea of which type of social class model is appropriate. The analysis so far suggests an urban community that consists of clusters of individuals connected internally by differing proportions of weak and strong ties, which in turn are connected to other clusters by predominantly weak ties. Middle-class groups will tend to be internally connected with a higher proportion of weak ties than working-class groups.

This conclusion is entirely consistent with Labov's finding that innovating groups are located centrally in the class structure, characterized by him as upper-working or lower-middle class (Kroch 1978; Labov 1980:254). For, in British and American society at least, close-knit, territorially based, kin-oriented networks are located most clearly in the lowest classes, but upper-class networks are in some respects structurally similar, being relatively dense, small, close-knit and kin-oriented. Consider Mills's (1956) description of the American power elite, and the close ties among British upper-class speakers acquired at a limited number of private schools and universities and subsequently maintained for life. The majority of social and geographically mobile speakers fall between these two points. Thus, if we extend a network analysis to include an examination of loose-knit network types, which are susceptible to outside (frequently standardizing) influences, it is evident that network-based and class-based analyses are not contradictory as is sometimes suggested; rather, they complement each other. Moreover, a network analysis can give us an idea of the interpersonal mechanisms giving rise to the observable language/class correlations that are such a prominent feature of research in the quantitative paradigm.

AN INTEGRATED MODEL?

At this point, we have a picture of various ethnic and class groups as *both* internally structured *and* connected to each other with varying proportions and numbers of strong and weak ties. For example, ethnic sub-groups in Britain such as the black speakers studied by V. Edwards (1986) have a predominantly strong-tie internal structure but seem to be linked by relatively few weak ties to white working-class groups. These white groups in turn might have a similar internal network structure but have *more* weak tie links with other white working-class groups. Vertical links to middle-class groups might be fewer (this seemed to be the case in Belfast) and moreover to be frequently institutional to such persons as doctors, lawyers, teachers, welfare personnel, and the like. Middle-class groups for their part – professional, neighborhood, and friendship groups – are characterized by a higher proportion of weak ties *internally* than working-class groups; hence the problems of studying them systematically in network terms in Zehlendorf and in outer-city Belfast. But however we interpret the concept of class and however we model these localized networks, Granovetter's concept of the weak tie can be used to link close-knit community level groupings to more abstract institutional structures.

Such an analysis attributes the behavior of speakers to the constraining effects of the network or to the diminution of those effects that enable the legitimized language to permeate networks, rather than by any direct effect of prestige as defined by the perceived attributes of speakers who are seen to "belong" to different status groups. Social class is not conceived of here as a graded series of pigeonholes within which individuals may be placed. Following the analysis of the Danish Marxist anthropologist Thomas Højrup (1983), a view of social class more consistent with network analysis conceives of it as a large-scale and ultimately economically driven *process* that splits populations into subgroups. The groups sharing certain social and economic characteristics and lifestyles that emerge from this split may loosely be described as classes, but as we shall see Højrup offered a more explicitly motivated description in terms of *life-mode*. The attraction of this analysis from our point of view is that different types of network structure emerge from the conditions associated with the life-modes of these subgroups, and local and individual social behavior is seen as mediated through these smaller scale structures rather than directly related to class.

Whereas network analysis of the kind we have outlined so far can delineate various economic, political, and subcultural groupings in society, it cannot say anything about the varying potentials of such networks to exercise the economic and political power that is the source of conflict and inequality in society. In linguistic terms, this means that powerful networks have the capacity to impose their linguistic and cultural norms on others, whereas powerless ones do not but can merely use the resources of the network to maintain and at best renew their own linguistic and cultural norms. Therefore, to supplement network analysis we need a social theory such as Højrup's, which can explicitly link a network analysis of subgroups within society to an analysis of social structure at the political, institutional, and economic levels.

Højrup's analysis is based on ethnographic work in Denmark and extensive analysis of social and economic structure in other western European countries. Although it begs as many questions as it offers solutions (see, e.g., Pedersen 1991, who questioned its applicability to women), it is particularly suggestive in helping to construct a model of sociolinguistic structure that integrates the variables of social class and social network. With specific reference to western Europe, he proposed a division of populations into subgroups that are described in terms of three life-modes. These life-modes are seen as necessary and inevitable constituents of the social structure as a whole. His conception of this larger social structure is Marxist, and the initial analysis is in terms of modes of production and consumption. Thus, crucially, these subgroups are not seen as socially or culturally arbitrary but as the effect of "fundamental societal structures which split the population into fundamentally different life-modes" (Højrup 1983:47). Class is thus seen as a dynamic process that gives rise to these life-modes. Højrup's analysis is particularly helpful in suggesting a further integration of the concepts of network and class, because the different types of network structure that we distinguished in the previous section can be seen to a considerable extent as springing from differences in the life-modes of different individuals. Although the argumentation supporting his analysis is lengthy and complex, Højrup used a limited number of straightforward concepts to distinguish the three life-modes. Life-mode 1 is the life-mode of the self-employed in small family-run businesses, Life-mode 2 [are ordinary wage earners with high network strength and solidarity if they earn little and weakening networks and solidarity if they earn more. Life mode 3 refers to higher professional or managerial employees with many loose-knit networks.] Of critical importance is the ideological orientation of the three groups to work, leisure, and family.

[. . .]

Life mode 1 workers distinguish little between work and leisure and have a strong solidarity ethic. Life mode 2 individuals see a job as a means to achieve a meaningful life in the worker's free time, while for life mode 3 members the boundaries between work and leisure are blurred. They are socially and geographically mobile and willing to work long hours in order to rise up through the hierarchy.

[. . .]

This seems to fit in with our general characterization of the differing role of loose-knit and close-knit knit network ties. The primarily loose-knit network of the Life-mode 3 individual ensures that the dominant linguistic market – as embodied in some form of legitimized or standard language – holds sway without hindrance from (in Woolard's

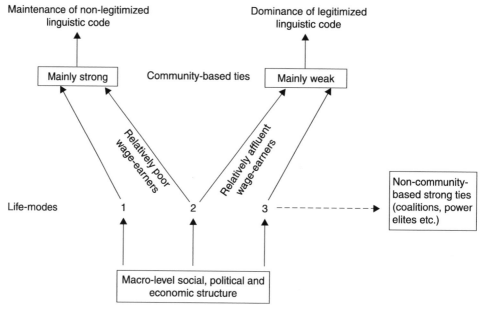

Figure 24.2   Macro- and microlevels of sociolinguistic structure.

terms) alternative vernacular markets. Figure 24.2 is a schematic representation of the relation of social network structure to these three life-modes.

It is important to emphasize that the concept of life-mode, like that of network, is a structural one, in that the ideological and cultural characteristics of a particular life-mode are determined by its contrast to the other life-modes in the social formation. The interrelationships among the three life-modes and the cultural practices associated with each one will therefore take different forms in, for example, Denmark, Ireland, England, and Germany. In each of these countries, the three fundamental modes of production that the life-modes reflect "will appear in different variants and in different combinations of opposition and independence" (Højrup 1983:47). One consequence of this chain of dependence running from political and socioeconomic structures through life-modes to network structure and ultimately to socio-linguistic structure (see Figure 24.2) is, as we have already suggested, that close-knit networks will be associated with Life-mode 2 individuals in some nation states more than in others. This seems to be the case if, for example, we compare Belfast with Copenhagen. In Copenhagen, these wage earners are apparently more mobile and prosperous and less inclined to live and work together in close-knit groups of the kind described in Belfast (Gregersen & Pedersen 1991). This in turn will give rise to sociolinguistic patterns that depend on varying local contingencies and hence to urban vernaculars varying in their degree of focusing and vitality.

CONCLUSION

The purpose of this article has been to work toward an integrated model of sociolinguistic structure that links in an explicit way the social variables of socioeconomic class and social network. Although these variables are often presented as unrelated or even contradictory, we have tried to demonstrate that, although they are at different orders of generality, it is useful to propose an interpretation of sociolinguistic space that conceives of them as interrelated. They are, of course, related in reality also. Particular configurations of network structure do not emerge accidentally for no particular reason – the form they take is dependent on the large-scale social, political, and economic structures that sociolinguists generally access in terms of socioeconomic class. Thus, an attempt to integrate class and network as interpretative categories is well motivated.

[. . .]

The analysis of higher level social structure that we have found most useful here treats social and cultural divisions as emerging ultimately from the economic inequalities produced by social class. Højrup (1983) assumed such a framework in his process-based model of life-mode, which we have used in conjunction with network analysis to develop an integrated model of sociolinguistic structure. By emphasizing in particular the importance of distinguishing between relatively strong and relatively weak network ties, we have suggested how these economically determined life-modes give rise not only to the social and cultural differences described by Højrup, but to different kinds of network structure. This will further enable us to specify the conditions in which the linguistic norms of the groups are likely to be focused or diffuse, and the conditions in which they are open to, or resistant to change.

REFERENCES

Ash, S. and J. Myhill (1986) Linguistic correlates of inter-ethnic contact. In Sankoff (1986), 33–44.

Bortoni-Ricardo, S. M. (1985) *The Urbanisation of Rural Dialect Speakers: A Sociolinguistic Study in Brazil.* Cambridge: Cambridge University Press.

Bott, E. (1971) *Family and Social Network* (2nd ed.). London: Tavistock.

Bourdieu, P. (1977) The economics of linguistic exchanges. *Social Science Information* 16(6): 645–668.

Bourdieu, P. (1984) Capital et marché linguistique. *Linguistische Berichte* 90: 3–24.

Brown, P. and S. Levinson (1987) *Politeness.* Cambridge: Cambridge University Press.

Cochran, M. (1990) Environmental factors constraining network development. In M. Cochran et al. (1990), 277–296.

Cochran, M., M. Larner, D. Riley, L. Gunnarsson and C.R. Henderson (eds) (1990) *Extending Tending Families: The Social Networks of Parents and their Children.* Cambridge: Cambridge University Press.

Cohen, A. (ed.) (1982) *Belonging.* Manchester: Manchester University Press.

Dittmar, N. and P. Schlobinski (1988) *The Sociolinguistics of Urban Vernaculars.* Berlin: Mouton de Gruyter.

Dittmar, N., P. Schlobinski and I. Wachs (1988) The social significance of the Berlin urban vernacular. In N. Dittmar and P. Schlobinski (1988), 19–43.

Edwards, V. (1986) *Language in a Black Community.* Clevedon: Multilingual Matters.

Edwards, W. (1990) *Social Network Theory and Language Variation in Detroit.* Paper presented at the Eighth Sociolinguistic Symposium, Roehampton, London.

Fischer, C. (1982) *To Dwell Among Friends: Personal Networks in Town and City.* Chicago: University of Chicago Press.

Gal, S. (1979) *Language Shift: Social Determinants of Linguistic Change in Bilingual Austria.* New York: Academic.

Gal, S. (1988) The political economy of code choice. In Heller (1988), 245–263.

Giddens, A. (1984) *The Constitution of Society.* Cambridge: Polity.

Granovetter, M. (1973) The strength of weak ties. *American Journal of Sociology* 78: 1360–1380.

Granovetter, M. (1982) The strength of weak ties: a network theory revisited. In P. V. Marsden and N. Lin (eds) *Social Structure and Network Analysis*. London: Sage, 105–130.

Gregersen, F. and I.L. Pedersen (1991) *The Copenhagen Study in Urban Sociolinguistics*. (Universitetsjubilaeets Danske Samfund, Serie A). Copenhagen: C. A. Reitzel.

Gregg, R. J. (1972) The Scotch-Irish dialect boundaries in Ulster. In M. F. Wakelin (ed.) *Patterns in the Folk Speech of the British Isles*. London: Athlone Press, 109–139.

Gumperz, J. (1982) *Discourse Strategies*. Cambridge: Cambridge University Press.

Guy, G. R. (1988) Language and social class. In Newmeyer (1988), 37–63.

Heller, M. (1988) *Code-Switching*. Berlin: Mouton de Gruyter.

Højrup, T. (1983) The concept of life-mode: a form-specifying mode of analysis applied to contemporary western Europe. *Ethnologia Scandinavica* 1–50.

Kroch, A. S. (1978) Toward a theory of social dialect variation. *Language in Society* 7: 17–36.

Labov, W. (1972) *Sociolinguistic Patterns*. Philadelphia: University of Pennsylvania Press.

Labov, W. (ed.) (1980) *Locating Language in Time and Space*. New York: Academic.

Labov, W. (1981) Resolving the neogrammarian controversy. *Language* 57: 267–309.

Labov, W. (1986) Language structure and social structure. In S. Lindenberg et al. (eds) *Approaches to Social Theory*. New York: Russell Sage.

Labov, W. and W. Harris (1986) De facto segregation of black and white vernaculars. In Sankoff (1986), 1–24.

Labrie, N. (1988) Comments on Berlin urban vernacular studies. In Dittmar & Schlobinski (1988), 191–206.

Lippi-Green, R. L. (1989) Social network integration and language change in progress in a rural alpine village. *Language in Society* 18: 213–234.

Lockwood, D. (1989) *The Black-Coated Worker: A Study in Class-Consciousness*. Oxford: Clarendon. (Original work published 1966)

Mewett, P. (1982) Associational categories and the social location of relationships in a Lewis crofting community. In Cohen (1982), 101–130.

Mills, C. W. (1956) *The Power Elite*. Oxford: Oxford University Press.

Milroy, J. (1981) *Regional Accents of English: Belfast*. Belfast: Blackstaff.

Milroy, J. (1991) The interpretation of social constraints on variation in Belfast English. In J. Cheshire (ed.) *English Around the World: Sociolinguistic Perspectives*. Cambridge: Cambridge University Press, 75–85.

Milroy, J. (1992) *Linguistic Variation and Change*. Oxford: Blackwell.

Milroy, J. and L. Milroy (1978) Belfast: change and variation in an urban vernacular. In P. Trudgill (ed.) *Sociolinguistic Patterns in British English*. London: Arnold, 19–36.

Milroy, J. and L. Milroy (1985) Linguistic change, social network, and speaker innovation. *Journal of Linguistics* 21: 339–384.

Milroy, L. (1987a) *Language and Social Networks* (2nd ed.). Oxford: Blackwell.

Milroy, L. (1987b) *Observing and Analysing Natural Language*. Oxford: Blackwell.

Mitchell, J. C. (1986) Network procedures. In D. Frick (ed.) *The Quality of Urban Life*. Berlin: de Gruyter, 73–92.

Newmeyer, F. (ed.) (1988) *Linguistics: The Cambridge Survey. Vol. 4*. Cambridge: Cambridge University Press.

Patterson, D. (1860) *Provincialisms of Belfast*. Belfast: Mayne Boyd.

Pedersen, I.-L. (1991) *Sociolinguistic Classification in a Gender Perspective*. Unpublished manuscript. University of Copenhagen, Institut for dansk dialektologi.

Rickford, J. (1986) The need for new approaches to social class analysis in linguistics. *Language and Communication* 6(3): 215–221.

Sankoff, D. (1986) *Diversity and Diachrony*. Amsterdam: John Benjamins.

Sankoff, D., H. Cedergren, W. Kemp, P. Thibault and D. Vincent (1989) Montreal French: language, class, and ideology. In W. Fasold and D. Schiffrin (eds) *Language Change and Variation*. Amsterdam: John Benjamins, 107–118.

Schmidt, A. (1985) *Young People's Djirbal*. Cambridge: Cambridge University Press.

Staples, J.H. (1898) Notes on Ulster English dialect. *Transactions of the Philological Society*, 357–387.

Surra, C. A. (1988) The influence of the interactive network on developing relationships. In R. M. Milardo (ed.) *Family and Social Networks*. Newbury, CA: Sage, 48–82.

Trudgill, P. (1983) *On Dialect*. Oxford: Blackwell.

Trudgill, P. (1986) *Dialects in Contact*. Oxford: Blackwell.

Williams, R. A. (1903) Remarks on Northern Irish pronunciation of English. *Modern English Quarterly* 6: 129–135.

Woolard, K. (1985) Language variation and cultural hegemony: toward an integration of linguistic and sociolinguistic theory. *American Ethnologist* 12: 738–748.

QUESTIONS

Content

1. What is the difference between social class and social networks?
2. What is Milroy & Milroy's criticism of the concept of social class as it is often used in sociolinguistics?
3. How do class and networks interact?
4. What is a close-knit network?
5. How can network strength be measured?
6. When is the network approach particularly useful?
7. What is one of the methodological problems of network analysis?
8. How do innovations enter a community?
9. What social group is /e/ raising and /a/ backing associated with in Belfast and what is the social meaning of these variables and their link to network strength?
10. What is the relationship between class and social networks and how can network analysis be linked to an analysis at the macro level?
11. What makes Højrup's view of social class so attractive for a combination with network analysis?

Concept

1. Collect the names of everybody in your class and put them on the board. Draw a social network of the class. Is it a strong or a weak social network? Why? What does this mean in respect to linguistic influence and norm enforcement?
2. Consider Figure 24.3 (page 408). Ash and Myhill interpret the figure in terms of prestige and dominance (the prestige of the localized innovator and the dominant dialect as opposed to the dominated). They considered four groups of speakers: a core white group, a core black group, and two marginal groups – a group of blacks who have considerable contact with whites (WBs) and a group of whites who have considerable contact with blacks (BWs). Let's focus on the marginal groups here. According to Ash and Myhill's interpretation of Figure 24.3, the WBs converge toward white morphosyntactic norms more markedly than BWs converge toward black norms. They claim that this is due to the dominance of the white dialect. It can be surmised from the authors' descriptions of the two marginal groups that their contacts with the respective other ethnic group are of a classic weak-tie type. The white-oriented blacks in particular are described as con men, hustlers, and political activists. Do we need to invoke a macro notion such as dominance in interpreting this data? How could this data be interpreted using social network theory

in particular keeping in mind the WBs' social roles and the capacity of the core black vernacular to alternate between black and white morphosyntactic variants?

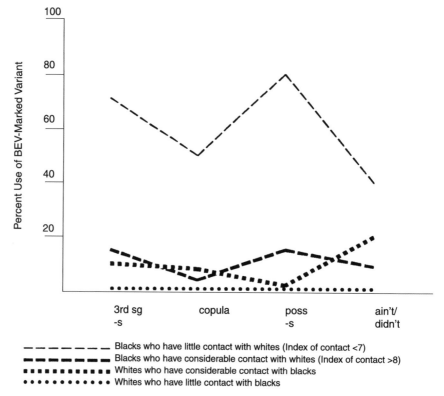

Figure 24.3   Average percentage use of black English vernacular-marked morphosyntactic variants by four groups of Philadelphia speakers (adapted from Ash & Myhill 1986: 39).

Chapter 25

Paul Kerswill and Ann Williams

MOBILITY VERSUS SOCIAL CLASS IN DIALECT LEVELLING: EVIDENCE FROM NEW AND OLD TOWNS IN ENGLAND

1. INTRODUCTION: CLASS, NETWORK AND LANGUAGE CHANGE

THIS ARTICLE ADDRESSES THE social context of internal migration as a force for the convergence of language varieties.[1] That migration should be such a force has long been recognised [. . .]. One of the most important contributions to the understanding of the social embedding of language change in recent years has been the proposal by the Milroys, in their 1992 article, to combine the two fundamental concepts of social class and social network into a unified social theory which will account for language variation and change. It is our aim in the present paper to show that the relationship between class and network that they propose needs modification to take account of highly mobile, but by no means socially marginal, groups of internal migrants whose sociolinguistic patterns are not normally considered in speech community studies (though see Kerswill 1993).

We begin by briefly presenting the Milroys' position. Linguists, they maintain, have been unreflecting and uncritical in their adoption of frameworks for stratifying and classifying groups within society. The consensus model (Durkheim and Talcott Parsons), favoured by Labov, is based on a view of society as an integrated whole in which the different parts work in harmony with one another. [. . .] The consensus view is limited, however, by its inability to account for the dynamic nature and continued vitality of non-standard vernaculars and therefore is unable to provide an explanation for linguistic change. Such phenomena can be better understood, according to the Milroys, by adopting as a framework the Marxian conflict model which takes account of the inequalities, divisions and opposing interests found within society. This model shows how varieties other than standard, legitimised varieties persist strongly and act as badges of identity for less privileged groups.

Source: Kerswill, Paul and Ann Williams (2000) Mobility and social class in dialect levelling: evidence from new and old towns in England. In Klaus Mattheier (ed.) *Dialect and Migration in a Changing Europe*. Frankfurt: Peter Lang, 1–13.

Social network theory also provides an explanation for the maintenance of non-standard dialects. [. . .] Strong [close-knit] networks both bind a local community together and reduce the possibility of changes in behaviour, including linguistic behaviour. The interaction between social network and social class can be seen when one considers that close-knit networks in the West are to be found mainly at the two extremes of the socio-economic scale. Thus, the least powerful and the most powerful maintain strong social networks – the former because of the *need* to maintain such ties for survival, the latter in order to reaffirm their exclusivity. The majority of speakers [. . .] come into contact with a wider range of people.

Within all groups in society, it is, according to the Milroys, individuals who establish large numbers of weak ties outside their immediate communities who are able to facilitate language change. [. . .] We would infer from this [. . .] that the spread of changes occurs more rapidly in socially and geographically mobile groups, especially migrants [. . .].

Finally, the Milroys propose an alternative to a social class analysis of society, using the Danish sociologist Thomas Højrup's model of *life-modes*. We have already mentioned the inverse correlation between social network strength and social class: a life-mode analysis is an attempt to explain why this should be so. [. . .]

Højrup's life-modes (after Milroy & Milroy 1992)
   Life-mode 1 groups workers who are self-employed in small family-run businesses [. . .]. Intent on maintaining a successful enterprise, they tend to make little distinction between work and leisure and have a strong solidarity ethic.
   Life-mode 2 comprises wage earners and employees. These workers do not share the strong commitment to work of the life-mode 1 members; for them a job is the means to the achievement of meaningful free time and leisure. There is no ideology of solidarity as in life-mode 1, but solidarity emerges in this group in the face of difficulties and lack of resources. These conditions give rise to the traditional close-knit neighbourhoods of the working class. If a family's income rises, the need for networks to provide support mechanisms is reduced. The family becomes materially better off and may move out of the neighbourhood to better accommodation. The solidarity ethic apparently disappears, only to surface again in times of industrial strife.
   Life-mode 3 members are also wage earners but they see their goal as rising up the hierarchy of the organisation for which they work. [. . .] [T]he individual is prepared to work long hours and move long distances to fulfil ambitions. As a result, their networks are primarily loose-knit.

Later, we argue that social mobility does not necessarily go hand-in-hand with a middle class (that is, life-mode 3) way of life: as we shall see, the effects on language of mobility and class can be separated, necessitating a more subtle model that includes a recognition of class-based cultural and attitudinal difference that cuts across network types and life-modes.

2. THE DIALECT LEVELLING PROJECT[2]

To illustrate these points, we present some [. . .] results from an ESRC [Economic and Social Research Council] project [. . .] which aims to elucidate the relationship between social class, demography and geographical distance from London in the promotion of the dialect levelling that is currently taking place in England.

The project has three premises:

1. In areas of high population movement there may be rapid changes in dialect and accent features, including levelling.
2. Membership of a close-knit, stable social network with strong local ties leads to linguistic conformity (i.e. not 'stepping out of line') and inhibits change.
3. Language change is most visible through the comparison of teenage language with (a) older adults' speech and (b) the speech of younger children.

The three English towns [Milton Keynes, Reading and Hull] chosen for the research differed in terms of the amount of inmigration they had experienced over the past 30 years and in their distance from London, which is held to be the origin of many of the phonological changes in English regional varieties today (see Table 25.1). [We focus here on Milton Keynes and Reading.] Our expectation was that the greater amount of social mobility in Milton Keynes, and consequent absence of close social networks, would correlate with more rapid dialect levelling than would be the case in Reading with its more stable population.

Choice of districts within each town

A major part of the research was the targeting of not one, but two districts in each town which corresponded to what might be roughly termed 'working class' and 'middle class' areas. The aim was to test the Milroys' assertion that more affluent groups would have qualitatively different network patterns from the less affluent. The initial selection of the districts was based mainly on our own detailed local knowledge of each town. Having chosen the districts, schools were then approached.

Table 25.1 Summary of demographic characteristics of Hull, Reading and Milton Keynes

	New town?	Close to London?	Pop. 1991	Pop. change 1981–91
Hull	no	no (340 km)	254,000	−8.7%
Reading	no	yes (60 km)	129,000 (not counting Wokingham)	−5.1% (an increase with Wokingham added)
Milton Keynes	yes, founded 1967 (pop. 44,000)	yes (70 km)	176,000	+39.2%

3. DEMOGRAPHIC DIFFERENCES BETWEEN OLD AND NEW TOWNS

[. . .] [I]nterviews and group discussions [were] conducted with 32 adolescents (8 boys and 8 girls from working class and middle class schools) in each town, as well as with elderly residents and young children. The adolescents read word lists and took part in discussions on linguistic issues. Information was collected on their lifestyles, in-school and out-of-school activities, family contacts, friendship patterns, tastes in music, magazines, clothes, sporting activities, and perceptions of different groups within the broader teenage culture. [. . .]

[. . .] [T]he middle class families have a good deal in common in that few of the parental generation were born in the town where they now live. These parents, almost all of whom were in the professions and senior managerial positions, had moved to Milton Keynes or Reading for work-related reasons. Most had higher education [. . .]. Few had extended family living locally. Such families would be typical of Højrup's life-mode 3.

In contrast, the Reading working class school is in an area where family ties are evidently closely maintained. The housing estate where it is located was developed from the 1920s onwards as an area with a high concentration of social housing. [. . .] This particular council estate could be seen as solidly life-mode 2 with some life-mode 1 families interspersed.

What can be said about the Milton Keynes working-class areas? [. . .] In a previous paper (Williams & Kerswill 1997), we discussed the low level of social cohesion and the high level of geographical mobility of the families studied. For example, we noted statements such as the following (taken from interviews with the mothers of the children we recorded):

> 'It took me about two years to even speak to someone. After the first year I was cracking up. I just wanted to go back. I hated it. Nobody had been born in Milton Keynes. Everybody had come from somewhere else. You had them from every-where – London, Scotland, Ireland. And if you didn't come down with them . . . they stuck to their own groups.'

[. . .]

We also noted the great willingness with which some people moved: while almost all families had moved at least once within Milton Keynes, three families had moved six, seven and nine times, respectively.

Despite this apparent lack of social cohesion, there was another tendency, albeit found among a minority of the families in our sample. This was the practice of moving to Milton Keynes as an extended family, with two adult generations, or perhaps siblings, moving together. These people were able to reproduce the family support mechanisms of their former home towns, the lack of which was noted by other people we interviewed.

Despite this presence of this practice, the picture of working-class Milton Keynes life is different both from middle-class life-styles in Milton Keynes and working-class life-styles in Reading, a fact which makes it difficult to fit this group into [one of Højrup's] life-modes. What the Milton Keynes working-class group does share with the middle-class groups, however, is an orientation towards people and places elsewhere – usually, home town and kin. Like the life-mode 3 professionals, they have moved considerable distances to live where they are now – although the motivation was usually better housing, not better employment prospects. Again, like life-mode 3 people, they do not seem to form close-knit territorially bounded groups with mutual dependency. However, [. . .] [i]n terms of occupation, they belong mostly to life-mode 2. Yet the formation of close-knit networks seems not to occur [. . .]. Thus, we have an economically deprived life-mode 2 group who seem to prefer the geographical mobility and the loose network patterns typical of people in life-mode 3.

This type of social network is common to migrants everywhere (Kerswill 1994), and as such should not surprise us. It is one which, if the Milroys' thesis is right, will lead to an openness to language change. We now consider some preliminary results.

4. LEVELLING VS. CONSERVATISM IN MILTON KEYNES AND READING

We begin by considering the vowel (aɪ), which occurs in words like *time*, *night*, etc. In vernacular speech in the south of England, it has a range of variants, including [ɑɪ] (similar to that used in Received Pronunciation, or 'RP'), [ɒɪ], [ɑɪ], [ɔɪ], [ʌɪ] and [ʌɪ]. There are also variants with a lengthened first element, which could be transcribed [ɑˑɪ], and a monophthongal [ɑ:] – both the latter associated with vernacular London speech. Table 25.2 shows the distribution of these variants in the speech of working-class subjects [. . .].

The table does not show that many of the teenagers' vowels have the lengthened onset characteristic of London (a point that could be investigated instrumentally). However, the most striking feature is the rather small overlap between the distributions of the older [native-born residents of Milton Keynes] and younger speakers; we return to this apparent lack of continuity below.

Table 25.3 shows the distribution of the same variants in Reading. By contrast with Milton Keynes, we see that there is rather little evidence of change over two generations. The predominant variant is a fully back, diphthongal [ɑɪ], with a small number of fronted and a larger number of back-raised variants. These variants are sometimes stereotyped as

Table 25.2   Percentage use of variants of (aɪ), Milton Keynes working-class group (interview with fieldworker)

	[ɑɪ]	[ɒɪ]	[ɑɪ]	[ɔɪ]	[ʌɪ]	[ʌɪ]
Girls (n=8)	25	45	29	1	–	–
Boys (n=8)	1	38	60	–	–	–
Elderly (n=4)	–	–	24	57	15	3

Table 25.3   Percentage use of variants of (aɪ), Reading working-class group (interview with fieldworker)

	[ɑɪ]	[ɒɪ]	[ɑɪ]	[ɔɪ]	[ʌɪ]	[ʌɪ]
Girls (n=8)	3	21	45	21	4	5
Boys (n=8)	1	19	64	14	3	–
Elderly (n=4)	–	12	48	22	2	16

'rural' in the south of England, and contribute to the perception of the Reading accent as coming from much further west, and therefore supposedly rural, than it does.

We turn now to (aʊ), as in *round*, *house*, *now*, which, unlike (aɪ), shows strong evidence of undergoing rapid levelling in southern England generally, with the attrition of regional variants in favour of the RP-like [aʊ]. Tables 25.4 and 25.5 show the distribution of variants found in our Milton Keynes and Reading samples, respectively.

For both towns, there is a near-categorical shift away from a localised form to a non-localised, standard-like one – a clear and dramatic instance of dialect levelling. [. . .] However, there is a crucial difference between the two towns: while the shift for (aʊ) is (we believe) total in Milton Keynes, this is not so in the working-class district of Reading, where perhaps 10 per cent of the children *occasionally* use the old variants. This difference is easily explainable in terms of differences in network structure, along the lines discussed earlier. [. . .] In new towns, there is no continuity across generations. This is clearly true of Milton Keynes: most youngsters there have no family contact with elderly native residents of the area, while this is not at all true of Reading, where we often find three generations living on the same estate.

The figures as presented above in fact obscure two other patterns. The first is that, in the intermediate generation of people native to the Milton Keynes area (those born between the 1940s and 1960s), the variant [æʊ], virtually absent in the oldest and youngest speakers, is the single most common variant (see Kerswill & Williams 1994: 22; Kerswill 1996b). Clearly factors we are not in a position to discover at the moment are at work. The second observation is that the transcription [aʊ] subsumes a number of potentially distinct variants. One of these we believe to be both innovative and socio-linguistically salient. The possibly new variant is a fully back [ɑu], or even [ɔu]. We noted it in both Milton Keynes and Reading, and we would speculate that it is used more by white children whose friendship groups include young people of African Caribbean origin.

Finally, we can mention two as yet unquantified observations relating to the vowels of Milton Keynes and Reading. The first concerns the vowel (ʌ), as in *cup*. [. . .] We have noted some very back variants in both towns, but especially in Milton Keynes. [. . .] The back vowel is, we believe, an innovation and, like the back variant of (aʊ), may be associated with peer groups which include African Caribbean speakers. [. . .]

Table 25.4   Percentage use of variants of (aʊ), Milton Keynes, interview style

	[ɛː]	[aːə]	[æʊ]	[aʊ]	[ɛʊ]	[ɛɪ]
Girls (n=8)	–	6	5	89	–	–
Boys (n=8)	–	12	4	83	–	–
Elderly (n=4)	10	–	1	–	63	26

Table 25.5   Percentage use of variants of (aʊ), Reading, interview style

	[ɛː]	[aːə]	[æʊ]	[aʊ]	[ɛʊ]	[ɛɪ]
Girls (n=8)	–	8	–	90	–	2
Boys (n=8)	–	6	–	87	4	3
Elderly (n=4)	3	–	4	1	53	38

The second observation concerns a conservative trait of Reading speech. This is a central pronunciation of /ɑ:/ in words like *last, bath, park*. This is fairly prevalent in the Reading teenagers' speech, who will often say [lɑ̈:s nɔɪʔ] for *last night*. Strangely, the fronting is less pronounced among the elderly speakers: it is almost as though this feature has been seized upon as a marker of local identity by the young – though we have no evidence yet that this is so.

5. CONCLUSION: SOCIAL NETWORK AND CLASS CULTURE AS INDEPENDENT INFLUENCES ON LANGUAGE CHANGE

In our previous project, we suggested that a number of phonological variables show evidence of levelling in Milton Keynes. For some features, especially vowels, the levelling is towards an RP-like norm; for others, especially consonants, it is towards a generalised southern non-standard norm. We suggested at the time that these results were due to (1) the mutual accommodation that comes about in a demographic melting-pot such as this, and (2) the continued contact that the town has had with other places since its initial establishment. The results we have presented in this article confirm these findings. The comparison of Milton Keynes with Reading allows us to say with more certainty that it is open networks with many links to people elsewhere that allow the levelling to take place.

But to return to the title of the paper: we believe that the data shows that mobility and social class are two separate influences. On the basis of the Reading data only, one might conclude that high mobility and low social class are mutually exclusive: both the social and the linguistic data are consistent with this conclusion. [. . .] The tendency towards non-regional norms perceptible in the working-class Milton Keynes youngsters, however, should not be over-estimated. In this group, non-RP phonology is still the norm, as is non-standard grammar. This occurs *despite* the open, looseknit networks with many contacts outside the town that are contracted by the Milton Keynes working-class subjects. We must then ask why non-standard forms persist in the speech of Milton Keynes youngsters as strongly as they do. We believe there is a difference in culture: ethnographic interviews with youngsters of both classes in both these towns and in Hull suggest a strong class awareness (Kerswill & Williams 1997). In fact, the main divide they perceived was 'class', with strong statements being made by the working-class teenagers against 'posh' people. Within such working-class families, mobility does not imply an openness to standardisation, despite the Milroys' claim: class-based cultural differences concerning literacy as well as relationships with schools, authorities and employers may be maintained in a migrant population such as that in Milton Keynes. Thus, we would like to argue that class-based norms directly affect a person's willingness to adopt standard English and RP pronunciations, without the necessary mediation of networks.

A life-mode analysis is clearly very useful; however, the link that the Milroys make between class and network is possibly more subtle than they had supposed. Class-based culture can have a direct effect on standardisation, quite independently of mobility and open networks.

REFERENCES

Højrup, T. (1983). The concept of life-mode: a form-specifying mode of analysis applied to contemporary western Europe. *Ethnologia Scandinavica* 1: 1–50.

Kerswill, P. E. (1993). Rural dialect speakers in an urban speech community: the role of dialect contact in defining a sociolinguistic concept. *International Journal of Applied Linguistics* 3: 33–56.

Kerswill, P. E. (1994). *Dialects Converging: Rural Speech in Urban Norway*. Oxford: Clarendon Press.

Kerswill, P. E. (1996a) Milton Keynes and dialect levelling in south-eastern British English. In D. Graddol, J. Swann and D. Leith (eds.) *English: History, Diversity and Change*. London: Routledge, 292–300.

Kerswill, P. E. (1996b) Divergence and convergence of sociolinguistic structures in Norway and England. *Sociolinguistica* 10: 90–104.

Kerswill, P. E. and A. Williams (1994) A new dialect in a new city: children's and adults' speech in Milton Keynes. Final report presented to the Economic and Social Research Council.

Kerswill, P. E. and A. Williams (1997) Investigating social and linguistic identity in three British schools. In U.-B. Kotsinas, A.-B. Stenström and A.-M. Malin (eds.) *Ungdomsspråk i Norden. Föredrag från ett forskarsymposium [Youth language in the Nordic countries. Papers from a research symposium]*. Series: MINS, No. 43. Stockholm: University of Stockholm, Department of Nordic Languages and Literature. 159–176.

Kerswill, P. E. and A. Williams (2000) Creating a new town koine: children and language change in Milton Keynes. *Language in Society* 29: 65–115.

Milroy, L. and J. Milroy (1992) Social network and social class: toward an integrated sociolinguistic model. *Language in Society* 21: 1–26.

Trudgill, P. (1986) *Dialects in Contact*. Oxford: Blackwell.

Williams, A. and P. Kerswill (1997) Investigating dialect change in an English new town. In Alan Thomas (ed.) *Issues and Methods in Dialectology*. Bangor: Department of Linguistics, University of Wales, Bangor. 46–54.

NOTES

1. This article is also published in *Cuadernos de Filología Inglesa*, vol. 8, 1999.
2. 'The role of adolescents in dialect levelling': 1995–98. ESRC ref. R000236180, award holders A. Williams, P. Kerswill and J. Cheshire. Research Fellows A. Williams and A. Gillett.

QUESTIONS

Content

1. What kinds of social networks are said to inhibit (or, conversely, promote) change?
2. What is *(dialect) levelling*?
3. To what extent do the working class kids in Milton Keynes and Reading behave the same? How are they different?

1. Kerswill & Williams claim that "the least powerful" need to maintain strong networks "for survival".

    a. What do you think they mean by "survival"?
    b. Do you agree that "the most powerful" groups need strong networks for reasons other than this?

2. How do Højrup's life modes compare with other measures of social class?
3. Kerswill & Williams's final conclusion is that "class-based norms directly affect a person's willingness to adopt standard English … without the necessary mediation of networks". Does this amount to the same thing as their earlier comment that the persistence of non-standard varieties is because they function as "badges of identity"?

Chapter 26

Terttu Nevalainen

MAKING THE BEST USE OF 'BAD' DATA: EVIDENCE FOR SOCIOLINGUISTIC VARIATION IN EARLY MODERN ENGLISH

1. INTRODUCTION

OVER THE LAST FORTY years, modern sociolinguists have established a number of external factors that correlate with linguistic innovations and processes of language change. They include [. . .] the age, social status and gender of the speaker [. . .].

As the study of language change largely falls within the purview of language history, sociolinguistic findings also provide testable hypotheses for language historians. [. . .] Historical linguists assume that human languages in the past were not in any principled way different from those spoken today. [. . .]

Even if possible in theory, extending sociolinguistics into the past has its limits. Historical sociolinguists will have to face the fact that their data are preserved only randomly and, what is more, that they are only indirectly related to everyday spoken communication, which is the primary source of modern research. The sociolinguist William Labov (1972, 1994) gives these material limitations the collective label of 'the bad-data problem'. [. . .][1]

In this article I explore the perspectives of English historical sociolinguistics in later stages of the language with a particular focus on the Early Modern period. My aim is to evaluate the relevance to long-term language change of two speaker variables: social status and gender. The empirical analysis proceeds from a small network of five individuals and extends to the evolving supraregional language community at large. The time period examined spans from the sixteenth to the seventeenth century. My data are drawn from the electronic *Corpus of Early English Correspondence*, the 1998 version of which covers the period from 1417 to 1681.[. . .] [Two] 16th-century morphosyntactic changes are discussed in quantitative terms.

Source: Nevalainen, Terttu (1999) Making the best of 'bad' data. *Neuphilologische Mitteilungen* 100: 499–533.

[One] of them, the spread of -(E)s in the third-person singular present indicative [is] associated in the literature with the spoken idiom in that [it was] first diffused in informal contexts of language use. The other [. . .], the generalization of simple over multiple negation [. . .] appear[s] to have spread from more formal contexts of language use and been associated with written rather than spoken registers. The difference between these two kinds of change may be related to, but need not be identical with, the distinction between changes 'from below' and changes 'from above' the level of social awareness that are identified by modern sociolinguists (Labov 1994: 78).

The results obtained indicate that present-day generalizations on the leading role of the intermediate social ranks and women in language change can partly be replicated for Early Modern English. Differences also emerge, however [. . .].

2. SOCIOLINGUISTICS AND LANGUAGE HISTORY

2.1 Sociolinguistics

[. . .]

Understanding language change is [. . .] one of the major goals that present-day socio-linguists set for themselves. One of the principal tenets of sociolinguists like Labov (1972, 1994) has long been that the present could be used to explain the past. It is argued that, as living languages continually vary and change in patterned ways, the principles of language change could be arrived at by studying the present. However, from a language historian's point of view, it is equally evident that present-day sociolinguistics cannot replace the study of linguistic variation in the past in its own right. In order to reconstruct actual processes of language change in their social contexts we need to combine the two approaches.

2.2 Language history and social history

One of my main arguments in this paper is that sociolinguistics generates testable hypotheses for language historians. Historical linguists do not in general expect human languages in the past to have been in any principled way different in terms of their structural potential from those spoken today. Historical sociolinguists similarly promote the uniformitarian principle to an axiom of sociolinguistic reconstruction.

[. . .]

The principle should not, however, be interpreted naively or simplistically. It does not justify a simple projection of modern social variables such as social class onto the past, any more than it implies that the same variables could be generalized across the board today. Analyses of social stratification in New York City or Norwich would hardly be appropriate for the study of an African metropolis or a small village in the north of Europe. Similarly, the social conditions of preindustrial societies obviously differed from those operating today. The social variables referred to by historical sociolinguists should therefore be based on an independent reconstruction of past societies (see Nevalainen and Raumolin-Brunberg 1989, Nevalainen 1996a, Raumolin-Brunberg 1996).

Just as modern sociolinguists have access to the research carried out by sociologists, historical sociolinguists will consult social historians. Not infrequently, this means adopting new concepts for testing the relevance of constructs such as social stratification in language change. If we want to find out whether social status correlated with language use in the past, we need to explore the extent to which a given society was hierarchically structured. To refer, for instance, to the middle classes in early modern England (1500–1700) without asking whether such notions are applicable to preindustrial societies, would be, as Wrightson (1994: 51) points out, anachronistic. Such constructs as social order are, of course, no less problematic in social history than they are in sociology today (Burke 1992: 58). The best that historical sociolinguists can do is to draw on models that have met with a certain level of consensus among social historians and historical sociologists (see 4.1).

2.3 The 'bad-data' problem

As pointed out above, historical sociolinguists are faced with the problem that their texts are preserved randomly and are only indirectly associated with typical spoken interaction. However, these shortcomings are described by William Labov (1994) as only part of the language historian's 'bad-data' problem. The other half of the problem, equally serious according to Labov, is concerned with the accessibility of social information prerequisite for historical sociolinguistics:

> Historical linguistics can then be thought of as the art of making the best use of bad data. The art is a highly developed one, but there are some limitations of the data that cannot be compensated for. Except for very recent times, no phonetic records are available for instrumental measurements. We usually know very little about the social position of the writers and not much more about the social structure of the community. Though we know what was written, we know nothing about what was understood, and we are in no position to perform controlled experiments on crossdialectal comprehension. (Labov 1994: 11)

While Labov's views are for the most part valid, he partly overstates his case. First, thanks to the empirical work done on historical genre variation over the last twenty years, much more is now known about the relationship between speech-like and literate texts than twenty-five years ago, when these problems were first considered. [. . .] Second, [. . .] it is not true [. . .] that the social position of individual writers was unknown. Even [. . .] where this is the case, the basic social structure of the speech community may often be successfully reconstructed on the basis of information provided by social historians (see section 4.1).

Although sociohistorical reconstruction may not be possible with all changes and all periods, where available, it can throw new light on a number of linguistic processes, some of which may still be in progress today. [. . .]

3. ENGLISH HISTORICAL SOCIOLINGUISTICS: SOURCES AND APPROACHES

3.1 Genre variation

The first monograph to apply sociolinguistic methods to language history was Suzanne Romaine's *Socio-historical linguistics* (1982). Empirically, it is a genre analysis of the relative pronoun system in Middle Scots. Genre variation has since then become one of the most researched areas in this field. [. . .]

The external variables besides genre that have been studied using computerized corpora are chronology and variety or dialect. Chronology here represents the important variable of real time, as opposed to apparent time, which is a way of displaying linguistic variation across different age groups at a particular point in time in modern socio-linguistic research. The variable of language variety may comprise either national varieties such as British and Scottish English, or regional variation within a national variety. Genre is, however, the pivotal variable in variation studies, because it also makes it possible for the researcher to chart the progress of a given change in apparent time on a scale of formality or speechlikeness (see Devitt 1989, Biber and Finegan 1997, Kohnen 1997, Rissanen et al. 1997a and b).

[. . .]

3.2 Social variation: a project

It is obvious that the key to understanding the social embedding of language changes in the past is to examine texts that come as close as possible to the day-to-day interaction between people. [. . .] [To this end], a project was launched in 1993 by Dr. Helena Raumolin-Brunberg and myself with the general aim of exploring the extent to which the models of language change suggested by modern sociolinguistics applied to the past.[2]

Our work began by creating a sufficient empirical data-base for the project. The result was a computer-readable corpus, the *Corpus of Early English Correspondence (CEEC)* [. . .]. The corpus contains letters written by 777 people between 1417 and 1681. Most of the writers represent the gentry and the intermediate social groups presented in Figure 26.1 in section 5.3, but the aim of the corpus team has been to establish as balanced a social coverage as possible with the resources available. [. . .]

Personal correspondence is the only interactive text type to supply a wide range of authentic communication from the early 15th century to the present day. Being able to conduct research in real time is one of the true advantages that historical sociolinguists using materials like this have over their colleagues working with present-day data. Also, unlike sociolinguists who interview their informants, language historians need not worry about being involved with the production of their data, the classical Observer's Paradox (Labov 1972: 61; L. Milroy 1987b: 59–60). Tedious though letter-writing must have been even to accustomed writers, it was, at the time of writing, free from the intrusion of a linguistic fieldworker.

This purely methodological point in no way implies that early modern letter writers would not have been mindful of their intended addressees and [. . .] even possible 'overhearers'. We therefore hypothesize that they would have accommodated to their audiences and used an idiom closest to their vernacular whenever addressing their immediate family and personal friends, but moved away from it when dealing with more distant recipients and corresponding in their purely professional capacity. The evidence that has accumulated on register variation in the *CEEC* supports this hypothesis. [. . .]

As to 'overhearers', letter-writing is no different from tape-recordings in that it is further regulated by external constraints that are not typical of everyday spoken inter-action. [. . .] The case in (1a) is a typical one: the addressee is asked to destroy the letter because of its confidential contents. In (1b) the addressee is anticipated, albeit jocularly, to (mis)use her husband's letters on later occasions.

(1a) My lord, I beseech you keep my letters close or burn them; for though I have sorrows, I would no creature should be partaker, nor of knowledge with me. (Honor Lisle 1538 (LISLE) V,319)

(1b) If you could read my lres [letters] your self I would have written largelie of your owne busisenes, And because I will have none acquainted wth them but who you thinke fitt besides your self, I have taken the paines to write it in Romaine hand in this inclosed paper, wch I thinke your self can read. (Anthony Antony 1615 (STOCKWELL) I,37)

Historical sociolinguists working with authentic materials such as letters will also have to accept the social limits of their evidence. Early modern people's ability to write was confined to the higher and intermediate social ranks and to professional men. In (1b), Anthony Antony, Sir Oliver Lambert's London agent, takes recourse to the italic hand ("Romaine hand"), which was easier to read than the professional secretary hand, to make his letter legible to its recipient, Captain Thomas Stockwell. [. . .] Stockwell must have [sometimes] relied on outside help even in his personal business. Antony's communication reveals his awareness of the presence of these outsiders.

4. SOCIAL HIERARCHY AND GENDER IN EARLY MODERN ENGLAND

4.1 Social stratification

All accounts of social stratification in any period will be theory-dependent, and may be expected to vary. One way of approaching the issue in the early modern period is through social historians' transition model of social status in the 16th and 17th centuries. [. . .] [T]he early modern society is more appropriately described with reference to ranks or degrees than to social classes [. . .].

The early modern model, presented in outline in Table 26.1, is based on landowner-ship, income, titles and lifestyle (Laslett 1983: 22–52, Wrightson 1982: 17–38; see also Nevalainen 1996a). It introduces a social hierarchy as a rank scale running from the nobility down to paupers. [. . .] Despite its insensitivity to social mobility and the

Table 26.1   Rank and status in Tudor and Stuart England

Estate	Grade	
GENTRY	**Nobility**	Royalty Duke, Marquess, Earl, Viscount, Baron *Archbishop*, Bishop
	Gentry proper	Baronet (1611–), Knight, Esquire Gentleman
	Professions	Army Officer, Government Official, Lawyer, Medical Doctor, Merchant (in foreign trade), Clergyman, Teacher, etc.
NON-GENTRY	Yeoman, Merchant (in domestic trade), Husbandman, Craftsman, Tradesman, Artificer Labourer, Cottager Pauper	

gradation of status groups in towns, the model may serve as a point of departure for testing the linguistic relevance of social status in the early modern period.

The major dividing line runs between the gentry and the non-gentry. This distinction is based on whether one would earn one's living by manual labour or not. [. . .]

As to social mobility, [. . .] [t]he terms 'social aspirer' and 'social mover' are here [both] used to refer to those professionals who moved up several steps on the social ladder. [. . .]

The position of women in Table 26.1 is derivative. Unmarried women are ranked on the basis of their fathers' status, but married women according to their husbands'. [. . .]

To the early modern people themselves the hierarchy sketched in Table 26.1 appears to have represented some measure of reality. Besides forms of address, seating order in church and placement in ceremonial processions, there were even attempts to regulate the external markers of social status by the Statutes of the Realm. The *Act agaynst Wearing of Costly Apparell*, passed in 1510, gives regulations on the appropriate dress code across the status hierarchy. As the extract in (2) shows, frequent reference was made to the distinction between those '*undre the Degre of a Gentilman*' and those above it.

(2) **AN ACT AGAYNST WEARING OF COSTLY APPARRELL.**

Be it ordeyned by the Auctoritie of this p~sent P~liament that no p~sone of whate estate condic~on or degre that he be use in his apparell eny Cloth of golde of Purpoure Coloure or Sylke of Purpoure Coloure but onely the Kyng the Qwene the Kyng~ Moder the Kyng~ Chylder [. . .] And that noo s~vyng ma~ne undre the Degre of a Gentilman use or were eny Goune or Coote or suche lyke apparrell of more Clothe then too brode yerdes and an halfe in a shorte Gowne and thre brode yerdes in a longe Gowne [. . .] And that no s~vaunte of Husbondy nor Sheparde nor comen Laborer [. . .] were any Clothe wherof the broode yerde passythe in pryce twoo shillyng~ [. . .] uppon payne of imprisonament in the Stokkys by thre days. (*Helsinki Corpus*, E1 STA LAW STKAT3 III,9)

[. . .]

Although the early modern status system is different both from the medieval and the modern ones, I hope to have made the point that a socio-economic hierarchy can be reconstructed for the period. The empirical task for a historical sociolinguist is to study the extent to which such a hierarchy might correlate with language variation and change in Early Modern English.

4.2 Gender

The other speaker variable that I shall use to illustrate the relevance of social variation in language history is *gender*. The choice of term suggests a more complex interpretation of the variable in terms of social practices than the purely biologically determined *sex*. There is no agreement to date as to the complex ways the two may be related (Walsh (ed.) 1997). Recent research, however, strongly suggests that gender identities vary in salience. Eckert and McConnell-Ginet (1998: 490) propose that this variation could be analysed locally in terms of *communities of practice*, i.e. "aggregates of people who come together around mutual engagement of some common endeavour".

Social historians' views of gender roles in the early modern period are similarly varied, depending on the approach adopted, primary sources used, and the social status of those analysed (Hitchcock and Cohen 1999). [. . .]

[. . .] [I]n early modern England an individual's sexual temperament was a question of the balance of bodily humours, independent of the sexual orientation of men and women. Human physiology was described in terms of four humours, but masculinity was associated with the dominance of hot and dry humours and femininity with cold and moist. [. . .] Foyster (1999: 28–31) stresses that femininity and masculinity were, however, always socially constructed. So reason and strength, for instance, the qualities associated with manhood, had to be acquired before they could be asserted to others. On a concrete level, Fletcher (1996: 412), too, concludes that the most far-reaching social differences between men and women in the early modern period derived from education. This point will be developed in 4.4.

The typical social roles that were assigned to men and women in the early modern era were those of breadwinner and head of household for men, and mother and housewife for women (Erickson 1993, Laurence 1994, Eales 1998: 60–85, Mendelson and Crawford 1998: 256–344). On the other hand, not all women were married, and according to some estimates about one fifth of the households in early modern England were headed by women, either widows or spinsters (Capp 1996: 119). [. . .] However, as Mendelson and Crawford (1998: 344) note, social status came from a woman's family position in the social hierarchy, not from her own skills as a professional.

[. . .]

4.3 Sociolinguistic hypotheses

A great deal of research has been carried out on the correlation between linguistic variables and social class over the last forty years (for overviews see L. Milroy 1987a, Chambers 1995). One historically relevant hypothesis that may be drawn from these studies is related to the evolution of standard language and the differences in social network structures of social groups. [. . .] Middle groups [in the social hierarchy] are expected to have more diffuse social networks, which more readily transmit linguistic changes (Milroy and Milroy 1985a, J. Milroy 1992: 211–214). We may therefore ask whether it was also the case in the Early Modern English period that the intermediate ranks were linguistically more innovative than either the very highest or the very lowest social strata.

Anticipating an answer in the affirmative, James and Lesley Milroy (1993: 69) particularly single out the mobile merchant group as an agency of change in earlier English. [. . .] There are, however, writers like H.C. Wyld (1936: 184), who argue that those changes that have made their way into colloquial English, both pronunciation and grammar, in the last one and a half centuries were all introduced from the lower social orders. [. . .]

The role of gender in language variation is another much researched area in present-day sociolinguistics (see Coates (ed.) 1998). [. . .] Labov (1990: 215) [. . .] argues that women are [. . .] often the innovators in changes from below, that is, processes operating below the level of social awareness [but that they also favour more standard forms in changes from above].

A number of different factors have been made to account for women's use of prestige forms. Most of them are, as James (1996: 99) remarks in her review, either social and economic, or related to power and status. [. . .] Working-class women, for instance, may have wider contacts with the standard language and more incentive at work to modify their speech towards it than men (L. Milroy 1987a). By contrast, the power-and-status approach relates to the fact that women are generally granted less status and power than men. By using prestige language forms, women wish to assert their authority and position, and to gain respect (e.g. Eckert 1989, Labov 1990). Avoidance strategies have also been proposed. Gordon (1997) argues that women's conspicuous use of standard-language forms might be related to modern society's double standard regarding sexual behaviour, which affects women more than men. [. . .]

On the other hand, gender is often raised above socio-economic class as a factor accounting for social differences in language use (e.g. Horvath 1985, Milroy and Milroy 1993, Holmes 1997). This is particularly the case with processes of language change, and Labov's (1990) point about change from below being led by women. So James and Lesley Milroy (1993), for instance, find that strictly localized linguistic forms tend to be preferred by males, while the high-frequency variants employed by females typically gain a supra-local status. Lesley Milroy (1998) [. . .] argues that men's heavier use of non-standard forms may be related to male susceptibility to peer constraint, "[. . .] they must not innovate because they fear the consequences" [. . .] [Milroy 1998: 375]

In historical sociolinguistics it remains to be seen whether women and men differ systematically with respect to language change or not. There are social factors suggesting that this could indeed be the case. As Eckert (1989: 255) points out, the domestication of female labour involves a clear division of roles, with men engaged in the public market-place and women's activities focused on the private, domestic sphere. This is also largely true of women in the early modern era, and suggests that their access to many aspects of the evolving standard language may have been restricted.

A direct comparison between the present and the early modern period will, however, be complicated by two facts. First, although emphasis on the polarization of social roles may be appropriate, the separate-spheres model ignores those public spheres where women's presence was prominent, and contribution to conversations central: in the street, in taverns, at the market, at church, and — in the case of noblewomen — at the Court. [. . .] The second point is a linguistic one: in an earlier period such as the early modern there was no stable linguistic norm that could be called a fully-fledged standard language. Although supralocal usages spread in all areas of grammar, the norms of the evolving standard variety were far from fixed (Nevalainen, 2000a).

Lesley Milroy's point about gender socialization and peer constraint may, however, be a relevant one in the early modern context as well. It is argued by Capp (1996: 130) and Foyster (1999: 58) that the early modern man's reputation always depended upon the opinion of others. [. . .] At the same time, one may note that the sexual double standard was much harsher on women than on men, which presumably made women no less susceptible to public opinion.

Whether gender differences are approached through traditional gender roles, mobility or social control, Eckert's (1989: 247) general point remains valid: "there is no apparent reason to believe that there is a simple, constant relation between gender and [linguistic] variation". Nevertheless, the gender hypothesis remains worth further testing with historical material. It may also be connected with the social status hypothesis discussed above. Considered together, they form a two-part research question focusing on the evolution of the standard language. We may assume either (1) that, to the extent they are relevant, the variables of social status and gender work independently from each other in language change, or (2) that their effects are combined. The first part of the question would predict, for instance, that future standard language norms were first diffused by women, regardless of social status. The second implies more complicated scenarios, basically, that women of the middling ranks were in the vanguard of linguistic change.

4.4 Constraints of literacy

In order to test the role of gender differentiation in language change, historical socio-linguists will, first of all, have to come to terms with the unequal representation of men and women in their primary data. As emphasized in the research on literacy in Renaissance England, women's average level of education and therefore their ability to write was much lower than men's. Even high-ranking women could not receive the same formal education as men.

[. . .]

However, general literacy figures tend to conceal the extent of social and regional variation in reading and writing skills. The division between the gentry and the non-gentry also surfaces in this case. While evidence shows that the overall literacy of women in the 17th century lagged considerably behind that of men, it is fairly safe to assume that the gentry, both women and men, could by this time read and write (see Cressy 1980: 141–174, Heal and Holmes 1994: 252–254, Jewell 1998: 146–154).

5. TESTING THE HYPOTHESES

5.1 The data

The *Corpus of Early English Correspondence* makes it possible to study a number of female correspondents even before 1600. Although secretaries and amanuenses [*Eds: 'scribes'*] were often used by these women, they also provide a fair amount of material [written by their own hand]. One of these writers is Sabine Johnson, the wife of John Johnson, a London wool merchant. Writing in the 1540s and '50s, Sabine Johnson's generation are mostly in their late twenties and early thirties (Winchester 1955). Their circle is well represented in the corpus, and will serve as a useful point of departure for analysing the language community at large. Their usage will be compared with the rest of the speaker-writers in the *CEEC* (1996 and 1998 versions; see Nevalainen and Raumolin-Brunberg (eds). 1996).

Table 26.2 in 5.2 compares Sabine Johnson with her immediate family, her husband John Johnson and brother-in-law Otwell Johnson. John was a merchant of the Staple and mostly active in London and Calais, while Otwell lived and worked in London. Two other people were added to the table for the sake of comparison, Anthony Cave and Richard Preston. Anthony Cave represents the older generation. He was a wealthy merchant of the Staple and had been John Johnson's master. Richard Preston was John Johnson's servant, and would come under the non-gentry in Table. 26.1. [. . .] Sabine Johnson, *née* Saunders, and Anthony Cave were both natives of Northamptonshire, whereas the Johnson brothers were born in Calais and apprenticed in London (Winchester 1955: 23–26).

5.2 Morphological changes: the Johnson circle

In order to test the sociolinguistic hypotheses [implicit in section 4] above, I shall present quantitative data on [two] morphosyntactic changes that were in progress or completed in the 16th century. These [. . .] were selected because they were all gradually becoming the property of a nationwide language community. Its written norms were reinforced by the print culture, officialdom and the system of education (J. Milroy 1992: 129–130). [Both] features were later codified as part of Standard English, and therefore serve as useful test cases for the study of gender and status differences in language change in the era before prescriptive grammar (Nevalainen, 2000a).

[. . .]

The [first] case is the transition from -(E)TH to -(E)s in the third-person singular present indicative. The sibilant form -(E)s was first attested in the Northumbrian dialect in the tenth century, both in the plural and in the singular. The form continued to predominate in the north in the 15th century, but also spread rapidly to the south in the course of the 16th century [Kytö 1993]. The process was practically completed in the course of the 17th century (Holmqvist 1922, Nevalainen and Raumolin-Brunberg, 2000). An example of the two variant forms by Sabine Johnson is given in (3). With two verbs, HAVE and DO, the recessive suffix -(E)TH prevailed longer than in other verbs. Both auxiliary and main verb forms of the two are excluded from the figures in Table 26.2.[3]

Table 26.2   The frequency of occurrence (%) of -(E)s and single negation in the Johnson family circle 1542–53 (*CEEC* 1996; for absolute figures, see the Appendix)

Frequency of use (%)	-(E)s (%) v. -(E)TH*	Single NEG (%) v. Multiple NEG
100%	Richard Preston	
90%		
80%		Anthony Cave
70%		
		Otwell Johnson
60%		John Johnson
		Richard Preston
50%		
40%	**Sabine Johnson**	
30%		**Sabine Johnson**
20%	Anthony Cave	
10%	John Johnson	
	Otwell Johnson	
0%		

(* excluding DO and HAVE)

(3) To apont the tyme, it **lyes** not in me, and whether it shal be befor Whetsontyd or after, Our Lord **knowth**, for I stand in doutt, wherefore I moest hartely desyre you to make all the sped hom that you can. (Sabine Johnson 1546 (JOHNSON) 673)

The [second] process examined is the decline of multiple negation. The process was well under way in the 15th century (Mustanoja 1960:340), and nearly completed in the standard language in the 17th (Barber 1976: 283). In this study, the linguistic variable of multiple negation is constructed so as to include all instances of multiple negation and those of single negation where multiple negation would have been possible, i.e., nonassertive environments involving an item from the ANY-paradigm [*Eds: anyone, any-thing etc.*] (Nevalainen 1998). Examples (4) and (5) illustrate the typical case that one and the same person could show both multiple and single negation side by side in the mid-16th century. One of the syntactic environments to preserve multiple negation later than others is the co-ordinate structure with NOR shown in (5).

(4) Har answar was that she wold **not** set har myend to **no** man tell she was delyvered and choirched, and than as God shall provyde for har; sayng it is but a whyell sense har husbond dyed, and that she thought **no** man wold by so hasty to move **any** setche thyng to har, . . . (Sabine Johnson 1545 (JOHNSON) 396)

(5) Of Mr. Wilmotte's mater I nede **not** to write **anything** that I have lerned by Ambrose aforesayd, . . . for all the Streat will **no**[t] so serve him, **nor no** man ellis: (Otwell Johnson 1544 (JOHNSON) 127)

[. . .]

Table 26.2 shows that Sabine Johnson's usage is more advanced than most of the others' in [. . .] the generalization [. . .] of -(E)s in the third-person singular indicative (for numerical details, see the Appendix). [. . .] Richard Preston leads -(E)s generalization, but Sabine Johnson comes next. [. . .] [H]er husband John and Anthony Cave are less advanced. At the same time Sabine Johnson appears more conservative than the others in the case of the incoming single negation as opposed to multiple negation [. . .]. Despite their differences in age and background, the four men largely agree on the use of single negation [. . .].

5.3 Change from below: -(e)th v. -(e)s

[. . .]

-(E)TH v. -(E)S. The case of the third-person singular present indicative is intriguing. Register variation does not explain the choice of variants in the merchant circle: there is almost none to speak of (Nevalainen, 2000a). We shall therefore return to the corpus for more data to find out whom Sabine Johnson and Richard Preston, in particular, were aligned with. Figure 26.1 presents the social stratification of the incoming form -(E)s in the *CEEC* in 1540–59. Only male writers are included; they represent the entire country, but only a few of them come from the North and East Anglia. HAVE and DO, both auxiliary and main verb, have been excluded from the figures.

It appears from Figure 26.1 that in the 1540s and '50s -(E)s was preferred by the non-professional non-gentry, men like Richard Preston in the Johnson circle. The incoming suffix must therefore have spread from below at least in the sense that it was promoted by people below the gentry line, whose use of -(E)s significantly differed from the rest (p < .0001). Professionals, whose category here includes the lower clergy, by contrast particularly disfavoured the incoming form, as did social aspirers, including Thomas Cromwell, the 1st Earl of Essex, Stephen Gardiner, the Bishop of Winchester, and William Paget, Lord Paget of Beaudesert. These upwardly mobile men all had non-gentry origins but reached the top of early modern English society. It looks as though -(E)s might have been marked as colloquial or even stigmatized in the mid-16th century, and was therefore avoided by those who wished to dissociate themselves from the lower ranks. [. . .]

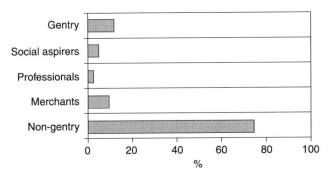

Figure 26.1 The use of -(E)s (%) as opposed to -(E)TH in the third-person singular in the whole corpus in 1540–59, excluding HAVE and DO (*CEEC* 1998, male writers).

The point to be noted here is that Sabine Johnson did not belong to the lower social orders herself. She was the wife of a reasonably well-to-do merchant. To throw some more light on the issue we could continue at the microlevel and construct her social networks in more detail. We could, for instance, compare her with her four brothers. Two of them, Ambrose and Blaise Saunders, were apprenticed as merchants, but Robert had studied law and Laurence was a clergyman. Only Ambrose Saunders used the -(E)s form to any extent, and even his frequency is extremely low, a mere 4% of the cases (3 times -(E)s as opposed to 64 times -(E)TH). This is at the same level as John and Otwell Johnson's usage.

One more argument, that of regional influence, could be advanced to distinguish Sabine Johnson's usage from her male next of kin. But the conclusion remains the same: if her usage reflected her native Central Midland origins, where -(E)s is likely to have occurred in the colloquial language at the time (Holmqvist 1922: 138–147), then her more educated brothers did not share this norm in their private correspondence, nor did Anthony Cave. However, Sabine Johnson was aligned with the other women writers in that -(E)s was generally more frequent in female than in male letters of the time (Nevalainen, 2000b).

The incoming form was gaining acceptance fairly rapidly in London, as can be seen from Figure 26.2. It presents the frequencies of -(E)s out of all inflected cases of the third-person singular present indicative twenty years later, 1580–1599. Only male writers are included here from the ranks of the nobility, gentry, and non-gentry. Their scores can be contrasted with Queen Elizabeth I's usage of the variable in her autograph letters to King James VI (1584–1596), shown at the top of the diagram. The Queen's score comes close to that of Robert Dudley, the Earl of Leicester, who here represents the hereditary nobility. Statistically, Queen Elizabeth differs significantly only from William Cecil, the 1st Lord Burghley, who was a social mover. Cecil's letters, both secretarial copies and autograph, interestingly contain no more than 1% of -(E)s (variable total = 163). As Queen Elizabeth did not restrict her use of -(E)s to her private correspondence but used it in her published work, we may assume that the form must have by now been regarded as an acceptable one in London, even in the highest circles.

[. . .]

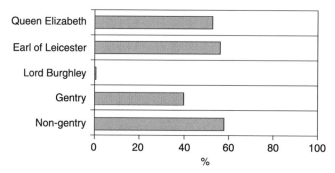

Figure 26.2 The use of -(E)s (%) as opposed to -(E)TH in the third-person singular in London in 1580–99, excluding HAVE and DO (*CEEC* 1998).

5.4 Change from above: multiple v. single negation

[. . .]

Multiple v. single negation. As appears from Table 3, the [. . .] process that Sabine Johnson did not promote was the replacement of multiple negation by the nonassertive NOT . . . ANY paradigm in the 16th century. If we compare male and female usage more generally, the results suggest a consistent trend aligned with gender. Figure 26.3 presents the distribution of multiple negation according to gender in the 16th and 17th centuries in the *CEEC*. In all three subperiods the disappearance of multiple negation was promoted by men. The difference between men and women is statistically significant in all three periods. These findings, therefore, again do not agree with what one would expect on the basis of present-day English, where women tend to favour standard language forms.

However, as the large majority of the women in the *CEEC* come from the upper ranks, the nobility and the gentry, social status differences should also be considered in the analysis. It will therefore be interesting to contrast noble- and gentlewomen's use of multiple negation with the average male usage in different ranks. The overall trends found in the *CEEC* in the 16th and 17th centuries are shown in Figure 26.4. The figure indicates that the social strata with the highest frequencies of multiple negation throughout the period are the upper ranks, the nobility and the gentry, on the one hand, and, more noticeably, what are called the lower ranks, on the other. This numerically under-represented category consists of the lowest ranks that we have access to, that is, the non-professional people below the gentry who could write.

By contrast, the people who lead the process of change from multiple to single negation belong to the ranks of professionals, the more substantial merchants, and social aspirers. The aspirers were born either to a rank below the gentry or the lower gentry but had highly successful professional careers and were raised to the peerage, either temporal or spiritual. Figure 26.4 shows that in the 16th century multiple negation was particularly avoided by men who were accustomed to communicating in writing, and were influenced

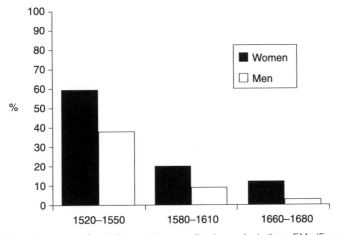

Figure 26.3   Relative frequency of multiple negation according to gender in three EModE periods: 1520–50, 1580–1610 and 1660–80 (*CEEC* 1998 and Supplement).

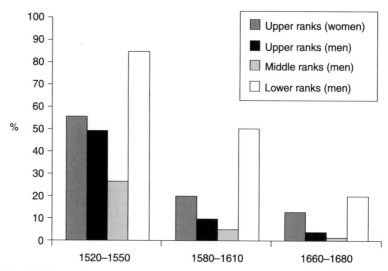

Figure 26.4   Multiple negation according to social rank. Upper ranks: royalty, nobility, gentry; middle ranks: professionals, merchants, social aspirers; lower ranks: other ranks below the gentry (*CEEC* 1998 and Supplement).

by the officialese of their time in their professional capacity. These results are supported by the fact that multiple negation was increasingly absent from the legal language of the day [. . .]. As to linguistic conditioning, my data in Nevalainen (1998) show that coordinate structures were the last to preserve multiple negation. No major differences could, however, be detected in the way the different syntactic environments correlated with the social rank order.

Statistically, the three male status groups presented in Figure 26.4 differ significantly from each other in the first subperiod (1520–50). Differences between the upper and middle groups even out in the second (1580–1610), where professional men come close to completing the change. The third subperiod (1660–80) in Figure 26.4 indicates that the change has nearly reached its completion in the first two social categories, whereas multiple negation to some extent still persists among the lower ranks. However, the data in the third category are scarce; it is included here merely because it is indicative of what we know about the social embedding of multiple negation in the 18th century (Knorrek 1938), and, for that matter, today.

Analysing the gender data in Figure 26.4 more closely, we find that the upper-rank women do not significantly differ from the highest status group men, the nobility and the gentry, in the first period. However, a significant difference between them emerges in the second period. Although the change is nearing its completion in the third period, the difference persists. As might be expected, the upper-rank women also differ significantly from the men in the middle ranks, who lead the change in all three subperiods, but they do not differ from the lower-ranking men. This pattern was anticipated by Sabine Johnson, herself a member of the middle group. Regardless of rank, women did not lead the process towards simple negation in the 16th and 17th centuries [. . .].

6. DISCUSSION

What do these results tell us about gender differentiation and real-time language change? [. . .] [T]he changes in progress studied here later found their way into Standard English. It is therefore obvious, first of all, that Sabine Johnson's usage does not unequivocally meet the expectations [. . .] of women tending to adopt standard forms more readily than men. Before beginning to look for idiolectal explanations for the differences, however, we need to consider the qualification Labov (1990: 213) adds to his Principle 1: "for women to use standard norms that differ from everyday speech, they must have access to those norms". [. . .] One reason for the discrepancy between our expectations and the Johnson data may indeed be a merchant's wife's limited or delayed access to forms of language that were chiefly propagated by professional networks, or through the written medium.

This was also more generally the case of women in the 16th century. The unequal educational opportunities which were directly reflected in the amount of writing produced by women were referred to in 4.4. [. . .] Although some individual women may have reached remarkable levels of academic achievement, these high achievers came from unusual circumstances (Jewell 1998: 11–12).

[. . .] What historical sociolinguists will therefore need to distinguish are innovations coming 'from below' and those coming 'from above'. Processes that spread from colloquial spoken interaction, and often below the level of social awareness, originate 'from below', and those that derive from the professional registers of educated people, 'from above'. The latter may include conscious borrowing from other speech communities (Labov 1994: 78). This distinction refines the working hypotheses presented in 4.3. by introducing the type of sociolinguistic process as one factor in language standardization and change. It further brings to the fore James's (1996) market-forces and social-network explanations for gender differences in this period.

As we have seen, early modern women were also active in adopting forms of language that were later codified as Standard English. If Labov's (1990:215) Principle 2 ("in change from below, women are most often the innovators") is not restricted to sound-changes and holds for the past, we may more generally assume that the vernacular features that found their way into Standard English *were* promoted by women. However, the role played by social rank in the diffusion of these changes should not be ignored. In the section of the male population accessible to us, it is those under the gentry-professionals line who seem to have been the first to spread a feature like the third-person singular -(E)s in the country at large.

[. . .]

[On the other hand, t]he *Sociolinguistics and Language History* project has also produced evidence to the effect that, as early as the 17th century, gentry women were more closely aligned with educated than uneducated men in promoting [other changes, such as] the generalization of the auxiliary DO in negative declaratives as opposed to the use of the simple form (Nurmi, 2000). At least two factors may account for these results. In the 17th century, women's rate of literacy was first of all considerably higher than in the early part of the 16th, and one may with some confidence assume that the vast majority of the gentlewomen in this period could both read and write (section 4.4). The second factor relates to the heightening awareness among the literate of the processes of standardization leading to supraregional norms in the 17th century (Milroy and Milroy 1985b: 29–48, Blake 1996: 172–271). The standardization of spelling in both printed works and private writings is a good example of the evolution of the standard in the 17th century. However, as Wyld (1936) amply demonstrates, this change was not led by women. More historical research is therefore needed to put a date on Labov's (1990: 213) Principle I: "in change from above, women favour the incoming prestige form more than men".

7. CONCLUSION

My findings suggest that we cannot single out the mobile merchant ranks as the obvious leaders of linguistic change in earlier English. Nor can we propose any simple gender-based model for the diffusion of language change in the 16th and 17th centuries. This was a time when a supraregional language community was only coming into existence. Perhaps partly for this reason, the linguistic data that I have discussed points to a rather complex scenario of gender differentiation in language change in early modern England.

First, not unlike today, changes differed in their register orientation. In those that originated in everyday, colloquial language, women could indeed emerge at the forefront. This was the case with the transfer from (. . .) -(E)TH to -(E)s. In a long-term process such as the third-person -(E)s women were found to lead the process over an extended period of time.

Unlike today, however, 16th-century women did not prove the leading influence in processes associated with professional language use and written registers. This was [. . .] shown clearly by the disappearance of multiple negation and the rise of the ANY-paradigm in negative sentences, which was promoted by social aspirers and other men from the professional ranks. The process also shows how a gender difference could persist for well over a century. The case of multiple negation further makes it evident that social status could override gender in a change emanating from networks of professionals. High-ranking women differed significantly from the men leading the change but not from men of their own ranks in the mid-16th century. Social status should therefore not be ignored in historical studies of gender differentiation.

In conclusion, the evidence provided by the *Corpus of Early English Correspondence* implies that, in some important respects, the role of women in language change must itself have changed between the 16th and the 20th centuries. While they did not promote the 16th-century professionally-led change away from multiple negation, women were in the vanguard of such changes from below as the generalization of -(E)s over -(E)TH in the third-person singular. The difference can be explained in terms of the two sexes' differential access to education in general and to professional specializations in particular. The question remains at what point in time women began to promote incoming prestige forms. There is some tentative evidence based on the *CEEC* to suggest that it may have been as early as the 17th century. This is one of the many historical issues that call for further sociolinguistic study.

NOTES

1. Quite a few general 'external' histories of the English language do exist, e.g., Leith (1983) and Fisiak (1993). Crystal (1995) also devotes a good deal of space to discussing the external circumstances under which English has evolved through time.

2. The *Sociolinguistics and Language History* project has been funded by the Academy of Finland and the University of Helsinki. I should like to thank the members of the team, Jukka Keränen, Minna Nevala, Arja Nurmi, Minna Palander-Collin and, in particular, Helena Raumolin-Brunberg for their various contributions to this paper. Thanks are also due to all those who generously commented on the first version of the paper presented at the 4th ESSE Conference in Debrecen in September 1997.

3. The quantitative information the figures and tables in the text draw on is tabulated in the Appendix. Whenever statistical inferences are made, they are based on chi-square tests at the 5%-level of significance or higher. The tests were carried out pairwise by contrasting one person (gender, rank) with another person (gender, rank) at a time. Continuity correction (Yates's correction) was applied in 2×2 contingency tables.

    In the illustrations cited from the *CEEC*, the name of the writer is followed by the year of writing and, in brackets, the collection of letters from which the material is drawn, followed by the page number. For a list of the collections, see Nevalainen and Raumolin-Brunberg (eds). (1996).

REFERENCES

Barber, Charles (1976) *Early Modern English*. London: André Deutsch.

Biber, Douglas and Edward Finegan (1997) Diachronic relations among speech-based and written registers in English. In Terttu Nevalainen and Leena Kahlas-Tarkka (eds) *To Explain the Present: Studies in the Changing English Language in Honour of Matti Rissanen* [Mémoires de la Société Néophilologique 52]. Helsinki: Société Néophilologique. 253–275.

Blake, Norman F. (1996) *A History of the English Language*. London: Macmillan.

Burke, Peter (1992) *History and Social Theory*. Cambridge: Polity Press.

Capp, Bernard (1996) Separate domains? Women and authority in Early Modern England. In Paul Griffiths, Adam Fox and Steve Hindle (eds) *The Experience of Authority in Early Modern England*. Houndmills and London: Macmillan. 117–145.

Chambers, J.K. (1995) *Sociolinguistic Theory*. Oxford: Blackwell.

Coates, Jennifer (ed.) (1998) *Language and Gender*. London and New York: Longman.

Cressy, David (1980) *Literacy and Social Order: Reading and Writing in Tudor and Stuart England*. Cambridge: Cambridge University Press.

Crystal, David (1995) *The Cambridge Encyclopedia of the English Language*. Cambridge: Cambridge University Press.

Devitt, Amy (1989) *Standardizing Written English: Diffusion in the Case of Scotland 1520–1659*. Cambridge: Cambridge University Press.

Eales, Jacqueline (1998) *Women in Early Modern England, 1500–1700*. London: UCL Press.

Eckert, Penelope (1989) The whole woman: sex and gender differences in variation. *Language Variation and Change* 1: 245–267.

Eckert, Penelope and Sally McConnell-Ginet (1998) Communities of practice: where language, gender, and power all live. In Jennifer Coates (ed.) *Language and Gender*. London and New York: Longman. 484–494.

Erickson, Amy Louise (1993) *Women and Property in Early Modern England*. London and New York: Routledge.

Fisiak, Jacek (1993) *An Outline History of English*. Vol. 1. External History. Poznań: Kantor Wydawniczy SAWW.

Fletcher, Anthony (1996) *Gender, Sex and Subordination in England 1500–1800*. New Haven and London: Yale University Press.

Foyster, Elizabeth A. (1999) *Manhood in Early Modern England: Honour, Sex and Marriage*. London and New York: Longman.

Gordon, Elizabeth (1997) Sex, speech, and stereotypes: why women use prestige speech forms more than men. *Language in Society* 26: 47–63.

Heal, Felicity and Clive Holmes (1994) *The Gentry in England and Wales 1500–1700*. London: Macmillan.

Hitchcock, Tim and Michèle Cohen (1999) Introduction. In Tim Hitchcock and Michèle Cohen (eds) *English Masculinities 1660–1800*. London and New York: Longman. 1–22.

Holmes, Janet (1997) Setting new standards: sound changes and gender in New Zealand English. *English World-Wide* 18: 107–142.

Holmqvist, Erik (1922) *On the History of the English Present Inflections, Particularly -th and -s*. Heidelberg: Carl Winter's Universitätsbuchhandlung.

Horvath, Barbara M. (1985) *Variation in Australian English: The Sociolects of Sydney*. Cambridge: Cambridge University Press.

James, Deborah (1996) Women, men and prestige speech forms: a critical review. In Victoria L. Bergvall, Janet M. Bing and Alice F. Freed (eds) *Rethinking Language and Gender Research: Theory and Practice*. London and New York: Longman. 98–125.

Jewell, Helen M. (1998) *Education in Early Modern England*. Houndmills and London: Macmillan Press.

Knorrek, Marianne (1938) *Der Einfluß des Rationalismus auf die englische Sprache: Beiträge zur Entwicklungsgeschichte der englischen Syntax im 17. und 18. Jahrhundert*. Dissertation Berlin. Breslau: Paul Plischke.

Kohnen, Thomas (1997) *Text – Textsorte – Sprachgeschichte. Englische Partizipial- und Gerundialkonstruktionen 1100 bis 1700*. Habilitationsschrift. Bonn.

Labov, William (1972) *Sociolinguistic Patterns*. Philadelphia: University of Philadelphia Press.

Labov, William (1990) The intersection of sex and social class in the course of linguistic change. *Language Variation and Change* 2: 205–254.

Labov, William (1994) *Principles of Linguistic Change: Internal Factors*. Oxford: Blackwell.

Laslett, Peter (1983) *The World We Have Lost – Further Explored*. London: Routledge.

Laurence, Anne (1994) *Women in England 1500–1700: A Social History*. London: Weidenfeld and Nicolson.

Leith, Dick (1983) *A Social History of English*. London: Routledge and Kegan Paul.

Mendelson, Sara and Patricia Crawford (1998) *Women in Early Modern England 1550–1720*. Oxford: Clarendon Press.

Milroy, James (1992) *Language Variation and Change*. Oxford: Blackwell.

Milroy, James and Lesley Milroy (1985a) Linguistic change, social network and speaker innovation. *Journal of Linguistics* 21: 339–384.

Milroy, James and Lesley Milroy (1985b) *Authority in Language*. London, Boston and Henley: Routledge and Kegan Paul.

Milroy, James and Lesley Milroy (1993) Mechanisms of change in urban dialects: the role of class, social network and gender. *International Journal of Applied Linguistics* 3: 57–77.

Milroy, Lesley (1987a) *Language and Social Networks*. 2nd ed. London and New York: Blackwell.

Milroy, Lesley (1987b) *Observing and Analysing Natural Language*. Oxford: Blackwell.

Milroy, Lesley (1998) Women as innovators and norm-creators: the sociolinguistics of dialect leveling in a northern English city. In Suzanne Wertheim, Ashlee C. Bailey and Monica Corston-Oliver (eds) *Engendering Communication: Proceedings from the Fifth Berkeley Women and Language Conference*. Berkeley, CA: Berkeley Women and Language Group. 361–376.

Mustanoja, Taunò F. (1960) *A Middle English Syntax*. Part 1. *Parts of Speech* [Mémoires de la Société Néophilologique 23]. Helsinki: Société Néophilologique.

Nevalainen, Terttu (1996a) Social stratification. In Terttu Nevalainen and Helena Raumolin-Brunberg (eds) *Sociolinguistics and Language History: Studies Based on the Corpus of Early English Correspondence*. Amsterdam and Atlanta: Rodopi. 57–76.

Nevalainen, Terttu (1996b) Gender difference. In Terttu Nevalainen and Helena Raumolin-Brunberg (eds) *Sociolinguistics and Language History: Studies Based on the Corpus of Early English Correspondence*. Amsterdam and Atlanta: Rodopi. 77–91.

Nevalainen, Terttu (1998) Social mobility and the decline of multiple negation in Early Modern English. In *Advances in English Historical Linguistics*, ed. by Jacek Fisiak and Marcin Krygier, 263–291. Berlin and New York: Mouton de Gruyter.

Nevalainen, Terttu (2000a) Processes of supralocalization and the rise of Standard English in the Early Modern Period. In Ricardo Bermúdez-Otero, David Denison, Richard M. Hogg and C.B. McCully (eds) *Generative Theory and Corpus Studies: A Dialogue from 10ICEHL*. Berlin and New York: Mouton de Gruyter.

Nevalainen, Terttu (2000b) Gender differences in the evolution of Standard English. *Journal of English Linguistics*, 38–59.

Nevalainen, Terttu and Helena Raumolin-Brunberg (1989) A corpus of Early Modern Standard English in a social perspective. *Neuphilologische Mitteilungen* 90: 67–110.

Nevalainen, Terttu and Helena Raumolin-Brunberg (1996) Social stratification in Tudor English? In Derek Britton (ed.) *English Historical Linguistics 1994*. Amsterdam and Philadelphia: John Benjamins. 303–326.

Nevalainen, Terttu and Helena Raumolin-Brunberg (2000) The changing role of London on the linguistic map of Tudor and Stuart England. In Dieter Kastovsky and Arthur Mettinger (eds) *The History of English in a Social Context : A Contribution to Historical Sociolinguistics*. Berlin: Mouton de Gruyter. 279–338.

Nurmi, Arja (2000) The rise and regulation of periphrastic *do* in negative declarative sentences: a sociolinguistic study. In Dieter Kastovsky and Arthur Mettinger (eds) *The History of English in a Social Context : A Contribution to Historical Sociolinguistics*. Berlin: Mouton de Gruyter. 339–362.

Raumolin-Brunberg, Helena (1996) Historical sociolinguistics. In Terttu Nevalainen and Helena Raumolin-Brunberg (eds) *Sociolinguistics and Language History: Studies Based on the Corpus of Early English Correspondence*. Amsterdam and Atlanta: Rodopi. 11–37.

Rissanen, Matti, Merja Kytö and Kirsi Heikkonen (eds) (1997a) *English in Transition: Corpus-based Studies in Linguistic Variation and Genre Styles*. Berlin and New York: Mouton de Gruyter.

Rissanen, Matti, Merja Kytö and Kirsi Heikkonen (eds) (1997b) *Grammaticalization at Work: Studies of Long-term Developments in English*. Berlin and New York: Mouton de Gruyter.

Romaine, Suzanne (1982) *Socio-historical Linguistics: Its Status and Methodology*. Cambridge: Cambridge University Press.

Walsh, Mary Roth, (ed.) (1997) *Women, Men and Gender: Ongoing Debates*. New Haven and London: Yale University Press.

Winchester, Barbara (1955) *Tudor Family Portrait*. London: Jonathan Cape.

Wrightson, Keith (1982) *English Society 1580–1680*. London: Hutchinson.

Wrightson, Keith (1994) 'Sorts of people' in Tudor and Stuart England. In Jonathan Barry and Christopher Brooks (eds) *The Middling Sort of People; Culture, Society and Politics in England, 1550–1800*. London: Macmillan. 28–51.

Wyld, Henry Cecil (1920/1936) *A History of Modern Colloquial English*. Oxford: Blackwell.

APPENDIX

Numerical information

For Table 26.2   The use of -(E)s, YOU, single negation (SN), and WHICH in the Johnson circle in 1542–1553 (*CEEC* 1996). Totals of each variable shown in brackets

Writer	-(E)s (-(E)s + - (E)TH)	Single NEG (SN + MN)
Anthony Cave	29 (128)	27 (35)
Sabine Johnson	16 (41)	3 (13)
John Johnson	14 (165)	30 (54)
Otwell Johnson	5 (90)	29 (44)
Richard Preston	36 (36)	7 (13)
Total	100 (460)	96 (159)

For Figure 26.1   The use of -(E)s as opposed to -(E)TH in the third-person singular in the whole corpus in 1540–59 excluding HAVE and DO (*CEEC* 1998). Variable totals shown in brackets

Social rank	-(E)s	%	-(E)s + -(E)TH
Gentry*	20	12%	(169)
Professionals	2	3%	(65)
Social aspirers	14	5%	(256)
Merchants	63	10%	(659)
Other non-gentry	44	76%	(58)
Women (all ranks)	19	33%	(58)
Total	162	13%	(1265)

* consisting of the nobility, upper and lower gentry

For Figure 26.2   The use of -(E)s as opposed to -(E)TH in the third-person singular in London in 1580–99 excluding HAVE and DO (*CEEC* 1998). Variable totals shown in brackets.

Social rank	-(E)s	%	-(E)s + -(E)TH
Nobility (Court)			
Queen Elizabeth	41	50%	(82)
Dudley, Robert	63	52%	(122)
Cecil, William	1	1%	(163)
Gentry*	51	38%	(134)
Professionals	(no data available)		
Merchants	(no data available)		
Other non-gentry	19	56%	(34)
Total	175	33%	(535)

* consisting of the upper and lower gentry

For Figure 26.3   Frequency of multiple negation (MN) according to gender in three EModE periods: 1520–50, 1580–1610 and 1660–80 (*CEEC* 1998 and Supplement). Totals of the variable (single + multiple negation) shown in brackets

Gender	1520–50 MN (SN + MN)	1580–1610 MN (SN + MN)	1660–80 MN (SN + MN)	
Women	27 60% (45)	24 20% (120)	12	12% (103)
Men	203 38% (528)	43 9% (493)	13	3% (415)
Total	230 40% (573)	67 11% (613)	25	5% (518)

For Figure 26.4   The frequency of multiple negation (MN) according to social rank in three EModE periods: 1520–50, 1580–1610 and 1660–80 (*CEEC* 1998 and Supplement). Totals of the variable (single + multiple negation) shown in brackets

Rank	1520–50 MN (SN + MN)	1580–1610 MN (SN + MN)	1660–80 MN (SN + MN)
Women			
Gentry*	18 55% (33)	24 20% (120)	11 13% (84)
Men			
Gentry*	111 49% (227)	29 10% (300)	9 4% (232)
Middle ranks	76 27% (282)	9 5% (183)	3 2% (178)
Other non-gentry	16 84% (19)	5 50% (10)	1 20% (5)
Total	221 39% (561)	67 11% (613)	24 5% (499)

* consisting of the nobility, upper and lower gentry, and upper clergy

QUESTIONS

1.   What is the 'bad-data' problem, and to what extent is it really a problem? How do historical sociolinguists work around it?
2.   Who led the change from 3s − ETH to − (E)S?
3.   Who led the change from multiple negation to single negation?

1.   Nevalainen suggests that the use of 'gender' rather than 'sex' implies a more complex interpretation of the variable.
     To what extent does the analysis of 3s –(E)S and multiple negation make use of the more complex, social and practice-oriented definitions of gender that she introduces in section 4.2?
2.   To what extent can the notion of a 'social aspirer' be translated into contemporary communities you are familiar with?
     What have you observed about the linguistic and social behaviours of 'social aspirers' that seems similar to or different from the linguistic behaviour of the social aspirers in the 16thC?
3.   The analysis of the switch from multiple to single negation involves a complex interplay of gender and social class over time.

Explain the social diffusion of single negation so that at each stage in its development, it is clear why different groups of speakers pattern alike.

4. Nevalainen raises questions about how much generalisations about who leads changes from above (Labov's Principle 1) can be extended into the historical record. Compare her arguments about the role of literacy among women in the 16thC and 17thC and the influence of literacy on their participation in these changes with Haeri's arguments about the interaction between literacy and gender in the variation she observed in Cairo.

Chapter 27

Penelope Eckert

VOWELS AND NAIL POLISH: THE EMERGENCE OF LINGUISTIC STYLE IN THE PREADOLESCENT HETEROSEXUAL MARKETPLACE

THE CHALLENGE OF A theory of linguistic practice is to locate the speaking subject within a social unit in which meaning is being actively constructed, and to investigate the relation between the construction of meaning in that unit and the larger social structure with which it engages. It is for this reason that Sally McConnell-Ginet and I (Eckert & McConnell-Ginet 1992) have called for using the community of practice as the site for the study of language and gender. A community of practice, as defined by its originators, Jean Lave and Etienne Wenger (1991), is an aggregate of people who, through engagement in a common enterprise, come to develop and share ways of doing things, ways of talking, beliefs, values—in short, practices. For the sociolinguist, the value of the construct "community of practice" resides in the focus it affords on the mutually constitutive nature of individual, community, activity, and linguistic practice. For the student of language and gender, it offers the possibility to focus on the local construction of gender—to see how gender is co-constructed with other aspects of identity, and to identify what one might abstract from this as gender.

In the following pages, I will briefly sketch a series of events and developments, as a community of practice within a cohort of preadolescents moves through fifth and sixth grades. Originating in a loosely assembled collection of childhood playmates and class-mates, this community of practice develops in the form of a heterosexual crowd. The crowd's membership and practices are in continual and rapid flux as its members jointly move towards adult social heterosexuality. I will focus on the emergence of a local style among the female participants in this crowd—a style that they see as "teen" style but that others, depending on their point of view, might see as reflecting gender, ethnicity, class, and attitude. Through an account of some day-to-day events, I hope to describe the

Source: Eckert, Penelope (1998) Vowels and nail polish: the emergence of linguistic style in the preadolescent heterosexual marketplace. In Natasha Warner et al. (eds) *Proceedings of the 1996 Berkeley Women and Language Conference*. Berkeley: Berkeley Women and Language Group, 183–190.

nature of stylistic development, the interconnection of language with style in action and appearance, and its role in the co-construction of gender, class, age, ethnicity, and a number of interrelated terms of identity. These events take place at Hines Elementary School, a school in Northern California serving a low income, ethnically heterogeneous student population composed primarily of Mexican Americans and Asian Americans, particularly Vietnamese, along with smaller numbers of African Americans, South Islanders, white Anglo Americans and other groups.

The passage from childhood to adolescence brings the emergence of a peer-dominated social order. In the process, the very meaning of gender is transformed since it brings, most saliently, a transition from a normatively asexual social order to a normatively heterosexual one, transforming relations among and between boys and girls. While heterosexuality is quite commonly viewed as an individual development, observing preadolescence makes it quite clear that heterosexuality is above all a social imperative (Rich 1980), and changes in individual relations between boys and girls are mediated by a cohort-based heterosexual market. In *Gender Play*, (1993) Barrie Thorne documents the beginnings of the heterosexual market in elementary school. She notes the frenetic engagement in pairing up, fixing up, and breaking up; and girls' engagement with the technology of femininity—coloring nails and lips, frequently with age-appropriate semi-pretend cosmetics such as lip gloss and felt-tip pens; and the rejection of childish games.

The transition into a heterosexual social order brings girls and boys into mutual and conscious engagement in gender differentiation, in the course of which boys appropriate arenas for the production of accomplishment, and girls move into the elaboration of stylized selves. Both boys and girls come to view themselves as commodities on the heterosexual market, but while boys' value on the market is tied to the kinds of accomplishment that they have been cultivating throughout childhood, the girls' value is tied to the abandonment of boys' accomplishment and to the production of style and interpersonal drama. Girls become engaged in the technology of beauty and personality, learning to use a range of resources in which language use is elaborated along with the adoption of other resources such as nail polish, lip gloss, hair style, clothing, and new walks. It is not uncommon in fifth grade to see girls and boys running around, making sudden movements, rolling on the floor or throwing themselves to the ground, using their bodies in much the same way. Increasingly in sixth grade, girls stop running and start monitoring their facial expressions, striking feminine and dramatic poses, adorning and inspecting their hands in a disembodied manner, arranging their breasts. And boys begin to subdue their facial expressions, control their hair, spread out their shoulders, develop deliberate tough or athletic walks and flamboyant moves on the athletic field or court, consciously deepen their voices. The process of objectification affects both boys and girls as they work to produce value as complementary commodities on the market. But the nature of this complementarity is not neutral but involves qualitative changes in girls' place in the world. As boys take over casual playground sports, girls replace vigorous physical playground activity with observing, heckling, and occasionally disrupting boys' games, and with sitting or walking around in small and large groups. The practice of walking around has in itself symbolic significance. Moving away from the crowd and walking around slowly, intensely engaged in conversation draws attention to those who do it, by contrasting with the fast movements of their peers, with play, with the larger groups engaged in games, and with the louder tone of children's talk. This walking, furthermore, is a visible occasion on which girls engage in intense social affiliation activities, negotiating heterosexual pairings and realigning friendships.

Not everyone is engaged in the heterosexual market. Indeed, the market is located locally within particular communities of practice—heterosexual "crowds." While any dyad or triad of girls can walk around and talk, only certain girls' walking and talking will carry status. The crucial ingredient is the public knowledge that they have something important to talk about—that the social relations they are exercising in their talk are important social relations—those of the emerging heterosexual crowd. The boundaries of the crowd are quite fluid, and part of community practice is the management of participation, marginality, and multiple membership. In particular, since among the girls much of the activity has to do with realignments, the management of fluidity is central to community practice. Thus it is not simple engagement in heterosexual social practice that signals the entrance into adolescence, but the cohort-wide co-construction of social status and heterosexual practice. Furthermore, the development of a "popular crowd" that is by definition heterosexual brings the cohort, simultaneously, into engagement with the world beyond the age cohort. Participation in the heterosexual market offers new possibilities for the construction of a public persona. The crowd dominates the public sphere, partially by inserting the private sphere into it. Heightened activity and style draw attention to those who are engaged in it, and makes their private affairs public events. In this way, they take on status as public people. This "going public" is a crucial component of the process of maturation taking place in this age group. Such things as girls' trips to the mall, and gang-oriented territoriality, are primarily about inserting and viewing the self as an independent agent in the public domain.

Both the negotiation of heterosexuality and relationships in general, and the technology of beauty and personality, become professional areas, in which girls are recognized as more knowledgeable than boys. Since it is still new and mysterious, this knowledge is respected and a source of status and admiration from both boys and girls. Heterosexuality is, in some important sense, a girls' pastime, engaging girls more among themselves than with boys. Boys play a more passive role in the process, leaving the girls to do much of the initiating, and frequently passively participating in girls' strategies. One boy, for example, broke up with his girlfriend of six months at the request of her friends, who wanted to punish her for being "a bitch." There is an excitement about all this realignment, about venturing into the unknown. Seeking legitimate agency, girls opt for power and excitement in the heterosexual market. Seeing that they won't gain recognition for the pursuits that boys are taking over, girls choose to call the shots, and to become experts in a whole new arena. Girls become heighteners of the social, breathing excitement into heretofore normal everyday people and situations, producing desire where none was before. The direction of all this energy to the sphere of social relations throws girls into a conscious process of stylistic production as they jointly construct group and individual styles, and in the process propel themselves into the public arena. This stylistic production brings together resources from a broad marketplace of identities, merging aspects of gender, ethnicity, age-appropriateness, heterosexuality, class, immigration status, etc., into one highly meaningful local style.

Linguistic style is a way of speaking that is peculiar to a community of practice—its linguistic identity (California Style Collective 1993). Briefly put, style is a clustering of linguistic resources that has social meaning. The construction of a style is a process of bricolage: a stylistic agent appropriates resources from a broad sociolinguistic landscape, recombining them to make a distinctive style. In this way, the new style has a clear individual identification, but an identification that owes its existence to its life in a broader landscape of meaning. Above all, that style is not simply a product of community practice—it is not just a way of displaying identification—it is the vehicle for the construction of this identification. It is precisely the process of bricolage that allows us to put together meanings to construct new things that are us and that place us in relation to the rest of the world. This process of bricolage takes place within communities of practice, and to a great extent is the joint work of the community and of the tensions between individual and community identities. I relate the following series of vignettes in order to illustrate the emergence of a complex style as the age cohort moves into heterosexual social practice. This emergence of style is accomplished in a complex interplay between group and individual identity and style (Wenger, 1999). In the following account, I focus on the interaction between Trudy, a stylistic icon, and the home girls, the community of practice that is most prominent in her school-based activities.

In February of fifth grade, as I walked out of the lunchroom onto the playground, Trudy and Katya, who normally played Chinese jumprope at recess, rushed over and invited me to come with them. They told me that they no longer always played at lunch time—sometimes they just talked instead. Katya said "just talk" with a hunch of her shoulders, wide eyes, and a conspiratorial grin. They led me over to some picnic tables, telling me behind their hands that what they talk about is boys, and that Trudy is "with" someone. Once we were seated on the picnic tables, Trudy and Katya hesitated, giggled, and looked around conspiratorially. Trudy then whispered behind her hands, informing me that it was Carlos that she was with, and then told us both that he had kissed her. Katya "ooooo"ed and looked wise. I asked where he'd kissed her and she laughed uproariously and pointed to her cheek. We sat for a few more moments, and then went off to play hopscotch.

A few weeks later, as I was playing Chinese jumprope with Alice and two other girls, Trudy, Katya and Erica came along and tried to join in. Alice, whose rope we were using, said they couldn't join. In a fashion reminiscent of the way in which boys occasionally disrupt girls' games Trudy and Erica jumped into the circle both at once, taking giant leaps onto the rope, creating chaos and laughter, simultaneously outjumping Alice and dismissing the game. Alice got upset and folded up the rope. This was the last time I ever saw Trudy play a "child's game." This is not to suggest that the transition away from kid stuff is abrupt—Trudy may well have played Chinese jumprope at home some more, as adolescent behavior is slowly incorporated into day-to-day practice. A year later, for example, Trudy reached into her low-slung baggy jeans to show me her new sexy lace underpants, saying, "Yesterday I wore kid pants" (meaning cotton pants).

Trudy moved quickly into the world of teen behavior, of heterosexuality, flamboyance, and toughness. She took to walking around the playground with a group of girls, talking and heckling a group of boys as they played football. Together, this group of girls and of boys came to constitute a highly visible, predominantly Mexican American, heterosexual crowd. Trudy became a key player in this crowd, flamboyant in her style and highly active in pursuing relationships among both girls and boys. As fifth grade drew to a close and sixth grade took off, crowd activity progressed fast and furiously, as male and female pairings were made and broken, as girls' friendships shifted, and as drama built with girls accusing each other—or girls outside the group—of "talking shit," and kissing or trying to steal their boyfriends. Trudy emerged as a stylistic icon: she had more boyfriends (serially) than anyone else, she was more overt in her relations with her boyfriends, she dressed with greater flair, she was sexier, tougher, louder, more outgoing, more innovatively dressed, and generally more outrageous than any of her peers. The highly prominent style that became Trudy's hallmark was simultaneously an individual and a group construction. The heterosexual crowd supported Trudy's activities, providing the social landscape, the visibility, and the participation necessary to make them meaningful. At the same time, Trudy made meaning for the crowd and for its members individually and severally, her actions drawing others into the adolescent world, taking risks in their name.

After school one day, a small group of girls fussed over Trudy, who was crying because her boyfriend had told someone that he wanted her to break up with him. "He won't do it himself, he wants me to do it," she sniffed. The assembled group of admiring and sympathetic girls criticized the boyfriend. "That's what he always does," said Carol. Sherry said "He just uses girls." Trudy sniffled, "I like him so: much." In her heartbreak, Trudy established herself as way ahead in the heterosexual world—as having feelings, knowledge and daring as yet unknown to most of her peers. At the same time, she gave Carol and Sherry the opportunity to comfort her, to talk knowingly about her boyfriend's perfidy—to participate in the culture of heterosexuality. In this way, her flamboyance propelled Trudy and those who engaged with her into a new, older, sphere.

After the breakup, Trudy "got with" Dan. "I love Da:n," she kept saying in my ear, the vowel nice and backed, "I love Da:n." During hands-on science, my tape recorder sat turning in the middle of the table. Every once in a while Trudy leaned forward to the microphone and whispered, "I love Da:n." Her group asked me later if I'd listened to the tape—they asked, with a frisson, if I'd heard what she was whispering. Her pronunciation of the vowel in Dan has special significance. In Northern California Anglo speech, /ae/ is splitting into two variants (Moonwomon 1991), raising before nasals and backing elsewhere. Latino speech is set apart from other local dialects with the lack of such a split—all occurrences of /ae/ are pronounced low and back, and this pronunciation is commonly foregrounded as a stylistic device.

One day, a group of girls sat at the edge of the playground complaining that there weren't any cute boys (i.e. the boys in their class hadn't become cute over the summer). As they talked, they kept their collective eye on the boys who were goofing around nearby. One of them pointed out that there was one cute boy, at which point they all called out in unison, "Sa:m!" As they intoned his name, pronouncing the vowel long and low, the girls attracted Sam's attention as well as that of the group of boys. They moved on to make humorous observations about other boys, and about each other's activities with boys, hooting loudly after each observation in a kind of call and response. The boys began to get agitated, and Jorge yelled something at them. Trudy stood up, stuck out her butt at him and called, "Kiss my ass, Jorge, you get on my nerves!" Linguistic devices, such as the pronunciation of /ae/, the meat of studies of variation, take on their social meaning in use—in the occasions on which they are given prominence in connection with social action. Trudy's use of language, like her use of other aspects of style, has a special status. Her flamboyance is a platform for the construction of meaning of all sorts. As other girls report her actions to each other, as they take on bits of her style, they are propagating sound change (the backing of /ae/) along with the meaning that Trudy and her community of practice have imbued it with. This meaning, though, is constructed not for the vowel in isolation, but for the larger style.

As sixth grade got under way, the girls' crowd expanded, and dubbed itself the "home girls." They took to greeting each other with a hug—in the morning as they arrived at school, and as they emerged from their different classrooms at recess, as they split up at the end of recess, and before they went home at the end of the day. At first awkward and self-conscious gestures among Trudy and a small handful of friends, the hugs spread and became stylized—a brief one-armed hug became the favorite. This greeting clearly indicated who was part of the crowd and who was not, at the same time that it endowed the crowd with an air of maturity. Fortuitously, in an attempt to regulate unwanted physical contact among students, teachers and administrators "outlawed" hugging when it began to spread, conveniently imbuing the hug with mild defiance as well. Hugging, therefore, had additional value as an act of defiance—particularly as the girls, on the way to the playground at recess, took to stopping by one classroom to give a quick hug to other home girls who were being kept in from recess because of unfinished work or misbehavior.

Girls' open defiance towards teachers was incorporated into home girl style in the course of sixth grade. But most girls found it difficult to display defiance in the classroom, and once again Trudy stepped in for them. Her defiance, however, only verged on being openly rude, and aimed to be an entertaining stylistic display. One day, for example, the teacher went around the class asking students how they rated a report they had just heard. Trudy was inspecting her long red fingernails, and clicking them loudly on her desk to the admiration of many in the room. The teacher called out, "Trudy?" Trudy answered, "What." The teacher, mishearing, said, "Did you say 'two'?" Trudy said, "No. I'm all 'what.' "

Trudy sprawled across her table, squirming and calling out unwanted answers and comments to the teacher. She told me she had had too much chocolate at lunch and she was feeling "hyperactive." When PE finally arrived, she burst onto the playground, jumping on and off a picnic table shouting "whassup? whassup? whassup?" She climbed onto the table, struck a pose with hips out, told me she'd beaten up Sylvia "because she's a bitch," and gave me a blow-by-blow story of the fight.

One day, Alicia entered the classroom, standing unusually tall. She strolled over and rested her fingertips on my table, tilted her head back, hand on hips, and said, "Whassup?" In this way she signaled to me that she was now hanging with the home girls.

All of these—the ritual hugs, the greetings, the songs, the accusations, the fight stories—are part of an emerging style. The transition into a heterosexual social order brings boys and girls into mutual and conscious engagement in gender differentiation, in the course of which girls move into the elaboration of flamboyantly stylized selves. The development of flamboyant linguistic style is a key part of this elaboration, and inseparable from the emerging use of other aspects of gendered style such as nail polish, lip gloss, hair style, clothing, and new walks. These stylistic endeavors are inseparable from the construction of meaning for the community of practice, and from the construction of an identity for the individual as a participant in that community. At the same time, they are what provide the emergence of the adult from the child—and for girls, the transfer of meaning and excitement from the physical to the social. What is particularly important about this entire process is that what will later be adult endeavors with grave consequences, are initially engaged in for a kind of childish excitement and then for a sense of power in the heterosexual market, with no clear view of the subordination that lies around the corner. The development of an adolescent persona is a gradual process that begins with playing with small stylistic components—nail polish, a watch, a hair arrangement, a pose, a dance step, a facial expression, a phrase, a pronunciation, a song. It begins with the development of "attitude" toward boys, transforming them into objects, in relation to which one can display new styles of behavior, and play out scenarios. Initially a terrain for the development of new initiative, it gradually transforms into a discourse of female objectification and subordination.

REFERENCES

California Style Collective (1993) Personal and group style. Paper presented at NWAVE 22 (Ottawa).

Eckert, Penelope and Sally McConnell-Ginet (1992) Think practically and look locally: language and gender as community-based practice. *Annual Review of Anthropology* 21: 461–490.

Lave, Jean and Etienne Wenger (1991) *Situated Learning: Legitimate Peripheral Participation*. Cambridge: Cambridge University Press.

Moonwomon, Birch (1991) Sound Change in San Francisco English. Unpublished dissertation, University of California, Berkeley.

Rich, Adrienne (1980) Compulsory heterosexuality and lesbian existence. *Signs* 5: 631–660.

Thorne, Barrie (1993) *Gender Play*. New Brunswick, NJ: Rutgers University Press.

Wenger, Etienne (1999) *Communities of Practice*. Cambridge: Cambridge University Press.

QUESTIONS

Content

1. What is a community of practice and why is it a useful concept?
2. Why is the age group of 5th to 6th grade particularly interesting?
3. How do girls' and boys' styles differ when transitioning into a heterosexual order?
4. What, according to Eckert, is style and how does it come about?
5. What is Trudy's role in style construction? What is the group's role?
6. What is the meaning of the lowered and backed /æ/ in this particular community of practice?
7. What features contribute to "home girl" style?

Concept

1. Is your class a community of practice?
2. Are you aware of changing styles in particular in male or female communities of practice yourself? What features contribute to this style?

Chapter 28

Janet Holmes and Stephanie Schnurr

'DOING FEMININITY' AT WORK:
MORE THAN JUST RELATIONAL PRACTICE

INTRODUCTION

RESEARCHERS IN THE AREA of language and gender have recently begun to examine the 'multiplicity of experiences of gender' (Eckert and McConnell-Ginet 2003: 47) in different social contexts and communities of practice. A number of researchers, for example, have explored the concept of masculinity, and indeed 'masculinities'(Connell 1995; Cameron 1997; Edley and Wetherell 1997; Johnson and Meinhof 1997; Kiesling 1998, 2004; Bucholtz 1999; Meân 2001; Coates 2003; Bell and Major 2004). Some attention has also been paid to 'the multiplicity of . . . femininities'(Eckert and McConnell-Ginet 2003: 48), that is, the dynamic and diverse ways in which people construct different kinds of femininity in social interaction in different contexts (e.g. Okamoto 1995; Livia and Hall 1997; Cameron 1997, 1998; Coates 1997, 1999; Cameron and Kulick 2003). This paper contributes to this enterprise by analysing some of the ways in which people construct and negotiate different femininities in white-collar New Zealand workplaces.

Femininity is an ambiguous concept with complex associations. It could even be argued that 'femininity' has been treated as something of a dirty word in gender studies, associated, from a feminist perspective, with a rather dubious set of behaviours. Most obviously, acting 'feminine' conjures up politically incorrect 'frilly pink party dresses'; femininity is associated with demureness, deference, and lack of power and influence (as discussed in Eckert and McConnell-Ginet 2003: 16ff, 184ff; see also Lakoff 2004). Femininity invokes a stereotype, and it is a negative one for many feminists, and a problematic and uncomfortable one for many academic women. Discussing this issue, Mills (2003) implicitly subscribes to this negative attitude: 'one of the many important advances made by feminism is to open up within the notion of what it means to be a

Source: Holmes, Janet and Stephanie Schnurr (2006) 'Doing femininity' at work: more than just relational practice. *Journal of Sociolinguistics* 10: 31–51.

woman a distinction between femininity and femaleness, so that one can be a woman without considering oneself to be (or others considering one to be) feminine' (Mills 2003: 188). Accepting such a claim entails subscribing to the view that 'feminine' and 'femininity' are dirty words which must be replaced by the euphemisms 'female' and 'femaleness'. But is this necessary? We argue that 'feminine' can be reclaimed as a positive attribute.

In contesting the denigration and rejection of the words 'feminine' and 'femininity', it is important to note that the basis for this negative stereotype is the *exaggeration* of features which are associated with the construction by women of a normative gender identity. The exaggeration evokes derision. As Mills herself notes, in the media 'the representation of stereotypically feminine women is rarely presented ... without mockery or ridicule'(2003: 187). But this should not mean that the enactment of normatively feminine behaviour should be a cause for embarrassment and apology by professional women (or men) in the workplace.

In what follows, we attempt to re-present the notion of femininity as a positive rather than a negative construction in workplace interaction. We analyse a number of specific examples which illustrate the negotiation of a range of femininities at work. We draw on the notion of a gendered community of practice (Holmes and Stubbe 2003a), in which certain kinds of gender performance are perceived as 'unmarked' (Ochs 1992: 343), or ' "normal" behaviour' (Kiesling 2004: 234), while others are regarded as marked or 'emphasised' (Connell 1987: 187). Building on the notion that – through their association with particular roles, activities, traits, and stances – certain socio-pragmatic, discursive and linguistic choices, or ways of speaking, 'index' (Ochs 1992, 1996) or culturally encode gender (Cameron and Kulick 2003: 57), we explore the different ways of 'doing femininity' identified in our workplace data.

In a recent paper examining the ways in which authority is constructed in workplace interaction, Kendall (2004) suggests that gender identity is often irrelevant in the workplace. She argues that in everyday interaction people focus on role construction rather than gender identity: 'women and men do not generally choose linguistic strategies for the purpose of creating masculine or feminine identities' (2004: 56) ... 'situations in which women and men consciously choose language options to create femininity and masculinity are rare' (2004: 76). Certainly gender is not frequently a *conscious* focus of identity performance at work (but see Hall 1995, 2003; Besnier 2003). Nonetheless, the distinction between two types of social identity is not always easy to make, especially when particular linguistic features are associated with more than one kind of identity (e.g. masculinity and leadership, femininity and subordination/server status). As Cameron and Kulick note, in some cases 'the same way of speaking signifies both a professional identity and a gendered identity, and in practice these are difficult to separate: the two meanings coexist, and both of them are always potentially relevant. The actual balance between them is not determined in advance by some general principle, but has to be negotiated in specific situations'(2003: 58).

In our view, then, gender is relevant at some level in every workplace interaction, an ever-present influence on how we behave, and how we interpret others' behaviour, even if our level of awareness of this influence varies from one interaction to another, and from moment to moment within an interaction. We are always aware of the gender of those we are talking to, and we bring to every workplace interaction our familiarity with societal gender stereotypes, and the gendered norms to which women and men are expected to conform (Eckert and McConnell-Ginet 2003: 87). Workplaces are simply one of many sites for gender performances which have the potential to strengthen the 'gender order' (Connell 1987); and while in some professions 'doing gender' is quite central to workplace performance, in all workplaces individuals unavoidably enact gendered roles, adopt recognisably gendered stances, and construct gender identity in the process of interacting with others at work.

In addition, there are situations in which people exploit their audience's familiarity with stereotypical concepts of femininity or masculinity in a more conscious fashion for particular effect, as we illustrate below. The concept of 'double voicing' (Bakhtin 1984) is relevant here, accounting for the ways in which speakers mingle components of different styles for particular effect. Talk which indexes gender in exaggerated or over-emphatic ways may be manipulated for the purpose, for instance, of parodying and even subverting established workplace norms and expectations about appropriate ways for professional employees to behave at work. The ability to interpret and appreciate the social meaning of such gender performances depends inevitably on recognition of what constitutes an unmarked gender performance or 'unmarked behaviours for a [particular] sex' (Ochs 1992: 343) in a particular community of practice. The first section of the analysis addresses, therefore, the issue of the construction of unmarked femininity in particular communities of practice.

The data we draw on was collected by the Wellington Language in the Workplace (LWP) Project (see http://www.vuw.ac.nz/lals/lwp; Holmes and Stubbe 2003b). The Project includes material from a wide variety of New Zealand workplaces, and uses a methodology which allows workplace interactions to be recorded as unobtrusively as possible. The LWP corpus currently comprises over 2500 workplace interactions, involving around 400 participants. In this paper, we draw on data from white-collar professional workplaces in order to explore the ways in which workplace participants, and especially workplace managers, construct complex femininities in different discourse contexts within particular communities of practice.

'DOING FEMININITY' IN A FEMININE COMMUNITY OF PRACTICE

We begin by considering what it means to behave in a normatively feminine way in a recognisably feminine community of practice. Holmes and Stubbe (2003a) explored the notion of 'gendered' workplaces, and examined some of the discourse features which people use to characterise the organisational culture of different workplaces as being relatively more 'feminine' or 'masculine'. Describing workplaces in this way does not indicate that everyone in a particular workplace behaves in a consistently gendered manner; rather these labels act as a shorthand, indicating the expectations and constraints on gender performances in some contexts in those workplaces. Indeed our analyses demonstrate that the characteristics stereotypically associated with such generalisations are often inaccurate, and that day-to-day interactions in particular communities of practice typically challenge the generalisations. Nevertheless, it was clear that those participating in our research, as well as members of the wider New Zealand community, were very willing to identify some workplaces as particularly feminine and others as very masculine. And such perceptions inevitably affect expectations about appropriate behaviour including ways of speaking. IT companies and manufacturing organisations typically tended to be labelled as more masculine workplaces, while organisations (and especially government departments) which dealt directly with clients, or with people-oriented, social issues, or with education, tended to be perceived as more feminine places to work.

Within such workplaces people draw from a range of linguistic and discursive resources to construct their identities as 'professionals' in workplace interaction, and to negotiate particular pragmatic functions, such as giving directives, criticising, disagreeing, approving, and so on. Their choices index particular stances (e.g. authoritative, consultative, deferential) which construct not only their particular professional identities or roles (e.g. manager, team leader, support person), but also their gender positioning (see, for example, Holmes, Stubbe and Vine 1999; Holmes and Stubbe 2003a; Kendall 2003, 2004). This is the most obvious way in which people enact conventional gender identities at work – through linguistic and discursive choices which indirectly index normative femininity whilst also instantiating a particular professional relationship. Example 1 illustrates this in a community of practice described by its members, as well as by outsiders, as a very feminine community of practice:

Example 1 [1]

Context: Ruth is the department manager. Nell is a policy analyst. Nell has prepared an official letter on which Ruth is giving her some feedback. [2]

1.	Ruth:	it's **actually** quite **I mean** it's
2.		it's well written [inhales] I **just** have
3.		I **just** think the approach is **could**
4.		should be a bit different in terms of see like
5.		the organisation wouldn't
6.		we wouldn't usually say something like this
7.		that **I mean** it's true but um we should **probably**
8.		put in there that um the organisation has
9.		what we did **actually** in terms of
10.		providing advice on other avenues of funding
11.		/but\ what the organisation =
12.	Nell:	/mm\
13.	Ruth:	= provides is a policy advice organisation
14.		and does not have um ++
15.		they **actually** have only limited funding for
16.		sponsorship + (and) I've **just** realised though
17.		that this is (like) that they go in a couple of weeks
18.		it **might** have been worth talking to Stacey
19.		about um funding through
20.		I **think** it's through [*name of funding agency*]
21.		( ) last year we got funding for [tut] a someone
22.		from [*name of organisation*] to attend
23.		an international conference [drawls]:in: India
24.		**I think** + I **can't remember exactly** the criteria

25.   but there is a fund there and it **may might** be **a bit** late
26.   but **just I mean** Stacey knows the contacts
27.   and I **think** it's in [*name of funding agency*]
28.   and whether or not it's worth having a talk to them about . . .

Ruth wants Nell to make some amendments to the letter, and the interaction is clearly potentially face threatening. Ruth's strategy for conveying her critical comments and her directives entails the use of a range of classic face-saving mitigation devices. In this short interaction, she uses a variety of hedges and minimisers (in bold above): *could*, *may*, *might*, *probably*, *just* (2), *actually* (3), *I mean* (3) and *I think* (5), and approximators, *a bit*, *I think it was*, *I can't remember exactly*, etc. These devices minimise the force of the face-threatening implicit criticisms and directive speech acts, and pay attention to Nell's face needs (Brown and Levinson 1987).[3]

Ruth also minimises the critical implications of her comments by emphasising the positive. So she begins by highlighting the fact that Nell's version of the letter is fine, *it's well written* (line 2). She also acknowledges that what Nell has said is true (line 7), but comments that it is not the *usual* way of doing things in the organisation. The shift from *the organisation* (line 8) to the use of the pronoun *we* (line 9) which is strategically ambiguous between exclusive and positively polite inclusive meaning (*we wouldn't usually say something like this*), allows Ruth to suggest that she and Nell are working on this together, thereby again saving both interlocutors' faces in a potentially tricky situation. On this interpretation, mitigation is clearly at the core of this array of strategies.

From an analyst's perspective, this is normatively feminine talk, characterised by features which have been described in decades of language and gender research (e.g. see Tannen 1993, 1994a, 1994b; Crawford 1995; Holmes 1995; Aries 1996; Coates 1996; Wodak 1997; Talbot 1998; Romaine 1999). In this section of her interaction with Nell, Ruth is making use of linguistic, pragmatic and discursive devices which signal considerateness and positive affect, stances associated with femaleness and feminine identity in New Zealand society. These are, of course, just some of the available strategies for fulfilling her role as manager, and in other contexts she draws on more confrontational, authoritative, and direct strategies to achieve her goals (see, for example, Holmes and Stubbe 2003b: 49). Example 1 serves, however, to illustrate an interaction in which a middle-class professional woman performs her managerial role in a way which also constructs a conventionally feminine gender identity. It also serves as a linguistic instantiation of classic 'relational practice' (Fletcher 1999), that is, off-record, other-oriented behaviour which serves to further workplace goals. In Fletcher's analysis relational practice is paradigmatically women's work, and thus a quintessential example of 'doing femininity' at work. In the community of practice in which these women worked, this gender performance was unremarkable and 'unmarked'. Being normatively feminine in this community of practice did not arouse derision, and nor did it require apology.

Importantly, however, the perception of such behaviour as acceptable and unmarked held true for professional women in many of the white-collar workplaces in which we recorded. Doing feminine gender using the kinds of strategies and linguistic devices described above was typically perceived as unmarked, as simply one component of performing their professional identity in particular interactions in a very wide range of communities of practice. Feminine behaviour, in other words, was regarded as normal behaviour in such contexts, and hence can be re-classified positively rather than derided.

When men 'do femininity' at work, however, the perceptions of, and reactions to, their behaviour are much more complex. For example, in our data, when men made use of discourse strategies and linguistic devices associated with normatively feminine behaviour, the responses varied significantly on different occasions in different communities of practice. In a relatively feminine community of practice, the use by a male of linguistic markers of considerateness and concern for the addressee's face needs, such as those identified in Example 1, when used in a similar professional context, occasioned no comment. Indeed, our ethnographic observations and interviews indicate that such behaviour was regarded as normal, appropriate and unmarked.

[. . .]

Using linguistic features and discourse strategies which attend to relational aspects of the interaction, and index normative femininity, is perfectly acceptable as a way of performing aspects of one's professional identity within these communities of practice. In other words 'doing femininity' is unmarked behaviour in such contexts, whether it is performed by a man or a woman. Thus defined, normative femininity can be regarded positively rather than treated as the focus of ridicule.

'DOING FEMININITY' IN A MASCULINE COMMUNITY OF PRACTICE

There are, however, workplace contexts where using a feminine style can evoke a very much less positive response. Especially in relatively masculine communities of practice, the effective use of a normatively feminine style was a much more complex and even hazardous enterprise. And men, in particular, tended to be the target of negative comment for using stylistic features which conventionally index femininity.

So, for example, the discursive behaviour of members of an IT team in a big commercial organisation contrasted sharply with the norms of the places [discussed previously]. There was, for instance, scarcely any conventional small talk among team members before or after meetings. Pre-meeting talk tended to be business-oriented, a chance to update on work which team members were doing together in other contexts. In the six meetings of this team that we videotaped in full, there is scarcely a single topic that is not directly related to some aspect of the team's work. And the humour among these team members was predominantly aggressive and sarcastic, and sometimes undeniably sexist (e.g. with references to nagging wives, and heavy drinking with the boys). Over 90 percent of the humorous comments which occurred in one meeting, for instance, were sarcastic and negative jibes, intended to put down the addressee or to deflate them. Behaviour which was perceived as 'soft' or conventionally 'feminine' elicited a very different reaction in this community of practice from the way it was treated by Ruth's colleagues [. . .], as Example 2 demonstrates:

Example 2

Context: Six men in a regular meeting of a project team in a large commercial organisation. They are discussing a technical issue related to a project for some clients. Callum's colleagues pretend to be horrified that he has actually talked face-to-face with the clients.

1.   Barry: but we can we can kill this/particular action\ point
2.   Marco: /well yep\ you can kill
3.   this particular action point
4.   Barry: and you/guys\
5.   Callum: /are\ you sure +++ I took the opportunity
6.   of talking with some of the users
7.   Barry: what again? [laughs]/[laughs]\
8.   Marco: /not again what are you doing talking to them\
9.   Barry: [laughs]: go on /Callum come on\
10. Marco: /[laughs]\
11. Callum: and th- and they th-++
12. Marco: they've still got /issues\
13. Callum   /(I I I)\ well + I don't think they're sure? +
14.   (   ) if they're really issues or not

The group of men here make fun of Callum for engaging voluntarily in 'communicative' behaviour with clients. Using stereotypically masculine language, Barry and Marco suggest that a proposed action, namely dealing with a specific technical issue, be *killed*, that is, dropped (lines 1–3), since it is peripheral to the main project. Callum interrupts with a protest, using a question *are you sure* (line 5), rather than a more aggressive form of challenge. Even so, the three-second pause suggests that his comment causes surprise. He goes on to point out that the proposed action emerged from his discussions with the people who will be using the programme (lines 6–7). Barry and Marco then proceed to mock Callum, ridiculing the notion that he should actually 'talk', that is verbally communicate face-to-face, with clients. Barry's tone of voice in his question *what again?* (line 7) conveys mocking astonishment, and Barry's *Callum come on* (line 9) is drawled with a rise-fall intonation indicating sardonic incredulity. Callum persists, despite the mockery, and maintains his relatively feminine approach, *I don't think they're sure? if they're really issues or not* (lines 13–14) with a high rising terminal on *sure*, a feature coded as feminine in New Zealand speech. He is also reporting behaviour that is stereotypically feminine, namely, these people don't know what they think, thus risking tarring himself with the same brush by association.

This short excerpt illustrates how this group of professional IT experts construct themselves as a very masculine community of practice; both in content (e.g. *kill this point*) and style: they contest each other's statements very directly, and the floor is a competitive site where they interrupt one another freely. In this context, Callum's verbal behaviour is clearly 'marked'. The underlying (only slightly facetious) assumption is that 'real men' (and especially computer experts) do not ever actually talk face-to-face with clients; talking to clients is rather the responsibility of the support staff at the user interface, many of whom are, unsurprisingly, women. Indeed, contributing more than the minimal amount of talk seems to be generally regarded as relatively feminine behaviour within the culture of this IT project team, where the most senior participant in the team meetings contributes the least talk. In this exchange, then, the team members imply that Callum has behaved in an unmasculine way, and mock his conventionally feminine approach.

[. . .]

Ways of talking which conventionally index femininity can function as unmarked in some communities of practice, while the same discourse strategies and linguistic features may be perceived as marked and comment-worthy in others. We turn now to the discussion of a rather different way in which women may exploit gendered norms of interaction at work, drawing on the conventional indices of femininity for particular, and sometimes subversive, purposes.

[. . .]

[Holmes and Schnurr then go on to show that the identification of particular types of behaviour as markedly feminine allows conversationalists to exploit these features for ironic self-quotation and parody of how women should behave in the workplace. Hence, language is not only used to enact and reinforce conventional gender positioning, but also to "subvert unacceptable socio-cultural norms, and contest restrictive concepts of professional identity at work" (quoted from original page 45).]

CONCLUSION

This paper has explored certain aspects of gender performance in the workplace. We have discussed different femininities or ways of 'doing femininity', and suggested that workplace interaction provides opportunities [. . .] for indexing normative femininity, a kind of gender performance which has been associated with 'relational practice' (Fletcher 1999) [. . .].

We have shown that the use of familiar and normative discourse resources for indexing femininity by both women and men may elicit different responses in different contexts within different communities of practice. We have suggested that, especially in relatively feminine communities of practice, such performances are frequently treated as 'unmarked behaviours' (Ochs 1992: 343), not just for women but for either sex. Indeed, in many contexts within such communities of practice, the ability to discursively index conventional femininity is regarded as an asset, and skill in adopting a feminine stance is positively construed. There is no evidence here for the negative conception of femininity which pervades much of the discussion of this concept. Feminine behaviour is regarded as normal and assessed positively in many contexts within such communities of practice.

On the other hand, we identified relatively low tolerance for aspects of behaviour perceived as normatively feminine in some contexts, and especially by men engaged in transactional, task-oriented interaction in more masculine communities of practice. Features which are conventionally associated with femininity may thus attract negative comment or derision in particular workplace interactions, within particular workplace cultures. Though often expressed in covert and implicit ways, such negative reactions could be regarded as evidence of sexism in such workplaces.

[. . .]

In conclusion, while professional identity might appear the most obviously relevant aspect of social identity in workplace interaction, the analysis in this paper demonstrates that people also discursively manage and interpret complex gender identities through workplace talk. Moreover, we suggest that our analysis provides a basis for recasting the concepts 'feminine' and 'femininity' in a more positive light, reclaiming the potential for women and men to behave in feminine ways, and make constructive but unremarkable use of conventionally feminine discourse strategies, 'even' at work.

NOTES

1.   This example is discussed in more detail in the context of an analysis of leadership strategies in Holmes, Schnurr, Chiles and Chan (2003). Tina Chiles, in particular, contributed to the analysis of this example.
2.   See Appendix for transcription conventions.
3.   We are not suggesting that indirectness should always be construed positively (or directness negatively). There are obviously occasions when indirectness can be unhelpful and counter-productive (see Holmes 2006 chapter 2). Such assessments can only be made in context; they require attention to participants' reactions, and often to the longer-term outcomes of an interaction insofar as these can be derived from the ethnographic detail collected in workplaces where we recorded.

REFERENCES

Aries, Elizabeth (1996) *Men and Women in Interaction*. Oxford, U.K.: Oxford University Press.

Bakhtin, Mikhail (1984) *Problems in Dostoevsky's Poetics*. Minneapolis, Minnesota: University of Minnesota Press.

Bell, Allan and George Major (2004) 'Yeah right': voicing kiwi masculinity. Paper presented at the New Zealand Language and Society Conference, Massey University, Palmerston North, New Zealand.

Besnier, Niko (2003) Transgenderism and language use in Tonga. In Janet Holmes and Miriam Meyerhoff (eds) *Handbook of Language and Gender*. Oxford, U.K.: Blackwell, 279–301.

Brown, Penelope and Stephen C. Levinson (1987) *Politeness: Some Universals in Language Usage*. Cambridge, U.K.: Cambridge University Press.

Bucholtz, Mary (1999) You da man: narrating the racial other in the production of white masculinity. *Journal of Sociolinguistics* 3: 443–460.

Cameron, Deborah (1997) Performing gender identity: young men's talk and the construction of hetero-sexual masculinity. In Sally Johnson and Ulrike Hanna Meinhof (eds) *Language and Masculinity*. Oxford, U.K.: Blackwell, 47–65.

Cameron, Deborah (1998) 'Is there any ketchup Vera?': gender, power and pragmatics. *Discourse and Society* 9: 435–455.

Cameron, Deborah and Don Kulick (2003) *Language and Sexuality*. Cambridge, U.K.: Cambridge University Press.

Coates, Jennifer (1996) *Woman Talk: Conversation Between Women Friends*. Oxford, U.K.: Blackwell.

Coates, Jennifer (1997) Competing discourses of femininity. In Helga Kotthoff and Ruth Wodak (eds) *Communicating Gender in Context*. Amsterdam, The Netherlands and Philadelphia, Pennsylvania: John Benjamins, 285–314.

Coates, Jennifer (1999) Changing femininities: the talk of teenage girls. In Mary Bucholtz, A. C. Liang and Laurel A. Sutton (eds) *Reinventing Identities*. New York: Oxford University Press, 123–144.

Coates, Jennifer (2003) *Men Talk*. Oxford, U.K.: Blackwell.

Connell, Robert W. (1987) *Gender and Power: Society, the Person and Sexual Politics*. Stanford, California: Stanford University Press.

Connell, Robert W. (1995) *Masculinities*. Berkeley, California: University of California Press.

Crawford, Mary (1995) *Talking Difference: On Gender and Language*. London: Sage.

Eckert, Penelope and Sally McConnell-Ginet (2003) *Language and Gender*. Cambridge, U.K.: Cambridge University Press.

Edley, Nigel and Margaret Wetherell (1997) Jockeying for position: the construction of masculine identities. *Discourse and Society* 8: 203–217.

Fletcher, Joyce K. (1999) *Disappearing Acts: Gender, Power, and Relational Practice at Work*. Cambridge, Massachusetts: MIT Press.

Hall, Kira (1995) Lip service on the fantasy lines. In Kira Hall and Mary Bucholtz (eds) *Gender Articulated: Language and the Socially Constructed Self*. New York: Routledge, 183–216.

Hall, Kira (2003) Exceptional speakers: contested and problematized gender identities. In Janet Holmes and Miriam Meyerhoff (eds) *Handbook of Language and Gender*. Malden, Massachusetts: Blackwell, 352–380.

Holmes, Janet (1995) *Women, Men and Politeness*. London: Longman.

Holmes, Janet (2000) Women at work: analysing women's talk in New Zealand workplaces. *Australian Review of Applied Linguistics* (ARAL) 22: 1–17.

Holmes, Janet (2005) Power and discourse at work: is gender relevant? In Michelle Lazar (ed.) *CDA and Gender*. London: Palgrave, 31–60.

Holmes, Janet (2006) *Gendered Talk at Work: Constructing Gender Identity Through Workplace Discourse*. Oxford, U.K.: Blackwell.

Holmes, Janet, Stephanie Schnurr, Tina Chiles and Angela Chan (2003) The discourse of leadership. *Te Reo* 46: 31–46.

Holmes, Janet and Maria Stubbe (2003a) 'Feminine' workplaces: stereotypes and reality. In Janet Holmes and Miriam Meyerhoff (eds) *Handbook of Language and Gender*. Oxford, U.K.: Blackwell, 573–599.

Holmes, Janet and Maria Stubbe (2003b) *Power and Politeness in the Workplace: A Sociolinguistic Analysis of Talk at Work*. London: Longman.

Holmes, Janet, Maria Stubbe and Bernadette Vine (1999) Constructing professional identity: 'power' in policy units. In Srikant Sarangi and Celia Roberts (eds) *Talk, Work and Institutional Order: Discourse in Medical, Mediation and Management Settings*. Berlin: de Gruyter, 351–385.

Johnson, Sally and Ulrike Hanna Meinhof (eds) (1997) *Language and Masculinity*. Oxford, U.K.: Blackwell.

Kendall, Shari (2003) Creating gendered demeanours of authority at work and at home. In Janet Holmes and Miriam Meyerhoff (eds) *Handbook of Language and Gender*. Oxford, U.K.: Blackwell, 600–623.

Kendall, Shari (2004) Framing authority: gender, face and mitigation at a radio network. *Discourse and Society* 15: 55–79.

Kiesling, Scott Fabius (1998) Men's identities and sociolinguistic variation: the case of fraternity men. *Journal of Sociolinguistics* 2: 69–99.

Kiesling, Scott Fabius (2004) What does a focus on 'men's language' tell us about language and woman's place? In Mary Bucholtz (ed) *Language and Woman's Place: Text and Commentaries*. Oxford, U.K.: Oxford University Press, 229–236.

Lakoff, Robyn Tolmach (2004) Language and woman's place revisited. In Mary Bucholtz (ed.) *Language and Woman's Place: Text and Commentaries*. Oxford, U.K.: Oxford University Press, 15–28.

Livia, Anna and Kira Hall (eds) (1997) *Queerly Phrased: Language, Gender, and Sexuality*. New York: Oxford University Press.

Meân, Lindsey (2001) Identity and discursive practice: doing gender on the football pitch. *Discourse and Society* 12: 789–815.

Mills, Sara (2003) *Gender and Politeness*. Cambridge, U.K.: Cambridge University Press.

Ochs, Elinor (1992) Indexing gender. In Alessandro Duranti and Charles Goodwin (eds) *Rethinking Context: Language as an Interactive Phenomenon*. Cambridge, U.K.: Cambridge University Press, 335–358.

Ochs, Elinor (1996) Linguistic resources for socializing humanity. In John J. Gumperz and Stephen C. Levinson (eds) *Rethinking Linguistic Relativity*. Cambridge, U.K.: Cambridge University Press, 407–438.

Okamoto, Shigeko (1995) 'Tasteless' Japanese: less 'feminine' speech among young Japanese women. In Kira Hall and Mary Bucholtz (eds) *Gender Articulated: Language and the Socially Constructed Self*. New York: Routledge, 297–325.

Romaine, Suzanne (1999) *Communicating Gender*. London: Lawrence Erlbaum.

Talbot, Mary (1998) *Language and Gender: An Introduction*. Malden, Massachusetts: Polity Press.

Tannen, Deborah (ed.) (1993) *Gender and Conversational Interaction*. Oxford, U.K.: Oxford University Press.

Tannen, Deborah (1994a) *Gender and Discourse*. London: Oxford University Press.

Tannen, Deborah (1994b) *Talking from 9 to 5*. London: Virago Press.

Wodak, Ruth (ed.) (1997) *Gender and Discourse*. London: Sage.

APPENDIX

yes	Underlining indicates emphatic stress
[laughs]::	Paralinguistic features in square brackets, colons indicate start/finish
+	Pause of up to one second
(3)	Pause of specified number of seconds
.../......\... .../......\...	Simultaneous speech
(hello)	Transcriber's best guess at an unclear utterance
?	Rising or question intonation
–	Incomplete or cut-off utterance
......	Section of transcript omitted
=	Speaker's turn continues
[*edit*]	Editorial comments italicized in square brackets

All names used in examples are pseudonyms.

QUESTIONS

1. Holmes' and Schnurr's introduction section includes the sentence below. What does this mean? What is the relation between linguistic choices, particular roles, and gender? What does it mean to 'do femininity'?

   'Building on the notion that – through their association with particular roles, activities, traits, and stances – certain socio-pragmatic, discursive and linguistic choices, or ways of speaking, "index" (Ochs 1992, 1996) or culturally encode gender (Cameron and Kulick 2003: 57), we explore the different ways of "doing femininity" identified in our workplace data.'

2. What does it mean to behave in a normatively feminine way in a recognisably feminine community of practice?

3. How are stances of considerateness and positive affect linked to gender?

4. What does it mean to behave in a normatively masculine way in a recognisably masculine community of practice?

5. What happened when markers of considerateness and concern for the addressee's face needs were used by men in a relatively masculine community of practice?

Concept

Consider the following two examples from Holmes and Schnurr. The first is taken from a recognisably feminine community of practice and the second from a recognisably masculine community of practice. Both include ways of talking which conventionally index femininity. What are these features? Are they marked or unmarked in the respective communities of practice? How do we know?

Example A

Context: Large project team meeting in commercial organisation. The project manager, Smithy, is reporting on the project's progress to the section manager, Clara.

1.	Smithy:	um service level team to produce
2.		a strategy document they've done +
3.		um Vita was to meet with I S to determine er
4.		an implementation plan for the recording device
5.	Vita:	yes done it +
6.	Smithy:	[*parenthetical tone*] Vita's done a um work plan
7.		just for that/um implementation\ and that
8.	Clara:	great/that'll make the plan easier\
9.	Smithy:	we can feed/(out what) you want\
10.	Vita:	/haven't actually\(heard anything …)
11.	Smithy:	Vita's going to meet with Stewart
12.		to determine how 0800 numbers
13.		come in to the call centre

Example B

Context: Meeting of the senior management team in middle-sized IT company. Neil apologises for not being able to attend the first monthly staff meeting to which he has been invited.

1.	Shaun:	okay but I think it's important
2.		you do go to the staff meeting
3.		and get introduced
4.	Neil:	yeah ………
5.		er I can't do it today unfortunately I've
6.		I've already booked in some time
7.		with someone else this afternoon
8.		but the next one I can come along to yeah
9.	Shaun:	we'll think about it
10.	Neil:	pardon
11.	Shaun:	we'll think about it
12.	Neil:	/[laughs]\
13.	Shaun:	/we don't take kindly to\ being rejected
14.	Neil:	oh I'm sorry I've got a yeah got a meeting
15.		this afternoon which I can't get out of
16.		if I'd have known I would've changed it yeah
17.	Shaun:	what is our formal position on Neil (5)

PART SIX

Gender

Editors' Introduction to Part Six

THIS READER CLOSES WITH a section on gender and creates a link to the first section on style and politeness. Research on language and gender has undergone similar changes as the research on style and politeness, with a current focus on speaker identities, and both concepts, style and politeness, are of great importance in current language and gender research.

The modern research tradition of language and gender was kicked off by Robin Lakoff in her 1973 article "Language and Women's Place". While pioneering at the time, empirical research conducted in the aftermath of Lakoff's study identified three major weaknesses of her work: the methodology, which consisted of casual observation and introspection; the problem of explanation; and the form and function problem, i.e. ignoring the possibility that the same form (e.g. a tag question) can serve a variety of different functions. Subsequent research on language and gender during the last four decades witnessed a shift in how gender was conceptualised and how potential differences and similarities in research studies were explained, from early research similar to Lakoff's (sometimes referred to as a deficiency approach, as "women's language" was suggested to be deficient when compared to "men's") to the so-called dominance approach (e.g. O'Barr & Atkins 1980), and the difference approach (e.g. Tannen 1990), to social-constructivist approaches. The latter focus on the diversity of male and female speech styles in more localised investigations of gender (Henley 1995, Bucholtz 1996, 1999, Eckert 2000, D. Cameron 1997, 2000, Holmes & Schnurr 2006, Schleef 2008), on a constructivist approach to identity, and the exploration of context and its constraints. The notion of indexicality is another important concept within this general group of approaches. Not surprisingly, questions asked within research on language and gender have also shifted during the last four decades from investigating whether women and men use different quantities of the same form, to an investigation of when, why, and how certain women and men use different linguistic strategies. A more detailed description of changes to approaches in language and gender research can be found in D. Cameron (2005).

In this section of the Reader, we have collected four articles which are particularly useful examples of various modes of analysis in current research on language and gender. Several other articles in this Reader also relate their findings to gender and will be briefly mentioned below. Haeri's article on language variation and change in Cairo is different from the other three in this section in that it was written in the variationist tradition of research on language and gender. Other articles in this Reader relevant to gender and written in a similar tradition include R. Cameron (2005), Sankoff and Blondeau (2007), Ito and Tagliamonte (2003), Nevalainen (1999), and Milroy and Milroy (1992). Haeri's article investigates the sociolinguistic variable of apical palatalisation in Cairene Arabic. Some students may need help with some of the descriptive phonetics in this paper, but the valuable findings can be appreciated without complete understanding of the phonetics. Palatalisation is an example of a stylistic resource that belongs to Cairene Arabic proper rather than Classical Arabic. Women in Cairo seem to have been the innovators of this sound change. This is interesting because other features, those which span the classical/nonclassical dichotomy, seem to be following a different pattern. Haeri's article is not only important because it provides evidence for patterns of sociolinguistic variation in a non-Western culture but it also enriches findings on the use of standard versus vernacular features by women. Early studies (e.g. by Trudgill in Norwich) found women using more features of the standard language. Subsequent research, however, has modified this generalistion as we now also know that women often use more of an incoming non-standard variant than men (see Meyerhoff 2006 for an overview of research).

In contrast to Haeri, the other three articles in this section are all social-constructivist in nature, as are Eckert 1998 and Holmes and Schnurr 2006 in the previous section. With the exception of Eckert 1998, all of these focus on discourse and conversational practice rather than the link of gender to standard and vernacular. They show very nicely what repercussions the paradigm shift discussed above has had for the way research is conducted. For example, while Haeri analysed data collected in sociolinguistic interviews, Ochs, Kiesling, Barrett, Eckert, and Holmes and Schnurr investigate naturally occurring language and focus on an analysis of style in their studies.

Ochs' article is a classic in language and gender research. It outlines one of the important points within post-structural approaches to language and gender, namely that gender is usually indexed indirectly, mediated by several factors: certain speech acts, association with certain stances, and particular social practices. The second part of Ochs' article exemplifies some of these theoretical claims using data on child-directed speech in the US and Samoa. This second part of the article has been quite heavily excerpted while at the same time including the main arguments.

Kiesling and Barrett both focus on the expression of speaker identities while, quite usefully, exploring other concepts as well; power in the case of Kiesling, and code-switching within the framework of markedness theory in the case of Barrett. Kiesling investigates issues of power and dominance as they relate to male identities by discussing the unique personal approaches and discursive strategies used by individual men. Barrett's exploration of the language style of African-American drag queens shows how unmarked and marked stylistic choices are used as rhetorical devices to highlight the instability, fleetingness and constant negotiation of social categories related to gender, ethnicity, class, and sexuality. Again, local analyses of language and speakers' negotiations of identity play a very important part here, as does the diversity of male and female speech styles in context – alongside indexicality, all issues very much at the heart of current language and gender research.

REFERENCES

Bucholtz, Mary (1999) 'Why be normal?': language and identity practices in a community of nerd girls. *Language in Society* 28: 203–223.

Bucholtz, Mary (1996). Black feminist theory and African American women's linguistic practice. In Victoria L. Bergvall, Janet M. Bing and Alice F. Freed (eds), *Rethinking Language and Gender Research: Theory and Practice*. London: Longman, 267–290.

Cameron, Deborah (1997) Performing gender identity: young men's talk and the construction of heterosexual masculinity. In Ulrike Hanna Meinhof and Sally Johnson (eds) *Language and Masculinity*. Oxford: Blackwell, 41–64.

Cameron, Deborah (2000) Styling the worker: gender and the commodification of language in the globalized service economy. *Journal of Sociolinguistics* 4: 323–347.

Cameron, Deborah (2005) Language, gender, and sexuality: current issues and new directions. *Applied Linguistics* 26: 482–502.

Eckert, Penelope (2000) *Linguistic Variation as Social Practice: The Linguistic Construction of Identity in Belten High*. Oxford: Blackwell.

Henley, Nancy (1995) Ethnicity and gender issues in language. In Hope Landrine (ed.) *Bringing Cultural Diversity to Feminist Psychology*. Washington: American Psychological Association, 361–396.

Lakoff, Robin (1973) Language and women's place. *Language in Society* 2: 45–80.

Meyerhoff, Miriam (2006) *Introducing Sociolinguistics*. London: Taylor & Francis.

O'Barr, William M., and Bowman K. Atkins (1980) Women's language or powerless language? In Sally McConnell-Ginet et al. (eds) *Women and Language in Literature and Society*. New York: Praeger, 98–110.

Schleef, Erik (2008) Gender and academic discourse: global restrictions and local possibilities. *Language in Society* 37: 515–538.

Tannen, Deborah (1990) *You Just Don't Understand: Women and Men in Conversation*. New York: Ballantine.

FURTHER READING

Cameron, Deborah (2008) *The Myth of Mars and Venus: Do Men and Women Really Speak Different Languages?* Oxford: Oxford University Press.

Cameron, Deborah and Don Kulick (2003) *Language and Sexuality*. Cambridge: Cambridge University Press.

Cameron, Deborah and Don Kulick (2006) *The Language and Sexuality Reader*. London and New York: Routledge.

Coates, Jennifer (1998) *Language and Gender: A Reader*. Oxford: Blackwell.

Coates, Jennifer (1993) *Women, Men and Language*. 2nd ed. London & New York: Longman.

Eckert, Penelope (1989) The whole woman: sex and gender differences in variation. *Language Variation and Change* 1: 245–267.

Eckert, Penelope and Sally McConnell-Ginet (2003) *Language and Gender*. Cambridge: Cambridge University Press.

Hall, Kira and Mary Bucholtz. (eds) (1995) *Gender Articulated: Language and the Socially Constructed Self*. London and New York: Routledge.

Holmes, Janet and Miriam Meyerhoff (2003) *The Handbook of Language and Gender*. Oxford and New York: Blackwell.

Smyth, Ron, Greg Jacobs, and Henry Rogers (2003) Male voices and perceived sexual orientation: an experimental and theoretical approach. *Language in Society* 32: 329–350.

Sunderland, Jane (2006) *Language and Gender: An Advanced Resource Book*. London and New York: Routledge.

Tannen, Deborah (1994) *Gender and Discourse*. Oxford: Oxford University Press.

Chapter 29

Niloofar Haeri

A LINGUISTIC INNOVATION OF WOMEN IN CAIRO

IN THIS ARTICLE, I introduce the sociolinguistic variable of apical palatalization in Cairene Arabic. My aim is to provide a detailed characterization of its linguistic and sociolinguistic features. The significance of palatalization as a sociolinguistic variable is its status as a stylistic resource of Cairene Arabic. The richness of the stylistic resources of *Classical* Arabic has tended to overshadow the sociolinguistic dynamics of nonclassical varieties in many studies.[1]

Depending on the complex interaction of a number of factors, some Egyptians use features of Classical Arabic while speaking in Egyptian Arabic. One example is the use of lexical items containing the phoneme /q/ (called the "qaf," a voiceless uvular stop), which historically belongs to Classical Arabic. Several studies have found that women use fewer such lexical items than men (Abdel-Jawad, 1981; Bakir, 1986; Sallam, 1980; Schmidt, 1974). What are the patterns of gender differences with regard to a stylistic resource such as palatalization which do not span the classical/nonclassical dichotomy? In what follows, I describe the variable and provide an analysis of its phonological characteristics. In the second half of this article, I provide data on the use of palatalization with regard to gender, age, social class, style, and education. The fieldwork for this study was carried out in 1987–1988. Out of a sample of 87 tape-recorded interviews, 49 were chosen, representing 25 women and 24 men. A total of 8,011 tokens was extracted.[2]

LINGUISTIC ANALYSIS

Palatalization in Cairene Arabic affects allophones of the dental stop phonemes /t, d/ and /T, D/, which are called "plain" and "emphatic," respectively. The emphatic stops of

Source: Haeri, Niloofar (1994) A linguistic innovation of women in Cairo. *Language Variation and Change* 6: 87–112.

Cairene Arabic are produced with accompanying pharyngealization, where the root of the tongue is backed. [. . .]

The two most favored environments for palatalization are a following high front vowel or glide. A segment may be weakly palatalized or strongly palatalized. In the first case, the effect is one of frication, whereas in the second, the segment becomes an affricate. For example, /mamti/ 'my mother' may be realized as [mamtʲi] or [mamči]. The release of weakly palatalized segments is often accompanied with aspiration so that a more narrowly transcribed representation of the example would be [mamtʰiˀ], where the final vowel is higher and produced with more lip spreading than if the segment were not palatalized. The phonetic environments in which palatalization occurred variably in the data are as follows:

Following Environments		
short high front vowel (word-final)	[i]	/faaDi/ 'empty'
word-medial	[-i-]	/tiktibi/ 'you write [fem.]'
long high front vowel	[ii]	/gidiid/ 'new'
long mid front vowel	[ee]	/sanateen/ 'two years'
palatal glide	[y]	/nadya/ 'Nadia' [female name]
epenthetic vowel		/ruHt gibt/ '(I) went and bought' (lit. 'brought')
other vowels		/uskutuu/ 'be quiet [plur.]'
consonant		/sitt ʔawi/ 'woman very'
pause		

A few of the environments bear explanation. The high front /i/ was coded separately, depending on whether it occurred word-finally or non-finally: for example, /ʕaadi/ 'normal' versus /tiktib/ 'write [masc. imperative]'. This is because there are differences in phonetic quality between the two so that, where /i/ occurs word-finally, I believe it is higher than when it occurs in other environments. The long [ii] belongs to a separate phoneme.

A following glide occurs most often when the next word starts with a glide, as in /bizzaat yaʕni/ 'in essence meaning . . .'. But it also occurs in words such as /nadya/ 'Nadia' [female name], /vidyo/ 'video', and so on. An epenthetic vowel is inserted when there is a sequence of three consonants (Broselow, 1976), as in /ʔomt baʔollaha/ [ʔomtəbaʔollæhæ], lit. 'I got up tell her', 'so I told her'. This environment then turns out to be a potential one for palatalization. The quality of the epenthetic vowel is variable. Some speakers, especially women, pronounce it as a short high front [ɪ], others pronounce it as a lower schwa [ə].

Turning now to the last three environments, the following should be mentioned. Although in the vast majority of cases, palatalization took place before a high front vowel (or glide), there were a few instances where the vowel was low front. The actual examples in my data are:

[bɪtæʕmɪlha] 'she does it'
[bæʕD æyyɪ] '. . . each other any . . .'
[bɪtæʕi] 'mine'

There were also three tokens, all repetitions of the same word, where palatalization took place when the following vowel was a high back [u]. The actual word was:

/uskutuu/ → [oskočʉ] 'be quiet [plur.]'

This vowel is generally not fronted, and it is similar to the French high back [u], as in the word *nous* 'we'. All three palatalized tokens occurred during an interview with a mother whose children were being noisy and preventing her from talking. It may be that the environment for palatalization is becoming more general, embracing not only high front vowels, but also low front and high back vowels. The examples of advanced palatalization involving [æ] and [u] were all uttered by women.

Palatalization occurs, though rarely, when the segment is followed by a pause: /bint/ → [bɪnč] 'girl'.[3] Finally, when the following segment is a consonant, palatalization occurs, but, again, rarely.

/itrabeet fil/ → [ɪtræbeeč fɪl] '(I) was brought up in'

There are also examples in the data of sequences of three consonants which are not broken up by an epenthetic vowel, as would be required by the phonotactics of Cairene. Yet in this environment, palatalization takes place.

/sitt ʔawi/ → [sɪč ʔæwi] 'woman very'[4]

ANALYSIS OF VARBRUL RESULTS

VARBRUL runs reported here are based on tokens of *strong* palatalization, that is, where palatalization resulted in the affricates [č, dž]. However, I will compare the results of weak and strong palatalization. In these runs, all and only the linguistic factor groups were run together. As can be seen from Table 29.1, voiceless segments in general have higher probabilities for undergoing palatalization than their voiced counterparts. Concentrating on the first four segments, we also see that the plain [t, d] have higher probabilities than the pharyngeal [T, D], respectively. [. . .] Impressionistically, the distinction between emphatic and plain consonants is neutralized, so that when both sets are palatalized, they are phonetically indistinguishable. [. . .]

Table 29.1 Percentages and probabilities of application of palatalization for dental stops

Segment	Percentage	Probability	N
t	22	.58	3,857
T	17	.53	185
d	18	.43	3,313
D	15	.36	221
tt	11	.38	106
dd	10	.36	329
Total			8,011

PALATALIZATION OF PHARYNGEAL SEGMENTS

Keating (1988) surveyed a variety of studies which have proposed phonological feature systems. She stated that palatals are classified as [−back], and pharyngeals as [+back], among other features used to classify these sounds (Ibid.:7). That is, whereas for pharyngeals the tongue root is retracted, for palatals, it is fronted (Keating, 1988; Royal, 1985). This contradiction in features is what renders the results puzzling. How can the same segment be both front and back? [However, there is] evidence to suggest that phonemically pharyngeal segments are often articulated without pharyngealization. Thus, when these segments are palatalized, they were probably produced without pharyngealization in the first place.

[. . .]

EFFECTS OF FOLLOWING ENVIRONMENT: TWO PUZZLING FINDINGS

The three following environments which have the highest probabilities for palatalization are a palatal glide [y], a high front [i], and a long high front [ii] (see Table 29.2). From an articulatory point of view, these results are expected. As we saw earlier, all studies of palatalization indicate that the position of the tongue in this process is high and front, assimilating to the tongue position for the following vowels.[5] Thus, the most favored environments for palatalization are high front vowels.

There are, however, two puzzling findings in Table 29.2. The first is the difference between the two allophones of /i/. Word-final [i] (e.g., /faaDi/ 'empty') has a probability of .68, whereas nonfinal [i] (e.g., /tiktib/ 'write [masc. imp.]') has a probability of .28. In addition, there is a considerable difference between both allophones of [i], on the one hand, and [ii], on the other. Why should there be a difference between long and short [i]? To discuss these questions further, let us first take a look at the entire Cairene vowel system (the chart is taken from Broselow, 1976, which is also based on Mitchell, 1956).

Table 29.2   Percentages and probabilities of application of palatalization for following environment

Environment	Percentage	Probability	N
[y] glide	29	.68	489
[i] (word-final)	24	.63	3,703
[ii]	18	.51	1,239
[ɪ] epenthetic	21	.49	344
[i] (nonfinal)	10	.28	1,573
[ee]	3	.10	113
Other vowel	6	.19	128
Consonant	5	.13	280
Pause	4	.12	142
Total			8,011

The Cairene Vowel Phonemes

i	u	ii	uu
		ee	oo
a		aa	

As can be seen from the chart, there is no phonemic short /e/ (or short /o/). In Table 29.2, we saw that the following vowel has to be high (and front) for palatalization to take place. Are all allophones of /i/ equally high? What are the articulatory features of the allophones of /i/? Where are they located on the vowel chart?

It seems that what crucially distinguishes these two allophones is height: word-final [i] is higher than nonfinal [i]. The latter is closer in quality to a mid-front [e]. For example, in a word such as /abtidi/ 'I begin', which would traditionally be transcribed as [æbtɪdi], the syllable [di] is more likely to undergo palatalization than [tɪ]. [. . .] We may also compare [ii] and [ee], whose probabilities are .51 and .10, respectively. These two vowels differ only on the basis of height. This is further evidence that vowel height is an important factor in explaining why a word-final [i] is a more favored environment than nonfinal [i].[6]

[. . .]

Let us now turn to the second question, namely, why is there a difference between [ii], on the one hand, and both allophones of /i/, on the other? Clearly, we are also dealing with vowel length as a potential factor. Length, in itself, does not discourage palatalization, as a comparison of [ii] with [ee] shows. So we should look at other factors. [. . .]

Wahba's (1991) study is an acoustic analysis of long and short vowels in closed syllables in Egyptian Arabic. This study provides us with a crucial finding. Wahba found that long [ii] is significantly higher than nonfinal [i] (Ibid.: 4). This strongly supports our claim that the important dimension explaining the difference among all the high front vowels is height.[7]

[. . .] Before we proceed to a sociolinguistic analysis of this variable, I should address one other question: namely, whether weak and strong palatalization are two separate phonological processes or one. The linguistic evidence points more strongly toward one process though not wholly conclusively, whereas the sociolinguistic evidence clearly shows two processes at work. Diachronic data showing real-time distribution are crucially needed here. In the absence of this kind of data, I offer the less convincing apparent-time data, showing the speakers' use of weak and strong palatalization according to their age. I begin with the linguistic evidence.

WEAK AND STRONG PALATALIZATION: ONE PROCESS OR TWO?

First, note that *palatalization* is a cover term embracing a number of phonological processes. In this regard, Bhat (1978) stated that this varied usage makes it difficult to come up with a satisfactory definition which would include all kinds of palatalization. [. . .] Bhat criticized earlier works that considered palatalization as a single process and argued that the three processes of fronting, raising, and spirantization can occur alone, and for this reason, they should be considered as "independent entities" (1978:51). [. . .]

Table 29.3 Comparison of following environments for weak and strong palatalization

Environment	Percentage		Probability	
	Weak	Strong	Weak	Strong
Glide	22	29	.69	.68
Word-final [i]	19	24	.57	.64
[ii]	15	18	.53	.51
Epenthetic [ɪ]	8	21	.40	.49
Nonfinal [i]	8	10	.37	.28
[ee]	7	3	.28	.10
Other vowels	2	6	.12	.19
Consonant	2	5	.17	.13
Pause	9	4	.45	.12

It seems that all three processes are at work in the palatalization of dental stops in Cairene Arabic, and there is no reason to separate them.

[. . .]

We can compare the probabilities of the dental stops involved in both kinds of palatalization to see if there are any differences. [. . .] Similarities in the effects of following environment provide [strong] evidence for a unitary treatment, as can be seen in Table 29.3. The order of environments in terms of their probabilities is remarkably similar for both weak and strong palatalization. The only large difference has to do with the probability for the category "pause," which has a probability of .45 for weak and .12 for strong palatalization. There are a total of 142 tokens in this category. Some speakers release their final dental stops, and when this stop is voiceless, there is considerable aspiration in the release. This aspiration is similar to that for weakly palatalized voiceless segments, and I coded them as such. This, I believe, is why "pause" has a much higher probability. Other than this difference, which I consider to be minor, there are no major differences that would argue for considering weak and strong palatalization as two separate processes. [. . .] I conclude tentatively that we are dealing with one process, namely, we have a gradient variable with three variants: not palatalized, weakly palatalized, and strongly palatalized.

Weak and strong palatalization do not seem to have come into the phonology of Cairene Arabic at the same time. It appears that weak palatalization came in first, and then for some speakers, the frication of weak palatalization turned into affrication. It is thus important to look at the social distribution of each separately so that we may better document the recent history of palatalization and the variety of social values it has come to represent.

A SOCIOLINGUISTIC CHARACTERIZATION OF PALATALIZATION

I begin the discussion with the most outstanding feature of the social distribution of the data. Palatalization, perhaps more than any other aspect of the Cairene phonology, distinguishes the speech of men and women. Women have frequent and advanced

Table 29.4 Probability and percentage differences of application of palatalization between men and women

	Weak		Strong		
	Probability	%	Probability	%	Total tokens
Women	.60	18	.77	31	4,418
Men	.38	10	.18	5	3,593

palatalization, whereas men have little palatalization in their speech. Table 29.4 shows the magnitude of this difference. Due to such large differences, most of the data here are presented for women and men separately. This is also in keeping with the suggestions made in Eckert (1989) and Labov (1990). Labov stated that multivariate analysis of the kind sociolinguists use most, namely VARBRUL, assumes independence among factors and was designed primarily for linguistic analysis where independence can be expected. For social factors, where we can expect interaction, separate runs for men and women are required, as is the use of cross-tabulations to locate possible interaction. I use cross-tabulations to report on the results. Chisquare tests are used to assess the significance of any apparent differences.[8]

IS PALATALIZATION A SOUND CHANGE IN PROGRESS?

Two questions need to be answered with regard to the status of palatalization: (1) How recent is it? (2) Is it a sound change in progress in the sense that it has neither gone to completion, nor stopped completely in its tracks due to overwhelming stigmatization? To answer the first question in the absence of real-time data, it would have to be shown that palatalization was not present during the childhood or adolescence of the oldest speakers in this data base. Figure 29.1 shows the use of strong palatalization among three age groups. Neither men nor women above age 50 have any strong palatalization. But in the next age group, there is a jump from 2% to 28% for women. [Eds: All differences reported in the remainder of the paper were shown to be significant at $p \leq 0.001$ unless specified otherwise.] This frequency goes up to almost 40% in the youngest age group. [. . .] The pattern in Figure 29.1 shows that strong palatalization probably did not exist for speakers above age 50 when they were children or adolescents. In other words, it was not part of the phonology of Cairene Arabic in the 1920s or 1930s. [. . .]

As for the second question, the systematically differentiated distribution of palatalization (both strong and weak) among women in particular shows that palatalization is a change in progress. As is discussed later, in addition to the data presented in Figure 29.1, data on education and social class also support this claim.

[. . .] Figure 29.1 provides a more complete picture by showing the age distribution for both kinds of palatalization. The youngest women have twice as high a frequency of strong palatalization as weak palatalization. More importantly, the oldest age group has 15% weak palatalization for women and 4% for men. Based on the linguistic behavior of the oldest group in terms of weak and strong palatalization, it seems that weak palatalization preceded strong palatalization. [. . .] Again, to be able to locate when weak palatalization came in, we would need diachronic data and speakers in their 70s and 80s.[9]

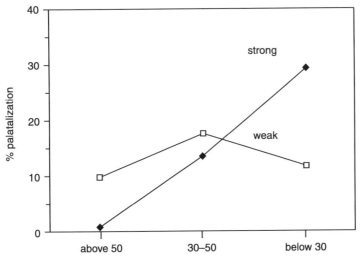

Figure 29.1   Weak and strong palatalization compared in three age groups.

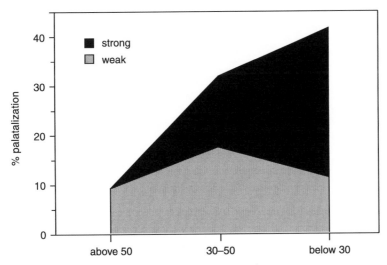

Figure 29.2   View of weak and strong palatalization in an area graph.

Restating the conclusions reached so far, it seems that palatalization is a sound change in progress, and that it started in the form of weak palatalization. Figure 29.2 shows that strong palatalization is replacing weak palatalization for the youngest age group.

LOCATING THE INNOVATORS OF PALATALIZATION

[. . .] [I]n Figure 29.3, where weak and strong palatalization among women in the four social classes are compared, it seems that [Lower Middle Class] LMC and [Middle Middle Class] MMC women took weak palatalization a step further, both in terms of going from frication to affrication [i.e. strong palatalization] and in terms of frequency. The evidence so far supports the claim that palatalization was an innovation of women;

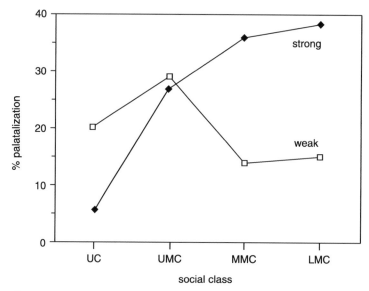

Figure 29.3 Percentages of weak and strong palatalization compared for women in four social classes.

Table 29.5 Percentage of weak and strong palatalization in four styles among women and men

	Women		Men	
	Weak	*Strong*	*Weak*	*Strong*
Narrative	18	31	12	4
Nonnarrative	19	31	8	5
Response	17	29	9	3
Word list	25	54	21	11

and if, as it seems to be the case, weak palatalization came in first, then it was an innovation of UC and UMC women.

The relation of style to social class has been discussed by a number of researchers, including Labov (1966, 1972), Bell (1984), Holmes (1992). Where a new, "nonstandard" variant is concerned, its use has been found to decrease in more formal styles. However, in the case of weak and strong palatalization, its use increases in Word List Style. This can be seen in Table 29.5. Although there is little consistent stylistic differentiation, the clearest pattern is that the highest amount of palatalization is used in Word List Style. Chisquare calculations show no significant differences among the first three styles ($p < .70$), but they are all different from Word List Style at the .05 level. The same pattern can be seen among men.

In Table 29.6, the same data are provided according to social class. LMC and MMC tokens are combined because I found no statistically significant differences between the two groups so far, though this does not mean that their linguistic behavior is always the same. Looking at the data in Table 29.6, we see that MMC (and LMC) women have almost twice as high a percentage of weak palatalization in Word List Style as in the other

Table 29.6   Cross-tabulation of social class and style for weak and strong palatalization among women (%)

	Narrative		Nonnarrative		Response		Word list	
	Weak	Strong	Weak	Strong	Weak	Strong	Weak	Strong
MMC[a]	12	34	16	38	15	36	21	68
UMC	31	30	29	32	24	16	33	17
UC	32	7	16	6	15	3	–	–

[a] LMC and MMC combined.

styles; UMC women have a higher percentage than the former groups. The "nonstandard" status of the palatalized variants seems to be overridden by some other social meanings. The innovators of most sound changes studied so far have not been from the upper classes. In the case of palatalization, which seems to be a change from above the social hierarchy, its status as an upper class way of talking is perhaps a factor in its increased usage in the most formal style.

In Table 29.6, we see that UC women seem to disfavor strong palatalization, and UMC women have less strong palatalization in the two formal styles. The general pattern is that, whereas weak palatalization is associated with women in the upper classes, strong palatalization is a feature of the speech of women in the (lower) middle classes. [. . .]

It could be argued that the lack of a consistent stylistic pattern is due to the fact that palatalization is still below the level of conscious awareness and therefore has not received widespread stigmatization. However, for a sound change to be below the level of conscious awareness does not mean that its use has no social meanings. The lack of linear and predictable patterns of usage, as reflected in the data on style, shows that consistent usage patterns are more often features of *stable* variables or those that are clearly associated with groups on the lower rungs of the social hierarchy. The social meanings of stable variables become conventionalized and established. On the other hand, the social meanings of sound changes in progress are multiple, changing, and *variable*. The data here show that the process through which sociolinguistic forms acquire widely agreed upon and conventionalized social meanings is not complete for palatalization (Haeri, 1991, 1992b).

For the sake of completeness and comparison, the same data on men are provided in Table 29.7. There is little social or stylistic differentiation among men. However, men in the LMC category have their highest frequencies in the Word List Style. As there is only

Table 29.7   Cross-tabulation of style and social class for weak and strong palatalization among men (%)

	Narrative		Nonnarrative		Response		Word list	
	Weak	Strong	Weak	Strong	Weak	Strong	Weak	Strong
LMC	9	8	10	11	7	8	22	31
MMC	11	3	6	3	12	0	11	6
UMC	16	2	7	1	7	1	28	0
UC	30	7	19	9	18	6	–	–

one man in the UC category, I cannot be sure that his relatively high percentages are generalizable to other men in the same social class.

Finally, in order to obtain an overall picture of the contour of this sound change from no palatalization to weak and then to strong palatalization, Figs. 29.4 and 29.5 are provided. Figure 29.4 shows a two-stage sound change, similar to the lenition of (ch) in Panama City, as described by Cedergren (1973). Strong palatalization is replacing weak palatalization for women below age 50 who are in the LMC and MMC groups. Figure 29.4 also shows that UMC women are not following this lead. Figure 29.5 provides the same data for men. Here, however, it is only LMC men who show any

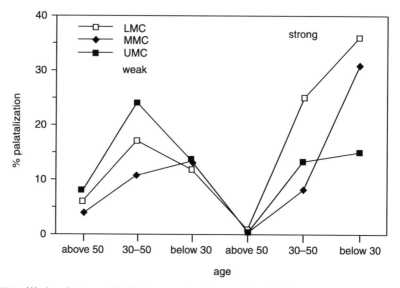

Figure 29.4　Weak and strong palatalization according to age and social class among women.

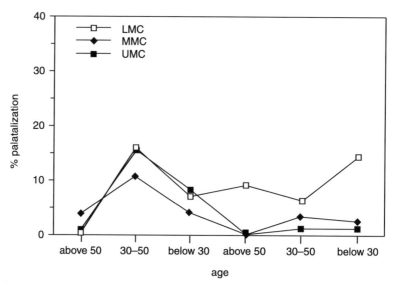

Figure 29.5　Weak and strong palatalization according to age and social class among men.

participation in the use of strong palatalization. In both graphs, the UMC category is highlighted to show better the probable origin of this sound change.

EDUCATION AND TYPE OF SCHOOL

One other piece of evidence that supports our conclusion that palatalization was an innovation of UMC women should be brought forth at this point. In the present sample, with the exception of one UMC woman and three UMC men, all of the UMC and UC speakers had attended private schools. None of the men and women in the other social categories had. If we can show that those who attended private schools have a significantly higher frequency of weak palatalization, then our claim about the source of this innovation is further confirmed. [. . .] [W]omen who attended private schools have twice as high a frequency of weak palatalization as those who attended public schools. The frequency of weak and strong palatalization is reversed, depending on the type of school the speaker attended. For strong palatalization, those who went to public schools have a higher frequency than those in the private school category. This is almost a replication of our data on social class, but not completely because four UMC speakers are in the public school category. But this factor, I believe, has some explanatory power in the differentiation of class-based linguistic differences that we have observed. [. . .]

[. . .][M]en who attended private school have the highest amount of weak palatalization, [but] the type of school does not seem to be relevant for men in terms of their participation in this sound change. Chi-square calculations for men show little statistical significance for weak palatalization ($p < .10$) or for strong palatalization ($p < .20$).

LEVEL OF EDUCATION

Figures 29.6 and 29.7 present data on education for women and men. Figure 29.6 is reminiscent of Figure 29.3 on social class because the patterns are reversed for weak and strong palatalization. That is, as the level of education goes up, so does the frequency of weak palatalization. Strong palatalization, however, decreases after high school. Women in high school have the highest amount of strong palatalization; men in the same category have the highest amount of weak palatalization (see Figure 29.7). What is interesting about both figures is that those speakers with the lowest level of education are not the ones with the highest amount of palatalization in their speech. Nor is strong palatalization a feature of highly educated speech. This is also consistent with previous results: UC women (i.e., those generally with more education than high school) have less strong palatalization in their speech than weak palatalization. Strong palatalization is a feature of middle and lower middle class, high school educated women. Such results play a role in explaining why the data on stylistic differentiation do not bear consistent patterns. *Strong palatalization, for example, is neither a feature of least educated, nor most educated speakers.*

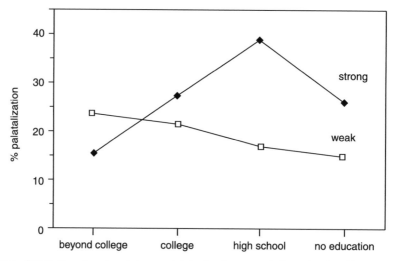

Figure 29.6   Distribution of weak and strong palatalization for women in four educational levels.

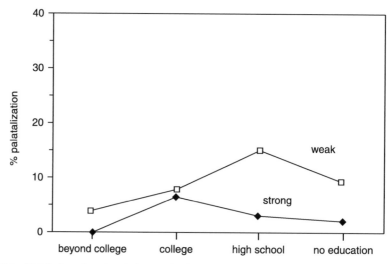

Figure 29.7   Distribution of weak and strong palatalization among men in four educational levels.

DISCUSSION

A large number of sociolinguistic studies in diverse speech communities have found that women are often the innovators of sound changes (see Eckert & McConnell-Ginet, 1992; Labov, 1982, 1990). I have shown here that, for palatalization in Cairene Arabic, women are the innovators and far ahead of men in its propagation. Because in comparison to older forms, newer ones are said to be "nonstandard," women have been said to use "nonstandard" variants of changing variables more frequently than men. In the case of Arabic, all *non* classical forms are automatically considered "nonstandard." Thus, with regard to palatalization, whether a form is not palatalized at all, weakly palatalized, or strongly palatalized, it would always be "nonstandard" so long as it belongs to Egyptian

Arabic and not to Classical Arabic. It is clear that the automatic equation of Classical Arabic with "Standard Arabic" is problematic (Haeri 1987, 1991; Ibrahim, 1986). The dialect of Egyptian Arabic, which is spoken in the capital, has itself a "standard" variety. This, of course, is not surprising when we look at many other countries in the world where the urban dialect of the capital is the standard variety of the national language. So, formulating the linguistic behavior of women and men with respect to palatalization according to general practice, I would say that women are the innovators of palatalization, using the "nonstandard" variant more than men. As we mentioned earlier, this replicates findings in many other speech communities.

Corroborating our results, I should also mention the relevant findings of Royal (1985). Pharyngeal phonemes exist both in the phonology of Classical and nonclassical Arabic varieties. However, strong pharyngealization is associated with the proper norms of the classical language. Royal carried out acoustic analyses of men and women in two neighborhoods in Cairo, one affluent and one belonging to the "popular quarters." In the first neighborhood, and among the younger generation of the second, she found that "Men display a higher degree and women a lesser degree of pharyngealization relative to each other in all circumstances, thereby sharply differentiating women's pharyngealization from men's" (Ibid.: 164). Thus, there seems to be another sociolinguistic variable and another sound change in progress where women are ahead of men in its propagation.

The presence of sociolinguistic variables such as palatalization [and] "de-pharyngealization" [. . .] as resources for style shifting point to the fact that variation in nonclassical varieties is possible without recourse to Classical Arabic. In other words, Cairene Arabic is not a monolithic "colloquial" entity, as this and all other nonclassical varieties have been called (Haeri, 1992a).

It is clear that the existence of diglossia does not render such communities transparent and predictable. I have shown the impact of social structure as represented by such factors as social class, gender, and education on Cairene Arabic. Thus, like languages serving other complex communities, Cairene Arabic reflects the heterogeneity of its speakers.

NOTES

1. The use of the term "Classical Arabic" is not meant to imply that this language since its codification in the eighth century has remained wholly unchanged. Because Classical Arabic has been used throughout the centuries as a medium of writing and because language academies in a variety of countries (e.g., Syria and Egypt) have been continuously coining scientific and technical terms, Classical Arabic is a language with a number of "versions," and some scholars prefer to distinguish between what they call "Modern Standard Arabic" on the one hand and Classical Arabic on the other. In fact, there are a number of terms (e.g., literary Arabic) that various scholars use. I justify the use of "Classical Arabic" on a number of grounds. Foremost among them is that speakers whom I interviewed categorized the linguistic varieties used in Egypt with the terms *il-lughat il-arabiyya* "the Arabic language" or *il-nahawi* to refer to the classical language and *ammiya* "common" or *masri* "Egyptian" to refer to Egyptian Arabic.

2. Two women and two men whose speech contained frequent and advanced palatalization were chosen to be coded first in order to establish the envelope of variation. Their interviews, three of which were nearly 2 hours long, were coded in their entirety. More than 400 tokens were extracted

from each of these interviews. On the basis of the speech of these four individuals, the rest of the interviews were coded impressionistically for six phonetic environments.

3. In this environment, gemination of the final consonant also occurs frequently, for example, [bitt] "girl". The possible interaction of these two processes is not explored here. This process is rather frequently commented on by many speakers as an example of "slangy" talk.

4. It is not clear what happens to the initial glottal stop in /ʔæwi/ "very". It may be that it gets elided and we get [sɪčæwi]. Broselow (1976:24) stated that glottal stops that are historically "derived" from the /q/ are "always present no matter what the environment." That is, they do not get deleted or are "never elided" (p. 25). On the other hand, a geminate followed by another consonant might not be considered as *three* consonants.

5. In words like /inti/ "you" [fem.], the final [i] is sometimes devoiced. There also seems to be a lowering rule being applied to the [i] *after* palatalization has taken place. Only in lexical items with a final [i] where palatalization occurs does final [i] sound to be lowered. If palatalization does not apply, the lowering does not take place either.

6. There is another issue to consider in this regard: the potential role of stress. To address this issue we would have to compare, for example, stressed word-final [i] with stressed nonfinal [i]. In my data, the only lexical item in which the [i] is word-final *and* stressed is the feminine demonstrative /di/ "this". Otherwise, the rules of stress, as described by Broselow (1976), do not result in its placement on the final syllable of a word. For all other lexical items that have final [i] (e.g., /ʕaadi/ "normal", /inti/ "you" [fem.], /mamti/ "my mother", etc.), the penultimate (or the antepenultimate) syllable receives primary stress. Leaving aside the word /di/, we have a group of tokens that all have final, unstressed [i] and a group of tokens that have both stressed and unstressed nonfinal [i]. As I did not code for stress in my original coding, I cannot at this point explore the matter fully. Bhat (1978) found that, in apical palatalization, unstressed front vowels are a more favored environment than stressed ones. If this is the case, then the difference in probability between word-final [i] and nonfinal [i] may also be due to the fact that the former tokens are unstressed. Still, the evidence presented earlier shows that height is crucial in predicting the application of palatalization.

7. Long [ii] occurs most frequently in closed syllables. Tokens of the form /šoftiih/ "you [fem.] saw him/it", where the final vowel is long, stressed, and in an open syllable, were very infrequent in my data.

8. Coding for the factors of age, education, and style was determined as follows. For the category of age, the clearest patterns could be seen when speakers were divided into three groups: below 30, 30–50, and above 50. For the factor of education, I originally divided the speakers into the following categories: no education, some elementary school, some high school, high school, college, and beyond college. However, as the differences between the first two categories and between the second two turned out to be either nonexistent or very small, I grouped them together. Thus, there are four educational levels: no education, high school, college, and beyond college. In addition, as the majority of the upper middle class and all of the upper class Cairenes in this sample had attended private schools where a language other than Arabic is the medium of instruction, I compared those who had attended such schools with those who had attended public schools, where the medium is Classical Arabic. Only private schools that used a language other than Arabic as the main medium of instruction were counted as "private." The factor of style was coded as: narrative, nonnarrative, response to questions, and word list. Tokens that were part of the personal narratives related by the speakers were coded as "narrative." "Nonnarrative" was defined as those stretches of speech where the speaker volunteered a discussion that was neither a narrative, nor a response to a question. Tokens that were part of the first two sentences of an answer to a question were coded as "response." All tokens that occurred during discussions on language, literature, and the section on experiments were also put in this category. Some speakers were asked to read a word list; therefore, all tokens obtained from this reading were categorized as "word list style."

A composite index of social class was constructed to stratify the speakers. Four factors were taken into account. In order of importance, they are: father's or mother's occupation, whether the speaker attended a private language school, or a public school, the speaker's neighborhood, and the speaker's occupation. Each factor received between 1 and 5 points, with 1 being the highest and 5 the lowest. The weight of each factor is, respectively, 0.5, 0.25, 0.15, and 0.1. Thus, the index of a person who gets a 1 in all categories is: $(1 \times .5) + (1 \times .25) + (1 \times .15) + (1 \times .1) = 1$.

9.   One can use old Egyptian movies to get diachronic data. I looked at some old movies such as *Alf Laila wa Laila* 'A Thousand and One Nights', by Ali El-Kassar, made in the late 1930s. The actress playing Sheherazade had some palatalization. But I did not systematically code the speech of the actors or actresses, so I cannot provide further information on this point.

REFERENCES

Abdel-Jawad, Hassan (1981). Lexical and phonological variation in spoken Arabic in Amman. Doctoral dissertation, University of Pennsylvania.

Bakir, Muhammad. (1986). Sex differences in the approximation to standard Arabic: a case study. *Anthropological Linguistics* 28: 3–10.

Bell, Allan. (1984). Language style as audience design. *Language in Society* 13: 145–204.

Bhat, D. N. S. (1978). A general study of palatalization. In J. Greenberg, C. Ferguson, & E. Moravcsik (eds.), *Universals of Human Language: Vol. 2. Phonology*. Stanford: Stanford University Press, 47–91.

Broselow, Ellen. (1976). The phonology of Egyptian Arabic. Doctoral dissertation, University of Massachusetts, Amherst.

Cedergren, Henrietta. (1973). The interplay of social and linguistic factors in Panama. Doctoral dissertation, Cornell University.

Eckert, Penelope (1989) The whole woman: sex and gender differences in variation. *Language Variation and Change* 1: 245–267.

Eckert, Penelope, McConnell-Ginet, Sally (1992) Think practically and look locally: language and gender as community-based practice. *Annual Review of Anthropology* 21: 461–490.

Haeri, Niloofar (1987) Male/female differences in speech: An alternative interpretation. In K. M. Denning, S. Inkelas, F. C. McNair-Knox, & J. R. Rickford (eds.), *Variation in Language: NWAV-XV*. Stanford: Stanford University, Department of Linguistics.

Haeri, Niloofar (1991) Sociolinguistic variation in Cairene Arabic: Palatalization and the qaf in the speech of men and women. Unpublished doctoral dissertation, University of Pennsylvania.

Haeri, Niloofar (1992a) Synchronic variation in Cairene Arabic: the case of palatalization. In E. Broselow, M. Eid, & J. McCarthy (eds.), *Perspectives on Arabic linguistics IV* (Current Issues in Linguistic Theory 85). Philadelphia: John Benjamins, 169–180.

Haeri, Niloofar (1992b) Above and beyond conservation and innovation: gender and negotiations of meaning. Paper presented at NWAV-XXI, University of Michigan, Ann Arbor.

Holmes, Janet (1992) *An Introduction to Sociolinguistics*. London: Longman.

Ibrahim, Muhammad (1986) Standard and prestige language: a problem in Arabic sociolinguistics. *Anthropological Linguistics* 281: 115–126.

Keating, Patricia (1988) A survey of phonological features. Distributed by the Indiana University Linguistics Club.

Labov, William (1966) *The Social Stratification of English in New York City*. Washington, DC: Center for Applied Linguistics.

Labov, William (1972) *Sociolinguistic Patterns*. Philadelphia: University of Pennsylvania Press.

Labov, William (1982) Building on empirical foundations: perspectives on historical linguistics. In *Perspectives in Arabic Linguistics IV*.

Labov, William (1990) The intersection of sex and social class in the course of linguistic change. *Language Variation and Change* 2: 205–254.

Mitchell, T. F. (1956) *An Introduction to Egyptian Colloquial Arabic*. London: Oxford University Press.

Royal, Ann-Marie (1985) Male/female pharyngealization patterns in Cairo Arabic: a sociolinguistic study of two neighborhoods (Texas Linguistics Forum 27). Austin: University of Texas, Department of Linguistics.

Sallam, A. M. (1980) Phonological variation in educated spoken arabic: A study of the uvular and related plosive types. *Bulletin of the School of Oriental and African Studies* 43.

Schmidt, Richard (1974) Sociolinguistic variation in spoken Arabic in Egypt: A re-examination of the concept of diglossia. Unpublished doctoral dissertation, University of Wisconsin, Madison.

Wahba, Kassem M. (1991) An acoustic study of vowel variation in colloquial Egyptian Arabic. Paper presented at the Fifth Annual Symposium of Arabic Linguistics, Ann Arbor, Michigan.

QUESTIONS

Content

1. What are the main variants of this variable?
2. What is the effect of style on the variable? Which variant do women use most frequently in the most careful Word List Style?

   a. Which social class of women uses this variant most of all?

3. Which women use more weak palatal variants, the ones who went to private or public schools? Which women use more strong palatals?

Concept

1. "The social meanings of sound changes in progress are multiple, changing and *variable*". Find independent evidence to support Haeri's claim in the articles by Zhang and Kiesling (or any others you are familiar with).
2. What is unexpected about the patterns for social class and style for this variable? Why are they unexpected? (You will need to compare Haeri's results with other studies to answer this.)
3. Consider the patterns for weak and strong palatalization for women of different ages. Explain the reasoning behind the conclusions that:

   a. palatalization is a change in progress
   b. weak palatalization precedes strong palatalization.

Chapter 30

Elinor Ochs

INDEXING GENDER

1. THE MICRO-ETHNOGRAPHY OF GENDER HIERARCHY

GENDER HIERARCHIES DISPLAY THEMSELVES in all domains of social behavior, not the least of which is talk. [. . .] This view embodies Althusser's notion that "ideas of a human subject exist in his actions" [. . .]. Mundane, prosaic, and altogether unsensational though they may appear to be, conversational practices are primary resources for the realization of gender hierarchy.

[. . .] I will argue that the relation between language and gender is not a simple straightforward mapping of linguistic form to social meaning of gender. Rather the relation of language to gender is constituted and mediated by the relation of language to stances, social acts, social activities, and other social constructs. [. . .]

With respect to gender hierarchy, the following discussion argues that images of women are linked to images of mothering and that such images are socialized through communicative practices associated with caregiving. Although mothering is a universal kinship role of women and in this role women have universally positions of control and power, their communicative practices as mothers vary considerably across societies, revealing differences in social positions of mothers. Mothers vary in the extent to which their communication with children is child-centered (i.e. accommodating). Differences in caregiver communicative practices socialize infants and small children into different local images of women. These images may change over developmental time when these young novices see women using different communicative practices to realize different social roles (familial, economic, political, etc.). On the other hand, continuity in women's verbal practices associated with stance and [. . .] the enactment of diverse social roles may sustain images of women that emerge in the earliest moments of human life.

Source: Ochs, Elinor (1992) Indexing gender. In Alessandro Duranti and Charles Goodwin (eds) *Rethinking Context: Language as an Interactive Phenomenon.* Cambridge: Cambridge University Press, 335–358.

The discussion will compare communicative practices of mothers in mainstream American households (Anglo, white, middle class) and in traditional Western Samoan households. [. . .].

2. SOCIAL MEANINGS AND INDEXICALITY

Before turning to the communicative practices of mothers and their impact on socialization of gender, let us turn our attention to a more general consideration of language and gender [. . .].

Sociological and anthropological studies of language behavior are predicated on the assumptions that (1) language systematically varies across social contexts and (2) such variation is part of the meaning indexed by linguistic structures. Sociolinguistic studies tend to relate particular structures to particular situational conditions [. . .]. Hence two or more phonological variants of the same word may share the identical reference but convey different social meanings, e.g. differences in social class or ethnicity of speakers, differences in social distances between speaker and addressee, differences in affect. [. . .] Competent members of every community have been socialized to interpret these meanings and can without conscious control orchestrate messages to convey social meanings. Sociological and anthropological research is dedicated to understanding these communicative skills, interpretive processes, and systems of meaning indexed through language.

[Current research] on indexicality [. . .] stresses the inherently social construction of written and spoken language behavior. Part of the meaning of any utterance (spoken or written) is its social history, its social presence, and its social future. With respect to social history, Bakhtin (1981) and Vološinov (1973) make the point that utterances may have several "voices" – the speaker's or writer's voice, the voice of a someone referred to within the utterance, the voice of another for whom the message is conveyed, etc. The voices of speaker/writer and others may be blended in the course of the message and become part of the social meanings indexed within the message. This perspective is a potentially critical one for investigating the relation of language to gender, where gender may generate its own set of voices.

A second tradition examining social indexicality of language is sociological and anthropological research on speech events and speech activities. Here Bateson's (1972) and Goffman's (1974) work on keying and frames for events, as well as [. . .] Silverstein (1976) on shifters and indexes are all useful in analyzing the social potential of language behavior. Silverstein provides further specification of indexes: [. . .] social conditions may be communicated through the referential content of a word, phrase, or clause or through some linguistic feature that has no reference. With respect to indexing of gender in English, referential indexes include such items as the third person pronouns "he" and "she," and the titles "Mr." and "Mrs.," "Sir" and "Madam," and the like. [. . .]

From a sociolinguistic point of view, however, referential indexes are far fewer than non-referential indexes of social meaning, including gender. Non-referential indexing of gender may be accomplished through a vast range of morphological, syntactic, and phonological devices available across the world's languages. For example, pitch range may be used in a number of speech communities to index gender of speaker. For example, research on pre-adolescent American male and female children indicates that young girls speak as if their vocal apparatus were smaller than young boys of the same age and same size vocal chords (Sachs 1975). Here it is evident that pitch has social meaning and that young children have come to understand these meanings and employ pitch appropriately to these ends. [. . .]

A concern with indexicality is also at the heart of linguistic and philosophical approaches to the field of pragmatics, [. . .] broadening the notion of presupposition beyond logical presupposition to include pragmatic presupposition, i.e. context-sensitive presupposition. Thus an utterance such as "Give me that pen" logically presupposes that there exists a specific pen and pragmatically presupposes that (1) the pen is some distance from the speaker and (2) the speaker is performing the speech act of ordering. From this perspective, we can say that utterances may pragmatically presuppose genders of speakers, addressees, overhearers, and referents. For example, in Japanese, sentences that include such sentence-final morphological particles as *ze* pragmatically presuppose that the speaker is a male whereas sentences that include the sentence-final particle *wa* pragmatically presuppose that the speaker is a female.

3. THE INDEXING OF GENDER

The notion of gender centers on the premise that [. . .] social groups organize and conceptualize men and women in culturally specific and meaningful ways. Given that language is the major symbolic system of the human species, [. . .] we should expect language to be influenced by local organizations of gender roles, rights, and expectations and to actively perpetuate these organizations in spoken and written communication (Bourdieu 1977). In relating sociocultural constructions of gender to social meaning of language, an issue of importance emerges: **few features of language directly and exclusively index gender**.

In light of this, we must work towards a different conceptualization of the indexical relation between language and gender. In the following discussion, I suggest three characteristics of the language—gender relation. The relation of language to gender is (1) non-exclusive, (2) constitutive, (3) temporally transcendent.

3.1 Non-exclusive relation

In looking at different languages and different speech communities, the most striking generalization is the paucity of linguistic features that alone index local concepts of men and women or even more minimally the sex of a speaker/addressee/referent (Brown and Levinson 1979, Ochs 1987, Seki 1986, Silverstein 1985). [. . .]

Rather, overwhelmingly we find that the relation between particular features of language and gender is typically non-exclusive. By non-exclusive, I mean that often variable features of language may be used by/with/for both sexes. Hence, strictly speaking we cannot say that these features pragmatically presuppose male or female. What we find, rather, is that the features may be employed more by one than the other sex. [. . .] Women in New York City, for example, overuse the postvocalic /r/ to the extent that they sometimes insert an /r/ in a word that has no "r" in its written form, e.g. instead of saying "idea," they hypercorrect to "idear" (Labov 1966). In this and other examples, the relation between language and gender is distributional and probabilistic.

In addition, non-exclusivity is demonstrated by the fact that many linguistic forms associated with gender are associated as well with the marking of other social information, such as the marking of stance and social action. Thus, for example, tag questions in English are associated not only with female speakers (Andersen 1977), but with stances such as hesitancy, and social acts such as confirmation checks. [. . .] [C]onveying multiple social meanings is highly efficient from the point of view of linguistic processing and acquisition (Slobin 1985). Further, the multiplicity of potential meanings allows speakers to exploit such inherent ambiguities for strategic ends, such as avoiding going "on-record" in communicating a particular social meaning (Brown and Levinson 1987, Tannen 1986).

A question raised by such facts is "Why this distribution?" How does the distribution of linguistic resources relate to rights, expectations, and other conceptions of men and women in society? [. . .]

3.2 Constitutive relation

By positing a constitutive relation between language and gender, I mean that one or more linguistic features may index social meanings (e.g. stances, social acts, social activities), which in turn helps to constitute gender meanings. [. . .]

Let me provide a few examples of constitutiveness. Many of the linguistic features that in the literature are associated primarily with either men or women have as their core social meaning a particular affective stance. [. . .][C]ertain linguistic features associated with men's speech in Japanese coarsely intensify the force of an utterance, while those associated with women's speech typically convey an affect of gentle intensity (Uyeno 1971, Seki 1986). We can say that the former features directly index coarse intensity and the latter a soft or delicate intensity. The affective dispositions so indexed are part of the preferred images of men and women and motivate their differential use by men and women. When someone wishes to speak like a woman in Japanese, they may speak gently, using particles such as the sentence-final *wa*, or to speak like a man they may speak coarsely, using the sentence-final particle *ze*.

Similarly, we can find particular linguistic features directly indexing **social acts** or **social activities**, such as the imperative mode indexing the act of ordering in English or respect vocabulary terms in Samoan indexing the activity of oratory. These acts and activities in turn may be associated with speaking like a male or speaking like a female and may display different frequencies of use across the two social categories.

It is in this sense that the relation between language and gender is mediated and constituted through a web of socially organized pragmatic meanings. Knowledge of how language relates to gender is not a catalogue of correlations between particular linguistic forms and sex of speakers, referents, addressees and the like. Rather, such knowledge entails tacit understanding of (1) how particular linguistic forms can be used to perform particular pragmatic work (such as conveying stance and social action) and (2) norms, preferences, and expectations regarding the distribution of this work *vis-à-vis* particular social identities of speakers, referents, and addressees.

[. . .]

A model displaying how linguistic forms help to constitute gender meanings is presented in Figure 30.1. In this model, linguistic forms are resources for conveying a range of social meanings. [. . .][T]he model indicates that constitutive relations obtain between stances, acts, and activities as well as between each of these and gender meanings.

This model indicates two kinds of relations between language and gender. The first and less common is the direct indexical relation, as when a personal pronoun indexes gender of speaker or a kin term **indexes** gender of speaker and referent. This relation is represented by radiating lines from linguistic resources to social meanings. The second relates gender to language through some other social meaning indexed. In this second relation, certain social meanings are more central than others. These meanings however help to **constitute** other domains of social reality. That is, a domain such as stance helps to constitute the image of gender. This sort of constitutive relation is represented by two-headed arrows.

[. . .]

A more complex representation of language and gender would specify which types of conversational acts, speech activities, affective and epistemological stances, participant roles in situations, and so on enter into the constitution or construction of gender within a particular community and across different communities. A more refined model would also introduce the notion of markedness. Certain acts, activities, stances, roles, etc. are frequently enacted by members of a particular sex, that is, they are unmarked behaviors for that sex. Others are less frequent behaviors, and yet others are highly unusual for that particular sex. These behaviors would be interpreted differently than unmarked behaviors. Where the behavior is highly marked, one sex may be seen as assuming the "voice" of another (Bakhtin 1981), or as acting like the other sex.

One of the major advances in language and gender research has been a move [. . .] [toward a focus] on what men and women do with words, to use Austin's phrase (Austin

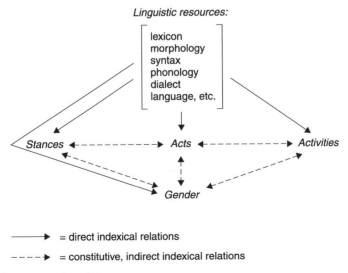

Figure 30.1   Language and gender.

1962), and have in this endeavor then isolated linguistic structures that men and women use to this end. [. . .]

We now have access to a range of studies that are stylistic and strategic in orientation (cf., for example, Gal 1989, Schieffelin 1987, Philips and Reynolds 1987, Brown 1980, Zimmerman and West 1975, West and Zimmerman 1987) Several studies have noted the tendency for men to participate more in speech activities that involve formal interactions with outsiders and women to be restricted to activities within family and village contexts. In these cases, men and women display different competence in particular genres, including, of course, their grammatical and discourse structures (cf., for example, Gal 1989, Keenan [Ochs] 1974, Sherzer 1987, Shore 1982).

Other studies have emphasized ways in which men and women attend to the "face" of their addressees in performing conversational acts that may offend the other. [. . .] Brown's (1979, 1980) study of Tenejapa Maya society [. . .] indicates that Tenejapa women talking with other women tend to be more polite than men talking with men. When women and men talk to one another, they are equally polite. Tenejapa women talking with other women tend to use different kinds of politeness features than do men with other men. They use linguistic structures that show support, approval of another, [. . .] whereas men tend to use linguistic forms that indicate a sensitivity to the other's need not to be intruded upon [. . .]

The association of women with greater politeness is not universal: [. . .] in a [. . .] study of men's and women's speech in Western Samoan rural society, I have not found that Samoan women are more polite than men of the same social status, except in one particular context. As listeners to narrative tellings, women tend to use more positive politeness supportive feedback forms than do men of the same status. In other contexts, however, the expression of politeness differs more in terms of social rank of speaker (e.g. titled person or spouse of titled person, untitled person) than in terms of gender. With the exception of Brown's study, research on men's and women's attention to face and expression of politeness needs to be pursued more systematically, taking into account a range of situational parameters (the speech activity, the speaker-addressee-author-audience-overhearer-referent relationships, the genre, etc.). A wider data base is needed to understand differences in men's and women's communicative strategies and to resolve contradictory findings within the same society (cf. for example Connor-Linton 1986 on politeness among American middle class adolescents).

3.3 Temporally transcendent relation

Thus far we have considered how linguistic forms may help constitute local conceptions of male and female at the time a particular utterance is produced or is perceived. Japanese speakers index femaleness as they use the sentence-final particle *wa*, for example. Language in this sense has the power to constitute the present context. The constitutive power of language, however, **transcends** the time of utterance production/perception, hence the property of temporal transcendence. Language can also constitute past and future contexts. [. . .] For example, [. . .] the practice of praising can recontextualize [Ochs 1990] a past act as an accomplishment, and accusations can recontextualize past acts as wrongdoings [. . .]. All conversational acts that function as first-pair parts of adjacency sequences (Sacks, Schegloff, and Jefferson 1974), e.g. questions, invitations, compliments, precontextualize the future in that they set up expectations for what the next conversational act is likely to be, e.g. answers, acceptances/declines.

The relevances of temporal transcendence to this discussion of language and gender is that societies establish norms, preferences and expectations *vis-à-vis* the extent to which and the manner in which men and women can verbally recontextualize the past and precontextualize the future. The roles and status of men and women are partly realized through the distribution of recontextualizing and precontextualizing acts, activities, stances, and topics.

[. . .] The status of women in mainstream American society and Western Samoan society is in part constituted through the particular ways women as mothers recast the past and precast the future in their interactions with infants and small children.

4. COMMUNICATIVE STYLES OF MOTHERS AND OTHER CAREGIVERS

4.1 Underrated mothers

One of the major concerns in gender research has been the social and cultural construction of gender in society. A logical locus to examine this process is interaction between young children and older members of society. By examining the kinds of activities and acts caregivers of both sexes engage in with children of both sexes and the manner in which these activities and acts are carried out, we can not only infer local expectations concerning gender but as well articulate how these expectations are socialized. One important tool of socialization is language. Not only the content of language but the manner in which language is used communicates a vast range of sociocultural knowledge to children and other novices. This use of language we call "language socialization" (Schieffelin and Ochs 1986a, 1986b; Ochs 1986, 1988, 1990). Language socialization includes both socialization through language and socialization to use language. In the following discussion, I will propose a relation between the position and image of women in society and language use in caregiver-child interaction.

Although mothering is a universal kinship role of women and in this role women have positions of control and power, their communicative styles as mothers vary considerably across societies. Such variation in the language of mothering reveals differences across societies in the social position of mothers *vis-à-vis* their young charges. The discussion here will contrast caregiving communicative styles among mainstream white middle class (WMC) Americans with Western Samoan caregiving styles. Based on research carried out with B. Schieffelin (Ochs and Schieffelin 1984; Schieffelin and Ochs 1986a, 1986b), I will argue that images of women in WMC American society are socialized through a communicative strategy of high accommodation to young children. A very different image of women is socialized in traditional Samoan households, where children are expected to be communicatively accommodating to caregivers.

In their ground-breaking volume on sexual meanings, Ortner and Whitehead (1981: 12) comment that "women's universal and highly visible kinship function, mothering, is surprisingly underrated, even ignored, in definitions of womanhood in a wide range of societies with differing kinship organizations." I will argue that the white middle class social scientists' dispreference for attending to the role of mothering is an outcome of the very language socialization practices I am about to describe.

In the analysis to follow I focus on cross-cultural differences in strategies associated with three pervasive verbal practices of mothers and other caregivers:

(1) verbal strategies for getting messages across to young children (**message production strategies**)
(2) verbal strategies for clarifying messages of young children (**interpretive strategies**)
(3) verbal strategies for evaluating accomplishments of children and others (**praising strategies**)

I will demonstrate that through each of these verbal strategies, mainstream American mothers, in contrast to traditional Samoan mothers, construct a low image of themselves. The strategies adopted by mainstream American mothers minimize their own importance by (1) lowering their status, (2) giving priority to the child's point of view, and (3) even denying their participation in accomplishing a task. The strategies to be discussed are represented in Figure 30.2.

4.2 Organization of caregiving

Before detailing these strategies, let us consider briefly the organization of caregiving in the two societies under consideration. In traditional Samoan households, caregiving is organized in a somewhat different manner from that characteristic of mainstream American households. First, caregiving is shared among a number of family members of **both genders**. Mothers are primary caregivers in the first few months of their infant's life, but they are always assisted, usually by siblings (both brothers and sisters) of the young infant. Once the infant is somewhat older, these sibling caregivers assume most of the basic caregiving tasks [. . .]. This type of caregiving arrangement is characteristic of most of the world's societies (Weisner and Gallimore 1977).

As is widely documented, Samoan society is hierarchically organized (Mead 1930, Sahlins 1958, Shore 1982). Social stratification is evident in the political distinctions of *ali'i* "chief," *tulaafale* "orator," and *taule'ale'a* "untitled person"; in titles within the rank of *ali'i* and within the rank of *tulaafale*; and among untitled persons along the dimensions of relative age and generation. Hierarchical distinctions are evident in domestic as well as public interactions.

[. . .] [C]aregiving is hierarchically organized. Untitled, older, higher generation caregivers assume a social status superior to younger untitled caregivers who are

	Mainstream American (child-centered)	Samoan (other-centered)
Production strategies	Extensive simplification	Little simplification
Interpretive strategies	Express guess and negotiate meaning	Display minimal grasp
Praising	Unidirectional	Bidirectional

Figure 30.2   Verbal strategies that constitute mothering.

co-present in a household setting. Further, caregivers enjoy a higher status than the young charges under their care.

Among the demeanors Samoans associated with social rank, direction of accommodation is most salient. Lower ranking persons are expected to accommodate to higher ranking persons, as in other stratified societies. Lower ranking caregivers show respect by carrying out the tasks set for them by their elders. They provide the more active caregivers, while others stay seated and provide verbal directives. Samoan caregivers say that infants and young children are by nature wild and willful and that accommodation in the form of respect is the single most important demeanor that young children must learn. A core feature of respect is attending to others and serving their needs. A great deal of care is taken to orient infants and young children to notice others. Infants, for example, are usually held outwards and even spoonfed facing the social group co-present.

4.3 Message production strategies

One of the outstanding observations of mainstream American mothers is that they use a special verbal style or register [. . .] often called "Baby Talk" or "Motherese" (Newport 1976) [. . .]. Characteristics of this register include the following: restricted lexicon, Baby Talk words (child's own versions of words), shorter sentence length, phonological simplification (such as avoidance of consonant clusters in favor of consonant-vowel alternation, e.g. *tummy* versus *stomach*), morphosyntactic simplification (e.g. avoidance of complex sentences, copula), topical focus on here-and-now versus past/future, exaggerated intonation, slower pace, repetition, cooperative proposition-making with child (e.g. expanding the child's utterance into adult grammatical form, providing sentence frames for child to complete.)

Baby Talk register has been a major area of investigation over the last decade or so in the field of language acquisition. The existence of such a register was argued by many to indicate that language acquisition was facilitated by such input. More recently, cross-cultural observations of caregiver-child communication indicate that simplified registers are not characteristic of this communicative context in all societies (Heath 1982, Ochs 1982, Ochs and Schieffelin 1984, Schieffelin and Ochs 1986a, 1986b, Ward 1971). We now know that the process of language acquisition does not depend on this sociolinguistic environment. Western Samoan, Kaluli New Guinea and black working class American children are not surrounded by simplified speech of the sort described above and yet they become perfectly competent speakers in the course of normal development. [. . .] [W]hy then do caregivers in certain societies choose to communicate in this fashion with their children whereas others do not?

In Ochs and Schieffelin (1984), we proposed that Baby Talk is part of a more pervasive cultural orientation to children among mainstream Americans. In particular, we proposed that mainstream American society is highly child-centered and that there is a very strong expectation that those in the presence of young children will **accommodate to children's perceived wants and needs**. [. . .]

In the domain of verbal communication, accommodation takes many forms. Beyond the use of Baby Talk register, a widely observed behavior of mainstream American mothers is their participation in conversation-like interactions with tiny infants. [. . .] To pull this off obviously requires quite a bit of communicative accommodation on the part of the mother. [. . .]

Throughout the course of their infancy, children are [. . .] participants in exchanges which are strongly scaffolded (Bruner 1975) by their mothers. Mothers are able to enter into and sustain communication with small children by not only speaking for them but as well by taking into consideration [. . .] a variety of other child-oriented conditions that may assist in the interpretation of children's gestures and vocalizations.

[. . .]

Such extensive verbal and non-verbal accommodation on the part of mothers and others in caregiving roles is expected as part of the mainstream American caregiving role. Being a "good mother" or "good teacher" is to empathize with and respond to the child's mind set. Once a caregiver believes that she or he understands this mind set, a good caregiver will either intervene or assist the child in carrying out her or his desired activity.

In [. . .] traditional Samoan households, where children are socialized to accommodate to others, it is not surprising to learn that mothers and other caregivers do not use a simplified register in speaking to infants and young children [. . .].

Accommodation is universally associated with demeanor of lower towards higher ranking parties. That mainstream American mothers use a simplified register pervasively has a constitutive impact on the image of women in that this practice socializes young children into an image of women as accommodating or addressee-centered in demeanor. In traditional Western Samoan households, mothers and other caregivers rarely simplify their speech to young children. This practice socializes young children to be accommodating, i.e. to attend carefully to, the non-simplified speech and actions of others.

4.4 Interpretive strategies

A second manifestation of child- versus other-centeredness or accommodating versus non-accommodating verbal practices is located in cross-cultural differences in mothers' and other caregivers' responses to children's unintelligible utterances (see Figure 30.2).

As with simplified registers, Western Samoan and mainstream American speech communities generally display similar verbal practices in responding to unintelligible utterances. However, important differences lie in the social conditions under which particular practices are preferred and appropriate. In both communities, unintelligible utterances may be (1) ignored, (2) responded to by indicating unintelligibility (e.g. "What?," "I don't understand," "Huh?," etc.), or (3) responded to by verbally guessing at the meaning of the utterance (Ochs 1984). The two communities differ in their preferences for using these strategies when speaking to young children. Overwhelmingly, mainstream American mothers prefer to respond to young children's unintelligible speech by verbally guessing. Overwhelmingly, Western Samoan mothers and other caregivers prefer to ignore or point out the unintelligibility of the child's utterance.

These differences reinforce different images of mothers and other caregivers in the two societies, i.e. more/less child-centered and more/less accommodating. Verbal guesses are more child-centered and accommodating than simply indicating unintelligibility in two senses:

(1) Expressed guesses entail greater perspective-taking, i.e. taking the child's point of view. [. . .] Pointing out that the child's utterance is not clear does not entail this kind of sociocentrism [. . .].

(2) Expressed guesses are hypotheses or candidate interpretations presented to the child for confirmation, disconfirmation, or modification. Expressed guesses thus [. . .] give the child the right to influence mothers' interpretations of the child's utterances. In contrast, displays of non-understanding do not engage the child in such negotiations.

[. . .]

Another way of analyzing message production practices and interpretive practices is to say that Samoan and mainstream American mothers define different goals in their interactions with young children and that these goals in turn entail different linguistic practices. Mainstream American mothers often set the goal of engaging infants and small children as conversational partners, and they do so from within hours of their child's birth for lengthy stretches of time (Ochs and Schieffelin 1984). Once they establish conversation as a goal, mothers are obliged to make enormous linguistic accommodation for that goal to be accomplished. Children who are a few hours old, for example, can hardly be expected to speak for themselves, therefore [. . .] mainstream American mothers systematically set goals that are impossible for a child to achieve without dramatic scaffolding by the mother.

The Samoan way is different, for Samoan mothers and other caregivers do not establish goals for the child that demand such extensive accommodation from others. [. . .] Samoan caregivers simply do not place infants in communicative contexts that demand this kind of verbal scaffolding. The Samoan way is to delay such communicative exchanges until the child displays more verbal and communicative competence.

4.5 Praising strategies

The final strategy relevant to the construction of gender meanings in society concerns mothers' and other caregivers' evaluative comments on an activity involving a child (see Figure 30.2). In this discussion, we attend to the property of language introduced earlier as "temporal transcendence," i.e. the capacity of language to recontextualize the past and precontextualize the future in addition to contextualizing the present. Among their many functions, evaluative comments reframe or recontextualize a past act or set of acts. Praising, for example, recontextualizes a past act/activity as an accomplishment. [. . .] Of interest to this discussion is the fact that (1) mainstream American and Western Samoan mothers and other caregivers recontextualize past acts/activities as **different** kinds of accomplishments, and (2) these different contextualizations help to constitute weak and strong images of the mothers and others.

From the discussion so far, you are aware that mainstream American mothers [. . .] heavily assist children in carrying out certain activities, e.g. constructing a toy, drawing a picture, tying a shoelace. [. . .] Such activities may be seen as "joint activities" (Vygotsky 1978), accomplished by mother and child. [. . .] However, mainstream American mothers typically recontextualize such activities [. . .] by directing praises at the child such as "Good!" or "Look at the beautiful castle you made!," with no mention of the mother's role [. . .]. In other words, these mothers deny their own participation; through their own praising practices, they make themselves invisible. [. . .]

In Ochs and Schieffelin (1984), we noted that this kind of behavior [. . .] serve[s] to minimize the asymmetry in knowledge and power between caregiver and child. Indeed we have claimed that caregivers in mainstream American society are uncomfortable with such asymmetry and [so] they mask differences in competence [. . . .].

In contrast to American middle class households, in traditional Samoan communities, activities are often recognized as jointly accomplished. [. . .] Whereas in mainstream American interactions, praising is typically unidirectional, in Samoan interactions, praising is typically bidirectional. There is a strong expectation that the first one to be praised will in turn praise the praiser. Typically the praise consists of the expression *Maaloo!* "Well done!" Once the first *maaloo* is uttered, a second *maaloo* is to be directed to the producer of the original *maaloo*. In these *maaloo* exchanges, each *maaloo* recontextualizes the situation. Like mainstream American praising, the first *maaloo* recontextualizes an act/activity of the addressee as an accomplishment. The second *maaloo*, however, recontextualizes the act/activity as jointly accomplished. [. . .] Children in Western Samoan households are socialized through such bidirectional praising practices to articulate the contribution of others, including mothers.

5. GENDER HIERARCHIES

In summary, I have suggested that mothering cannot be taken for granted in assessing gender identity across societies. [. . .] When I examine transcripts of children's interactions with others, I see a set of cultural meanings about the position of mother, hence about women, being conveyed to children hundreds of times in the course of their early lives through linguistic forms and the pragmatic practices these forms help to constitute. [. . .] From a sociolinguistic standpoint, [. . .] Samoan mothers enjoy a more prestigious position *vis-à-vis* their offspring than do mainstream American mothers [. . .]. On a communicative level, they are accommodated to more often by children [. . .]. Further, they socialize young children to recognize the contribution of caregivers and others to achieving a goal, in contrast to American middle class mothers, who tend to socialize their children to ignore or minimize the role of the mother in reaching a goal. Finally, Samoan mothers have command over human labor in that they are typically the highest status caregivers present and have the right to delegate the more time-consuming and physically active caregiving tasks [. . .]. Thus even among caregivers they are the least accommodating, and the linguistic record indexes this demeanor in numerous ways.

[. . .]

We are now in a better position to evaluate Ortner and Whitehead's remark that the role of mothering "is surprisingly underrated, even ignored, in definitions of womanhood" (1981: 12). This state of affairs is precisely what we would predict from the language socialization practices in mainstream American households in the United States and much of middle class Western Europe as well. "Mother" is underrated because she does not socialize children to acknowledge her participation in accomplishments. "Mother" is ignored because through her own language behavior, "mother" has become invisible.

REFERENCES

Andersen, Elaine (1977) Learning how to speak with style. Unpublished Ph.D. dissertation, Stanford University.

Austin, J. L. (1962) *How to Do Things with Words*. Oxford: Oxford University Press.

Bakhtin, Mikhail (1981) *The Dialogic Imagination*, ed. M. Holquist. Austin: University of Texas Press.

Bateson, Gregory (1972) *Steps to an Ecology of Mind*. New York: Ballantine Books.

Bourdieu, Pierre (1977) *Outline of a Theory of Practice*. Cambridge: Cambridge University Press.

Brown, Penelope (1979) Language, interaction and sex roles in a Mayan community: a study of politeness and the position of women. Unpublished Ph.D. dissertation, University of California, Berkeley.

Brown, Penelope (1980) How and why women are more polite: some evidence from a Mayan community. In Sally McConnell–Ginet, Ruth Borker and Nelly Furman *Women and Language in Literature and Society*. New York: Praeger. 111–36.

Brown, Penelope and Stephen Levinson (1979) Social structure, groups, and interaction. In K. Scherer and H. Giles (eds) *Social Markers of Speech*. Cambridge: Cambridge University Press. 292–341.

Brown, Penelope and Stephen Levinson (1987) *Politeness: Some Universals of Language Usage*. Cambridge: Cambridge University Press, 56–289.

Bruner, Jerome (1975) The ontogenesis of speech acts. *Journal of Child Language* 2: 1–21.

Connor-Linton, Jeff (1986) Gender differences in politeness: the struggle for power among adolescents. In Jeff Connor-Linton, Christopher J. Hall, and Mary McGinnis (eds) *Southern California Occasional Papers in Linguistics*. Vol. II: *Social and Cognitive Perspectives on Language*. Los Angeles: University of Southern California, 64–98.

Gal, Susan (1989) Between speech and silence: the problematics of research on language and gender. *Papers in Pragmatics* 3(1): 1–38.

Goffman, Erving (1974) *Frame Analysis*. New York: Harper and Row.

Heath, Shirley (1982) What no bedtime story means: narrative skills at home and school. *Language in Society* 11: 49–77.

Keenan (Ochs), Elinor (1974) Conversation and oratory in Vakinankaratra, Madagascar. Unpublished Ph.D. dissertation, University of Pennsylvania.

Labov, William (1966) *The Social Stratification of English in New York City*. Washington, DC: Center for Applied Linguistics.

Newport, Elissa (1976) Motherese: the speech of mothers to young children. In N. Castellan, D. Pisoni and G. Potts. Hillsdale (eds) *Cognitive Theory, Vol. II*. NJ: Lawrence Erlbaum Associates.

Ochs, Elinor (1982) Talking to Children in Western Samoa. *Language in Society* 11: 77–104.

Ochs, Elinor (1986) From feelings to grammar. In Bambi B. Schieffelin and Emilnor Ochs (eds) *Language Socialization across Cultures*. Cambridge: Cambridge University Press.

Ochs, Elinor (1987) The impact of stratification and socialization on men's and women's speech in Western Samoa. In S. U. Philips, S. Steele, and C. Tanz (eds) *Language, Gender and Sex in Comparative Perspective*. Cambridge: Cambridge University Press.

Ochs, Elinor (1988) *Culture and Language Development: Language Acquisition and Language Socialization in a Samoan Village*. Cambridge: Cambridge University Press.

Ochs, Elinor (1990) Indexicality and socialization. In G. Herdt, R. Shweder and J. Stigler (eds) *Cultural Psychology: Essays on Comparative Human Development*. Cambridge: Cambridge University Press, 287–308.

Ochs, Elinor and Bambi Schieffelin (1984) Language acquisition and socialization: three developmental stories. In R. Schweder and R. LeVine (eds) *Culture Theory: Essays in Mind, Self and Emotion*. Cambridge: Cambridge University Press.

Ortner, Sherry and Harriet Whitehead (1981) *Sexual Meanings: The Cultural Construction of Gender and Sexuality*. Cambridge: Cambridge University Press.

Sachs, Jacqueline (1975) Cues to the identification of sex in children's speech. In B. Thorne and N. Henley (eds) *Language and Sex: Difference and Dominance*. Rowley, Mass.: Newbury House, 152–171.

Sacks, Harvey, Emanuel Schegloff and Gail Jefferson (1974) A simplest systematics for the organization for turn-taking in conversation. *Language* 50: 696–735.

Schieffelin, Bambi (1987) Do different worlds mean different words?: an example from Papua New Guinea. In S. Philips, S. Steele, and C. Tanz (eds) *Language, Gender and Sex in a Comparative Perspective.* Cambridge: Cambridge University Press, 249–260.

Schieffelin, Bambi and Elinor Ochs (1986a) Language socialization. In B. Siegel, A. Beals and S. Tyler (eds) *Annual Review of Anthropology*, Vol. 15. Palo Alto: Annual Reviews, 163–246.

Schieffelin, Bambi and Elinor Ochs (eds.) (1986b) *Language Socialization across Cultures.* Cambridge: Cambridge University Press.

Seki, Minako (1986) Gender particles and linguistic/non-linguistic context. MS, Department of Linguistics, University of Southern California.

Sherzer, Joel (1987) A diversity of voices: men's and women's speech in ethnographic perspective. In S. Philips, S. Steele, and C. Tanz (eds) *Language, Gender and Sex in a Comparative Perspective.* Cambridge: Cambridge University Press, 95–120.

Shore, Bradd (1982) *Sala'ilua: A Samoan Mystery.* New York: Columbia University Press.

Silverstein, Michael (1976) Shifters, linguistic categories, and cultural description. In K. Basso and H. A. Selby (eds) *Meaning in Anthropology.* Albuquerque: University of New Mexico Press. 11–56.

Silverstein, Michael (1985) Language and the culture of gender: at the intersection of structure, usage and ideology. In Elizabeth Mertz and Richard Palmentiers (eds) *Semiotic Mediation.* New York: Academic Press, 219–59.

Slobin, Dan (1985) Why study acquisition crosslinguistically. In *The Crosslinguistic Study of Language Acquisition, Vol. 1.* Hillsdale, NJ: Lawrence Erlbaum Associates, 3–24.

Stern, Daniel (1977) *The First Relationship: Infant and Mother.* London: Fontana/Open Books.

Tannen, Deborah (1986) *That's Not What I Meant!: How Conversational Style Makes or Breaks Relationships.* New York: Ballantine Books.

Uyeno, T. (1971) A study of Japanese modality: a performative analysis of sentence particles. Unpublished Ph.D. dissertation, University of Michigan.

Vološinov, V. N. (1973) *Philosophy and the Philosophy of Language*, trans. L. Matejka and I. R. Titunik. New York: Seminar Press. Original publication in Russian, 1929.

Vygotsky, Lev (1978) *Mind in Society.* Cambridge, Mass.: Harvard University Press.

Ward, M. C. (1971) *Them Children.* New York: Holt Rinehart and Winston.

Weisner, Thomas, and Ronald Gallimore (1977) My brother's keeper: child and sibling caretaking. *Current Anthropology* 18(2): 169–90.

West, C., and D. Zimmerman (1987) Doing gender. *Gender and Society* 1(2): 125–51.

Zimmerman, Donald, and Candace West (1975) Sex roles, interruptions and silences in conversation. In B. Thorne and N. Henley (eds) *Language and Sex: Difference and Dominance.* Rowley, Mass.: Newbury House, 10–129.

QUESTIONS

Content

1. What do Japanese sentence-final particles like *ze* and *wa* directly index: stances, speech acts, or gender of the speaker?
2. What does it mean to say there is a "constitutive" relation between language and gender? How does this differ from assuming a direct index between language and gender?
3. What are some of the important differences between the way caregivers socialize children in Samoa and the US?
4. How does Ochs claim mothers in white, middle class American families are silenced?

1. Which of the following terms are direct indexes of gender? Which are direct indexes of age?

    a. *she*
    b. *godparent*
    c. *vixen*
    d. *sheep*
    e. *uncle*
    f. *you*
    g. *cub*
    h. *person*

2. How does **direct indexing** help to create and **constitute social categories?**
3. Ochs claims that gender roles are partly differentiated by how much women and men can "recontextualise" and "precontextualise" events. Give an example of a speech act, or social activity, that recontextualizes events. To what extent do you think men and women are equally likely to engage in this speech act/social activity?

Chapter 31

Scott Fabius Kiesling

POWER AND THE LANGUAGE OF MEN

INTRODUCTION

POWER IS USUALLY CITED as the most important factor when discussing the ways in which men's identities are constructed.[1] For example, in 'Men, inexpressiveness, and power', Jack Sattel argues that: 'the starting point for understanding masculinity lies, not in its contrast with femininity, but in the asymmetric dominance and prestige which accrues to males in this society' (1983, p. 119). In this chapter, I aim to show how issues of power and dominance as they relate to male identities are more complex than previously suggested. I will provide examples of some of the discursive strategies used by individual men in order to create and demonstrate power, showing how each man adopts a unique and personal approach when doing so. In particular, I will demonstrate how sequentiality and activity type must be taken into account when exploring the construction of men's identities through language.

It cannot be denied that men have more power than women in modern Western society. Men still dominate the upper echelons of government and business, and women continue to perform most of the unpaid labour of housework and child care. In addition, women still frequently earn less than men for comparable work, and professions dominated by women are less valued monetarily than those dominated by men (see Hewlett, 1986). Along with the freedom brought by power, however, comes the expectation (or requirement) that a man will somehow embody this power in his identity. This expectation is by no means as restrictive as those which obtain where women's identities are concerned; when a man constructs a powerful identity, it is usually connected in some way to 'real' power. Thus, the expectation of a 'powerful' identity for men is not symmetrical to the expectation of a 'powerless' identity for women, since a

Source: Kiesling, Scott Fabius (1997) Power and the language of men. In Ulrike Hanna Meinhof and Sally Johnson (eds) *Language and Masculinity*. Oxford: Blackwell, 65–85.

man's powerful identity is *rewarded* (with power), whereas a woman's non-powerless identity may be *punished*.

Following Sattel's suggestion, therefore, I take the power of men as a starting point for investigating how men construct their identities through language; I unpack the concept, describe different kinds of power, and show how these work with specific regard to four individual men.

My analysis is based on data gathered during a continuing ethnographic study of a fraternity in the United States. A fraternity is an all-male social club at a university, in which membership is selective. Typically, the fraternity becomes the central organization around which members structure their college lives, especially socially. It is a 'community of practice' (Eckert and McConnell-Ginet, 1992), defined sharply from the rest of the university through various means – initiation rituals, secret ceremonies and exclusive social events. Cynthia McLemore (1991) has worked on intonation in the female counterpart to the fraternity – the sorority. She showed that this type of community is ideal for studying language and society, especially the language of society's privileged members, because it is an intensely social, well-defined community, and its activities are based primarily on talk (e.g. meetings and parties). In addition, fraternities exhibit processes typical of other social groups more intensely: entrance into the community is carefully guarded, its members change completely every four years, and yet it manages to retain a unique history and ideology. Finally, fraternities are important to study because they prepare their members for the world of work after college. By analysing the strategies that men learn in fraternities, we can therefore gain insights into how men acquire, construct, and reproduce certain social practices in anticipation of dominance over others in later life.

In this chapter, I will explore how the fraternity's ideology and the immediate speech situation work together to constrain the members' identities. I use the term 'constrain', rather than 'affect' or 'determine', because identity construction is, to some extent, a creative endeavour. In theory, the men are free to create any identity they want, but in practice, they are pushed (and push themselves) towards identities which do not challenge the perceived values of the fraternity or of dominant US society. Each man also has different discursive resources (e.g. storytelling ability, joking ability, a powerful structural role, a loud voice, etc.) in order to draw upon disparate types of power. And crucially, each member has his own personal history within the fraternity, which further constrains the kind of identity he can display at any given time. Each time he speaks, then, the man must produce an utterance (and posture, gaze, etc.) that satisfies these constraints as far as possible. At the same time, he must make the utterance coherent within each current speech situation.

Because I am focusing on power, I will begin by outlining the framework of power used in my analysis. I will then discuss the specific ideology of power at work in the fraternity in question, exploring, for example, the kinds of constraints which the community places on a member's presentation of self. Finally, I will analyse excerpts from my corpus in order to illustrate how men draw upon, and construct, different types of power through their use of language.

A FRAMEWORK FOR POWER

Before applying a concept to any analysis, it should be well defined. When power is used as an explanation in sociolinguistic analyses, however, it is frequently undefined and unanalysed. Because I am taking power as the starting point for my work, I will briefly sketch the theoretical approach which is to be employed.

Following Foucault (1982), power is action that modifies action. The effect of this action need not be immediate, direct or even real. So, for example, because power takes place in actions, it is exercised to the extent that people *believe* that they should perform an action because of another action. However, power is not something that individuals may suddenly pull out and use. It must be salient to the situation; the people being acted on must believe in it. Thus, illusions can be powerful motivators. People believe that they should act in certain ways with certain people because they feel that not acting in these ways would have serious consequences. The reasons for performing a given action might therefore seem irrational, such as the avoidance of embarrassment, or the appearance of foolishness or 'weakness'. But what constitutes a serious consequence is, in turn, dependent on the community in question and its own particular values. This means that any analysis exploring issues of power must be based on a primary analysis of the local community's values and its ideology.

Whilst this view of power is flexible, it lacks analytical force. At a practical level, therefore, I assume that people have power because they occupy roles – some so enduring as to seem eternal and necessary, some fleeting and unnoticed, and some newly created within specific interactions. People place themselves in roles by using language because different ways of speaking are associated with such roles. A new role may be thrown together out of bits of others, and, in some cases, a single role may dominate a personality. But such roles can only really be discovered by analysing the discourse of community members, and by examining the community's formal and informal structures through ethnographic observation and interviewing.

On the basis of my own study, I have identified seven types of power processes from which local roles may be built: physical (coercive and ability), economic, knowledge, structural, nurturant, demeanour and ideological. I distinguish between two types of physical power: *coercive physical power* is the power of the mugger, while *ability physical power* is an action made possible by physical ability or skill. *Economic power* is the process that rewards one action (e.g. labour) with the possibility of another action (e.g. purchasing goods). *Knowledge power* is the process of gaining knowledge in order to perform an action. *Structural power* is the power of a place within a structure, classically (but not necessarily) a hierarchy. *Nurturant power* is the process of helping another, as in teaching or feeding. *Demeanour power* is the power of solidarity: moral authority, being liked, being 'a good guy'. The process of demeanour is not normally addressed by views of power, because the actions in this type of power act on emotions. Thus a person exhibits demeanour power when others feel happy, entertained, involved, respectful, etc.

But it is the ideological process which is the most important. This is a 'defining process', because individuals evaluate the other types of power processes through the ideological process. This defining process – which I will refer to as *ideological power* – ratifies certain traits as powerful, and determines which of the other processes are available (i.e. identifies the roles in the community). Within each of the other processes, ideological power identifies what is, and what is not, powerful. Thus, ideological power is the process of power whereby ways of thinking about the world are naturalized into a community's behaviour.

Each of the seven types of power outlined is not isolated from the others, but all are closely connected to form what Foucault refers to as: 'a net-like organization [. . .] something which circulates, or rather (as) something which only functions in the form of a chain' (1980, p. 98). In this way, an ideology such as the competitive, hierarchical group ideology frequently identified as typical of all-male interaction is likely to affect the way in which men structure their groups, change their demeanour and learn disciplines. Men may be inclined to form hierarchical communities, act in ways that always seem competitive, and see education and work as a competition. The success with which they learn to think and act in these ways will, in turn, affect their ability to use economic, structural, physical, knowledge and demeanour processes of power.

Power is therefore a way of viewing local practices globally: an etic framework filled in by emic values. Power in this view (as a role focused on – or created in – a community-defined structure) is similar to concepts of footing and alignment (see Goffman, 1981). However, by using the framework I have outlined, we can identify the types of roles which are available and created vis-à-vis power. As a consequence, we will not be limited to analyses using broad, universal categories. Moreover, we can approach some comparability across communities by looking at the ways in which different communities deal with similar ideologies of power, and similar communities deal with different ideologies of power.

'IDEOLOGY POWER' IN A FRATERNITY

In the light of the framework I have outlined, I need to discuss the ideology of the fraternity in question before analysing how power works in the fraternity's discourse. The way a man presents himself within a fraternity is of ultimate importance because he becomes a member of and gains status in the fraternity by projecting the right kind of identity.

Gaining membership to a fraternity is contingent upon successfully negotiating the process of 'rush', which is not unlike courtship. In this process, current members meet prospective members (known as 'rushes') at organized social functions; they also socialize informally, for example, by talking in dormitory rooms. Prospective members gauge whether they want to be a part of the fraternity, and current members consider whether they want to invite the prospective members to join. The rushes selected by the current members are then offered an invitation for membership, and can accept or reject the 'bid', as the offer is known. Once they have accepted a bid, the rushes become probationary members, or 'pledges'. During the 'pledge period', which lasts for six to eight weeks, pledges learn the fraternity's traditions, and pledge education activities take place in unofficial secret ceremonies, which are similar to military 'boot camps'. Pledges are treated as second-class citizens, subordinating their autonomy and identities to the fraternity as an institution, and to individual older 'brothers', as members are called. Pledges 'earn respect' and the privilege to become members themselves. They also learn the fraternity's customs, traditions and oral history. During this time, a strong bond tends to form between so-called 'pledge brothers', who are members of the same 'pledge class', because of their common adversity as second-class citizens.

The pledge period culminates in initiation, a formal clandestine ceremony where the secrets, rights and responsibilities of membership are imparted. However, the newly initiated brother – known by the acronym 'nib' – is still inexperienced in the eyes of the fraternity. He lacks knowledge and past accomplishments in order to prove that he will function well in a fraternity office. In the social sphere, nibs normally follow the older brothers' lead, show respect to them, and defer to their judgement. But nibs still have more latitude here than in the fraternity's 'business' sphere, which will be discussed below. As a brother becomes older, he has a chance to prove himself by performing services for the fraternity. Also, simply by becoming older, he gains the respect of younger 'generations' of members.

In the fraternity I studied for over a year, which I will call Gamma Chi Phi (ΓΧΦ), almost all of the men were Caucasian. Out of fifty-seven members, one was Korean-American, and four were Arab-American. Most were of college age (17–22 years old); three alumni members were in their late twenties. By comparison, the university as a whole is 88 per cent Caucasian, 10 per cent Asian and 6 per cent African-American.

[. . .]

The names of the fraternity and all members are aliases.

At ΓΧΦ, there is an overt distinction between the formal, governing sphere of the fraternity, on the one hand, and the social sphere, on the other. However, the border between the two is fuzzy; older, office-holding members tend to associate together, and personality plays a large role in deciding who is elected into fraternity offices. Nonetheless, the ideological organization is the same throughout the fraternity, and can best be described as hierarchic.

The hierarchical nature of the fraternity is already evident in the stages of acquiring membership outlined above. First, because only certain men are accepted into membership, the fraternity experience begins by valuing one identity over another. In ΓΧΦ, demeanour and physical power are highly valued. If someone is rich, caring or gets good grades, they are not more likely to be offered membership. The current members value skill at playing sports – so a prospective member who played baseball in high school will be highly respected because he can help the fraternity win at intramural softball. Demeanour power is, however, most important in terms of gaining membership.[2] Members told me in interviews that the main reason they joined was because they thought the fraternity was 'a good group of guys'; similarly, bids are offered because a prospective member seems like 'a good guy'.

But what is 'a good guy'? Members themselves had difficulty defining this characteristic. For them, a good guy would seem to be someone who others enjoy being with, and someone who would appear to exemplify the members' own ideology. Thus, it may be someone who tells funny stories, or who is the subject of funny stories. Because of the hierarchic, competitive ideology of the organization, a man who acts strong, competitive and quick is valued. Friendship and community is shown through what seems like competitive talk filled with insults, boasts, orders, and embarrassing jokes and stories. A 'good guy' is someone who exemplifies powerful, competitive traits in all spheres: he works hard, gets things accomplished, is seen as a leader, and is verbally skilled in the 'competitive cooperative' style through which the men build solidarity. By selecting only men with certain characteristics, the fraternity creates a hierarchy between its members and outsiders (although non-members are also ranked).

Once access to the fraternity has been gained, there is still an implicit hierarchy evident in all stages of membership. The pledges begin their fraternity experience by being treated as unknowledgeable, childlike servants, and even when the pledges become full members, they are still not valued as highly as older members. Usually, only after at least one year of membership does a man have the power to affect, through his own actions, the actions of the fraternity and its members. When attempting to influence the fraternity in this way, ability and demeanour power are highly valued, along with knowledge power. This is especially evident during elections, for example, where members evaluate candidates' work ethic, experience, personality and skills.

Thus, the main constraint that the men place on each other is to present a competitive, successful, confident identity. The fraternity ideology also values hard work, especially work that promotes the good of the group. In this way, members are taught to protect and care for each other.

DATA ANALYSIS: POWER AND IDENTITY IN PRACTICE

In this section, I will explore how four men employ different discursive means in order to construct powerful identities. The excerpts I analyse come from an election meeting involving the entire fraternity membership. Ordinary meetings are held every Sunday evening in a campus classroom, but elections are held only once a year, usually in the autumn.

Because they are speaking in a meeting, the four men in question have much at stake. Initially, they must show that they have the authority to speak. But because their identities are on public display in the business sphere, the men are more constrained than usual by the competitive, hierarchic ideology of the fraternity. Through the varying employment of mitigation, mood, pronoun use and personal experience, these members orient themselves towards different processes of power. The processes they draw upon are consistent with the identities that they have constructed previously in the fraternity, but are nevertheless specific to the time of speaking.

The excerpts I analyse are taken from a discussion during elections for the office of chapter correspondent, whose job it is to communicate with the national fraternity through letters published in the fraternity's national magazine. The position traditionally goes to a younger member because it requires little experience or knowledge of how the fraternity works. After the four candidates – Kurt, Ritchie, Mullin and Ernie – give their speeches, they leave the room so that other members can discuss the candidates' strengths and weaknesses. The four members I shall focus on are: Darter, Speed, Ram and Mack.

Darter

The first speaker I consider is Darter, a newly initiated brother. He no doubt still feels deferential to those men who, until a few weeks ago, had almost total control over his life. Although he was the president of the pledge class, and is recognized as a possible future leader of the fraternity, he is not in a position to exercise demeanour or structural power because he is a nib, and does not hold a high position. In his comments, the first he has made in the elections, Darter bases his argument on his knowledge of the candidates' abilities. Two of the candidates are his pledge brothers, Ritchie and Ernie. Kim is Korean-American; Speed is an older brother.

Excerpt 1

48	DARTER:	Um *Ri:tchie* may come off like he's really like a dumb ass
49		and everything but uh
50		he's like one of the smartest people
51		I know y'know
52		I went to high school with him
53		and he was like ranked *fifth* in our class.
54		and he can he can write like rea:lly well
55	KIM:	He's *A*:sian man, what
56		do you expect?
57	SPEED:	(sarcastic) Is he really?
58	DARTER:	I mean he he *types* like unbelievably . . . quick.
59		um I just think this would be a good position for him
60		to hold because he's a really good writer,
61		I mean I've read a lot of papers of his.

Because he is young and a new brother, Darter does not normally speak in meetings. But in this comment Darter draws from his specialized knowledge – his high school friendship with Ritchie – to assert his right to speak. He begins by acknowledging the identity that Ritchie has in the fraternity (line 48).[3] Darter then contrasts this identity with the identity he remembers from high school (lines 50–4). He then states his position: 'I just think this would be a good position for him to hold.' He mitigates his statement through the use of 'I just think', which suggests his opinion is not very valuable. By using 'I think' and the conditional 'would', he frames his statement as a suggestion, rather than a fact (e.g. 'this is a good position for him'). Instead of simply making this more direct statement, he includes a dependent clause that explicitly highlights his reasoning ('because he's a really good writer'), which is implicit from his statements in lines 50–4. (I show below that the older brothers do not need to provide this kind of justification.) Darter then emphasizes once again how he knows that Ritchie is a good writer. He thus explicitly justifies his support for Ritchie through his knowledge of the latter's writing abilities. His power is therefore not based on his demeanour or position in the fraternity, but on knowledge, which he is careful to highlight extensively. He presents himself as holding information important to the debate, but as unsure of its worth.

Speed

The next speaker I introduce is Speed, a third-year member. Of the four men I am considering, he speaks next in the meeting. His statement is short and to the point.

Excerpt 2

83	MICK:	Speed
84	SPEED:	Ri:tchie. I like Ritchie 'cause he's smart
85		and he probably writes really good too:
86		so let him do it dude.

Speed at first does not justify his statement. He merely states Ritchie's name. Then he notes that Ritchie is smart and (extrapolating from line 84) that Ritchie is capable of doing the job. His short statement indicates that for him the choice, based on Ritchie's ability, is simple. It is just a matter of 'letting him do it'. In addition, by first only uttering Ritchie's name, Speed implies that members should be swayed by the mere fact that he is for Ritchie.

Ram

Ram presents his powerful identity in a different way. An older brother, he has just finished a year as treasurer. He creates a fatherly, 'wise elder' identity through his comment:

Excerpt 3

119	Ram:	um I'd like to endorse David here, surprisingly
120		I mean the kid –
121		I don't want to see him fall into another –
122		and I'm not saying that he would
123		Kevin Fierst type thing,
124		I think we need to make him –
125		We need to strongly involve him *now*
126		I think he's pretty serious about it, y'know
127		and with a little guidance I mean he'll do a fine job.

Ram creates a powerful identity by putting himself in the role of a person with age and experience: he refers to David as 'the kid', and he shows off his knowledge of past members of the fraternity (Kevin Fierst was a member who dropped out of school because of substance abuse problems). He further highlights his position through his use of the phrase 'with a little guidance', suggesting that he is qualified to give that guidance. He also shows concern for David ('I don't want to see him fall into another . . . Kevin Fierst type thing'), which suggests a fatherly position. Thus, he draws on the part of the fraternity ideology that stresses 'looking out for' another brother. Finally, he also uses the device of speaking on behalf of the fraternity ('we need to strongly involve him now'), although he mitigates his statement more than Mack, in the next section, by embedding it in 'I think'.

Mack

Contrast Darter and Speed's comments with those made by Mack, a fourth-year member, who was Darter's pledge educator (in charge of the programme and activities during the pledge period). Mack affects actions through his demeanour, using little mitigation in his statements, and through the imperative mood. Mick is the president, Pencil is the graduate advisor.

Excerpt 4

184	MICK:	Mack.
185	MACK:	*Okay* . . .
186		This is *it* . . .
187		Somebody said something about=
188	PENCIL:	=Again, we need to reorganize (?).
189	MACK:	yeah somebody's –
190		we need to look at what we have left here,
191		and there are certain positions
192		that everybody fits into perfectly.
193		Ernie does *not* fit into this: (0.1)
194		I'm not sure where Ernie fits in just yet.
195	?:	historian
196	MACK:	*but* I: a:m afraid that we are going to *waste* uh
197		one of the few brains *left*. in someplace that that
198		uh historian has potentially been a
199		non-existent position. uh I think for a couple
200		semesters yahoo took some pictures,
201	PENCIL:	We're talking about chapter correspondent now
202	MACK:	what's that? I know
203	PENCIL:	and he can hold *both* positions
204	MACK:	I understand that. (0.3)
205		But he won't.
206		(0.5)
207		I see- I see *Kurt*- I see Kurt- I see *Kurt*-
208	PENCIL:	Then talk about chapter correspondent.
209		point of order.
210	?:	we have we have four left.
211	PENCIL:	point of order.
212	MACK:	I see Kurt as chapter correspondent.
213		not Ritchie damn it.

Mack begins by serving notice that his word is gospel: 'This is it'. It is unmitigated and imperative. Unlike Darter, Mack does not justify his statement at all. This non-mitigation and non-justification presents a role of someone who can make a proclamation – someone with power. In line 190, he emphasizes this view by instructing the members on how to go about making a decision ('We need to look at what we have left'). He does this by using the first person plural subject without any hedges (or 'I think', as Darter does), and by using 'need' instead of 'should'. Contrast his statement with what might be termed its 'opposite': Mack might have said 'I think we should look at what's left'. By using a bald imperative, then, Mack implicitly puts himself in a role of structural power. However, Mack is not constructing a new place for himself in the fraternity, but continuing in a carefully constructed role: that of the elder, wise, behind-the-scenes manipulator. In an interview, he indicated this manipulator role was the one he seeks for himself. Although he has held few fraternity offices, he goes to other members before elections, and suggests that they run for certain positions, then makes comments in their favour during elections.

Mack was also the pledge educator for the newly initiated brothers, which may affect his comments in two ways. First, he has had a position of supreme authority over the new members until recently – he was their teacher and 'drill sergeant' – so that they perceive him as an authority within the fraternity. Second, he can claim to know the new members better than any other member (except perhaps the new members themselves). Thus, he can claim to be qualified to make these pronouncements. He can use his structural and demeanour power to influence the new members, many of whom will vote in the election, and he can employ his knowledge power to influence older brothers.

Mack also demonstrates his role by where he sits in the classroom in which the meeting is held. Older members sit on the right-hand side of the room, and Mack sits as far to the right as possible. Darter, in contrast, sits on the 'younger' left-hand side, towards the middle (the extreme left-hand side is empty). Mack's cadence is also significant. Though not evident in the transcript, he speaks with a slow, pause-filled cadence that gives the impression of thoughtfulness and wisdom, while Darter speaks very quickly.

Mack continues to use unmitigated, authority-laden devices throughout his comments. In lines 191–4, he sets up a system in which each member has his place, and Mack knows who belongs where. He presents his statements as axiomatic truths by using 'there are' without any indication that he is actually voicing a personal opinion. Had he used modality markers, such as 'may', he would be implying that members can decide the issue for themselves. Instead, he leaves no room for doubt. In line 196, he presents himself as advisor to the fraternity ('I am afraid'). In contrast, instead of using these devices to speak for the collective in a leader-like role, he might have said something like 'I think Ritchie is overqualified for this position'. It is unclear where his argument is going from line 197 forward, because he stops his sentence, and begins to discuss the historian position. It looks as if he planned to highlight his age, by discussing the past worth of the historian position in lines 198–200 ('historian has potentially been a non-existent position'). Pencil then argues with him about discussing one position at a time (lines 201–11), which prompts Mack to finish his statement. Mack ends by simply stating that 'he sees' Kurt as correspondent, again without any justification (in fact, with less justification than at the beginning of his comments). This construction, 'I see', is used by other brothers to create a similar air of authority, as though the speaker were a visionary, who speaks with the wisdom of the ages.

Thus, there is a large difference between the way in which the older brothers and a younger brother present themselves. The older brother has a position of experience and respect that he can implicitly draw upon, while the younger brother, lacking this structural and demeanour power, is explicit about his reasoning to sway votes in his direction. While both are under similar general pressures to present a 'powerful' identity, each has different resources and solves the problem in his own way.

Speed

Now contrast Mack and Ram's remarks with a later comment by Speed. After Mack speaks, other older members have taken up the discussion of finding offices for the newly initiated brothers. Speed responds to this trend, and returns to his utilitarian theme. Speed's comments are given in a hurried, shouting voice, as if he is angry.

Excerpt 5

245	SPEED:	All right look.
246		first of all, you guys need to realize we do *not*
247		*ha:ve* to ne- necessarily make a:ll the new
248		brothers, put them in positions right away.
249		a *lot* of the new brothers already have positions.
250		they can get elected next year *or* next semester.
251		there *are* some positions that are semesterly.
252		we don't have to make sure that every one of them
253		has a position. they need time to *learn* and grow-
254		it's better that : they're- that they're=
255	?:	I need an assistant
256	SPEED	= shut the fuck up.
257		it's better that they're-
258		that they're almost like I was with Tex.
259		I was Tex's like little bitch boy . . . graduate
260		affairs, and I learned a lot more there,
261		than I would if I got stuck in some leadership
262		role, *so fuck 'em,*
263		I don't care if *any* of 'em don't get a position.
264		but I'm telling you right now,
265		I think Ritchie should do it because like Kim
266		said, people are gonna read this shit,
267		Kurt might get *ha:mm*ered and write some shitty . . .
268		fuckin' letter, Ernie *can't* write,
269		fuckin' Mullin already has a position,
270		so put Ritchie in there,
271		and stop fuckin' trying to . . . set everybody up in
272		a position. Christ.
273	MICK:	Alex.
274	SPEED:	I:'d like one
275		(laughter)

Speed is an older brother, but he has created an adversarial identity in the fraternity, resisting those in formal offices. He relies on a different presentation of power, one that sets him up in opposition to others. Even though he is a third-year member, he always sits on the 'non-powerful' left-hand side, in the back of the room, thus showing his contempt for the fraternity hierarchy. Speed's argumentative identity is evident in this speech, but he uses some of the same linguistic devices as Mack. Like Mack, Speed uses the imperative. He begins by saying 'All right look', which is similar in tone to Mack's 'This is it'. In line 246, Speed states that 'you guys need to realize', which is similar to Mack's 'we need to look at what we have left'. Speed then shows his knowledge of the fraternity, continuing in an imperative mood, saying 'we don't have to make sure that every one of them has a position', which contrasts with Mack's 'we need to look at what we have left here'.

Speed then draws on his personal experience (as Ram did) in the fraternity for an example in lines 259–62 (notably in a low position – 'I was Tex's like little bitch boy'). This statement disparages 'leadership positions', and implicitly the organizational structure of the fraternity. Next, he uses an aggravated, bold statement to show his indifference to the brothers' aspirations in lines 262–3 ('so fuck 'em . . .'). Speed then again presents a utilitarian argument for voting for Ritchie by pointing out why other candidates are unqualified (lines 264–70). In line 264, he uses a pedagogic tone similar to Mack's ('I'm telling you right now'). Note that this rhetoric is consistent with his argumentative, impatient identity: he sums up each person quickly, with aggravation and profanity. Then, at the very end (line 274), he injects some self-directed humour. Throughout the elections, he has been unable to get elected, and this has become a running joke. When he says 'I'd like one', he adds to his demeanour with a joke making fun of himself. Ending with a joke is a common device used by the members in these comments; it builds demeanour power by easing the tedium that accompanies the election meetings.

Thus Speed, while staying within the constraints of the hierarchic fraternity ideology, manages to construct an identity that appears to reject the manipulative structural power used by some of the older brothers. He accomplishes his identity by focusing on the value of competing against a structure of power; rebellion and independence are consistent with the fraternity's competitive ideology. He also focuses on the need to do what is best for the group by highlighting why Ritchie is best qualified for the position. Thus, Speed, Mack and Ram, while using similar linguistic devices to convince the members and present their identities, nevertheless construct very different identities. Because he is younger, Darter, on the other hand, has different constraints on the identity he presents in the meeting. He does not have a demeanour or structural power process working in his favour, so the problem presented to him – of creating an identity consistent with the fraternity ideology – is much different than the problem presented to Speed, Mack and Ram. Darter must create a means of influencing voting (an action that will affect other actions) without any prior history of being able to do so. He must also construct a role for himself that fits within the constraints of being a nib, but nevertheless convinces people to vote for his favoured candidate. Darter therefore draws on his specialized knowledge of the candidate.

It is important to notice also that Speed was genuinely impatient with the discussion at the time of his second statement, as seen by a comparison of his two utterances. In the first statement, he simply says why Ritchie is qualified for the position. In the second, however, he is arguing *against* other members – especially Mack – as much *for* Ritchie, in addition to arguing about the progress of the debate generally. This place in the discussion (he is nearly the last speaker) sets up a context in which he can position himself as the defender of ability power over structural power for its own sake. In other words, he can make clear his dislike of voting members into structural positions without any clear functional reason for doing so. This secondary argument was not possible in Speed's first comments because none of the older members had suggested considering all the new members, and what offices they should occupy. His identity construction in the second statement therefore shows the situated, sequence-dependent nature of identity.

[. . .]

All the men discussed create powerful identities, but they each use disparate strategies in order to achieve a different kind of power. Differences can be seen in how the men orient themselves to various features of the fraternity ideology. Most appeal to what will be best for the fraternity. Darter and Speed focus on the ideology of being rewarded for ability. They both argue that Ritchie is simply the most qualified candidate, and voting for him will benefit the fraternity the most. They therefore appeal to the part of the ideology that puts the group before the individual. Ram also appeals to this value, but in another way. He argues that the fraternity will lose Kurt if they don't involve him in it. Mack, however, focuses on the fraternity's hierarchical nature; for him, some jobs are more important than others, and must be 'assigned' to more important members. Thus, he wants Ritchie to have a job other than chapter correspondent. Mack also sees his own role as that of manipulator, and uses his structural position of age to put members in the offices that he 'sees' for them. Finally, Speed fights against this focus on structural power.

The elections are very important to the members. They care deeply about the fraternity and its future. Who they elect very much affects what happens in the fraternity. In addition, the outcomes affect their own power within the fraternity and, even more important perhaps, their ability to affect the actions of others in the future.[4]

DISCUSSION

I have thus shown how four men employ both similar and varied discursive devices in order to construct a particular kind of identity, given certain constraints on that identity. All four manage to present some kind of identity valued by the competitive, hierarchic fraternity ideology. Darter had to justify his statements overtly. Ram created a fatherly image. Mack spoke with a voice of the elder. Speed 'resisted' the dominance of structural power over ability, and the good of the fraternity and its members over trying to control every detail of the fraternity's future. While being men in a fraternity affected their language in similar ways, their individual solutions in time and space were unique. It is worth pointing out, however, that I have only had sufficient space to consider one speech activity here; in fact, the men's identities vary even more when other speech activities are analysed.

Sociolinguists often group people together based on criteria external to the community, and focus on how people of certain groups use language in a similar way. Generalizations about men and women are among the most common. But within these generalizations we find many variations. Within the fraternity community, for example, we can group older members together, because they tend to use less mitigation and justification and, more importantly, because age is one way the members group themselves. Clearly, then, it is essential, when considering the language of men, to explore how gender is mediated by age, status, and so on, in the same way that this has been necessary when analysing the speech of women. But even grouping Speed, Ram and Mack together as elder members of the fraternity ignores their very different individual presentations of self.

Meaningful generalizations are, however, still possible and necessary. We can still say that, in some general sense, many men in the United States construct powerful, competitively oriented identities. Moreover, due to the ideology of difference in US society, the motivation for men to construct these identities is of a different nature than for women, and the outcomes for 'resistance' are different for each of the two sexes. Men who construct the 'preferred' gender identity are rewarded with power, while women are not rewarded in the same sense when they construct the identity that society 'prefers' for their gender. In fact, a 'powerless' identity that many researchers have shown to be the 'preferred' identity for a North American woman could actually be seen as punishing women. Real resistance to the gender order, for instance a 'powerful female' identity or a 'powerless male' identity, may have similar consequences. But many men arguably have little motivation for such resistance. Speed, for example, appears to be resisting 'the establishment', but he is nevertheless using that 'resistance' as an alternative way of constructing a powerful, individualistic identity that is ultimately ratified by the fraternity ideology.

The way in which the fraternity men create different yet powerful identities suggests that particular roles, such as workplace and family roles, may be the specifics that make up what people idealize as 'masculinity' and 'femininity'. The men discussed here adopt elements of archetypal male roles: loyal friend, concerned father, wise elder, pragmatic individualist. In addition, two of the men identify *themselves* as having the identities they present in the election.

As Sattel (1983) points out, many men are expected to take on positions of leadership. But the direction of the indexing of men's identities and leadership is not clear; we might also say that society expects leadership positions to be held by men. Work such as Bonnie McElhinny's (1993) study of female police officers in Pittsburgh similarly highlights the importance of work and family roles in society's view of masculinity and femininity. [. . .]

CONCLUSION

In this chapter, I have explored the way in which the identities of four fraternity members are constructed through interaction in an election meeting. My findings have, however, a number of implications for work on language and gender in more general terms. For example, I have shown how the four men construct their own identities, drawing upon both the same, and different, types of power processes through the language they use. Thus, although all the men manage to evoke some type of power with their language, it would be extremely difficult to draw specific conclusions on the types of linguistic structures (e.g. tag-questions, hedging etc.) used by men 'as a group' on the basis of my data since their usage is highly contextualized. [. . .]

NOTES

1.   I have chosen the term 'men's identities', rather than 'masculinity', for several reasons. First, 'masculinity' is not a neutral term; it connotes a single stereotype of male identity, for example, John Wayne and Arnold Schwarzenegger in their movie roles. However, the majority of men in Western culture do not present themselves as copies of these movie heroes (Kessler and McKenna, 1978; Segal, 1990). Some men even contradict this view of men's identities. Thus, masculinity, as I use the term, is but one possible (idealized) type of male identity. Similarly, that there is no 'natural', single identity to which men aspire is an important point; hence, I use the plural 'identities'. Men's (and women's) identities are constructed, negotiated and changing, but they are also constrained by social structures that value some types of identities over others. Furthermore, I use the term 'men' rather than 'male' or 'masculine' in order to highlight the fact that the identity is a social as opposed to biological construction; it is gender, not sex. 'Identity' is an intersection between a social presentation of self, and a psychological understanding of that self.
2.   The fact that demeanour is of primary importance in the fraternity supports its inclusion as a type of power, and not something other than power.
3.   Line numbers match those from a complete transcript.
4.   Ritchie won the election.

REFERENCES

Eckert, Penelope and Sally McConnell-Ginet (1992) Think practically and look locally: language and gender as community-based practice. *Annual Review of Anthropology* 21: 461–90.

Foucault, Michel (1980) *Power/Knowledge: Selected Interviews and Other Writings*. New York: Pantheon Books.

Foucault, Michel (1982) The subject and power. *Critical Inquiry* 8: 777–95.

Goffman, Erving (1981) *Forms of Talk*. Philadelphia: University of Pennsylvania Press.

Hewlett, Sylvia Ann (1986) *A Lesser Life: The Myth of Women's Liberation in America*. New York: Warner Books.

Kessler, Suzanne J. and Wendy McKenna (1978) *Gender: An Ethnomethodological Approach*. New York: John Wiley & Sons.

McElhinny, Bonnie (1993) We all wear the blue: language, gender and police work. Unpublished Ph.D. dissertation. Stanford, CA: Stanford University.

McLemore, Cynthia (1991) The pragmatic interpretation of English intonation: sorority speech. Unpublished Ph.D. dissertation. Austin: University of Texas at Austin.

Sattel, Jack (1983) Men, inexpressiveness and power. In Barrie Thorne, Cheris Kramarae and Nancy Henley (eds) *Language, Gender and Society*. Cambridge, MA: Newbury House, 119–24.

Segal, Lynne (1990) *Slow Motion: Changing Masculinities, Changing Men*. London: Virago.

TRANSCRIPTION CONVENTIONS

Turn-taking

:	Bounds simultaneous speech.
=	Connects two utterances that were produced with noticeably less transition time between them than usual.
(number)	Silences timed in tenths of seconds.
(.)	Noticeable silence less than 0.2 second.
#	Bounds passage said very quickly.

Sound production

∧	Falsetto.
TEXT	Upper-case letters indicate noticeably loud volume.
*	Indicates noticeably low volume, placed around the soft words.
text	Italics indicate emphatic delivery (volume and/or pitch).
-	Indicates that the sound that precedes it is cut off, stopped suddenly and sharply.
:	Indicates that the sound that precedes it is prolonged.
,	Indicates a slight intonational rise.
?	Indicates a sharp intonational rise.

Breathiness, laughter, comments

h	An audible outbreath.
'h	An audible inbreath.
he, ha	Laughter.
(text)	Transcript enclosed in single parentheses indicates uncertain hearing.
((comment))	Double parentheses enclose transcriber's comments.

QUESTIONS

Content

1. What is power? How do people have power? How is ideological power different from the other types of power that Kiesling outlines?
2. Why is a fraternity particularly suited to study power?
3. How are powerful identities presented here, in particular when comparing the younger to the older speakers?
4. What are the identities the four speakers construct and what does Kiesling mean by 'sequence-dependent nature of identity'?
5. What discursive devices do these speakers use to construct particular identities?
6. What generalizations can be drawn from Kiesling's analysis in respect to gender?

Concept

Kiesling points out that it would be difficult to draw specific conclusions on the type of linguistic structures used by men 'as a group' to characterize 'male speech', as such structures are highly contextualized. Have another look at excerpts 1 and 5. What might such structures be and how are they contextually dependent?

Chapter 32

Rusty Barrett

MARKEDNESS AND STYLESWITCHING IN PERFORMANCES BY AFRICAN AMERICAN DRAG QUEENS

THIS CHAPTER CONSIDERS THE ways in which African American drag queens (AADQs) use language style in their performances, particularly the ways in which they use choices that would be considered "marked" under the markedness model (Myers-Scotton [Scotton] 1988; 1993, [. . .]). After discussing *drag queen* as a social category, I consider the concept of *style*, and some of the confusion surrounding the terminology used for linguistic varieties. [It is the main point of this article to show that the markedness model can be a helpful tool for understanding the ways in which the performers' stylistic choices indicate their attitudes about the issues they bring up during their performance.] I use examples from AADQ speech to demonstrate how AADQs use both unmarked and marked choices as rhetorical devices in their performances to highlight the instability of social categories related to gender, ethnicity, class, and sexuality.

DISTINGUISHING DRAG QUEENS

First, it is important to clarify the meaning of *drag queen*. Basically, the social category of drag queens is gay men who dress as women, especially those who perform in gay bars. As a social group, drag queens are often confused with other groups: transsexuals, transvestites, cross-dressers, and female impersonators.[1] *Transsexuals* are individuals who feel that the sex they were assigned at birth does not correspond with their true gender identity. The term *transvestite* is used to refer to those who wear the clothing of the opposite sex (i.e., opposite from the sex they were assigned at birth). Unlike transsexuals, transvestites (or cross-dressers) categorize themselves as members of the gender

Source: Barrett, Rusty (1998) Markedness and styleswitching in performances by African American drag queens. In Carol Myers-Scotton (ed.) *Codes and Consequences: Choosing Linguistic Varieties*. New York and Oxford: Oxford University Press, 139–161.

corresponding to their assigned sex. *Cross-dressing* refers to anyone who wears the clothing associated with the opposite sex/gender, regardless of their sexual orientation. Neither transsexualism nor transvestitism/cross-dressing is a specifically gay/lesbian phenomenon. In contrast, *drag* is specifically part of lesbian and gay culture. Although it is possible to say that heterosexuals such as Milton Berle or Dustin Hoffman (in *Tootsie*) are "in drag," these men would not be considered drag queens.

The term *female impersonator* is closer to drag queen than any of the other terms considered here. Many professional drag queens refer to themselves as female impersonators or illusionists as a means of distancing themselves from nonprofessional drag queens. For example, one participant in Esther Newton's ethnography of gay female impersonators said that the term *drag queen* sounded "sort of like a street fairy puttin' a dress on" (1972: 17). However, female impersonators generally attempt to produce the illusion of being a "real" woman, usually performing as a specific celebrity (e.g., Marilyn Monroe, Liza Minnelli, or Cher).

Professional drag queens typically have their own unique persona (as opposed to only reproducing the persona of a single celebrity). In addition, most drag queens generally make no pretense about not being male but, rather, use their performances as a means of playing on the irony of crossing genders. Finally, although there are self-described female impersonators who claim to be heterosexual, drag queens are openly (and proudly) gay.

African American drag queen performances generally include lip synching to records and emceeing a variety of shows, including lip synching by other drag queens, male strippers, or talent shows. The emcee usually presents comedic monologues that involve interaction with the audience. Performances often encode direct information about the relationship between language (and performance as a whole) and social and cultural issues. As Turner noted, the relationship between performance genres and society is "reciprocal and reflexive—in the sense that the performance is often a critique, direct or veiled, of the social life it grows out of" (1986: 22). This is true of AADQ performances, which often present critiques of social structure and are often highly political. As Briggs argues, "performers are not passive, unreflecting creatures who simply respond to the dictates of tradition or the physical and social environment. They interpret both traditions and social settings, actively transforming both in the course of their performances" (1988: 7). Building on the work of Bauman (1975) and Hymes (1981), Briggs (1988: 8–9) notes that one of the primary components of performance is the responsibility of the performer to his or her audience. The audience evaluates a performer not only on the content of the speech but also on the performer's communicative competence in accordance with the criteria for a specific performance genre. A primary goal of drag performance is to highlight mismatches between the performer's "perceived" identity (as a woman) and her "biographical" identity (as a man). A successful drag performance is dependent on the ability to use language in a way that demonstrates that categories based on gender, ethnicity, class, and sexuality are indeed performances (cf. Butler 1993) and cannot be taken as obvious or constant reflections of some "authentic" identity.

DRAG QUEENS IN THIS STUDY

The drag queens in this study all belong to the class of *glam(or) queens*, that is, drag queens who attempt a highly stylish image of glamour, dressing up like movie stars at the Academy Awards or contestants in the evening gown competition at a beauty pageant. "Glam" queens typically wear evening gowns with lots of beads or fringe, exaggerated jewelry (such as big earrings or wide flashy bracelets), and big-haired black wigs.[2] Their clothing is often fairly revealing, with very short skirts or high slit dresses and bare arms. Although they dress in a way to accentuate their ability to look "feminine," they often undermine that image of femininity in their performances. Thus, instead of producing humor through their appearance, they play off the irony that a man could create the believable image of a woman.

Most of the language examined in this chapter is taken from public performances by AADQs in gay bars in Texas. From January to May 1993, I observed between six and ten AADQ performances per month. In addition to dealing with drag queens in Texas, some of the data in this study come from television appearances by RuPaul [two talk show appearances and a speech given at the 1993 March on Washington], a drag queen originally from Atlanta whose dance song "Supermodel (You'd better work!)" became very popular in early 1993. RuPaul recorded two albums, appeared in several films, and was on numerous television shows and even wrote her[3] autobiography (RuPaul 1995).

[. . .]

LANGUAGE STYLE AND THE MARKEDNESS MODEL

I take *style* to be an overarching term for all linguistic varieties below the level of *language*, namely the types of variation that Ferguson (1994) categorizes as *dialect, register*, and *genre*.[4] Ferguson states that "identifying markers of language structure and language use" (1994: 18–21) set apart one dialect from another, one register from another, and one genre from another. Among themselves, the three varieties differ in this way: (1) dialects distinguish one *social group* from another; (2) registers distinguish one *communication situation* from another; and (3) genres distinguish one *message type* from another. I follow Ferguson in distinguishing the three types of varieties in this way.

Whether a given set of linguistic variables (on any of the levels of phonology, morphosyntax, or lexicon) is classified as dialect, register, or genre is determined by the discourse (i.e., through usage). For example, for speakers with multiple group identities (i.e., with more than one dialect), a given dialect may be reserved for speech in a particular communication situation (e.g., with particular interlocutors). However, because that dialect is also a feature of the situation, that dialect functions as a register for those speakers. This means that in different interactions the terms *dialect, register*, and *genre* may apply to the *same* set of linguistic variables. For this reason, I use the term *style* to represent all the sets of linguistic variables included in any of the three categories. Thus, I employ the following definition of *style*:

Style: The set of linguistic variables that are characteristic of a given dialect, register, or genre.

[. . .]

MOTIVATIONS FOR SWITCHING BETWEEN STYLES

Myers-Scotton's markedness model (Scotton 1988; 1993) analyzes switches between different codes (languages or styles) of a given language based on the relationship between the code and the rights and obligations sets (RO sets) indexed by the code. Sets of linguistic variables may be seen as indexing the particular RO set associated with a given group identity, situational context, or speech event. Thus, individual dialects, registers, and genres index particular RO sets. Within the markedness model, each type of interaction has an unmarked RO set. According to the model, "the unmarked RO set is derived from whatever situational features are salient for the community for that interaction type" (Myers-Scotton 1993: 84). Paramount among those features are the identities of participants. Speakers use codes to index the RO sets that are unmarked for a given interaction or to attempt to change or explore the nature of the RO set present in an interaction. Thus, the RO set is dynamic: At the outset of an interaction an unmarked RO set is in place, but it is open to change as well.

In regard to motivations for codeswitching, Myers-Scotton (1993) claims that there are four major types of switches: sequential unmarked code switching, codeswitching itself as the unmarked choice, codeswitching as the marked choice, and codeswitching as an exploratory choice. [Three of] these are described in the discussion that follows. By analyzing all switching as one of [. . .] four types, the markedness model enables us to explain the choices of stylistic variables speakers make from their linguistic repertoires to achieve specific goals in the course of particular interactions.

In addition, however, the markedness model could provide a means for exploring the relationships and distinctions among the fuzzy sets comprising style: dialect, register, and genre. For example, consider sequential unmarked codeswitching, which refers to switches from one code to another as unmarked when the unmarked RO set changes within an interaction. That is, with a change in situational factors, the unmarked RO set changes, and with this change comes a change in unmarked code to index the new RO set. This type of switching would be predicted for both dialects and registers. For dialect switching, sequential switches from one dialect to another as unmarked would be predicted when there are changes in the group identities that are salient; for register switching, sequential unmarked switching would be predicted when there are changes in the situational context.

The second type of switching, codeswitching as the unmarked choice, would be predicted to occur with dialects. This type of switching consists of a pattern of switching back and forth between two styles in the same conversation, with the overall pattern carrying the message of multiple identities for the speakers. However, such switching is not predicted when styles function as registers. By definition, a register occurs in a particular situational context and therefore we cannot speak of a change of register without a change in situation. Switching as the unmarked choice takes place *without a change of situation* and therefore cannot involve registers. However, we would predict that the third and fourth types of switching, marked switching and exploratory switching, would occur with register rather than dialect in the majority of cases. Codeswitching as a marked choice is a switch to a code that is not the unmarked choice for the current RO set and therefore is a call for another RO set in its place. Codeswitching as an exploratory choice occurs when an unmarked RO set (and therefore an unmarked choice) is not clear. In such cases, speakers use switching to propose alternate choices as candidates for an unmarked choice and thereby as an index for the RO set which they favor. I suspect that all types of switching can occur between genres.

[. . .]

STYLISTIC CHOICES OF AFRICAN AMERICAN DRAG QUEENS

Although AADQs usually employ a wide variety of styles, three basic styles recur in their speech, reflecting membership in three different social groups. These are an AAVE style, a gay male style, and a style based on stereotypes of white women's speech. The AAVE and gay male styles index the identities of AADQs as African Americans and as gay men, respectively. The *white woman style* indexes their identity as drag queens while also indexing the RO set associated with actual white women and implying a variety of social attributes associated with white women, including stereotypical notions of femininity and glamour (cf. Barrett 1994).

When used by AADQs, each of these styles reflects a stereotype of the linguistic behavior for the prototypical member of the social groups indexed by the style. As Le Page and Tabouret-Keller note, when speakers construct their identities through language, "what they recognize and imitate are stereotypes they have created for themselves" (1985: 142). As linguists, we often pride ourselves on the fact that we study language as it is actually used, often attempting to demonstrate the falseness of stereotyped attitudes. When discussing choices of linguistic style, however, it is important to remember that speakers often base their linguistic behavior on stereotypes (as they do not have our privileged access to detailed sociolinguistic studies). Thus, each of the styles I am presenting does not reflect the *natural* speech of any actual white woman, gay man, or African American. Rather, the styles reflect prevailing stereotypes concerning the speech of members of these three social groups and are used by AADQs to index the RO sets of those social groups.

Because each of these styles indexes a social group, each constitutes dialects in Ferguson's (1994) framework.[5] Nevertheless, because each can serve to index a particular situation, each also can be considered as a register as well as a dialect (depending on usage). This is why I use the broader term *style* as a cover term. As is often the case with styles, there is a certain amount of overlap in the sets of linguistic variables making up these three styles. Although I will not arrange the variables in a given style in a hierarchy of "salience," it is important to keep in mind the fact that the degree of indexicality is not constant across variables. In addition, it should be noted that not all variables will be present in any given style at any given moment (and the presence/absence of variables will not be constant across speakers). Speakers may even choose a subset of linguistic variables from a style to index specific attributes associated with speakers of that style. For example, Sunaoshi (1995) demonstrated that Japanese women in managerial positions choose particular features (but not the complete set of variables) from the "Motherese" style in Japanese to index the authoritative status of mothers. By not using the full set of variables associated with Motherese, these women are able to assert their authority without fully indexing the powerful differential between mothers and children (which might be seen as condescending to their employees).

In the data that follow, I generally classify a particular utterance as belonging to a given style according to the following (rather arbitrary) criteria: (1) a linguistic variable represents a particular style if the variable's distribution does not overlap with it in some other style and (2) a particular style is present if two linguistic variables from that style are present that do not both overlap with another style (although they may each individually overlap with two different styles). The basic features of each of these styles are outlined in the following sections. Those features characterizing the white woman style come from Lakoff (1975), because Lakoff's description reflects a stereotyped image of how white women should speak (cf. Barrett 1994; Bucholtz and Hall 1995). The features associated with stereotypes of gay men's speech are those I have discussed elsewhere (Barrett, 1997); they are compiled from a variety of sources (Lakoff 1975; Rodgers [1972] 1979; Hayes 1981; Walters 1981; Goodwin 1989; Moran 1991; Gaudio 1994). The features of AAVE have been widely studied by linguists; the list presented here is primarily that of Walters (1992). Wyatt provides a similar list (1994).

In the remainder of this chapter, I present examples that demonstrate the ways in which AADQs choose particular stylistic variables from this repertoire to enhance their performances.

White Woman Style (Lakoff 1975: 53–56)

- Specific lexical items related to their specific interests, generally relegated to them as "woman's work": *dart* (in sewing) and specific color terms (*ecru*, *magenta*)
- "Empty" adjectives like *divine, charming, cute* . . .
- Question features for declaratives: tag questions (*It's so hot, isn't it?*), rising intonation in statement contexts (*What's your name, dear? Mary Smith?*)
- The use of hedges of various kinds (e.g., *well, y'know, kinda*)
- The intensive use of *so*
- Hypercorrect grammar, superpolite forms, and euphemisms: women are not supposed to talk rough.
- Women don't tell jokes.

Gay Male Speech Style (Barrett 1997)

- The use of lexical items and structures included as part of Lakoff's women's language, e.g., specific color terms and the "empty" adjectives (*marvellous, adorable,* etc.), as well as hedges and boosters.
- The use of a wider pitch range for intonational contours than in speech of straight men.
- Hypercorrect pronunciation; the presence of phonologically nonreduced forms and the use of hyperextended vowels (the probable source of the "lisping" stereotype).

- The use of lexical items specific to gay language (Rodgers [1972] 1979 gives a somewhat dated lexicon of many such expressions).
- The use of a H*L intonational contour, often co-occurring with extended vowels (as in *FAAABulous*).

African American Vernacular English (AAVE) Style (Walters 1992)

AAVE Realizations of Standard English Phonological Features:

- Interdental fricatives as labiodental fricatives: "teeth" [tʰijf], "other" [ʌvə]
- Final consonant reduction: /r/ deletion, "sister" [sɪstʰə]; /l/ palatalization or deletion, "all" [ɑ]; /l/ cluster vocalization or reduction, "film" [fɪm] or [fɪ.lm]; unreleased stops as glottal stops, "cat" [kʰæʔ]; cluster simplification, "best" [bɛs]
- Intervocalic weakening: /r/ deletion, [v] → [β] "every" [eβij]
- Strident cluster metathesis or modification: "ask" [æks], "stray" [ʃtrej]
- Prenasal raising of [ɛ] to [ɪ], "pen" [pʰɪn]; or lowering to [æ]: "thing" [θæŋ]
- Monophthongization of [ai]: "my" [ma]
- Stress fronting: "police" [pʰów:lijs]

AAVE Morphological and Lexical Innovations and Realizations of SE Features:

- Absence of nonsyllabic inflectional endings: third person singular {-s}, noun plural {-s}, possessive {-s}
- Reduction of unstressed syllabic inflections {ing}: [ɪn], or [.n], and {to}: [ə] "going to" [gʌnə]
- Lexical verbs as aspect markers: perfective "done," *I done finish my work*; inceptive "come" *don't come coming in here . . .;* future perfect *be done;* intensive continued progressive *be steady;* habitual copula: *she be nervous* vs. *she nervous* (non-habitual) (Green 1994)
- Negation: multiple negation, *didn't do nothing; ain't* as negative of forms of *to* be and *to have*
- "You" plural distinctions: *y'all* and *y'all's*
- Special intonation patterns, e.g., H*HL in rhetorical speech

CONTEXT AND UNMARKED CHOICES

For in-group communication outside performances, AADQs typically exhibit style-switching as the unmarked norm. This switching consists of all three of the styles discussed here, mirroring the fact that AADQs are all African American, gay men, and drag queens. Thus, by unmarked switching between styles, they index these three aspects of their group identities.

This continuous switching between the three styles is typical of AADQ speech, so much so that the styles may even co-occur, with phonological variables from one style overlapping with syntactic variables from another style. In the utterance in [1] (from RuPaul on the *Arsenio Hall Show*), the phonology is that of the white woman style (i.e., it is typical of Standard English, but not the hypercorrect pronunciation sometimes associated with the speech of African American women or gay men). The syntax, however, is typical of the AAVE style.

[1]   You know, in my mind's eye I always been a superstar, you know. And nobody couldn't tell me no differen[t].

The white woman phonology occurs up until the final word *different*, which is pronounced [dɪfrɪn] (i.e., without the final [t]). After the word *different*, the speech continues in AAVE style, so that the switch actually occurs before the end of the sentence. This meshing of styles is possible because of the fuzzy boundaries between styles and points to a problem that was not addressed by purely quantitative studies of language style. A quantitative analysis would most likely misanalyze the utterance in [1] as belonging to only one style, depending on whether the coding was for syntactic or phonological characteristics. This suggests that possible cases of styleswitching as the unmarked norm may have gone unnoticed because the styles were studied as closed sets that can be easily isolated from one another.

Consider the following example, a speech given by RuPaul at the 1993 March on Washington for Lesbian, Gay and Bisexual Rights:

[2]   Speech given by RuPaul
  1   Hello America
  2   My name's RuPaul
  3   Supermodel of the worl[d]
  4   [begins chant, audience joins in] Hey . . . Ho . . . Hey . . . Ho . . . Hey . . . Ho
  5   You know people ask me all the time
  6   Where I see myself in ten years
  7   And I say I see myself in the White House, baby!
  8   Miss Thing goes to Washington
  9   Can you see it? Wha- we gonna paint the mother pink, OK?
  10 We put one president in the White House, I figure you can do it again.
  11 Everybody say love! [audience responds, "love!"]
  12 Everybody say love! [audience responds again, "love!"]
  13 Now drive that down Pennsylvania Avenue!
  14 Peace, love and hairgrease!
  15 I love you!

In this example, RuPaul moves back and forth between each of the three styles, often allowing the styles to overlap. For this reason, and the fact that the situational context does not change, this type of switching would be referred to as dialect, as a subset of style, switching as the unmarked choice.

RuPaul begins her speech with typical standard, albeit feminized, English pronunciation reflecting the white woman style. The phrase *supermodel of the world*, however, is produced without a final [d] on the word *world*, a form typical of the AAVE style. The chant in line 4 reflects the call-response tradition, a genre often associated with African American preachers (and frequently used by drag queens). After the chant, RuPaul returns to a white woman style up until line 7 and the phrase *in the White House, baby*. This phrase is spoken with an increasingly widening pitch range, typical of the gay male speech style ending with the word *baby* spoken with an extended vowel and long falling (H*L) intonation (typical of the gay male style). In line 8, RuPaul refers to herself as *Miss Thang*, a term that indexes gay male identity and/or African American identity. She pronounces the word *thing* with standard English [ɪ], however, rather than with the [ei] or [æ] vowels typical of both the gay and AAVE pronunciations. Thus, a term related to both gay and African American identity occurs with a "white woman" phonology, letting the various styles overlap. In line 9 the question *Can you see it?* is spoken with a white woman phonology. The phonology then switches to AAVE with the word *mother*, which is pronounced without the final [r] and ends with the exaggerated H*L gay male style intonation on the word *OK*. RuPaul's phonology returns to a white woman style in lines 10 and 11. Although line 11 has white woman phonology, it begins a call-response routine, thus again indexing African American identity. In lines 12 and 13, the intonation becomes more like that found in African preaching (cf. Queen 1992). Through the use of codeswitching as the unmarked norm, RuPaul uses the speech to simultaneously index her membership in several different social groups.

Even though codeswitching as the unmarked norm is typically used for in-group communication and some performance contexts, a change in the situational context may mean a change in style. In this case, we can say that the performer is switching registers from one context to the next. For example, the table below compares the speech of RuPaul during her first appearances on the *Joan Rivers Show* and on the *Arsenio Hall Show*. These two televised interviews occur about one year apart from each other. The *Arsenio Hall* episode aired in March 1993; the *Joan Rivers* episode aired in May 1994. The *Arsenio Hall* interview was RuPaul's first appearance on national television. Although both were recorded before live audiences, the two programs constitute quite different contexts. The *Arsenio Hall Show* was hosted by an African American male, aired late at night, and was generally targeted to young adults. The *Joan Rivers Show* was hosted by a white woman, aired during the morning, and was generally targeted to women (especially women who do not work outside the home). The differences in context on the two programs can be seen in the stylistic choices made by RuPaul on the two programs. Table 32.1 compares

Table 32.1   Stylistic variation in the speech of RuPaul on two television talk shows

Style	Joan Rivers		Arsenio Hall	
	N	%	N	%
WW	70	81.4	38	50.6
GM	8	9.3	7	9.3
AAVE	0	–	10	13.3
WW/GM	8	9.3	6	8
GM/AAVE	0	–	4	5.3
WW/AAVE	0	–	2	2.6
AA/AAVE/GM	0	–	2	2.6
Totals	86	100	75	99.8

WW = white woman style, GM = gay male style, AAVE = African American Vernacular English style, N = number of utterances in a given style or combination of styles.

RuPaul's use of the three styles discussed above on each of the two programs. Because the styles overlap a great deal and may co-occur (as already noted above), the table compares utterances (rather than particular phonological or syntactic linguistic variables). The utterances are sorted according to those that occur exclusively in a given style, those in which a switch between two styles occurs or in which two styles overlap, and those in which all three styles occur. The tokens were collected from the first six minutes of the interviews.

On the *Joan Rivers Show*, which has a predominantly white studio audience, RuPaul does not use the AAVE style at all. More than 80% of the time, she uses the white woman style exclusively. This can be seen as a form of accommodation (cf. Giles, Coupland, and Coupland 1991) to the speech of Joan Rivers, an actual white woman. Nevertheless, RuPaul does continue to reference gay identity, demonstrating that drag queen identity must, at the very least, combine some elements of gay male speech with stereotyped women's speech.[6] In contrast, on the *Arsenio Hall Show*, RuPaul used the white woman style exclusively only half of the time and used the AAVE style exclusively 13.3% of the time. Thus, although the white woman style continues to predominate, it co-occurs with the AAVE style, reflecting the context and shared African American identity between RuPaul and Arsenio Hall. Although some of the stylistic choices on the *Arsenio Hall Show* reflect marked choices, it is clear that the context of the program allows for a much wider range of stylistic choices. Thus, context in a broad sense may influence what is the unmarked choice as well as the general range of stylistic choices possible. Moreover, although switching as the unmarked norm is quite common among AADQs, the styles may also occur in isolation, acting as registers indexing the RO set of a given situation. This is the case with the absence of the AAVE style on the *Joan Rivers Show*, in which RuPaul does not index her African American identity, reflecting the RO set of the interaction with a white woman.

Because each style may work individually, switches between any of the three styles may be a marked switch or a sequence of unmarked styles. Recall that unmarked sequences are predicted with changes in audience, topic, or context. A number of unmarked sequences occur in a specific genre of comedic monologues, that which offers critiques of the political and economic situations of African Americans. In this genre, certain comments may be directed to certain members of society, whether or not they are present in the audience. The white woman style is used to index the power held by whites, whereas the AAVE style is used to index the social situation of African Americans. The following example is from a drag queen performing in a gay bar. The style shifts correspond to a change in topic; as such they are changes in register. The AADQ is posing as a salesperson trying to sell rat traps to the audience. She offers three different types of rat traps for use in three different neighborhoods.

[3]   Segment of performance by African American drag queen in Texas
   1   OK! What we're gonna talk about is, um, rat traps, um . . .
   2   [holds up a mouse trap] This is a rat trap from <name of upper-class white neighborhood>
   3   It's made by BMW. It's real compact.
   4   It's, thank you . . . <obscured> . . .
   5   It's really good, it's very convenient, and there's insurance on it.
   6   And this is from <name of same white neighborhood>

7   OK, now for the <name of housing project> . . . [holds up a large rat trap]
8   This rat trap is made by Cadillac, it's a big mother fucker.
9   [holds up a gun] Now for the <name of inner city area>
10   You just don't need no rat trap.
11   Cause those mother fuckers look like dogs out there.
12   Shit!
13   I put in a piece of cheese, the mother fucker told me,
14   "Next time put in some dog food."

This example begins in the white woman style, switching to the AAVE style beginning in line 7. The sentences in 1–7 all end with a final rising tone, typical of the white woman style (Lakoff's "question intonation"). The phonology and intonation switch to AAVE in line 7, although the first syntactic features of AAVE do not occur until line 10, when the speaker begins to talk about the third location (which has the strongest reputation as a primarily African American low-income area). Thus, the number of linguistic variables used to index African American identity increases when discussing the neighborhood that is the strongest representative of the social conditions stereotypically associated with African Americans. This increase supports the claim of the markedness model that linguistic choices are indices of particular RO sets. In addition, it demonstrates that the density of variables from a particular style may increase with an increased desire to index the RO set corresponding to that style.

[. . .]

MARKED CHOICES IN AADQ PERFORMANCES

Although off stage AADQs generally use styleswitching as the unmarked norm for ingroup communication, in their performances they make more use of marked stylistic choices to draw attention to their speech. The performers use language style to play on the audience's assumptions surrounding issues of gender, ethnicity, and sexuality. A major part of the communicative skill displayed in AADQ performances relies on the speaker's ability to anticipate audience members' interpretations of the situation and then to use marked stylistic choices to disrupt the audience's assumptions.

Often, these marked choices reflect instances of *signifyin(g)*, an African American speech event in which the full meaning of an utterance cannot be understood from referential meaning alone (cf. Gates 1988; Mitchell-Kernan 1972). In signifyin(g), an utterance takes on special value through indexing a particular rhetorical figure or a speaker's skill at verbal art. In particular, the examples of signifyin(g) in these marked stylistic choices are cases of what Morgan (1994) discusses as "reading dialect," in which the linguistic style itself may be crucial in conveying the full meaning of a given utterance.

AADQs often directly address particular audience members, using marked stylistic choices to put the addressee "on the spot." This technique is quite common in drag performances. For example, this device is used by The Lady Chablis, a Savannah, Georgia, drag queen discussed in the best-selling *Midnight in the Garden of Good and Evil* (Berendt 1994). In her autobiography, The Lady Chablis describes how she approaches audience members during performances:

Whenever I performed my monologue, I made sure to comb the audience for a "victim." I'm always gonna pick on someone—that's part of my act. Still is. I'll usually find somebody in the front row who's got a certain *afraid* look on their face, like "Oh my God, please don't say nothing to me." *That's when I move in for the kill.* If I see a woman, and she's draped in diamonds, I might ask, "Girl, what didja do to get those jewels? Didja suck dick that good? Share y'secrets with The Doll!" (The Lady Chablis 1996: 103)

Here, The Lady Chablis uses a highly marked stylistic choice for comic effect. The highly informal style and coarse language directed at a woman "draped in diamonds" is unexpected, indexing a (false) closeness and familiarity between the drag queen and the audience member. As such, it represents both a dialect switch (imaginary change in participant identity) and a register switch (imaginary change in type of interaction). For example, discussing sexual exploits and using the term *girl* would normally be reserved for conversations with a close friend (most likely another gay man or another drag queen). The drag queen suggests that the audience member is not a wealthy upper-class woman but someone who simply received her jewels as a reward for her sexual abilities. As Myers-Scotton argues, such a marked choice is often a powerful feature of language "because it deviates from the expected and because its motivations may not be clear, therefore leaving the addressee off balance and unable either to predict the RO set in effect for the rest of the exchange or to explain the speaker's precise motivations" ([Myers-Scotton] Scotton 1985: 112). By using a marked choice, AADQs disrupt the expected RO set between audience and performer. Such marked choices are most often used to address white audience members, especially if they are clearly heterosexual or upper middle class. In these cases the marked choice produces comic effect because the AADQ used stylistic language choices to assert power over individuals belonging to more dominant social groups.

[. . .]

In the next example a Texas drag queen uses a marked choice to undermine the image of femininity indexed by the white woman style. The switch here is from one dialect to another, as if the drag queen belongs first to one social group and then to another.

[6]   Drag queen in Texas introducing a male stripper in a gay bar
1 Are you ready to see some muscles?
2 (audience yells) Some dick?
3 Excuse me I'm not supposed to say that, words like that in the microphone,
4 Like shit, fuck, and all that, you know?
5 I am a Christian woman.
6 I go to church.
7 I'm always on my knees.

In this example, the AADQ uses the white woman style in line 1. After using the word *dick* in line 2, she apologizes for using words that aren't "lady-like" (cf. Lakoff's "women don't talk rough"). Here the apology emphasizes the fact that the use of obscenities is a marked stylistic choice (given that it occurs within the white woman style). The performer further undermines the white woman style by explaining the apology in line 4 by using even more obscenities. These marked choices disrupt the RO set indexed by the white woman style, emphasizing the fact that the drag queen does not actually hold claim to the image of genteel femininity that the style indexes. The remainder of this example further exploits this irony with a joke about the drag queen being a *Christian woman* who is *always on her knees*. Here, the reference to being on her knees carries the dual meaning of "always praying" and "always performing fellatio," thus playing off of the stereotypes of white women and drag queens, respectively. The stylistic choice highlights the fact that the audience cannot assume that the "performed" identity of an upper-class, sophisticated woman is "authentic" because the chosen style produces inferences (about the character of the drag queen) that violate the expected behavior associated with the white woman style.

In example [7], RuPaul uses a marked switch into the AAVE style to emphasize her identity as a biologically male African American. Hall is using the standard dialect of American English, but RuPaul switches to AAVE.

[7]   RuPaul during her first appearance on the Arsenio Hall Show
      Arsenio Hall: I'm sure there're some people who would like the question answered do you . . . would you have rather been born a woman?
      RuPaul: No. No no. I'm very happy with being (.) a big o' black man.

Up to this point, RuPaul uses primarily the white woman style, indexing an RO set associated with a high level of sophistication and femininity. Following the pause after *being*, however, she switches into the AAVE style to say *a big o' black man*. This marked switch enhances the referential content of the utterance by using a linguistic style associated with being black. In addition, the choice undermines the audience's assumptions concerning RuPaul's performance of a sophisticated feminine identity by reminding them (both referentially and stylistically) that she is indeed both African American and male.

[. . .]

As these examples demonstrate, the use of marked choices disrupts the status quo during a given performance. By using such marked stylistic choices to call the prevailing RO sets into question the performers can draw attention to themselves and their communicative skills. In addition, these marked choices highlight the various questions of social difference brought out in the performances by indexing disunities between perceived/performed and "actual" (biographical) identity.

CONCLUSION

One of the goals of glam drag is to present an image that is as "real" as possible. Through the use of clothing, jewelry, hair, and cosmetics glam queens create an external image of exaggerated femininity, often taking great pride in how much they appear to be "real women." The Lady Chablis, for example, often announces that she is not only a real woman, but "a pregnant uptown white woman" (Berendt 1996). Thus, glam queens often make a specific effort to create the illusion of a femininity associated with upper-class white heterosexual women. Language style plays a crucial role in the construction of this image of femininity. AADQs demonstrate their ability to draw on the power and prestige of white society through the creation of an external image of a wealthy woman (i.e., clothes, jewelry, and makeup) and the use of the white woman style of speaking. The white woman style is thus crucial in creating a real, believable presentation of uptown white womanhood.

While the use of the white woman style adds to the external image of femininity in drag performances, styleswitching into AAVE or stereotyped gay male speech undermines the rich white feminine persona indexed by the white woman style. By switching into these other language styles, AADQs demonstrate that although they are capable of creating the visual and linguistic symbols of white upper-class society, they are not actually attempting to create a personal identity associated with white society. In AADQ performances, demonstrating pride in one's African American identity is usually as important as the ability to produce white women's language. AADQs who wear blond wigs or who prefer to lip-synch to songs by white artists are often criticized as "trying to be white." Styleswitching thus demonstrates that although an AADQ is capable of producing language that fits into white society (and thus, take on the prestige associated with white society), she consciously chooses to maintain her identity as an African American gay man (see Barrett 1994, 1995). The white woman style of speaking is thus used both to index the power and prestige of white upper-class society and to produce a critique of the social inequalities associated with white society.

AADQs use styleswitching to undermine audience assumptions concerning the personal identity of the performer. Marked switches are often used to renegotiate assumptions concerning AADQ identity, demonstrating that the performer refuses to be categorized according to a single, given set of social attributes. Styleswitching thus plays a crucial role in AADQ performances, keeping the audience aware that the performer cannot be tied down to a single identity. In turn, interest in the performance is heightened by the awareness that the current persona of the performer could change at any moment through a change in language style.

The examples presented here demonstrate the ways in which AADQs choose from sets of linguistic variables to attune their language to particular social settings. Using their knowledge of what the unmarked or marked code choice will be in a given interaction, they choose linguistic forms to produce specific effects. The markedness model provides a means of understanding the ways in which these stylistic choices convey the performers' attitudes about the issues brought up in the course of a performance. In some cases, they may choose the unmarked choice, whether that be a particular style or codeswitching as the unmarked norm. It is the marked choices, however, that are used to add emphasis and rhetorical force to AADQ performances. By using marked choices, AADQs tune their performances to undermine audience assumptions concerning issues of social difference such as ethnicity, sexuality, class, or gender.

NOTES

1.   The terms *transgender person* or *transgenderist* are often used as umbrella terms for various social groups. (For discussion see Bullough and Bullough 1993; Devor 1989; MacKenzie 1994; and Feinberg 1996.)

2. Unlike all of the other drag queens in this study, RuPaul almost always wears a blond wig.

3. I generally use feminine pronouns to refer to drag queens, especially in drag. The use of *he* to refer to a drag queen may be insulting as it insinuates that her performance is somehow flawed. (For a study of uses of *she* among gay men in general, see Rudes and Healy 1979.)

4. Here I depart from Ferguson's use of the term *conversational variation* in his definitions of variation. For me, conversation is a particular mode of discourse (or genre) included under the cover term style.

5. Traditionally, style and dialects are differentiated as follows. *Dialect* is used for specific social groups (differentiated along ethnic, regional, and sometimes class divisions). *Dialect* also often connotes an opposition to the *standard dialect*. Typically two styles differ from each other by fewer linguistic variables than two dialects do.

6. For example, as noted by Queen (1997), the actors in the film *To Wong Foo . . . Thanks for Everything, Julie Newmar* do not sound like actual drag queens, largely because they use white women's speech (and in the case of Wesley Snipes, AAVE), but they do not employ gay male speech as would an actual drag queen.

REFERENCES

Barrett, Rusty (1994) "She is *not* white woman!": the appropriation of white women's language by African American drag queens. In Mary Bucholtz, A. C. Liang, Laurel Sutton, and Caitlin Hines (eds) *Cultural Performances: Proceedings of the Third Berkeley Women and Language Conference*. Berkeley, Calif.: Berkeley Women and Language Group, 1–14.

Barrett, Rusty (1995) Supermodels of the world, unite!: political economy and the language of performance among African American drag queens. In William L. Leap (ed.) *Beyond the Lavender Lexicon: Authenticity, Imagination and Appropriation in Lesbian and Gay Languages*. Newark, N. J.: Gordon and Breach, 203–223.

Barrett, Rusty (1997) The "homo-genius" speech community. In Anna Livia and Kira Hall (eds) *Queerly Phrased: Language, Gender, and Sexuality*. New York: Oxford University Press.

Bauman, Richard (1975) Verbal art as performance. *American Anthropologist* 77: 290–311. Revised and expanded as *Verbal Art as Performance*. Prospect Heights, Ill.: Waveland Press, 1977.

Berendt, John (1994) *Midnight in the Garden of Good and Evil*. New York: Random House.

Berendt, John (1996) Chablis and me. In The Lady Chablis with Theodore Bouloukos *Hiding my Candy: the Autobiography of the Grand Empress of Savannah*. New York: Pocket Books, 12–18.

Briggs, Charles (1988) *Competence in Performance: The Creativity of Tradition in Mexicano Verbal Art*. Philadelphia: University of Pennsylvania Press.

Bucholtz, Mary and Kira Hall (1995) Introduction: twenty years after *Language and woman's place*. In Kira Hall and Mary Bucholtz (eds) *Gender Articulated: Language and the Socially Constructed Self*. New York: Routledge, 1–22.

Bullough, Vern L. and Bonnie Bullough (1993) *Cross Dressing, Sex, and Gender*. Philadelphia: University of Pennslyvania Press.

Butler, Judith (1993) *Bodies that Matter: On the Discursive Limits of "Sex."* New York: Routledge.

Devor, Holly (1989) *Gender Blending: Confronting the Limits of Duality*. Bloomington: Indiana University Press.

Feinberg, Leslie (1996) *Transgender Warriors: Making History from Joan of Arc to RuPaul*. Boston, Mass.: Beacon Press.

Ferguson, Charles A. (1994) Dialect, register, and genre: working assumptions about conventionalization. In Edward Finegan and Douglas Biber (eds) *Sociolinguistic Perspectives on Register*. New York: Oxford University Press, 15–30.

Gates, Henry Louis, Jr. (1988) *The Signifying Monkey: A Theory of African-American Literary Criticism*. New York: Oxford University Press.

Gaudio, Rudolf P. (1994) Sounding gay: pitch properties in the speech of gay and straight men. *American Speech* 69: 30–37.

Giles, Howard, Nikolas Coupland and Justine Coupland (1991) Accommodation theory: communication, context, and consequence. In Howard Giles, Justine Coupland, and Nikolas Coupland (eds) *Contexts of Accommodation: Developments in Applied Sociolinguistics*. Cambridge: Cambridge University Press, 1–69.

Green, Lisa (1994) Study of verb classes in African American English. *Linguistics and Education* 7: 65–81.

Goodwin, Joseph P. (1989) *More Man than You'll Ever Be: Gay Folklore and Acculturation in Middle America*. Bloomington: Indiana University Press.

Hayes, Joseph J. (1981) Gayspeak. In James W. Chesebro (ed.) *Gayspeak: Gay Male and Lesbian Communication*. New York: Pilgrim's Press, 45–57.

Hymes, Dell (1981) *"In Vain I Tried to Tell You": Essays in Native American Ethnopoetics*. Philadelphia: University of Pennsylvania Press.

[The] Lady Chablis, with Theodore Bouloukos (1996) *Hiding my Candy: The Autobiography of the Grand Empress of Savannah*. New York: Pocket Books.

Lakoff, Robin (1975) *Language and Woman's Place*. New York: Harper and Row.

Le Page, R. B. and Andrée Tabouret-Keller (1985) *Acts of Identity: Creole-based Approaches to Language and Ethnicity*. Cambridge: Cambridge University Press.

MacKenzie, Gordene Olga (1994) *Transgender Nation*. Bowling Green, Oh.: Bowling Green State University Popular Press.

Mitchell-Kernan, Claudia (1972) Signifying and marking: two Afro-American speech acts. In John J. Gumperz and Dell Hymes (eds) *Directions in Sociolinguistics*. New York: Holt, Rinehart & Winston, 161–179.

Moran, John (1991) Language use and social function in the gay community. Paper presented at NWAVE 20 (New Ways of Analyzing Variation). Philadelphia.

Morgan, Marcyliena (1994) No woman no cry: the linguistic representation of African American women. In Mary Bucholtz, A. C. Liang, Laurel Sutton, and Caitlin Hines (eds) *Cultural Performances: Proceedings of the Third Berkeley Women and Language Conference*. Berkeley, Calif.: Berkeley Women and Language Group, 525–541.

[Myers-Scotton, Carol] Scotton, Carol Myers (1985) "What the heck, sir": style shifting and lexical colouring as features of powerful language. In R.L. Street, Jr., and J. N. Cappella (eds) *Sequence and Pattern in Communicative Behaviour*. London: Arnold, 103–119.

[Myers-Scotton, Carol] Scotton, Carol Myers (1988) Codeswitching and types of multilingual communities. In P. Lowenberg (ed.) *Language Spread and Language Policy*. Washington, D.C.: Georgetown University Press, 61–82.

[Myers-Scotton, Carol] Scotton, Carol Myers (1993) *Social Motivations for Codeswitching: Evidence from Africa*. Oxford: Oxford University Press.

Newton, Esther (1972) *Mother Camp: Female Impersonation in America*. Chicago: University of Chicago Press.

Queen, Robin M. (1992) Prosodic organization in the speeches of Martin Luther King. *Proceedings of the IRCS Workshop on Prosody in Natural Speech*. Philadelphia: Institute for Research in Cognitive Science, University of Pennsylvania, 151–160.

Queen, Robin M. (1997) "I don't speak spritch": locating lesbian language. In Anna Livia and Kira Hall (eds) *Queerly Phrased: Language, Gender, and Sexuality*. New York: Oxford University Press.

Rodgers, Bruce (1972) *The Queen's Vernacular*. Reprint as *Gay talk: A (Sometimes Outrageous) Dictionary of Gay Slang*. New York: Paragon Books, 1979.

Rudes, Blair A. and Bernard Healy (1979) Is she for real?: the concepts of femaleness and maleness in the gay world. In Madaleine Mathiot (ed.) *Ethnolinguistics: Boas, Sapir and Whorf Revisited*. The Hague: Mouton, 49–61.

RuPaul (1995) *Lettin' it All Hang Out: An Autobiography*. New York: Hyperion.

Sunaoshi, Yukako (1995) Your boss is your "mother": Japanese women's construction of an authoritative position in the workplace. In Pamela Silberman, and Jonathan Loftin (eds) *SALSA II: Proceedings of the Second Annual Symposium about Language and Society–Austin (Texas Linguistics Forum 34)*. Austin: University of Texas Department of Linguistics, 175–188.

Turner, Victor (1986) *The Anthropology of Performance*. New York: PAJ Publications.

Walters, Keith (1981) A proposal for studying the language of homosexual males. Master's thesis, University of Texas at Austin.

Walters, Keith (1992) Supplementary materials for AFR 320/LIN 325: Black English. Master's thesis, University of Texas at Austin.

Wyatt, Toya A. (1994) Language development in African American English child speech. *Linguistics and Education* 7: 7–22.

QUESTIONS

Content

1. What is a drag queen?
2. Which of the three approaches to style is Barrett's concept of style most in line with: Labov's attention to speech model, Bell's audience design or the speaker design approach?
3. What is the markedness model and how can it explore the relationship and distinctions among dialect, register, and genre?
4. Barrett discusses three styles. What group identities do these styles index in his study?
5. Reread example 1. How would a purely quantitative study of language style deal with this data? Would it misanalyse it?
6. What is the difference between a marked and an unmarked switch and what functions do marked switches have?

Concept

1. Consider the following excerpt. Is this a marked or unmarked switch (consider the setting)? What does the choice imply? What does the stylistic change index?

   An African American drag queen approaches a white couple sitting near the stage during a performance in a gay bar. The bar has a predominantly African American clientele. When speaking to the white couple, the drag queen switches to the white woman style. The actual switch does not occur within the example below but precedes it.

   1 Oh, hi, how are you doing?
   2 White people. Love it.
   3 I . . . I'm not being racial cause I'm white.
   4 I just have a <obscured> . . . I can afford more sun tan.

2. Consider the following excerpt. Is this a marked or unmarked switch? What does the choice imply? What does the stylistic change index?

   A drag queen introduces a male stripper in a bar with a predominantly white clientele. A young African American man enters the bar and walks past the front of the stage. Lines 1 to 6 are primarily in white woman style. In line 7, the performer makes a switch to AAVE style to address the newcomer. In lines 9 to 11, the drag queen switches back to white woman style.

1   Please welcome to the stage, our next dancer,
2   He is a butt-fucking tea,[1] honey.
3   He is hot.
4   Masculine, muscled, and ready to put it to ya, baby.
5   Anybody in here (.) hot (.) as (.) fish (.) grease?
6   That's pretty hot, idn't it?
7   (Switches to exaggerated low pitch) Hey what's up, home boy?
8   (Switches back) I'm sorry that fucking creole always come around when I don't
    need it.
9   Please, welcome,
10 hot, gorgeous, sexy, very romantic,
11 and he'd like to bend you over and turn you every which way but loose.

---

[1] *Butt-fucking tea* refers to anything that is exceptionally good.

NOTES ON CONCEPT QUESTIONS

Chapter 1: Sociolinguistic methods for data collection and interpretation
(Schleef and Meyerhoff)

Exercise 1 (questionnaire design)

This questionnaire is good in some ways but bad in others. It is good in that it includes a variety of question types and examples. The questionnaire is well structured and has a clear end and beginning. The most negative aspect of this questionnaire is that the research question cannot really be answered with it. Quite often students design a questionnaire without really thinking through their research objective and how to analyse the data. Other negative aspects are that the introduction is a little short and should probably give more information. It is unclear what the adjectives 'always', 'often', 'sometimes', etc. mean (e.g. how often is 'sometimes'?) and why the particular adjectives in section four were chosen. No contact details of the researcher are given at the end of the questionnaire.

Exercise 2 (sampling technique)
1. Random or stratified random sampling
2. Ethnographic approach, social networks and the 'friend of a friend' technique
3. Ethnographic approach, social networks and the 'friend of a friend' technique

Exercise 3 (data collection)

Various ways to tackle these problems are possible here. The purpose of this exercise is to make students think about data collection issues rather than coming up with a correct answer. The group A project has more choices when it comes to data type and sampling technique, depending on exactly what aspects the group wants to focus on. A data grid is certainly appropriate as it would help getting an idea how much data is needed. For the group B project, the collection of naturally occurring data using a social network or ethnographic approach would be most suitable, although such an approach could certainly be complemented with interviews and focus groups.

Exercise 4 (ethics)
An informed consent form is of course appropriate in many cases. However, under certain circumstances the use of such a form may seem inappropriate. Especially when researchers have developed a close relationship with those studied, it may seem redundant or inappropriate to ask them to sign a form. Long-term research projects may also need special consideration. Informed consent should be a continuous process since the research relationship and the contexts of investigation may change. The limits of the relationship must be negotiated carefully throughout the project. These are all aspects a consent form, signed at the beginning of field-work, cannot take into consideration.

Exercise 5 (data interpretation)
Table 3 above lists existential constructions. Other potential variables include the discourse marker *like*, passive verb forms, past verb forms, copula presence/absence, negation, and many more. There are also several potential phonetic variables but they are not visible in this transcript. Choose past tense as a variable for further investigation. This is interesting because some forms can be classified as creole-like and others as non-standard English forms. The former include the preverbal marker *did* while the latter comprise bare stem forms of the verb or copula absence. As for constraints, tense, mood, voice, aspect, subject type and verb type could be included. Findings could be relevant for linguistic theory in regards to different settlement patterns on the island and the influence of different inputs on language change and the estab-lishment of community norms. For those interested in qualitative data analysis, the recordings offer good data to explore style shifting or the expression of different identities on the island. The pragmatic functions of some of the linguistic structures, e.g. *like*, could also be explored qualitatively.

Exercise 6 (data collection)
Eckert uses naturally occurring data. Her research is of an ethnographic nature, and she uses the concept of the community of practice as her framework of analysis. She uses this type of data collection and analysis because she is interested in finding out how meaning is actively constructed within a small social unit. A focus on a small group of speakers and a flexible approach to data analysis are therefore very important. Apart from linguistic variables, Eckert also investigates extralinguistic variables such as ritual hugs, the use of make-up and facial expressions. She chose those because they are important features that contribute to the style under investigation. These features emerged during data collection and out of her analysis rather than being pre-determined before the beginning of fieldwork.

Exercise 7 (working with spontaneous and natural data)
This exercise is of an exploratory nature. If students experience difficulties determining the functions of *oh*, ask them how the pragmatic meaning of a particular utterance changes without the *oh*. This may help them accessing the functions of the word.

Chapter 2: Back in style
(Bell 2001)

1. These questions are intended to highlight the tension between what the speaker may be doing and how it is interpreted by others. For example, there are cases where people initiate a shift but what other people identify them as is very different to what they may

be trying to identify with. I once attended a play where one character habitually put on an American accent. In the play it was clear that the character was trying to project a worldly, and experienced, professional persona. I asked the actors afterwards what the use of the accent meant to them, and they said that it reinforced what an idiot the character was in the eyes of the rest of the characters. It's not hard to imagine situations where this kind of mismatch plays out in real life too.

2. We might expect that this will be an additional constraint on the extent to which people can alter their speech. This might apply at many levels. If women spend more time talking to other women (and men to men) then this proviso would predict that women will end up talking more like each other (and men likewise). There have been recent attempts to investigate this in the independently motivated framework of Exemplar Theory. Exponents of Exemplar Theory don't seem to be aware of Le Page as their precursor. At a grosser level, you will have observed the effect of this when people try and perform a speech variety they don't have much exposure to – most Northern Hemisphere speakers of English have a couple of features that they turn on to imitate 'Southern Hemisphere' varieties and fail to distinguish between Australian, New Zealand and South African English. Conversely, Antipodeans usually have one generic 'North American' accent that is a macaronic blend of features typical of many discrete varieties of North American English.

3. To answer this, you need to work out what the difference between different social groups is and then compare that with the intra-speaker variation of Green Lantern and Silver Fox. Subtract the lower frequency for /t/ flapping from the higher frequency (and then do the same for /æ/ raising). Now see how much each speaker shifts on each variable. The Style Axiom predicts that an individual's style shifting will be derived from (i.e. be less extreme than) style shifting between social groups.

Chapter 3: Oprah and /ay/
(Hay, Jannedy and Mendoza-Denton 1999)

1. The quantitative evidence might suggest this – even with an African American referee, she uses more diphthongs than monophthongs, but note that her **audience** is the US viewing public, and most of her viewers are non-African Americans. This makes it hard to know what her norm is, since we've got several uncontrolled variables at play within an audience design model. An additional factor is that Oprah is on record as not being an advocate of widespread public use of AAVE.

    Depending on your perspective on phonetics and phonology, it is also debatable whether [aː] is reduced, relative to [ai]. In which case, the apparent frequency effect (like short-I raising, discussed in the paper) is unmotivated on linguistic grounds.

2. Probably we would expect a change in progress to be more sensitive to lexical frequency effects than a (relatively) stable variable is. For instance, the (ing) variable doesn't seem to show frequency effects – high frequency words are not more likely to occur with the alveolar nasal than low frequency words are. Discussions of lexical frequency effects and variation generally predict high frequency words will be in advance of low frequency words with respect to a linguistic change. Frequent use is predicted to favour reduced, lenited or less marked forms, and this provides directionality to a change. Debates about the role of frequency effects in variation and change have been around for a long time: you can learn more by researching the terms *Neogrammarian* and *lexical diffusion* in any good linguistics encyclopedia. In brief, the Neogrammarian hypothesis states that a change affects all relevant contexts at the same time (though

some contexts may favour the change more than others during the entire unfolding of a change, cf. Kroch 1989); the lexical diffusion hypothesis says variation and change starts in some words or word classes before spreading to others. It seems pretty clear that both kinds of change exist. This means that (socio)linguists need to determine two things before they can make sensible hypotheses: first, whether they are looking at a stable variable or a change in progress; second if it is a change in progress, what kind of change it is.

Chapter 4: A Chinese yuppie in Beijing
(Zhang 2005)

1. Yes, because this study shows that the Chinese yuppies' linguistic style in the local site of Beijing cannot be separated from developments in the transnational Chinese community and the global market. The yuppies regard themselves as belonging to several communities at the same time: Beijing, mainland China, and the international business world. This sense of belonging is reflected in their speech.

2. Various answers are possible here. For example, students will most likely use some kind of academic style when speaking in class. They will avoid the use of vernacular features. They will answer and ask questions. They may use many features to express negative politeness, e.g. hedges, subjunctive forms and phrases like 'I wonder' to limit the threat to their face. Outside of the classroom, when talking to fellow students, they will use a casual speech style which may include vernacular features. They may use more positive politeness strategies. For example, male students may address each other as 'dude' (in the US) or 'mate' and 'pal' (in the UK). There will be many humorous remarks, laughter, backchannelling but possibly also more conversational overlap.

Chapter 5: Linguistic routines and politeness in greeting and parting
(Laver 1981)

1. Results will vary here, so it will naturally be very hard to include it in a flowchart, but this is the point of the exercise. First, the use of the term varies by region. It seems to be more widely used in the US than in the UK. Second, many people have only a very vague understanding of what exactly the term means, and they are not aware of the fact that it was supposed to function as a counterpart to Mr, i.e. replace Mrs and Miss. So based on this idea, the box 'married' should be replaced by 'female' with an example that lists only Ms and no mention of Mrs and Miss should be made. However, this is not how most people understand this word. For many, it is merely an alternative choice. It is often understood as an indication of age (i.e. not a Miss). Some people believe only feminists and lesbians use it. It is linked to unmarried women who live with a partner, or those who do not want to disclose their marital status.

2. Various avenues of discussion can be entered here. We will only mention two points. In most cases, the polite norm is one of negative politeness. This is reflected in terms of address, greetings, partings, and the minimal occurrence of small talk. Terms of address such as 'sir' show this very well. Example (2), however, shows that these norms are negotiable and terms that would suggest the use of positive politeness strategies ('dear') are possible too, if circumstances permit. While it is perfectly all right for an older female to use such a strategy with a younger male server, the opposite may not necessarily be true without generating additional implicatures. Similar re-negotiation is

apparent in example (4). The self-oriented small talk initiated by the customer threatens the customer's own negative face by being revealing about herself. At the same time the customer attends to her positive face by presenting herself as interesting to the listener while also attending to the potential face threat to the server, due to the lack of prompt service, with humour.

Chapter 6: Formal forms and discernment
(Ide 1989)

1. to 3. Only excerpt (1) includes honorifics ('sir'). It is not entirely clear whether this form is used to raise the addressee (as Brown and Levinson would argue) or to acknowledge a status difference. Considering that there are no such forms in the other three excerpts, the former is probably the more appropriate explanation. Very few Americans will assume that there is truly a status difference between server and customer. We are most likely dealing with face wants here, not wants of roles and settings, as the polite forms and strategies used in these four excerpts vary quite considerably in spite of the fact that roles and settings are almost identical. Your Majesty or titles prefixing a person's name are other examples of honorifics in English, e.g. Miss, Ms., Mr, Mrs, Dr and Lord.

Chapter 7: Language with an attitude
(Preston 2002)

1. Different answers are possible here. One would have to expect that the most extreme evaluations of correctness and friendliness should be nearly opposites. If this is the case (for at least some varieties), then Preston's idea of investment and symbolic capital can indeed be applied; i.e. a particular group invests its symbolic capital in either friendliness or correctness, but not both. Most likely, there will be many answers that will be in between these two evaluations, so it may make sense to suggest the existence of continua of friendliness and correctness and that only the most extreme cases will yield the results Preston found for the American North and the American South. In the UK, for instance, Received Pronunciation is usually rated high on correctness but low on friend-liness, rural accents tend to be rated high on friendliness and low on correctness; however, non-standard accents of industrial cities (e.g. Birmingham) tend to receive intermediate results or are rated low on both dimensions.

Chapter 8: The 'L'il Abner' syndrome
(Preston 1985)

1. The purpose of this question is to encourage you to think about what kinds of social attributes are valued negatively in the particular community you come from, or where you might be conducting your research. We have seen studies of language attitudes that have used questions about likely employment prospects for a speaker, likely smoking patterns, clothing and music tastes, and so forth as ways of eliciting how positive or negative the perceptions of a particular speech variety are. You can probably think of others that would be meaningful in your own community.

2. It's well-known that the norms for CMC and texting allow for creative respellings and include some quite conventionalised abbreviations. This being so, it is possible that

people who participate a lot in online communities or who text a lot might have different attitudes to the kinds of eye dialect respellings that Preston was investigating. Eye dialect might be less likely to trigger a negative response from them. On the other hand, you can imagine a situation where the kind of data Preston used would trigger just as negative reactions: people who are used to using respelling and conventionalised abbreviations in new media might have very strong feelings about when and where it is appropriate to use them (and react negatively to their use outside of CMC etc.).

3. Writers probably aren't aware of the kinds of demotions of social status that the use of eye dialect and respellings can trigger. In most cases (and you can find evidence of this in interviews with writers; see, for example, the interview with Lois Ann Yamanaka in Johnson 2004), writers are struggling with the difficulties of transforming lived and primarily spoken experiences into text. For many writers, some respelling is what Preston would presumably consider an attempt to 'honestly' and accurately represent the different voices, characters and histories of the people they are creating on the page.

We have never seen any writers' responses to this kind of research. This would be interesting because even if a writer's attempts at eye dialect are well-meaning, should s/he ignore the impact it is likely to have on readers?

Incidentally, you can find related debates about respelling and the kinds of perceptions they trigger in many of the discussions about orthographies for creole or dialectal variants of a standardised language. Some people favour an orthography that is clearly distinguished from the standard language as a way of establishing a separate and distinct identity; some people favour an orthography closer to the standard language norm because they feel the alternatives trigger negative stereotypes (see Schieffelin and Doucet 1994, Rajah-Carrim 2008).

Chapter 9: Perceptual and phonetic experiments on American English dialect identification
(Purnell, Idsardi & Baugh 1999)

1. Researchers ought to carefully consider what the first words are in the matched guise stimulus. A strongly marked variant in the initial stages of the sample sentences being evaluated might bias the final results. The importance of first tokens of a variant seems (for some variables at least) to be quite significant. Listeners may effectively 'switch off' after hearing a first token of a sociolinguistically marked variant. This may cause problems for researchers who try and manipulate tokens embedded in a larger text.

2. The question here is really whether you can generalise very much about societal attitudes from the attitudes of university students, since students are probably younger, more geographically mobile, and more socially mobile than the population as a whole.

Another consideration (related to their age) is whether university students have fully acquired the sociolinguistic competences and evaluations typical of older speakers. Some research suggests that the acquisition of the norms of variation continues well into adulthood (Guy & Boyd 1990). If that's the case, then university students might still be learning what the social meaning of a particular variant is and their responses might be less consistent than older respondents' would be.

Other research on attitudes gives respondents more flexibility in how they answer. An advantage of forced choice questions is that the results are easier to conduct statistical tests on. A disadvantage is that your respondents may hold attitudes that you have neglected to ask about – you'll miss out on those.

Chapter 10: Language education policy and the medium of instruction issue in post-colonial Africa
(Ferguson 2006)

1.   It might be helpful to discuss the fact that the experience of many students in Europe and Asia is that they have to become used to functioning academically in English by the time they finish university. The issue is not confined to Africa.
2.   The purpose of working on this in small groups is to foster debate among the group members as you weigh up different options and evaluate each other's opinions. The discussion process, as well as the final recommendations, would be good material to report back to the class after a few days.

Chapter 11: Social stereotypes, personality traits and regional perceptions displaced
(Buchstaller 2006)

1.   Words on these lists are all evaluated negatively. *Go* appears well before *be like*. A possible discussion point might be whether you think negative attitudes to *go* might have softened the ground for *be like* to take hold.
2.   It's hard to mask the sex of a speaker in spoken form because there are a lot of cues to speaker gender (speech rate, pitch, intonation patterns, frequency of other socio-linguistically stratified variants …). Similarly, a regional accent is marked by many features: if you want to focus on regional ascriptions of *be like* it's hard not to bias the respondents if they hear US or British English vowels in the carrier sentences.
3.   All her respondents were from the UK, so it's possible the results were confounded in the same way that spoken stimuli would have been, i.e. the default variety that respondents assumed for the text was an abstract variety of British English. If so, this might account for the very high number of 'No Idea' responses as to where the different forms come from – what people were evaluating as they read came from themselves!

Chapter 12: Bilingualism in Paraguay
(Choi 2005)

1.   The main advantage is that the data is relatively easy to get hold of. There are several disadvantages. Not all speakers have the kind of introspection required for filling in such a questionnaire and may give inaccurate information. There may also be a danger of over- or under-reporting of one or other language due to political investment. When using a questionnaire, the same questions are used for all respondents. It is not possible to react to individual circumstances or ask follow-up questions. For example, some of the questions are somewhat socioeconomically biased. Asking about the housekeeper, doctors and the curandero makes only sense for those who can afford such services. It is also not clear to what extent public schooling is taken up.
2.   There are several similarities in these studies. In both studies, who you talk to plays an important role. Use of Guarani and Hungarian decreases from generation to generation,

when comparing Gal's table with Table 12.1 in Choi for example; 52.4% of respondents speak Guarani with their grandparents, 40% with their parents, and only 3.3% with their children. In both studies, formality also plays a role, with doctors more likely to be talked to in Spanish/German. However, there are also many differences. Gal's study represents a very advanced point in a language shift situation, while it is still unclear what exactly may happen in Paraguay. Location seems to play an important role in Paraguay with rural and urban areas developing into different directions. There also seems to be much more bilingual use than there is in Gal's study. The political support that Guarani receives has already increased the use of Guarani in schools and there is evidence for a substantial ethnolinguistic pride associated with Guarani. Such factors did not play a role in Austria which is normally considered – by its population and abroad – a German-speaking monolingual country.

Chapter 13: Code-switching in Gapun
(Kulick and Stroud 1990)

1. In situational code-switching codes, are switched in reaction to changes in the situation. Metaphorical code-switching can occur without changes in the situation as such. It refers to the tendency to switch codes in order to discuss a topic that would normally fall into another conversational domain. Metaphorical code-switching often enriches a situation, allowing for allusion to more than one social relationship within the situation. Blom and Gumperz (this volume) introduced the idea of topic related or 'metaphorical' code switching following a study they conducted in Norway. Generally speaking, most of Kulick and Stroud's functions can be covered by Blom and Gumperz' terminology if we accept a wide definition of topic. There is ample room for disagreement, though (for example in respect to code-switched repetitions), which can form the basis for a discussion.

Chapter 14: Social meaning in linguistic structure
(Blom and Gumperz 1972)

1. Various answers are possible here. Students will have noticed code-switching, or may even code-switch themselves, but they may have problems explaining what social meaning the different varieties have. If that is the case, it may help to ask students how the social meaning would change if no code-switching occurred.

Chapter 15: Dialect contact, focusing and phonological rule complexity
(Britain 1997)

1. Interdialectal [ɤ] is a phonetically intermediate form between [ʌ] and [ʊ] that has emerged as the norm in the central Fenland. Britain suggests that this interdialectal form has only recently focused from a wider range of variants. He also points out that the interdialectal form has only focused among young speakers who live in and around the central Fenland town of Wisbech. Why it has emerged is not entirely clear, so there is some room for discussion and hypothesising, all of which, however, should take into consideration that the variants under discussion are not very salient to speakers in the

Fens. Britain suggests that the focusing of the variant in question may be due to ongoing changes in Southern British English, where /ʊ/ class words are often unrounded and are begun to be lowered. So it is most likely younger speakers who will lead this change in the future. The question Britain brings up at the end of his article, though, is what group of young speakers will be leading the change (what social class and what gender?). Considering what students have learned about gender, one would expect women to lead this change as it seems to be a change in progress that is below the level of awareness. In such cases, women often use more of the new non-standard variant than men (see Meyerhoff 2006: 214). In respect to class, if we assume that this change represents a change from below, making predictions about class is difficult. Such changes may be introduced by any social class (Labov 1994:79), although they are most frequently introduced by the upper working class and young people.

Chapter 16: Legitimate language in a multilingual school
(Heller 2001)

1. and 2. Elsewhere, Heller points out that less overt attention is paid to mastery of spoken standard French in other than French classes but that it remains important in the evaluation of written work in those classes. Many students consider this to be unfair as they feel that these classes should mainly focus on content rather than the mastery of written French. This excerpt shows this very well. For this student, French, i.e. standard French, seems to be a subject rather than a language that plays a vital role as a means of communication in everyday school life at Champlain. Standard French is constructed as the legitimate language, yet also something alien, not the student's language in any way, which is (illegitimate) Ontarian French. We have to keep in mind, though, that this is a mockery — of the student himself but also of the school's linguistic standards. The student does in fact know a lot about French. He knows what a bad mistake is and can make such mistakes on purpose. Nonetheless, the example shows very nicely the general ideology students are confronted with at Champlain and the repercussions of this ideology for the student's idea of what a legitimate language is.

Chapter 17: Language crossing and the redefinition of reality
(Rampton 1998)

1. Rampton (1998: 296) analyses this exchange as follows:

> Lines 1–9 involve a verbal tussle in which Asif and Alan use questions to under-mine the positions that Ms Jameson stakes out in what she says. Asif's question in line 2 treats the account she gives of her late arrival as inadequate; she rebuts his inquiry as illegimate in line 3 but this is then undermined by Alan in lines 4 and 5; and in lines 6–8, Ms Jameson is delayed in the departure she announced in line 5 by a question that upgrades the query over her initial excuse into an explicit challenge. All this time, she has been locked into the interaction by the adjacency structures set up by the boys' questions, but at line 10, she breaks out of this pattern, ignores Asif's line 9 repair initiation, again announces her departure and leaves without saying anything more. With the cooperative exchange structure now disrupted and Ms Jameson apparently disattending to him, Asif launches into some 'muttering' 'afterburn' [...] In this refusal to submit to the unjust Miss

Jameson, Asif uses some Creole/Black English. Admittedly, it can sometimes be hard trying to distinguish Creole from the local multiracial vernacular, and Asif's stopped / θ / in 'dat's sad man' is ambiguous. But in lines 16 and 17, he uses a characteristically Creole unrounded front open vowel in 'not' (cf. Wells 1982:576; Sebba 1993: 153–154), and the stretched [1] in his first 'lunch' maybe connects with a black speech feature noted by Hewitt in south London (1986: 134).

Language crossing occurs in lines 16 and 17, possibly also in line 12. It can be considered language crossing because Asif uses a variety that he doesn't normally use and has full and easy access to. Rampton points out that constraints on the use of Creole are evident among Panjabi youngsters since they usually avoid using it in the company of Black peers, who would normally use Creole. This example of language crossing occurs in a moment when the routine assumptions about social reality were partially suspended. Asif's muttering is addressed to a person not actually present. In the normal social order of things, Asif would most likely not tell Ms J that she doesn't need any lunch as it may have serious disciplinary consequences. The use of crossing, therefore, not only marks this 'loosening of routine assumptions about social reality' (Rampton 1998: 298) but helps create it by deconstructing the categories of ethnicity considered normal in the dominant social structures.

Chapter 18: The globalisation of vernacular variation
(Meyerhoff and Niedzielski 2003)

1.   The authors were able to show that there are clearly distinct subsets of lexical pairs. Some are spreading but are perceived as exotic, while others are spreading but appear to be localising. This is important because it informs our theoretical explanations for the spread of innovative lexical items. For example, it would be wrong to argue that localising lexical items are used by speakers to sound American or British or that they are spreading because they evoke particular social meanings associated with one nation or another. Conversely, if forms are perceived to be American, for example, this would strengthen claims that such variation is due to an increasing global influence of U.S. English. Whether a variant is perceived to be local or exotic may also shed light on the different histories or paths of diffusion of such lexical items, which may in turn inform the study of language change and research into the linguistic expression of localised identities. In principle, this study of lexical pairs could be replicated for phonetic variables, testing how differing pronunciations of the same word are perceived by speakers of a particular variety of English.

Chapter 19: The social motivation of a sound change
(Labov 1972)

1.   (a) This is a matter of considerable debate – What do people pay attention to? What kinds of variables (phonetic versus syntactic versus lexical) have social meaning ascribed to them? The idea that what people pay attention to are clusters of variables (and that's what makes a style) is probably closer to what lay people actually tell us, e.g. the observation that heavily Northern Cities-shifted speakers sound 'nasal' describes a range of effects of the NCS on a number of vowels (see work by Preston and others in Part 2 of this volume).

Alternately, though, there is some suggestion that only specific variables get indexed even in chain shift scenarios. The distinction between stereotypes, markers and indicators is probably relevant here.

(b) It might mean that we want to collect more data about clusters of variables than we usually do. Note that this fits in well with his suggestion that sociolinguists should be looking at variables that have something to say about linguistic systems.

2. We would expect to find a peak in the same age group (by birth year) that he did. No prediction about what happens in subsequent age groups can be made because of the complex history of advance and retreat of centralised variants in this area (cf. Pope et al. 2007). Note that some of the real time studies Labov reviews in later work (Labov 1994) show peaks among the teenagers in subsequent generations, indicating that there is some age-grading even with changes in progress. Sankoff's (2006) review article offers a concise summary.

Chapter 20: Layering and recycling in English intensifiers
(Ito and Tagliamonte 2003)

1. Robin Lakoff (1975, 2004) argued that features of 'women's language' were associated not only with women, but also with academic and gay men. Her larger generalisation was that there is a link between social power and certain ways of talking. Perhaps a similar association of 'powerlessness' underlies Stoffel's observation.

2. The switch always goes to real(ly), one of the two most common intensifiers, and the one that I & T argue has been subject to most extreme recycling. It seems plausible that when reformulating a phrase with an intensifier, the more common variants will be preferred as they are seen to be 'better' examples of intensification. This may carry with it additional emphasis, but we can't tell from these examples, and it's not clear why the recycled variant really would be perceived to be a better way of signalling additional emphasis, rather than the perennial favourite very.

3. A stable variable is likely to show greater use of the conservative or prestige variant by women and by people with higher education. Sankoff & Blondeau's study of (r) in Montreal (and many other studies of changes in progress) shows more frequent use of the innovative variant by women, and different results for education. There is no single answer for this question: depending on what study people choose to look at, an interesting relationship between sex and education is likely to emerge; the point of the exercise is to encourage discussion of what these interesting relationships are and how society is organised so that such associations are produced.

Chapter 21: Language change across the lifespan
(Sankoff and Blondeau 2007)

1. The answer to this is in the article — generational change and age-grading might show up in trend studies; age-grading and lifespan change might show up in panel studies. The important issue here is to understand the different profiles of variation/change.

2. Speakers must be able to acquire new frequencies (at least) over the lifespan and beyond the so-called Critical Period. Whether this involves acquiring new structural constraints, e.g. allophonic conditioning favouring phonetic variants, syntactic structures favouring certain grammatical variants, is an open question. The full text of the article indicates that if Montreal (r) speakers **do** significantly change the frequency of a variant

over time, they simultaneously acquire/change the phonological constraints on the variation. It's not clear how general this pattern is because it's so poorly studied as yet; see
Boberg (2004) for some thoughts.

3. The full text of the article cites a number of studies, some of which show stability of
individual systems over time, some of which show change, some of which show changes
in frequency without changes in underlying constraints. As Sankoff & Blondeau
note, there is a need for lots more information about how labile (i.e. changeable) adult
linguistic systems are.

Chapter 22: Norwich revisited
(Trudgill 1988)

1. Trudgill undertook a trend study because it was not a resampling of the same individuals.
2. In the full version of the article Trudgill discusses the possible role of the media in more
detail. Although it is attractive to think of the media as being the vector for the transmission of some variation and change, it is hard to reconcile this with the gradual
geographical diffusion of some variables. If the mass media plays an important role in
transmission of the changes, we might expect changes to show up at the same time
across an entire viewing region (perhaps a whole country). Yet the evidence suggests
changes often spread between metropolitan areas first.
3. Trudgill's study distinguished styles on the basis of the speaker's activity (e.g. casual
conversation versus reading aloud). This approach focuses on how much attention
the speaker may be paying to the speech activity they're involved in. Presumably, in
the 1968 study, the centralisation of (e) lagged in reading passage and word list
styles because speakers were more attentive to their pronunciation in these activities
than they were in casual conversation. But over time, the attention appears to wane
as the centralised variant becomes more entrenched and normal in the community.
Trudgill suggests that the nature of the variable is important for determining whether
it will move gradually through different styles. Perhaps this is because the potential
confusion caused by a merger of two phonemes (here: /ɛ/ and /ʌ/) is something
that only arises when you are reading words out of context. Context tells you if
someone said *bell* or *bull* (most of the time). But in a word list, speakers might be
inclined to really concentrate on keeping these words distinct, until such time as the
merger has become part of what's normal in the speech community. At that point, it
would be hard for someone, even when they're concentrating, to keep the phonemes
distinct.

Chapter 23: Aging and gendering
(Cameron 2005)

1. A key factor must be that Cameron says (d) is stable, like the other canonical ones are.
In the full version of the article he shows that his hypotheses are complicated if a
change is new or mid-way to completion. An implication of this parallelism is that the
patterns we see in the (d) data might well show up in an individual's life history. Previous
work on stable variables suggests that the drop in non-standard forms in middle-age is
due to integration in the linguistic marketplace (this is discussed more in Cheshire
1987, Downes 1995, Holmes 2008, Meyerhoff 2006). Maybe this shows that the
effects of integration in the linguistic marketplace are not only due to exposure to the
prestige norms, but also to broader cross-gender associations.

2. (a) We should be paying attention to network ties and people's individual life histories more in how we categorise them in social class terms (cf. Weber).

   (b) We should ensure that our age cohorts are based on socially and interactionally meaningful divisions based on who associates with whom, i.e. generations of 15–25 years are one way of organising our data, but may not be the most appropriate one for answering certain questions.

3. In the full version of this paper, Cameron responds to and discusses a question that was put to him about whether certain activities constrain interaction between the sexes at different ages (in people's teens and adulthood). One suggestion is that if you pursue a career as a professional athlete or in merchant finance, you might end up with a network as gender-segregated as small children have. This is an empirical question that could only be answered by long-term, (probably) participant-observation. Cameron responds to this question by suggesting that older people whose activities or careers involve a high degree of gender segregation (e.g. involvement in single-sex sports teams) would also show a higher degree of gender-differentiation in their speech.

Chapter 24: Social networks and social class
(Milroy and Milroy 1992)

1. Most likely it is a weak social network as not everyone knows everyone else. For simplicity's sake, it is best to base this classroom connection on whether or not students talk to each other; if they do, they have a network link. Those who also socialise outside of the classroom will receive a second link and will have a multiplex connection. Most likely there will not be many such cases, and the network will have to be characterised as neither dense nor multiplex, i.e. weak. As a consequence, mutual linguistic influence and norm enforcement within this particular network will be minimal.

2. Milroy and Milroy (1992: 13–15) argue that the data can be interpreted in terms of weak ties rather than prestige and dominance:

> Two patterns are particularly noticeable in the language of these two contact groups (white-oriented blacks and black-oriented whites). First, on morpho-syntactic variation their scores average about the same, and on copula deletion and 'ain't' for 'didn't', the whites actually outperform the blacks on 'black' variants. Second, whereas the core black group uses these features quite variably (pre-sumably also using the 'white' variants), the core white group does not use the black variants at all. So in their convergence pattern, the BWs and the WBs have different starting points. In ethnic group terms, the white group starts much further back on the black English dimension than the black group on the white dimension. And it follows [...] that the core black vernacular incorporates a resource not available to mainstream white speakers – the capacity to alternate between black and white morphosyntactic variants according to occasion of use. To this extent, these speakers resemble the inner-city Belfast speakers, who also have at their disposal alternating forms that carry different symbolic functions according to occasion of use. Typically, one of these alternants has in-group functions and belongs to the vernacular, whereas the other has out-group functions and is more standardlike. [...]
>
> From this perspective, the convergence of WBs toward white norms is not so remarkable, as these white norms are already available to them within an existing

pattern of core black vernacular variation. The reason why the white-oriented blacks use the white norms more often than other blacks is accessible through a theory of weak ties, as it is clear from the authors' descriptions of these speakers that their contacts with whites are of a classic weak-tie type. They are described as con men, hustlers, and political activists, and it is hardly plausible that con men (for example) could successfully practise on persons with whom they had contracted strong (dense and multiplex) ties. The degree to which these speakers use the white norms is increased by the range and number of situations in which they have weak-tie contacts outside their core community, and for them the adoption of more white usage is functional in their weak-tie contacts. The suggestion by Ash and Myhill (1986: 41) that prestige is the explanation for this shift toward white norms seems to be quite a weak explanation, which simply begs the question of what is meant by prestige in such a context (for a discussion of prestige-based arguments, see J. Milroy 1987).

The convergence of black-oriented white speakers to black norms is in a sense more remarkable, as the core white dialect does not possess the new variants (copula deletion, etc.) that they adopt (to a certain extent) in carrying out what must presumably be an act of linguistic accommodation. These outside variants have to be acquired, and so some affirmatory effort is involved. Although the researchers do not give precise information as to the strength of these speakers' participation in black culture, the model of linguistic diffusion and change we have outlined in [the preceding article] would predict that their ties with both communities are likely to be relatively weak. On the basis of the information provided by Ash and Myhill, we assume that it is this group, and not the WB group, who most resemble the peripheral characters who Rogers and Shoemaker (1971) argued are typical of the innovating individual.

Chapter 25: Mobility versus social class
(Kerswill & Williams 2000)

1. This is a difficult contrast to understand: survival is opposed to exclusivity. Yet at the level of the group, one way to understand exclusivity is that it ensures the continued maintenance of socially valued distinctions (like class). Kerswill & Williams may be thinking of 'survival' in more individualised ways. They mention the practical benefits to working class people in being able to draw on each other for help, where needed.

   You might also want to talk about how the word 'survival' implies a certain agentiveness and suggests that members of all social classes are active in the definition and maintenance of boundaries between different classes. In doing this, it offers an interesting contrast to a more top-down approach, which might highlight the ways institutional structures enforce social norms and define membership in categories like social class, independently of individuals' desires.

2. They are very different to definitions based solely on control of capital, but have more in common with the aspirational and attitudinal measures discussed in Meyerhoff (2006).

Chapter 26: Making the best of 'bad' data
(Nevalainen 1999)

1. To answer this question, you will need to look for evidence that Nevalainen has considered the kinds of practices and activities women and men engage in. What is their

access to formal education? How constrained are their movements? What is their role in their family or community?

2. The notion of 'social aspirers' is hardly unique to this period in history. I would probably call such people upwardly mobile. The most famous sociolinguistic story of a social aspirer (in English) is the story of Eliza Doolittle, told by Shaw in *Pygmalion* (and the movie *My Fair Lady*).

3. Both Nevalainen and Haeri want to impress on us the contingent nature of prestige. People without access to, or training in, the rites of the standard language marketplace will have trouble orienting to the norms that are prestigious in that part of society. This frees them up to lead changes. This reminds us that generalisations such as Labov's Principle 1 are themselves contingent – in this case, on the fact that in most Western cities men and women have roughly equal access to education.

Chapter 27: Vowels and nail polish
(Eckert 1998)

1. It could be, but, especially if your class is of a larger size, most likely it isn't. You could argue that the class is developing a shared repertoire as the whole class is learning to talk about sociolinguistics using appropriate vocabulary. One could also argue that there is a jointly negotiated enterprise, if joint class discussions are included under the label of 'jointly negotiated enterprise'. However, there would also have to be mutual engagement, which is probably the criterion hardest to fulfil in a classroom situation. Large classes without discussions and without much contact with other students would therefore not qualify as a CoP. Smaller classes with true mutual engagement in a common enterprise that develop a shared repertoire might be.

2. Various individual answers are possible.

Chapter 28: 'Doing femininity' at work
(Holmes and Schnurr 2006)

1. *Example A* is a good example of cooperative talk, with Smithy, the male project manager, engaging in facilitative behaviour. He draws attention to Vita's work, which merits praise (lines 6 and 7). Clara also makes an appreciative comment in line 8. Smithy's move is made very discreetly but Clara picks it up right away. This is a very nice example of relational practice in a work team. While praising and acknowledgement are features that conventionally index femininity, it is unmarked in this community of practice as the conversation moves on right away. This is different in *excerpt B*, which also includes features that conventionally index feminity, but they are marked. They are commented on and made fun of. Neil's apologetic and mitigating language in lines 4 to 8 and 14 to 16 has associations with relatively feminine ways of talking. In this team, relational practice is expressed through contestive humour, jocular insult and extensive teasing (e.g. lines 9, 13 and 17), which Neil misinterprets as true criticism.

Chapter 29: A linguistic innovation of women in Cairo
(Haeri 1994)

1. The important thing to focus on in this exercise is that variants seldom index one and only one social property (or interpersonal stance, cf. Ochs reading). It should be relatively

easy to demonstrate this even in older, and more deterministically expressed social dialect surveys. Sociolinguists, like Kiesling and Zhang, who are very interested in how variation is **used**, provide very rich detail on the multiplicity of meanings that different variants (therefore by extension the variable itself) have for the speakers.

2. We don't expect to find evidence of the upper classes initiating changes. Usually it is the 'inferior' social classes: upper working class and/or lower middle class. Though note that even in this unusual case, it is **women** who are the leaders of the change in progress, not men. This is consistent with other research on vernacular changes in progress at the earlier stages of the change.

3. Apparent time evidence (steady increase of palatalisation in each generation surveyed) supports (a); a combination of apparent time evidence and the distribution of variants by social class supports (b).

Chapter 30: Indexing gender
(Ochs 1992)

1. Some of the terms can only refer to adult or grown people/animals. Some can only refer to female/male animals/people. These are words that *directly* index age and gender.

2. This is Ochs' important theoretical point. Her claim is that most linguistic features directly index stances (e.g. hesitancy) or activities (e.g. directing subordinates) and these stances and activities are conventionally associated with different genders in different communities. So there is an indirect (or 'mediated') relationship between gender and the linguistic features.

Chapter 31: Power and the language of men
(Kiesling 1997)

1. Excerpts 1 and 5 are particularly interesting because they show very different constructions of identities and the use of different linguistic features as a consequence. Darter (excerpt 1) is a newly initiated brother who still feels deferential to many of the other men in the group. Darter uses phrases that suggest that his opinion is not very valuable (line 59: *I just think*). He uses discourse markers that introduce justifications for his statements (lines 51 and 58: *you know, I mean*) and provides factual information to justify his support for Ritchie. Speed, on the other hand, speaks in a way that could be perceived as competitive and aggressive, a kind of discourse that may be regarded as stereotypically masculine. According to Kiesling, Speed creates an adversarial identity which results in linguistic features such as imperatives (e.g. lines 245, 246 and 256), swear words (line 256, 262, 266, 267, 268 and 271), he interrupts another speaker quite aggressively (line 256) and ends with a joke (line 274). The comparison of these excerpts shows very nicely how much the features used by these two speakers differ and that a quantitative analysis of any of those features would not have been able to uncover the findings made by Kiesling. The use of these structures, therefore, has no direct link with the category of men; they are contextually dependent. They may be used in certain styles, to express certain stances, and they may contribute to the construction of certain identities, which of course are also contextually dependent and negotiated in interaction.

Chapter 32: Markedness and styleswitching in performances by African American drag queens
(Barrett 1998)

1.   Switching to white woman style is a marked choice as the bar has a predominantly African American clientele. The switch implies that the white couple must be spoken to in white English. Barrett argues that this stylistic change indexes power issues. These issues are created by the white heterosexual couple 'invading' a space for gays and lesbians, particularly gay African Americans. Through humour at the expense of the white heterosexual couple, the African American drag queen 'makes it clear that their decision to come and "observe" (and appropriate) gay African American culture is, at the very least, problematic.' (Barrett 1998: 155)

2.   The switch to AAVE is a marked switch as it happens in a bar with a predominantly white clientele. The switch creates solidarity with the African American man who has just entered the bar. The apology for using AAVE in line 8 makes this switch even more salient as a marked choice. Note, however, that the apology itself includes AAVE features (the verb 'come' occurs without the Standard English-*s* inflection). This choice undermines the sincerity of what is being said and expresses solidarity with the African American clientele.

References

Ash, S. and J. Myhill (1986) Linguistic correlates of inter-ethnic contact. In David Sankoff (ed.) *Diversity and Diachrony*. Amsterdam: John Benjamins, 33–44.

Barrett, Rusty (1998) Markedness and styleswitching in performances by African American drag queens. In Carol Myers-Scotton (ed.) *Codes and Consequences: Choosing Linguistic Varieties*. New York and Oxford: Oxford University Press, 139–161.

Boberg, Charles (2004) Real and apparent time in language change: late adoption of changes in Montreal English. *American Speech* 79: 250–269.

Cheshire, Jenny (1987) Age and generation-specific use of language. In Ulrich Ammon et al. (eds) *Sociolinguistics: An International Handbook of the Science of Language and Society*. Berlin: Walter de Gruyter, 760–767.

Downes, William (1998) *Language and Society*. 2nd edition. Cambridge: Cambridge University Press.

Guy, Gregory R. and Sally Boyd (1990) The development of a morphological class. *Language Variation and Change* 2: 1–18.

Hewitt, Roger (1986) *White Talk Black Talk*. Cambridge: Cambridge University Press.

Holmes, Janet (2008) *An Introduction to Sociolinguistics*. 3rd edition. London: Longman.

Johnson, Sarah Ann (2004) *Conversations with American Women Writers*. Hanover, NH: University of New England Press.

Kroch, Anthony (1989) Reflexes of grammar in patterns of language change. *Language Variation and Change* 1: 199–244.

Labov, William (1994) *Principles of Linguistic Change: Internal Factors*. Oxford: Blackwell.

Lakoff, Robin T. (1975) *Language and Woman's Place*. New York: Harper & Row.

Lakoff, Robin T. (2004) *Language and Woman's Place: Text and Commentaries*. Revised and expanded edition, Mary Bucholtz (ed.). Oxford: Oxford University Press.

Meyerhoff, Miriam (2006) *Introducing Sociolinguistics*. London: Routledge.

Milroy, James (1987). The concept of prestige in sociolinguistic argumentation. *York Papers in Linguistics* 13: 215–226.

Milroy, Leslie and James Milroy (1992) Social network and social class: toward an integrated sociolinguistic model. *Language in Society* 21: 1–26.

Pope, Jennifer, Miriam Meyerhoff and Robert Ladd (2007) Forty years of language change on Martha's Vineyard. *Language* 83: 615–627.

Rajah-Carrim, Aaliya (2008) Choosing a spelling system for Mauritian Créole. *Journal of Pidgin and Creole Languages* 23: 193–226.

Rampton, Ben (1998) Language crossing and the redefinition of reality. In P. Auer (ed.) *Code-switching in Conversation: Language, Interaction and Identity*. London and New York: Routledge, 290–317.

Rogers, E. M. and F.F. Shoemaker (1971) *Communication of Innovations* (2nd ed.). New York: Academic Press.

Sankoff (2006) Age: apparent time and real time. In Keith Brown (ed.) *Elsevier Encyclopedia of Language and Linguistics*, Volume 9, 2nd edn. Oxford: Elsevier, 110–116.

Schieffelin, Bambi B. and Rachelle Charlier Doucet (1994) The 'real' Haitian Creole: ideology, metalinguistics and orthographic choice. *American Ethnologist* 21: 176–200.

Sebba, M. (1993) *London Jamaican: A Case Study in Language Interaction*. London: Longman.

Wells, J. (1982) *Accents of English*, 1–3. Cambridge: Cambridge University Press.

INDEX

by age/predication **332**
distributional analysis 327–34
by modified adjectives/age **330**, **331**
voices, sets of 484
volition **99**, 99–100
volitional aspect, politeness 98
Vološinov, V.N. 484

Wahba, K.M. 470
wakimae 98
Watam 202
Watts, R.J. 30
weak-ties model, networks 400–2
Wellington Language in the Workplace (LWP)
    Project 450
Western Samoa 488, 490
White Woman Style 519
women

and language change 434, 464, 477–8
and power 511
Woolard, K. 394
word frequency, and non-reductive processes 56 *see
    also* lexical frequency
workplace
    as feminine/masculine 450–1
    and femininity 448–56
World Bank
    and linguistic Africanisation 158–9
    structural adjustment policies 164n.9

York 326, 327, 329
York English corpus **326**
yuppies, Chinese 62, 66, **67**, 67, 69–70,
    72–4

Zambia 154, 163n.1

Reprint of #877662 - C0 - 246/189/31 - - Lamination Gloss - Printed on 04-Feb-19 09:46